OXFORD WORLD'S CLASSICS

SELECTED SPEECHES

DEMOSTHENES of Athens (384–322 BC) is widely regarded as
the best of the Attic orators, above all for his forcefulness and his
professionalism. He was a master of all the available styles, so that
he could adapt his writing and delivery to the circumstances of the
speech, whether he was delivering it himself or had written it for
a client. Demosthenes came from a wealthy family, but his father died
young, and the orator's first appearances in Athenian public life came
with a series of private speeches attempting to recover his inheritance.
Having earned a name for himself as a speech-writer, he then wrote
speeches for others in both public and private cases, as well as some
more for his own use in court cases. But he is best known for his political
speeches, written in opposition to the growing power of Macedon in
northern Greece, under first Philip II and then his son, Alexander the
Great. Demosthenes saw through Philip's imperialist machinations
and spent his political career trying to warn the Athenians and other
southern Greeks about the Macedonian menace. But his opponents
were too strong for him, and in the end forced him to suicide. Sixty-
one speeches are extant under his name, but the authenticity of about
twenty of these is disputed.

ROBIN WATERFIELD is a writer, living in Greece. His previous
translations for Oxford World's Classics include Plato's *Republic* and
five other editions of Plato's dialogues, Aristotle's *Physics*, Herodotus'
Histories, Polybius' *Histories*, Plutarch's *Greek Lives* and *Roman Lives*,
Euripides' *Orestes and Other Plays* and *Heracles and Other Plays*,
Xenophon's *The Expedition of Cyrus*, and *The First Philosophers: The
Presocratics and the Sophists*.

CHRIS CAREY is Professor of Greek at University College London.
He has published on Greek oratory, rhetoric, history, drama, lyric,
and law.

OXFORD WORLD'S CLASSICS

*For over 100 years Oxford World's Classics have brought
readers closer to the world's great literature. Now with over 700
titles—from the 4,000-year-old myths of Mesopotamia to the
twentieth century's greatest novels—the series makes available
lesser-known as well as celebrated writing.*

*The pocket-sized hardbacks of the early years contained
introductions by Virginia Woolf, T. S. Eliot, Graham Greene,
and other literary figures which enriched the experience of reading.
Today the series is recognized for its fine scholarship and
reliability in texts that span world literature, drama and poetry,
religion, philosophy, and politics. Each edition includes perceptive
commentary and essential background information to meet the
changing needs of readers.*

OXFORD WORLD'S CLASSICS

═══

DEMOSTHENES

Selected Speeches

═══

Translated by
ROBIN WATERFIELD

With Introductions and Notes by
CHRIS CAREY

OXFORD
UNIVERSITY PRESS

OXFORD
UNIVERSITY PRESS

Great Clarendon Street, Oxford, OX2 6DP,
United Kingdom

Oxford University Press is a department of the University of Oxford.
It furthers the University's objective of excellence in research, scholarship,
and education by publishing worldwide. Oxford is a registered trade mark of
Oxford University Press in the UK and in certain other countries

Published in the United States of America by Oxford University Press
198 Madison Avenue, New York, NY 10016, United States of America

British Library Cataloguing in Publication Data

Data available

Library of Congress Control Number: 2013948415

ISBN 978-0-19-959377-4

Printed in Great Britain by
Clays Ltd, Elcograf S.p.A.

CONTENTS

INTRODUCTION

Demosthenes' life and times

DEMOSTHENES was born in 384 BC into a wealthy mercantile family. We are unusually well informed about the family wealth because of the litigation which followed the death of his father (also named Demosthenes). The estate (at least according to Demosthenes himself) was worth about 15 talents, in a society where a man with property of 3 talents counted as moderately wealthy. Despite his wealth, his father's family was undistinguished. His mother's family, however, had a tradition of involvement in politics. Our contemporary source for the mother's family is his enemy Aeschines,[1] who has every reason to distort. So we have to treat the information we are given with some suspicion. But it is clear that Demosthenes' maternal grandfather Gylon was politically active at the end of the fifth century BC. He seems to have been exiled at one stage to the Black Sea area.[2] Aeschines has Gylon marry a 'Scythian' woman, that is, a member of one of the non-Greek nomadic tribes indigenous to the region. This kind of allegation was part of the rough-and-tumble of Athenian politics (a tough environment by any standards) and the slur cannot be literally true, since Demosthenes never faced a serious challenge to his citizen status. The allegation could be plucked out of the air; the distance from Athens to the Black Sea made it impossible in practice to test the claim and Athenian slander laws were sufficiently permissive to make the claim risk-free even if false. Or it may mean no more than that Gylon's wife was of non-Athenian colonial Greek stock. From the middle of the fifth century a man needed two Athenian parents in order to be a citizen himself; but this law seems to have fallen into abeyance during the latter part of the Peloponnesian War (431–404). Though it was reinstated after the restoration of democracy in 403, this was not retroactive, and provided that Demosthenes' mother was born before 403 his citizen status would be unaffected.

---

[1] Aeschines 3.171–2.

[2] Aeschines alleges treason. He may actually be correct about the charge, since the Athenian Assembly was always ready to attribute failure to betrayal when it might be due to error, incompetence, or just bad luck.

The consummate skill already evident in his earliest speeches suggests that Demosthenes had a good training in rhetoric. Since the fifth century, training in the art of speaking had formed an essential part of the education of a wealthy Athenian.[3] It was also an important part of any training for politics, given the need to address mass audiences in the Assembly and in the courts. Ancient biographies like to link famous names as teacher and pupil, and in Demosthenes' case our sources make him the pupil of Isaeus, a speechwriter for the courts, who was active in Athens in the first half of the fourth century. There is nothing implausible in the statement.[4]

Demosthenes' first opportunity to put his training to the test came early. His father had died while Demosthenes was still a boy. Though his mother was still alive, he was in Athenian terms an *orphanos* and his father's estate was managed by guardians appointed by his father in his will. The will arranged for the management of the property and also (in a manner not uncommon in Athens) for the marriage of his widow and his daughter, Demosthenes' sister. Neither marriage eventually took place, and when on coming of age Demosthenes received the accounts from his three guardians for the management of the estate, the amount remaining was sufficiently low to convince him that he had been defrauded. This began a series of successful legal disputes with his guardians.

It may be at this time that he began work on training his voice. There were, of course, no microphones and the large numbers to be addressed either in the courts or in the Assembly placed a considerable demand on voice and breathing. According to a later biographer Demosthenes had a weak voice and a lisp. To overcome both he practised speaking with pebbles in his mouth, running or walking uphill. Ancient biographical traditions are rich in myth and one can never be quite sure of the reliability of statements they make; but this one has some claim to credibility, since it came from Demetrius of Phalerum,

---

[3] Plutarch, writing in the Roman period (*Life of Demosthenes* 4.4), claims that Demosthenes missed out on schooling because he was a sickly child. We do not know the authority for the statement; but even if true this would not rule out training in rhetoric, which came in adolescence.

[4] D. M. MacDowell, *Demosthenes the Orator* (Oxford, 2009), 21, suggests that Demosthenes consulted Isaeus specifically in relation to the inheritance suit against his guardians; this is entirely possible, since Isaeus was a specialist in this kind of litigation.

a generation younger than Demosthenes, who claimed to have heard it from Demosthenes himself.[5]

Recovering property adjudicated in court was not straightforward in Athens, where the litigant himself had to follow up the court ruling (there were no official bailiffs to assist in private cases). We know from subsequent litigation that his guardians worked hard to frustrate his attempts to regain his property by disputing the status of some of the items claimed. It is therefore uncertain how far he was able to reconstitute his father's estate. This may in part account for his decision to write speeches for hire for delivery by litigants in the law-courts. Business was probably not slow in coming. The precocious rhetorical skill displayed in the battle with his guardians showcased Demosthenes' ability for potential clients. We need to bear in mind that this was a world without newspapers or advertising, and so proven success, word of mouth, and recommendation (together with published speeches on sale in the booksellers' stalls) were probably the primary factors in generating business for the budding speechwriter (Greek *logographos*, 'logographer').

An additional factor in shaping Demosthenes' decision to become a logographer was that either before the lawsuits with the guardians, or as a result of his discovery of his talents, he decided on a career in politics. Though there was (limited) pay for some administrative offices, there was no regular salary for politicians.[6] To be able to devote time to politics at state level private wealth was necessary. The need for money was accentuated by the role of the courts in Athenian politics, since it was common for political debate to spill over into legal challenges and charges in court, with the potential of huge and financially crippling fines, and even exile or death. The speechwriting must have helped him to build a political war-chest.

But speechwriting for the courts was more than a means of financial preparation. It gave Demosthenes an arena in which to hone his rhetorical skills and polish his style. The speeches written for delivery by clients included in this volume give some sense of the range of cases

---

[5] Plutarch, *Life of Demosthenes* 11.1-2. Demetrius served as the pro-Macedonian governor of Athens for ten years from 317 and so he is not an objective source for the life of an enemy of Macedonia; but since the story is not discreditable to Demosthenes, it cannot simply be dismissed as biased. Demosthenes himself cheerfully (18.180) acknowledges a nickname (Battalus), which probably refers to a stammer, though his opponent Aeschines (1.131, 2.99) claims it had an obscene and degrading meaning.

[6] For Athenian political life, see further pp. xviii–xx.

which a successful speechwriter might handle, from violence (*Against Conon*, speech 54) through commerce (*Against Lacritus*, speech 35) to inheritance and other property issues (*For Phormion*, speech 36; *Against Callicles*, speech 55) and beyond. Writing for the courts also offered a means of building and sustaining political alliances. By the 350s at least Demosthenes was certainly writing speeches to be delivered by others in political trials, including the speeches against Androtion (speech 22 in the modern editions), Leptines (speech 20), Timocrates (speech 24), and Aristocrates (speech 23, included in this volume). The earliest of these, *Against Androtion* of 355/4, is relatively modest in scale, though scintillating in style (if weak in substance), and it looks as though Demosthenes was testing his skills before embarking on more substantial and demanding cases. The earliest extant political speeches of his own date to the late 350s, and at this point his logographic speeches peter out. It seems that he was too busy with his own political career to spare time to write for others; possibly also the style of his political oratory was too distinctive for anyone else to pass it off as his own.

Greece in the classical period was largely divided into autonomous city states. For politicians not just in Athens but elsewhere in Greece the defining issue of the period after 350 was the Macedonian question. By the late 350s Demosthenes had concluded that Philip of Macedon was a threat to Athenian interests and to Greece as a whole. Certainly he was a problem for Athens from the very start. Macedonia had been a marginal territory in mainland Greek history. It was fissile, unstable, and difficult to control, and Greek states had long exploited Macedonian discord for their own purposes. The accession of Philip to the kingship in 357 changed all that. Energetic, imaginative, unusually astute, and utterly ruthless, he managed to establish firm control over Macedonia itself and then began to expand Macedonian territory and influence. Athens had strong interests in the north both in the islands and on the Thracian Chersonese (modern Gallipoli peninsula). Athens was also heavily dependent on grain imported by sea from the Black Sea to feed its large (by ancient Greek standards) population; the limited amount of open flat land in Attica was inadequate for this. So the rise of a militarily strong and expansionist power in the north was cause for concern.

The clash was not long in coming. In 357 Philip gained control of the city of Amphipolis and in the next few years encroached further on Athenian interests in the north. The capture of Amphipolis was especially galling. Athens had not actually controlled Amphipolis (an Athenian colony) since the 420s, when it was detached from the empire by the Spartans during the Peloponnesian War. But the Athenians always regarded it as theirs and the city had enormous strategic importance, since it was close to the gold-mines of Mount Pangaeum. It was also at the confluence of trading routes, as its earlier name Nine Roads (*Enneahodoi*) indicates. The disgruntlement was exacerbated by the fact that Philip had prevented Athens from intervening by promising to hand the city over to Athens once captured.

Athens was therefore formally at war with Philip from 357, but this amounted to very little in practice, since Athens was incapable of mounting serious opposition in the north; from 357 to 355 the city was busy dealing with the revolt of her subject allies (the so-called Social War, from the Latin word for 'ally', *socius*), which sapped finances and left little enthusiasm for long-distance war. This was mirrored in the cautious defensive policy favoured by the most influential political group, headed by Eubulus, the dominant political figure in mid-fourth-century Athens. Athens was not entirely inactive, however. From 356 central Greece was embroiled in a war fought for control of the temple at Delphi (the Third Sacred War) which dragged on for ten years. In 353 Philip was invited by the Thessalians to intervene to break the deadlock. A decisive victory by Philip over a Phocian army left him in control of Thessaly. He followed up the success by advancing on Thermopylae, the narrow pass which formed the gateway to central and southern Greece, but was blocked by an Athenian force.

Another chance to foil Philip, this time in the far north, came in 349 when Philip moved against the city of Olynthus in the Gulf of Torone, a major power in the region. Olynthus appealed to Athens for help. It was in this context that Demosthenes delivered his three Olynthiac speeches (speeches 1–3, all in this volume), urging the Athenians to send aid. The strategic significance of Olynthus was clear to all, though the fact that Demosthenes had to worry away at the issue indicates that there was still scepticism about Athens' capacity to intervene at such a distance against an enemy campaigning on his own doorstep. Athens did send aid, but without success; Olynthus fell in 348.

By now it was clear that Philip's expansionism was not confined to the extreme north. Aware that their military and other resources made it impossible for the Athenians to oppose Philip unaided, Eubulus and his associates sent ambassadors to various Greek states to try to assemble an anti-Macedonian coalition, but without success. The competing interests of the Greek states, which made failure almost inevitable, were reinforced by a number of factors: exhaustion in the Peloponnese after recent inter-city wars; astute diplomacy from Philip (who was always good at dividing his enemies); uncertainty about the extent of Philip's territorial ambitions (which he was good at playing down); and probably distrust of Athens' own recent expansionist past. Athens' problems were compounded by doubts about the reliability of their main allies in central Greece, the Phocians, whose seizure of Delphi had precipitated the Sacred War. The Phocians were in a position to control the pass at Thermopylae and a change of allegiance on their part would give Philip access to the south.

At this point politicians in Athens with very different views on the Macedonian question concluded that peace with Philip was the only sensible course. The extent of the rapprochement can be seen from the fact that when the main proponent of peace with Philip, Philocrates, was prosecuted, Demosthenes, the inveterate enemy of Philip, spoke in his support. The reasons and strategic aims of those involved in this marriage of convenience varied; there were those who concluded that peace was the best way to secure Athens' interests in the long term, and those for whom it offered time to recoup and regroup in preparation for a renewal of hostilities. Philip had himself put out feelers to Athens. A number of diplomatic missions to Philip in 346 resulted in the conclusion of the Peace of Philocrates (named after its proposer). Immediately afterwards, Philip consolidated his influence in central Greece by settling the Sacred War on terms which, despite the (probably sincere but certainly misguided) assurances of those who desired a lasting peace, favoured Thebes over Athens.

Not all Athenians had wanted peace. Some hawks had argued against negotiations with Macedon and then against the proposal of peace. The collusion of the other factions and the general recognition that Athens was cornered prevented them from blocking the peace. But for most Athenians the treaty was no more than a pragmatic necessity and dissatisfaction set in very early, when it became clear that few practical benefits would emerge for Athens beyond the absence of war, while Philip was free to continue scheming to expand his influence.

Demosthenes himself, having served on the first two embassies to Philip, was working against the peace almost from the start. With his political ally Timarchus he mounted a legal attack on Aeschines, one of the key proponents of peace, immediately after its conclusion. The attack was foiled by a devastating counter-attack from Aeschines on Timarchus. But Demosthenes and his associates used the courts to attack leading proponents of the peace and their supporters in the period after 343; two of the speeches in this volume (Demosthenes 19 and pseudo-Demosthenes 59)[7] were delivered in this courtroom campaign. They were only partially successful, but the effect was to shift the debate towards a more anti-Macedonian agenda.

In the last few years of the 340s Athens and Macedon competed for influence, by diplomacy and armed conflict, sometimes direct, sometimes through proxies, in the Peloponnese, western Greece, Euboea, and the Black Sea area. It was in the last area that the crunch-point finally came, when Philip seized the Athenian Black Sea grain fleet in 340 and the two states found themselves at war. After a sluggish start, the war culminated in 338 at the battle of Chaeronea in Boeotia. Demosthenes had by this time finally achieved his goal of uniting Athens with Thebes, both a powerful military ally and a buffer immediately to the north of Athenian territory. Philip won. Thebes was destroyed, but Athens was treated generously. Philip was assassinated in 336 and replaced by his son Alexander, soon to become 'the Great'. But neither then nor a few years later when Alexander crossed to Asia to invade the Persian empire did Athens make any serious attempt to contest the still-growing power of Macedon. No convincing opportunity offered itself and peace was proving economically beneficial. Only on Alexander's death in 323 did the Athenians seize the opportunity to revolt against Macedon. In the brief Lamian War of 323–322 Athens was eventually defeated by the Macedonian general Antipater. A garrison was imposed and the democracy dramatically restricted. Demosthenes, who had played an active part in fomenting revolt, was captured and committed suicide.

Between Chaeronea and the Lamian War we are relatively badly briefed on Demosthenes' political life. In the period running up

---

[7] For the authorship of Demosthenes 59 see p. xxii.

to Chaeronea he was proposed for honours by supporters, who in turn were attacked in court by his opponents. So the political fight over Macedonian policy overflowed into the courts. The most important of these incidents was the proposal by Ctesiphon that the people honour Demosthenes with the proclamation of a public crown, a common means of rewarding service. Ctesiphon was prosecuted by Aeschines in retaliation for Demosthenes' prosecution of Aeschines in 343 for corruption and treason in his service as one of the ambassadors to Macedon in 346. The case came to court in 330. In Ctesiphon's defence Demosthenes delivered what is regarded by many as his greatest work, speech 18 in modern editions, *On the Crown*. Aeschines lost and lived in exile from Athens for the rest of his life.

The Athenian Courts

Since many of the speeches in this volume were written for the courts, for Demosthenes' own use and for use by others both in public and in private cases, something must be said about the Athenian legal system.

Unlike many modern jurisdictions, classical Athens (indeed Greece more generally, as far as we can see) made no use of state bodies for the detection and prosecution of crime. These tasks were left to individuals. In private cases (i.e. wrongs committed against an individual), the onus was on the alleged victim of an offence to sue; in public cases (those which were felt to impact on society as a whole or those committed against the state) any Athenian (and in some cases non-Athenians resident in Athens) could prosecute.[8] It was for the litigants (both prosecutor and defence) to assemble evidence and witnesses and to conduct the case in court.

All cases were heard by large panels of jurors, in private cases either 201 or 401 (depending on the sum at issue) and in public cases a minimum of 501, rising in units of 500; the odd number was needed to avoid a tied vote. Many sources attest the volubility of Athenian juries, which unlike their modern counterparts did not sit in respectful silence but made their views known; a hostile jury must have been

---

[8] The categories are not absolutely watertight, since there was some overlap; some offences against the individual could be pursued either through a public or through a private action; Demosthenes 54 (*Against Conon*) in this volume is a good example.

intimidating. There was always a presiding magistrate, but his job was largely to control proceedings; he gave no legal guidance to the jury, which had to decide for itself questions not just of fact but also of law. Timing (to ensure equal voice to each party) was governed by the water-clock, a pot with a hole in the bottom; hence the reference to 'water' for 'time' in some of the speeches in this volume. A case had a certain amount of water (i.e. a number of pots) allocated and when the water ran out the speaker had to stop. More time was allowed public than private cases, reflecting the relative importance of the issues at stake.

Unlike trials in modern systems, where the litigant usually takes a back seat, in Athens each party presented his case by continuous speech, prosecution first followed by defendant; the speech was interrupted by witnesses and other evidence.[9] It was possible to introduce a supporting speaker (*synēgoros*), and on rare occasions we find the supporting speaker conducting the whole case. But there is usually a good practical reason advanced (such as the nature of the case, the age/experience or the language limitations of the litigant, as in speeches 36 and 59 in the Demosthenic corpus, both in this volume) and the relative rarity of such cases suggests that jury panels were not well disposed to people who did not speak for themselves. It was illegal to work as a supporting speaker for pay, which effectively prevented the rise of the professional advocate. But the law will always attract professionalism; in Athens it took the form of writing speeches to be delivered in court by litigants, a trade which we can trace back at least to the last third of the fifth century. We have no idea how much a speech would cost but common sense suggests a market in which quality and reputation played an important role in regulating demand and price. Since the price, whatever it was, probably placed the services of a speechwriter beyond the reach of Athenians of modest means, unsurprisingly those surviving speeches which provide evidence for the status of the speaker point to a mon-eyed background, and this probably applies to all the speeches we

---

[9] In the fifth and early fourth centuries witnesses deposed orally, but by the 380s this had been replaced by written depositions which seem generally to have been drafted by the litigant for the witness to approve; the witness in court then simply confirmed the testimony and took responsibility for its factual content, or declined to testify, taking an oath of disclaimer that he was not present or had no direct knowledge of the facts in question.

have, even where this is not immediately apparent. Though we cannot conclude, as some moderns have, that litigation was confined to the elite, then as now people of modest means were less likely to go to law.

Litigants swore to keep to the point. And in fact in surviving speeches the emphasis in most cases is firmly on the main issue. This is not the whole story, however. There were no explicit rules of evidence and so relevance was not fixed but fluid, amounting to what the jurors were prepared to accept as useful for their decision-making. Ancient rhetorical theory (and oratorical practice) from the start recognized that the character projected by a speaker and the emotional state he could generate in the audience were an important part of the task of persuasion. Greek rhetoric also relied heavily on argument from probability. This was especially valuable in the courts in the absence of anything resembling forensic evidence and the lack of a state investigative body. All of this meant that there was considerable scope to introduce extra-legal material such as personalities, appeals to emotion (explicit or covert), references to a speaker's past civic record, and allegations of an opponent's past misconduct, all potentially tangential to the main issue. Whether such material is felt to be irrelevant depends to a large extent on the presentational skill of the speaker. The impact of extra-legal issues was particularly felt in the case of political trials, where the current climate, the standing of individuals, and collective prejudices (as most notoriously in the case of Socrates) could have a profound influence on the verdict.

After the parties had presented their case, the jurors both decided between litigants and (where the penalty was not fixed by law) decided the penalty in case of conviction; in practice they had less choice than this suggests, since the two litigants offered alternative penalty proposals and the jurors chose between them. Voting in the fourth century was done with metal ballots. Each juror had two ballots, one for prosecution and one for defence, and there were two urns, one for the vote cast, the other for the discarded vote. To win, a litigant needed a simple majority of votes cast. And since there was no objective standard of legal proof, that meant simply that a majority of the jurors needed to be more persuaded by A than by B. There was no formal opportunity for discussion (impossible to organize anyway with panels on this scale), though jurors presumably exchanged views among themselves on the way to vote. The verdict of an Athenian jury was final. There was no mechanism for appeal; only verdicts which had been given by default (due to failure of a litigant to appear) could be overturned. A litigant with a grievance arising from the case against him could, however, bring a suit for false testimony (*dikē pseudomartyriōn*) against his opponent's witnesses, provided that he declared his intention to do so before the verdict.

The system required a large number of potential jurors to make it work and the state enrolled 6,000 jurors a year. The qualification for jury service was to be a male citizen over thirty years of age. The jurors swore an oath at the beginning of the administrative year, then simply turned up to be selected and were paid on those days when they were selected to serve. In the fifth century jurors seem to have served in the same court for their year but in the fourth century they were allocated to the court on a daily basis by an elaborately randomized process, to prevent bribery. There was no formal training and some moderns on this basis describe the jurors as amateurs. The term is a little misleading, and not just because the jurors were paid; jurors could serve indefinitely and so some at least must have had considerable experience. The pay (three obols, half a drachma) was at best half a day's wage for a labourer; so it amounted more to a (still useful) compensation for lost time rather than a living wage. The pay did not change in the century from the 420s to the 320s, a period when inflation eroded the spending power of the currency and pushed up other wages, which suggests that there was no difficulty in attracting people to serve.

A lot of the business coming before the courts was political. The courts played a role in some of the routine administrative business of the democracy. For instance, officials were subject to an examination (an 'assessment', *dokimasia*) after election to office; if they were rejected, they could appeal to a court. In such cases the court was acting as a complement to the sovereign Assembly. At the end of his period of office, an official was subject to an audit (*euthynai*) to check for financial or other misconduct; any alleged dereliction would go to a court. The courts also had a key role in the legislative process, in that anyone bringing a proposal to the Assembly which breached proper procedure or conflicted with existing laws was liable to prosecution through the public action for illegal proposals (*graphē paranomōn*), with heavy fines on conviction. And politicians regularly brought other kinds of prosecution for alleged offences (such as corruption) against their opponents.

Athenian politics

Like the law-courts, Athenian democracy shares features and principles with modern systems, but in structure and operation is unlike anything familiar to the modern reader with the sole exception of the Swiss. By about 500 BC Athens had a broadly democratic government, and the process of democratization continued after the two Persian invasions of 490 and 480/79. At the end of the fifth century two successive political coups placed the city in the hands of oligarchic groups (in 411/10 and 404/3), but the democracy was restored in 403 and continued unhindered until the end of the Lamian War.

Power in the democracy lay with the Assembly (Greek *ekklēsia*, though our sources mostly speak just of the people, *dēmos*), which in the fourth century met forty times a year. The Assembly decided all major policy issues. In the fifth century it also legislated by decree, though from the end of the fifth century the specifics of legislation were delegated to large panels of 'law-makers' (*nomothetai*), chosen from those who had sworn the juror's oath, as part of a larger tendency to make the legislative process both more cumbersome and more focused. The Assembly met on the hill of the Pnyx near the Areopagus and the Acropolis. Membership was open to all Athenians who had reached the age of majority (eighteen). In theory any Athenian (perhaps as many as 30,000 citizens) could attend, though the Pnyx itself probably never had room for more than 6,000 and in practice regular attendance must have been easier for those who lived in or near the city; citizens from more remote areas of Attica (or from the island of Salamis, for instance) were presumably more infrequent attenders. Pay for attendance was introduced at the end of the fifth century or early in the fourth; the pay was gradually increased during the fourth century, which suggests that in the Assembly, unlike the courts, maintaining attendance was a problem.

Athens had no government in the modern sense of a formally constituted group of people delegated to decide policy for a designated period. The people in session on the Pnyx were the government of Athens. And it had no term of office; speakers addressing the

Assembly regularly treat those addressed as identical with all other assemblies past (however remote) and present. In practice a body of thousands cannot direct public business and the Assembly relied on the various boards of magistrates of different sizes, holding office for a year and chosen by lot (a selection method favoured by democracy) to handle routine business, of which the most important was the Council of Five Hundred (the *Boulē*). The business for the Assembly was prepared by the Council.

Though a large group can debate and vote, individuals are needed to initiate policy discussion and the Assembly sessions were dominated by public speakers (*rhētores*) who relied on experience, persuasive skills, and political networks to influence the people. The mass of citizens who attended would vote (by show of hands, unlike the secret ballots used in the courts), but it takes confidence and experience to address a mass audience and few ordinary Athenians spoke at Assembly meetings. As noted above, these speakers were not paid. But they were professional in the sense that they devoted much of their time to politics. Since there was no job and no job description, a politician could remain powerful as long as he could still sway the *dēmos*, and we have evidence for political careers stretching over several decades. This in part explains the importance of litigation in the Athenian political system. The only effective way to put an end to a rival's political career was through a trial on a political charge resulting in a crippling fine, exile, or death. In practice, for public speakers neutralization was through huge fines; the more severe penalties were more likely for generals and ambassadors who were more obviously open to charges of treason. Though politics was a zero-sum game, not all trials had such seismic consequences; lesser fines would leave defendants bruised but still active, and so the system, harsh as it was, also allowed for policies to be tested and adjusted or reversed, and for the standing of individuals to be evaluated.

There were no parties in the modern sense of formally structured groups with shared programmes. But groupings there were, and Athenian politicians usually worked within relatively informal groups sharing a political agenda. We rarely know the number of groups operating at any one time, but at the beginning of the fourth century scholars have identified at least six, and we can see at least three in action during the debate on the peace with Macedon in 346. So the bipartisan structure which operates in many modern systems

does not apply. An aspiring politician would usually attach himself
to the group around a prominent political figure and work his way
up to prominence, if he was lucky, astute, and tough enough. The
lesser players would play their part by offering noisy support in the
Assembly, acting as supporting speakers in Assembly debates and
trials, and bringing prosecutions against opposing politicians. When
we first meet Demosthenes in the Assembly he is a middleweight
player. By the time of our last speech, *On the Crown* (Demosthenes
18), he is the biggest politician in Athens.

Demosthenes' style

For later writers Demosthenes was the most versatile of the Athenian
orators, a master of what ancient students of rhetoric would class as
the middle style, neither too ornate nor too simple, but able to move
across the stylistic range. Context also matters, since a private case in
the courts called for a more simple style than a public case. The same
applied to personalities. A high-profile public trial in the courts with
a politically active speaker allowed for a greater emotional range and
a more formalized style than a private case with an obscure speaker
claiming to be a stranger to litigation. The opportunity for overt
stylistic mastery is at its most visible in those big public cases where
Demosthenes spoke in his own person at the height of his career,
where the known experience of the speaker and the appreciation of
a good performance by the audience allowed for a more overt use of
the various stylistic devices which had been formalized and categor-
ized by teachers of rhetoric since the fifth century.

   A feature emphasized by ancient critics is the force with which
Demosthenes expresses himself. One striking feature of his style is
a gift for the vivid and well-judged image to get across a point economically, often with devastating wit. Demosthenes has an excellent
ear for what will work with an audience.[10] To avoid tedium he moves
between short and staccato utterances and long, elaborately con-
structed sentences.[11] As his career progressed, he became more sensi-
tive to the impact of rhythm. The avoidance of hiatus (the collision of

---

[10] Demosthenes himself is said, when asked about what made a good orator, to have
said 'delivery, delivery, and delivery'; Cicero, *On the Orator* 3.213.

[11] The longest of these have, however, often been broken up in the translations that
follow, for the sake of good, comprehensible English.

a word ending in a vowel with another beginning with a vowel) makes for a much more fluent delivery, while the avoidance of runs of short syllables makes for a weightier manner and (probably) a steadier pace. Both of these have profound implications for the hearer's perception of the speaker, though it is unlikely that any but the aficionados of rhetoric were conscious of the fine details.

The variety which we find in sentence structure can also be seen in the construction of his speeches, where the order and shaping (even omission) of elements reflects his sense of the needs of the moment rather than any technical principles. Perhaps the most interesting example of this flexibility is speech 19 (*On the Dishonest Embassy*), where he divides up his (very brief) account of Aeschines' alleged crimes between different sections of the speech instead of offering a single section devoted to narrative in line with rhetorical theory and general practice.

Demosthenes and Posterity

Orators and speechwriters had been publishing speeches since at least the last quarter of the fifth century. And we can be reasonably sure that some at least of Demosthenes' oratorical output was published in his lifetime. Scholars have long suggested that the speeches delivered in the two great duels between Aeschines and Demosthenes (Aeschines 2 and 3, Demosthenes 18 and 19) in the form in which we have them have been edited for publication. These were, however, for both authors the culmination of and testimony to their careers and policies.

We cannot be sure how much of the rest of his corpus was published during Demosthenes' lifetime, but it is likely that many speeches, both public and private, were in the public domain by the end of the fourth century. For Demosthenes was evidently already an established classic by the early third century, when scholars working in the newly founded library at the court of the Ptolemies in Egypt set about the task of acquiring the great texts, prose and verse, from archaic and classical Greece. Among the texts acquired and edited by the library were those of Demosthenes. The corpus which reached Alexandria was already contaminated. We have sixty-one speeches which claim to be by Demosthenes. But it was already recognized in antiquity that the corpora of the orators contained speeches which had been erroneously attributed, though no attempt was ever made to create an 'expurgated' edition of genuine speeches. Some of the speeches in the Demosthenic corpus cannot have been written by him on grounds of content, and others are suspected on grounds of style. In particular, there is a group of speeches probably or certainly written by Apollodorus, the son of the ex-slave banker Pasion, which probably found their way into the Demosthenic corpus at an early date; one of these ('Demosthenes' 59, *Against Neaera*) has been included in the present volume for the remarkable insights it gives into Athenian life and politics.

The scholars of the Hellenistic period carefully selected authors in each literary genre for editing and study. These selections never amounted to formal lists (though the authority of the Alexandrian scholars was such that they are often so treated in our ancient sources), but they did have the effect of privileging certain authors and texts. We have evidence by the Roman period for a list of ten 'canonical' Athenian orators. The list was not stable (we get other numbers, and there is some small variation in the names included), but Demosthenes is always there. For Dionysius of Halicarnassus, writing in the Roman period, he is one of the three best Athenian orators (*On the Ancient Orators* §4). Cicero (*Brutus* 35) pronounces him the complete orator. Cicero's admiration was not confined to praise and precept. His own series of speeches attacking Mark Antony were inspired by Demosthenes' speeches warning of the threat to Greek liberty from Philip of Macedon (the *Philippics*); the name was given to them by Cicero himself (*Letters to Brutus* 2.3.4), and for a man like Cicero, devoted to a political system which was being destroyed by men of violence, the inspiration was as much about spirit and principles as about rhetoric. These attacks ironically were to cost Cicero his life, just as Demosthenes had died for his resistance to Macedon. Cicero's judgement is echoed by the rhetorician Quintilian (10.1.76), for whom Demosthenes is by far the greatest of the ten Athenian orators. He was also widely admired in the Renaissance, his status reinforced by the fact that so many other oratorical texts failed to survive into the modern era. Many modern readers of Greek oratory share the view of Cicero and Quintilian that Demosthenes was the greatest of the ten canonical orators.

Politically too Demosthenes has fared well over time. As was noted above, the highly confrontational and competitive nature of Athenian political life, combined with the tendency of the Assembly to smell betrayal in defeat and failure, encouraged public and politicians alike to view political opposition in stark terms of honesty and loyalty versus deviousness, venality, and treason. Since the culture, both in Athens and in Greece more generally, was one in which the giving of gifts was a normal part of public life, there was fertile ground for accusations of selling the national interest. This was the stance taken by Demosthenes in his attacks on the party which favoured peace with Macedon. There was probably some truth in the allegations, to the extent that some at least of his fellow ambassadors were less scrupulous—and less smart—than they could and should have been in responding to Philip's largesse.

The contrast between unimpeachable patriotism and unpatriotic venality was a line which found favour with the Athenian Assembly and courts, as we can see from Demosthenes' continuing influence after the disaster at Chaeronea and his success in his last great encounter in court with Aeschines. Demosthenes' claims for himself were certainly true, at least to the extent that his unflagging devotion both to Athens and to a particular vision of its destiny eventually cost him his life. And the picture which Demosthenes and his ally Hypereides give of a Greece riddled with the corruption of men who had sold out to Philip does reflect Philip's astute use of the enormous wealth of Macedon to acquire support in the various cities of Greece. But you did not have to be a traitor to conclude that peace was in Athens' best interests. The Athenians themselves recognized this, or at least enough of them to make a difference. Demosthenes failed to convict Aeschines in 343, and any subsequent attack on Aeschines for treason or corruption, if there was one, was equally unsuccessful.

The Demosthenic reading of fourth-century history has proved popular with subsequent readers, including moderns. Since Macedonian domination did in some ways signal the end of a way of life, certainly the end of the small independent city state which had been the model of Greek geopolitics since the archaic period, Demosthenes was right about the threat posed by Macedon. But it remains questionable what Athens could ever have achieved alone against the resources available to Philip and Alexander, in a context where combined Greek resistance was as difficult to create as it had been in previous threats to Greek autonomy. And the tale of corruption is a reading which gives

TRANSLATOR'S NOTE

THE text used as the basis for this translation is the Oxford Classical Text of M. R. Dilts. Dilts's OCT comes in four volumes, published by Oxford University Press respectively in 2002, 2005, 2008, and 2009. Volume 1 contains Orations 1–18, volume 2 Orations 19–24, volume 3 Orations 25–40, and volume 4 Orations 41–61. Those few places where I have adopted a different reading from Dilts have been marked in the translation with an obelus (†), which refers the interested reader to the Textual Notes (pp. 513–14); an asterisk (*) in the text means that there is a note on that section of the text in the Explanatory Notes (pp. 431–512).

The speeches that have come down to us attributed to Demosthenes are sixty-one in number. Their order and numbering was fixed by Alexandrian scholars late in the third century BC, largely on the basis of their content, but it was soon recognized that not all the speeches were authentic works of Demosthenes. Probably about twenty of them are spurious. For this volume we simply chose those which showcased Demosthenes' skills and shed the most light on the public and private lives of Athenian citizens living at a critical time of European history, on the rise of Philip of Macedon, and on Demosthenes' own life and career.

A few words should be said about the documents that are found embedded in many of Demosthenes' speeches. The reader will often come across an italicized 'stage direction' stating that a document was read out.[1] The received Greek text sometimes, but far from always, follows this stage direction with the purported text of the document. Not all of these documents are genuine. Over the centuries forgers filled many of the gaps, so that where they received a text stating that some document was read out, if no document accompanied the text they not infrequently did the best they could to supply one out of their own historical research and imagination. Sometimes these forgeries are easy to spot, but not always, because many of the documents are

---

[1] The received text itself often contains no more than a bare indication, such as 'Testimony', that a document featured at that point of the speech. The expanded 'stage directions' in these places, and all other embedded stage directions, have been written by me.

too short to supply a statistically significant number of clues. Again, I have basically translated Dilts's text, so that where he marks a document as spurious I have not included it. Occasionally, however, I have differed from Dilts, especially in speech 59, where many of the documents are too short for certainty. As usual, I have commented on all departures from Dilts's text.[2]

[2] See now M. Canevaro, *The Documents in the Attic Orators: Laws and Decrees in the Public Speeches of the Demosthenic Corpus* (Oxford, 2013), a book that was published too late for consideration by us in the preparation of this volume.

SELECT BIBLIOGRAPHY

Career, biography, and style

Harris, E., *Aeschines and Athenian Politics* (Oxford and New York, 1995).

MacDowell, D. M., *Demosthenes the Orator* (Oxford, 2009).

Pearson, L., *The Art of Demosthenes* (Meisenheim am Glan, 1976).

Pickard-Cambridge, A. W., *Demosthenes and the Last Days Of Greek Freedom* (London, 1914).

Sealey, R., *Demosthenes and His Time: A Study in Defeat* (New York, 1993).

Worthington, I. (ed.), *Demosthenes, Statesman and Orator* (London and New York, 2000).

Worthington, I., *Demosthenes of Athens and the Fall of Classical Greece* (Oxford, 2013).

History, society, and politics

Bauman, R. A., *Political Trials in Ancient Greece* (London, 1990).

Carey, C., *Democracy in Classical Athens* (Bristol, 2001).

Cawkwell, G., *Philip of Macedon* (London, 1978).

Christ, M. R., *The Bad Citizen in Classical Athens* (Cambridge, 2006).

Cox, C. A., *Household Interests: Property, Marriage Strategies and Family Dynamics in Ancient Athens* (Princeton, 2001).

Dover, K. J., *Greek Popular Morality in the Time of Plato and Aristotle* (Oxford, 1974).

Davies, J. K., *Wealth and the Power of Wealth in Classical Athens* (New York, 1981).

Ellis, J. R., *Philip II and Macedonian Imperialism* (London, 1976).

Fisher, N. R. E., *Social Values in Classical Athens* (London, 1976).

Gabrielsen, V., *Financing the Athenian Fleet: Public Taxation and Social Relations* (Baltimore, 1994).

Hammond, N. G. L., *Alexander the Great*, 2nd edn. (Bristol, 1989).

——*Philip of Macedon* (London, 1994).

Hansen, M. H., *The Sovereignty of the People's Court in Athens in the Fourth Century B.C., and the Public Action against Unconstitutional Proposals* (Odense, 1974).

——*Eisangelia: the Sovereignty of the People's Court in Athens in the Fourth Century B.C. and the Impeachment of Generals and Politicians* (Odense, 1975).

——*Athenian Democracy in the Age of Demosthenes* (Oxford, 1991).

Herman, G., *Morality and Behaviour in Democratic Athens: A Social History* (Cambridge, 2006).

Hornblower, S., *The Greek World 479–323*, 4th edn. (London and New York, 2011).

Just, R., *Women in Athenian Law and Life* (London, 1989).

Lacey, W. K., *The Family in Classical Greece* (London, 1968).

Liddel, P., *Civic Obligation and Individual Liberty in Ancient Athens* (Oxford and New York, 2007).

Ober, J., *Mass and Elite in Democratic Athens* (Princeton, 1989).

Osborne, R., *Athens and Athenian Democracy* (Cambridge, 2010).

Rhodes, P. J. (ed.), *Athenian Democracy* (Edinburgh, 2004).

——*A History of the Classical Greek World, 478–323*, 2nd edn. (Oxford, 2010).

Tritle, L. A. (ed.), *The Greek World in the Fourth Century: From the Fall of the Athenian Empire to the Successors of Alexander* (London and New York, 1997).

Worthington, I., *Philip II of Macedonia* (New Haven and London, 2008).

Wycherley, R. E., *The Stones of Athens* (Princeton, 1978).

Law

Arnaotoglou, I., *Ancient Greek Laws: A Sourcebook* (London and New York, 1998).

Christ, M., *The Litigious Athenian* (Baltimore and London, 1998).

Gagarin, M., and Cohen, D. (eds.), *The Cambridge Companion to Ancient Greek Law* (Cambridge, 2005).

Harrison, A. R. W., *The Law of Athens*, 2 vols. (Oxford, 1968, 1971).

Hunter, V. J., *Policing Athens: Social Control in the Attic Lawsuits, 420–320 B.C.* (Princeton, 1994).

Johnstone, S., *Disputes and Democracy: The Consequences of Litigation in Ancient Athens* (Austin, Tex., 1999).

Lanni, A., *Law and Justice in the Courts of Classical Athens* (Cambridge, 2006).

MacDowell, D. M., *Athenian Homicide Law in the Age of the Orators* (Manchester, 1963).

—— *The Law in Classical Athens* (London, 1978).

Todd, S., *The Shape of Athenian Law* (Oxford, 1993).

Oratory

Edwards, M., *The Attic Orators* (London, 1994).

Kennedy, G. A., *The Art of Persuasion in Greece* (Princeton, 1963).

Pernot, L., *Rhetoric in Antiquity*, trans. W. E. Higgins (Washington, DC, 2005).

Schaps, D., *The Economic Rights of Women in Ancient Greece* (Edinburgh, 1979).

Usher, S., *Greek Oratory: Tradition and Originality* (Oxford, 1999).

Commerce

Cohen, E. E., *Ancient Athenian Maritime Courts* (Princeton, 1973).
——*Athenian Economy and Society: A Banking Perspective* (Princeton, 1992).
Isager, S., and Hansen, M. H., *Aspects of Athenian Society in the Fourth Century B.C.* (Odense, 1975).
Millett, P., *Lending and Borrowing in Ancient Athens* (Cambridge, 1991).

Commentaries

Carey, C., *Apollodoros: Against Neaira* (Warminster, 1992).
——and Reid, R. A., *Demosthenes: Selected Private Speeches* (Cambridge, 1985).
Kapparis, K. A., *Apollodoros, 'Against Neaira' [D.59]* (Berlin, 1999).
MacDowell, D. M., *Demosthenes: Against Meidias* (Oxford, 1990).
——*Demosthenes: On the False Embassy (Oration 19)* (Oxford, 2000).
McQueen, E. I., *Demosthenes: Olynthiacs* (Bristol, 1986).
Pearson, L., *Demosthenes: Six Private Speeches* (Atlanta, Ga., 1972).
Usher, S., *Demosthenes: On the Crown* (Warminster, 1993).
Wooten, C., *A Commentary on Demosthenes' Philippic I, with Rhetorical Analyses of Philippics II and III* (Oxford, 2008).
Yunis, H., *Demosthenes: On the Crown* (Cambridge, 2001).

Further Reading in Oxford World's Classics

Cicero, *Defence Speeches*, trans. D. H. Berry.
——*Political Speeches*, trans. D. H. Berry.

CHRONOLOGY

All dates are BC.

404   Athens surrenders to Sparta; end of Peloponnesian War.

404/3   Regime of the Thirty at Athens.

384   Birth of Demosthenes.

378   Foundation of Second Athenian League.

371   Thebes defeats Sparta at the battle of Leuctra.

369   Thebes invades the Peloponnese; Athens sends aid under Callistratus.

364/3   *Against Aphobus* (speeches 27–8).

359   Philip II becomes king of Macedonia.

357   Philip captures Amphipolis and Pydna; Athens blocks Theban intervention in Euboea.

357–355 Athens at war with members of the Second Athenian League (Social War).

356   Start of the Third Sacred War; Philip captures Potidaea.

352   Philip defeats Phocians at battle of Crocus Field; he marches on Delphi but is blocked by an Athenian force at Thermopylae.

351   *Against Aristocrates* (speech 23); *First Philippic* (speech 4).

350/49 *For Phormion* (speech 36); *Against Lacritus* (speech 35).

349   Philip threatens Olynthus; Olynthus allies with Athens and Athens sends relief force.

349/8   *Olynthiacs* (speeches 1–3).

348   Fall of Olynthus; Athenian expedition to Euboea; *Against Boeotus* (speech 39).

347/6   Demosthenes *Against Meidias* (speech 21).

346   Athenian embassies to Macedonia; conclusion of the Peace of Philocrates; Philip ends the Third Sacred War; Timarchus and Demosthenes indict Aeschines for misconduct as ambassador to Philip; Aeschines prosecutes and convicts Timarchus; *On the Peace* (speech 5).

343   Philocrates is indicted by Hypereides and flees; Demosthenes brings his prosecution of Aeschines to court; *On the Dishonest Embassy* (speech 19).

343   (possibly 342 or 341) *Against Neaera* (speech 59, by Apollodorus).

342–340   Philip in Thrace versus Cersobleptes.

341   Diopeithes' activities in the Chersonese lead to protest from Philip, as ally of Cardia; *On the Situation in the Chersonese* (speech 8) and *Third Philippic* (speech 9).

340   Philip seizes Athenian grain ships; Athens declares war on Philip.

339   Accusation of Amphissans against Athens at Delphi leads indirectly to the Fourth Sacred War; Athens allies with Thebes; Philip becomes head of the opposing Amphictyonic forces.

338   Defeat of anti-Macedonian axis at Chaeronea; Philip creates the League of Corinth with himself as its leader.

336   Ctesiphon proposes a crown of honour for Demosthenes and is indicted by Aeschines; Philip assassinated, accession of Alexander to Macedonian throne.

335   Thebes revolts and is captured and razed by Alexander.

334   Alexander invades Asia.

330   Aeschines' prosecution of Ctesiphon comes to court; Demosthenes' *On the Crown* (speech 18); Aeschines leaves Athens.

323   Death of Alexander; Athens takes the lead in the (unsuccessful) Lamian War against Macedon.

322   Death of Demosthenes.

MAP I Greece and the Aegean Sea

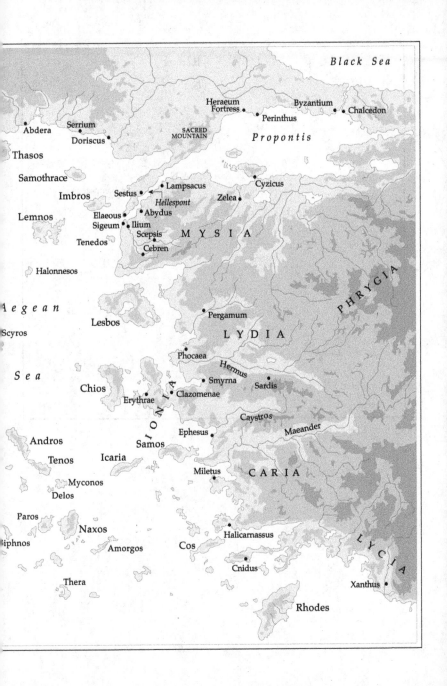

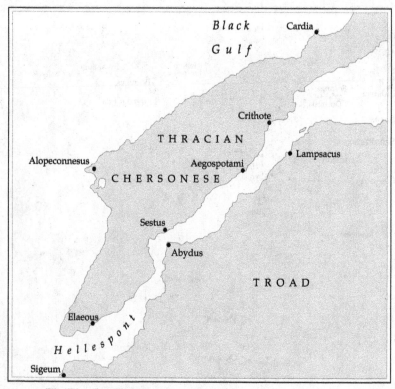

MAP 2 The Thracian Chersonese

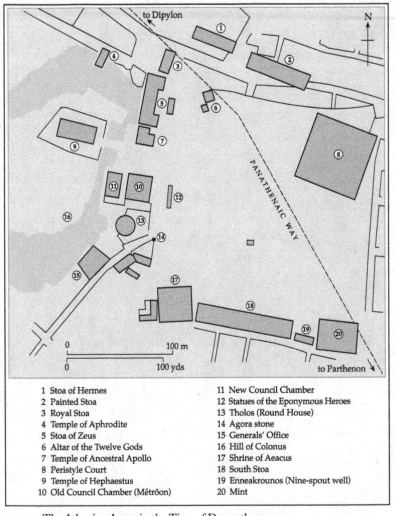

1 Stoa of Hermes	11 New Council Chamber
2 Painted Stoa	12 Statues of the Eponymous Heroes
3 Royal Stoa	13 Tholos (Round House)
4 Temple of Aphrodite	14 Agora stone
5 Stoa of Zeus	15 Generals' Office
6 Altar of the Twelve Gods	16 Hill of Colonus
7 Temple of Ancestral Apollo	17 Shrine of Aeacus
8 Peristyle Court	18 South Stoa
9 Temple of Hephaestus	19 Enneakrounos (Nine-spout well)
10 Old Council Chamber (Mêtrôon)	20 Mint

MAP 3 The Athenian Agora in the Time of Demosthenes

DELIBERATIVE SPEECHES

THE 'OLYNTHIAC' SPEECHES

The 'Olynthiacs' is the title given to three speeches delivered by Demosthenes in the Assembly the year 349/8. The title was already in use in late antiquity.[1] Olynthus was the head of a confederation of cities in the Chalcidice, the three-pronged peninsula in the far north of Greece. Olynthus had approached Athens for support in 357 when Philip began to expand his territory. Athens rejected the advances and the Olynthians were forced to enter into an uneasy alliance with Macedon. In 349 Philip found an excuse to wage war on Olynthus. Demosthenes spoke repeatedly for vigorous action in aid of the city; only three speeches are preserved, but he may have made more. Despite (limited) Athenian intervention, the city fell in 348. Philip razed Olynthus and sold the population as slaves, a not uncommon phenomenon in Greek warfare.

The order of the Olynthiacs in this translation follows that in the medieval manuscripts and modern editions. But ancient scholars debated the order in which they were delivered. Dionysius of Halicarnassus, writing in the Roman era, argued for the order 2, 3, 1. The debate has continued into modern times. The evidence is inconclusive. The third certainly seems to be the last in the sequence. But the first seems more urgent than the second and there is something to be said for the view of the great nineteenth-century historian George Grote that the actual order was 2, 1, 3.

---

1. FIRST OLYNTHIAC

[1] I'm sure you would give a good deal, Athenians, to know which of the courses of action currently under consideration will be best for the city. Under these circumstances, then, anyone's advice should be welcome. After all, not only are you in a position to listen and attend to a speaker who has come prepared with practical recommendations, but it's your good fortune, as I see it, that there are also speakers who are capable of coming up with plenty of important ideas on the spur of the moment. This will make it easy for you to select the best course from among the proposals.

[1] For the fluctuation in ancient labels see introduction to speech 4.

[2] Despite the fact that the present crisis in the north, Athenians, all but cries out for you to take matters there into your own hands, if you care about the safety of the region, I'm still not sure what our position is on the matter. My view is that you should avoid repeating your past mistakes. You should immediately vote to despatch a force and ensure its earliest departure from here, and you should send envoys there to announce this intention and watch the situation. [3] My main worry, you see, is that, by a combination of concessions and all-too-plausible threats, and by misrepresenting us and our absence, an unscrupulous opportunist like Philip might turn the situation to his advantage and take something of ours for his own.

[4] Nevertheless, Athenians, one may with some justification claim that the point at which Philip is at his most unassailable is also the point at which your interests are best served. It's true that when it comes to swift and timely military action, the advantage is his: he, a single individual, is responsible for every policy decision, whether it was reached with or without consultation; he combines the functions of general, sovereign, and paymaster; and wherever he goes he has his army with him. But these same factors put him at a disadvantage in relation to the Olynthians and the peace accord he would like to make with them. [5] They are in no doubt what they are fighting for: not glory or even a bit of land, but to save their country from ruin and slavery. They know how he treated the Amphipolitans who betrayed their city to him and the Pydnaeans who opened their gates for him.* And the truism that free states are wary of a tyranny applies especially when the states involved share a border.

[6] Once you see that I'm right, Athenians, and you bear in mind all the other relevant factors as well, I would have you prosecute the war with renewed determination and resolution—without resenting the war levies,* or getting others to serve in your place, or leaving *anything* undone. There's no longer any reason, let alone any excuse, for refusing to do your duty. [7] After all, everyone has been going on for a while about how important it was for the Olynthians to be set at odds with Philip, and now this has happened of its own accord, and in a way that particularly helps you. I mean, if you had argued them into embarking upon the war, they'd probably by now be unreliable and half-hearted allies. But since they have their own personal reasons for hating him, their hostility is likely to be solid, based as it is on their fears and experiences.

[8] Don't squander this opportunity, Athenians, now that it has come your way. Don't behave as you so often have in the past. After the Euboean expedition,* for instance, Hierax and Stratocles came from Amphipolis and stood on this very platform, asking us to sail and take possession of the city; if we had shown the same degree of commitment to our own interests as we did to the security of Euboea, we'd have gained Amphipolis then* and been spared all our subsequent troubles. [9] Or again, when news arrived of the sieges of Pydna, Potidaea, Methone, Pagasae, and so on*—I don't want to waste time over a complete list—if we had immediately despatched Athenian forces, as we should have, to help any one of these cities in the first instance, we would now find Philip more compliant and far less arrogant. But in fact our constant habit of neglecting the present and imagining that the future will turn out well all by itself means that Philip's strength is our fault, Athenians. It is we who have made him the most powerful Macedonian king ever. Well, an opportunity has dropped into our laps now, through the Olynthians, and it's at least as good as any of the past ones.

[10] It seems to me, Athenians, that anyone who undertakes a fair appraisal of the benefits the gods have bestowed on us would have plenty to be grateful for, despite the fact that many things are not as they should be. And quite right too. After all, while our many losses in the northern war should rightly be attributed to our own negligence, I for one would count it as a manifestation of divine favour that the losses are recent and have already been offset by the chance of an alliance, if we're willing to avail ourselves of it. [11] Our situation is analogous to the acquisition of wealth, I think. If a man gets to keep what he's made, he's profoundly grateful to Fortune, but if he accidentally loses it, he also loses his sense of gratitude. The same goes in politics too: those who fail to make proper use of opportunities also forget the favours the gods have done them. Past blessings tend to be judged in the light of the eventual outcome. It follows that we must take considerable thought for the future, Athenians; if we get it right, we shall wipe out the bad name our past actions have earned us.

[12] If we let these people down too, Athenians, and Philip destroys Olynthus, what is there to stop him subsequently going wherever he pleases? Can anyone tell me? Have you ever reckoned it up, Athenians? Do you see how Philip, despite his original weakness, has become powerful? First he took Amphipolis, and then in turn

Pydna, Potidaea, and Methone, and then he invaded Thessaly. [13] Next, after he had settled Pherae,* Pagasae, and Magnesia to his satisfaction, off he went to Thrace. He removed some of the chieftains and installed others, and then fell ill. Once he had recovered, he didn't sink into complacency, but immediately attacked Olynthus. And I haven't mentioned his campaigns against the Illyrians, the Paeonians, Arybbas, and so on.*

[14] 'All right,' someone might say, 'but what's the point of telling us this now?' There are two reasons, Athenians. I want you to see how unprofitable your consistent negligence has been; and I want you to appreciate that Philip's restless energy is second nature to him. There's no way it will let him stay inactive and rest on his laurels. But if Philip's intention is always to improve his status, and ours is to avoid addressing the situation, what do you think the final outcome is likely to be? [15] By the gods, are you too dense to see that, if we remain negligent, the war is going to come here next, after Olynthus? And, if that happens, Athenians, I'm afraid that we will resemble people who casually borrow at high interest. A brief period of prosperity is followed by their losing even what they started with, and the cost of our complacency might very well prove to be just as high. As a result of our self-indulgence, we may later find ourselves compelled to do all sorts of difficult and unwelcome things, and we may find Attica itself at risk.

[16] 'Criticism is easy,' you might say. 'Anyone can do it. But an adviser's job is to tell us what to do in any given situation.' Now, I'm well aware, Athenians, that, when you suffer disappointment, it's often not those who are responsible who feel your anger, but those who most recently touched on the matter in their speeches. All the same, I don't think it's right for a politician to be so focused on his personal safety that he refrains from saying what, I believe, is in your best interests. [17] In my opinion, then, there are two campaigns you should undertake in these circumstances. First, you should save the Olynthians' towns for them and despatch troops for this purpose; second, you should have the fleet and another army ravage Philip's territory. Failure to launch either one of these expeditions will, I fear, make the entire effort a waste of time. [18] I mean, if you only ravage his territory, he'll sit it out until he's reduced Olynthus, and then it will be easy for him to go and defend his homeland. And if you send just the expedition to Olynthus, he'll maintain a close siege and

keep the situation locked up tight, seeing that there's no risk to his homeland, and eventually he'll prevail over the besieged inhabitants. In other words, the action you take must be adequate and twofold.

[19] So much for my view about what steps to take. As for finances, you do have money, Athenians, more than anyone else. I'm referring to the funds you appropriate as you want.* The money could be used for paying troops; there's enough for that. Otherwise, you don't have enough or rather, you don't have anything at all. 'So are you actually proposing that these funds should be used for military purposes?'* Good heavens, no! [20] But I do believe that troops should be made ready, that there should be a military fund, and that there should be a single system whereby men are paid in return for service.* You, however, prefer the status quo, and believe that these funds should be readily available for you to use for festivals. In that case, the only remaining option, as far as I can see, is for everyone to pay a war levy—a heavy one if we need a great deal of money, a light one if we need little. But we do need money; without it, it will be impossible for us to meet even one of our obligations. Various further proposals have been tabled for how to raise money, and it's up to you to choose the one that seems best. Please address the matter while there's still time.

[21] It's worth bearing in mind and considering Philip's situation at the moment. Despite appearances, and whatever a careless observer might say, he is ill prepared and his situation is not particularly good. He'd never have embarked on this war if he had thought that he'd actually have to fight. He was hoping at the time that he would carry all before him at his first approach, but he has been proved wrong. This disappointment has rattled him and severely dented his confidence, and then there are the Thessalians as well. [22] As you know, untrustworthiness is their national characteristic; no one has ever been able to rely on them. Philip is simply finding them now to be exactly as they've always been in the past. They've officially resolved to demand the restitution of Pagasae, and they've stopped him fortifying Magnesia.* I've even heard it said that they would like to deprive him even of the revenue from their harbours and markets, on the grounds that they need this money to administer Thessaly, and that it's not Philip's to take. But if he loses this source of income, he'll be extremely hard pressed to maintain his mercenaries.

[23] Furthermore, we are bound to believe that the average Paeonian and Illyrian—well, absolutely all of them, in fact—would

prefer self-determination and freedom to slavery. They aren't used to subservience, and Philip is a hard master. That's what people say and there's surely no reason for us to doubt it. After all, when foolish people meet with undeserved success, it triggers folly in them; in many cases, this seems to make it harder for them to protect their assets than it was to acquire them. [24] So I'd like you, Athenians, to see his difficulty as your opportunity. You should be ready to play your part by sending embassies as necessary, by taking to the field yourselves, and by urging everyone else to do likewise. Look at it this way. If Philip were granted the same kind of opportunity against you—if we were involved in war with our neighbours—do you think he'd hesitate to attack you? Doesn't it embarrass you, then, to shrink from doing to him, now that you have the chance, exactly what he would do to you if he could?

[25] One more thing, Athenians. Don't forget that you are currently faced with a choice between fighting him there or having him fight you here.* If the Olynthians hold out, you'll fight there and it will be his territory that suffers, while you remain secure in the enjoyment of the land you hold and call home. But if Olynthus falls to Philip, who will stop him coming here? [26] The Thebans? This may be a very harsh thing to say, but they won't hesitate to make it a joint invasion. What about the Phocians, then? But they can't even protect their own homeland without your help. Anyone else? 'But he won't want to attack us, my friend.' I disagree. It would make no sense at all for him to turn down the chance to carry out the threats he's been called a madman for blurting out in the first place.

[27] Well, I'm sure I don't need to tell you the great difference between fighting here and fighting there. Suppose you had to be abroad for no more than thirty days: if you took with you from the countryside (which I'm assuming to be free of hostile forces) everything you needed for camp life for this period of time, I'm sure that the losses incurred by those of you who are farmers would be more severe than for the entire previous war.* But if war came here, think of the scale of the losses then. And that's not taking into account the ignominy and disgrace, which are just as damaging if you look at things right.

[28] Bear all this in mind, please, all of you, and then take to the field and drive the war north. To those of you who are well off, I say it won't cost you much to protect the great wealth your good

fortune has brought you, and then you'll be able to enjoy all that's left in perfect security. As for those of you who are of military age, the experience of warfare in Philip's territory will make you formidable guardians of the homeland you'll have kept from harm. And politicians will meet with no difficulties when they come to be audited for their actions while in office, in the sense that you will judge their conduct in the light of how your affairs stand. I pray, then, for a good result for everyone!

2. SECOND OLYNTHIAC

[1] As I see it, Athenians, the current situation is a good example of the kindness the gods often display towards the city. People have emerged who are prepared to fight Philip; their land borders his and they are not without military strength; and, most importantly, they are so committed to war that they don't just see peace with him as risky, but regard it as the ruin of their country. Is there any aspect of this that does *not* seem out of the ordinary, and suggest the favour of the gods? [2] Our job now, therefore, Athenians, is to make sure that we aren't found to have treated ourselves less well than circumstances have treated us. After all, it would be disgraceful—an utter disgrace, I should say—if we were to betray not only cities and places that were once under our sway,* but also the allies and opportunities afforded us by Fortune.

[3] It would be a mistake, I think, Athenians, to list Philip's strengths as a way of impressing upon you how important it is that you do your duty. Why? Because I think it would be a catalogue of his successes and our blunders. Admiration increases for him in all quarters, precisely because he has accomplished more than he deserves; but your mishandling of matters has brought shame upon the city. [4] Anyway, I won't go into that, because objective enquiry would reveal that he gets his strength from us, not from himself. I don't see this as an occasion to talk about how Philip should feel grateful to those politicians who have been doing his job for him, and how you should be punishing them. But there are other facts available, which all of you really should be acquainted with, and which, seen in the proper light, Athenians, would redound greatly to *his* discredit. These facts are what I shall try to talk about.

[5] To describe him as an untrustworthy liar without providing evidence might well be regarded as empty abuse. But as a matter of fact it will take hardly any time to go through everything he has ever done and prove his falseness in every case. Besides, the exercise is worthwhile for two reasons, I think. First, it will reveal him in his true colours as a crook; second, those who have been panicked into the belief that Philip is somehow invincible will be able to see that he has already exhausted every trick that enabled him earlier to gain strength, and that from here on his career can only decline.

[6] I myself, Athenians, would certainly regard Philip as an object of awe and admiration if I saw that he had grown great by honest means. But in fact, if I stop to think about it, I find that originally, when the Olynthians were wanting to negotiate with us, and some of our politicians were trying to drive them away, he won us over in our stupidity by saying that he would surrender Amphipolis and by fabricating that famous open secret.* [7] Then, in an act of aggression against former allies, he gained the friendship of the Olynthians by taking Potidaea, one of your possessions, and handing it over to them. Finally, he recently won over the Thessalians by promising to give them Magnesia and by undertaking to fight the Phocian War on their behalf.* In short, he has duped everyone he has had dealings with. Every time he came across someone who didn't know what he was like, he deceived him and added him to his alliance, and that's how he became strong.

[8] Just as he used deceit to gain power, when everyone imagined that he was going to act in *their* interests, so this same deceitfulness is bound to be the means by which he is brought low again, now that he has been exposed as nothing but a *self*-interested agent. This is the critical situation Philip finds himself in, Athenians. If I'm wrong, let someone step up and prove it to me, or rather to you. He would have to argue either that people who have once been lied to will still be trusting in the future, or that people who have been ignominiously enslaved won't welcome their freedom.

[9] Now, someone here might basically agree with me, but still think that Philip will be strong enough to maintain his position, because of all the strongholds and harbours and so on he has already taken. But this is a mistake. I mean, when a coalition is sustained by mutual loyalty, and the interests of everyone taking part in the war coincide, people are prepared to share the hardships, suffer the setbacks, and

still remain firm. But when, as in Philip's case, a man has been raised to power by greed and underhand dealings, the slightest pretext, the merest stumble, is enough to make the whole thing crumble and collapse. [10] It's impossible, Athenians—impossible, I say—for a crooked cheat and liar to gain enduring power. Power gained by such means lasts for an instant, a brief span. It may bloom vigorously in the soil of others' hopes, but in time it is seen for what it is and it withers away. Just as the lowest parts of houses, ships, and so on have to be strongest, so every action should be founded on and motivated by truth and honesty. But these qualities are completely absent from Philip's conduct.

[11] We must help the Olynthians. That is my view, and the more efficiently and rapidly we deliver that help, the more I approve. And we should send an embassy to the Thessalians, partly to explain what we're up to, and partly to stir them to action, since they've now officially resolved to demand the restitution of Pagasae, and to negotiate about Magnesia.* [12] But you must make sure, Athenians, that the ambassadors you send don't just make speeches. They should also be in a position to point to something concrete that you've achieved as a result of having taken to the field in a manner worthy of Athens—as a result of being actively involved. Speech without action is always empty and meaningless, but especially when it comes from Athenians. Our words are more likely to be distrusted in all quarters, precisely because we're famous for our exceptional facility with speech.

[13] You must prove yourselves changed and reformed, then; you must pay a war levy, take to the field, and do everything without dragging your heels, if anyone is to take you seriously. If you're prepared to move matters forward as you should, not only, Athenians, will the fragile and unsound state of Philip's coalition be revealed, but the weakness of his rule and authority at home will also be exposed.

[14] Generally speaking, the strength and dominance of Macedon have no more than a supplementary role to play in events. As such, they may make quite a difference, as they did, for instance, in supporting you in Timotheus' time against Olynthus. Then again, joint action with Macedon turned out well for the Olynthians in their dispute with Potidaea; and it did for the Thessalians too, not long ago, when their struggle against the tyrant house was endangered by dissension and disarray.* But of course the addition of even a small force is always helpful, even if on its own it is weak and riddled with

deficiencies. [15] And the fact is that all those wars and campaigns of his—the foundation of his power, one might think—have worked against him by making Macedon less secure than it needs to be. For it would be wrong to suppose, Athenians, that Philip and his subjects have the same likes and dislikes. His goal, his desire, is glory. He has decided to accept the consequences, come what may, of a life of action and danger. He has rejected a risk-free life in favour of the glory of achieving what no other Macedonian king has ever achieved.* [16] But his subjects gain none of the credit that his actions bring. Worn out by his constant campaigning here and there, their lives are filled with pain and misery. They're allowed no time for their own businesses and affairs; with the local ports closed by the war, they can't even dispose of any goods they are somehow able to produce.

[17] It's not hard to infer from this how most Macedonians feel about Philip. It's true that his mercenaries and the Foot Companions* have the reputation of being excellent, battle-hardened troops, but I was told by someone who had visited the country, a man whose honesty is completely beyond question, that they are no better than the next man. [18] The point is, my informant told me, Philip's lust for glory is such that he always keeps any of his men who are skilled campaigners and fighters at a distance, because—one of his many flaws being monstrous ambition—he wants to take the credit for every achievement himself. At the same time, any of his men who are fundamentally decent and honest cannot abide Philip's daily wantonness, drunkenness, and obscene cavorting, and find themselves marginalized and scorned. [19] All the rest of his entourage, my informant said, are brigands, flatterers, and the kind who get drunk and indulge in dances whose very names I refuse to mention today in your presence.*

There can be no doubt that he was telling the truth. The people Philip welcomes and keeps by his side are those who used to be driven by common consent out of our city for outdoing street entertainers in their obscenity—men like that public slave Callias,* and others of his ilk: actors in low comedies, composers of disgusting songs that raise laughter by degrading one's companions. [20] For all their apparent triviality, Athenians, intelligent people will find these cases significant as indicating the delusional cast of his mind. The trouble is, of course, that his achievements make this harder to discern. Success is good at disguising defects, but the truth about him will be revealed as soon as he suffers the slightest setback. And my feeling, Athenians, is that it won't take long for the truth to emerge, if the gods will it and you want it. [21] A medical analogy might help. As long as a person is well, he feels nothing; it's only when he falls ill that things start to ache—fractures or sprains, or some other pre-existing unsoundness. Something similar goes for states and tyrants: as long as they're fighting away from home, their weaknesses aren't apparent to most people, but when they become involved in war with a neighbour, all is revealed.

[22] Is there anyone here who sees Philip's luck as the reason he's so formidable an opponent? That's sound and sensible thinking. In human life Fortune is indeed a powerful—no, a decisive force. All the same, if I had to choose, I'd prefer our city's Fortune to his, as long as you, for your part, are prepared to do even a fraction of your duty. I mean, I see far more reasons for the gods to look benevolently on us than on him. [23] But we sit here doing nothing, and a lazy man can't ask even his friends to act on his behalf, let alone the gods. So it's hardly surprising that Philip, with all his campaigning, his hard work, his personal presence at every endeavour, and his exploitation of every opportunity and season, is getting the better of us, with our delaying, deliberating, and information-gathering. That's not what surprises me. The opposite would be surprising—if we proved superior to him, even though we're doing none of the things people at war are supposed to do and he's doing them all.

[24] No, what I find surprising, Athenians, is this. In the past you defended the rights of the Greeks against the Spartans.* There were many occasions when you could have gained considerable personal advantages, but you refused them. In order to secure justice for everyone else, you paid war levies that drained your coffers and you bore the brunt of the fighting, but now you hesitate to take to the field and you postpone the introduction of a war levy. Your own possessions are at stake. Often in the past you've saved everyone else—either all at once or one after another—yet now you placidly endure the loss of your own property. [25] That's what puzzles me.

There's another thing too. Why is it, Athenians, that none of you is capable of seeing how long you've been at war with Philip, and what you've been doing all that time? You must surely be aware that you've spent the entire period putting things off, waiting for others to act, blaming one another, taking one another to court, and resorting once again to wishful thinking. In other words, much the same as what you're doing now. [26] Are you so misguided, then, Athenians, that you expect our situation to change from bad to good by applying the same policies which made it bad in the first place? That's not just illogical; it flies in the face of nature. It's a natural law that keeping something is far easier than getting it in the first place, but now the war has left none of our former possessions in our keeping, so we must get them back. That's the immediate task before us, and it's one we must undertake ourselves.

[27] My recommendations are as follows. You must pay a war levy. You must take to the field in person and with determination. You must avoid blaming anyone until you have the situation under control; only then should you honour those who deserve commendation and punish the wrongdoers, letting the facts guide your verdicts. You must banish excuses and rid yourselves of your failings, because there's no way you can criticize others' conduct unless you're first doing your duty yourselves.

[28] I mean, why, Athenians—to inject a little reality into our discussion of the generals—why do you think that all the generals you've put in command of expeditionary forces avoid this war and find their own private wars instead? It's because, in the war against Philip, the officers run all the risks for no reward. Any prizes to be won are yours; for instance, if Amphipolis falls, it's you who will immediately take it over. In their own private wars, however, there's less danger and the profits go to the officers and men—Lampsacus, Sigeum, the shipping they capture.* Everyone always goes where it pays them to go. [29] But you—first you notice how bad things are and take the generals to court; then you listen to the defence they use at the hearing, that they had no choice, and acquit them! The upshot is that you quarrel and fall out among yourselves, with different factions convinced of different points of view, and meanwhile the state suffers.

In days gone by, Athenians, the practice of syndication* was introduced to pay the war levies, but now syndication rules our political life. Each faction has a politician at its head, a general as his subordinate, and some of the Three Hundred as hecklers. All the rest of us are assigned to this or that faction. [30] I'd like to see an end to this. Even now, you must take responsibility for yourselves and see that everyone equally has a share in deliberation, speech-making, and action. If you let one section of society lord it over you like tyrants, while the members of another group are compelled to be trierarchs, to pay war levies, and to serve in the army, and a third group has nothing to do except sit in judgement on the rest, nothing that needs to be done will get done on time. Whichever section of society is currently feeling aggrieved will let you down, and then you'll be busy punishing them instead of your enemies.

[31] To sum up, I urge *everyone* to pay a war levy, each according to his means. I urge you to take to the field in rotation, until *everyone* has served. And I urge you to allow *everyone* who steps up a chance to speak, and to choose the best recommendations from those you hear, rather than favouring what one or another particular person says. If you do this, you'll find yourselves thanking the speaker straight away, and yourselves later, when your general situation improves.

3. THIRD OLYNTHIAC

[1] The thoughts that occur to me when I consider our situation, Athenians, are very different from those suggested by the speeches I've been listening to. Punishing Philip is the express theme of the speeches that are being delivered, but our situation has got so bad that we need to make sure we don't first come to harm ourselves. The only way I can describe the mistake these speech-makers seem to me to be making is that they're offering you an illusory subject for deliberation. [2] Speaking for myself, I'm perfectly well aware that there was a time when we could have safely held on to our possessions *and* punished Philip. Not long ago, within my own lifetime, we could have done both these things. But I'm convinced that now our first step should be to make sure that our allies survive. Once this has been secured, it will then be possible for us also to think about who is to be punished and how. But until we've made a proper beginning, I can't see the slightest point in discussing the end.

[3] If ever there was an occasion that demanded considerable and careful deliberation, this is it. It's not that I think it particularly hard to know *what* advice to offer under the circumstances. No, the only thing I'm uncertain of, Athenians, is *how* to express what I want to say to you. What I've seen and heard here today has led me to conclude that our objectives have slipped from our grasp not so much because we don't know what we should be doing, but because of a reluctance

to do it. I ask you, then, to bear with me if I speak candidly, and to consider only whether I'm telling the truth, and whether my intention is to secure a better future for us. For you can see that the reason our situation has got so utterly wretched is that some of our politicians are concerned only with saying what they think you want to hear.

[4] It's essential, I think, for me first to remind you a bit of the past. You remember, Athenians, when you heard—it was three or four years ago—that Philip was in Thrace and had Heraeum Fortress* under siege. It was Maemacterion* at the time. After all the speeches and uproar in the Assembly you formally resolved to launch forty triremes, to conscript crews from those under the age of forty-five, and to raise sixty talents by means of a war levy. [5] That year went by, and then it was Hecatombaeon . . . Metageitnion . . . Boedromion. At last, during Boedromion, after the Mysteries,* you unenthusiastically despatched ten unmanned ships under Charidemus, and five talents of money. For after receiving the news that Philip was ill or dead (both rumours reached us), you decided that the crisis for which you needed to despatch troops had passed, and you abandoned the expedition, Athenians. But that was the perfect opportunity. If we had wholeheartedly taken to the field then, as we had resolved to do, Philip would not have survived to trouble us now.

[6] Well, what's done can't be undone. But now another war is upon us, and that's why I've brought up the past. I don't want to see the same thing happen again. So what use shall we make of the present opportunity, Athenians? If you don't take to the field with all the strength you can muster, don't you think your whole approach to the war will have played into Philip's hands? [7] The Olynthians were, at the beginning, not without military strength, and the situation was such that neither they nor Philip could feel confident of winning. We made peace with the Olynthians and they with us. This—that a major city, an Athenian ally, was lying in wait for any opportunity he might provide—inconvenienced Philip and more or less stopped him in his tracks.

We regarded it as of critical importance that they were set at odds with Philip. That's what everyone kept going on about, and now it's fortuitously happened. [8] What else can we do, then, Athenians, but send help, wholeheartedly and in strength? As far as I can see, we don't have a choice. It's not just a matter of the disgrace we'd incur if we betrayed our interests. It would also be dangerous, Athenians.

I can see the consequences being pretty alarming, given the Thebans' attitude towards us, the Phocians' now-parlous financial state, and the fact that there's nothing to stop Philip turning his attention here once he's finished crushing his current opponents.* [9] So delaying doing your duty until then amounts to wanting to see danger at your door when you could hear about it elsewhere. It amounts to seeking help when at the moment you could supply it. After all, surely there can hardly be any doubt that this is how matters will end if we pass up the present opportunities.

[10] 'But we all recognize the importance of sending help,' some-one might say in response, 'and we shall do so. Just tell us how.' Now, don't be taken aback, Athenians, if what I say strikes most of you as odd. Appoint legislators. But don't let them use their sessions for *making* any laws: you already have enough. Have them, instead, get rid of the laws that are currently harming you. [11] Not to beat about the bush, I'm talking about the laws governing the Theoric Fund, and some of those governing military service.* The former distribute military funds as theatre-money to those who stay at home, while the latter give immunity to those who shirk military service and so dis-courage people who do have a sense of duty. Once you've got rid of these laws—that is, once you've made it safe for people to offer the best advice—then find someone who will propose what you all know to be the right course. [12] But until you've done that, don't bother to look for someone to offer advice that's in your best interests and risk ruin-ation at your hands. You won't find any such person, above all because there's only one likely outcome: it will be a miscarriage of justice, but anyone making such speeches and proposals will suffer. And so far from having improved the situation, he will in fact have made it even more dangerous in the future than it is now to offer the best advice.

Yes, and moreover, Athenians, you must get the original authors of the laws to repeal them.* [13] After all, it's wrong for them to garner the popularity of a law that has been harming the entire population, while the one whose advice is sound is penalized by unpopularity, when his proposals would improve everyone's lot. Until you've set this right, Athenians, it will be unrealistic of you to expect to find anyone in Athens strong enough to break these laws with impunity, or stupid enough to commit himself to certain ruin.

[14] There's something else I'd like you to appreciate, Athenians. A decree is worthless unless it's accompanied by a willingness on

your part to implement its provisions without dragging your heels. If decrees were self-sufficient—if by themselves they either compelled you to do your duty or accomplished their own agendas—you wouldn't be in the position of passing many decrees but acting on few if any of them, and Philip wouldn't have lorded it over you for so long either. If decrees were all it took, he'd have been punished ages ago. [15] But that's not how things work. Speaking and decision-making may precede action, but in terms of effectiveness and importance action comes first. All that's missing, then, is action. Everything else is already in place, in that there are people here with the competence to tell you what you need to do, Athenians, and there's no one in the world quicker than you at judging such proposals. And, if you do the right thing, you'll be in a position to act now.

[16] What, after all, are you waiting for, Athenians? Are you expecting to find a better opportunity than the present? When are you going to do what has to be done, if not now? Hasn't the fellow already taken over all our strongholds? What about the absolute disgrace we should suffer if he gains Olynthus too? Aren't the very people we promised to protect without demur in the event of war now at war? Isn't he our enemy? Aren't our possessions in his hands? Isn't he a barbarian?* Isn't he . . . *whatever* one might call him? [17] By the gods, after letting him take all these places—after practically handing them to him on a plate—are we going to look for people to blame? I'm quite certain that we won't hold ourselves responsible. No one who flees from battle blames himself; he blames the general or the next man— anyone, rather than himself—despite the fact that the defeat was, of course, due to *everyone* who ran away. For the soldier who's blaming others could have stood his ground, and if everyone had done that, they'd have won.

[18] So, now, if A's advice is unacceptable, let B stand up and speak, but without blaming the first speaker. If B's advice is better, act on it, and may Fortune smile on you! If the advice is unpleasant, that's not the speaker's fault, unless he omits the requisite prayers. Prayers are easy, though, Athenians; it's not hard to bundle together all one's desires in a few words. But making a decision when a matter of practical policy is on the agenda—that's nowhere near as easy. One has to choose the best course, not the pleasant one, if they're incompatible.

[19] 'What if someone finds a way to leave the Theoric Fund alone?' it might be asked. 'What if he points to other sources of military

funds? Wouldn't he carry the day?' I don't deny it, Athenians—*if*
such a thing is possible. But I wonder if it ever has been or ever
will be possible for a man first to spend what he has on trifles and
still have enough in his depleted coffers to spend on necessities.
No, the only substance that proposals like this have is given to them
by people's desires. That's why there's nothing easier than self-
deception: opinions are always formed by desires, but the real world
is rarely so accommodating. [20] What I'd like you to do, Athenians,
is face reality, and consider what you need to do to be able to take to
the field and be paid for it. People who are prudent and principled
don't find themselves neglecting any of their military functions due
to financial hardship and putting up with the consequent criticism.
Nor do they snatch up arms and march against the Corinthians and
Megarians,* while being prevented by lack of money for the troops
from stopping Philip enslaving Greek cities.

[21] Now, these words of mine have not been chosen for the idle
purpose of making myself unpopular in certain quarters. I'm not so
foolish or misguided as to want to be disliked when there's nothing to
be gained by it. No, but I do regard it as the mark of an honest citizen
to value the security of the state over his popularity as a politician. I'm
told, as you presumably are too, that this was typically the way politics
was practised by Athenian statesmen of the past. I'm talking about
the great Aristeides, Nicias, my namesake,* Pericles—the statesmen
every speaker in this Assembly praises and utterly fails to emulate.
[22] But politicians nowadays do nothing but ask you 'What do you
want? What shall I propose? What is your pleasure?', and ever since
they've been doing that, the interests of the city have been frittered
away on momentary gratification, and the upshot is that while everything's all right for them, it's all wrong for you. [23] But suppose one
had to summarize our past achievements and our present ones. What
would the headlines be, do you think, Athenians? My account will be
short and familiar to you, because you don't have to look abroad for
exemplary men to imitate. Athenian paradigms will bring you success.

[24] Our forefathers, then, who, unlike you, were not flattered
and pampered by their politicians, won the willing obedience of the
Greeks for forty-five years. They banked more than ten thousand
talents on the Acropolis.* The Macedonian king was their subject, as
a barbarian should be of Greeks. They erected many glorious trophies
as a result of the battles they fought in person on land and at sea.

Their achievements were such that they are the only people in history who have left behind a reputation that is proof against envy.

[25] That was their position in the wider Greek world. What about at home, in their domestic affairs, public and private? In the public sphere, they gave us buildings and artefacts—temples and the dedications they contain—of such quality and grandeur that no one subsequently has been able to come close. In the private sphere, they were so moderate and so passionately democratic [26] that their houses were no grander than the next man's. If any of you actually knows the kind of houses the celebrities of the time had, men such as Aristeides and Miltiades, you can confirm this. For them, you see, politics wasn't a way of lining their own pockets; each of them just wanted to see Athens flourish. They were trustworthy in their dealings with the Greeks, carried out their religious obligations, and treated one another as equals: hence, not surprisingly, their remarkable success.

[27] That's how matters stood in the days of our forefathers, under the leaders I mentioned. But what are things like now, thanks to the worthy statesmen of today? Is there any similarity at all? Under them—well, of the many things I could mention, I'll say only this. Everyone here recognizes that we had a perfectly clear field. The Spartans were destroyed, the Thebans were otherwise engaged, and there was no one else capable of challenging us for first prize. We were in a position not only to hold securely on to our own possessions, but to arbitrate others' claims. [28] But now we've lost our own territory; we've spent over fifteen hundred talents on trifles; we've lost in peacetime the alliances we gained during the war;* and we've trained up a formidable foe for ourselves. If anyone thinks I'm wrong, let him step up here and tell me how Philip became strong, if it wasn't our own doing.

[29] 'But listen, my friend. We might be badly off in terms of the wider world, but in the city itself things have improved.' But where's the evidence for this claim? The battlements we're whitewashing, the roads we're repairing, the fountain-houses and the follies? Look at the men whose policies led to these 'improvements'. Some of them have exchanged poverty for wealth, or obscurity for distinction; others have had houses built for themselves that are grander than our public buildings. The more the city's fortunes have declined, the more theirs have increased.

[30] How did all this come about? Why are things in such a mess now, when they were fine in the past? Because in those days the people had the courage to see to their own business and carry out their military duties themselves, and so politicians were their servants. Benefits were in the hands of the people themselves, and every politician was content to receive from them his share of honour or authority or whatever. [31] Nowadays, though, it's the other way around. Benefits are controlled by the politicians and they are responsible for all business. You, the people, have been emasculated and stripped of funds and allies; you have become servants, extras, content if the politicians give you a portion of the Theoric Fund or arrange a parade for the Boedromia.* The most manly action you can muster is when you thank them for what is already yours. Meanwhile, they pen you in the city and offer you these treats as a way of making you tame enough to feed from their hands. [32] But then, it's impossible, of course, for people who are taken up with mean and paltry matters to acquire a noble and vigorous cast of mind. Men's characters are determined by their occupations.

By Demeter, I shouldn't be surprised if I suffered more at your hands for this speech than the original instigators for their actions. There are some things one cannot say freely here in the Assembly; in fact, I'm surprised I've got away with it today.

[33] So, if you were prepared even at this late date to change your ways—to do your military duty and act like true Athenians—and if you used your domestic surpluses to help improve your situation abroad, then perhaps—just perhaps, Athenians—you might gain some decisive and substantial benefit. You'll have lost those hand-outs, of course. They remind me of the diets doctors prescribe, which neither make the patient strong nor allow him to die; in the same way, the 'benefits' you receive are neither large enough to make a lasting difference, nor so small that you can refuse them and get on with something else. All they do is increase the apathy of each and every one of you.

[34] Am I talking about paid service? Yes, Athenians, and I also recommend the immediate adoption of a single, universal system, which will allow each man to receive his share of the common funds and to serve in whatever capacity the state requires.* If war can be avoided, he's better off at home, where he's no longer driven by poverty to demeaning work. If there's a crisis on, like now, it's better for him

to serve in person as he should, in defence of his country, with his service paid for by these funds. If his age exempts him from military service, let him oversee and manage everything that needs to be done, and receive, from within the same system, what he currently gets unsystematically and without performing a useful function. [35] In short, without increasing or decreasing costs, or hardly at all, I would do away with the current chaos and introduce systematic order to the state's finances. There would be a single system for handouts, for military service, for jury service, and for everyone who did whatever he could, depending on his age and the demands of the situation.

Note that I'm not for a moment suggesting that we should be giving the indolent money owed to the active. Nor have I said that we should ourselves remain idle, passive, and hesitant, while hearing of the successes of our mercenaries under so-and-so's leadership, which is what happens at the moment. [36] I'm not, of course, criticizing anyone who takes on any of your duties for you, but I am urging you to do by yourselves what you respect others for doing, and not to surrender the position of honour, bequeathed to you by your forefathers, who won it by many a glorious struggle.

I've said pretty much what needed to be said. It's up to you now to choose the course that will best serve the interests of Athens and everyone.

4. FIRST PHILIPPIC

The title 'Philippics' is given to four speeches (numbers 4, 6, 9, and 10 in modern editions) delivered by Demosthenes in the Assembly.[1] Though Philip had been encroaching on Athens' interests in the north from his capture of Amphipolis in 357, Macedonian kingship was notoriously precarious and there was some reason to hope that Philip would be added to the list of powers which had sought, but failed, to carve out a large sphere of influence in the highly unstable early decades of the fourth century. But by the late 350s it was becoming clear to many, including Demosthenes, that Philip was a different kind of Macedonian ruler and that his ambitions extended far beyond control of regions adjacent to Macedonia. The speech is dated by Dionysius of Halicarnassus (writing towards the end of the first century BC) to the year 352/1; if so, it must have been late in this year (see the first note on 4.17). The immediate occasion for the speech is unclear. There is no sense of crisis and the background seems to be simply the relentless activity of Philip in areas, especially the Chersonese, where Athens had interests.

_____

[1] If the topic before us today were unfamiliar, Athenians, I wouldn't have spoken until most of the usual speakers had given their views.* Then, if any of their suggestions had met with my approval, I'd have kept quiet, and otherwise I'd have tried at that point to say what I think. But in fact the issue is one they've often addressed in the past, and so, even though I am the first to get to his feet, I think I may reasonably crave your indulgence. After all, if their past advice had been sound, you wouldn't have to be debating the matter again today.

[2] The first thing I want to say, Athenians, is that there's no need for gloom at the current situation, however bad it seems. In fact, the worst aspect of the past is precisely what should give us the most hope for the future. What do I mean? The situation is bad, Athenians, because of your complete failure to do your duty. There'd be no hope

---

[1] The fourth of these has been viewed by some moderns as spurious in whole or in part. Ancient scholars used the title 'Philippic' more widely to designate the first eleven speeches in our corpus, though by the third century AD the term 'Olynthiac' was also in use to distinguish (what we too call) the three Olynthiac speeches.

of improvement only if it had got like that when you *were* doing all you should.

[3] Next, you should recall something you already know, from hearsay if not from personal experience. Not long ago, when the Spartans were at the height of their power, the nobility and sense of duty with which you behaved were exactly what one would expect of Athenians.* You endured war against Sparta to see justice done. Why bring this up? Because I want you to see and appreciate, Athenians, that just as nothing is alarming when you're careful, so nothing goes according to plan when you're remiss. Think of how you overcame Sparta, for all its might, because you gave the matter your best attention; then think of Philip, whose insolent aggression alarms us now because of our failure to have taken the slightest interest in doing our duty.

[4] Some of you may be thinking, Athenians, that Philip is bound to make a difficult foe, considering how powerful he is at the moment and the loss of all our strongholds. You'd be right, but look at it this way. There was a time, Athenians, when we held as our own possessions Pydna, Potidaea, Methone, and the whole of the region in question. Many of the peoples who are currently on his side were free and self-governing, and preferred to be on good terms with us than with him.* [5] Now, suppose that back then Philip had decided that Athens would make a formidable foe, given that we commanded his territory with so many fortresses and that he had no allies. If he'd thought like that, he'd never have embarked on the course he's been pursuing; he'd never have got so strong. But he clearly saw all those places as available war prizes, Athenians. He understood that the possessions of the absent naturally belong to those who are present, and that the possessions of the careless belong to those who are prepared to work and take chances.

[6] All his conquests and takeovers, then, have been direct results of this attitude of his. Some places he captured by normal military means, while with others he entered into treaties of alliance and friendship. For everyone freely gives their friendship and respect to those who show themselves ready and willing to do all that needs to be done. [7] The same goes for you too, Athenians. If you resolve to adopt this attitude now, since you didn't earlier; if to a man you stop prevaricating and serve the state as you ought, without demur and to the best of your abilities—the rich by paying the war levies,* and those of military age by serving; if, to put it plainly and simply, you resolve to take responsibility for yourselves and you stop, each

of you, hoping to do nothing while his neighbour does it all for him; then, the gods willing, you'll recover your own possessions, regain what your apathy has lost you, and punish Philip.

[8] Philip is no god: you shouldn't think that what he has at the moment is his immutably and for ever. He's vulnerable to fear and loathing, Athenians, and to envy, even from those who seem to be especially close to him. There's no reason to think that the people around him aren't liable to all the feelings that are found in other men. But at the moment all such feelings are being repressed because your tardiness and apathy have left them no outlet. Listen to me: you must shed this indifference *now*. [9] I mean, you can see what's happened, Athenians: the man has become brutally aggressive. He's not even leaving you a choice, to act or not to act. He issues ultimatums couched, I hear, in the most arrogant language. He's incapable of remaining content with the conquests he's already made: he's always surrounding himself with fresh acquisitions, hemming you in on all sides while you delay and sit idle.

[10] When will you do your duty, Athenians? When? What are you waiting for? Some emergency, I suppose. But what about what's happening right now? I always thought it was the mark of a free man to regard any situation that dishonoured him as an emergency. Or tell me, each of you: do you want to spend your lives asking one another for news? What could be more newsworthy than the fact that a man from Macedonia is doing well in a war against Athens and is directing Greek affairs? [11] 'Has Philip died?' 'No, by Zeus, but he's ill.'* But what difference does it make to you? Whatever happens to him, you'll soon create a second Philip if you remain as negligent as you are at the moment. Even this Philip owes his rise to your indifference rather than to his own strength. [12] And here's another thing. Suppose something were to happen to him; suppose Fortune, which always takes better care of us than we do of ourselves, were to do even this for us.* You must see that, if you were close at hand, you could intervene while conditions were chaotic and arrange things as you wished. At the moment, however, even if the opportunity presented itself, you would be incapable of gaining Amphipolis. You're nowhere near ready, either practically or mentally.

[13] I'll say no more about this. I'll assume that I've made my case and you've come to recognize the necessity of doing your duty willingly, all of you, without demur. But what kind of levy do I think

it would take to extricate us from our troubles? How large a force? Where's the money coming from? What's my thinking on how we can best and most quickly get ourselves into a general state of readiness? I'll tell you, but I have just one thing to ask of you first, Athenians. [14] Don't be too quick off the mark. Listen to all I have to say, and then make up your minds. And if I seem to be talking about a whole new military effort, don't think that I'm prevaricating. In any case, those who call for 'prompt and immediate action' are in danger of missing the point that despatching troops right now won't make the slightest difference to what's already happened. [15] No, what's needed is an explanation of what kind of levy—how large? how financed?—will be capable of staying the course until we've either negotiated an end to the war or got the better of our enemies. That's how we'll stay safe from harm in the future. Now, I think I'm capable of giving just such an explanation, though of course I won't stand in the way of anyone else's proposals. I'm making a big promise here, but the proof of the pudding lies in the eating. It's up to you to judge its worth.

[16] My first proposal, then, Athenians, is that you should get fifty triremes ready for service. My second is that you should resolve to man them and serve on them yourselves, when the time comes. In the third place, I urge you to organize horse-transports and enough other vessels for half the cavalry.* [17] The importance of these measures, as I see it, is that they will enable us to combat these sudden sorties that Philip is currently making from his homeland at whim against places such as Thermopylae, the Chersonese, and Olynthus.* We must make him realize that you just might pull yourselves out of the slough of indifference and get moving, as you did when you went to Euboea, Haliartus (or so I hear: it was some time ago), and, not to prolong the list, Thermopylae, just the other day.*

[18] Even if you don't actually stir from Athens, these proposals of mine are not unimportant. When he sees that you're well prepared—and he'll receive accurate information, because there are people here in Athens, too many of them, who tell him everything—either he'll be cowed into inactivity, or, if he ignores what's going on, we'll catch him napping, since there'll be nothing to stop us sailing against his homeland whenever he gives us the chance.

[19] These are the measures that should, in my opinion, meet with your unanimous approval; these are the practical steps that I think should be taken. But first, Athenians, I strongly recommend that you

put together a force to fight him unceasingly,* to be a constant thorn in his side. I'm not talking about ten thousand or twenty thousand mercenaries. I'll have none of such paper armies. No, the force I'm thinking of will be Athenian, and it will be unswervingly obedient, whether you appoint a single general or more, and whichever particular individual or individuals get the job. And you must, of course, make provisions for its maintenance.

[20] But what kind of force will it be? How large? How supplied? How will we ensure that it does what it's supposed to do? I shall address each of these points separately.

Now, my position on mercenaries* . . . well, please try to avoid the mistake that has so often injured you in the past. You have a constant habit of overestimating what is required, and so you vote for the largest possible scheme, but then, when it comes to action, you fail to take even the smallest measures. No, you should scale down the measures you take and the money you provide, and then add more if it turns out to be too little. [21] I'm talking about a force of two thousand men in all, of whom five hundred should in my view be Athenians, drawn from whichever age-group you think appropriate. They should serve for a fixed term*—not a long one, but its length would be decided by you—and then the next batch of citizens should take their place. The rest of the force, I think, should be made up of mercenaries. The infantry should be supplemented by five hundred horse, of whom at least fifty should be Athenians, with the same conditions of service as the infantry.

[22] All right, then, what next? Ten swift warships. Given that Philip has a fleet, we need swift warships as well, to guarantee our expeditionary force safety at sea. How will these troops be provisioned? I'll tell you. I'll explain, but first let me say why I think such a small force will suffice, and why, in my opinion, Athenian citizens should serve. [23] The reason for the small size of the force, Athenians, is that we can no longer hope to come up with an army to meet him in pitched battle. At first, we must wage a guerrilla war. Our force shouldn't be bloated, then—we don't have any way to fund or provision a large body of men—but it shouldn't be insignificant either.

[24] To understand why I'm insisting on the presence and participation of Athenian citizens, we only have to look to the past. It's said that once upon a time Athens maintained a mercenary force in Corinth* (under the leadership of various generals, including

Polystratus, Iphicrates, and Chabrias) and you served alongside them. And it's said that this combined force of mercenaries and citizens, fighting side by side, used to defeat the Spartans.* But ever since your mercenaries began operating independently, they've been inflicting defeats on our friends and allies, while our enemies have become far too strong. After a casual glance at whatever war we're engaged in, off the mercenaries sail against Artabazus or someone—anyone rather than our enemies.* And the general follows, which is hardly surprising, given that it's impossible for him to command obedience without money for his men.

[25] What do I want, then? I'd like to see you make it impossible for either general or men to evade their responsibilities, by coming up with their pay and by having Athenians serve alongside them to supervise, so to speak, their conduct as soldiers. After all, the way we go about things at present is absurd. Suppose someone were to ask you: 'Is this a time of peace for you, Athenians?' 'Zeus, no,' would be the reply. 'Not for *us*. We're at war with Philip.' [26] But haven't you been electing, from the citizen body, ten taxiarchs, ten generals, ten phylarchs, and two hipparchs?* And what do they get up to? You send just one man out to the war, while the rest help the festival commissioners organize parades! Just like sculptors of terracotta figurines, you elect your officers for display in the Agora, not for military purposes. [27] But in the field, Athenians, shouldn't the infantry commanders be Athenian citizens? Shouldn't the hipparch be Athenian? Shouldn't the officers be our men, if the army is to be genuinely Athenian? Instead, you require your hipparch to sail to Lemnos,* while the cavalry commander responsible for defending Athenian possessions is Menelaus. I've got nothing against the man, but the holder of this commission should have been chosen by you.

[28] Now, it may be that you agree with what I've been saying, but would very much like to hear about the financial side: how much money is involved, and where's it coming from? I'll get on to that now. Here are the figures. For the maintenance of the force (rations alone), a little over ninety talents will be required, as follows:

For the ten swift warships: 40 talents, at 20 mnas per ship per month.
For 2,000 soldiers: 40 talents, each man receiving 10 drachmas a month in rations.
For the 200 cavalrymen: 12 talents, assuming 30 drachmas a month for each man.*

[29] It would be a mistake to see the provision of rations alone for the troops as a poor beginning. I'm absolutely certain that, with their rations in place, the war itself will provide the men with everything else. They'll be able to top their pay up to its full amount, without injuring any Greeks or allies of ours. If I'm wrong, I'm prepared to join the expedition as a volunteer myself, come what may.

Now, how to raise the money I'm asking you to find? I'll answer this straight away.

A budget statement is read out.

[30] This is what we've been able to come up with, Athenians. When you've made up your minds and it comes to a vote, vote for it, if you approve of it. Then you'll be fighting Philip not just with decrees and letters, but with practical measures too.

[31] I think you'll be in a much better position to think about the war and our arrangements in general, Athenians, if you consider the location of the land we're fighting against. You'll see that most of Philip's successes are due to the fact that the winds and the course of the seasons help him to pre-empt us. He waits for the etesian winds or winter,* and attacks when it's impossible for us to get there. [32] Since this is so, we must wage war not by sending out expeditionary forces (none of which would ever arrive in time), but by creating a permanent force, a standing army. There are islands up there we can use to quarter the troops in winter, such as Lemnos, Thasos, and Sciathos, with harbours and grain and everything an army needs. Then, in the summer, when there's no risk from the winds and no difficulty in maintaining a position offshore, it will be easy for our troops to hover just off his coastline, at the mouths of his ports.

[33] Anyway, the disposition of the troops and the timing of their activities will be decided on the spot by whoever you put in charge. What I've covered in my proposal is what has to come from you. Athenians, if you supply these troops—if you first find the money I've mentioned and then put together the full complement of infantry, triremes, and cavalry—they'll be under a legal obligation to stay where they are and persevere with the war. By making yourselves the treasurers and the dispensers of the funds, and by requiring the general to be answerable to you for his actions, you will no longer find yourselves caught in the vicious circle of debating the same issues over and over again.

[34] And that's not all, Athenians. Most importantly, you'll deprive Philip of his greatest source of income. What is that? Your own allies are the source he relies on to make war on you, since he plunders their shipping. And a further benefit is that he'll no longer be able to harm *you*, unlike when his raids on Lemnos and Imbros netted him Athenian citizens as prisoners of war, or when he captured your ships at Geraestus and stole an incalculable amount of money, or, finally, when he landed at Marathon and left your shores with the sacred trireme.* You were unable to stop these depredations and equally incapable, for all your good intentions, of getting help to these places on time.

[35] But why is it, Athenians, that the Panathenaea and the Dionysia are always celebrated at the right time, whether experts or amateurs are chosen to manage them? These festivals cost more money than any given expedition, and involve more fuss and preparation than anything else I can think of, and yet they take place on time, while every single one of your expeditions is late—to Methone, to Pagasae, to Potidaea.* What is the reason for this, do you think? [36] It's because every aspect of the festivals is regulated by law. Each of you knows well in advance which member of his tribe is going to be chorus-producer or gymnasiarch.* You know what these men have to do, when they're supposed to do it, what they are to receive, and where it's coming from. Everything is taken care of, every avenue explored, nothing left uncertain.

But when it comes to war and our preparations for it, nothing is regulated or revised, and everything is vague. That's why we wait for news, and then appoint trierarchs,* and then institute the exchange procedure, and then think about how to raise the money. After that, we decide to conscript metics and independent slaves*—but then decide on citizens, and then on proxies,* [37] and then, with all these delays, there's no longer any point to the expedition. We spend the time for action on preparation, and while we delay and prevaricate, the critical opportunities for action slip by. Meanwhile, the interim forces we think we have prove incapable of handling the crisis,* and Philip has the appalling insolence to send the Euboeans letters like this:

A letter of Philip to the Euboeans is read out.

[38] Most of this letter is true, Athenians—which it shouldn't be.* It does not, of course, make pleasant hearing. But complaisant

speech would be appropriate only if the things one might suppress, to avoid unpleasantness, were also suppressed in the real world. If, on the other hand, inappropriately honeyed speech actually injures us, it's our disgrace if we deceive ourselves, if we postpone uncomfortable issues and thereby miss every opportunity for action, [39] and if we prove incapable of learning even the simple lesson that to handle a war correctly we mustn't lag behind, but be ahead of the game. Just as a general is supposed to be at the head of his men, so decision-makers should be ahead of events; otherwise, their decisions can never be implemented and they are bound always to be following the trail of things that have already happened.

[40] No one, Athenians, can match your resources. You have triremes, hoplites, cavalry, and income, yet to this day you have never used them as you should. The way you fight Philip is exactly how barbarians box. In these contests, every time a boxer is hit, he claps his hands to the place struck, and if you hit him on the other side, there go his hands again. He lacks the skill or the instinct to put up his guard or look straight at his opponent. [41] The same goes for you too. If you hear that Philip's in the Chersonese, you vote to send troops there; if you hear he's at Thermopylae, that's where you send them. You chase him to and fro in response to news of his whereabouts. You are at his command. You've never made any strategic decisions on your own and for your own good, and you never look to the future until you hear that something has happened or is in the process of happening. You might have been able to get away with this before, but the situation is critical now, and evasion is no longer possible.

[42] It seems likely to me, Athenians, that one of the gods, embarrassed at our behaviour, implanted this restlessness in Philip. Had he been content with what he had already taken and won, and taken no further action, I think that would have satisfied some of you, even though it would have brought disgrace upon the city and earned us a reputation for cowardice and every other weakness in the book. In fact, though, his constant aggression and greed just might stir you to action, if you still have even a little spirit. [43] Speaking for myself, your utter lack of concern or anger amazes me, when I consider that a war which began with the aim of punishing Philip is ending, now, with the aim of avoiding ruin at his hands.

Now, he's not going to stop—that's clear—unless someone stops him. So should we wait around until that happens? Do you think that despatching triremes filled with nothing but the hopes some politician has raised makes everything all right? [44] Why don't we man the ships? Despite our failure to date, why don't we now despatch a force consisting in part, at least, of Athenian troops? Why don't we attack his territory? I hear the question: 'Where will our ships find anchorage?' The war itself, Athenians, will reveal his weak points, if we make the effort. But if we sit at home, listening to politicians slandering and criticizing one another, we'll never achieve anything important.

[45] It's my belief that whenever we despatch a levy that includes citizen soldiers, even if it's not wholly Athenian, both the gods and Fortune look favourably upon the enterprise and fight on our side. But whenever we despatch only a general, supported by a futile resolution and vain hopes, nothing important takes place. That kind of expedition is greeted with scorn by our enemies and mortal terror by our allies. [46] It's impossible, quite impossible, for one man ever to be able to fulfil all your desires. All he can do is make promises, give assurances, and criticize this or that colleague, and as a result our policies have come to nothing. What else could one expect from a general, when he's in command of miserable, unpaid mercenaries, when there are people here who don't hesitate to lie to you about his 'achievements', and when you vote at whim, on the strength of what you're told?

[47] How are we to put a stop to all of this? Only when you arrange things, Athenians, so that the same people serve as a commander's troops, as witnesses of his generalship, and, when they get home, as judges at his audit.* Then you'll not only *hear* how your affairs are going, but you'll be there in person to see it. But at the moment things have reached such a state that, while every general faces two or three trials for his life here in Athens, none of them has the courage to risk his life even once in battle. They'd rather die like slave-traders or robbers than as they ought. I mean, it's criminals who are sentenced to death in court; generals are supposed to die on the field of battle.

[48] Various rumours are making the rounds in Athens, with each of us busily inventing different things to say—that Philip is negotiating with the Spartans for the overthrow of Thebes, for instance, and intends to break up the free states;* or that his ambassadors are on their way to the Persian king; or that he's fortifying towns in Illyris. [49] Now, Athenians, I do believe—by the gods, yes—that Philip has become intoxicated by his stupendous achievements, and I believe

that, because he sees a clear field before him and has been fired up by his successes, he often dreams of further conquests. But, by Zeus, I absolutely cannot believe that he's choosing to act in such a way that the greatest fools in Athens can know what he intends to do. And there's no greater fool than a rumour-monger.

[50] But never mind all that. We have to focus on the facts, which are as follows. The man is our enemy; he's stealing from us and has been lording it over us for years; every time we hoped that someone would do something for us, we've come off badly; in the future, we can depend only on ourselves; and if we pass up the present opportunity to make war there, in all likelihood we'll be forced to do so here. Recognition of these facts will lead us to make the right decisions and to dismiss idle talk. After all, there's no need to wonder what the future will be like: you can be sure that it will be bad, unless you shed your apathy and willingly do your duty.

[51] In the past, I've never deliberately courted favour by recommending a course of action that I was not convinced was also good for you. Today is no different: I've spoken my mind fully, freely, and frankly, without keeping anything back. I know it's good for you to receive the best advice, but I can only hope that offering the best advice is also good for the adviser. If I were sure of that, I'd be a lot happier. Nevertheless, even though it's uncertain what the consequences will be for me, I have chosen to speak, because I'm convinced that it will be in your best interests to act on my proposals. May the policy adopted be the one that will benefit us all.

5. ON THE PEACE

This speech is dated by our ancient sources to 346 BC. Earlier in the year Athens had completed the Peace of Philocrates with Philip. The peace was unsatisfactory for Athens from the start. Philip had used the intervals between Athenian peace missions to mop up their ally, the Thracian king Cersobleptes. His resolution of the Third Sacred War, though more generous than it might have been (the Phocian cities were destroyed and the population resettled in villages, the funds they had stolen from the Delphic temple to finance the war were to be repaid in instalments), had strengthened Thebes, Phocis' enemy and Athens' main rival in central Greece. The Amphictyonic Council, a consortium of states which oversaw the shrine at Delphi, had reallocated the Phocian membership to Philip, who in autumn 346 presided over the Pythian games, which had been suspended during the war. Athens refused to be represented at the games and Philip sent envoys demanding that Athens acknowledge his membership of the council. Demosthenes (who had already started proceedings against his fellow ambassador Aeschines; see speech 19) was probably working against the peace himself. But it would be dangerous for Athens to provoke the whole of the Amphictyonic League. So his task in this speech is to persuade the Athenians to adopt a pragmatic approach. The perceived discrepancy with Demosthenes' uncompromising attitude to Philip elsewhere led some readers to doubt the authenticity of the speech, according to one ancient commentator, who rightly observes that Demosthenes' view of Philip is unchanged, and that his argument simply reflects his concern for Athens' interests. The discrepancy with Demosthenes' claim at 19.113 (three years later) that Aeschines alone argued for acceptance of Philip's membership of the Amphictyonic Council led the rhetorician Libanius in the fourth century AD to suggest that the speech was written by Demosthenes but never delivered. But this (genuine) contradiction reflects Demosthenes' reliance on his audience's faded memory and is part of the memory games in which both he and Aeschines engaged on the issue of past dealings with Philip.

---

[1] It goes without saying, Athenians, that things are extremely perplexing and confusing at the moment. We've lost a lot, and there's no point in wasting fine words on it, but there's also absolutely no agreement about what we should do with what's left. Some say this, and

some say that. [2] Deliberation is tough enough as it is, but you've made it far harder, Athenians. Whereas the universal norm is to deliberate ahead of events, you do so afterwards, and this means that, for as long as I can remember, criticizing your past mistakes has been a way for politicians to become popular and gain reputations as good speakers, and meanwhile you never get to grips with the actual business, the matter under discussion. [3] Even so, despite all this, I believe, strongly enough to have got to my feet today, that if you resolve to listen without heckling and without nitpicking—as is only right when the topic of discussion is the good of Athens and matters as weighty as those before us—I shall be able to suggest a way to improve things and save the situation.

[4] I am perfectly well aware, Athenians, that those who are brazen enough to cite their own past speeches and beat their own drums always profit from it here in the Assembly, but it strikes me as such a vulgar and offensive practice that I can hardly bring myself to do it, even though I don't see that I have any choice. But I think you'll be in a better position to assess what I'm going to say today if I first remind you of a couple of things I've said on earlier occasions.

[5] The first example that comes to mind, Athenians, is when Euboea was in turmoil and you were being advised to help Plutarch—that is, to embark on an inglorious and costly war. I was the first on my feet and the only one to object to the proposal, and I was almost torn to pieces by those who, for meagre takings, had persuaded you to commit a series of grave errors.* And then a short time later, after the ignominy of worse treatment than anyone anywhere has ever received from people they had gone to help, you unanimously recognized the perniciousness of these policies and the superiority of my advice.

[6] Another occasion on which I stepped up and addressed you, Athenians, was when I saw that Neoptolemus was hiding behind his profession as an actor to gain immunity, and was doing the city a great deal of harm by handling and directing Philip's business for him here in Athens.* As subsequent events made clear, I wasn't motivated in the slightest by personal enmity nor was I misrepresenting the facts. [7] Now, in this case I can't blame the politicians who supported Neoptolemus, since he found no such support at all, but you yourselves. I mean, you could hardly have displayed more partiality towards him and against me if you'd been watching tragedies in the Theatre of Dionysus, rather than discussing the security of the state.

[8] Nevertheless, by now, of course, you've all come to see the truth. Although he claimed that the purpose of his journey to Macedonia at the time was to recover some money he was owed there and bring it here to fulfil his liturgical obligations, and although his main argument was how inexcusable it would be to reproach a man for transferring funds from there to here, nevertheless, as soon as peace afforded him immunity, he converted all the real estate he had acquired here into cash and off he went to Philip, taking the money with him.

[9] So these two occasions when I spoke out testify that the views I expressed in my speeches at the time were right and fair, and that I was simply stating the facts. I'll mention just one further case, Athenians, and then I'll come straight to the point. The occasion I'm thinking of was when we ambassadors returned after receiving the oaths to the peace treaty.* [10] At the time, you were being assured that Thespiae and Plataea would be refounded, that if Philip got his way he'd save the Phocians and scatter the population of Thebes, and that you'd receive Oropus and get Euboea back in compensation for Amphipolis. Beguiled by such illusory hopes, you acted imprudently and perhaps dishonourably too, and did nothing about the Phocians. But you'll find that I wasn't taken in by any of these tricks, and didn't keep quiet either. I warned you, as I'm sure you remember, that this was all news to me, a bolt from the blue, and said that in my view these claims were nonsense.

[11] There have been a number of occasions, then, when I've displayed superior foresight to anyone else. But I'm not attributing this to intelligence, Athenians, or any other special gift. The only way I can explain my knowledge and foresight is by reference to the following two factors. The first is good luck, Athenians, which in my opinion is a more potent force than all human cleverness and intelligence. [12] The second is that my verdicts and opinions are not for sale. No one could argue that my policies and proposals depend on handouts. This allows me to see without bias where our advantage lies in the light of the actual facts. But as soon as money enters the equation, it upsets the balance, like a pair of scales, and drags reasoning down with it. Objectivity and sound thinking on any matter are completely incompatible with taking money.

[13] My first recommendation, then, is that anyone who intends to equip the city with allies or revenue or anything should do so without jeopardizing the current peace.* I say this not because I admire

the peace—in fact, it demeans us—but because its character is now irrelevant. It may indeed have been better, given the circumstances, for it never to have been made, but now that it's in place it would be better for it not to be broken as a result of our actions, because we've lost a lot that would at the time have made the war safer and easier for us than now.

[14] My second recommendation is that we should take care not to give the board that is currently calling itself the Amphictyonic Council a compelling or at least plausible reason for raising a common war against us.* The point is that if we were to find ourselves once more at war with Philip over Amphipolis or some such private bone of contention, which doesn't concern the Thessalians or the Argives or the Thebans, I doubt any of them would fight us, and least of all—no heckling, please, until you've heard what I'm going to say—[15] least of all the Thebans. It's not that they like us, or that they wouldn't want to ingratiate themselves with Philip, but they see clearly, however dense one might think they are,* that they'll bear the brunt of any war against us in which they're involved, while someone else sits back and waits to reap the benefits. They're unlikely to make such a sacrifice, then, without a common cause and reason for war.

[16] Or again, if war broke out once more between us and the Thebans over Oropus or some other local issue, I don't think it would turn out at all badly for us. I think our respective allies would play their part to resist an invasion of our home territory, but I doubt they'd support an act of aggression. This is the spirit of any worthwhile alliance, and it means, of course, that [17] none of the allies feels such loyalty towards us or the Thebans that they see no difference between our survival and our dominance. They all want us to survive, because their own security depends on it, but not one of them wants either of us to become the dominant power and rule over them.

So where's the danger? What we have to guard against, in my view, is the possibility that the coming war has everyone pooling their grievances and finding reasons to unite against us. [18] Argos, Messene, Megalopolis, and their sympathizers among the other Peloponnesian states will be hostile because of our embassy to Sparta and because, as they see it, to some extent we approve of what the Spartans did.* The Thebans, we hear, are already angry with us, and the fact that we take in those who are in flight from them and never miss an opportunity to display our dislike of them will only exacerbate their hostility.

[19] The Thessalians are angry about our protection of the Phocian exiles;* and Philip is angry because we're trying to block his entry to the Amphictyonic Council. What concerns me, then, is the possibility that, even though they each have their own personal reasons for hostility, they might unite to make war on us, using the Amphictyonic decrees as a pretext. And then they'll be sucked into a war with us, beyond what is good for them individually, as they were with the Phocians.

[20] After all, it can't have escaped your notice that the Thebans and Philip and the Thessalians all joined forces for the recent war, despite having markedly different concerns. The Thebans, for instance, were unable to stop Philip entering Greece and securing the pass,* and equally unable to stop him coming in at the end and taking the credit for all *their* efforts. [21] I mean, the situation now is that the Thebans may have gained a little territory,* but they've done their prestige and reputation terrible harm, in the sense that they wouldn't have won a thing if Philip hadn't come south. This wasn't the outcome they wanted, but their desire for Orchomenus and Coronea, combined with their weakness, forced them to put up with it all. [22] As for Philip, there are those who go so far as to suggest that he didn't really want to hand Orchomenus and Coronea over to the Thebans, but had no choice. Good luck to them, say I, but I'm sure that his overriding concern was to occupy the pass. He wanted the glory of people thinking that the war had been decided by him, and he wanted to manage the Pythian festival—that was what he longed for above all.* [23] And the Thessalians' motives were different again. They didn't want either the Thebans or Philip to become strong, which they saw as contrary to their best interests. The two prizes they were after were the Pylaea and Delphi, and it was their desire to control the Council and the shrine that induced them to throw in their lot with the others. You can see, then, that each of them, for his own personal reasons, ended up sacrificing his own interests. And that's exactly what we must guard against.

[24] 'Should we then act on your recommendations out of fear of this happening again? Is that what you, of all people, are suggesting?' Not a bit of it. What I'm suggesting is that we maintain our high standards, avoid war, and demonstrate to the world our intelligence and the justice of our claims. As for those who dare to think that we shouldn't give an inch,† and who fail to see that war will follow,

I'd like to mention the following considerations. We're already letting the Thebans keep Oropus, and our answer, if anyone were to ask us to tell him truly why, would be: 'To avoid war.' [25] We've already surrendered Amphipolis to Philip as we were required to by the terms of the treaty; we're letting Cardia be excepted from the rest of the cities on the Chersonese;* we're letting the Carian occupy the islands—Chios, Cos, and Rhodes;* we're letting the Byzantines detain our shipping.* And we're doing all this, obviously, because we regard the peace afforded by the treaty as better for us than conflict and strife over these issues. Given, then, that we've already dealt like this with each of our potential enemies one by one, over matters of the greatest importance that touch us personally, it would be outright stupidity and folly for us now to go to war with all of them at once over the shadow in Delphi.*

8. ON THE SITUATION IN
THE CHERSONESE

The speech was delivered in 341 BC. The year before, the Athenians had sent out fresh colonists to the Thracian Chersonese (modern Gallipoli peninsula), all of which was under Athenian control except for the city of Cardia. The Athenian general Diopeithes was supporting the colonists, who almost inevitably found themselves in dispute with Cardia. Like most Athenian generals in the north, Diopeithes had to find the money for his mercenaries by various acts of freebooting, including an incursion into the part of mainland Thrace controlled by Philip, who retaliated by putting a Macedonian garrison in Cardia and made a formal complaint to Athens. Diopeithes' activities were divisive in Athens, where some argued that he was violating the peace and should be recalled. This is what Demosthenes is responding to here. The tone and tenor contrast sharply with *On the Peace*. Where just a few years earlier Demosthenes was trying to restrain the hotheads, here he is consciously urging a policy which will put Athens on a collision course with Philip. The confident and assertive tone reflects several factors. The series of trials against proponents of the peace in the late 340s both reflected and promoted a change in the dynamics of Athenian politics, leaving the opponents of Macedon, especially Demosthenes, increasingly in the ascendant. The presence of Philip's forces in the Chersonese made it easier to argue that Athens' interests were directly under threat. And Demosthenes was becoming more confident about the prospects for acquiring allies for a conflict which Athens could not sustain alone.

---

[1] Neither malice nor favour, Athenians, should ever motivate a political speech. Politicians should stick to telling you what they think it best for you to do, especially when major issues affecting the state as a whole are on the agenda. But since a few of them feel compelled to speak because they've got a bone to pick or something, it's your job, Athenians, as constituting the majority, to ignore everything else and consider, as you vote and act, what you think will do Athens good.

[2] What we need to focus on today is the situation in the Chersonese and Philip's Thracian campaign,* which is now in its eleventh

month. But Diopeithes' doings and designs have dominated most of the speeches. Now, it seems to me that, when there are charges to be brought against someone you can legally punish whenever you feel like it, you have the option of considering the case either now or later, as you see fit, and there's no real need for me or anyone else to make out that it's urgent. [3] But when our standing enemy has a sizeable army in the Hellespontine region and is trying to take over there, and when the slightest delay will make it impossible for us to save the situation, it seems to me that we should complete our deliberations and preparations as quickly as possible, and not let ourselves be distracted by irrelevant clamour and accusations.

[4] I'm often surprised at the things that tend to get said here, but I've never been more astonished than I was at a recent Council meeting, when I heard someone saying that a choice between simply going to war or simply keeping the peace is all any politician should be offering you. [5] But look at it this way. If Philip is doing nothing—if he's keeping his hands off our possessions, as stipulated by the treaty,* and isn't forming the whole world into a coalition against us—then words are redundant, and we must simply keep the peace. And I can see that you, at any rate, would be happy with that. On the other hand, if a written record of our oath and the terms of the treaty is available for inspection, [6] and if it turns out that right from the start (before Diopeithes and the cleruchs, the people who are now being denounced as warmongers, even left Athens) Philip has been illegally seizing a number of our possessions (and there are decrees of yours, still in force, complaining about this), *and* is spending the whole time continually stealing from everyone else there, both Greeks and barbarians, *and* is forming a coalition against us, what do they mean by saying that we must either go to war or keep the peace? [7] It's not as if we have a *choice* in the matter: the only course open to us is perfectly justified and perfectly unavoidable, though they deliberately overlook it. And what is it? To defend ourselves against his aggression.

But, by Zeus, perhaps they mean that Philip isn't wronging us or making war on us as long as he stays away from Attica and Piraeus. [8] Well, if that's how they define 'wrong' and understand 'peace', then, first, I'm sure you can all see the monstrous iniquity of their position, how it exposes Athens to risk, and, second, what they're saying is in fact inconsistent with the charges they're bringing against Diopeithes. I mean, why on earth would we let Philip do whatever he likes, as long as he stays away from Attica, while Diopeithes isn't even allowed to go to the assistance of people in Thrace without our accusing him of warmongering?

[9] 'All right, by Zeus, but even if they're wrong in this respect, it remains true that it's appalling for the mercenaries to ravage the Hellespont, and wrong for Diopeithes to detain shipping. We should stop him.' All right, fine, you won't hear any argument from me on this. [10] But if this advice of theirs is motivated entirely by considerations of justice, it seems to me that, as well as trying to break up our army by filling your ears with slander of its commander and paymaster, they should also show that Philip's army will be disbanded, if you're to find their advice persuasive. Otherwise, I'm afraid that the course they're setting the city on is no different from the one that has already brought us to the brink of disaster.

[11] After all, I hardly need to remind you that Philip owes his victories to nothing so much as the fact that he gets to the scene of action before us. Anyone who has a standing army and plans his actions in advance is capable of suddenly pouncing on whoever he decides to attack. But in our case, it's only when news arrives that we panic and make our preparations. [12] And in the end, of course, he has plenty of time to achieve his objectives, while we drag our heels and waste every penny we spend. For all our display of enmity and the desire to check him, we incur the disgrace of arriving too late for the action.

[13] You must see, Athenians, that all the rest is just words and evasion. The real point of all Philip's manoeuvring and planning is to make sure that, while you stay at home with no army out in the field, he has all the time in the world to arrange everything as he wants. Consider, first, what's going on at the moment. [14] He's in Thrace now with a sizeable army, and eyewitnesses report that he's sending for considerable reinforcements from Macedonia and Thessaly. Now, suppose he waits for the etesian winds and then goes and puts Byzantium under siege.* Do you think, first, that the Byzantines would persist with their current folly and wouldn't turn to us for help? [15] I doubt it. Rather than surrender to him, they'll open their gates even to people they trust less than us—unless the city falls to him first. So if we're unable to launch an expedition and there's no help available there, there'll be nothing to prevent their ruin. [16] 'That's because they're crazy, by Zeus, the Byzantines!

They're behaving like complete imbeciles!' Quite so, but they must still be protected, because that's what is good for Athens.

Then again, we can't be sure that he's not going to attack the Chersonese. In fact, to judge by the letter he wrote to you, he *is* going to take 'defensive measures' against the settlers there.* [17] Now, as long as the army that has been formed there is in existence, it will be able to protect the region and hurt Philip a bit as well. But if it's disbanded, what will we do if he attacks the Chersonese? 'We'll put Diopeithes on trial, by Zeus!' And how will that help? 'All right, we'd better launch an expedition ourselves.' What if the winds stop us? 'All right, by Zeus! But he won't do it.' And who can possibly guarantee that? [18] Face facts, Athenians. Bear in mind that it's almost the time of year when certain people feel obliged to clear the Hellespont of your presence and hand it over to Philip.* Now, suppose he leaves Thrace, stays away from the Chersonese and Byzantium (we have to take this possibility into consideration as well), and assaults Chalcis and Megara, just as he did Oreus not long ago.* Is it better for us to resist him here, letting war draw near Attica, or to keep him busy up there? The latter, surely.

[19] A concerted effort is needed from you now, given these facts and considerations. But, by Zeus, instead of trying to disparage and disband the army that Diopeithes is trying to assemble for Athens, you should be assembling another one yourselves, helping him out financially, and generally offering him your cooperation and friendship. [20] Look, suppose Philip were asked: 'Which would you prefer? To see Diopeithes' current troops thrive?'—whatever they're like: you won't hear any argument from me on this—'To see their value recognized in Athens and their numbers increased by official support? Or would you prefer to see them dispersed and destroyed, brought down by the accusations of a few detractors?' He'd choose the latter option, of course. From which it follows that, if those few detractors were successful, they would be answering Philip's prayers. And yet you still wonder how the city has reached the brink of ruin?

[21] I'd like to carry out a candid review of our current situation, to try to see what we're making of it, what we're up to at the moment. We're refusing to pay a war levy or raise a citizen contingent;* we can't keep our hands off public money; we refuse to support Diopeithes financially; [22] we disapprove of him providing for

himself, begrudge him what he gets, and worry about his sources, intentions, and so on; we refuse, in other words, to mind our own business. We mouth praises of politicians who display true Athenian values, but our actions support their opponents.

[23] The usual question you ask every politician who steps up to address you is 'What should we do?' But the question I'd like to ask you is: What should I say? If you refuse to pay the levy, or raise a citizen contingent, or keep your hands off public money, or support him financially, or let him provide for himself, or mind your own business, I don't know what I'm supposed to say. When people allow so much licence to critics and detractors that they listen even when their accusations concern things they claim he's going to do in the future—well, what can one say?

[24] Now, there may be people here who need to learn what the effect of this behaviour of yours is likely to be. I shall speak candidly— not that I could do otherwise. Every single general who has ever left Athens at the head of an expeditionary force from Athens—if I'm wrong, punish me as you see fit—takes money from Chios or Erythrae or wherever he can—from the inhabitants of Asia, that is. [25] Those with only a couple of ships take less, and those with a larger force take more. And the givers don't give their greater or lesser amounts for nothing. They're not crazy: they buy for their merchant navy immunity from depredation or robbery, or the right to have ships convoyed, or something of this sort. They say, however, that their gifts are acts of kindness, and so these donations are known as 'benevolences'.

[26] So now it's Diopeithes who has an army up there and, of course, they'll all give him money. How else is a man to pay his troops, do you think, when he was given nothing by you and has no other source of income? From the sky? No, he lives on what he can gather, beg, and borrow. [27] Those who denounce him here in the Assembly, then, are in effect telling everyone not to give him a penny more, on the grounds that he's going to be punished just for what he plans to do, let alone for anything he may have done or achieved. That's what they mean when they say: 'He's preparing a siege,' or 'He's betraying the Greeks.' But do any of these grousers care for the Asiatic Greeks?* Then they must care more for everyone else than for their own country.

[28] That's also the effect of sending a second general to the Helles-pont.* After all, Athenians, if Diopeithes is committing atrocities

and detaining shipping, just one little document is all it would take to stop him in his tracks.* The laws tell us to impeach men who commit these crimes; they don't tell us to go to all the expense of launching a whole fleet just to watch over our own men, by Zeus. That's a completely crazy thing to do. [29] It's for *enemies* that we need to maintain troops, launch a fleet, and raise money through war levies, because they can't be apprehended under our laws. But for *ourselves* we have decrees, the impeachment process, and the *Paralus*.* That's how decent people go about it, as opposed to the destructive malice of these grousers today.

[30] If only the existence of these malcontents were the worst of it. But in your sessions here your attitude by now is such that, if a speaker tells you that Diopeithes is responsible for all your troubles (or Chares, or Aristophon, or whichever fellow citizen they pick on), you agree straight away and the air rings with cries of 'You're right!' [31] But if someone comes and tells you the truth—if he says: 'This is nonsense, Athenians. It's *Philip* who's responsible for all your trials and tribulations. If he'd done nothing, the city wouldn't be in any trouble at all'—even though you can't deny the truth of what he's saying, it still makes you cross, I think, and feel rather as though you'd lost something. [32] Now, the reason for this—and, please, in the name of the gods, let me speak candidly when I have the city's best interests at heart—is that certain politicians have trained you to be menacing and dangerous in assembly, but to put pathetically little effort into warfare. So if the 'guilty party', according to some speaker or other, is someone you know you can apprehend here in Athens, you agree with his denunciation and are in favour of apprehending the alleged culprit. But if he names someone you'll be able to punish only if you first defeat him by military means, you're stymied, of course, and your frustration makes you cross.

[33] It should be the other way round, you see, Athenians. Every politician in Athens should accustom you to be calm and polite in assembly, where you legislate for yourselves and your allies, but to show the menacing and dangerous side of yourselves in warfare, where you do battle with enemies. [34] As it is, however, their outrageous demagoguery and courting of your favour has created a situation where you're spoiled and pampered in your assemblies by only ever hearing what you want to hear, when in the real world you're already teetering on the brink of disaster.

What if the people of Greece were to demand an explanation for all the opportunities you've wasted recently through apathy? What if they were to say: [35] 'You know how you send us envoys once in a while, telling us that Philip has designs on us and Greece as a whole, warning us to take precautions, and so on?'* To this we can only agree and say yes, because that is what we do. 'Well, then, you hypocrites, during the ten months he was away,* constrained by illness, winter, and warfare, unable to return home, [36] why did you fail either to liberate Euboea or to regain any of your lost possessions? While you stayed at home, taking your ease and free of illness (unless hypocrisy is an illness), how come he set tyrants up in two places in Euboea, entrenching one on the coastline directly across from Attica and the other threatening Sciathos?* [37] However little zeal you have at the moment, how come you did nothing about even these problems and just ignored them? It looks very much as though you're avoiding confrontation with Philip, and you've made it plain that, even if he died ten times over, you still wouldn't stir yourselves. So what's the point of your envoys and your denunciations? Why are you making trouble for us?' What should we reply, Athenians? *I* have no idea.

[38] Now, there are people who imagine that they silence a speaker the instant they ask 'So what should we do?' The most honest and truthful answer I can give them is: 'Stop doing what you're doing at the moment.' But I shall give a more detailed response as well. And I trust that they'll be as ready to act as they are to ask questions.

[39] First, Athenians, you should be absolutely clear on this: Philip is at war with Athens and it is he who has broken the peace. Please stop accusing fellow Athenians of this. You must fix in your mind the fact that Philip is hostile to the city as a whole and means to do it harm. His hostility extends to the very foundations of the city, [40] and I should say that it extends to every inhabitant of the city as well, even those who imagine that they are in his good books. If they don't believe me, they should consider Euthycrates and Lasthenes from Olynthus,* who supposed that their betrayal of the city gave them entry to his inner circle, and have been utterly and terribly ruined. But primarily he has declared war on our democracy; the primary goal of all his plotting and planning is to find a way to dissolve it.

[41] There's a sense in which this should occasion no surprise. He's perfectly well aware that even if his takeover is otherwise complete, it will have no security as long as Athens is a democracy. He knows that

it would take just a single stumble—a not-infrequent occurrence in human life—for all the factions that are currently repressed to turn to Athens for help. [42] For while being disinclined yourselves to the greedy course of imperialism,* you're brilliant at stopping others from gaining power and at taking it from those who have it. In short, you never hesitate to make life difficult for would-be imperialists or to free the oppressed everywhere.

Now, he doesn't want to have democratic freedom waiting to pounce at the slightest opportunity he might provide—not a bit of it—and he's quite right to think that it would; this is no idle fancy. [43] So the first thing you have to do is take as given his implacable hostility towards our democratic constitution. Unless this conviction takes root in your minds, you'll remain reluctant to take the situation seriously.

Second, you should appreciate that his current endeavours and schemes are all designed to harm Athens, and that therefore any resistance offered to him anywhere works in our favour. [44] I mean, no one is stupid enough to suppose that Philip wants those miserable Thracian possessions—how else could one describe Drongilus, Cabyle, Masteira, and the places he's currently taking from us?—and endures hard labour, foul weather, and deadly peril to get them, [45] and yet has no interest in Athens' harbours, ship-sheds, triremes, silver mines,* and substantial revenues. No one is stupid enough to think he doesn't begrudge us these things, while he winters in hell for the sake of Thracian silos with their millet and spelt.* No, the point of all his endeavours, in Thrace and elsewhere, is to gain control of our assets.

[46] What, then, is the sensible course of action? You need to recognize and appreciate the truth of what I've been saying, shed your excessive and intolerable indifference, pay a war levy, require your allies to do likewise, and take practical steps to ensure the continuance of this army, the one already assembled there. Then you'll have a force ready to protect and aid everyone in Greece, to counter the one Philip has ready to attack and enslave them all. [47] Nothing important is ever achieved by sending out expeditionary forces. No, you must conscript an army, provide for its maintenance, find bankers and slaves for it, and make sure that the closest possible watch is kept over its finances. And then your next job will be to audit the financial officers for the money, and the general for the campaign. If you do all

that, and truly do it wholeheartedly, you'll either force Philip to keep an honest peace and confine him to his own borders, which would be the greatest of all blessings, or you'll fight him on equal terms.

[48] Now, if I'm giving anyone the impression that this will cost a lot in terms of money, work, and effort, he's absolutely right. But if you consider the consequences for Athens if we refuse to act, you'll find that we're better off choosing to do our duty. [49] After all, suppose some god (the task being beyond the powers of a mere mortal) were to guarantee that, after all your inactivity and negligence, Philip wouldn't in the end come against Athens. Even so, by Zeus and all the gods, it would be inexcusable for your selfish apathy to condemn everyone else in Greece to slavery. You'd be letting yourselves down, failing to live up to Athenian traditions, and falling short of your ancestors' achievements.

Personally, I'd rather die than recommend this course of action. All the same, if someone else does, and you find him persuasive, so be it. Don't put up a fight. Don't do a thing. [50] But if the idea is quite unacceptable—if we all foresee, on the contrary, that the more we allow Philip to take over, the stronger and more difficult an enemy he becomes for us—how long do we go on hesitating? What are we waiting for? When shall we resolve to do our duty, Athenians? [51] 'When there's an emergency, by Zeus,' you say. But what free men would recognize as an emergency is not just already upon us, but has been for a long time, and our prayer now should be that we don't meet what *slaves* would recognize as an emergency. What's the difference? For a free man, there's no greater emergency than a situation that dishonours him; I don't know of anything that could exert greater pressure on a free man than this. But for a slave blows and physical abuse constitute an emergency, and I pray that it doesn't come to that. It doesn't even bear thinking about.

[52] I'd be happy to give you the full picture and show you precisely how certain politicians go about their subversive task, but I'll restrict myself to just one point. Whenever the topic of Philip comes up, someone or other leaps to his feet to sing the praises of peace and remark on how painful it would be to maintain an army of any size. 'Certain people', he says, 'want to plunder the treasury,' and more along the same lines, the effect of which is to slow you down and give Philip time to do what he wants. [53] And the upshot is idle leisure for you, for the time being (though I suspect you'll find that it has

come at a high price), and for them, the politicians, popularity and pay for these services of theirs. But their persuasive talk about peace is wasted on you, I think; here you sit, fully persuaded. They should direct it at the man who's committing acts of war. After all, if he were persuaded, he'd find you ready.

[54] We shouldn't see spending money on our safety as painful; just think how we'll suffer if we don't spend it. As for 'plundering the treasury', that should be stopped by proposing protective measures to safeguard our finances, not by undermining Athenian interests. [55] But that's another thing I want to protest about, Athenians. The thought of the treasury being plundered upsets some of you, though you can act to protect it and punish any wrongdoers, yet you're not upset by the fact that step by step Philip is plundering the whole of Greece, when you are the target of his depredations.

[56] Here's a puzzle, Athenians. On the one hand, we have a man whose campaigns, acts of aggression, and seizure of cities are plain for all to see—yet we never hear them described as acts of war by any of this clique. On the other hand, when someone advises you not to give up, not to abandon these places, they accuse him of warmongering. Why is this, do you think? I'll tell you. [57] It's because they want to divert the anger you naturally feel every time you suffer in the war on to the people who are actually giving you the best advice. They want you to put these men on trial instead of resisting Philip; they want to prosecute cases, because otherwise they'd be prosecuted for what they're doing now. That's the meaning of their talk of 'certain people in Athens who want war'; that's the real point of their wrangling. [58] But I know for a fact that, before anyone in Athens has formally proposed a declaration of war, Philip has already taken many of our possessions and now he's sent help to Cardia.* If, despite this, we are willing to pretend that he's not at war with us, he is not such an utter fool as to disabuse us.

[59] What shall we be saying, however, when he marches on Athens? He'll give us the same assurances of his peaceful intentions that he gave to the people of Oreus when his troops had already invaded; that he gave earlier to the people of Pherae when he was assaulting their city walls; and that he gave to the people of Olynthus—they were the first—until he appeared with an army of invasion right there on their land.* Even with him moving against us, even then, shall we be calling anyone who advises us to resist a warmonger? Then our only

option is slavery; there's no other choice if we're denied both resistance and peace.

[60] And yet you have more at stake than anyone else. Philip doesn't want to subdue Athens; he wants to obliterate it.* He knows perfectly well that you'll never tolerate slavery and that, even if you did, your past as leaders would make you terrible slaves. He knows that, given the opportunities, you could make more trouble for him than anyone. [61] You must appreciate that this is a life-and-death struggle. You must hate and crucify* those who have sold themselves to him. There's no way, no way at all, for you to prevail over external enemies until you've punished the enemies within. [62] Why do you think Philip bullies you so much these days? I don't see how else to describe it. Why do you think he's good to everyone else, even if he does always have a hidden agenda, but is already threatening us? He seduced the Thessalians into their current subjection,* for instance, by being a generous benefactor, and it was incredible how he tricked the wretched Olynthians, by giving them first Potidaea and then a great deal more.* [63] Now he's seducing the Thebans by handing Boeotia over to them and freeing them from a hard-fought, major war.* Each of them did well out of it—but some of them have already suffered, as everyone knows, and the rest will suffer in their turn.

But you—I won't mention all that you've lost to date, but see how thoroughly you were duped just during the peace process. [64] Didn't you lose Phocis, Thermopylae, the Thraceward region, Doriscus, Serrium, and Cersobleptes himself?* Isn't Philip now admitting that Cardia is his?* So why does he single you out for special treatment? It's because Athens is the only place in the world where it is permissible for people to speak for the enemy, and where a man who's been corrupted can safely address you in person, even though you're the ones who've been robbed of your own property. [65] It wasn't safe for anyone in Olynthus to take Philip's part, until the general populace of the city had shared in the advantages of possessing Potidaea. It wasn't safe for anyone in Thessaly to take Philip's part, until Philip had done the general populace of Thessaly the favour of expelling the tyrants and returning the Pylaea to them. It wasn't safe in Thebes either, until he gave them back Boeotia and destroyed Phocis.

[66] But in Athens, even though Philip has stolen Amphipolis and Cardia from you, even though he's making Euboea a fortress to threaten you, and is now advancing on Byzantium,* it's safe to speak

for him. And see how some of those who do so suddenly exchange poverty for wealth, and anonymous obscurity for prominence and distinction, while the opposite happens to you and you end up dishonoured and impoverished. For, as I see it, allies, trust, and goodwill make up the city's capital, and you've lost all of these. [67] As a result of your negligence and carelessness, however, Philip has prospered. He has become powerful enough to be a threat to everyone, both Greeks and barbarians, while you've become isolated and insignificant, far-famed for your overflowing shops, but scorned when it comes to providing what's important.

I see a marked difference between the advice some of our politicians are giving us, and what they tell themselves. They tell us to keep the peace even when we're the injured party, but they're incapable of keeping the peace here in Athens even when they've got no cause for grievance. [68] And so one or another of them steps up and says: 'Demosthenes, you refuse to make proposals or take any chances. You're timid and weak.'* Well, it's true that I'm not bold or corrupt or unprincipled, and I hope never to be, but actually I think I have more courage than many of our more reckless statesmen. [69] It takes no courage for a man to ignore the city's interests and busy himself with prosecuting cases, confiscating property, handing out money, and bringing charges. His safety is guaranteed by the fact that his words and measures are designed to please you; his boldness comes without risk. But a man who often opposes your will if it's in your best interests that he does so; a man who says nothing just to please you, but only ever offers the best advice; a man who, if his preferred policy depends more on Fortune than on rational considerations, still accepts responsibility in either case—[70] this man has courage and is a useful member of society, unlike those who for the sake of ephemeral popularity have wreaked terrible damage on Athens.

I don't find them admirable in the slightest, and so little do I consider them valuable members of society that if someone were to ask me, 'Tell me, what good have *you* done our city?', I wouldn't mention my trierarchies, even though I could, or the choruses I've produced, the war levies I've paid, the prisoners I've ransomed, and all my other benefactions.* [71] No, I'd reply that I've consistently practised a different kind of politics from theirs. Although I could, I suppose, prosecute cases as well as the next man, and court popularity and confiscate property and in general behave just like them, I've never taken a single step down that path, nor have I been seduced by the prospect of either wealth or advancement. Instead, I persist in delivering speeches that may make me in your eyes a lesser man than many, but will make you a greater power than you are today, if you take the advice they contain. I think I may say this much without giving offence. [72] I don't see it as my job, as an honest member of society, to invent policies that would shoot me to the top of the pile in Athens, while dashing you to the bottom in the wider world. No, the city should prosper along with the policies of good citizens, and every politician should offer the best advice, not the easiest. Nature inclines of its own accord towards what is easy, but it's the job of a good Athenian to enlighten his fellow citizens and point them towards what is best.

[73] In the past I've heard people complain that even excellent advice such as mine consists of nothing but words, when what we need is action, some definite achievement. I'll go right ahead and tell you how I feel about this. In my view, the job of an Athenian politician consists in fact of nothing except offering the best advice, and I think this is a point I can easily prove. [74] I'm sure you remember how the great Timotheus once addressed you on the importance of despatching an expedition to save the Euboeans from enslavement by the Thebans.* In the course of the speech he said something like this: 'I can't believe you're still debating what the best course of action is under the circumstances, when there are already Thebans on the island. Will you not cover the sea with triremes, Athenians? Will you not rise and go straight down to Piraeus? Will you not launch the fleet?' [75] That's what Timotheus said, you acted on his advice, and the combination of advice and action brought success. But however excellent his advice (and certainly it was the best possible), if you'd been too lazy to take it, the city would have gained none of the advantages that subsequently came its way, would it? Of course not. The same goes in my case too: look to yourselves for action, and look to your politicians for the best advice.

[76] I'd like now to sum up what I've been saying, and then I'll sit down. My advice is that you should raise a war levy. You should keep the existing army together, making improvements where needed, but not disbanding it entirely on the strength of adverse criticism. You should send envoys everywhere to explain, rebuke, and negotiate. In addition to all these measures, I think you should punish politicians

who take bribes and execrate them wherever you find them, because then the good advice of decent men, who go about their work honestly, will be seen for what it is by everyone, not just by themselves. [77] If you attend to the situation and stop ignoring it altogether, perhaps, just perhaps we might see improvement even at this late date. But if you sit here and limit your involvement to heckling and applause, while hesitating to act when action is called for, I can't see how the city can be saved. Words alone are not enough; you must act!

9. THIRD PHILIPPIC

The *Third Philippic* was delivered in 341 BC, not long after the Chersonese speech (Demosthenes 8). The theme is again the aggression of Philip and the need for decisive action against him. But where the earlier speech is devoted to a very specific local situation, the current speech deals with larger strategic issues. The difference of focus makes for a more generalized rhetoric, giving the present speech a grandeur to which the Chersonese speech rises only intermittently. While attacking Philip, accusing his political opponents as usual of corruption and treason, and criticizing his audience for inaction and lack of a sense of urgency, he downplays his partisanship in favour of a rousing vision of incorruptibility, a claim to be acting for Greece and not just Athens, and a plea for integrity in public life. The speech survives in two forms in the medieval manuscripts. The most authoritative manuscript lacks some short passages which occur in others. Though it is entirely possible that these are spurious additions, perhaps by a later rhetorician, they have a Demosthenic ring and it has been suggested that the variants result from Demosthenes himself. They could either go back to options marked in the pre-delivery script or to different revisions made with a view to publication. At any rate, the translation below is of the fuller version of the text.

————

[1] In almost every Assembly, Athenians, speaker after speaker denounces the unjustified aggression with which Philip has been acting against us and everyone else ever since the peace treaty.* All of them, I'm sure, would agree, even if they don't actually say so, that everything we say and do should be designed to put an end to his insolence and punish him. Nevertheless, it's clear to me that carelessness and thoughtlessness have reduced us to such a state that . . . however offensive it may be to say it, the truth is, I'm afraid, that even if all the speeches and all the measures you voted for had been deliberately intended to reduce us to as pitiful a state as possible, it's hard to see how we could be worse off than we are now.

[2] Now, there are presumably a number of reasons for this; the situation is not the result of just one or two factors. But if you look at things properly, you'll find that responsibility lies above all with those who make it their job to say what you like to hear rather than

recommend what is in your best interests. Some of these men are so concerned with trying to preserve their own prestige and power, Athenians, that they take no thought for the future and expect you to be equally irresponsible. Others criticize and malign anyone who tries actually to *do* something about the situation—which can only ensure that while we're busy finding fellow citizens to punish,* Philip will get away with saying and doing whatever he likes.

[3] However familiar this kind of politics may be to us, it is directly responsible for our troubles—and I would ask you, Athenians, to pardon my candour in speaking the truth. Here's what I want you to consider. In general, you acknowledge the right of everyone in Athens to speak his mind. You even grant the right to foreigners and slaves; many servants here are allowed to speak with greater candour than full citizens in some other states. But you've completely banished freedom of speech from your public assemblies. [4] And the upshot is? You're spoiled and pampered in your assemblies by only ever hearing what you want to hear, when in the real world you're already teetering on the brink of disaster. If that's the way you feel today, I have nothing to say. But if you're prepared to listen to the best advice, even if it comes unadorned by flattery, I'm ready to give it. For, however bad things are, however much we've lost, we can still make a full recovery if you resolve to do your duty.

[5] Now, what I'm about to say might seem paradoxical, but the truth is that the worst aspect of the past is precisely what should give us the most hope for the future. What do I mean? The situation is bad, Athenians, because of your complete and utter failure to do your duty. There'd be no hope of improvement only if it had got like that when you *were* doing your duty. But, as things are, although Philip has prevailed over your indifference and neglect, he has not prevailed over Athens. *You* are undefeated—but then you haven't made the slightest effort!

[6] If we all agreed that Philip has broken the peace treaty and is at war with us, all a speaker would have to do is recommend the safest and simplest way of resisting him. Now, Philip is taking cities, holding a number of your possessions, and threatening the whole world. Despite this, there are those among you who are absurdly inclined to countenance the idea, so often voiced in this Assembly by some of our speakers, that it's some of *us* who are responsible for the war.* So I need to correct this impression—and to take care

while doing so. [7] I mean, there's a distinct possibility that anyone who proposes and recommends a course of resistance will incur the charge of warmongering.

The very first point I want to clarify, then, is whether we're even in a position to discuss if we should remain at peace or go to war. [8] So let's start with the question whether peace is a realistic option for us, and whether the decision is up to us. If it is, then peace is certainly my preferred option, and I call upon any speaker who agrees not to dissemble, but to draw up proposals and act. But if there's someone else in the picture, an armed man with a sizeable force at his side, and he offers you 'peace' as a screen while behaving like a man at war, what alternative do we have except to resist?

It doesn't bother me if you want to *pretend*, as he does, that we're at peace. [9] But to describe as 'peace' an arrangement that enables him to take over the rest of Greece and then move against us is crazy, to start with. Moreover, it's a unilateral peace, observed by you towards him but not the other way around. This is precisely what Philip buys with all the money he spends*—the right to fight you while not being fought by you.

[10] Now, there could be nothing more stupid than for us to wait for him to admit that he's at war. Even if he's marching on Attica and Piraeus he'll deny it. His past behaviour towards others proves it. [11] He told the Olynthians, when he was forty stades* from their city, that the only options were the abandonment of Olynthus by them or of Macedonia by him, even though previously, whenever he was accused of hostile intentions, he always waxed indignant and sent envoys to plead his case.* He also pretended that the Phocians were his allies while he was marching against them. There were even Phocian representatives in his train, and most people here were insisting that it was the Thebans who would suffer from his march south.* [12] Then again, when he entered Thessaly not long ago it was as a friend and ally—and he took Pherae, which he now holds. Finally, what about those wretches in Oreus?* The line he spun them was that he had sent his troops to pay them a goodwill visit, because he'd heard that they were suffering from internal discord, and he claimed that in such circumstances it was the job of true friends and allies to be at their side.

[13] Now, although these people would presumably have put up a defence, they couldn't actually have caused him any real harm. But he still chose to trick them, rather than declare his hostility. Do you

think, then, that he'll give *you* advance notice before making war on you, especially when you're perfectly content to be deceived?* [14] Of course he won't. Given that you, the targets of his aggression, aren't accusing him of any wrong, but in fact are laying charges against some of your fellow citizens, he'd be the biggest fool in the world if he were to reconcile the various warring factions among you, give you enough warning to turn against him instead, and deprive his hirelings here of the opportunity to continue delaying you with the argument that 'It isn't *Philip* who's making war on the city'.

[15] By Zeus, would anyone in his right mind make words rather than deeds his criterion for deciding who is at peace and who is at war with him? Of course not. Well, Philip wasted no time. As soon as the peace treaty had been concluded, before Diopeithes' command and before the cleruchs who are currently in the Chersonese had been sent out,* he set about taking Serrium and Doriscus. In the process, he drove from Serrium castle and the Sacred Mountain the troops installed there by your general.* [16] But what was he doing when he did this? After all, he had committed himself on oath to the peace.* Don't say: 'So what? Are these places any concern of ours?' The relative or even total insignificance of these places to us isn't the issue. Morality and justice are equally relevant whether a man's crime is great or small.

So tell me, when he sends mercenaries to the Chersonese, which the Great King of Persia and all Greeks recognize as yours—when he admits in writing that he's sending help there*—what's he doing? [17] I mean, he *says* he's not at war. But I find it completely impossible to see this as the behaviour of a man who's observing the peace with us. By the same token, I also consider his intervention at Megara, his establishment of tyrannies on Euboea, his current advance into Thrace, his scheming in the Peloponnese,* and every military endeavour of his, as violations of the treaty and as acts of war against us—unless you believe that people who erect siege engines are keeping the peace until they bring them right up to the walls. But you can't think that. After all, if a man is actively preparing the means for my capture, he's making war on me even before his engines fire a single shot or his archers a single arrow.

[18] Look at how vulnerable you are, should anything happen. The Hellespont might fall into other hands; the enemy might gain control of Megara and Euboea; the Peloponnesians might side with

him. How can I suppose that the man behind this strategy of hostility towards Athens is observing the peace with us? [19] Of course he isn't. He has been at war with us, by my reckoning, since the day when he destroyed the Phocians.* As for you, the sensible course, in my opinion, would be for you to take defensive measures immediately; if you let him be, I think you'll find later, when you want to resist, that it's no longer possible. The extent to which I differ from all your other advisers, Athenians, may be measured by the fact that I don't think the Chersonese or Byzantium should even be up for debate today.* [20] Go to their defence and see that they come to no harm—but in your deliberations remember that *every* Greek city is in terrible danger.

I'd like to tell you what it is about our situation that makes me so afraid. Then, if I'm right and you see things the way I do, you can at least take thought for your own future, even if you're reluctant to do so for others; but if my thinking seems ridiculous or deranged, you can ignore me, both now and in the future, and treat me as someone not quite right in the head.

[21] There are a number of disturbing facts I could mention: Philip's rise from mean and humble beginnings; the mutual suspicion and disunity of the Greeks; how much more surprising his rise to power was than the completion of his takeover now that he has already made so many gains. I shall keep all such concerns to myself. [22] But it's clear to me that absolutely everyone has followed your lead in conceding to him something that has been the issue in every Greek war in history. What do I mean? The right to act as he pleases, to pillage and plunder the Greeks one after another, to attack and enslave the cities.

[23] Now, your leadership of Greece lasted seventy-three years, Spartan hegemony for twenty-nine, and more recently the Thebans too gained a certain amount of power after the battle of Leuctra.* But neither you nor the Thebans nor the Spartans was ever given total freedom of action by the Greeks, Athenians. Not a bit of it. [24] On the contrary, if *anyone* thought that you, or rather the Athenians of the time, were taking undue liberties, *everyone*, even those with no cause for complaint, sided with the injured party and went to war. Or again, after the Spartans had inherited your position of dominance and become the leaders of Greece, when they showed signs of going too far and of disturbing the status quo more than they should, everyone took up arms against them, even those who had no cause for complaint.

[25] There's no need for me to multiply the examples. Just think of us and the Spartans. Even though neither side could claim to have been wronged by the other, we still thought it right to go to war to defend others against the wrongs we saw being done to them. And yet, Athenians, all the wrongs committed by the Spartans during their thirty years of dominance, and by our ancestors during their seventy-year hegemony, fall short of those that Philip has committed against the Greeks in less than thirteen years of ascendancy.* Did I say they fall short? They don't even come close.

[26] It won't take long to prove the point. I'm not going to bring up Olynthus, Methone, Apollonia, and the rest of the thirty-two Thraceward communities,* all of which he destroyed with such savagery that it's hard for a visitor to tell if the places were ever inhabited. I make no mention of the destruction of the powerful Phocian League. But how are the Thessalians doing? Hasn't he stripped them of their cities and constitutions, and established tetrarchies instead, to ensure his mastery over every region as well as every city?* [27] What about Euboea? Aren't the cities there—an island that's close to Thebes and Athens—now ruled by tyrants? Doesn't he explicitly write in his letters: 'There can only be peace between me and people who are willing to obey me'?* And he acts on this principle; it's not just words to him. He's gone to the Hellespont; before that he went to Ambracia;* in the Peloponnese, he holds the important city of Elis; not long ago he tried to gain Megara by underhand means. Neither Greece nor foreign lands can contain the man's greed.

[28] In Greece, we all know what's going on; we see it and we hear about it. But we don't send indignant delegations to one another to discuss it. We're in such a pitiful state, so entrenched in our separate cities, that even today we find it impossible to act in our own interest or do the right thing. We remain disunited, incapable of combining in mutual support and friendship. [29] We stand by and watch the man growing stronger, and the only explanation I can find for this is that each city is purposely ignoring, in its deliberations and actions, the security of Greece as a whole, and regarding the time it takes for others to be ruined as personal gain. After all, everyone knows that, like a relapse or a sudden onset of fever, Philip is going to attack even those who seem at the moment to be well out of reach.

[30] You should also bear in mind that, however much the Greeks suffered under the Spartans or us, they were at least being wronged by

legitimate sons of Greece. Here's an analogy. Suppose the legitimate
son of a wealthy household mishandles or mismanages his estate; he
certainly deserves censure and criticism for doing so, but it cannot be
denied that, as the heir of the estate, it was his business he was engaged
in. [31] But if the estate was being ruined and wrecked by a slave
or a foster-brother, when it was none of his business: by Heracles!
Horror and anger would be the universal reaction. But Philip's current manoeuvres don't meet that kind of reaction, and he's not only
not Greek* or even akin to Greeks, but he's not even a barbarian from
a land one could be proud of; he's a damned Macedonian, and even
the slaves we used to buy from there were worthless.

[32] Nevertheless, his insolence knows no bounds. On top of his
destruction of Greek cities, he presides over the Pythian games, an
exclusively Greek event, and if he can't attend in person, he sends
some of his minions to organize the festival.* He holds Thermopylae
and the passes into Greece, and maintains that control with garrisons and mercenaries. He has even elbowed his way past us, the
Thessalians, the Dorians, and all the rest of the Amphictyons, and
gained the right of precedence in consulting the oracle, a privilege
that's denied even to some Greeks.* [33] He writes down for the
Thessalians the new constitution they are to adopt. He sends mercenaries to Porthmus to expel the democrats from Eretria, and others to
Oreus to set Philistides up as tyrant.*

But the Greeks connive at all this. They look on it like a hail-
storm, I think: everyone prays it won't come his way, but no one lifts
a finger to stop it. [34] Not only does his insolence against Greece as
a whole go unopposed, but—and this is the absolute limit—no one
resists even personal injury. He wronged the Corinthians by attacking Ambracia and Leucas. He wronged the Achaeans by promising to give Naupactus to the Aetolians. He took Echinus from the
Thebans, and now he's marching on Byzantium, which is supposed
to be an ally of his.* [35] As for our own grievances, I shall confine
myself to mentioning just the fact that Cardia, the most important
city of the Chersonese, is in his hands.* In spite of this treatment, we
hesitate and act like weaklings. We look askance at our neighbours
and distrust one another, rather than the man who is wronging us
all. But given that he treats us as a whole with such aggression,
what do you think he'll do when he gains mastery over each of us
separately?

[36] How has this come about? There must be some reasonable and fair explanation of the fact that in times past the Greeks were partial to freedom, and now they're partial to slavery. In those days, Athenians, most people shared a particular attitude. It's no longer with us, but it defeated the wealth of Persia, kept Greece free, and never lost a battle on land and at sea. The current parlous and chaotic state of our affairs is due entirely to its loss. [37] What was this attitude? A universal loathing of the practice of taking money from anyone who wanted to rule over or destroy Greece. It was a very serious matter to be caught taking bribes, and those who did so were most severely punished.

[38] There was no question of buying, from politicians or generals, the critical moment for any particular action (which Fortune often affords even careless people against attentive opponents), or civic concord, or distrust of tyrants and barbarians, or in short anything like that. [39] But now all these things are treated like marketable commodities and sold abroad, and the attitudes that are imported instead have infected Greece with a deadly sickness. What attitudes am I talking about? All the various attitudes that bribery brings in its train. A man is envied for having taken a bribe, dismissed with a smile if he admits having done so, forgiven if he's convicted, hated if he criticizes this conduct, and so on and so forth. [40] The point is that, by any criterion of strength—warships, a plentiful supply of men and money, an abundance of all other materials—every city nowadays is far better off than it was in the past. But thanks to those who traffic in them, these resources lose their utility, their potential, their value.

[41] But I'm sure you don't need me to tell you how things stand nowadays; you can see it for yourselves. What I want to do now, however, is prove that in the past things were quite different. In order to do so, I shall draw not on arguments of my own devising, but on your ancestors' words, as inscribed by them on a bronze stele and placed on the Acropolis.* The inscription was not designed to be of use to *them*; they had the appropriate attitude without it. No, they set it up so that *you* would have a model to remind you that you're supposed to take bribery seriously. [42] So, what does the inscription say? 'Arthmius the son of Pythonax, citizen of Zelea, is to be an outlaw and enemy of the Athenian people and of their allies, himself and all his kin.' And it goes on to give the reason for this: 'Because he introduced Persian gold into the Peloponnese.' That's what the inscription says.

[43] In the name of the gods, please stop and think what made the Athenians of the time do this. What was their motive? Arthmius, a citizen of Zelea—and therefore a subject of the Persian king, since Zelea is in Asia—was proclaimed an enemy of the Athenians and their allies, himself and his kin, and they were all outlawed, for having, in the course of a mission for his master, introduced gold, not into Athens, but into the Peloponnese. [44] And this was not the usual kind of outlawry. Why should a man of Zelea care if he's to be banned from taking part in Athenian public life? That's not what the inscription means. But think about our homicide laws. In cases where prosecution for murder isn't feasible, but killing is still sanctioned, the law states: 'And let him die an outlaw.' In other words, the killer of such a person remains unpolluted by the killing.*

[45] They felt, then, that the security of all Greece was their concern. Otherwise, if that wasn't their assumption, they wouldn't have cared about bribery and corruption in the Peloponnese. And anyone they found out about was severely punished, with his name even recorded on a stele. Naturally, this made Greece an object of fear to the barbarian, rather than the other way around. But that's no longer the case. You look at everything differently now, not just bribery. What do I mean? [46] You already know; I don't have to list all your faults. In any case, everyone else in Greece is pretty much as guilty as you. That's why I say that the present situation calls for a great deal of care and sound advice. What would I advise? Do you want me to tell you? And you won't get angry?

[47] There's an ingenuous argument that we hear from those who want to reassure us. It goes: 'Philip isn't yet as powerful as the Spartans. The Spartans were unbeatable at sea and ruled over the whole world; they had the Persian king as their ally; nothing stood in their way. But Athens still resisted them without being crushed.' But here's what I think. There have been great developments in almost every sphere, but nothing has changed and developed as much as warfare. [48] In the first place, I hear that everyone in those days, including the Spartans, used to invade for four or five months while the weather was good, ravage the enemy's farmland with their hoplites and citizen contingents, and then return home.* Their approach was so old-fashioned, or rather they were such good citizens, that bribery never came into it: war was carried out openly, according to certain rules.

[49] Nowadays, however, as I'm sure you're aware, traitors are the most destructive factor, and regular, pitched battles are totally ineffective. If you hear that Philip marches where he pleases, it's not because he has a phalanx of hoplites in his train, but because an army consisting of light-armed troops, horsemen, bowmen, mercenaries, and so on stretches out behind him. [50] And then, when he attacks a city that is riven by internal strife, and the inhabitants are too suspicious of one another to come out and defend their farmland, he sets up engines and puts the city under siege. It goes without saying that he doesn't differentiate between summer and winter; there's no time of year that he sets aside for a break.*

[51] I urge you all to keep these facts in mind and think about them. Then you'll see the importance of keeping the war away from Attica. If you take as your model the simple kind of warfare from the days of the war with Sparta, you'll find yourselves in a lethal stranglehold. No, your defensive strategy should be to keep the war as far from Athens as possible by all means, both political and military. Try to ensure that he stays bottled up in Macedonia, and avoid any decisive engagements.* [52] For a war, you see, we have many natural advantages—if we're willing to do our duty, Athenians. As one example among thousands, consider the nature of Macedonia, much of which can be plundered and devastated. But he has more experience of battle than us.

[53] I urge you, then, to act on my suggestion and resist him by military means. But that alone is not enough. Heart and mind, you must come to condemn those Athenians who speak for him. You must see that you'll never prevail over our enemies until you've punished those among you who serve their interests. [54] But, as Zeus and all the gods are my witnesses, you won't be able to do this. Your folly or madness, if that's what it is—for the terrifying thought has also occurred to me that some supernatural agency might be driving you to ruin—has become so extreme that you call on hirelings to speak (some of whom wouldn't even deny the label) because you want to hear abuse, envy, scorn, or whatever, and you laugh at their every gibe. [55] As if that wasn't bad enough, what's worse is that you've made it safer for them to pursue their policies than it is for patriotic politicians. But you know how terrible the consequences can be of giving such men a hearing. The facts I'm going to mention are familiar to you all.

[56] In Olynthus, some politicians were devoted to Philip and his every wish was their command, and others were true patriots and were trying to prevent the enslavement of their fellow citizens. Which of them doomed their homeland? That is, which of them carried out the act of treachery that sealed Olynthus' doom and took the cavalry over to the other side?* It was Philip's sympathizers. And, in the days when there still was such a place as Olynthus, they actually managed to persuade the popular assembly, with their innuendos and lies about the patriots, to send Apollonides into exile.*

[57] Olynthus wasn't the only place; the same practice has been utterly ruinous elsewhere too. In Eretria, after Plutarch and his mercenaries had been ousted and the democrats got possession of the city and of Porthmus, the city was divided between those who wanted to be under Athenian protection and those who preferred Philip.* The wretched and ill-starred Eretrians generally listened more to the members of this latter faction, and they were eventually persuaded to banish the politicians who were defending their own interests. [58] And look what happened then. Philip, their ally, sent them Hipponicus with a force of a thousand mercenaries, demolished the walls of Porthmus, and installed three tyrants: Hipparchus, Automedon, and Cleitarchus.* Twice since then the democrats have tried to save themselves, but he's had them banished, sending a mercenary force each time, first under Eurylochus' command and then Parmenion's.

[59] I'll mention only a few of the many other cases. In Oreus Philip's interests were being looked after by Philistides, Menippus, Socrates, Thoas, and Agapaeus, the very people who are now in control of the city (and it was no secret what they were up to), while a man called Euphraeus,* a former resident of Athens, was trying to ensure that they would retain their freedom and call no man their master. [60] It would take too long to explain all the various ways in which he was foully and despicably treated by his fellow citizens, but a year before the fall of the city he found out what Philistides and his accomplices were up to and formally denounced them as traitors. But a large mob formed, orchestrated and arranged by Philip, and hauled Euphraeus off to prison for disrupting the city.

[61] And what did the people of Oreus do when they saw this? So far from helping Euphraeus and crucifying the others, they calmly, even happily, accepted what was happening, saying that Euphraeus

deserved everything he got. After that, there was nothing to stop Philistides and his cohorts from doing exactly as they pleased. They began to intrigue for the capture of the city, and proceeded to put their plan into effect. If any ordinary citizen of Oreus realized what they were up to, he was cowed into silence by the memory of what had happened to Euphraeus. Things got so bad that no one dared to speak out about the looming disaster until the enemy was right by the city walls in battle array. And then the pro-Macedonian group betrayed the city, even while the loyalists were defending it. [62] Ever since the fall of the city in this shameful and underhand fashion, Philistides and his friends have been ruling as tyrants. Those who protected them before and connived at Euphraeus' treatment have been banished or killed, while Euphraeus himself committed suicide, an act that epitomized the honesty and integrity with which he had worked for the good of his fellow citizens by resisting Philip.

[63] You might be wondering why the citizens of Olynthus, Eretria, and Oreus were happier with the pro-Macedonian faction than with the patriots. The explanation is the same as here in Athens. Sometimes, however much they'd like to, it's impossible for people who have their fellow citizens' best interests at heart to say anything that their audience wants to hear, because they're compelled to consider the safety of the state. Their political opponents, however, serve Philip's interests in the very act of gratifying their audience. [64] The patriots were busy explaining the necessity for a war levy,* while their opponents were saying it was completely unnecessary. One side was recommending war and mistrust, the other peace, until the trap was sprung. And so on and so forth, of course; I don't need to dwell on particulars. One lot was offering advice that would make them popular, the others advice that would save the city. But eventually the people were for the most part won over, not so much because they'd been flattered or because they didn't know any better, but because they believed they'd been decisively defeated, and gave up.

[65] What I'm afraid of, by Zeus and Apollo, is that the time may come when you look around and find that you've run out of options, and then you might give up just as they did. But let's pray that it doesn't come to that, Athenians! Better to die ten thousand deaths than to grovel to Philip! See how well the people of Oreus have now been repaid for rejecting Euphraeus and entrusting themselves to Philip's friends! [66] See how well the people of Eretria have been repaid for

expelling your envoys and surrendering to Cleitarchus! They're being whipped and slaughtered, like the slaves they are! And how well and leniently he treated the Olynthians, who had elected Lasthenes* as their cavalry commander and had banished Apollonides!

[67] It's the worst kind of folly to entertain hopes of lenient treatment, to take bad advice, to shirk one's duty, to listen to those who speak for the enemy, and to assume that the city one inhabits is so powerful that, come what may, it can suffer no harm. [68] And that's not all. It's also contemptible to say, at some later point in time, 'Who would have thought it? If only we'd done things differently, by Zeus!' The people of Olynthus could think of plenty of things now which would have saved them from destruction if they'd looked ahead then. So could the people of Oreus and Phocis; so could the inhabitants of each and every place he has laid low.

[69] But what good would that do them? Whatever the size of the vessel, big or small, it's when the boat is in no danger that every man on board, from crewman to helmsman, has to be alert, to see that no harm comes to it, deliberate or accidental. By the time the sea is over the gunwales, there's no point in trying. [70] The same goes for us, Athenians. At the moment, we're safe and in possession of a city with unrivalled power, resources, and international standing. What are we to do, then? There are probably people seated here today who have long been wanting to ask this question. I shall give you an answer, by Zeus. I shall even draft a proposal, for you to ratify, if you wish, by a show of hands.

First, then, we must resist. We must make sure that we have what we need in the way of triremes, money, and troops. For surely, even if everyone else succumbs to slavery, *we* must still fight for our freedom. [71] Once we're fully ready ourselves and our course is clear, we issue a general appeal and send envoys everywhere to explain what we're up to—to the Peloponnese, I mean, and to Rhodes and Chios, and to the Persian king too, because it's certainly in his interest for us to curb Philip's world-conquering ambitions.* If these missions are successful, you won't have to face the danger and expense alone, when the time comes, and if they aren't you'll at least have created a delay. [72] Since our opponent in the war is a single individual, who lacks the strength of a united city, even delay serves our purpose. The mission that toured the Peloponnese last year to denounce Philip is a case in point. The envoys—who included myself, the excellent Polyeuctus, and Hegesippus—travelled from city to city and forced Philip to postpone his expeditions against Ambracia and the Peloponnese.

[73] But as long as you lack the resolve to work for your own defence, you should not, I think, issue that general appeal. It makes no sense for you to profess a concern for others while neglecting your own safety—to make others fear the future while you remain unperturbed about the present. That's not what I'm suggesting. What I'm saying is that we should send money to the troops in the Chersonese and do all that they ask of us;* we should make our preparations; we should summon and convene a general meeting of the Greeks, to clarify things for them and tell them off. This is suitable work for a city with the international standing of Athens. [74] If you imagine that the Chalcidians or Megarians are going to save Greece, while you evade your duty, you're mistaken. They'll be content if they can each secure their own safety. No, this is your job. Your ancestors fought long and hard for this privilege, and they bequeathed it to you. [75] If we sit idly by, looking after our own selfish interests and doing our best to do nothing ourselves . . . well, first, there's no one else to do the job and, second, if we do nothing now, I wouldn't be surprised if we find ourselves later having to carry out a whole load of unpleasant tasks all at once.

[76] That is my advice; that's what I propose. And I believe that even now we can still make a recovery if you do as I suggest. If someone has better advice to offer, let's hear it. And I pray in the name of all the gods that you make the right decision.

TRIALS IN PUBLIC CASES

18. ON THE CROWN

The hostility between Aeschines and Demosthenes continued unabated through the war against Philip, which culminated in the crushing defeat at Chaeronea, and beyond. Part of the continuing struggle between the rival factions centred on honorary decrees voted by the assembly to Demosthenes for his service to the state. Honorary decrees, as well as forming part of the democratic system of rewards and punishments by which the people maintained control over the politicians, also offered a means of testing policies, since the move by one group to propose an honour for one of their members or foreign associates could be contested by their opponents through the action for illegal legislation (*graphē paranomōn*); this action could be brought against the proposer of a decree which was in procedure or substance in breach of existing legislation. Demosthenes was voted a crown three times during and after the period of renewed hostility against Philip, in 340, 338, and 336. Each time the proposer was indicted by a political opponent. The present case concerns the last of the three proposals, by Ctesiphon, who was indicted by Aeschines. The charge was based partly on alleged technical breaches in the proposal, partly on the claim that the decree was flawed in content on the ground that Demosthenes was unworthy of the award. Aeschines could be sure that Demosthenes would appear as supporting speaker for Ctesiphon to defend both an associate and his own political record; so the stage was set for a showdown between the old enemies. The case did not come to court until 330. We are never told why it took so long, but it is likely that both sides were looking for the right moment to face a popular audience and were happy to acquiesce in adjournments. The world in which Athenian politics was conducted had now changed radically. Macedon was in control of Greece and Athens had lost its independence. Since Demosthenes had overseen a policy which had lost many lives and ended Athenian independence, Aeschines had good reason for optimism. In the event he lost by a crushing margin and quit Athenian politics. Evidently the jurors felt that Demosthenes' policies were right in principle and that the alternative represented by Aeschines, though less costly both in lives and in money, was less palatable. The speech was widely admired in antiquity, as it has been in the modern era, and is regarded by many as Demosthenes' finest. It is probably too long to have been delivered in this form in court. It and the prosecution speech of Aeschines (which survives as the third in his collection) were evidently revised for publication, as each sought to re-enact the courtroom battle before the bar of history. On the question who was right the jury is still out.

---

[1] I pray first to all the gods and goddesses that for this trial, Athenians, I may find you as well disposed towards me as I have always been towards Athens and all of you. My second prayer is for something that concerns you very much, in the sense that it bears very greatly on your piety and your reputation—that the gods move you to reject my opponent's advice as to how you should listen to me.* It would be quite wrong of you to do otherwise. [2] You should take your lead from the law and your oath, a document designed throughout to guarantee justice, one of whose provisions is that you should give both sides an equal hearing. This means, of course, that you should not have prejudged the case in any respect, and that you should be equally well disposed towards both parties. But it also means that you are obliged to allow every litigant to arrange his arguments as he wants and defend himself as he chooses.

[3] Aeschines has me at many disadvantages in this trial, Athenians, two of which are really serious. First, the stakes are unequal: it's far worse for me to lose your favour at this moment in time than it is for him to fail to make his case. After all, for me . . . well, I don't want to say anything disagreeable at the start of my speech, but my accuser has me at a disadvantage.* The second point is a fact of human nature: everyone enjoys listening to abuse and accusations, but has a low tolerance for self-praise. [4] So he gets the job of pleasing you, and I'm left with annoying almost everyone! If I hold back in this respect and don't talk about my achievements, I doubt I'll be able to mount a successful defence or show why I deserve the crown. But if I embark on an account of my record as a statesman, I'll be forced to talk about myself a lot. I shall endeavour to do so as modestly as possible; but whatever the case forces me to do is his fault, really, since it was he who initiated the trial on these terms.

[5] You would all agree, I'm sure, Athenians, that this case concerns me no less than Ctesiphon, and therefore demands just as much effort from me. It's unpleasant and annoying to lose anything, especially when it's an enemy who takes it from you, but there's nothing worse than losing your goodwill and respect, precisely because there's nothing more important than having them. [6] Since these are the terms of the trial, I ask every one of you to give me a fair hearing as I defend myself against the charges. That is what the law demands of you, and Solon, the original author of our code of laws, was a loyal democrat.* If he thought that laws should be given authority not only by being

written down, but also by jurors being required to swear an oath, [7] I'm sure this didn't mean that he mistrusted you. It was because he realized that the only way for a defendant to escape the prosecutor's slanderous aspersions, which give him the advantage because he speaks first, is if each of you jurors observes his sacred obligation and listens favourably to the second speaker's defence; and if each of you reaches a verdict on the case as a whole only after listening fairly and impartially to both sides.

[8] It looks as though today I shall be submitting my entire private life for scrutiny, as well as my achievements as a statesman, and so I'd like once again to call on the gods and pray in your presence, first, that for this trial I may find you as well disposed towards me as I have always been towards Athens and all of you, and, second, that the gods move each and every one of you to reach a verdict in this case that will be sure to enhance the good name of the city as a whole and your piety as individuals.

[9] Now, if Aeschines had confined his prosecution speech to the official charges, I too would get straight down in my defence to addressing the Council's decree.* But since he spent just as much time raising extraneous matters, mostly lies about me, it seems both necessary and fair, Athenians, for me briefly to address those issues first. I wouldn't want anyone here to be led by mere irrelevancies to listen less sympathetically to the justice of my response to the indictment.

[10] As far as my private life is concerned, see how straightforwardly and fairly I can respond to all his slanderous aspersions. I've never lived anywhere but here in Athens, so you would know if I was the kind of person he was making me out to be. If he's right, then, don't listen to another word from me, however exceptional and constant my public service has been, but get up and cast your vote against me right now. But if the conclusion and opinion you've reached is that I and my family are far better and better born than him and his family, and just as respectable—I won't put it any more contentiously than that—as any of our fellow citizens, then don't take his word for anything else either, because it's obviously all equally false. Just remain as well disposed towards me today, please, as you have always been on all my earlier appearances in court.

[11] [*To Aeschines*] For all your bloody-mindedness, Aeschines, it was utterly simple-minded of you to imagine that I would give up talking about my achievements as a statesman and turn instead to

your insults. No chance! I'm not so stupid. What I'll do is examine your lies and allegations about my political career, and only later, with the jury's approval, will I turn to the personal insults you so liberally hurled at me.

[12] [*To the jurors*] Despite the fact that among the many crimes he has imputed to me are at least some for which the law prescribes severe penalties—the most severe penalties, in fact—the purpose of the present trial is just this: it is an opportunity for him to express hostile rancour, insult, abuse, defamation, and so on, all at once, even though it is impossible for the state to exact an appropriate or even approximately appropriate punishment for the crimes with which he has charged me, if his accusations are true.* [13] I mean, it's unnecessary to deny a person access to the people and the chance of a hearing, especially if the attempt is motivated by malicious spite: as the gods are my witnesses, Athenians, that is untoward, un-Athenian, and unfair. No, if, in his opinion, I was committing crimes against the city that were as grave as he was just describing in his melodramatic fashion, he should have had me punished as stipulated by law at the time the crimes were committed. He should have impeached me, if he found me doing things that warranted impeachment, or he should have indicted me, if he found me making illegal proposals. After all, if he's prepared to prosecute Ctesiphon in order to get at me, surely it's inconceivable that he wouldn't have indicted me if he had thought he would gain a conviction.

[14] The same goes for every other crime that he mentioned in the course of the slanderous account you've just heard, or any other crime against you that he might claim to have found me committing. Every single one of them is punishable under the law; in every case, conviction in court entails harsh and severe penalties. He could have used these legal instruments against me. If that's what he had in fact done—if he had gone about it like that—his accusation of me today would be in keeping with his past practice. [15] But no, he stepped off the straight, legally sanctioned road; he had no interest in putting it to the test at the time of the events. And so, after all these years he struts on stage with an assortment of accusations, gibes, and insults—and then takes Ctesiphon to court, when I am his target. Although the entire trial displays his hostility towards me, he assiduously avoids open confrontation with me and comes to court to try to deprive someone else of citizenship.* [16] And yet, whatever else one might

say in favour of Ctesiphon's acquittal, Athenians, it would, I think, be perfectly fair to say that Aeschines and I should contest our hostility between ourselves. There's no justice at all in sidestepping our confrontation and trying to do someone else harm.

[17] All this suggests that every single one of his charges is a baseless lie, bearing no relationship to the truth. But I shall consider them one by one, and especially the fabricated version of the peace and the embassy that he used against me. He attributed to *me* the things *he* did with the help of Philocrates!* I don't have any choice in the matter, Athenians, but I don't think it's inappropriate anyway: I shall remind you how things stood at the time, so that you can consider every point in its proper context.

[18] First, then, at the start of the Phocian War*—which I had nothing to do with, since it pre-dated my entry into politics—your position was that you wanted the Phocians to survive, even though you appreciated that they were in the wrong, and you'd have been delighted to see the Thebans suffer. Your hostility towards the Thebans was neither unreasonable nor unjustified, because they had been taking undue advantage of their success at Leuctra.* Second, the entire Peloponnese was divided, with those who hated the Spartans too weak to eliminate them, and those who had formerly held power thanks to the Spartans struggling to retain control of their cities. The upshot for the Peloponnesians and for everyone else in Greece was unending strife and turmoil. [19] There was no way of disguising this, and once it came to Philip's attention he bribed his collaborators in every city, and set about sowing discord and internal conflict everywhere. Then, while others' policies were astray and awry, he strengthened his own position and made himself the supreme power in Greece.

Meanwhile, luck had run out for the once-dominant Thebans. The length of the war was wearing them down, and it became perfectly clear that they would be forced to turn to you for help. Philip didn't want that to happen, an alliance between the two cities, so he offered you peace and them military assistance.* [20] He found you almost willing dupes, which would have been impossible, except that the rest of the Greeks displayed . . . I don't quite know whether to call it cowardice or stupidity or both at once. Even though you were involved in a war that went on and on without interruption—even though, as events have made clear, you were fighting for the common good—they offered you no assistance at all: no money, no troops, nothing. Your anger was perfectly reasonable and fair, and it made you willing to listen to Philip. *That* was how the peace treaty came about at the time; it had nothing to do with me, as he alleged. Anyone who looks into the matter impartially will find that it was Aeschines and his cohorts, with their wrongdoing and bribe-taking while the terms of the peace were being drafted, who were responsible for our present troubles.*

[21] In the interests of truth, I'll give a detailed account of all this. For however clearly we might find evidence of criminal activity there, it has nothing to do with me. The first person to make a speech and raise the topic of peace was Aristodemus, the actor;* then Aristodemus was followed by Philocrates of Hagnous—your associate, Aeschines, not mine, however strenuously you deny it—who introduced a formal proposal and had been bribed, along with Aristodemus, for this purpose. And, whatever their motives, which I won't go into just now, the proposal was supported by Eubulus and Ctesiphon. At no point did I have anything to do with it.

[22] That's what happened. There can be no doubt about it, because it's the truth. But Aeschines, deep-dyed in depravity, doesn't stop at claiming that I was responsible for the peace; he also dares to say that I made it impossible for us to convene a general meeting and make peace along with all the other Greek states.* [*To Aeschines*] And then, you . . . Words fail me. I don't know what to call you. Can you name any occasion when you were present, and you saw me trying to stop the city embarking on such a venture, an alliance as important as you were just describing, and you protested at what I was doing? Did you ever come forward with information and denounce me for the crimes you're attributing to me now? [23] But if I had accepted money from Philip to stop the Greeks joining forces, so far from saying nothing, your only option was to shout it from the rooftops, to call the world to witness, to explain the facts to these men here. But you did nothing like that; no one got to hear your famous voice.*

[*To the jurors*] The fact of the matter is that we had no envoys out and about in Greece at the time; we had sounded everyone out long before. His account of the matter is completely untrue. [24] And as if that weren't enough, I can't conceive of anything more defamatory of you than these lies of his. If you were encouraging the Greeks to go to war, while at the same time sending ambassadors to Philip to negotiate peace, you were acting like Eurybatus,* not like a proper city or decent people. But in fact it's all completely and utterly false. What possible reason could you have had for convening the Greeks at that moment in time? To make peace? But everyone already had that. To make war? But you were in discussions about peace.

As it turns out, then, not only was I not the original instigator or author of the peace, but everything else he said about me is demonstrably false as well. [25] Then again, consider the policies each of us pursued after the city had ratified the peace. This will show you who was collaborating with Philip, and who was working for you, with the city's welfare at heart. What I did was propose, as a member of the Council, that the ambassadors should find out where Philip was, sail there as quickly as possible, and receive his oaths.* Aeschines and his cohorts, however, refused to do so, even after my proposal had been passed. [26] And what was the significance of their refusal, Athenians? I'll tell you. The longer the interval before the oaths, the more it suited Philip and the worse it was for you. Why? Because you had suspended all military activities not just from the moment you committed yourselves on oath to the treaty, but from the first moment you began to anticipate peace.

Philip, however, was extremely busy throughout the entire period. He believed—and it turned out to be true—that he would be able to keep all the places he seized from us before swearing to the treaty, because no one would revoke it for their sake. [27] But I guessed what he would do, Athenians, and that was precisely why I drafted the resolution I just mentioned, that we should sail to wherever Philip was and get him to commit himself on oath to the treaty as soon as possible. I wanted the treaty to be secured by his oaths while your allies, the Thracians, still held Serrium, Myrtenum, and Ergisca—the strongholds Aeschines mocked just now in his speech.* I didn't want to see him seize the critical places, make himself master of Thrace, and gain all its wealth and troops. That would make it easier for him to succeed in all his future endeavours.

[28] Aeschines omitted to mention this decree of mine, or to have it read out. Instead, he attacked me for suggesting, as a member of the Council, that Philip's ambassadors should be introduced to the Assembly. What was I supposed to do? Formally object to the introduction of men who had come for no other reason than to talk to you? Tell the theatre-manager not to reserve seats for them?* They'd have sat in the two-obol seats, were it not for my decree! Should I have

acted like Aeschines and his cohorts, and tried to save the city trivial sums of money after having sold all its assets? No way. [*To the Clerk of the Court*] Please take this decree and read it out, to make up for Aeschines' omission, though he was well aware of its existence.

Demosthenes' decree is read out.†

[30] [*To the jurors*] That's what I proposed at the time. My aim was to do Athens good, not Philip. But those fine ambassadors of ours more or less completely disregarded the decree and sat in Macedonia for three whole months, until Philip returned from completing his conquest of Thrace. We could have reached the Hellespont in ten days, or three or four if we'd taken ship,†* and we'd have saved the strongholds by receiving his oaths before his takeover. He'd hardly have laid a finger on them if we'd been there. If he had, we wouldn't have received his oaths, and then he'd have failed to get the peace he wanted. He'd have had neither the peace nor the strongholds.

[31] That was just the first instance during the embassy of Philip's thieving ways and the first fruit of the bribes those villains had accepted. And I admit that my undying hostility and enmity towards them dates from this event. But let's consider their next crime, which was even worse. It followed hard on the heels of the first. [32] After their failure to comply with my decree had enabled Philip to seize Thrace, and he had committed himself on oath to the treaty, he bought another favour from them. This time their job was to stop us leaving Macedonia until he was completely ready for his campaign against the Phocians. He was worried that, if we returned to Athens and told you of his intentions and preparations, you would mount an expedition, take the sea route to Thermopylae in your triremes, and close the pass as you had done before.* He intended to be past Thermopylae by the time you heard from us what he was up to, and then there would be nothing you could do about it. [33] But even if he occupied Thermopylae, he was still afraid that you might spoil his plans by voting to help the Phocians before he had finished them off. This worried him so much, in fact, that he hired this despicable creature here [*Demosthenes points to Aeschines*]—this time on his own, not along with the other ambassadors—to unleash an orgy of destruction by means of the speeches and reports he delivered.

[34] Now, there's something I need you to bear in mind, Athenians, please, throughout this trial. If Aeschines hadn't made charges that

were irrelevant to the indictment, I wouldn't be bringing up extraneous matters either. But his reliance throughout on slanderous allegations forces me to respond briefly to each of his charges.

[35] So what was it that he said all those years ago to bring about an orgy of destruction? He said that Philip's advance past Thermopylae was no cause for concern, because 'You'll get everything you want. Do nothing, and in two or three months' time you'll hear that Philip is on good terms with those whose enemy he had been when he arrived, and on bad terms with his former friends.* Words are no guarantee of good relations,' he said, rather pompously, 'but common interests are. And it's in everyone's interests—Philip's, the Phocians', and yours—to get rid of the obdurate oppressiveness of the Thebans.'

[36] These words of his met with a warm welcome in certain quarters, because there was a vein of hostility towards the Thebans at the time.* But what happened next—not *long* afterwards, but straight away? The Phocians were ruined, their cities razed to the ground, and you, who had been persuaded by him to do nothing, soon found yourselves bringing your goods and chattels in from the countryside.* Meanwhile, Aeschines had his money, and on top of everything else we incurred the hostility of the Thebans and Thessalians, while Philip gained their gratitude for what he had done.* [37] [*To the Clerk of the Court*] To corroborate what I've just been saying, please read first Callisthenes' decree, and then Philip's letter. Both documents are quite explicit about all this.

Callisthenes' decree is read out.

[38] [*To the jurors*] When you made peace, was that what you expected? Was that what this hireling promised you? [39] [*To the Clerk of the Court*] Now read the letter that arrived afterwards from Philip.*

Philip's letter is read out.

[40] [*To the jurors*] The letter may be addressed to you, but you can see the clear and precise message it contains for his allies. 'I've done all this', it implies, 'against the will of the Athenians, and they aren't best pleased about it. So if you Thebans and Thessalians are sensible, you'll treat them as your enemies and put your trust in me.' That was the message he wanted to get across, even if he didn't use those actual words. It enabled him to win them over so thoroughly that they failed

to look ahead and see any of the consequences, but let him take over completely. Their current misfortune and misery are direct results.

[41] And the man who helped Philip gain their trust, his accomplice, who brought his lies back here to Athens and duped you by repeating them in his report, now laments what has happened to the Thebans and goes on about it in heart-rending terms! But he is responsible for it all—the Theban catastrophe, the disaster in Phocis, and the general wretched situation in Greece. [*To Aeschines*] Of course you're upset at what happened, Aeschines; of course you feel sorry for the Thebans. You own property in Boeotia and farm their land.* And what a lot of pleasure the Theban catastrophe gave me, considering that my surrender was immediately demanded by the person who was responsible for it!* [42] [*To the jurors*] But I find myself touching here on a topic that will perhaps be more appropriate later. I'd better go back to proving that the present situation is a direct result of the crimes committed by Aeschines and his cohorts.

Once you had been tricked by Philip—by these hired men of his, who sold themselves while serving as ambassadors and told a pack of lies in their reports—and once the poor Phocians had been tricked and their cities destroyed, what happened next? [43] The loathsome Thessalians and the stupid Thebans began to regard Philip as their friend, their benefactor, their saviour. He was their be-all and end-all, and they wouldn't hear a word spoken against him. You had misgivings and doubts about what he had done, but you kept the peace. You had no choice in the matter. Everyone else in Greece as well, who had been duped and cheated of their hopes no less than you, was glad to keep the peace, even though they had long been indirectly under attack.

[44] Philip was busy conquering the Illyrians, the Triballians, and some Greeks as well,* which was adding substantially to the forces under his command; at the same time, there was a trickle of people from the Greek cities, who were using the opportunity created by the peace to travel to Macedonia and get themselves corrupted. Under these circumstances, everyone who was affected by these preparatory moves of Philip's was under attack. They may not have realized it, but that's another matter. It's certainly not my fault, [45] because I was constantly issuing warnings and raising the alarm, not only here in Athens, but wherever I was sent. But the Greek cities were diseased: their politicians and agents were accepting bribes or being tempted

by the prospect of money; few private citizens were concerned about the future, while the majority were seduced by the calm and leisurely pace of their daily lives; and everyone was suffering from the delusion that the threat would pass them by and supposed that the risks run by others would keep them safe from harm.

[46] What has happened, of course, is that ordinary people have paid for all their inopportune negligence with their freedom, while those in power, who imagined they were betraying everything apart from themselves, have come to realize that they betrayed themselves first. At the time, when they were accepting bribes, they were called 'Philip's friends and intimates', but now they hear the proper terms applied to them: 'damned toadies' and the like. [47] The point is, Athenians, that when someone spends money on a bribe, it's not the traitor's interests he's trying to advance; and once he's got what he paid for, he has no further use for the traitor's advice. Otherwise, no one would be better off than a traitor!

But that's not what happens, of course. Far from it. An imperialist who gains control of a state also becomes the master of those who sold it to him; and from that moment on, knowing how corrupt they are, he treats them with loathing, suspicion, and contempt. [48] Even if the time for action has passed, understanding such things is always timely and sensible, so look at the facts. For a while, Lasthenes was known as one of Philip's friends—until he betrayed Olynthus. So was Timolas, until he doomed Thebes. So were Eudicus and Simus of Larisa, until they let Philip take over Thessaly. You'll find these men all over the world—banished, humiliated, plagued by every kind of misfortune. What happened to Aristratus in Sicyon, or to Perilas in Megara? They became outcasts, didn't they? [49] These cases show with perfect clarity that Aeschines and his cohorts need a loyal patriot who vigorously opposes their policies! [*To Aeschines*] Without such a person, Aeschines, you traitors and hirelings would never meet with the conditions for being bribed! It's because there are plenty of people here who stop you getting your way that you and your cohorts are alive and drawing your pay. Left to yourselves, you'd never have lasted this long.

[50] [*To the jurors*] There's plenty more I could say about the past, but I've probably already gone on too long about it. It's his fault for spraying me, so to speak, with the dregs of his own corruption and wrongdoing. Some of you are too young to remember what happened,

and so I had to clear my name, but I might have irritated those who knew, even before I'd said a word about it, how venal he had been back then. [51] Not that he calls it 'venality', of course: he calls it 'friendship and intimacy'. In fact, at one point in his speech just now he used the phrase 'the man who taunts me for being Alexander's friend'.* [*To Aeschines*] But why should I taunt you for friendship with Alexander? What 'friendship'? What makes you so special? I wouldn't call you the 'friend' of either Philip or Alexander—I'm not that crazy—unless we're to call seasonal labourers and other hired hands the friends and intimates of those who hired them. [52] No, I call you a 'hireling', first of Philip and now of Alexander, and all these men here agree with me. If you don't believe me, ask them—or perhaps I should do so for you. [*To the jurors*] Tell me, Athenians, do you regard Aeschines as Alexander's hired hand or as his friend? [*To Aeschines*] You can hear what they say.*

[53] [*To the jurors*] Anyway, I'd like now to respond to the charges contained in the actual indictment as well. I shall have to describe my achievements, because Aeschines needs to hear—as if he didn't already know—why, in my opinion, I deserve not only the honours mentioned in the Council's decree, but much more besides. [*To the Clerk of the Court*] Here, take this indictment and read it out.

The indictment is read out.

[56] [*To the jurors*] Those are the parts of the decree he thinks are illegal, Athenians. If I take them first, I'm sure you'll see that I'll be going about my defence in the right way, since throughout I'll be following the same order as his indictment. I'll address each point in turn, without missing anything out, if I can help it.

[57] So, the decree states that I always acted and spoke in the best interests of the people, was always determined to do the best I could, and was officially commended for doing so. It seems to me that your assessment of these statements by Ctesiphon depends on my public career, in the sense that their truth and appropriateness, or their falsity, will emerge from considering my policies. [58] And I think the same goes for the facts that he proposed the crown without adding 'once he has submitted to his audit',* and recommended that the award should be proclaimed in the theatre. That is, I think my record as a public servant is again the factor that should determine whether or not I deserve the crown and proclamation before the people. But

I agree that I should also point to the laws that allowed Ctesiphon to make these proposals.

That's my plan, Athenians, for a fair and straightforward defence, and I shall therefore move on to my achievements. [59] But I wouldn't want anyone to think I'm digressing from the indictment if I find myself mentioning general Greek affairs and issues. In finding fault with the decree for stating that by word and deed I promoted your best interests, in charging that this statement is false, he made discussion of my entire career as a statesman relevant and necessary. There are many fields of public service. I chose Greek affairs as mine, and this means that I am entitled to refer to them in the course of my defence.

[60] I shall not be speaking about the places Philip seized and secured before I embarked on my career as a politician and public speaker, on the grounds that none of them had anything to do with me. I will, however, mention and supply an account of all the setbacks he endured from the moment I gave my attention to these matters. But first, I just want to point out that [61] Philip had a huge advantage, Athenians. The Greek cities—not just some of them, but absolutely all of them—produced a more abundant crop of damnable traitors and bribe-takers than had ever been seen before in living memory. The situation in Greece was already bad, as a result of political feuding, but with these men as his accomplices and collaborators he made it even worse, using trickery or bribery or whatever it took to doom cities to destruction. Even though they all shared a common interest in checking his growth, he managed to divide them into many factions.

[62] This was how things stood in Greece; no one was aware of the gathering, growing evil. What you have to do, then, Athenians, is consider what course of action the city should have chosen under these circumstances, and, since it falls under the field of politics I assigned myself, it's appropriate that you should hear about it from me. [63] [*To Aeschines*] What should Athens have done, Aeschines? Should we have renounced our pride and dignity, aligned ourselves with the Thessalians and Dolopians, helped Philip become master of Greece, and undone the glorious and honourable achievements of our ancestors? But perhaps that would truly have been too shocking. Should we instead, then, have sat back and watched events unfold, even though it was obvious what was going to happen if

Philip met with no opposition and we had, of course, seen it coming for a long time?

[64] [*To the jurors*] But now that it's all over I'd love to ask the severest critic of my policies which group he'd have liked the city to have joined. The one that must share the blame for the humiliating disasters that have happened in Greece, and includes, let's say, the Thessalians and their associates? Or the one that watched events unfold in the expectation of profiting from the outcome, a category that includes the Arcadians, Messenians, and Argives? [65] But many of these cities, perhaps all, have ended up worse off than us. If Philip had taken his leave as soon as his conquests were over, and then had done nothing, and specifically nothing to harm any of his allies or anyone else in Greece, it would make a kind of sense to find fault with, and prosecute, those who opposed what he was doing. But if Philip stripped everyone in Greece of their prestige, their regional supremacy, their freedom, and even, where he could, their systems of government, then, of course, in following my advice you made exactly the right decision.

[66] But, as I was saying, [*to Aeschines*] what should Athens have done, Aeschines, when it saw Philip working towards making himself master and tyrant of Greece? Or, more to the point, what was a statesman here in Athens to say in his speeches or write in his proposals? [*To the jurors*] I had always been aware, all my life, before ever I set foot on the speaker's platform, that it was the Athenian way to fight for distinction, honour, and glory, and that your commitment to promoting the common Greek good cost you more, in terms of both money and men, than any other state in Greece spent on its *own* interests. [67] At the same time, I saw that Philip himself, our opponent, in his pursuit of imperial power, had lost an eye, broken a collar-bone, maimed an arm and a leg, and was prepared to sacrifice any body part that Fortune cared to remove if it meant he would live the rest of his life renowned and honoured.*

[68] No one, surely, would have dared to suggest that it was appropriate for someone raised in Pella—an insignificant little place at the time—to harbour ambitions on a scale that would move him to desire dominion over Greece and to dedicate himself to that goal, while you, who are Athenians and are reminded on a daily basis of your ancestors' virtue in every speech you hear and spectacle you see, cravenly surrendered your liberty to Philip of your own free will. That would

have been a preposterous suggestion. [69] The only remaining alternative, therefore—the only *possible* alternative—was to oppose, in the
name of justice, all his acts of unwarranted aggression against you.
That's what you did from the start, quite rightly and properly, and
that's the policy—I freely admit it—that I've been proposing and
promoting throughout my political career. But what was I to do? [*To
Aeschines*] I put the question to you now, leaving everything else out
of it. Amphipolis, Pydna, Potidaea, Halonnesos—I have no memory
of these places. [70] Serrium and Doriscus, the sack of Peparethos,
and all the other crimes committed against Athens—I deny knowledge even of their existence.* And you know your claim that I stirred
the people of Athens to hostility towards Philip by talking about
these crimes? The decrees came from Eubulus, Aristophon, and
Diopeithes, not from me. But you . . . you just go right ahead and say
whatever you want, don't you?

[*To the jurors*] Anyway, let's leave all that aside. [71] But when Philip
annexed Euboea and made it a bastion against Attica; when he intrigued
against Megara; when he seized Oreus; when he razed Porthmus;
when he installed Philistides as tyrant in Oreus and Cleitarchus
in Eretria; when he subjugated the Hellespontine region and put
Byzantium under siege; when he destroyed some Greek cities and
forced others to take back their exiles*—when he did all these things,
was or was he not acting illegally, breaking the treaty, and violating the
terms of the peace? And was there or was there not a need for someone in Greece to come forward and stop him doing these things? [72]
If not—if Greece was to be seen as the proverbial 'Mysian plunder'*
while there were still Athenians alive and walking the earth—then my
speeches on these issues were pointless, it was equally pointless of you
to have taken my advice, and everything we've done might as well be
counted as crimes and blunders and attributed to me. But if someone
had to come forward and put a stop to Philip's aggression, who better
than the people of Athens? That was the policy I recommended. The
sight of Philip enslaving the whole world moved me to oppose him,
and I never stopped issuing warnings and giving reasons for us not to
give in. [73] [*To Aeschines*] But it wasn't we who violated the terms of
the peace treaty, Aeschines; it was Philip, when he seized our ships.*

[*To the Clerk of the Court*] Fetch the actual decrees and Philip's
letter, and please read them in order. They'll show who is responsible
for what.

Eubulus' decree is read out.

[75] [*To the jurors*] It was Eubulus, not me, who proposed this decree. The next one came from Aristophon, the next from Hegesippus, then Aristophon again, then Philocrates, then Cephisophon, and then all of them together.* I played no part in these matters. [*To the Clerk of the Court*] Go ahead, read them.

The remaining decrees are read out.

[76] [*To Aeschines*] These decrees constitute my evidence. Why don't you do the same, Aeschines? Why don't you produce one that was drafted by me and shows that I was responsible for the war? But you can't. If you could, that would have been your prime exhibit. What's more, even Philip doesn't hold me responsible for the war; he blames others for it. [*To the Clerk of the Court*] Please read Philip's letter.*

Philip's letter is read out.

[79] [*To the jurors*] Not a word about Demosthenes in this letter; he doesn't attribute *anything* to me. But why does he make allegations against others and fail to mention anything I've done? Because in doing so he'd have brought up his own crimes, which I was relentlessly opposing. First, I proposed the mission to the Peloponnese, when he was originally trying to worm his way into there. Then I proposed the mission to Euboea, when he was after Euboea. Then I proposed the expedition to Oreus—no diplomatic mission this time—and the one to Eretria, after he had installed tyrants in those cities. [80] Later I was solely responsible for sending out the naval expeditions which saved the Chersonese, Byzantium, and all our allies there. These missions and expeditions did the city nothing but good, with eulogies, expressions of esteem, honours, crowns, and gratitude coming its way from the beneficiaries. Meanwhile, among Philip's victims, those who listened to us at the time gained their safety, while those who neglected our advice often recall our warnings, appreciate our kindness towards them, and see Athenian citizens as men of wisdom and clairvoyance, because everything turned out as we predicted.

[81] Now, Philistides would have given a great deal of money to keep Oreus, as would Cleitarchus for Eretria. Philip himself would have spent lavishly to have these places as his dependencies, ranged against you, and at the same time to conceal his widespread acts of

unwarranted aggression and prevent anyone from investigating them. But everyone knows this [*to Aeschines*]—and no one better than you, Aeschines, [82] since you were Cleitarchus' and Philistides' proxy* in Athens, and their envoys used to stay with you when they visited Athens in those days. The city sent them packing, on the grounds that their intentions were hostile and their proposals neither just nor expedient, but they were *your* friends. So nothing turned out as Philip wished, for all your slanderous allegation that I keep silent after pocketing money and raise my voice only when it's gone.* That's not your way, is it? No, you raise your voice once you're in pocket, and you'll never stop, unless this court today shuts you up by stripping you of your citizenship.

[83] [*To the jurors*] Anyway, my exploits then gained me a crown from you. In his proposal, Aristonicus said the same things, word for word, as Ctesiphon in his just now, and the crown was proclaimed in the theatre. Aeschines was there, but he didn't raise any objections, and he didn't indict the proposer either. [*To the Clerk of the Court*] Please take this decree and read it out.

Aristonicus' decree is read out.

[85] [*To the jurors*] What slur, I ask you, has Athens incurred as a result of this decree? Has it been mocked or ridiculed in the slightest, as far as anyone here is aware? Yet this is the outcome Aeschines just predicted if I were crowned. Now, when an event is recent and everyone knows the facts, they respond with gratitude if it turned out well, and if not with punishment. Well, as you can see, I was thanked at the time, not censured or punished. [86] So up to and including the time of these events, it was recognized that I was acting in the city's best interests. My advice and proposals prevailed in debate; my proposals were put into practice and led to crowns for the city, for me, and for everyone; and you marked my successes with sacrifices to the gods and with processions in their honour.

[87] When Philip had been forced off Euboea by a combination of your weaponry and my policies and decrees (though my contribution is strenuously denied in some quarters), he began to look for another bastion to use against you. It came to his attention that we are the largest consumers of imported grain, so he decided to gain control of the grain-shipment routes. He descended on Thrace and started by demanding that the Byzantines, who were his allies, should

support his war against Athens. When they refused, on the legitimate grounds that these were not the terms of their alliance, he surrounded the city with a palisade, brought up engines, and put it under siege. [88] There's no point in my asking what you should have done under these circumstances, because it's blindingly obvious, but who was it who came to the help of the Byzantines and saved them? Who was it who stopped the Hellespont becoming enemy territory at that time? It was you, Athenians, and when I say 'you', I mean the city. And who was it who addressed the city, drafted proposals, took practical measures, and dedicated himself wholeheartedly and unstintingly to the matter? That was me.

[89] But you don't need me to tell you how much everyone bene-fited from this; you experienced the reality of it. Besides enhancing your reputation, the war that broke out then brought you all the ne-cessaries of life in greater quantities and at a better price than during the present peace—the peace which these fine fellows protect, to the detriment of the city, in the expectation of future benefit. May they be cheated of their hopes! May *your* prayers to the gods be answered, because you have the city's welfare at heart, and may they share in that future, rather than you in the future they'd like to see. [*To the Clerk of the Court*] Please read out to the jury the Byzantine decree awarding a crown to the city, and the decree of the people of Perinthus to the same effect.

The decrees are read out.

[92] And now please read the crown decree of the Chersonesians as well.

The decree is read out.

[93] [*To the jurors*] In other words, my programme and policies not only managed to save the Chersonese and Byzantium, and stop Philip gaining control of the Hellespont—actions that brought Athens hon-our and distinction—but also displayed to the world Athenian mag-nanimity and Philip's villainy. Within the plain view of everyone, he put Byzantium under siege, despite having an alliance in place with the city. What could be more disgraceful or disgusting than that? [94] You, however, who had plenty of valid reasons for complaint against the people of Byzantium after the dishonourable way they had treated you before,* didn't bear a grudge against them and didn't abandon

them, despite the wrong they had done you. In fact, you went on to prove yourselves their saviours, which won you fame and friendship everywhere. Now, everyone knows that in the past the city has often awarded crowns to statesmen, but I'm undeniably the first—the first of Athens' advisers and politicians, that is*—to have gained a crown for the city.

[95] I shall now prove that his tirade against the Euboeans and Byzantines, in the course of which he reminded you of all the occasions when they behaved badly towards you, was malicious in intent. It's not just that it bore little relation to the truth—*that*, I think, is something you can't help but know; it's also that, even if it were perfectly true, it was more expedient for the situation to be handled as I handled it. In order to prove this, I'd like to give a brief account of one or two of Athens' recent good deeds. For both individuals and states should always try to model their future conduct on the best deeds of their past.

[96] Let's return, Athenians, to when the Spartans were dominant on land and sea,* and Attica was surrounded by territory they controlled with harmosts and garrisons—Euboea, Tanagra, all Boeotia, Megara, Aegina, Ceos, and the rest of the islands. Despite the fact that the city had no fleet or fortifications at the time, you still mounted an expedition to Haliartus and then, very shortly afterwards, to Corinth. Your predecessors could well have borne a grudge against both the Corinthians and the Thebans for their actions during the Decelean War,* but they didn't. Far from it.

[97] [*To Aeschines*] You'll notice, Aeschines, that in neither case were these actions carried out to help benefactors, nor were they unaware of the risks involved. But they didn't see these as reasons to abandon people who had looked to them for help. No, the prospect of danger meant less to them than the distinction and honour they would win, which was right thinking—the thinking of good people. No one can escape the fact that life has death as its limit, even if he keeps himself locked away in a cubbyhole, and good men, with good hope as their shield, are bound always to undertake every noble exploit and to bear with courage whatever comes their way from the gods.*

[98] [*To the jurors*] That's what your predecessors did; that's what the more senior of you did after the Thebans' victory at Leuctra, when they tried to destroy the Spartans.* The Spartans were neither our friends nor our benefactors; in fact, they had often done us

terrible harm. But you thwarted the Thebans, without being deterred by their formidable strength at the time and the fearsome reputation they had earned, and without taking account of what the men for whom you were going to risk your lives had done in the past. [99] And this showed all Greeks everywhere that, while anger is of course your response to any and every wrong done you by others, yet when they are at risk of annihilation or loss of freedom, you don't bear grudges or hold the past against them.

Nor were these the only occasions when you displayed this attitude. When the Thebans were trying to annex Euboea,* you didn't stay aloof; you didn't let the wrong Themison and Theodorus had done you at Oropus influence your behaviour. No, you helped them too. This was the first time, by the way, that the city obtained the services of volunteer trierarchs, and I was one of them. But more on that later. [100] Just saving Euboea was a good and noble deed, but there was far better yet to come. After you had gained control of the cities and their inhabitants, you restored them, in the interests of justice, to the very people who had wronged you, without letting any of the injuries you had suffered influence your judgement in a matter where trust had been placed in you. I pass over the countless other cases I could mention. I could draw on the past or our own times for sea battles and military expeditions undertaken by Athens, always for the sake of the freedom and security of the rest of Greece.

[101] And so, having witnessed Athens' willingness to engage time and again in major conflicts to protect others' interests, what course of action was I to suggest or recommend when what was at stake was in a sense the city itself? Oh, yes, by Zeus: that you should bear a grudge against people in their hour of need, and should seek plausible reasons for total surrender. But if I had made even a verbal attempt to dishonour the noble traditions of our city, a death sentence would have been the right response, whoever the prosecutor was. I say 'even a verbal attempt', because I'm certain you wouldn't have put such advice into practice. After all, if you had wanted to, what was to stop you? It wouldn't have been difficult. Weren't Aeschines and his lot already on hand with precisely such advice?

[102] Anyway, let's turn now to the bill I introduced next. I'd like you once again to consider it in the light of what was in the city's best interests. It was clear to me, Athenians, that your fleet was falling apart.* The rich were gaining exemptions after spending hardly

anything, while citizens of moderate or slender means were being bankrupted, and the deterioration of the fleet meant that the city was slow off the mark. I therefore proposed a law which enabled me to force the first group, the rich, to do their duty, thus ending the exploitation of the poor. It also made it possible for the fleet to be in a seaworthy condition when it was needed, which was of critical importance for the city.

[103] I was indicted, stood trial before you on this issue, and was acquitted, with my prosecutor failing even to gain the required proportion of the votes.* But how much money do you think I was being offered by the leaders of the syndicates, or by those in the second or third ranks?* They mainly wanted me not to propose this law in the first place, but, failing that, they wanted me to let it drop while the issue was *sub judice*. You'd be shocked to hear how much I was being offered, Athenians. [104] But it was hardly surprising, coming from them. The earlier legislation allowed them to fulfil the liturgy in groups of sixteen,† which meant that they could ruin their less well-off fellow citizens while paying little or nothing themselves. Under my law, however, the amount each person was required to pay was determined by a means test, and the upshot of this was that a man who had previously contributed a sixteenth of the cost of just one trireme might now be required to take responsibility for the costs of two ships. They had even taken to calling themselves 'contributors' rather than 'trierarchs'. So they offered me the earth to have the law cancelled and to avoid being compelled to do their duty.

[105] [*To the Clerk of the Court*] Please read first the decree which led to my indictment and trial, and then the registers, starting with the one drawn up under the previous law and then the one drawn up under my law.

The decree is read out.

[106] Now that admirable register.

The first register is read out.

And now, for the sake of comparison, the register compiled under my law.

The second register is read out.

[107] [*To the jurors*] Was it just a trivial amount of relief I gave those of you who are poor?* Was it just a trivial amount of money the

rich would have spent to get out of their obligations? I pride myself not only on my resistance to their advances and my acquittal from the indictment, but also on having introduced a law that was good for the city and has proved its value in practice. Throughout the war our naval forces were managed in accordance with my law, and not one trierarch ever presented you with a suppliant's branch because he felt hard done by, or took up residence in the temple at Munychia,* or was thrown into prison by the Naval Commissioners; nor was a single trireme abandoned abroad and lost to the city, or left behind here because it wasn't seaworthy. [108] But all of these things happened under the earlier versions of the law. And why? Because the poor were carrying the burden of the liturgy and that created all sorts of problems. Thanks to me, the trierarchies were transferred from the poor to the rich and everything went as it should.

Another reason why I deserve gratitude, then, is that throughout my political life I have done nothing but increase the glory, honour, and power of Athens. No measure of mine is motivated by malice or anger or ill will; none is petty or un-Athenian. [109] You will find that the same principles guide both my domestic and my foreign policies. At home I never preferred the blandishments of the rich to the rights of the general populace, and abroad I never prized Philip's gifts and friendship over the common good of all Greeks.

[110] Moving on, then, I think I should speak about the proclamation and the audit. I think I've said enough to show that I acted in the best interests of the state, and that I've always been a loyal democrat and committed to your welfare. It's true that I've said nothing about my most important measures and activities,* but I should respond next to the alleged illegalities, and in any case, even if I say nothing more about my political activity, I can still rely on the fact that each of you already knows about it. I shall go ahead on that basis.

[111] Now, Aeschines served up such a garbled account of the laws that apply to Ctesiphon's decree that I swear he must have left you confused, and I didn't understand much of it myself either. But I shall give a simple and straightforward account of the legal issues. I mean, it would never cross my mind to claim, as he maliciously insists I did, that I had no need to submit to an audit. In fact, I acknowledge a life-long liability to account for everything I've done as an administrator or public servant. [112] I do, however, claim not to be liable, on any day of my life, to account for private funds I have freely given to the

people—are you listening, Aeschines?—and I claim that the same goes for anyone else as well, even if he happens to be one of the nine Archons. Is there any law in our constitution that is so riddled with injustice and spite that, when a man has altruistically and generously contributed some of his own money, it denies him a vote of thanks, hauls him before the Board of Sycophants, and gives them the right to audit his donation?* Of course not! If Aeschines says there is, let's see it. That would be enough, and I would say no more.

[113] There's no such law, Athenians. Like a true sycophant, he says that, because I was responsible for the Theoric Fund when I made my subvention, 'Ctesiphon proposed an official vote of thanks for a man who had an audit pending'. But this misrepresents the facts: Ctesiphon wasn't referring to auditable funds, but to my benefaction. 'But you were also one of the Supervisors of the City Walls.' And that was exactly why I deserved the official vote of thanks, because I financed the project from my own pocket, without drawing on public funds. It's the public account that needs a final audit and investigation, but a donation deserves gratitude and recognition, which is why Ctesiphon proposed a vote of thanks in my case.

[114] I maintain, in fact, that this distinction isn't just enshrined in your laws, but is typically Athenian. This is easy to prove; many examples come to mind. I think first of Nausicles, who has often been crowned by you for benefactions he made while serving on the Board of Generals. Then there was Diotimus with his gift of shields, and Charidemus likewise; they were both crowned. Or take Neoptolemus here: he had wide official responsibilities, but was rewarded for his subventions. It would be harsh if a public official were prevented by his position from making a private donation to the city, or if his generosity led to an audit rather than thanks. [115] [*To the Clerk of the Court*] To verify what I've been saying, get the actual decrees that were passed in these cases and read them out. Go ahead, please.

Two decrees are read out, one after the other.

[117] [*To Aeschines*] Every one of these men was auditable for his conduct while in office, Aeschines, but not for what he did to earn a crown. Nor am I, then, either. At any rate, I suppose the same rules apply to me as to others, under the same circumstances. I gave money to the city from my own funds; I'm being thanked for that, but I'm not liable to be audited for these gifts. I held public offices, and of

course I've been audited for them, but not for my subventions. And, by Zeus, if I had done wrong while in office—well, you were there when the accountants submitted my accounts to the court. Why didn't you accuse me of wrongdoing then?

[118] [*To the jurors*] In actual fact, Aeschines himself supports my claim that I was crowned for things that are not liable to audit. [*To the Clerk of the Court*] Here, take the decree that was proposed in my honour, and read it in its entirety. [*To the jurors*] You will see that the parts of the resolution drawn up by the Council which he failed to mention in his indictment prove the trumped-up nature of the charges he's bringing. [*To the Clerk of the Court*] Go ahead.

The resolution is read out.

[119] [*To Aeschines*] So, even though none of these benefactions of mine is mentioned in your indictment, you're treating the rewards the Council says I deserve for them as indictable. In other words, you agree that it's legal for the gifts to be given, but you indict as illegal any expression of gratitude for them! [*To the jurors*] By the gods, what sort of man would do such a thing? A damned, villainous, malicious crook, that's who!

[120] Now for the question of the proclamation of the award in the theatre.* I won't mention the tens of thousands of people who have been proclaimed there before, including myself on several occasions. [*To Aeschines*] But, by the gods, Aeschines, are you too dense and stupid to realize that it makes no difference where the proclamation is made—that the crown still brings its recipient just as much admiration? It's those *conferring* the crown who are benefited by a proclamation in the theatre, because it encourages everyone in a mass audience to serve Athens well. The onlookers' applause is more for the exhibition of gratitude than for the person receiving the crown. That's why we have this law. [*Demosthenes hands the document to the Clerk of the Court*] Here's the law I mean; please read it.

The law is read out.

[121] [*To Aeschines*] Did you hear that, Aeschines? There's no ambiguity about the wording: 'Except for any person specified in a decree of the people or the Council, who is to be proclaimed.' So much for your trumped-up charges and your pathetic fabrications. I recommend hellebore for your problem.* Do you feel no shame at taking

someone to court out of malice rather than for any crime? Doesn't it bother you to alter laws, to remove some of their clauses, when they should be read out in their entirety to jurors who are under oath to uphold the laws with their vote? [122] And then, in the course of doing this, you list the qualities proper to a democrat, as if you'd taken possession of a statue you'd ordered and then found to your disappointment when it was delivered that it had not been made according to specification,* or as if democrats were recognized by their theoretical attributes, and not by their actions and policies. The names you call me, many of them obscene, that you bawl out as though you were standing on a cart,* may apply to you and your family, but they don't apply to me.

[123] [*To the jurors*] This raises another point, Athenians: the difference between accusation and abuse. As I see it, accusation presupposes crimes that are punishable under the law, whereas abuse presupposes the kind of slanderous allegations enemies typically make about one another. Now, it doesn't seem likely to me that our ancestors built these courts of law for us to hurl personally motivated obscenities at each other in front of an audience; they were built to convict those who commit crimes against the city. [124] Aeschines knows this as well as I do, but he preferred vilification to accusation. By rights, he should get as good as he gave, even where this is concerned. I'll come to that presently, but in the meantime I have a question for him. [*To Aeschines*] What are we to say of you, Aeschines? Are you the city's enemy or mine? Mine, obviously. Why, then, did you pass up opportunities to do the people a favour and punish me by legal means for my crimes, by audit or indictment or some other legal procedure? [125] Why today, when *I* am utterly unassailable—unassailable by law; because of the passage of time; thanks to the statute of limitations; because I've previously been tried more than once on all the relevant issues; and because of my proven innocence of any crimes against the city—but the *city*'s reputation is bound to be affected to a greater or lesser extent by something that was, after all, the people's doing – why do you confront me on such an issue? It seems likely that you might be just pretending to be my enemy, when you're really an enemy of the people.

[126] [*To the jurors*] Anyway, the verdict that is demanded by your oath and by justice is now obvious. But it seems that I must respond to his many lies; it goes against the grain for me to speak ill of others,

but his allegations leave me no choice. Since I have to give you at least the most essential facts about him and show what sort of person, from what sort of family background, so readily launches into abuse and ridicules my words, even though he himself used language that no decent person would ever have used [127] . . . Well, had my prosecutor been Aeacus or Rhadamanthys or Minos,* and not a tittle-tattler, a pettifogger, and a damned clerk, I'm sure none of them would have spoken that way or come up with such offensive pomposities. None of them would have cried out what sounded like a line from a tragedy, 'O earth! O sun! O virtue!', or anything like that; they wouldn't have invoked 'intelligence and education, by which we tell good from bad'. But that's what you got from Aeschines, as you know.* [128] [*To Aeschines*] But what have you, you piece of trash, or your family to do with virtue? People like you can't even tell the difference between good and bad. What virtue? What makes you so special? And what gives you the right to talk about education? A truly educated person would never talk about himself like that, and would blush to hear someone else doing so. But people like you, who lay claim to an education they don't have, are so obtuse that they're painful to listen to and don't come across as educated at all.

[129] Where you and your family are concerned, the difficulty is not knowing what to say, but where to start. Should I begin with your father, Tromes, a slave who worked in the school of Elpias near the temple of Theseus, and wore heavy fetters and a wooden collar? Or with your mother, who regularly engaged in 'midday marriage' in the lean-to near the shrine of the hero Calamites, while bringing up her handsome manikin, the quintessential third-string actor, you? But everyone already knows about your mother, without my saying a word. So should I start with the naval piper Phormion, the slave of Dion of Phrearrioi, who raised her up from her noble trade? But as Zeus and all the gods are my witnesses, this worries me. If I'm to describe your background properly, it will look as though I've deliberately chosen improper language!*

[130] [*To the jurors*] So I'll leave his background out of it, and start with his own life. It has indeed been extraordinary: it has made him an accursed enemy of the people. It wasn't long ago—no, what am I saying? It was just the other day—when he became, at one and the same time, an Athenian citizen and a public speaker. He lengthened his father's name by two syllables, changing it from 'Tromes'

to 'Atrometus', and reinvented his mother as the very dignified 'Glaucothea', although everyone knows her as 'Empousa',* a name she came by, obviously, because there was nothing she wouldn't do or allow to be done to her. How else would she get such a name? [131] [*To Aeschines*] But gratitude and decency are so alien to you that, even though the Athenians were responsible for your transformation from slave to free man, and from pauper to plutocrat, so far from feeling obliged to them, you sold your services and promote policies that do them harm. [*To the jurors*] All right, there are some slightly ambiguous cases, where it might be argued that his proposals were in the city's interests; but, leaving those aside, I'll mention instances where it has been proved beyond the shadow of a doubt that he was acting in our enemies' interests.

[132] Everyone here knows how Antiphon, who was struck off the register of citizens, returned to the city after promising Philip that he would set fire to the dockyards.* I found him hiding in Piraeus and brought him before the Assembly, but Aeschines, with his usual malignancy, screamed and shouted that what I was doing was intolerable in a democracy—that I was assaulting fellow citizens who had fallen on hard times and entering homes without a warrant—and procured his release. [133] If it were not for the clear-sightedness of the Areopagus Council, who realized what a bad mistake you were making and reopened the investigation, this traitor would have been snatched from your grasp unpunished, and would have been allowed to leave the city thanks to Aeschines' bombast. As things turned out, though, the Areopagus Council had him arrested and brought before you once again, and this time you had him tortured on the rack and executed.

[134] The Areopagus Council, then, knew that Aeschines was responsible for what had happened. That's why, when you appointed him as your advocate in the matter of the temple of Apollo on Delos—an act prompted by the same blindness that has often led you to betray your own interests—as soon as you brought the Areopagus Council in too and put it in charge of the affair, it immediately sacked Aeschines, on the grounds that he was a traitor, and gave Hypereides the job. This was done by a vote from the altar,* and not a single vote was cast for this piece of filth. [135] [*To the Clerk of the Court*] To verify what I've been saying, please call the relevant witnesses.

The witnesses' deposition is read out.

[*To the jurors*] Sacking Aeschines, then, and giving his job to someone else was the Council's way of pronouncing him a traitor and no friend of the democracy.

[136] The Antiphon affair is just one example of the kind of thing this lout got up to as a politician. It's rather similar, don't you think, to what he's accusing me of?* But let's remind ourselves of another occasion, when Philip sent Python of Byzantium, accompanied by delegates from all the rest of his allies, to try to shame the city and show that we were in the wrong.* With his confidence high, Python bore down on you with a flood of words, but I stood firm. I got to my feet, argued against him, and so far from conceding that the city's position was unjustified, I so convincingly proved Philip to be in the wrong that even his allies stood up and admitted it. Aeschines, however, supported Python and testified—falsely, I might add—against his country.

[137] As if that were not enough, some time later Aeschines was caught meeting with the spy Anaxinus in Thrason's house.* Now, anyone who is in the habit of holding one-to-one meetings and conversations with an enemy agent is surely a born spy himself and an enemy of his country. [*To the Clerk of the Court*] To verify what I've been saying, please call the relevant witnesses.

The witnesses' deposition is read out.

[138] [*To the jurors*] I could tell countless such stories about him, but I won't. The situation is pretty much as follows. I could produce a great deal more evidence to prove that in those days he was working for the enemy and trying to browbeat me. But you tend not to commit these things accurately to memory, nor assign them the indignation they deserve. Instead, when someone wants to trip up and persecute a rival speaker who's trying to do you good, you've proved to have the perverse habit of more or less entirely letting him get away with it. You trade the good of the city for the pleasure you feel at listening to insults. And this means that it's always easier and less dangerous to hire one's services out to the enemy than it is to choose the path of patriotic politics.

[139] It's bad enough that Aeschines helped Philip before the war. By Earth and all the gods, of course it is! It was treachery! All the

same, let's say we don't hold that against him. But once our ships had been openly seized, once the Chersonese was being ravaged, once the man was marching on Attica, there was no ambiguity about the situation: we were at war. Even then, however, this malicious mumbler of verse can't dispute the fact that he never acted in your interests, nor does he have to his credit any decree of greater or lesser importance that was designed to do the city good. If he says he does, he's welcome to use some of my water to prove it.* But no such decree exists. Now, there are only two possibilities: either he didn't propose any measures to counter mine because at the time he found nothing wrong with my policies; or the reason he made no attempt to improve on my policies is because he was working for the enemy.

[140] But what about when there was destructive work to be done? Was he silent then? Did he propose no measures? On the contrary: no one else could get a word in! Now, of course, up to a certain point the city could tolerate what he was doing and he could get away with it, but there was one final thing he did, Athenians, which set the seal on everything he had done before. He devoted a lot of his speech to it—to an account of the Amphissan decrees,* that is. It was all an attempt to distort the truth, but that's just impossible in some cases. [*To Aeschines*] You don't have words enough to free you of the taint of what you did then.

[141] [*To the jurors*] With you as my witnesses, Athenians, I call on all the gods and goddesses who protect this land of Attica, and especially on Pythian Apollo, the city's ancestor,* to hear my prayer. If I'm telling you the truth now, and if I also told the truth in the speech I delivered straight away at the time in the Assembly, as soon as I saw that this blackguard had an interest in the business—for I knew what he was up to; I knew straight away—may the gods grant me good fortune and freedom from danger. But if my charge against him is false, motivated by hostility or personal rivalry, may they see that nothing good ever comes my way.

[142] Why have I uttered this curse? Why do I express myself so forcefully? Because although there are documents in the public archive that will allow me to make an irrefutable case, and although, of course, you remember what happened, I'm still afraid that Aeschines might be dismissed as too insignificant to have wreaked such havoc. That's what happened before, when the lies he told in his ambassadorial report doomed the poor Phocians to destruction.* [143] But in

fact the Amphissan War, which brought Philip, the bane of all Greece, to Elatea* and led to his election as leader of the Amphictyons, was Aeschines' work. All our worst misfortunes are to be laid at the door of this one man. Back then, I immediately raised the alarm and cried out in the Assembly: 'You're bringing war to Attica, Aeschines, an Amphictyonic war!' But he had packed the meeting with his supporters, who made it impossible for me to carry on, while others were so taken aback that they thought I must be motivated by personal hostility and that the charges I was bringing against him had no substance.

[144] You shall hear now, Athenians, the true nature of the business, what the point of the exercise was, and how it was executed. You were prevented from hearing the truth at the time by what was, as you'll see, a carefully contrived scheme. Understanding this will greatly enhance your understanding of political life. You shall see now just how cunning Philip was.

[145] Philip was never going to bring his war against you to any kind of conclusion unless he made the Thebans and Thessalians enemies of Athens. Despite the pitifully poor performance of your generals against him, the mere fact of war, compounded by piracy, was causing him immense difficulties: he could neither export his country's produce nor import what he needed; [146] he wasn't at the time stronger than you at sea, nor was he able to invade Attica by land unless the Thessalians joined him and the Thebans gave him passage; and although he defeated the various generals you sent out against him (I'll say no more than that),* sheer geography and the relative resources of the two sides were still making things difficult for him.

[147] Now, it seemed to him that no one in Thessaly or Thebes would listen if he tried to persuade them to march against you in support of his own private quarrel. However, if he could find a common cause with them and be elected their leader, he expected it to be easier to trick or persuade them. So what did he do? He set about— and see what a good job he did!—sowing confusion in the Pylaea and involving the Amphictyons in war, on the assumption that they would immediately ask for his help.* [148] Well now, if the move came from one of his or his allies' sacred delegates, the Thebans and Thessalians would smell a rat and the whole council would be on the alert. But if his agent was an Athenian, an enemy delegate, no one would have any idea that he was complicit. And they didn't.

[149] So what did he do? He hired Aeschines. Since, of course, in your usual slipshod way, no one here foresaw what would happen or took precautionary measures, Aeschines was nominated to be your official delegate at the Pylaea, and was pronounced elected after three or four hands had gone up.* When he joined the Amphictyons, bringing with him the high reputation of Athens, he set aside and ignored all his other obligations in order to focus on the task for which he had been hired. He had written a fair-seeming speech, including an account of how the Cirrhaean plain came to be consecrated land,* which he recited to the sacred delegates. Now, these were men with no experience of rhetoric and no idea what to expect, [150] so he won them over, and they voted to inspect the land which the Amphissans maintained was theirs to farm, but which he alleged was part of the sacred plain. Aeschines justified himself with the pretext that the Locrians were bringing a suit against us or something, but that was simply untrue. This becomes obvious when you consider that of course the Locrians couldn't initiate a suit against the city without citing us. But who subpoenaed us? Before what authority? [*To Aeschines*] Tell us who has the answers; point him out to us. But you can't. This pretext of yours has no substance or reality to it.

[151] [*To the jurors*] So the Amphictyons carried out the land survey he had suggested, and while they were doing so the Locrians fell on them. The whole party came close to being massacred, and some of the sacred delegates were seized. In the ensuing buzz of activity, formal complaints were followed by war being declared against the Amphissans. At first, Cottyphus was the commander-in-chief and the forces were raised from the Amphictyons themselves. But some of them failed to turn up, and the rest were so ineffective that they might as well not have turned up. At that point, those who had been primed to do so—men from Thessaly and elsewhere who had long been suborned—began to make arrangements for Philip to take over as leader at the next Pylaea. [152] They came up with a plausible argument: either the Amphictyons themselves would have to raise money, maintain a mercenary force, and fine those who refused to cooperate, or they could elect Philip. To cut a long story short, the upshot was that Philip was elected.

He was quick to act. After calling up his troops, he entered Greece as though he were making for Cirrhaea, but then ignored the Cirrhaeans and Locrians, and seized Elatea instead. [153] If this hadn't immediately induced the Thebans to change their minds and join us, the entire force of Philip's endeavour would have descended on Athens like a flash flood. But the Thebans managed to check his impetus for a moment, at any rate. This was due, Athenians, mainly to a kindly god, but then also to me, in so far as it depended on any one man. [*To the Clerk of the Court*] Please hand me those decrees and the record of the dates when each of these events happened. [*To the jurors*] You'll see what this monster got away with—the terrible havoc he set in motion. [154] [*To the Clerk of the Court*] Go ahead, read the decrees.

Two Amphictyonic decrees are read out.

[155] And now please read the record of the dates when these things took place. [*To the jurors*] It was while Aeschines was our official delegate at the Pylaea. [*To the Clerk of the Court*] Go ahead.

The dates are read out.

[156] Now give me the letter which Philip sent to his allies in the Peloponnese when he was faced with the defection of the Thebans. [*To the jurors*] This too will make it perfectly clear that Philip was concealing the real reason for his enterprise, which was to target Greece, the Thebans, and you. He was only pretending to carry out the wishes of the Amphictyonic council. And the man who made it possible for Philip to justify his actions in this way was Aeschines. [*To the Clerk of the Court*] Go ahead, read it.

Philip's letter is read out

[158] [*To the jurors*] You can see that he avoids any mention of his own reasons for the campaign, and takes refuge in those provided by the Amphictyons. But who paved the way for him? Who handed him these excuses on a plate? Who must bear the bulk of the responsibility for the catastrophe? Aeschines, of course. It follows, Athenians, that you shouldn't keep blaming the disasters that have befallen Greece on just one man. It wasn't just Philip: corrupt men in every state were involved, as Earth and the gods are my witness. [159] Aeschines was one of them, and if I am to speak the truth with no holds barred, I for one wouldn't hesitate to say that he was the curse of all Greece, responsible, on the principle that the sower of the seed is responsible for the crop,† for all the lives that came to be lost, the ravaged land,

the ruined cities. It's strange that you didn't avert your gaze as soon as you caught sight of him;* but it seems that deep darkness tends to come between you and the truth.

[160] Having dealt briefly with the ways in which Aeschines harmed Athens, I turn next to the measures I took to oppose him. There are a number of good reasons why you should hear an account of what I did, not least the fact that, after all the real effort I put in on your behalf, Athenians, it would be wrong of you to refuse to listen to the mere words of my account. [161] I couldn't help noticing, for example, how influential Philip's corrupt partisans were in Thebes and, to a lesser extent, here in Athens. Under their influence, despite the danger and the urgent need for caution, the two cities were not only ignoring Philip's growing power, without taking any precautions, but were even ready to fall out and fight each other. I therefore devoted all my time to making sure this didn't happen. It wasn't just that I had my own reasons for thinking this the most expedient course; [162] I also knew that Aristophon, and later Eubulus, were constant in their desire to see the two cities on good terms, and that, although they were often on opposite sides where other issues were concerned, they always saw eye to eye on this. [*To Aeschines*] These are men you flattered and fawned on during their lifetimes, you phoney, but now that they're dead you speak ill of them, without even realizing that you're doing so! I mean, your condemnation of my Theban policy applies much more to them than to me, since they saw the advantages of alliance with Thebes before I did.

[163] But, as I was saying, once Aeschines had brought about the Amphissan War, and he and his accomplices had succeeded in arousing your hostility towards Thebes, Philip marched on Athens. That was why they had been busy setting the two cities at odds with each other, and they had made such headway that, if we hadn't roused ourselves in the nick of time, the situation would have been beyond repair. But once you've listened to the decrees I have here, and to the responses they met with, you'll see how things stood at the time between the two cities. [*To the Clerk of the Court*] Here, please read these out.

The decrees are read out.

[166] And please read the responses as well.

The responses are read out.

[168] [*To the jurors*] These documents show how things stood between
Athens and Thebes, thanks to Philip and these agents of his. The tone
of the decrees and the responses gave him good reasons to think that,
come what may, we and the Thebans would never join forces. And so
he and his army took to the field and occupied Elatea.

Now, you all know the chaotic effect the fall of Elatea had on us
here, but I'd like to run briefly through the most important incidents.
[169] Evening had come, when a messenger reached the Executive
Committee with the news that Elatea had fallen. They immediately
interrupted their dinner and got up. Some of them began to clear the
stall-holders out of the Agora and burnt the booths,* while others
sent for the generals and summoned the public trumpeter. The city
was in turmoil.

At dawn the next day, the Executive Committee summoned the
Councillors to their chamber, while you began making your way to
the Assembly. Before the Council had finished its deliberations or
framed any draft proposals, the entire population was sitting up on the
hill.* [170] The Councillors arrived, and the Executive Committee
announced the news it had received and introduced the messenger.
After the messenger had delivered his report, the herald asked, 'Does
anyone wish to speak?' No one came forward. He repeated the invitation time and again, but still no one got to his feet, even though all the
generals and public speakers were there, and our country was calling
for suggestions as to how it might avoid destruction. For the voice
of the herald doing his duty is rightly taken to be the voice of the
country as a whole.

[171] No one came forward. But if the invitation had been for anyone who wished Athens to survive to step up, all of you here and every
other Athenian citizen would have risen and approached the speaker's
platform, since the city's safety is something we all desire, of course.
If the invitation had been for the richest, the Three Hundred* would
have come forward. If the invitation had been for people with both
attributes, both patriotism and wealth, the people who came forward
would have been those who subsequently made substantial benefactions. I mean, it took both wealth and patriotism for them to do
that. [172] But apparently that moment, that day, was calling for
a man who was not only patriotic and rich, but had also followed the

course of events from the start and understood Philip's motives and intentions. After all, even a wealthy patriot would still not know what to do or what advice to give you, unless he had studied the situation for a long time and knew what Philip was up to. [173] And so, as it turned out, the man who was needed on that critical day was me. It was I who stepped up and addressed you.

Now, there are two good reasons why you should take careful note of what I said. First, it will show you that I was the only one of the speakers and policy-makers who stood his patriotic ground in the face of danger. It was I whose advice and proposals proved to be right for you under the terrifying circumstances. The second reason is that, at the cost of just a little time, you will learn a great deal that will help you in your future political activity.

[174] So this is what I said. 'Those who are unduly alarmed because they are assuming that Philip can count on the support of the Thebans are, in my opinion, failing to understand the situation. Surely, if they were right, we wouldn't be hearing that Philip was in Elatea, but on our borders. Nevertheless, there's no doubt in my mind that he has come to arrange Theban affairs to his liking. But let me tell you how things stand in Thebes. [175] Philip already has in his pocket all the Thebans he could bribe or trick, but he's finding it completely impossible to win over those who have resisted him right from the start and are still his opponents. What does he want, then? Why has he taken Elatea? To display his strength and demonstrate his military resources close to Thebes. He hopes that this will give his friends there courage and confidence, and overwhelm his opponents, who will either be frightened or forced into making reluctant concessions.

[176] 'So if at this juncture,' I said, 'we deliberately recall every Theban offence against us, and suspect them of being in the enemy's camp, we'll be answering Philip's prayers. But that's not all. If his opponents in Thebes give up their resistance, everyone there, without exception, will be on his side. And then, I fear, we would face a joint invasion of Attica. But if you do as I suggest—if you *think* about what I'm saying, instead of just trying to pick holes in it—I'm sure you'll see that my ideas are right and will disperse the danger that currently threatens the city.

[177] 'What am I suggesting, then? First, that you dismiss the fear you feel at the moment and transform it, all of you, into fear for the

Thebans, who are much closer to the danger than we are and effect-ively in the front line. Second, that you send the men of military age and the cavalry to Eleusis, so as to leave no one in any doubt that you are under arms. This will make it possible for the pro-Athenian fac-tion in Thebes to speak up in defence of justice with no less freedom than their opponents enjoy, because they'll see that, just as the army in Elatea is there to support Philip's traitors, so you are standing by in readiness to support those who are willing to fight for freedom, and will help them if they are attacked.

[178] 'The next step would be for you to elect ten ambassadors and give them joint responsibility, along with the generals, to decide when they should go to Thebes and what use to make of the expedition-ary force. But when the ambassadors reach Thebes, what strategy do I recommend? Please pay close attention now. They should not ask the Thebans for anything; it would be disgraceful to do so at this junc-ture. What they should do, on the understanding that the Thebans are desperate and we are better prepared, is promise to respond to a request for help. Then, if the Thebans welcome our approach and follow our lead, we'll have got our way while acting from motives that reflect well on the city; and if the plan comes to nothing, the Thebans will only have themselves to blame for their mistakes, and we'll have done nothing disgraceful or demeaning.'

[179] That was the substance or at least the gist of my speech, and then I stepped down. Since my words met with universal approval and there were no objections, I followed the speech with a proposal, the proposal with ambassadorial service, and ambassadorial service with convincing the Thebans. I was involved throughout, from start to finish; I devoted myself unstintingly in your service to the danger-ous situation the city found itself in. [*To the Clerk of the Court*] Please bring me the decree that was passed at the time. [180] [*To Aeschines*] But how should we see our respective roles that day, Aeschines? Shall I be Battalus, the name with which you insult and taunt me, and you no ordinary hero, but one of those we see on the stage—Cresphontes, or Creon, or Oenomaus, whom you once foully murdered in Collytus? If so, then I, Battalus of Paeania, proved at that time to be of greater value to his country than you, Oenomaus of Cothocidae.* But you've never been of service to the city in your life, whereas I did everything that was expected of a good citizen. [*To the Clerk of the Court*] Go ahead, read the decree.

Demosthenes' decree is read out.

[188] [*To the jurors*] That was how the rapprochement between Athens and Thebes first came about, when previously the two cities had been drawn by Aeschines and his cohorts into mutual hostility, hatred, and mistrust. As a result of this decree of mine, the danger threatening the city at the time vanished like a passing cloud.

Now, an upright citizen would have let everyone know at the time how, in his view, my measures could be improved on; he wouldn't have reserved his criticisms until now. [189] A statesman and a sycophant are poles apart, but the chief difference between them is that a statesman reveals his views before the event and doesn't try to shift responsibility on to those who followed his advice, or Fortune, or circumstances, or anyone other than himself. A sycophant, however, keeps silent when he should speak and cavils whenever anything turns out less than satisfactory.

[190] Anyway, as I said, the circumstances at the time called for honest speaking from someone who cared for Athens. Now, I will go so far as to admit my culpability if anyone today can suggest a better plan than mine, or show that there was *any* viable alternative. For if any course of action has occurred to anyone today that would have been expedient then, I agree that I should have seen it at the time. But if there neither is nor was any alternative, and even today no one has suggested one, what was a statesman to do at the time, if not promote the best of the available possibilities? [191] [*To Aeschines*] So that's what I did, Aeschines, because the herald was asking, 'Does anyone wish to speak?', not 'Does anyone wish to assign blame for the past?' or 'Does anyone wish to stand surety for the future?' You sat speechless in every Assembly at the time, while I repeatedly stepped up and spoke. Well, since you failed to do so then, why not speak your mind now? Tell us what speech I ought to have had to hand, or what opportunity I missed to further Athenian interests. What alternative alliance should I have recommended? What alternative course of action should I have advised the people of Athens to take?

[192] But bygones are everywhere treated as bygones. No one ever offers advice about the past; it's the future or the present that calls for the profession of adviser. At the time in question, although some of the dangers could be presumed to lie in the future, others were already upon us. You should consider my policy in the context of

these dangers, Aeschines, without picking on future developments. The end of everything is in the lap of the gods, but a statesman's intentions are exactly revealed by his policies. [193] So don't treat Philip's victory as a crime of mine: in such cases, the outcome is up to the gods, not me. But if you can disprove my claim to have actively pursued every expedient suggested by human reason, and to have acted throughout with integrity and dedication, exhausting myself in the process; or if you can prove that the events I initiated disgraced and demeaned the city, and were unnecessary; then you may accuse me, but only then.

[194] Since the storm that broke out overwhelmed not just Athens, but all Greece, what options did I have? Imagine a thoroughly security-conscious ship-owner who fitted out his ship with safety in mind. Blaming me is like blaming him when his equipment gets stressed and broken in a storm. 'But I wasn't the captain,' he'd say, just as I would point out that I wasn't a general. 'Besides, the whole thing was Fortune's doing, and Fortune wasn't mine to command.' [195] What I'd like you to realize, after due consideration, Aeschines, is this. If what happened to us was inevitable when we had the Thebans fighting alongside us, what do you think would have happened if Philip had attained the objective on which he expended all his powers of persuasion, and they had sided with him instead of us? And look at how threatened and endangered we felt when the battle was fought three days' journey away: what do you think would have happened if the same disaster had struck within Athenian territory? Don't you realize that, as it turned out, those three days made a vital contribution towards our survival, giving us the space to make a stand, muster our forces, and catch our breaths? Don't you realize that, had it been otherwise . . . but I shouldn't mention an experience we were spared by a kindly god, and by the protection of our alliance with Thebes, the very alliance you're denouncing.

[196] [*To the jurors*] The whole of this lengthy argument, jurymen, has been for your benefit, and for the bystanders listening outside. All I need for the despicable Aeschines is a few clear words. [*To Aeschines*] If you were the one and only person who knew what the future held, Aeschines, it was your duty to warn us when the matter was up for discussion. But if you lacked such foresight, you were constrained by the same ignorance as the rest of us—and so why are you holding against me something I might just as well accuse you

of? [197] For the extent to which I'm a better citizen of Athens than you—I'm confining myself here to the matter at hand; I'll come to the rest presently—is shown by the fact that while I devoted myself to what was by common consent good for the city, without hesitation or compromise, whatever the personal risks, you neither improved on my measures (otherwise they wouldn't have been adopted), nor made the slightest contribution towards promoting the city's best interests. Instead, you've been found after the event to have acted as the worst and most malign enemy of the city might have done. At the same time that Aristratus on Naxos and Aristoleos on Thasos,* whose hostility towards Athens is in no doubt, are taking Athenian sympathizers to court, Aeschines is bringing charges in Athens against Demosthenes. [198] But a man who used the misfortunes of the Greeks as stepping-stones to personal glory deserves death; he shouldn't be accusing someone else. And a man who profited from the same set of circumstances that did the enemies of Athens good cannot possibly be a patriot. Your lifestyle, your actions, your policies—and, again, your lack of policies—all show you for what you are. [*To the jurors*] When business is being conducted that is widely held to be good for you, Aeschines has nothing to say. When a setback happens and things go wrong, Aeschines is on hand. Like an old fracture or sprain, it's only when something bad happens to the body that he starts to ache.

[199] Since Aeschines lays so much stress on subsequent developments, I should like to say something rather strange. If my claim seems extravagant, I would ask you, by all that's sacred, not to be surprised, but to consider it in a favourable light. Suppose everyone already knew what was going to happen; suppose it was common knowledge and [*to Aeschines*] you, Aeschines, were busy warning us about it; suppose that, instead of keeping completely silent, you had raised the alarm at the top of your voice and shouted it from the rooftops. [*To the jurors*] Even then, it would have been wrong for the city to have abandoned its position, if it cared for reputation, ancestors, or the ages to come. [200] Now, it's true that the city is held to have come off badly—but then, in this, along with all other human beings, we are subject to the will of the gods. But if, while claiming to be the leader of Greece, Athens had ceded that position to Philip, we'd have been charged with betraying the common Greek cause. If we had given up without a struggle the position our ancestors endured every kind of danger to secure, the contempt of all Greeks would have

been directed at . . . [*to Aeschines*] you, Aeschines! Not at the city, I'm sure, nor at me.

[201] [*To the jurors*] In the name of Zeus, how could we have looked visitors to Athens in the face if events had turned out as they have and Philip was appointed to overall leadership and command, but it was others who fought to stop this happening, without our help, despite the fact that in the past the city had never chosen inglorious safety over the perils of a noble cause? [202] The whole world over, everyone knows that the Thebans, and the Spartans (as the dominant power prior to the Thebans), and the Great King of Persia would have been absolutely delighted to give us whatever we wanted, as well as allow us to keep what we had, as long as we surrendered our leadership of the Greeks to someone else. [203] But that, of course, was not the Athenian way; it would have been morally repugnant and out of character. From the beginning of time, no one has ever been able to persuade us to side with a strong but unjust power and seek safety in slavery. No, throughout history Athens has always, whatever the risks, fought for distinction, honour, and glory.

[204] This is a matter of pride for you, and you see it as an essential part of the national character, so much so that you reserve your highest praise for those of your ancestors who put these principles into practice. Quite right too. Who could fail to admire the courage of men who abandoned their city and took to their triremes rather than submit? Who chose as their general Themistocles, the man who had urged this course on them, and stoned Cyrsilus to death for suggesting acquiescence?* And it wasn't only Cyrsilus himself: your wives did the same to his wife. [205] The Athenians of that time weren't looking for a politician or general who would gain them prosperous slavery; the only life they considered worth living was a life of freedom. Each of them saw himself as the child not just of his parents, but of his country. What's the difference? A man who sees himself as the child only of his parents expects to die of natural causes when his time comes, whereas someone who sees himself as the child of his country will sacrifice his life to prevent his country losing its freedom. He fears the degradation and dishonour that would be his lot in an enslaved city more than he fears death.

[206] Now, of course, if I were trying to claim that it was at my urging that you adopted your ancestors' values, no one would let me get away with it, and with good reason. But in fact my claim is that these

kinds of principles are *yours*—that they were the city's values even before I was born. What I *do* claim for myself, however, is to have been of service for particular events. [207] Aeschines, however, denounces the whole enterprise and is asking you to deal harshly with me on the grounds that, if it were not for me, the city would never have felt fear or faced danger. In the short term, he's intent on depriving me of the crown, but he's also denying you the praise of all future generations, because if you condemn Ctesiphon for any alleged defects in my policies, people will attribute what happened to an error on your part, not to an implacable Fortune. [208] But there's no way, Athenians, no way at all that the decision to ignore safety, and fight for the freedom and preservation of all Greece, was a mistake. This I swear by your ancestors—those who bore the brunt of the fighting at Marathon, and those who served in the phalanx at Plataea, or fought at sea off Salamis and Artemisium.* And I swear it also by the rest of the brave men who lie in our public tombs, [*to Aeschines*] all of whom the city honoured with burial in the state cemetery, Aeschines, whether or not they were successful or victorious. Rightly so, because they had all equally displayed bravery, and each of them had met the particular fate assigned him by his guardian spirit.

[209] And then, you miserable, hunched little clerk, when *you* spoke of trophies and battles and great deeds of old—not that any of the events you mentioned had the slightest relevance to the current trial*—it was only in an attempt to deprive me of the crown, the token of my fellow citizens' respect. But as for me, what should my values have been, as I stepped up to mount the speaker's platform? Why don't you, an undistinguished actor, tell me, whose policies have always aimed at winning distinction for the city? Should I have modelled myself on a speaker whose advice would have betrayed Athenian ideals? [210] [*To the jurors*] In that case, I really would have deserved to die. After all, Athenians, no one should use the same criteria to judge cases where only private interests are at stake and those which affect the common good. You should consider the ordinary transactions of everyday life in the light of the statutes and practices that are specific to them, but when assessing political policies you should refer to your ancestors' values. If you intend to live up to their standards, each of you has to believe, when he enters a court to judge a case of public interest, that along with his staff and token* he bears the reputation of the city.

[211] But touching on your ancestors' achievements has diverted me from mentioning some relevant decrees and incidents. I'd like to return, then, to where I broke off.* When we reached Thebes, we found representatives there from Philip, the Thessalians, and the rest of his allies. Morale was high in Philip's camp, while our supporters were terrified. To prove that I'm not saying this today just to help my case, [to the Clerk of the Court] please read the letter that we envoys sent off straight away at the time. [212] [To the jurors] But Aeschines is such a consummate sycophant that he attributes everything that went well to circumstances, not to me, and blames me and my attendant misfortune for everything that went wrong. In his opinion, despite being known as an adviser and speaker, I made no contribution towards anything that was effected by speaking and consultation, but am solely responsible for all our failures on the battlefield and in generalship. It's hard to imagine a more vicious or damnable form of sycophantic harassment. [To the Clerk of the Court] Go ahead, read the letter.

The letter is read out.

[213] [To the jurors] The Thebans held an assembly and introduced the other envoys first, since they were formally their allies. They stepped up and delivered a speech full of praise of Philip and condemnation of you, in the course of which they reminded the Thebans of every hostile act you had ever carried out against them. The gist of the speech was that they wanted the Thebans to repay Philip for his benevolence towards them, and to punish you for the wrong you had done them. There were two ways, they said, that the Thebans could do this: either by giving them passage through to you, or by invading Attica alongside them. And they argued, at least to their own satisfaction, that, if the Thebans followed their advice, there would be an influx of assets such as livestock and slaves out of Attica and into Boeotia, while if they followed the advice we were going to give, Boeotian assets would be plundered by the enemy. They said plenty more besides, but the point was always the same. [214] As for our response, I would give my life to be able to recount it in detail, but it's past history, and I'm worried that you might think that since then a kind of deluge has overwhelmed the world, making an account of past events a boring waste of time. But listen at least to what we persuaded them to do and how they responded to us. [To the Clerk of the Court] Here, take this and read it.

The Thebans' response is read out.

[215] [*To the jurors*] So next the Thebans began to write and invite you to join them. To cut a long story short, you took to the field and went to their assistance. They were so welcoming that they took the hoplites and cavalry, who had been outside, into their homes and city, among their children, womenfolk, and all that they held most dear. On that day the Thebans displayed for all to see their admiration of three qualities of yours: courage, justice, and self-restraint. For by choosing to fight alongside you rather than against you, they acknowledged your superiority to Philip and recognized that your claim on them was more just than his; and by allowing you among their womenfolk and children—the possessions that they and all of us feel most protective about—they showed that they trusted you to act with self-restraint. [216] And events proved them right, Athenians, as far as you were concerned, anyway. The army came inside the city, but not a single complaint, justified or unjustified, was brought against a single soldier. What a credit to your self-restraint! And in the early battles, the one by the river and the winter one,* you displayed an exemplary, not to say remarkable degree of discipline, preparation, and commitment. This gained you praise from everyone else and the gods sacrifices and processions from you.

[217] There's something I'd really like to ask Aeschines.* When all this was going on, and the city was full of pride, joy, and thanksgiving, I wonder whether he participated in the sacrifices and shared the general joy, or whether he sat at home moping and mourning and sulking at the city's success. For if he joined in and didn't keep his distance, it's terrible, or rather sacrilegious of him to be asking you today, when you are under oath, to condemn as not in your best interests a policy which he himself had acknowledged, with the gods as his witnesses, to be in your best interests. But if he didn't join in, surely he deserves to die many times over for finding what made everyone else happy a source of grief. [*To the Clerk of the Court*] Please read these decrees for me now.

The sacrificial decrees are read out.

[218] [*To the jurors*] So for you it was a time of sacrifices, and for the Thebans a time to appreciate that we had been their saviours. As it turned out, then, those who had seemed to need help because of the intrigues of Aeschines and his cohorts were in a position to help

others because they followed my advice. Philip's response was to write repeatedly to the Peloponnese, and his letters reveal his tone of voice and how disturbed he was. [*To the Clerk of the Court*] Here, take these letters and read them. [*To the jurors*] You'll see how effective my persistence, my travels, my labours, and my many decrees were, for all that Aeschines mocked them just now in his speech. [219] Think of all the renowned and eminent statesmen there have been in Athens before me, Athenians: Callistratus, Aristophon, Cephalus, Thrasybulus, and countless others. But none of them ever devoted himself wholeheartedly to the city. One would draft proposals, but not serve as an ambassador; another would serve as an ambassador, but failed to make proposals. Each of them left himself time off and a loophole in case of accidents. [220] 'Are you implying', someone might ask, 'that your strength and determination were so superior that you could do everything yourself?' No, that's not what I mean. What I'm saying is that I was so certain of the seriousness of the danger gripping the city that I found it impossible to make any space for considerations of personal safety. Nothing would satisfy me except doing what had to be done, and doing it thoroughly. [221] I may perhaps have been blinkered, but I was absolutely certain that, whether it was a matter of advice or implementation or ambassadorial duty, no one would do a more committed and honest job than I would. That's why I took on every job myself. [*To the Clerk of the Court*] Read Philip's letters.

Philip's letters are read out.

[222] [*To Aeschines*] You can see how Philip was affected by my policies, Aeschines. You can see the tone of voice he adopted, even though previously he had often confidently addressed the city in threatening terms. In return, I was deservedly awarded a crown by my fellow citizens. You were there, but you raised no objections, and the man who brought the indictment, Diondas, failed to gain the required proportion of the votes. [*To the Clerk of the Court*] Now please read these decrees, bearing in mind that they have been found innocent of any wrong, and that it wasn't even Aeschines who brought the indictment against them.

The decrees are read out.

[223] [*To the jurors*] These decrees, Athenians, are identical, word for word, with the earlier decree proposed by Aristonicus and with

the one Ctesiphon here recently drafted. Now, Aeschines neither prosecuted them himself nor spoke in support of Diondas' indictment. But if his current denunciation of me is valid, rather than prosecuting Ctesiphon now, it would have been far better for him to have initiated a prosecution then, against Demomeles, the original proposer, and Hypereides.* [224] Why? Because Ctesiphon can refer to these precedents; to the verdicts of the courts; to the fact that it wasn't Aeschines who prosecuted Demomeles and the others, even though their proposals were identical to Ctesiphon's; to the illegality of retrying any case that has been settled, as these have; and so on and so forth. At the time, however, the case could have been decided on its own merits, before the intrusion of these issues.

[225] But, of course, it wasn't possible at the time for Aeschines to do what he's been doing today. He couldn't have taken a bunch of old episodes and decrees and selected from them, for slanderous purposes, things that no one knew about before or were of dubious relevance to today's proceedings. He couldn't have tried to make a plausible case by altering dates and attributing events to motives other than the true ones. [226] That was impossible at the time. The entire debate would have been conducted on the basis of the truth, since the events had only recently taken place. You still remembered what had happened and had the details practically at your fingertips. That's why he had no interest in putting the matter to the test at the time of the events, and has come before you now instead. As I see it, he expects you to view the trial as a rhetorical contest rather than an examination of policy; he'd like your verdict to be influenced by eloquence rather than what is good for Athens.

[227] What next? He cunningly suggested that you should disregard what you thought of us when you left home this morning, and behave like auditors:* when, sitting as auditors, you expect to find someone with a surplus, but see that the figures balance and there's nothing left over, you concede. He wants you to do the same now, to be swayed by the apparent force of his argument. Well, this will enable you to see how every unjust action turns out to contain the seeds of its own destruction. [228] For this clever analogy of his amounts to an admission from him today, at any rate, that we do already have reputations—I for promoting Athens' interests, he for promoting Philip's. If this wasn't how people already thought of each of us, he wouldn't have tried to change your minds. [229] But I shall easily

demonstrate that he's wrong to ask you to change your minds in this respect. This won't be a matter of totting up figures, which is no way to assess facts, but I shall briefly remind you of the details, and treat you, my audience, simultaneously as auditors and witnesses.

As a result of my policies, maligned by Aeschines, instead of the Thebans' joining Philip for an invasion of Attica, which was what everyone expected, they formed up alongside us to stop him. [230] Instead of war in Attica, it took place seven hundred stades away,* on the far borders of Boeotia. Instead of Euboean pirates plundering our land, Attica remained unmolested from the sea throughout the war. Instead of Byzantium falling to Philip and giving him control of the Hellespont, the Byzantines fought alongside us against him. [231] [*To Aeschines*] Do you think such achievements can be reckoned up like counters? Are we supposed to offset these events and delete them from the record? Shouldn't we be trying to ensure, rather, that they are remembered for all time? [*To the jurors*] I'm not even including on the credit side the fact that it was other people who came to experience the savagery which manifests itself once Philip has them in his power, while you have had the good fortune to enjoy the fruits of the humanity that he feigned while securing the remainder of his objectives. I'm not going to make anything of this.

[232] [*To Aeschines*] I have no hesitation at all, however, in saying that anyone who wanted to build a fair, unbiased case against a politician would not have included the kind of charges you brought against me just now in your speech, supported by false analogies and imitation of my words and gestures. Of course, the fate of Greece hinges on whether I used this word or that, or moved my hand one way or the other! How could you doubt it? [233] No, anyone wanting to build a fair case against me would consider, on the basis of the facts alone, the means and resources Athens had at the start of my political career, the resources that were subsequently accumulated under my direction, and what the situation was in the enemy camp. And then, if I weakened the city, he would prove that I was the guilty party, and if I considerably strengthened it, he wouldn't try to misrepresent the facts. But since you ducked the issue, I shall do it for you. [*To the jurors*] It's up to you to decide whether or not the account I give is fair.

[234] So, the city's resources consisted of the islands, but only the weaker ones: Chios, Rhodes, and Corcyra weren't with us. Contributions gave us an annual income of a mere forty-five talents,

and this had been collected in advance.* We had no hoplites or cavalry apart from our own. But the most terrifying thing of all, and the greatest help for the enemy, was that Aeschines and his cohorts had arranged matters so that all our neighbours—the Megarians, Thebans, and Euboeans—were inclining more to hostility than friendship. [235] That was the situation in which the city found itself; it's an exact description. Now consider our opponent Philip's circumstances. First—and this is of critical importance in warfare—he was the absolute ruler of his subjects. Second, he had a standing army. Third, he had plenty of money. Fourth, he did whatever he wanted, without having to state his intentions in preliminary decrees, without having to make his thoughts public, without being persecuted in the courts, without being prosecuted for making illegal proposals, without being answerable to anyone. In short, he had absolute sovereignty, absolute power, and absolute authority.

[236] Then there was me, who had the job of resisting him. It's fair to ask what power I had. None. Consider first just the right to address the Assembly: this was the only privilege I had, but it was available to Philip's hirelings just as much as to me. And whenever they got the better of me (a not infrequent occurrence, for one reason or another), at the end of the day the decisions you had made favoured our enemies. [237] Nevertheless, despite starting with these disadvantages, I arranged alliances between you and Euboea, Achaea, Corinth, Thebes, Megara, Leucas, and Corcyra. This gained you an army of fifteen thousand mercenaries and two thousand cavalrymen, not counting the citizen contingents. I also ensured as large an income from contributions as I could.

[238] [*To Aeschines*] Now, Aeschines, raising the question of the fairness of our agreement with Thebes or Byzantium or Euboea, and talking as you did today about equity, just displays your ignorance.* You're forgetting, first, that there was an earlier occasion too when a fleet of triremes, three hundred in number, fought in defence of Greece, and that two hundred of these were provided by Athens.* On that occasion, the city obviously didn't feel hard done by. We didn't put those who had recommended this course on trial, and we didn't resent the situation. So far from disgracing itself like that, the city thanked the gods that, with all Greece in danger, its contribution towards the removal of the threat was twice as large as everyone else's. [239] Second, it is futile to try to ingratiate yourself with the jury by

slandering me. I mean, why are you telling them now what I should have done? You were here in Athens and you attended the Assembly. Why didn't you come up with a proposal along these lines then? That is, if you'd been able to given the crisis we were living through at the time, when we had to accept what the circumstances made possible, even if that fell short of what we wanted. After all, the rival bidder was ready to snap up those we alienated and to enrich them as well.

[240] [*To the jurors*] If I am being denounced *now* for my policies, what do you think Aeschines and his godless associates would have said or done *then*, if, while I was haggling over details, the cities had gone and joined Philip, giving him control of Euboea, Thebes, and Byzantium? [241] They'd have talked of betrayal, wouldn't they? They'd have said that those potential allies of ours had been snubbed. And then: 'Thanks to the people of Byzantium, Philip has gained control of the Hellespont and command of the grain shipments to Greece. Thanks to the Thebans, catastrophic war has come to Attica from just across the border. Pirates operating from Euboea have closed the sea.' That's what they'd have said, and plenty more along the same lines, don't you think?

[242] Athenians, a sycophant is a pernicious creature—pernicious, malignant, and poison-tongued in all he ever does. And this apology for a human being was born a phoney; he's never acted sincerely or independently. He's a consummate tragic ape, a rustic Oenomaus, a counterfeit orator. [*To Aeschines*] What good has your clever way with words done the country? And *now* you talk to us of the past? [243] Imagine a doctor who says nothing when he visits sick patients and gives no indication of how they might recover, and then, when one of them dies and is being buried according to custom, he joins the funeral procession and gives his prescription: 'If only this poor fellow had done such and such, he wouldn't have died.' You're just like that, Aeschines. You imbecile, is now the time for you to speak up?

[244] [*To the jurors*] Now, as for the defeat the city suffered—[*to Aeschines*] the defeat that you greet with joy, damn your eyes, when you should weep—[*to the jurors*] you'll find that I had nothing to do with that either. Look at it this way. There was never a single occasion when I served abroad as your ambassador and was bested by Philip's representatives. I returned undefeated from Thessaly and Ambracia, from Illyris and the Thracian kings, from Byzantium, and from everywhere I went, including, finally, Thebes. Now, on each of these

occasions, after his diplomats had failed, Philip resorted to force of arms, attacked the place, and conquered it. [245] [*To Aeschines*] Is that my fault, would you say? Don't you feel any qualms at mocking a man for cowardice,* while simultaneously expecting him to defeat Philip's army singlehandedly? And to do so by force of words, which are my only province? I have no influence on a soldier's courage, the hazards of battle, or command decisions—despite the fact that you're trying to hold me accountable for them. But that just shows how perverse you are.

[246] [*To the jurors*] But do, please, conduct a thorough examination of everything for which a speaker is responsible. I expect nothing less. What does fall within a speaker's province? Spotting emerging situations, recognizing them in advance, and warning everyone else. I did that. But there's more: reducing to their minimum, whenever they occur, those universal and inevitable failings of political life—sluggishness, hesitation, ignorance, and rivalry—and by the same token encouraging concord, friendship, and devotion to duty. I did all that too, and demonstrably left nothing undone that I could have done. [247] Now, ask anyone how Philip attained most of his successes, and the answer will always be the same: by force of arms, and by bribing and corrupting politicians. Well, I had no troops answerable to me or under my command, and so I cannot be held accountable for any military matters. And as for accepting or resisting corruption, I defeated Philip. For just as the acceptance of a bribe by someone constitutes victory for the briber, so refusal constitutes defeat. And so, as far as lay within my power, Athens remained undefeated.

[248] So far—and I could produce numerous other arguments to the same effect—I've been justifying Ctesiphon's proposal with arguments of my own. I shall now continue with arguments supplied by all of you! Immediately after the battle the Athenian people, who were fully aware of my policies from the evidence of their own eyes and were beset by immediate fears and terrors, so that it wouldn't have been surprising if there had been a strong vein of antipathy towards me, first adopted my recommendations for securing the city (in fact, every single protective measure that was taken—the disposition of sentries, the entrenchments, the fortification funds—was a result of decrees proposed by me), and, second, chose me out of the entire citizen body to take charge of the Emergency Grain Fund. [249] Subsequently, those who were determined to see me fall joined forces

and brought the whole range of legal instruments to bear against me—indictments, audits, and impeachments. At first, though, they didn't do so in their own names, but made use of people they supposed would ensure them anonymity. I'm sure you know what I'm talking about. You'll remember that in the immediate aftermath of the battle I was on trial every day, and that they left no expedient untried. In their attempt to bring me down, they sent against me the unscrupulous Sosicles, the sycophant Philocrates, the fanatics Diondas and Melantus. But I survived all their assaults, thanks mainly to the gods, but also to you and the rest of my fellow citizens. And it's only right that I should have survived, because that's what the truth required, and it does credit to the jurors whose verdicts kept faith with the oath they had sworn. [250] And so, whenever I was impeached, your verdict of innocence, and my prosecutors' inability to extract from you the required proportion of the votes, confirmed that my policies were in the city's best interests. And whenever I was acquitted on an indictment, my proposals and measures were thereby proved to be legal.* And every time you approved my accounts, you were admitting that I had acted throughout with integrity and without accepting bribes. Under these circumstances, what was the right and proper language for Ctesiphon to use of my political career? Wasn't it what he heard from the lips of the Athenian people and sworn jurors, and which the truth confirmed for all to see?

[251] 'All right,' says Aeschines, 'but what about that proud boast of Cephalus, that he was never once indicted?' A proud boast indeed, by Zeus, if also a lucky one! But why is it more reprehensible to have been indicted often and never once convicted of wrongdoing? In any case, Athenians, as far as Aeschines is concerned, I could repeat Cephalus' boast, because *he* never drew up an indictment against me or prosecuted me for illegal proposals. [*To Aeschines*] In other words, in your eyes I'm just as upstanding a citizen as Cephalus.

[252] [*To the jurors*] Aeschines' malicious antagonism is evident in everything he said, but especially in his remarks on luck. In general, I judge any human being who casts another's bad luck in his teeth to be a fool. A man may think that everything is going splendidly and that he has exceptional luck, but for all he knows it will have changed by evening. So what is to be said about it? How can he deride someone else's luck? But since Aeschines used his speech as an opportunity to sound off arrogantly about this, among many other things, let's

consider luck, Athenians. Let's see how much more realistic and unpretentious a discussion of it I can provide.

[253] In my opinion, Athens enjoys good luck, and I see that the oracle of Zeus at Dodona agrees.* But the prevalent luck of human beings in general at the moment is fearfully harsh. Is there anyone in the world today, Greek or barbarian, who has not experienced a raft of troubles? [254] Now, I count as signs of Athens' good fortune the excellence of our policies and the fact that we are better off than those very Greeks who thought that abandoning us was the path to prosperity. And in so far as we've suffered setbacks and things haven't turned out exactly as we wanted, I regard this as our appointed share of the general bad luck of mankind. [255] But I think my personal luck, or the luck of any single individual, must be viewed in the context of his private circumstances. That, in my opinion, is the right and proper way to consider luck, and I think you agree. But Aeschines claims* that my personal luck is more influential than the luck of the city as a whole—as if something slight and trivial could be more powerful than something great and good. That's just impossible.

[256] [*To Aeschines*] Now, if you intend to carry out a thorough investigation of my luck, Aeschines, you'd better compare it with yours; and if you find that mine is better than yours, stop deriding it. Let's go back to the start. [*To the jurors*] It's not my fault, by Zeus, if this seems tasteless in any way. To my mind, denigrating someone for poverty and boasting about a privileged upbringing are equally stupid. But the snide and unwarranted allegations of this pest make it impossible for me not to respond. I shall do my best, however, to keep the account within reasonable bounds of modesty.

[257] [*To Aeschines*] When I was a child, Aeschines, I was able to go to the right schools, and I had means enough to avoid the degrading effects of poverty. Likewise, as an adult, I was in a position to fund choruses, take on trierarchies, and pay war levies. I seized every opportunity to act altruistically in private and in public, to make myself useful to my city and my friends. When I decided to embark on a career in politics, the policies I espoused earned me many crowns, not just from my country, but from many other places in Greece as well, and made it impossible for even you and your cohorts, my enemies, to deny the value of my political activities.

[258] That's the kind of luck I've met with in my life. I could say a lot more besides, but I won't, in case my pride causes offence. But

why don't you, with your high-and-mighty ways and contempt for others, think about what kind of luck you have enjoyed, compared to me? Your childhood was one of considerable hardship. You used to sit alongside your schoolteacher father, grating the ink, sponging the benches, and sweeping the classroom. Your rank was that of a slave, not a free-born child. [259] Once you were an adult, you used to read the scripts in your mother's cult and assist her in all the rest of her hocus-pocus.* At night, you would cloak the initiates in their fawn-skins, mix them their wine, purify them, and wipe them clean with mud and bran. After the purification, you had them get to their feet and say: 'I have escaped evil; I have found the better way.' It was a source of pride to you that you were the loudest howler—[to the jurors] and I believe him, since anyone with such a big voice must surely emit the most wonderful howls! [260] [To Aeschines] By day, you led the bands of gorgeous revellers through the streets, crowned with leaves of fennel and white poplar, while you gripped the broad-headed snakes and waved them over your head, crying 'Euoi Saboi' and dancing to the mantra hyes attes, attes hyes. You were known to the old hags as their leader and guide, the bearer of their caskets and baskets. Your rations were lentil tarts, plaited cakes, and fresh-ground biscuits. Who wouldn't count himself truly fortunate and thank his lucky stars for such a life?

[261] Somehow or other (I won't go into how it happened), you got yourself registered as an Athenian citizen, and you immediately chose the most noble of occupations, clerking and assisting minor officials in their duties. Throughout this phase of your life you committed every crime that you denounce in others, but eventually you moved on and into something that certainly did no discredit to your previous career. [262] You hired yourself out to Simyccas and Socrates, those loud-lamenting men of the stage, as their third-string actor,* but your major source of income was harvesting figs and grapes and olives, as a fruit merchant, from others' fields. You earned more that way than you did from the dramatic competitions in which you and your colleagues took part—competitions you entered at mortal risk, because the war between you and your audiences was truceless and unremitting. But I suppose all the wounds you received at their hands have given you the right to mock as cowards those who haven't faced such dangers.

[263] Anyway, I shall pass over those aspects of your life that may be attributed to poverty, and turn to your actual character flaws.

Once it had occurred to you to take up a career in politics, you chose
a platform which entailed that, when the country was prospering, you
lived the life of a hare—fearful, trembling, constantly expecting to
be beaten for the crimes you knew you were committing—but when
misfortune prevailed, your cheerful face was everywhere to be seen.
[264] [*To the jurors*] I ask you, how should the living punish a man
who is cheered by the deaths of thousands of his fellow citizens?

There's plenty more I could say about him, but I shan't. There
are further aspects of his character that I could expose in all their
ugliness and vulgarity, but I don't think I should lightly list them all.
It's better if I restrict myself to those I'm not embarrassed to mention. [265] [*To Aeschines*] So compare your life and mine, Aeschines,
without losing your temper, please, while you do so. And then ask
the jurors which any of them would prefer—your luck or mine. You
taught at school; I attended school. You conducted initiations; I was
initiated.* You worked as an Assembly clerk; I attended the Assembly.
You were a third-string actor; I was in the audience. You were hissed
off the stage; I was hissing. Throughout your career as a politician,
you worked for our enemies; I worked for my country. [266] I won't
bother with the rest of it, beyond this. Today I'm being assessed to
see whether I deserve a crown, and I've been found to have a spotless
record. You, however, have long had a reputation for sycophancy, and
the issue for you is whether you are to continue behaving in this way,
or whether you'll be brought to an abrupt halt by failing to gain a fifth
of the votes. What good luck you've enjoyed in your life! How could
you doubt it? It's no wonder you cast aspersions on mine!

[267] [*To the jurors*] So let's also hear the depositions that testify to
the liturgies I performed. [*To Aeschines*] Why don't you too, by way of
contrast, recite the lines you used to ruin: 'I have come from the gates
of darkness, where the dead lie hidden.'* Or what about 'Know me as
the unwilling bearer of bad news'? And then there's 'You wretch, may
you wretchedly' perish, at the hands of the gods, of course, but also
by the unanimous verdict of these jurors, seeing that you're as poor
a citizen as you are an actor. [*To the Clerk of the Court*] Please read the
depositions.

The depositions are read out.

[268] [*To the jurors*] My public record, then, speaks for itself. As for
my private life, if there's anyone here who is unaware of my kindness

and generosity, and my friendship to those in need, you won't hear about it from me. I'm not going to bring it up or provide any witnesses to confirm, for instance, that there are men whom I ransomed from the enemy,* or men whose daughters' dowries were supplemented by me, or anything like that. This is how I look at it: [269] I think that the decent thing for the recipient of a favour to do is remember it for ever, but that the giver should forget it immediately if he is to avoid pettiness. I don't see much difference between reminding someone of your personal kindness towards him and insulting him. So I'm not going to do anything like that and I'm not going to be goaded into it either. Whatever opinion people already have of me in this respect is all right with me.

[270] I'd like to move on now from the private to the public sphere, and say a few words to you about that. [To Aeschines] Aeschines, if you can name any person on this earth, Greek or barbarian, whose life has not been negatively affected by first Philip's, and now Alexander's regime, all right: I'll admit that my luck—or misfortune; call it what you will—is responsible for everything that has happened. [271] But if suffering and misery are widespread and not restricted to those who have set eyes on me and heard my voice*—if not just individuals, but whole cities and peoples are affected—don't you think it would be much more fair and honest to blame this on what appears to be the common luck of all mankind, and a rough and unwelcome tide in the affairs of man?

[272] But such considerations don't bother you at all. You blame me, even though my political activity has been restricted to Athens, and even though you know perfectly well that some, if not all, of your slanderous allegations redound on to every Athenian, and especially you. If I had been an absolute ruler and the sole decision-maker, it would make sense for you and your political cronies to blame me. [273] But since you and they attended all the Assemblies, and the city has never stopped anyone contributing to discussion of where its interests lie, and since at the time everyone—and you in particular, Aeschines—agreed that the policy in question was indeed in the city's best interests, what could be more unfair and unjustifiable than your condemnation now of policies that you couldn't improve on at the time? I say that this goes for you in particular, Aeschines, because it certainly wasn't friendship for me that moved you to deny yourself all the optimism and pride and prestige that my policies attracted at

the time. No, the truth, and your inability to come up with better ideas, were too strong for you.

[274] [*To the jurors*] Everywhere else in the world I see a specific system for such cases. A man does wrong on purpose, and meets with condemnation and punishment; a man does wrong accidentally, and is pardoned rather than punished. So when a man is innocent of any crime or wrongdoing, and devotes himself to what is by common consent good for the city, but comes to grief along with everyone else, he doesn't deserve censure or criticism, but compassion. [275] This distinction isn't only to be found enshrined in law, but, as a naturally occurring phenomenon, it's also reflected in the unwritten laws and customs of mankind. Aeschines is such an extraordinarily vicious sycophant, however, that he blames me for things he himself referred to as disastrous accidents.

[276] And that's not all. Posing as one who has always spoken in a frank and friendly manner, he kept warning you to be careful of me, and to be on your guard against my devious tricks. He called me a cunning speaker, a wizard, a sophist, and so on. He seems to think that if a man pre-emptively ascribes his own attributes to someone else, that will be taken as gospel, and his audience will be diverted from thinking about the character of the speaker himself. But I'm sure he's known to all of you, and that you regard him as far more of a devious wizard and so on than me. [277] I'm also sure that my skill at speaking . . . well, let's assume that I have it. But it's obvious to me that you, the audience, exercise a considerable degree of control over a speaker's success. Whether or not a particular speaker's advice is taken to be sound depends on how receptive you are and how much you warm to him. So if I do in fact have a certain way with words, you'll all find, if you think about it, that it's always at your service in the public domain, and that I never use it to do you harm or for my own private purposes. By contrast, Aeschines not only puts his skill at the service of our enemies, but also wields it against anyone who annoys him or crosses him in any way. He doesn't use it honestly or for the benefit of Athens.

[278] An exemplary citizen shouldn't expect jurors, who are in court on public service, to confirm any personal emotions such as anger or hostility; that should never be his motivation in addressing you. Ideally, such emotions should play no part in his character, but if he has no choice, he should at least keep them within reasonable

bounds. When is passion permissible for a political speaker? When any of the city's critical concerns is threatened, and when dealing with enemies of the democracy, that's when. That's no more than one would expect from a high-minded and dutiful citizen. [279] But Aeschines has never demanded my punishment, either in the name of the city or in his own name, for any public crime, nor, I might add, for any private crime either.* Instead, he's come to court with a ragbag of reasons why it would be wrong for me to receive a crown and a public vote of thanks, and has gone on and on about it. This doesn't smack of honourable citizenship, but of personal hostility, rancour, and pettiness. Moreover, the fact that he has consistently avoided taking me to court, and has now proceeded against Ctesiphon instead, shows what a complete coward he is.

[280] [*To Aeschines*] This leads me to conclude, Aeschines, that you went ahead with this trial not with the intention of punishing any crime, but because you wanted to display your eloquence and skill at declamation. But what counts, my friend, is not a politician's eloquence or the volume of his voice, but whether or not his principles coincide with those of the Athenian people, whether he has the same friends and enemies as his country. [281] With this disposition, a man will always speak as a patriot, but anyone who courts people the city regards as potentially dangerous is not moored at the same anchorage as the majority, and cannot share their view of where safety lies either. None of which applies to me. How could you doubt it? For I share my fellow citizens' principles and preferences, and I've never acted for exclusive or self-interested reasons.

[282] Can the same be said of you? Of course not. Straight after the battle, you made your way to Philip as our ambassador. This was the man who was directly responsible for the disasters that befell our country in those days, and previously, as everyone knows, you had consistently declined the job. Now, who deceives the city? A man who doesn't speak his mind. And who is the legally designated object of the herald's curse? A deceiver.* What greater crime could one lay at the door of a politician than that he thinks one thing but says another? But we now know you to be exactly that kind of politician. [283] And yet you don't keep silent, and you brazenly look your fellow citizens in the eyes. Do you think they don't know what you're like? Do you think they're so dozy and forgetful that none of them remembers the speeches you made during the war, when you asserted with oaths and

imprecations that you had nothing to do with Philip, and that my suggestion that you had was an outright lie, motivated by personal hostility? [284] Yet no sooner had news of the battle arrived than, ignoring all that, you admitted the truth, and laid claim to friendship and intimacy with him—which is just another way of saying that you were in his pay. But what fair or honest reason could there be for Aeschines, the son of Glaucothea, a drumming priestess, to be on intimate or even casual terms with Philip? None that I can see. In fact, you were hired to undermine your fellow citizens' interests. But even though your treachery has been exposed for all to see, and even though you subsequently informed against yourself,* you still bring slanderous and insulting charges against me, when I'm the last person in the world who's guilty of such things.

[285] Many of the city's noble and important ventures were due to me, Aeschines, as were many of its successes, and the city did not forget it. Witness the fact that, just after the battle, when the people were to choose someone to deliver the funeral oration,* they didn't choose you from among the candidates, despite your magnificent voice, nor Demades, the author of the recent peace, nor Hegemon, nor any other member of your clique. They chose me. Then Pythocles and you stepped up—ye gods, how vicious and shameless can men be?—and made the same insulting accusations against me that you're making now, which made my fellow citizens even more ready to choose me!

[286] You already know why, but I'll tell you anyway. They were well aware of both sides of the coin—the loyalty and commitment I brought to my political activities, and your dishonesty, which was evident in the fact that, after the city's setbacks, you and your cronies admitted what you had denied under oath when things were going well. So they concluded that people who treated the general catastrophe as an opportunity to speak their minds with impunity had been their enemies for a long while, even if they were only then exposed as such. [287] They thought that the job of delivering the funeral speech and acclaiming the courage of the dead should be denied to someone who had shared a roof and table with those who had fought their fallen fellows. They found it inappropriate that someone who had got drunk in Macedonia along with the murderers, and had sung paeans in celebration of the Greek catastrophe, should then be awarded this honour on his return home to Athens—someone whose tears for the dead were feigned and superficial, and who felt no grief for them in

his heart. They recognized this grief in themselves and in me, but found no trace of it in you. That's why they chose me and not you or any of your cronies.

[288] Nor was this attitude confined to the assembled people: the fathers and brothers of the dead, the ones who had been chosen by the people to see to the funeral on that occasion, felt the same way too. It was their job to arrange for the funeral banquet to be held, as normal, at the house of a close relative of the dead, and they held it at my house. This was perfectly appropriate. Although each of them had closer family members among the dead than I did, no one was closer to all of them at once. For the person who had been the most closely involved in trying to gain them safety and success also grieved most acutely for them all and for their untimely deaths.

[289] [*To the Clerk of the Court*] Read him the epitaph which the city chose for their monument and had inscribed at public expense. [*To Aeschines*] This will show you, Aeschines, how in this matter too you are behaving like a foul, callous sycophant. [*To the Clerk of the Court*] Go ahead.

The epitaph is read out.†

[290] Did you hear that, Aeschines? 'Never to fail and ever to succeed is a mark of the gods.' The epitaph ascribes the power of ensuring success in battle not to politicians, but to the gods. So why do you cast the defeat in *my* teeth, damn you? I pray that the gods may turn your abuse of me back on to your head.

[291] [*To the jurors*] Among all his lies and accusations, Athenians, what surprised me most was his attitude when he mentioned what happened to the city then. He didn't behave like a loyal and upright citizen: he shed no tears, felt no grief in his heart. His voice was strong, booming with joy. He thought he was accusing me, of course, but in fact by showing that his attitude towards the disaster was different from everyone else's he was giving evidence against himself. [292] But surely the minimum requirements for anyone who claims, as he did in his speech,* to care for the law and the state, are that he should like and dislike the same things as the general populace, and should not be working for the enemy. [*To Aeschines*] But that's plainly what you've been doing today, in making out that I'm responsible for everything and that the city's troubles are due to me, [*to the jurors*] even though your policy of helping fellow Greeks preceded

my political and administrative activity. [293] I mean, if you were to say that your opposition to the empire that was threatening to engulf Greece was my doing, that would be an honour greater than all those you've ever awarded others. But I'm not about to claim that for myself, because I'd be doing you an injustice, and I'm sure you're not about to concede it. If Aeschines were behaving honourably, he wouldn't be damaging and distorting your most important and noble achievements out of hostility towards me.

[294] But why am I bothering to criticize him for this, when he has accused me in his lying way of far more reprehensible conduct? By Earth and all the gods, he accused *me* of being on Philip's side! If he can say that, he's capable of saying anything! But I swear by Heracles and all the gods that if you were to discard his lies and hostile bias, and consider in all honesty which men really and truly deserve to carry the blame for what happened, wherever you looked you'd find the culprits to be the very image of him, not of me. [295] When Philip was still weak and relatively insignificant, we were the ones who issued frequent warnings, who spoke words of encouragement and pointed out the best courses of action. They were the ones who were busy profiting from the betrayal of their countries' interests, and tricked and corrupted their fellow citizens into slavery. In Thessaly, it was Daochus, Cineas, and Thrasydaus; in Arcadia, Cercidas, Hieronymus, and Eucampidas; in Argos, Myrtis, Teledamus, and Mnaseas; in Elis, Euxitheus, Cleotimus, and Aristaechmus; in Messenia, Neon and Thrasylochus, the sons of the godforsaken Philiades; in Sicyon, Aristratus and Epichares; in Corinth, Deinarchus and Demaretus; in Megara, Ptoeodorus, Helixus, and Perilas; in Thebes, Timolas, Theogeiton, and Anemoetas; in Euboea, Hipparchus, Cleitarchus, and Sositratus. [296] But there aren't enough hours in the day for me to complete the list. All of them, Athenians, pursued the same aims within their own countries as Aeschines and his cohorts did here. All of them are foul flatterers and fiends, who have mutilated their own countries and thrown away their freedom, first to Philip and now to Alexander. They measure happiness by their stomachs and the basest criteria; they have overturned the standard of freedom and self-determination, which used to be the criterion of goodness in Greece.

[297] Thanks to my statesmanship, everyone in the world acknowledges that Athens had nothing to do with this disgraceful and shocking conspiracy of criminals—or rather, not to beat

about the bush, Athenians, this betrayal of Greek freedom—just as
everyone here acknowledges that I had nothing to do with it. [*To
Aeschines*] And you ask me what good I've done that makes me think
I deserve the crown? I'll tell you. When all the politicians in Greece
had been corrupted, starting with you, [298] nothing—no beckon-
ing opportunity, no conciliatory words, no extravagant promises, no
hopes or fears—induced or tempted me to betray what I took to be
the honourable and expedient course for my country. And none of
the advice I offered my fellow citizens was ever prompted, as yours
was, by a bias towards easy money; my motives were always upright,
fair, and unsullied by corruption. I was in a position of authority
for the most momentous events of our times, and my administration was sound and fair throughout. *That*'s why I think I deserve
the crown.

[299] As for my work on the city's defensive walls and trenches,
which you ridiculed, I think it deserved the gratitude and commendation I received—how could it not?—but I count it as far less significant than what I achieved in the political sphere. It was not with
stones and bricks that I fortified the city; stones and bricks are not
what I particularly pride myself on. *My* fortifications, if you care to
take an impartial look at them, consist of weaponry, cities, land, harbours, ships, horses, and troops to defend my fellow citizens. [300]
These are the materials with which I afforded Attica the best protection that human reason could devise; I ringfenced the entire region,
not just Piraeus or the city. And in the planning and preparation
phase, I never suffered defeat at Philip's hands. Quite the opposite,
in fact. But then the allied commanders and the army were beaten by
his good fortune.

[*To the jurors*] Can I prove these assertions? Without the slightest
difficulty. Look at it this way. [301] What was a patriotic citizen to do,
who was trying to manage his country's affairs with all possible care
and commitment and justice? Shouldn't he have created bulwarks for
Attica—Euboea from the sea, Boeotia from the interior, our neighbours to the west from the Peloponnese? Shouldn't he have taken
steps to ensure that the grain ships had friendly territory to skirt all
the way to Piraeus? [302] Shouldn't he have secured the city's existing
possessions—Proconnesos, the Chersonese, Tenedos—by despatching levies, addressing the issue in his speeches, and drafting proposals? And shouldn't he have arranged for other places—Byzantium,

Abydus, Euboea—to be our friends and allies? Shouldn't he have deprived the enemy of his most important resources and used them to supplement Athens' deficiencies? All this was achieved by my decrees and my measures.

[303] An unbiased look at my measures will also show, Athenians, that they were properly debated and legally executed, that no opportunity was ever wasted by carelessness or ignorance or treachery, and that nothing that lay within the resources and intelligence of one man was left undone. If a superior power such as a deity or Fortune, or if poor generalship, or the villainy of Aeschines and his fellow traitors, or all of these things at once caused fatal and decisive damage, how was this Demosthenes' fault? [304] If one man in every Greek city had taken up his post as I did here in Athens, or rather if Thessaly and Arcadia* had each had just one man whose principles were the same as mine, all Greeks, north and south of Thermopylae, would have been spared the troubles that afflict them now. [305] They would have their freedom and self-determination; they would inhabit the lands of their birth in safety and prosperity, free from all fear; they would be aware that they owed all these blessings to you and to Athenians in general; and all this would have been my doing.

But I'd like you to appreciate that, for fear of causing resentment, these words of mine fall far short of doing justice to events. [*To the Clerk of the Court*] So please take this document and tell them just how many expeditions were sent out as a result of my decrees.

The list is read out.

[306] [*To Aeschines*] These are the typical actions of an exemplary citizen, Aeschines. If things had gone well, we would indisputably—and, I might add, justly—have been the greatest power in Greece. Things didn't turn out well, but at least we still have our good reputation. No one blames the city or its policies; they curse Fortune for having decided matters this way. [307] What an exemplary citizen most certainly does not do, by Zeus, is distance himself from the city's interests, hire himself out to our opponents, and facilitate matters for the enemy rather than for his country. He doesn't slander a man for his determination to recommend and propose measures that match the city's dignity, and for sticking to his task. He doesn't remember and cling on to personal grievances. He doesn't maintain a dishonest and treacherous silence, as you commonly do.

[308] [*To the jurors*] True, there are times when it's right to be silent, when it serves the city's interests, and that's the kind of silence most of you keep, with no hidden agendas. But that's not at all Aeschines' kind of silence. He withdraws from public life whenever he feels like it (as he often does), and waits for a time when you're fed up with your regular speaker, or when you've suffered an unfortunate setback, or when some other difficulty has arisen—a common occurrence in human life. And then, when he sees his chance, he appears like a sudden gust of wind and presents himself as a speaker, reeling off words and phrases from his collection clearly and fluently in his trained voice. But his words are unprofitable and serve no good purpose; all they do is make trouble for one or another of his fellow citizens, or bring shame on the whole community.

[309] [*To Aeschines*] Now, if all this preparation and care stemmed from the honest heart of one who was committed to his country's welfare, Aeschines, they would have produced a rich crop of genuine benefits for everyone—alliances with cities, increased revenues, opportunities for trade, valuable legislation, ways to counter professed enemies. [310] In times past, people looked for all of these from a statesman, and history has provided exemplary citizens with many opportunities to display their usefulness. But you won't be numbered among them—not first, second, third, fourth, fifth, sixth, or anywhere, at any rate not for measures that did Athens good. [311] Have you negotiated any new alliances for the city? Have you despatched any levies or gained us friends or glory in any other way? As ambassador, or in any other position of service, have you enhanced Athenian prestige? Did any of your projects go well, here in Athens, elsewhere in Greece, or further abroad? What triremes have you gained us? What weaponry? What shipsheds? What repairs to the walls? What cavalry? Have you done any good at all in any sphere? What aid have you ever arranged for either the rich or the poor out of a concern for your fellow citizens and the common good?† None.

[312] 'Well, you may be right, my friend, but I've displayed loyalty and commitment.' Where? When? This is a downright lie! You didn't step up and make a contribution even when everyone who had ever delivered a speech from the speaker's platform donated something towards the city's safety, ending with Aristonicus' donating the money he had saved for redeeming his citizenship.* And it's not that you're poor. How could you be? You inherited more than five talents

from your brother-in-law Philon, and you were holding a 'loan' of
two talents from the leaders of the syndicates, for sabotaging the trierarchic law.* [313] But I'll say no more about that episode; I don't
want to be knocked off course by extra arguments. It's already clear
from what I've said that it wasn't poverty that stopped you contributing; no, you were making sure that you didn't create any problems
for those whose interests determine all your policies. So when do you
spring into action? When do you shine? When there's work to be done
damaging Athenian interests—that's when you're the man with the
clearest voice and the best memory, a superlative actor, a Theocrines
of the tragic stage.*

[314] What next? You mentioned noble Athenians of the past—and
quite right too. [*To the jurors*] But it's unfair, Athenians, for him to
exploit the affection you feel for the dead and evaluate me by comparison with them, when I'm still living here among you. [315] I mean, it's
common knowledge that everyone alive is subject to a greater or lesser
degree of malice, while the dead are no longer hated even by their
enemies. Since this is how things are, am I to be judged and evaluated today by comparison with my predecessors? Of course not. [*To
Aeschines*] That would be unjust and unfair, Aeschines. It would be
fairer to compare me with you, or with anyone else you like, provided
that his political principles are the same as yours and that he's alive.
[316] Here's another point for you to consider. Which is better, and
better for Athens? To use the benefactions of past times—enormous
as they were, too great for words to tell—to induce ingratitude and
scorn for those of today, or to allow everyone who acts as a loyal citizen his share of the respect and goodwill of these men here?

[317] Now, this is something else I don't want to have to say, but
anyone who looks at my policies and principles will see that they are
similar to or the same as those of our celebrated forebears. Yours,
however, resemble those of the sycophants who harassed such men.
For even in those days there were of course people who ridiculed their
contemporaries while singing the praises of their predecessors—
a malicious practice, and no different from what you're doing. [318]
According to you, I bear no resemblance to my predecessors. Well, do
you, Aeschines? Or your brother? Or any contemporary politician?
Not one of them, I'd say. No, my friend, compare a living politician
with his living contemporaries—that's all I'm saying—as we do in
all other spheres: poetry, dancing, athletics. [319] Philammon wasn't

denied a crown at the Olympic games because he was weaker than
Glaucus of Carystus or any other athlete from the past;* he won
a crown and was acclaimed victor because he was a better fighter than
those who entered the ring against him. So you too should compare
me with contemporary politicians, with yourself, with anyone you like
out of the entire citizen body. I'll take on all comers.

[320] When the city was in a position to pursue its best interests,
and anyone could take part in the competition of showing loyalty
towards Athens, I was the acknowledged leading politician and everything depended on my decrees and laws and diplomatic missions. You
and your cohorts were nowhere to be seen, except when you felt the
need to harass your fellow citizens. After the disaster, when there was
no longer any need for statesmen, and the search was on for lackeys,
men who were prepared to accept money to harm their country and
felt no aversion to fawning on others, *then* you and all your colleagues
lined up. You constitute a powerful and brilliant group, members of
the horse-owning class, while I'm not afraid to say that I'm weak—
but I am more loyal to the democracy than you and your lot.

[321] [*To the jurors*] There are two qualities, Athenians, that
a respectable citizen needs to have; I can describe myself like that
without risk of causing offence. First, when in power, he should
maintain to the end a policy designed to win distinction for Athens;
second, at every opportunity and in everything he does he should
act with patriotic goodwill. For that depends on his character, while
other factors determine whether he succeeds and prevails. And you'll
find that such loyalty has been a stable quality of mine. [322] Look
at it this way. My loyalty towards you never wavered—not when my
surrender was demanded, not when they tried to haul me before the
Amphictyons,* not when they threatened me, not when they tempted
me with offers, not when they set these wild beasts on me. Right from
the start, the political path I chose was straight and honest: to foster,
further, and fight for my country's honour, power, and glory.

[323] Others' victories don't make me go around in the Agora with
a joyful grin on my face, greeting and proclaiming the good news to
men I think will report my behaviour to the king. Nor do I shudder
and groan and hang my head at news of Athenian successes, as these
godless men do. They treat Athens with contempt, as if they were not
thereby making themselves contemptible. Their attention is focused
abroad, and whenever someone else succeeds at the expense of the

Greeks, they approve and say we should try to prolong the situation for ever.

[324] I call on all the gods: may none of you look favourably on their wish! Above all, may you implant even in them better hearts and minds; but if, after all, they are incurable, destroy them, and them alone, completely and utterly, on land and sea; and grant the rest of us the earliest possible deliverance from the fears that hang over us, and enduring safety.

19. ON THE DISHONEST EMBASSY

It required no prescience, as the peace of 346 was finalized, to see that it would not deliver major benefits to Athens, while Philip was able to use the interval between the Athenian vote for peace and his own swearing of the oaths to consolidate his position in Thrace, an area where any military activity would inevitably threaten Athenian interests, and then to use his settlement of the Sacred War to gain credibility and influence in central Greece. After the second mission to Macedonia in 346 Demosthenes, whose support for peace had probably been purely pragmatic, joined another opponent of peace, Timarchus, to prosecute one of the Athenian envoys to Macedonia, Aeschines, for his role in the negotiations. Aeschines had originally been hostile to Philip, but had served with Demosthenes as envoy to Philip to negotiate the peace. He never wavered afterwards in his support for peace and had evidently concluded that this was the best, perhaps the only, option. Philip had managed to keep everyone in the dark about his intentions for the settlement of the Sacred War, but had been making encouraging noises (without explicit commitment) to all sides. It seems that Aeschines had in turn, mistakenly as it turned out, encouraged the Athenians to expect a settlement favourable to them. This, together with his *volte-face* from anti- to pro-Macedonian, probably explains the decision to target him. He was not an easy target, however, and he retaliated by prosecuting Timarchus with devastating effect. Timarchus lost his citizen rights. In 343 Demosthenes resumed the prosecution. The moment was a good one for the opponents of Philip. There was general dissatisfaction with the peace. Demosthenes' associate Hypereides prosecuted the proposer of the peace, Philocrates, who fled the city, evidently recognizing that for him the treaty was now a political suicide note.[1] Aeschines stood his ground, and Demosthenes used the audit he had to undergo as a returning ambassador to launch his attack. Aeschines won, but by a narrow margin. This was probably all that Demosthenes needed. The verdict exonerated Aeschines from treason and corruption, but also confirmed the shift in the balance of power between opponents and supporters of peace. Demosthenes evidently felt no need to return to the attack. We have (unusually) the speeches for both sides (Aeschines' defence speech is the second in modern editions of his works). As with the speeches in the big contest of 330

---

[1] The prosecution of Neaera by Stephanus belongs to the same initiative; see introduction to speech 59.

(Demosthenes 18 and Aeschines 3), they appear to have been revised for publication to allow the opponents to offer the case for their policy in pamphlet form.

---

[1] I doubt that many of you can fail to be aware, Athenians, how much concern and lobbying this trial has aroused, since you've just had the experience of being pestered and harassed by people during your allocation.* Nevertheless, I shall be asking all of you not to let any influence or any individual take precedence over justice and the oath under which each of you has come into court.* Of course, this is a favour people should receive without having to ask, but I want you to bear in mind that justice and your oath serve you and the city as a whole, whereas the appeals and efforts of these lobbyists serve private interests, which you who are assembled here are supposed by law to curb, not to validate for the offenders.

[2] Now, in my experience, other people—those who approach state affairs honestly—make themselves available for continuous accountability even after they've been audited. Aeschines here, however, does pretty much the opposite. Even before coming before you and giving an account of his conduct, he has eliminated one of those who had offered to give evidence against him at his audit, and he's busy threatening others.* In doing so, he has introduced into the state a particularly pernicious practice, one that hugely harms your interests. A government official who employs fear of himself and illegal means to suborn his accusers threatens to leave you, the people, completely and utterly powerless.

[3] I'm confidently and firmly convinced that I shall prove Aeschines guilty of numerous crimes and demonstrate that he deserves the severest penalty. All the same, despite this certainty, there's something that worries me, and I'll go right ahead and tell you what it is. My impression, Athenians, is that in all trials in your courts timing is as critical as the facts, and so my worry is that the length of time that has passed since the embassy* might have made you forget the crimes, or find them less reprehensible. [4] I'll tell you, then, how I think you can still see that justice is done under these circumstances and reach the correct verdict. Take a moment, jurymen, to consider what factors the city ought to take into account when assessing an ambassador. First, there are his reports; second, his recommendations; third,

your instructions to him; fourth, his timing; and last, but not least, whether bribery influenced his conduct at all.

[5] Why these factors? His reports are important, because you base your practical deliberations on them: if he gives you accurate information, you know what you have to do, and otherwise you don't. Second, you take an ambassador's recommendations to be especially reliable, because you assume that the person you're listening to is expert in the issues relevant to his mission. It follows that an ambassador ought never to be found to have given you poor or inexpedient advice. [6] Third, he should have spoken or acted as you expressly voted, and carried out all your instructions.

All right, but why is his timing important? Because important business, Athenians, often has a very narrow window of opportunity, and if such a window is deliberately surrendered to the enemy, it cannot be recovered, try as one might. [7] The final consideration is whether or not he has accepted bribes, and here I'm sure you would all agree that for someone to profit from a situation that harms the city is absolutely intolerable. The legislator, however, left things vague, and simply said that under no circumstances were gifts to be accepted. His reasoning, I think, was that *anyone* who accepts bribes and is corrupted by money immediately ceases to be a reliable judge of what is good for the city.

[8] Well, then, if I demonstrate and prove beyond the shadow of a doubt that Aeschines' report was a pack of lies, that he prevented the Assembly from hearing the truth from me, consistently recommended policies that are detrimental to your interests, carried out none of the instructions he received for the embassy, threw away many opportunities that held great promise for the city, and, with his cohort Philocrates, accepted gifts and money for all this—if I make my case, bring in a guilty verdict and punish him as his crimes deserve. But if I fail to make my case even in part, think the worse of me and acquit him.

[9] These are far from being the only crimes I could charge him with, Athenians; there are others too, that would give anyone good grounds for condemning him. But, by way of preface, I'd like to remind you, although I'm sure most of you remember, of the political stance Aeschines took up at first, and of the speeches he felt moved to make denouncing Philip. His original actions and words, as you shall see, clearly convict him of accepting bribes.

[10] He was the first man in Athens, or so he claimed at the time
in a speech, to have realized that Philip had designs on Greece and
was in the process of corrupting some of the leading men of Arcadia.
With Ischander,* Neoptolemus' second actor, as his second actor,
he addressed both Council and Assembly on these matters, and prevailed upon you to send envoys all around Greece to convene a sum-
mit meeting here to discuss the question of war against Philip. [11]
Later, after returning from Arcadia, he told us how he defended you
at brilliant length against Philip's man Hieronymus before the Ten
Thousand in Megalopolis,* and went on about the terrible harm
people who accept gifts and money from Philip do not only to their
own states, but to all Greece. [12] So, since this was his political
position at the time, and since he had made himself exemplary in
this way, he became a member of the delegation you were persuaded
to send to Philip to discuss the possibility of peace—persuaded by
people such as Aristodemus, Neoptolemus, and Ctesiphon, with their
completely unreliable reports about the situation in Macedonia.* He
was chosen not to betray your interests, nor to believe Philip's lies,
but to watch over the other delegates. After all, those speeches of his,
and his hostility towards Philip, had naturally made you think of him
as trustworthy.

[13] He subsequently approached me with the suggestion that we
should work together on the embassy, and was particularly insistent
that we should both watch over that 'foul crook' Philocrates. And until
we returned here after the first embassy, I for one, Athenians, had no
idea that he had sold his services and been corrupted. First, there
were those earlier speeches of his, which I've already mentioned, and
then he stood up at the first of the two Assemblies that met to discuss
the terms of the peace treaty, and—I think I can remember his exact
words—began as follows: [14] 'My fellow Athenians, if Philocrates
had spent ages thinking how best to *thwart* the peace, I doubt he
could have come up with a better way than the present proposal. Even
though I do think we should enter into a peace treaty, I shall never, as
long as a single Athenian remains alive, advise the city to accept peace
on *these* terms.' And he went on to deliver a short, sensible speech
along those lines.

[15] You all heard this speech of his at the first Assembly. The
next day, the peace was due to be ratified. I was supporting our allies'
resolution and trying to ensure that the terms of the treaty should be

equitable and fair; this met with your approval, and you were refusing
to listen to a word from the vile Philocrates.* Then Aeschines stood
up and spoke in support of Philocrates! By all that's sacred, that was
a speech for which he deserves to die many times over! [16] He told
you to forget your ancestors and ban talk of trophies and sea battles,
and suggested that you should draft and enact a law forbidding you
from helping any Greek state that had not previously helped you.
And the most shocking and despicable thing was that he even dared to
make this speech while the representatives of the Greek cities, whom
you had invited at his instigation (before he was bribed), were standing by and listening!

[17] You again chose him to represent you, Athenians, this time
for the oaths,* and I shall tell you presently how he wasted time and
did nothing but harm the city's interests, and how often my wish to
stop him brought us into conflict over these matters. But when we
returned from this mission (the one to receive the oaths, which is the
subject of today's audit) without having attained a single one of the
goals, great or small, that were mentioned and promised when you
were drafting the peace treaty—completely and utterly frustrated,
because Aeschines and his cohorts had once again acted and conducted themselves as ambassadors in a manner that ran contrary to
their actual instructions—we duly presented ourselves before the
Council.*

Now, what I'm about to say is already widely known, since the
Council chamber was filled with onlookers. [18] I stepped up and
gave a full and honest report to the Council. I denounced Aeschines
and his cohorts, and told the whole story, from those first hopes
raised by Ctesiphon's and Aristodemus' reports, to the substance of
Aeschines' speeches while you were drafting the peace treaty and the
hopes he had dangled before us. There remained the Phocian question and Thermopylae, and I advised the Council not to neglect these
matters and not to make the same mistakes all over again—that is, not
to cling to one hope and promise after another and let the situation
go from bad to worse.

My words met with a receptive audience in the Council, [19]
but when it was time for the Assembly and we had to address you,
Aeschines here was the first of us to step up—and I implore you by
all that's sacred to help me out by endeavouring to recall whether
I'm telling the truth. He didn't even come close to reporting any of

our negotiations or mentioning anything that had been said in the
Council. We had no chance to see whether or not he disputed the
truth of what I had said there. Instead, he made such an impressive
speech, offering such huge advantages, that he held you all in thrall.
[20] He said that he had managed, while abroad, to persuade Philip
to do nothing that harmed the interests of Athens in any matter,
even in the business with the Amphictyons;* he described the long
speech criticizing the Thebans that he said he had made to Philip,
and recapitulated the main points; and he calculated that, as a result
of his negotiations, in two or three days, without stirring from home
or mounting a campaign or suffering any inconvenience, you would
hear that Thebes—just Thebes, not any other Boeotian city—was
under siege, [21] that Thespiae and Plataea were being resettled,*
and that repayment of the sacred funds was being demanded not
from the Phocians, but from the Thebans, for having planned to seize
the temple.* He said that he personally had explained to Philip that
planning the deed was no less impious than physically carrying it out,
and he told us that the Thebans had consequently put a price on his
head. [22] He also reported that some Euboeans, who were frightened
and disturbed by the new friendship between Philip and Athens, had
said to our ambassadors: 'Sirs, we are aware of the terms of your
peace accord with Philip. We know that you have given Amphipolis
to him, and that he has agreed to hand Euboea over to you.' And
there was another matter he had arranged, he said, although he
didn't yet want to say what it was, because some of his fellow envoys
were already jealous of him. This was meant to be a veiled allusion
to Oropus.*

[23] Not surprisingly, this speech went down well, and he made
a majestic descent from the platform, with everyone regarding him as
a superb speaker and a remarkable man. Then I got up. I said that this
was all news to me, and I tried to tell you something of what I had told
the Council. But Aeschines and Philocrates stood on either side of
me, and their boos and hisses eventually turned to jeers. This amused
you, and you refused to listen to what I had to say, or to believe any
information that differed from what Aeschines had said. [24] I think
this was a perfectly natural reaction. When a man expects to gain
such marvellous benefits, how can he bear to hear someone either
telling him that they aren't going to happen, or casting doubt on
what Aeschines and Philocrates had achieved? At the time, I suppose,

everything else took second place to the expectations and hopes that
were on offer. Any counter-argument could only seem an irritating
distraction, motivated by spite, while what these men had achieved
seemed so wonderful, and a solid gain for the city.

[25] So why have I started now by reminding you of these facts
and summarizing these speeches? First and foremost, Athenians,
I wanted to make sure that when you feel appalled and outraged on
hearing from me some of the things these men have done, none of
you exclaims in surprise: 'Why on earth didn't you say this straight
away at the time? Why didn't you tell us what was going on?'* [26]
I want you to remember that every time someone else might have
made himself heard, these men shut him out with their promises.
I want you to remember the fine assurances Aeschines gave you.
Then you'll realize that one of the many ways in which he worked
against you was that he stopped you learning the truth straight away,
when it was critical, and that he did this by holding out hopes, dup-
ing you, and making promises. [27] This, as I said, is my primary and
principal purpose, but my second reason is no less important. What
is it? I want you to remember that, before he started taking bribes,
his policy was to be wary and distrustful of Philip, and to think about
how he suddenly began later to trust him and treat him as a friend.
[28] Then, if the information he gave you has proved accurate and
everything has gone well, you can judge his change of heart to have
been honest and motivated by the good of the city; but if things have
turned out to be quite different from what he said, and have involved
the city in considerable disgrace and great danger, you will realize
that it was prompted by his own avarice and that he sold the truth
for cash.

[29] While we're on the subject of these speeches of theirs, I'd like
to begin by explaining how the whole Phocian business was taken
out of your hands by Aeschines and his cohorts. But I wouldn't want
any of you, jurymen, to think that, in view of the magnitude of the
affair, I am attributing to Aeschines crimes and offences that are
too great for a man of his standing. No, you should appreciate that
whoever you might have appointed to the post and put in charge
of developments would have caused just as much trouble, if, like
Aeschines, he had been bribed and set out to mislead and dupe
you. [30] After all, the fact that you often entrust public business to
second-rate men does not mean that the undertakings which the rest

of the world judges to be Athens' prerogative are second-rate too.
Far from it. It's true, of course, that it was Philip who destroyed the
Phocians, but these men were his allies. What you have to consider is
whether they deliberately ruined and threw away every chance that
came the embassy's way to save the Phocians, not whether Aeschines
achieved the impossible and destroyed them by himself.

[31] [*To the Clerk of the Court*] Give me the resolution drawn up
by the Council in response to my report, and the deposition of the
person who drafted it at the time. [*To the jurors*] This will prove that
I am not denying responsibility now for something I kept quiet about
at the time. No, I denounced Aeschines and his cohorts straight away
and foresaw the outcome. And precisely because the Council was not
prevented from hearing the truth from me, it refrained from thanking
these men and chose not to invite them to the Prytaneum—something
which, in all the city's recorded history, has never happened to any
other ambassadors. Not even Timagoras was refused these cour-
tesies, and he was condemned to death by the Assembly.* But they
were refused to these men. [32] [*To the Clerk of the Court*] But please
read out first the deposition, and then the draft resolution.

The deposition and the draft resolution are read out.

[*To the jurors*] Not a word of thanks here from the Council to the
envoys, nor any invitation to the Prytaneum. If Aeschines disagrees,
it's up to him to prove it and produce the evidence, and I will concede. But he can't.

Now, if all of us envoys had behaved in the same way, the Council
would have been right to refuse to commend any of us, since we
would all have behaved terribly. But if some did right and others
wrong, it seems likely that the honourable ones have become tainted
by this disgrace thanks to the wrongdoers. [33] So is there an easy
way to make it absolutely clear who the villain is? Yes: bring to mind
who it was who denounced the business from the start. Plainly, it
suited the villain to keep quiet and then, if he got away with it at
the time, to evade any further discussion of what had happened. The
one with a clear conscience, however, became concerned that silence
would make him seem a party to terrible crimes. Well, it was I who
denounced them from the start, while none of them denounced me.

[34] Anyway, the Council drafted the resolution you've just heard,
but by the time the Assembly met* Philip had already occupied

Thermopylae. This, you see, was the very first of their crimes: they put Philip in control, and although you should first have received a situation report, and then discussed it, and then acted as you saw fit, Philip was already there by the time you received the report, and it was hard to say what the right course of action was. [35] Moreover, no one read out the Council's draft resolution to the Assembly. Instead of a reading of the resolution, Aeschines got up and gave the speech I recounted to you a short while ago, about how he had managed, while abroad, to win from Philip a package of beneficial concessions and how the Thebans had consequently put a price on his head. The upshot was that, although at first you felt threatened by Philip's occupation of Thermopylae and were angry with these men for failing to warn you about it in advance, the expectation of getting everything you wanted made you as meek as meek can be, and you refused to listen to a single word from me or anyone else.

[36] Next, the letter from Philip was read out. This letter had been composed by Aeschines after we had left him behind, and was, as you shall see, an undisguised, explicit defence of these men's misconduct. It includes the assertion that, when they wanted to go to the towns and cities to receive the oaths, it was he, Philip, who stopped them and kept them back to help him arbitrate a dispute between the people of Halus and the Pharsalians.* He takes all their failings upon himself and personally accepts responsibility for them. [37] But the letter contains not a single word about the Phocians, or Thespiae, or any of the other matters Aeschines mentioned in his report to you.

It was no accident that things were presented in this way. Philip accepts responsibility for the misconduct for which you should have been punishing Aeschines and his cohorts—their failure to carry out their instructions or see to any of the matters you charged them with—and I don't think you'll be able to punish him. [38] And the lies and falsehoods Philip wanted Athens to hear were included by Aeschines in his report, which means that later you'll never be able to accuse Philip or implicate him in anything, since these matters were not mentioned in any letter or other form of communication from him. [*To the Clerk of the Court*] But please read out the letter [*to the jurors*]—the letter written by Aeschines, but sent by Philip. And notice that it's exactly as I've described it. [*To the Clerk of the Court*] Go ahead, read it.

Philip's letter is read out.

[39] [*To the jurors*] You can hear what a fine, polite letter it is, Athenians. But there's not a peep about the Phocians or the Thebans or anything else that was in Aeschines' report. In fact, it's a pack of lies, as I shall prove straight away. He says that he detained these men to help him reconcile the people of Halus with their neighbours. Well, the 'reconciliation' consisted in the expulsion of the inhabitants and the forced abandonment of the town! As for the prisoners,* even while wondering what he might do to please you, he claims that the idea of ransoming them for money had never crossed his mind. [40] But you've heard testimony often enough in Assembly meetings to the effect that I took a talent with me to ransom them, and that is hereby confirmed. That's why Aeschines persuaded Philip to include this statement in the letter—because he wanted to deny me the credit for my public-spirited act.

This is a critical point. In the first letter that we brought back, Philip wrote: 'I would write openly of the great benefits I intend to confer on you, if I were certain of obtaining the alliance as well.' But now that the alliance is in place, he says that he has no idea what he might do to please you. In other words, he has no idea of his own promises! But he must have, obviously—unless he was trying to mislead you all along. [*To the Clerk of the Court*] But to show that this is what he wrote then, please take just that section of the first letter and read it from here. [*Demosthenes points to the passage*] Go ahead.

An excerpt from Philip's first letter is read out.

[41] [*To the jurors*] So, before he secured a peace agreement, he promised to write a letter detailing the great benefits he would confer on us, if he also secured an alliance with us. But now that both peace and alliance are in place, he claims to have no idea how to please you, and says that all you have to do is tell him what you want and he will do it, as long as it is neither disgraceful nor dishonourable. This last clause is his let-out: if you did in fact tell him what you wanted and were induced to make a formal request, he has left himself a fall-back position.

[42] All this, and plenty besides, could have immediately been proved at the time. You could have been told what was going on and prevented from sacrificing your interests, if 'Thespiae' and 'Plataea'

and 'the imminent punishment of Thebes' had not robbed you of the truth. In fact, such statements make sense only if the point was for them to be heard and to give us false hopes; if they were to be acted on, it would have been better to have said nothing. I mean, if matters were so well advanced that forewarning the Thebans was no help to them, why has nothing happened? But if the plan came to nothing precisely because they were forewarned, who was the one who spilled the beans? It was Aeschines, wasn't it? [43] Actually, no. Since he had no intention or desire or expectation that his promises would be fulfilled, bean-spilling is one charge of which he may be acquitted. The idea, rather, was for you to be duped by what he said, to refuse to hear the truth from me, and to stay home; the idea was for the kind of decree to be passed that would ensure the destruction of the Phocians. Hence this web of lies; hence that speech of his.

[44] Anyway, when I heard him making all these fine promises, I knew perfectly well that he was lying, and I shall tell you how I knew. First, because when Philip was about to commit himself on oath to the peace treaty, it was Aeschines and his cohorts who had the Phocians excluded from the treaty. If the Phocians were to be saved, they would of course have said nothing and have let things stand as they were. Second, because it was Aeschines—not Philip's envoys, nor Philip's letter—who was making the promises. [45] Armed with this evidence, I stood up, came forward, and tried to respond; but you refused to listen to me, so I kept my peace, apart from protesting—and I beg you in the name of Zeus and the gods to remember this—that this was all news to me and was none of my doing. And I added that I found the promises implausible anyway.

You became angry at my finding them implausible, and I said: 'Just be sure, then, Athenians, to thank these men for any of their promises that come true, and to exclude me from any privileges and crowns you award them. But if things turn out differently, be sure to vent your anger on them. I give up.' [46] 'No, don't,' Aeschines replied. 'No need to give up now, but make sure that you don't take credit later.' 'Of course I won't,' I said. 'That wouldn't be fair to you.' Then Philocrates got up and said, with considerable rudeness, 'It's hardly surprising, Athenians, that Demosthenes and I hold different views. He drinks water, and I drink wine.' You found this amusing.

[47] Consider the decree that Philocrates subsequently drafted and presented. It sounds wonderful at first hearing, but if you take

into account the circumstances under which it was written, and the promises that Aeschines was making at the time, you'll see that their sole purpose was to surrender the Phocians, with their hands more or less tied behind their backs, to Philip and the Thebans. [*To the Clerk of the Court*] Please read the decree.

Philocrates' decree is read out.

[48] [*To the jurors*] You can see, Athenians, how the decree is filled with courteous and careful language. Note also the words 'the peace treaty shall be binding for Philip, and for his descendants as well, as shall the alliance', and 'Philip is to be thanked for promising to act in accordance with justice'. Actually, *he* made no promises. Quite the contrary: he said that he had no idea what he might do to please you. [49] Aeschines was the spokesman for his promises. Then, when Philocrates saw that you were fired up by Aeschines' words, he included the following clause in the decree: 'If the Phocians fail to do their duty and hand the sanctuary over to the Amphictyons, the Athenian people shall take action against them for trying to prevent this from happening.' [50] So, Athenians, since you stayed at home without taking to the field, and since the Spartans, after realizing that a trick was being played, had returned home,* and since no other Amphictyons were there except the Thessalians and Thebans, Philocrates' most carefully phrased clause has handed the sanctuary over to them. He wrote that the sanctuary was to be handed over to the Amphictyons, but to which Amphictyons? There was no one there except the Thebans and the Thessalians. He didn't write 'the Amphictyonic Council is to be convened'; he didn't write 'no action is to be taken until the Council meets'; he didn't write 'Proxenus is to lead an expedition to Phocis'; he didn't write 'the Athenians are to take to the field', or anything of this sort.*

[51] It's true that Philip also wrote two letters inviting you to take to the field, but it was not his intention that you should do so. Not a bit of it! Otherwise, he would never have waited until after he had used up all the time when you might have been able to mount an expedition before inviting you. By the same token, he wouldn't have stopped me from sailing back here when I wanted to,* nor would he have ordered Aeschines to make the kind of speech that was bound to discourage you from mounting an expedition. No, his intention was for you to think that he was going to do exactly what you wanted, so

that you wouldn't pass any resolutions that might obstruct his plans, and for the Phocians to end any resistance or opposition that the prospect of help from you might have encouraged, and surrender to him in utter despair. [*To the Clerk of the Court*] But please let the jurors hear Philip's actual letters.

Philip's letters are read out.

[52] [*To the jurors*] These are indeed letters of invitation—urgent invitation, by Zeus!—but if the invitation had been at all sincere, the very next task for Aeschines and his cohorts would have been to recommend that you take to the field and propose that Proxenus (who was near by, as they knew) should immediately go to Philip's assistance. Plainly, however, they did exactly the opposite. Of course they did, because the wording of the letters meant nothing to them. They knew what Philip had in mind when he wrote the letters, and that was the project for which they were acting as his assistants and his allies.

[53] Anyway, when the Phocians heard of the decisions you had taken in the Assembly—when they received a copy of Philocrates' decree and learnt what Aeschines had said in his report and the promises he had made—they were utterly undone. Think about it. There were people there, intelligent people, who distrusted Philip. They were induced to trust him. Why? Because, while they had plenty of experience of Philip's deceitfulness, it never occurred to them that Athenian ambassadors might dare to deceive their fellow Athenians. They assumed, then, that Aeschines' report was true and that it would be the Thebans, not themselves, who would meet with destruction. [54] Then there were others who thought that, whatever it took, they should fight back. But they too had the wind taken out of their sails by the assertion that Philip had been persuaded to take their part, and that if they didn't comply you would march against them, when they had been hoping for help from you. Yet others had been imagining that you were regretting your peace accord with Philip. When it was pointed out to them that you had voted for the peace to remain in force for his descendants as well, they gave up any hope of your ever helping them.

That is why the decree was made to bear so much—[55] which, in my view, is the worst of all their crimes against you. They drew up a peace accord with a mortal man, who owed his power to mere circumstances, that committed the city to immortal shame; they robbed the city of everything, even of the chance of being benefited by Fortune;* they drew on such immense depths of iniquity that they injured not just existing Athenians, but those not yet born. What could be more reprehensible than that? [56] Anyway, you'd never have tolerated the subsequent insertion into the peace treaty of the clause 'and for his descendants as well' if at the time you hadn't believed the promises Aeschines made, just as the Phocians did. In their case, the belief led to their destruction, and so, when they surrendered to Philip and voluntarily entrusted their cities to his protection, they met with the complete opposite of what Aeschines had promised in his report to you.

[57] It will help you to be certain that I'm right in saying that Aeschines and his cohorts encompassed the destruction of Phocis if I reckon up the dates on which the various events took place. If any of them wants to respond at all, he's welcome to get up and use some of my water for what he has to say.* So, the peace was made on 19 Elaphebolion, and we were away for three whole months for the oaths. The Phocians were safe throughout this period. [58] We returned to Athens from the mission for the oaths on 13 Skirophorion, by which time Philip had occupied Thermopylae. He was giving the Phocians assurances, but they were disinclined to believe a word of them, as is proved by the fact that otherwise they wouldn't have come here and appealed to you.

The next Assembly, at which all the damage was done by these men's lies and false assurances, took place on 16 Skirophorion. [59] I reckon that the news of your decisions reached Phocis four days later, since there were Phocians here on official business, who were anxious to hear the reports and see how you voted. It was on the 20th, then, four days after the 16th, that we may assume the Phocians heard about your decisions. The 21st, 22nd, 23rd—that was when the truce was made and Phocis was utterly doomed and lost.* [60] We can establish this date by the fact that on the 27th the Assembly met in Piraeus to discuss the shipyards, and Dercylus* arrived from Chalcis with the news that Philip had put the Thebans in charge of the entire business. Dercylus reckoned that the truce had been entered into four days earlier, so we have the 23rd, 24th, 25th, 26th, and the 27th is four days later. So the dates, the reports, the proposals—everything goes to show that these men were Philip's allies and are implicated in the destruction of Phocis.

[61] Moreover, the fact that none of the cities of Phocis fell to siege or assault, but that the treaty alone was enough to encompass their

total destruction, is the most convincing proof that this happened because they had been persuaded by these men that Philip was going to protect them. It must have been them, because the Phocians knew Philip too well. [*To the Clerk of the Court*] Fetch both the treaty of our alliance with the Phocians, and the resolution that authorized the dismantling of the Phocians' defences.* [*To the jurors*] These documents will show how matters stood between Phocis and Athens, and what happened in Phocis thanks to these godless men. [*To the Clerk of the Court*] Go ahead, read them.

The treaty of alliance between Athens and Phocis is read out.

[62] [*To the jurors*] These, then, were the terms of the relationship between Athens and Phocis: friendship, alliance, military help. Hear now what happened to the Phocians because Aeschines stopped you from sending them help. [*To the Clerk of the Court*] Go ahead, read.

The pact between Philip and the Phocians is read out.

[*To the jurors*] What could be clearer, Athenians? 'A pact between Philip and the Phocians'—not between the Phocians and the Thebans, or the Thessalians, or the Locrians, or anyone else who was there. And again, it says that the Phocians are to surrender their cities to Philip, not to the Thebans or the Thessalians or anyone else. [63] Why? Because you were told by Aeschines that Philip had come to protect the Phocians. They completely trusted Aeschines, looked to him for everything, and made peace because of him. [*To the Clerk of the Court*] Now read the rest of the document. [*To the jurors*] Consider what the Phocians were led to expect and what happened to them. Is there any similarity between what actually happened and what Aeschines said was going to happen? Are they even close? [*To the Clerk of the Court*] Go ahead.

The resolution of the Amphictyonic Council is read out.

[64] [*To the jurors*] Athenians, nothing that has happened in Greece within living memory is more frightening or more serious than this. I doubt that any event from even further back in history can compare with it. A single individual has been helped by Aeschines and his cohorts to gain control of so much, and to wield enormous power, despite the existence of our city of Athens, which traditionally champions the Greeks and refuses to let such things happen.

Nor is it only these decrees that allow us to see how the poor Phocians met their doom; the actual events that transpired do the same. [65] It's a terrible thing to see, Athenians; it would make you weep. Not long ago, when we were on our way to Delphi, we couldn't help seeing everything: houses razed to the ground; fortifications demolished; no adult males to be seen on the land, but only a few women, young children, and wretched old folk. Words are inadequate to describe the appalling state of affairs there at the moment. And yet, as you might well all remind me, these are the people who once voted in our favour against the Theban proposal to enslave us.* [66] Athenians, if your ancestors came back alive, how would they vote, do you think? What verdict would they bring against the people responsible for this destruction? It seems to me that they would consider themselves undefiled even if they stoned the guilty men to death with their own hands. It's a disgrace—though that is too weak a word—for those who saved us then and cast the vital vote in our favour to have met with the opposite fate thanks to these men, and to be allowed to suffer as no other people in Greece have ever suffered. And who is the guilty party? Who was it who duped them into this situation? Aeschines.

[67] There are plenty of reasons for thinking Philip lucky, Athenians, but one reason stands out above all. In fact, I swear by all the gods that I can't think of anyone else alive today who is so lucky in this particular respect. Achievements such as capturing great cities and annexing large stretches of land are, of course, enviable and glorious. Why not? But there are many others who have such achievements to their name. [68] The piece of good fortune I'm talking about, however, is unique to Philip and has never come anyone else's way. What is it? When he required unscrupulous men for his purposes, he found men who had even fewer scruples than he needed! Can anyone doubt that this is the right way to think of these men? Look how much Philip had at stake, but still there were certain lies he balked at telling himself. They occurred in none of his letters, nor in any of his envoys' speeches. These were the lies Aeschines and his cohorts were paid to try to deceive you with. [69] Even Antipater and Parmenion,* though they serve a master and wouldn't have to face you afterwards, still made sure that they wouldn't be used as the agents of your deception. But Aeschines and his cronies—who were Athenians, citizens of the city which is a byword for freedom, and

officially appointed ambassadors—undertook to deceive you, even though they were bound to meet you face to face, had to live with you for the rest of their lives, and would have to submit to an audit of their actions. Could men sink lower than this? Could anything be more depraved?

[70] You should appreciate too that Aeschines lies under your curse, and that to acquit such a liar is irreligious and contravenes your sacred obligation. A reading of the curse will prove this.* [*To the Clerk of the Court*] Please take the statute and read out the part of it that contains the curse. [*Demosthenes points to the passage*] Here it is.

The curse is read out.

[*To the jurors*] This is the legally prescribed curse, Athenians, that the herald pronounces on your behalf at every meeting of the Assembly, and when the Council is in session he does the same again there. Aeschines cannot claim ignorance of it, because as under-secretary to the Assembly and assistant to the Council it was his job to dictate it to the herald. [71] Would it not be extraordinarily inconsistent of you if today, when you have the power to do on your own exactly what you enjoin, or rather expect, the gods to do on your behalf, you fail to do it? That is, if you yourselves acquit the man whom you ask the gods to obliterate, 'himself and his family and his house'? Don't do it! You can leave it up to the gods to punish undetected crimes, but when you have the criminal in your hands, don't make it their business to deal with him.

[72] I hear that Aeschines is going to have the unmitigated impudence to disown everything he did—his report, his promises, his lies—as if he were on trial before strangers, and not you, who are perfectly aware of the facts. Instead, I hear, he's going to blame first the Spartans, then the Phocians, and then Hegesippus. How ridiculous of him—or, rather, how shameless! [73] I mean, whatever he's going to say today about the Phocians or the Spartans or Hegesippus—that they didn't let Proxenus do his job,* that they are impious, that . . . But it doesn't matter what he accuses them of, because it was all over and done with before the ambassadors returned here to Athens, and therefore couldn't have got in the way of saving the Phocians. Who says it couldn't? Aeschines here himself! [74] When he delivered his report, he didn't say that the Phocians would have been saved 'if it weren't for the Spartans', or 'if they'd let Proxenus do his job', or 'if

it weren't for Hegesippus', or 'if it weren't for this or that'. No, rather than anything like that, he explicitly said that he had managed, while abroad, to persuade Philip to protect the Phocians, settle Boeotia, and do nothing that went against your interests; that this would take two or three days; and that in response the Thebans had put a price on his head.

[75] So don't listen or let him get away with talking about things that happened before he delivered his report, and don't let him accuse the Phocians of having done wrong. In the past, when, as you often did, you saved the Spartans or those damned Euboeans or anyone else,* it wasn't because of their merits, but because their survival was in the city's interest, as is the case with the Phocians now. Besides, how can he shift the blame on to the Phocians or Spartans or you or anyone else? Have any of them done anything wrong, subsequent to his speech, that made it impossible for the promises he made to you then to be fulfilled? This is the question to ask. But he won't be able to reply, [76] because his lying report to you, your acceptance of it, the Phocians' learning of it, surrendering, and perishing, all took place within only five days.* It's perfectly clear, then, that every possible trick or ruse for the destruction of Phocis was already in place. After all, it was while Philip was unable to move because of the peace negotiations (though he was busy getting ready) that he sent for the Spartans and promised, as a way of stopping the Phocians gaining their support with your help, to arrange everything in the Phocians' interest. [77] When he reached Thermopylae, and the Spartans realized that they had been duped and withdrew, he next unleashed Aeschines to trick you. He wanted to guard against the possibility that, when you discovered he was acting in the Thebans' interest, he might be held up and have to spend time combating resistance by the Phocians, backed by you. He wanted to ensure that his takeover was completed without a struggle, and he got what he wanted. Should you, then, let Aeschines get away with tricking you, just as Philip tricked the Spartans and the Phocians? No, that would hardly be right.

[78] If he tries to tell you that our retention of the Chersonese compensates us for the Phocians and Thermopylae and all the rest of our losses, don't let him get away with it, jurymen, I beg you in the name of Zeus and all the gods. He has done enough damage already as ambassador, so don't let him make matters worse in his defence speech by disgracing the city with the suggestion that you sacrificed

the safety of your allies in an underhand deal to secure one of your possessions. You did no such thing. For four whole months after the treaty that ensured the safety of the Chersonese, the Phocians were in no danger. It was only later that the lies he told you brought about their destruction. [79] In any case, you'll find that in fact the Chersonese is in more danger now than it was then. I mean, when would it be easier to punish Philip for aggression against the Chersonese—*before* he seized any of these places, or now? Much easier then, surely. What does retaining the Chersonese amount to when the would-be aggressor no longer needs to feel fearful or threatened?*

[80] But there's something else that I hear Aeschines is planning to say. Why, he will ask in puzzlement, is his accuser Demosthenes? Why did no Phocian take him to court? It will be better if you hear an explanation of this from me first. The best and most sensible of the Phocian refugees are living quietly in exile after their terrible ordeal. None of them would wish to make himself a target of personal animosity for the sake of the disaster that struck them all. And although there are other Phocians who might be prepared to do anything for money, there's no one to pay them. [81] I certainly wouldn't have paid for someone to stand beside me here and decry their ordeal. The facts of what happened tell their own story, loud and clear. But the people of Phocis have been brought so pitifully low that none of them is interested in bringing charges at audits in Athens. All they have time for is enslavement and a terrified death at the hands of the Thebans and Philip's mercenaries, whom they are forced to feed, while they themselves have been disarmed and dispersed throughout their villages.

[82] So don't let him say this. Have him prove instead that the Phocians escaped destruction, or that he didn't promise that Philip would keep them safe. The point of auditing an embassy is to ask 'What happened?' and 'What was in your report?' If the report was true, go in peace; if false, pay the penalty. [*To Aeschines*] There's no point in asking why there are no Phocians here. The part you played, as I see it, was to reduce them to a state where they can neither help their friends nor resist their enemies.

[83] [*To the jurors*] Now, leaving aside the taint of disgrace and dishonour about his actions, the city also faces great danger because of them. This is easy to demonstrate. All of you know that the Phocian War and the Phocians' control of Thermopylae kept us safe from

the Thebans, and stopped Philip from invading the Peloponnese, Euboea, or Attica. [84] But this safety, afforded us by geography and events themselves, was thrown away by you under the influence of the lies and falsehoods told by Aeschines and his cohorts. Although it was assured by armed forces, constant warfare, substantial allied cities, and extensive territory, you let it go. Your earlier expedition to Thermopylae, at a cost of more than two hundred talents, including the personal expenses of the troops, was just wasted effort;* your hopes for Thebes too were vain.

[85] But of all the many terrible things Aeschines has done as Philip's servant, there's one that shows just how little regard he has for the city and every single one of you. Listen to me. Philip's decision right from the start always was to do for the Thebans everything that he has done, but by telling you the opposite in his report and exposing your disapproval of the situation, Aeschines has increased the enmity between you and the Thebans, and brought about their rapprochement with Philip. Could any man have acted with greater disloyalty?

[86] [*To the Clerk of the Court*] Get the decrees of Diophantus and Callisthenes* and read them out, please. [*To the jurors*] These decrees will show that when you were on the right track you earned thanksgiving sacrifices and praise not only here but abroad, but when you had been led astray by these men, you brought your families in from the countryside and voted to celebrate the Festival of Heracles within the city walls, even though we weren't at war. I fail to see how you could let Aeschines go unpunished, when he has made it impossible for even the gods to be worshipped in the traditional fashion. [*To the Clerk of the Court*] Please read the decree.

Diophantus' decree is read out.

[*To the jurors*] That was the decree which you thought appropriate to the circumstances then, Athenians. [*To the Clerk of the Court*] Now read the next one.

Callisthenes' decree is read out.

[87] [*To the jurors*] This later decree was a direct result of the actions of Aeschines and his cohorts, and runs quite contrary to the hopes you entertained when you first entered into the peace treaty and the alliance, and later when you were persuaded to add the clause 'and

for his descendants as well'. No, at the time these men had led you to expect marvellous benefits to come your way. But all of you know how many times since then you have been alarmed at the news that Philip's forces and mercenaries were at Porthmus or Megara.* It may be true that he has not yet set foot on Attic soil, but it would be wrong to make that a reason for complacency. What you need to ask your-selves is whether, thanks to these men, Philip has gained the ability to do so whenever it suits him. And, bearing that inexcusable fact in mind, what you need to do is condemn and punish the guilty party, the man who gave Philip this freedom of action.

[88] Now, I'm sure Aeschines will avoid addressing the charges brought against him. He will want to divert your attention as far as possible from the facts, so he'll describe all the ways in which the entire world benefits from peace, and he'll catalogue the horrors of war, and his 'defence' will consist mainly in his singing the praises of peace. But in fact even this tells against him. If something that is responsible for such great benefits to others has made things so difficult for you, the inevitable conclusion is that Aeschines and his cohorts accepted bribes and turned something that is in itself good into something bad.

[89] 'What?' he might say. 'Isn't it thanks to the peace that you possess and will continue to possess three hundred triremes, plus the necessary equipment and financial resources?' If he does say this, your response must be to point out that Philip's position too has been greatly improved as a result of the peace, in terms of weaponry, territory, and the income he now has available to him. His income especially has hugely increased. 'But so has ours, to a certain extent.' [90] Yes, but what enables men at any time to gain good things, whether they themselves or their superiors are the beneficiaries, is the condition of their affairs and their allies. As a result of these men's venality, our situation in these respects has deteriorated and weak-ened, while Philip has grown stronger and more formidable. Since Philip's alliances and his revenues have *both* increased thanks to these men, it's wrong to offset what we should rightly have gained from the peace against what these men have sold. Our gains are no compensa-tion for our losses. Far from it: we'd have made the gains anyway, and we'd have had what we've lost as well, if it weren't for these men.

[91] Surely you'd agree, Athenians, that in general justice lies in neither taking your anger out on Aeschines if, despite all the

calamities that have happened to the city, he was responsible for none
of them, nor in letting him be saved by some important achievement
that was actually someone else's doing. No, you must think about
what he is actually responsible for, and then express your gratitude
or your anger, whichever he turns out to deserve. [92] How will you
know which is appropriate? If you stop him jumbling everything up
together—the generals' offences,* the war against Philip, the benefits
of the peace—and consider everything separately. For example, were
we at war with Philip? Yes. Is anyone bringing any charges against
Aeschines in this context? Does anyone want to suggest that he's
responsible for what happened in the war? No. He has no charge
to answer on this score, then, and there should be no mention of
the war in his speech. A defendant should provide witnesses and
evidence on disputed issues, but he should not try to obfuscate matters by defending himself on issues where there's no disagreement.
[*To Aeschines*] So make sure you avoid talking about the war; no one
blames you for that.

[93] [*To the jurors*] Next, we found ourselves urged to make peace,
and we were persuaded that this was the right thing to do. We sent
ambassadors, and they brought back Philip's men to conclude the
peace. Again, is anyone blaming Aeschines in this context, accusing
him of responsibility for any of this? Is anyone saying that he was the
instigator of peace, or that he was wrong to have brought Philip's men
back here? No. So he shouldn't bring this up either, the bare fact of
our having made peace, because it wasn't his doing.

[94] Someone might ask me, 'So what are you getting at, my friend?
At what point did Aeschines' wrongdoing begin, do you think?' It all
started, Athenians, not when you were discussing the pros and cons of
making peace, because you had already made up your minds to do so
anyway, but when you were trying to decide on the terms and conditions. He argued against perfectly equitable points and, because he
had been bribed, spoke in support of a man whose proposals were for
hire.* Next, after he had been chosen to represent you for the oaths,
he completely ignored the instructions you had given him, destroyed
those of our allies who had managed to keep themselves safe during the
war, and told greater and worse lies than anyone ever has in the past or
will in the future. At first, up until the time when Philip entered into
the peace negotiations, it was Ctesiphon and Aristodemus who took
it upon themselves to dupe you, but once matters had progressed

and it was time for action, they passed the job on to Philocrates and Aeschines. They accepted the task and did their lethal best.

[95] So now he has to give an account of his actions and face the consequences. Because he is, of course, a damned, unscrupulous clerk,* he will defend himself as though he were on trial for the peace. He'll do this not because he wants to add to the number of charges to which he has to respond—no one is that crazy!—but because he's aware that his actions were criminal from start to finish, with no redeeming features. Defending the peace will at least enable him to pose as a nice person. [96] But I worry about the peace, Athenians. I worry that the peace might be as expensive to maintain as a high-interest loan. After all, the safety and security of the peace depended on the Phocians and Thermopylae, and they were sold by Aeschines and his cohorts. But if Aeschines wasn't responsible for our making peace in the first place, who was? Now, what I'm about to say is strange, but perfectly true. Anyone who is really happy with the peace has the universally reviled generals to thank for it! If under their command the war had gone as you wished, you wouldn't have tolerated any talk of peace at all!

[97] The generals were responsible for the peace, then, but we have Aeschines and his fellow bribe-takers to thank for its precariousness, instability, and fallibility. So stop him—stop him talking about the peace and restrict him to talking about his actions. He's not on trial for the peace, not at all. But he spoiled the peace. Look at it this way. If there had been a state of peace, and you hadn't subsequently been duped, and none of your allies had been destroyed, the peace would have been perfectly innocuous. The only bad aspect of it would have been the damage to your reputation. For this, it is true, Aeschines must share the blame, since he spoke in support of Philocrates. But no irreparable damage would have been done. As things stand, however, a great deal of irreparable damage has been done, in my opinion, and he is responsible for it.

[98] Anyway, I'm sure none of you is in any doubt about the despicable and vicious way in which these men ensured all this destruction and ruin. But I bring absolutely no malice to this case, jurymen, nor do I expect it from you. Far from it. If he acted out of stupidity or naivety or some other form of ignorance, I absolve him, and I advise you to do so too. [99] But actually none of these excuses is justified in public life. It's not as if you command or compel anyone to become a politician. No, when someone steps up, because he feels that he

has what it takes, you act with decency and respect. You grant him a favourable hearing, and so far from resenting his offer, you elect him to official positions and entrust your affairs to him. [100] If he's successful, he will be honoured for it and attain a prominent position in society. If he fails, is he to make excuses and try to shift the blame? That wouldn't be right. It's no consolation—how could it be?—for anyone, let alone our ruined allies or their families, to learn that their ruination was due to *stupidity* on my part, to say nothing of his. [101] All the same, you should acquit Aeschines, however appalling and outrageous his crimes, if he turns out to have committed them out of naivety or some other form of ignorance. But if he's simply a bad man who accepted cash and gifts, and if the facts themselves prove this, then you must put him to death, if possible, or, failing that, make an example of him for future generations. The question you need to ask yourselves, then, is what would constitute a fair proof in this case.

[102] Let's go back to those speeches Aeschines made to you about the Phocians and Thespiae and Euboea. If he wasn't deliberately misleading you because he had taken bribes, there are, logically, only two possibilities. Either Philip made, in his hearing, explicit promises about what he would do and how he would act, or else Aeschines was beguiled and duped by Philip's habitual courtesy into hoping that this is how he would act. There are no other possibilities. [103] Now, on either alternative, Philip should be the man Aeschines hates most in the world. Why? Because it was Philip, then, who was responsible for all the worst and most terrible things that have happened to him. He has lied to you and fallen out of your favour, and now he's on trial. By all rights, he should have been impeached long ago, but in fact, thanks to your innocent leniency, he's undergoing a mere audit, and at a time of his choosing.* [104] So, then, has any of you heard a single critical word from Aeschines about Philip? Or found him trying to expose Philip, or saying anything at all? No, not a bit of it. He's slower to criticize Philip than anyone else in Athens; even ordinary citizens who have never suffered personally denounce him more.

Not knowing that he had let himself be corrupted, I was expecting to hear Aeschines make a different kind of speech: 'Deal with me as you wish, Athenians. I was credulous and gullible; I made mistakes and I admit it. Beware of this man, Athenians: he is a villain, treacherous and cunning. Don't you see what he has done to me, how he took me in?' [110]† I haven't heard anything like that from him, and neither have you. Why? Because he wasn't duped or misled: he sold his services. He took money and then made his speech and betrayed us to Philip. As Philip's hired man, he was upstanding and honest, but as your ambassador and fellow citizen he was a traitor, and he deserves to die three times over, not just once.

[111] Nor is this the only proof that all those speeches of his were paid for. Not long ago a Thessalian delegation arrived here, accompanied by Philip's envoys, asking you to vote for Philip's admission to the Amphictyonic Council.* Now, there was one person above all who ought to have spoken up against this proposal. Who do I mean? Aeschines. Why? Because Philip's actions had given the lie to his report. [112] Aeschines said that Philip was going to fortify Thespiae and Plataea, and that, rather than destroy the Phocians, he would teach the Thebans a lesson. But what Philip actually did was make the Thebans excessively strong and eliminate the Phocians. He didn't fortify Thespiae and Plataea, and he added Orchomenus and Coronea to the states he had enslaved. No two sets of events could be more completely opposite! But Aeschines didn't argue against the proposal, and didn't even open his mouth to voice any objections. [113] Nor was that the worst of it: he was the only man in the city to speak in support of the proposal! Not even the foul Philocrates dared to do that, but Aeschines did. You heckled him and refused to listen, and then, as he stepped down from the platform, wanting to ingratiate himself with Philip's envoys who were there, he said (I'm sure you remember): 'Many are the hecklers, but few those who take up arms when required to.' As though *he* were such an amazing soldier, by Zeus!*

[114] Now, next, if there were no way to prove that any of the ambassadors had been bribed—if it weren't plain for all to see—we would resort to considering the testimony of tortured slaves, for instance.* But in fact Philocrates not only often used to admit his guilt in the Assembly, but even paraded it before your eyes by dealing in wheat, building houses, offering to go off to Macedonia even without official appointment, importing timber, and openly changing gold coins at the banks.* There's no denying that *he* took bribes, then, since he himself admits it and makes no secret of it. [115] Now, imagine a man who, when he could have been counted among the innocent, chooses to join Philocrates against them and allows himself to be taken to court. Is anyone so stupid or delusional that he would

let Philocrates get rich while he himself sacrificed his good name and put himself at risk? I hardly think so. All this, Athenians, strongly and clearly suggests, if you look squarely at the facts, that Aeschines did accept bribes.

[116] Take the most recent event. It shows as clearly as anything that he has been bribed by Philip. You know, of course, that the other day, when Hypereides was starting the process of impeaching Philocrates, I stepped up and said that there was one aspect of the impeachment that worried me—the idea that Philocrates alone had been responsible for so many hideous crimes and the other nine ambassadors for none. I argued that this was impossible, and that Philocrates would have got nowhere by himself, without the help of some of his colleagues. [117] 'It's not up to me', I said, 'to say who is and who isn't guilty. No, the facts themselves will expose the guilty and absolve the innocent. Anyone who wants to has the opportunity now to stand up and step forward to declare his innocence before you and state that he disapproves of Philocrates' conduct. And I for one will count anyone who does so as innocent.' I'm sure you remember this.

Well, no one came forward and made any such declaration. [118] The rest of them had various excuses: one was not liable to audit;* another might not have been there; a third was related to Philocrates by marriage. But Aeschines had no excuse, because the fact of the matter is that he has been completely corrupted. The services he has already rendered are not the end of it; if he is acquitted today there can be no doubt that he will continue to work for Philip against you. This is why, rather than speak a single word against Philip, he passes up the opportunity to be let off. He'd rather be disgraced and put on trial; he'd prefer whatever punishment this court imposes to doing anything that might displease Philip.

[119] But what is this bond between him and Philocrates? Why does Aeschines take such good care of him? Suppose that Philocrates' ambassadorial services had been of the highest quality and that he had worked throughout for the good of the city. Even so, if he admitted that he had profited from the mission—and he did admit it—you'd think that any of his fellow ambassadors who had remained uncorrupted would carefully have distanced himself from precisely this aspect of the mission and protested his own innocence in this regard. But Aeschines failed to do so. What could be more transparent, Athenians? Doesn't this fact proclaim, loud and clear, that Aeschines was bribed and that the

constant factor in his wrongdoing is money, not stupidity or ignorance or incompetence?

[120] 'So,' he'll say, 'where are the witnesses to my taking bribes?' That's the key question. [*To Aeschines*] The facts, Aeschines, the most reliable of all witnesses! You can't accuse facts of having been suborned, or suggest that they are what they are because they're doing someone a favour. What they are, as any inspection reveals, is the product of your treachery and corruption. But the facts are not the only witnesses: you will shortly bear witness against yourself. Stand up here and answer my questions. . . . Surely you won't claim that inexperience has made you tongue-tied. I mean, you prosecute new cases as readily as you take on new roles in plays, and win them even without the help of witnesses, in trials that have been allotted an entire day each.* This proves what a thoroughly clever fellow you are.

[121] [*To the jurors*] I'm sure you all agree that Aeschines has behaved unscrupulously throughout, but of all the terrible things he's done, none is worse, to my mind, than what I'm going to mention now. It will also bring into sharper relief the flagrancy of his bribe-taking and his out-and-out venality. For the third mission to Philip—the mission to secure the wonderful benefits he had dangled before you—you appointed most of the same ambassadors, including him and me. [122] I immediately stepped up and took the oath of exemption.* Some people shouted out that I should go, but I refused. Aeschines took up the appointment, however.

Later, after the Assembly had broken up, the ambassadors met to choose one of their number to stay behind in Athens. For everything was still up in the air, no one knew what was going to happen, and all kinds of different views were being aired at the time in the Agora by various groups. [123] What worried the ambassadors was the possibility that an extraordinary Assembly might suddenly be convened, and that then, once you had heard the truth from me, you would decide to do your duty by the Phocians, and Philip would lose control of the situation. For all it would have taken was a vote from you offering the Phocians a little hope, and they would have been saved. There was no way, no way at all, for Philip to stay where he was unless you remained deceived. There was no grain in the fields, which had been left unseeded because of the war, nor could he supply himself with grain because your triremes were near by and controlled the sea. And he was faced with a large number of Phocian cities which would have

been hard to take, except by protracted siege warfare. Even if he'd
been able to take one a day, there were twenty-two of them in all.

[124] All these factors made them decide to leave Aeschines here,
with the job of seeing that you didn't become undeceived and change
your minds. Now, for him to take the oath of exemption for no reason was very strange—and very suspicious: 'What's going on? First
you tell us about all the marvellous benefits that are coming our way,
and then you choose not to go as a member of the mission to secure
them?' But he had to stay, so what could he do? He made out that
he was ill, and his brother brought Execestus before the Council as
a medical witness, swore that Aeschines was ill, and was appointed in
his place. [125] Five or six days later, after the Phocians had met their
doom, Aeschines' job came to an end just as any job does. Dercylus
turned back from Chalcis and came and told you, at the Assembly in
Piraeus, about the downfall of the Phocians. Naturally, the news made
you sorry for the Phocians and terrified for yourselves. You decided
we should bring our families in from the countryside, repair our out-
lying fortresses, fortify Piraeus, and celebrate the Festival of Heracles
inside the city.

[126] Under these circumstances, with the city in the grip of all
this chaos and commotion, this clever, cunning, eloquent man took
himself off as ambassador*—without appointment by either Council
or Assembly—to the man who was responsible for all the turmoil.
He forgot the illness which had gained him his exemption earlier,
ignored the fact that someone else had been selected in his place, and
disregarded the law that ordains the death penalty in such cases. [127]
He took no notice of the fact that it was utterly strange for the man
who had announced that there was a price on his head in Thebes to
be going off to the Theban heartland and army headquarters just at
the time when the Thebans had gained control of Phocis as well as all
Boeotia. He was so deranged, so focused on profit and the bribes he
had taken, that none of this was of the slightest concern or importance to him, and off he went.

[128] As if that were not enough, what he did when he got there
was worse, far worse. Here in Athens you—all of us—were so upset
by the appalling things that had happened to the poor Phocians
that you decided not to send any members of the Council or the
Thesmothetes as official observers to the Pythian festival.* But while
you dispensed with this age-old practice, he went and feasted on

the victims sacrificed by the Thebans and Philip to celebrate their
political and military victories. He joined in the libations and prayers
offered by Philip in thanks for the destruction of the fortifications
and farmland and military potential of your allies. He wore a garland
and sang paeans along with Philip, and toasted Philip's health. [129]
There's no way for him to deny this and tell a different story. His
taking the oath of exemption is a matter of public record, stored in
the *Mētrōon* under the supervision of the public slave, in a decree
that mentions him directly, by name.* As for what he did in Thebes,
the other members of the embassy who were there will bear witness
against him; they were the ones who told me what went on, because
I wasn't involved in that mission, having taken the oath of exemption.
[130] [*To the Clerk of the Court*] Please read the decree and call the
witnesses.

The decree and the ambassadors' deposition are read out.

[*To the jurors*] What prayers do you suppose Philip and the Thebans
offered as they poured out their libations? Can there be any doubt
that they asked the gods to grant them and their allies victory and
military supremacy, and to destroy the Phocians' allies? In other
words, in joining in these prayers, Aeschines was wishing destruction
on the land of his birth. It is your duty now to turn this curse back on
to him.

[131] So: he broke the law by going there and became liable to the
prescribed death penalty; his behaviour there clearly merits the same
penalty many times over; and death would also be the right penalty
for his earlier conduct as ambassador. What you have to do, then,
is try to find a punishment of sufficient weight to seem appropriate
for so many crimes. [132] All of you, Athenians—the entire population, in fact—officially condemn all the consequences of the peace.
You also refuse to have anything to do with the Amphictyons, and
treat Philip with hostility and suspicion for his impious crimes, which
were as unjust as they were harmful to your interests. Under these
circumstances, wouldn't it be inexcusable, now that you've come to
court to judge the relevant audits, under an oath to act in the interests
of the city, to acquit the man who is responsible for all our troubles
and whom you know for a fact to be guilty? [133] Any of your fellow citizens—any of your fellow Greeks, even—would be justified
in rebuking you for condemning Philip, whose behaviour could be

excused on the grounds that he was putting an end to hostilities by simply buying collusion that was on offer, and then acquitting this man here, who brazenly betrayed you for money, when the law prescribes the severest punishment for anyone who does that.

[134] Anyway, perhaps Aeschines and his cohorts will argue that convicting one of the peace negotiators will provoke Philip's hostility. If this is true, I can't think of a more serious crime to impute to Aeschines. If the bribes Philip gave to secure the peace have enabled him to become so terrifyingly powerful that you're actually considering how to keep him happy, despite the fact that this makes you oath-breakers and puts you in the wrong,* what punishment would be appropriate for the person responsible for putting you in this position? [135] All the same, I think I can also demonstrate that, in all probability, punishing Aeschines is more likely to lead to overtures of friendship from Philip, which will be to your advantage.

You should be aware, Athenians, that Philip does not underrate you; his preference of the Thebans was not due to his belittling your effectiveness compared to theirs, but to his listening to the advice given him by Aeschines and his lot. I told you about this advice of theirs on an earlier occasion, in fact, in the Assembly, and none of them denied the truth of what I said. [136] There's nothing, they told him, less stable or solid than democracy; it's like a restless wind blowing on the sea and moving at random. One man comes and another man goes, and none of them cares or thinks about the common good. Philip needs constant friends, they told him, to negotiate and manage particular items on your agendas—friends such as Aeschines himself. With this arrangement in place, Philip's every objective would easily be secured in Athens.

[137] Now, it seems to me that if Philip heard that those who had given him this advice at the time were promptly executed on their return here, he would react in the same way as the Persian king did. What did the king do? When he found out that Timagoras, who had conned him out of a reputed forty talents, had been put to death by you—in other words, that he couldn't even guarantee to save his own life, let alone get the results he had earlier promised—he realized that the person he had paid was not the one in charge. So, first, he let it be known that Amphipolis would be restored to you, which at the time was registered as an ally and friend of his, and then he never bribed anyone ever again.

[138] That is what Philip would have done too, if he had seen any of these men being punished—and it's what he will do, if he sees it happening now. But what is he to do on hearing that their speeches meet with your approval, and that they prosecute others rather than suffer prosecution? Should he spend a lot when he can spend less? Why would he want to pander to all of you when he can pander to two or three? That would be crazy. It's not as if he chose to be a public benefactor of Thebes either. Not a bit of it. He was prevailed upon by their envoys, and I'll tell you how. [139] We were already at Philip's court on our mission when a Theban delegation arrived. He offered them money—a very great deal of money, they told us. But the Theban envoys stood firm and rejected the offer. Later, during a banquet following a sacrifice, Philip was in a generous mood in his cups, and after offering them considerable quantities of war booty and so on, he eventually tried to make them a present of silver and gold goblets. But they resolutely refused everything. [140] Finally one of the Theban envoys, a man called Philon, delivered a speech, Athenians, that should have been spoken by your representatives, not the Thebans'. He said how pleasing and gratifying it was to find Philip treating them with generosity and respect, but that he had their loyalty and friendship even without these gifts. They would like him instead, he said, to direct this benevolence towards the city as a whole, whose affairs were their concern at the moment, by doing something that would honour both himself and the Thebans; and they assured him that in this way he would gain the support of the whole city, not just themselves.

[141] So let's consider what happened to the Thebans as a result of this, and what the outcome was for us. The facts themselves will show you how important it is for a city's interests not to be bought and sold. First, they gained peace just when the war, which they were losing, was causing them a great deal of difficulty and hardship. Second, their enemies, the Phocians, were utterly destroyed, their fortifications and cities demolished. Anything else? Yes, indeed. They also got Orchomenus, Coronea, Corsia, Tilphosaeum, and all the Phocian land they wanted. [142] What the Thebans got from the peace, then, was more than they could have dreamt of. What about the Theban envoys? What did they get? Nothing, apart from the fact that it was thanks to them that their country did so well. But what a fine and noble way, Athenians, for them to enhance their virtue and prestige! Aeschines and his cohorts, however, sold theirs for cash.

Now let's compare what Athens got from the peace with what the Athenian ambassadors got, and you'll see if they and the city did equally well. [143] You lost all your possessions and allies, and swore to Philip that you would stop anyone who ever showed an interest in trying to save them. You are obliged by this treaty to regard anyone who might want to restore them to you as an enemy, and the man who stole them from you as a friend. [144] These are the terms that Aeschines supported and his colleague Philocrates proposed. Although I prevailed on the first day, and persuaded you to ratify our allies' resolution and send for Philip's envoys, Aeschines succeeded in gaining an adjournment until the next day and then persuaded you to adopt Philocrates' proposal, which included not just the terms I've described, but many even worse conditions.*

[145] So that is what the city got from the peace, and it's hard to imagine anything more demeaning. But what about the ambassadors, who were responsible for this disgrace? There's no need for me to mention what you've seen with your own eyes—the houses, the timber, the wheat—but there are also the countless farms and endless acres in the territory of our ruined allies, which bring Philocrates an income of a talent, and Aeschines thirty mnas. [146] But this is appalling, Athenians. It's scandalous for your ambassadors to profit from your allies' disasters. What else should one call it when one and the same peace entails, for the city which commissioned the ambassadors, the destruction of its allies, the loss of its property, and humiliating dishonour, and brings those of the ambassadors who were responsible for all this an income, prosperity, farmland, and wealth, instead of abject poverty? [*To the Clerk of the Court*] But please call the witnesses from Olynthus, who will verify what I've been saying.

The witnesses' deposition is read out.

[147] [*To the jurors*] I wouldn't be surprised if Aeschines had the effrontery to claim in some form or another that it was impossible to make the kind of honourable peace I wanted, since the generals had mishandled the war. If he does include this assertion in his speech, I implore you in the name of the gods to remember to ask him whether he was acting as a representative of Athens or of some other city. If he says he was working for another city, which had competent generals and won the war, it was perfectly reasonable for him to take Philip's

money.* But if he was working for Athens, why did he, as it turns out, accept gifts for terms which have caused the city that commissioned him to lose its assets? The outcome should have been the same for both the commissioning city and its ambassadors, if the matter had been handled fairly.

[148] There's another point for you to consider, jurymen. Who do you think was doing better, the Phocians in their war against the Thebans, or Philip in his war against you? As I see it, the Phocians certainly did better against the Thebans. They held Orchomenus, Coronea, and Tilphosaeum; they pinned a Theban force inside Neones; they killed two hundred and seventy at Mount Hedylium and erected a trophy; they had cavalry supremacy; the Thebans were beset by an *Iliad* of woes.* [149] Nothing like this happened to you, and I hope it never will. The down side of your war against Philip was that you were unable to injure him as much as you'd have liked, but you never felt in any danger of being injured by him. Why on earth, then, did the peace enable the Thebans, who were doing so badly in the war, to recover their own possessions and gain those of the enemy as well, while in peacetime you have lost even what you had kept safe during the war? The answer is that the Thebans' ambassadors did not accept bribes, whereas yours did.

If you still have any doubts about this, what I have to say next will remove them. [150] Philocrates' peace was finalized, with Aeschines' support, and Philip's ambassadors received your oaths and were satisfied. So far, no irreparable harm had been done because, although the peace was demeaning and unworthy of Athens, this was offset by the marvellous benefits that were due to come our way. I recommended to you, and mentioned also to Aeschines and his cohorts, that we should send a fleet at the earliest possible opportunity to the Hellespont—that we shouldn't neglect any of our strongholds there or let Philip occupy them in the meantime. [151] I was well aware how utterly disastrous careless neglect can be during the transition from war to peace. Once a man has been persuaded that it is in his overall interest not to take military action, he's never prepared to go to war over places that were never considered anything but negligible. No, whoever gets them first keeps them. Besides, it was my view that, if we launched a fleet, the city would gain one of two advantages. Remember that the envoys would be in Macedonia to receive his oaths, as officially instructed by you. Either Philip would return what he had taken from us and keep his hands off the rest, [152] or, if he didn't, we would immediately come back here and tell you. In the latter case, once you were aware of his greed and untrustworthiness over places that were far off and relatively insignificant, you wouldn't neglect those closer and more important places—Phocis and Thermopylae, I mean. And if Philip kept his hands off them, and you weren't tricked by anyone, your overall position would be safe, and he would of his own accord be treating you fairly.

[153] These expectations of mine were not unreasonable. As long as the Phocians were safe, as they were at the time, and held Thermopylae, there was no danger Philip could have threatened you with that might have made you forgo anything that was rightfully yours. After all, he wasn't in a position to force the pass by land, nor did he have control of the sea, and so Attica was safe. You, on the other hand, could immediately respond to any act of unwarranted aggression on his part by closing his ports and blockading him once more into financial and general hardship. Under these circumstances, the peace would give you the upper hand, not him. [154] This is not a retrospective fiction, something I'm making up now. I conceived the plan at the time, foresaw what the future held for you, and mentioned it to Aeschines and his cohorts. I can prove this. The ambassadors hadn't set out, but were wasting time here in Athens. No more meetings of the Assembly were scheduled—they had all been used up*—but since the Assembly had given the Council the authority to see to this matter, I, as a member of the Council, drafted a decree to the effect that the ambassadors should leave as soon as possible, and that one of the generals, Proxenus, should find out where Philip was and convey them to him. What I'm telling you now is exactly how I worded the decree then. [*To the Clerk of the Court*] Please take the decree and read it.

Demosthenes' decree is read out.

[155] [*To the jurors*] So I managed to get the embassy under way, but their subsequent actions showed beyond the shadow of a doubt that my colleagues weren't happy about it. When we reached Oreus and met up with Proxenus, rather than carrying out their instructions and travelling by sea, they took a roundabout route. We spent twenty-three days getting to Macedonia. And on top of the time we'd spent en route, there was a further delay while we were in

Pella, waiting for Philip to arrive, making a total of about fifty days. [156] Philip spent this time of peace and armistice taking Doriscus, Thrace, the area of the fortresses, the Sacred Mountain*—the whole kit and caboodle—and putting his own administrative structures in place there. Meanwhile, I went on and on, repeating the same points over and over again. My tone at first was that of someone airing a suggestion for shared consideration; later, it was as though I were teaching a class of ignoramuses; in the end, I was no longer prepared to compromise, and I treated them as out-and-out villains who had sold themselves. [157] My most vociferous opponent, the one who argued against every point I raised and everything you had voted for, was Aeschines; as for the other ambassadors, you'll find out in due course of time whether or not they approved of what Aeschines was doing. I have nothing to say about any of them at the moment, and I'm not accusing them of anything. None of them is under any *obligation* today to prove his integrity, but he can do so of his own accord, assuming he was not involved in the wrongdoing. You all appreciate by now the shocking and dreadful nature of what happened, and that money changed hands; the facts will show which of them were involved.

[158] 'Surely this time was spent receiving the oaths from Philip's allies, or on their other duties.' Far from it. Although they were abroad for three whole months and had an official allowance of a thousand drachmas, they didn't go to a single city, either on their way to Macedonia or on their way back, to receive the oaths. The oath-swearing took place at the inn in front of the sanctuary of the Dioscuri—if anyone here has been to Pherae you know the one I mean—when Philip was already on his way here with his army. What a disgrace! What a dishonour to Athens! [159] From Philip's point of view, however, it was critically important that the matter should be managed in this way. First, since Aeschines and his cohorts had been thwarted in their attempt to include the qualification 'except for the people of Halus and the Phocians', and Philocrates had been forced by you to delete that and write simply 'for the Athenians and the allies of the Athenians', without the qualification, Philip didn't want any of his allies to commit themselves on oath to the treaty, because they'd have been able to use it as an excuse not to support his campaign against the territories of yours that are now his. [160] Second, he didn't want there to be witnesses to the promises he was making in order to secure

peace, and he didn't want it to become public knowledge that in fact Athens was not losing the war, and that it was he who wanted peace and was making all kinds of promises to Athens in order to get it. In other words, it was because it helped him to conceal these facts that he preferred the ambassadors not to travel anywhere. And Aeschines and his cohorts indulged his every whim and employed gross flattery to ingratiate themselves with him.

[161] Now, faced with all these proven facts—that they wasted time, betrayed your Thracian territories, carried out none of your instructions, did nothing to promote your interests, and, back in Athens, told a pack of lies in their reports—how can any right-minded member of the jury, who takes his oath seriously, fail to convict the defendant? [*To the Clerk of the Court*] But to verify what I've been saying, please read first the decree giving us our instructions for receiving the oaths, and then Philip's letter, and then Philocrates' draft decree and the one actually passed by the Assembly.

The decree, Philip's letter, the draft decree, and the final decree are read out.

[162] Next, to prove that we'd have caught Philip in the Hellespont, if my advice and your official instructions had been followed, call the witnesses who were there.*

The witnesses' deposition is read out.

And please read out the other deposition too, which shows how Philip responded to Euclides' subsequent mission there.*

The witnesses' deposition is read out.

[163] [*To the jurors*] There's no way for them to deny that they were working for Philip, and here's further proof. When we set out on our previous mission, to negotiate the terms of the peace, you sent a herald on ahead to arrange truces for us.* Well, on that occasion, as soon as they reached Oreus, without waiting for the herald and without wasting any time, they sailed straight for Halus, even though it was under siege. Then they left Halus and visited Parmenion, who was directing the siege; then they set out through the enemy encampment for Pagasae, from where they carried on to Larisa, where they met up with the herald. Do you see how rapidly and resolutely they proceeded on that occasion? [164] But when it was peacetime and

perfectly safe to travel, and you had instructed them to hurry, it never crossed their minds that they should find a fast route or take ship. Why not? Because whereas earlier it had been in Philip's interest that the peace be concluded as rapidly as possible, now his interest was best served if they wasted as much time as possible before receiving the oaths. [165] [*To the Clerk of the Court*] But to verify this assertion of mine as well, please take and read this deposition.

The deposition is read out.

[*To the jurors*] How could people more clearly show that they were acting throughout in Philip's interests, than by the fact that on the same journey they stayed put when haste would have served you best, and hurried when they shouldn't even have moved before the herald arrived?

[166] The next consideration is how he and I chose to spend our time of idleness there in Pella. I tried to rescue the prisoners of war. I made enquiries, spent some of my own money, and asked Philip to use the accommodation allowance he was offering us for freeing them. I'll tell you in a moment how Aeschines passed the time, but, first, what was Philip doing offering us money as a group? [167] Let there be no doubt in your minds on this score either: Philip was sounding all of us out. How? He approached each of us separately and offered us money—a great deal of money, Athenians. But since someone refused his offer—I don't need to mention what happened in *my* case when the facts and events themselves will make it clear—he began to wonder whether we might all innocently accept a collective gift. He thought that, if we all took a slice, however small, of the collective pie, this would protect those who had already accepted the individual bribe. Hence the offer, under the guise of an accommodation allowance. [168] But when I thwarted that scheme, Aeschines and his cohorts divided the money up among themselves instead. When I asked Philip to put this money towards ransoming the prisoners, he could hardly denounce my fellow ambassadors and say, 'Oh, but it's already gone to so-and-so and so-and-so,' and at the same time he could hardly refuse to spend the money as I was asking either. So he agreed to my request, but deferred the matter by saying that he would send the prisoners back in time for the Panathenaea. [*To the Clerk of the Court*] Please read Apollophanes' deposition, and then those of the others who were there.

Apollophanes' deposition is read out.

[169] [*To the jurors*] Let me tell you also how I came to ransom some of the prisoners myself. While we were in Pella, waiting for Philip to arrive, some of the prisoners who were out on their own recognizances said that they would prefer to be personally responsible for their own ransoms, without being under obligation to Philip for this. In actual fact, I think, they doubted that I would succeed in persuading Philip to release them at his own expense. So they borrowed from me three or five mnas, or whatever the ransom was in any given case. [170] When Philip agreed to free the rest of the prisoners, then, I met with those who had borrowed from me and apprised them of the situation. I didn't want them to think that their impatience had left them in a worse position, and I didn't want people who weren't well off to have ransomed themselves out of their own resources while the rest were expecting to be released by Philip. So I gave them their ransom money as a gift. [*To the Clerk of the Court*] Please read out their testimony, which will verify what I've been saying.

The deposition is read out.

[171] [*To the jurors*] That's how much money I spent, then, or rather gave to my fellow citizens in their hour of need. Now, when it's his turn to speak, Aeschines will ask me this: 'Demosthenes, can you explain why, even though you claim to have realized from my support of Philocrates that we were up to no good, you still accepted the appointment as a member of the next embassy, the one for the oaths? Why didn't you take the oath of exemption?' When he says this, please remember that I had promised the prisoners I freed that I would bring their ransom money and do all I could to look after their interests. [172] In all decency, then, I couldn't go back on my word to men in their hour of need; I couldn't let down my fellow citizens. And if I took the oath of exemption it would have been improper, as well as dangerous, for me to have made my way there on my own. But if I hadn't wanted to rescue the prisoners, not even the prospect of substantial profit would have tempted me to join that lot on the mission. May I perish completely and utterly if this is not the whole truth! And I can prove it. For the third embassy, I took the oath of exemption twice, each time you appointed me to

it; and throughout this second mission I did all I could to thwart their designs.

[173] So that was how those aspects of the ambassadorial mission went for which *I* had sole responsibility, but wherever their numerical superiority gave them the upper hand the outcome was complete failure. But if my advice had been taken, all the rest of our business would also have gone just as well. I mean, how stupid or deranged would I have to be to take a loss for the good of the city, while watching others profit, and yet not try to see to fruition matters that would do the city far more good and wouldn't cost a thing! That would be extreme stupidity, Athenians! But I'm afraid that Aeschines and his cohorts were too much for me.

[174] What I'd like you to do now is have a look, against this background, at what Aeschines and Philocrates got up to. The contrast between my actions and theirs will be instructive. First, they transgressed your express instructions and contradicted their own promises to you by excluding from the treaty the Phocians, Halians, and Cersobleptes.* Second, they tried to make radical changes to the terms of our mission as decreed by you. Third, they added Cardia* to the list of Philip's allies and voted to send to you a completely distorted version of what had happened, of their own composition, rather than the letter I had written. [175] I was shocked by what they were doing, and I was also worried that I would be caught up in their ruin, so I resisted them—and then this fine fellow here accused me of having promised Philip that I would overthrow your democratic constitution! In actual fact, it was he who was constantly and continuously having private meetings with Philip. I won't mention any other instances, but one night in Pherae, when Dercylus was keeping an eye on him with the help of this slave here of mine, he caught him coming out of Philip's tent. I wasn't there, but he told the slave to tell me about it and to remember it himself. And then in the end this perfidious crook here, Aeschines, stayed with Philip for a night and a day after we had left. [176] To verify what I've been saying, I shall draw first on my own written testimony, for which I have made myself duly accountable.* Then I shall call on all the rest of the envoys one by one, and they will have only two options: either to testify to the truth of my deposition or to affirm on oath that they have no knowledge of the matter.* And if they take the oath, I shall provide you with clear proof that they are perjuring themselves.

Demosthenes' and the ambassadors' depositions are read out.

[177] Now you see how challenging and difficult things were for me throughout the mission! Seeing that they behave like this in front of you, the very people who have the power to reward or punish them, you can imagine what they got up to there, with their paymaster at hand.

Anyway, I'd like to recapitulate the charges, to show that I've done everything I promised I'd do at the beginning of my speech.* I've shown, not by argument but by reference to the facts, that Aeschines' report was a pack of lies designed to mislead you. [178] I've shown that your refusal to listen to the truth from me was his fault, because at the time he captivated you with his promises and assurances for the future; that he consistently recommended inappropriate policies by arguing against the peace as proposed by our allies and by supporting the terms proposed by Philocrates; that he wasted time in order to make it impossible for you to mount an expedition to Phocis even if you wanted to; and that while abroad he behaved in a thoroughly unscrupulous fashion, was treacherous throughout, sold his services, took bribes, and missed no opportunity to make trouble. That is what I originally promised I would show, and I have shown it.

[179] What now? The next point I want to make is perfectly straightforward. You are under oath to cast your votes in accordance with the laws and the decrees of the Assembly and the Council of Five Hundred, and now it turns out that, while acting as ambassador, Aeschines consistently broke the law, contravened decrees, and violated justice. It follows that any right-minded member of the jury is duty bound to convict him. Even if he had committed no further crimes, two of the things he did are enough to earn him the death penalty. I mean his betrayal to Philip of the Phocians and of Thrace. [180] But no one could point to any two places in the world that are more important to us than Phocis and Thrace; as Thermopylae is on land, so the Hellespont is at sea. Aeschines and his cohorts did an unforgivable thing when they sold both these places into Philip's sway, to the detriment of Athens. If the abandonment of Thrace and its fortresses were the sum total of his crimes, that total would still be enormous, and it would be very easy to show how often you have put men to death or fined them heavily for this. I'm thinking of Ergophilus, Cephisodotus, and Timomachus; earlier there were

Ergocles, Dionysius, and others. But it's hardly an exaggeration to say that all of them together harmed the city less than Aeschines.*

[181] But in those days, you see, Athenians, you still used to look ahead and take rational precautions against threats. Nowadays, however, you ignore anything that doesn't cause you immediate bother and daily distress, and then you make futile resolutions here in Athens: 'Philip is to give his solemn promise to Cersobleptes'; 'Philip is not to become a member of the Amphictyonic Council'; 'Philip is to improve the terms of the peace treaty.' But none of these resolutions would have been necessary if Aeschines had been prepared to take ship and do his job. Instead, by insisting on travelling by land, he has destroyed what could have been saved by taking ship, and by telling lies he has destroyed what could have been saved by the truth.

[182] I've heard that, when it's his turn to speak, he will forcefully complain at being the only person ever to find himself liable to an audit for speeches delivered in the Assembly. Leaving aside the fact that, of course, anyone who has been bribed to make a speech would be held accountable for his words, this is what I'd recommend. If Aeschines was not acting in an official capacity and just threw out some random and ill-considered words, don't be too particular about it. Let him go. Pardon him. But if, while acting as your ambassador, he took money and deliberately deceived you, dismiss the idea that he should not be accountable for what he said, and do not let him off. [183] I mean, what else should ambassadors be held accountable for if not their words? Ambassadors are not responsible for triremes or territory or troops or citadels. No one entrusts these things to ambassadors. No, words and opportunities are their province. Aeschines, then, is innocent if he did not deny the city opportunities for action, but guilty if he did. And he should be acquitted if his reports were truthful and served your interests, but if they were dishonest, if they had been paid for, and if they harmed your interests, he should be found guilty. [184] There's no greater wrong that anyone could do you than tell you lies. When a political system depends on words, how is it to survive unless the words are true? When a man speaks in support of policies that favour the enemy because he has been bribed to do so, how can he fail to put your regime at risk?

Moreover, squandering opportunities is nowhere near as serious a crime in an oligarchy or a tyranny as it is in a democracy. Far from it. [185] In those systems of government, of course, everything happens promptly at the word of command. But in your case, first the Council has to be fully informed and issue a draft resolution (and it can't do this whenever it likes, but only when a meeting is scheduled for heralds and embassies),* and then you have to convene an Assembly (but only on one of the days stipulated by law). And then the proposers of the best policies have to overcome and make their case against those who are opposing them out of ignorance or iniquity. [186] As if that weren't enough, once a policy has been agreed to be advantageous and a decision has been reached, time has to be granted, given widespread lack of resources, for people to come up with whatever they need to execute the chosen policy. So if a man deliberately fails to take advantage of these windows of opportunity in your kind of political system, he hasn't just wasted time; no, he has made you completely powerless.

[187] There's an expression that comes easily to the lips of anyone trying to dupe you: 'Political trouble-makers who stop Philip benefiting the city.' I'm not going to respond to the people who wield this slogan, except to read Philip's letters to you and remind you of all the occasions on which you were deceived. This will prove that, when it comes to misinformation, Philip has 'gone well over the top', as the overused cliché has it.

Philip's letters are read out.

[188] After having done nothing as ambassador but work against your interests in so many despicable ways, Aeschines now goes around asking 'What *can* one say about Demosthenes, prosecuting his fellow ambassadors?' By Zeus, yes, I am prosecuting a colleague. It's not as if I have any choice in the matter. [*To Aeschines*] Your constant intrigues against me, throughout the mission, have left me with only two options: either I seem to be your accomplice or I denounce you. [189] But I wouldn't even describe myself as your colleague, since you used the mission to wreak havoc, while I worked in the best interests of the city. Philocrates was your colleague, and so was Phrynon, in the sense that the three of you saw eye to eye and had the same objectives.

'Where does that leave the salt, the shared table, the libations?'* [*To the jurors*] This is his constant refrain, as if it were those who do right who betray these things, not those who do wrong. [190] The members of the Executive Committee all sacrifice together, dine together, and pour libations together, but I'm sure the good ones don't make this a reason for acting like the bad ones. No, if they find one of their colleagues doing wrong, they inform the Council and the Assembly. The same goes for the Council: after the inaugural sacrifice, the feast is shared. The generals perform their libations and rituals together, and so do almost all government officials. Do they use this as a reason for granting any miscreant colleagues immunity? Not a bit of it! [191] Leon chased his ambassadorial colleague Timagoras through the courts for four years; Eubulus prosecuted Tharrhex and Smicythus, though they had shared a table; in days gone by, the great Conon prosecuted his fellow general Adeimantus.* [*To Aeschines*] So who betrays the salt and the libations, Aeschines? Is it the traitors, the false envoys, the bribe-takers? Or is it their accusers? It's those who do wrong, obviously, and, like you, they betray not only their particular libations but those of the entire state.

[192] [*To the jurors*] I'd like to tell you a little story. It has nothing to do with the embassy, but it will demonstrate that, of all the people who have ever visited Philip, on public business or for their own private purposes, there have never been worse or more reprehensible villains than Aeschines and his cohorts. After his capture of Olynthus, Philip was organizing the festival of Olympian Zeus, and he issued a general invitation for actors to come and attend the festivities and celebrations. [193] While he was entertaining them and presenting crowns to the victors, he asked Satyrus, the comic actor—[*pointing*] there he is now—why he was the only one who hadn't asked for a favour. Had he detected a mean streak in Philip, or some antipathy towards him? Satyrus is said to have replied that, although he didn't want what other people wanted, there was a request he'd like to make—a favour Philip would find no difficulty at all in granting, but which he still doubted he would get. [194] Philip told him to speak up and even claimed, rather rashly, that there was nothing he wouldn't do for him. So Satyrus told him that he had been the friend and intimate of Apollophanes of Pydna. After Apollophanes' assassination, his terrified relatives arranged for his daughters, who were children at the time, to be taken to safety in Olynthus. 'Well,' he went on, 'these girls, who are now of marriageable age, were taken prisoner after the fall of Olynthus and are in your hands. [195] These girls are what I'd really like to give me. But listen, please: I want you to understand what kind of a gift you'll be giving me—assuming you grant my request, that is. Possession of it won't enrich me one bit, I shall

attach a dowry to it and give it away—and I won't let anything happen to them that would disgrace either me or their father.' At this, the assembled guests at the symposium all clapped and shouted and cheered so much that Philip was moved and granted the request—despite the fact that this Apollophanes had been one of the killers of Philip's brother Alexander.*

[196] By way of contrast with this symposium of Satyrus', let's look at the one that took place in Macedonia and was attended by Aeschines and his cohorts. Let's see if there's any similarity or resemblance. They were invited to the house of Xenophron, the son of Phaedimus (once one of the Thirty),* and they accepted. I didn't go. Just as the drinking was about to start, Xenophron introduced an Olynthian woman; she was good-looking, but, as events showed, free-born and respectable.* [197] At first, apparently, according to what Iatrocles* told me the next day, they merely forced her to sit quietly and have some food and drink. Later, however, things began to get heated, and they asked her to recline on a couch and sing something as well. This caused the lady a great deal of distress, since she neither wanted nor knew how to sing. At this point, Aeschines and Phrynon called her insolent and said that it was intolerable for a damned, infernal Olynthian slave like her to put on airs. 'Call a slave,' they said, and 'Have him bring a whip'. A slave arrived with a strap, and since the men were drunk, I suppose, and therefore easily provoked, when she said something and burst into tears, the slave ripped open her clothes and thrashed her repeatedly on the back. [198] Out of her mind with outrage at what was going on, the woman jumped up and fell at the feet of Iatrocles, upsetting the table in the process. If he hadn't taken her out of there, she'd have been killed in a drunken frenzy; this scum is a bad drunk. The woman's story came up even in Arcadia, at a meeting of the Ten Thousand. You heard it from Diophantus, whom I shall compel to testify in a moment; and the tale was repeated in Thessaly and everywhere.

[199] This obscene brute knows full well what he's done—and yet he still has the gall to look you in the eyes and tell you about the life he's lived. That's what he's going to do very soon, with that brilliant voice of his. It makes me sick. [*To Aeschines*] Do you think these jurors don't know that you started life as a reader in your mother's cult, and hung out as a child with inebriated revellers?* [200] That you worked next as an under-secretary in government offices and would bend the

rules for two or three drachmas? And that you ended up just recently being happily fed in others' rehearsal rooms as a third-string actor? When everyone knows what kind of life you've lived, what sort of fantasy life are you going to describe? The high life, I suppose! [*To the jurors*] This is the man who took someone else to court for prostitution! I'll come back to that, but for the time being [*to the Clerk of the Court*] please read these depositions.

The depositions are read out.

[201] [*To the jurors*] Look at the long list of terrible crimes he's known to have committed against you, Athenians, crimes riddled with every kind of iniquity. Bribe-taker, lickspittle, accursed for his lies, betrayer of his friends—the list includes all the most appalling crimes imaginable! He will have no defence against a single one of them—or at least no honest and straightforward defence. What he's planning to say instead, according to my information, is almost insane—but then I suppose he has no choice: lacking an honest defence, he'll try anything. [202] According to my information, you see, he's going to say that I was a party to all the crimes I'm accusing him of! That I approved of and colluded in all his schemes, but then suddenly had a change of heart and so here I am prosecuting him! But this is a lie, as well as irrelevant as a defence of his actions. It's no more than a way of casting aspersions at me. I mean, if I've acted as he says, I'm a bad man—but that makes not the slightest bit of difference to the iniquity of his actions.

[203] All the same, I feel I should address both issues and show you, first, that he'll be lying if he says this, and, second, what an honest defence is like. An honest, straightforward defence would establish either that the crimes of which he is accused never took place, or that what happened was good for the city. But neither of these options is open to him. [204] First, he can hardly claim that the city is better off with the Phocians destroyed, Thermopylae in Philip's hands, Thebes resurgent, Euboea garrisoned, Megara plagued by intrigue, and the peace unsecured by oaths.* This line of defence is ruled out by his report to you at the time, when he promised that exactly the opposite would happen and would be good for Athens. Second, he will find it impossible to convince you that these things never happened, since you've seen them yourselves and are well aware of the truth. [205] It only remains for me to show, then, that I was not their accomplice

in any of this. So why don't I omit all the rest of the evidence—my objections in the Assembly, my resistance while we were abroad, my constant opposition—and have Aeschines and his cohorts themselves testify that we never saw eye to eye, and that I refused the bribes they took while working for you?

Look at it this way. [206] If you had to name the most immoral, unscrupulous, and haughty person in Athens, who would it be? I'm sure that none of you would even accidentally name anyone but Philocrates. And who has the loudest voice and gets his points across most clearly? 'Aeschines' would of course be your reply. And who is it who, when faced with crowds, displays what they call timidity and cowardice, and I call caution? Me. I've never aroused your impatience or pushed you against your will. [207] Well now, what happens whenever these men are the topic of discussion in the Assembly? As you know, I take every opportunity to denounce them and expose them for what they are—that is, I bluntly accuse them of taking bribes and of betraying the city for cash. But none of them ever responds and argues against me. They don't even open their mouths or ask permission to speak. [208] Why is it, then, that the most immoral men in the city, with the loudest voices, are so thoroughly cowed by me, the most timid and soft-spoken? It's because truth is strong and consciousness of corruption is weak. It robs them of their boldness, binds their tongues, stops their mouths, chokes them, reduces them to silence.

[209] The most recent incident took place not long ago in Piraeus.* I'm sure you remember. You were refusing to appoint him ambassador, and he was yelling that he would prosecute me in this court and that court, and crying 'Ooh-la-la!' Many protracted trials and lengthy speeches might have resulted from this, when all that was needed were a few simple words which even a slave bought yesterday could cope with: 'Athenians, this is completely inexcusable. This man here is accusing me of crimes in which he was complicit. He says that I took bribes when it was he who was bribed, or at least was one of those who were bribed.' [210] Well, he said nothing of the kind, not a word of it, within your hearing. All he did was issue threats. Why? Because he knew what he had done and cowered before those few words. His mind couldn't draw near them, but shrank back. His conscience stopped his mind, until abuse and slander were all he could manage.

[211] But the strongest evidence comes from the realm of actions rather than words. Since I had served on two separate missions, it was only right and proper that I should submit to a second audit, and that's what I was trying to do, when up came Aeschines with a horde of witnesses and tried to tell the auditors that there was no need for me to appear before them, since I had already submitted to an audit and was now exempt.* How absurd! What was he up to? He had already been audited for the first embassy, and had got away without being accused of anything, so he didn't want to find himself in court again for this second embassy (the one for which he is on trial now), because it was then that he committed all his crimes. [212] But my second audit was going to force him to return to court as well, and that's why he tried to stop me appearing.

Two points emerge clearly from this action of his, Athenians. First, it's as good as a confession, and this means that to acquit him would be to contravene your oath. Second, whatever he says about me is going to be false. Otherwise he'd have spoken up and denounced me then, by Zeus, instead of trying to stop me appearing. [213] [*To the Clerk of the Court*] But please call the witnesses, who can verify what I've been saying.

[*To the jurors*] Now, if Aeschines' slanderous allegations against me include anything from outside the embassy, you have plenty of good reasons for refusing to pay attention. I'm not the defendant in today's trial and I shan't be assigned any more time afterwards.* So this tactic could only mean that he doesn't have any legitimate arguments. After all, what defendant in a trial would choose to cast aspersions if he had a proper defence to offer? [214] And you should bear this in mind too, jurymen. Imagine a trial with me as the defendant, Aeschines as the prosecutor, and Philip as the judge. If I had no proper defence to make against the charges, and merely slandered Aeschines and tried to blacken his name, don't you think Philip would protest at just that, at having his supporters slandered in front of him? So don't cede the moral high ground to Philip, but force Aeschines to stick in his defence to the actual charges. [*To the Clerk of the Court*] But please read the testimony.

The witnesses' deposition is read out.

[215] [*To the jurors*] My conscience was clear, and I thought it my duty to submit to an audit and to comply in all respects with my legal

obligations. He did the opposite, however, which makes nonsense of the suggestion that he and I were partners in crime. Besides, is he even allowed to bring up fresh accusations that he's never mentioned before? Of course not. But he'll do so all the same. Not that this is at all unexpected. After all, as you know, in the whole history of the human race, no criminal in court has ever admitted his guilt. They always bluster, protest their innocence, lie, make excuses, and do whatever it takes to avoid punishment. [216] Today, don't let any such ploys distract you. Judge the case on the basis of the facts. Pay no attention to what either of us says, and please ignore his witnesses, who will have been coached by him, at Philip's expense (and you'll see how ready they'll be to testify), to play whatever part he has assigned them. Pay no attention even to the magnificence and clarity of his voice, or to the feebleness of mine. [217] It would be wrong of you to think that your job here today is to judge a speaking or speech-making competition. No, the issue today is the shameful and scandalous ruination of your affairs, and you need to consider the actual facts, which are known to all of you, and then deflect the disgrace on to those who are responsible.

But what are the facts? Not that you need to hear them from me and Aeschines; you already know them. [218] If he and his cohorts told you exactly what would happen as a result of the peace; if you admit to being so thoroughly defeatist and cowardly that you were happy to make peace when you were under no immediate threat—your territory hadn't been invaded, for instance, nor were you subject to a naval blockade—and in fact grain prices were good and your general situation was no worse than it is now; [219] if before you entered into the peace, you already knew and had been forewarned by them of everything that was going to happen, such as the destruction of your allies, the resurgence of Thebes, Philip's seizure of the Thraceward region, and the fortification of Euboea against you; then you should acquit Aeschines and avoid compounding your terrible disgrace by breaking your oath too. For in that case he has done you no wrong, and I must be deranged and deluded to be prosecuting him now. [220] However, if what they said was quite different, and filled with nice promises; if what they said was that, out of goodwill towards Athens, Philip would protect the Phocians and humble the Thebans, *and*, if he got the peace he wanted, would more than compensate you for Amphipolis, *and* would return Euboea and Oropus; if all these words and promises were just a pack of lies designed to dupe you and almost make you lose Attica, condemn him. Otherwise, you will compound the insult—I don't know what else to call it—of their corruption, by carrying the taint of curse and perjury back home with you.

[221] I'd also like you to consider, jurymen, whether I could conceivably have had any personal reason for prosecuting Aeschines if he and his cohorts were innocent of any crime. You won't find any such reason. Is it pleasant to make so many enemies? No, nor safe either. Was there a history of enmity between us? No. Well, what about this?—an idea of his, I gather: 'You had a coward's reason: you thought you were in danger and that this was the way to save your skin.' [*To Aeschines*] But, Aeschines, if no offence or crime had been committed, as you claim, what did I have to be afraid of? [*To the jurors*] If he brings up this idea of his, jurymen, please consider: if I was supposed to have been afraid of being ruined along with them, despite being completely innocent, what does that imply about their guilt, and the punishment they deserve? [222] So, no, that's not the reason either.

[*To Aeschines*] Why am I prosecuting you, then? By Zeus, I must be a sycophant, hoping you would buy me off! [*To the jurors*] But which course of action would profit me more? To accept the generous amount of money Philip was offering, which was no less than what they got, and earn both his and their friendship? For they would certainly have been my friends if I'd joined them; their current hostility towards me isn't a relic of the past, but is due to my refusal to cooperate. Or to demand from them a fraction of what they got and incur Philip's and their enmity? In which case, I'd have spent my own money on ransoming the prisoners, and ruined my good name, and become an object of loathing, all for the sake of the trivial amounts of money I could expect from them.

[223] No, what actually happened was that, in the interests of justice and truth, and because I had the rest of my life to think of, I told you the facts and refused the money. I thought that I too would earn the respect you usually give men of integrity, and that my devotion to you should not be for sale at any price. I hate these men for their pernicious and godless conduct as ambassadors, and their corruption has also robbed me of my special privileges* by making you unhappy with the entire embassy. My prosecution of this case and involvement in this audit are precautionary measures: I want to use the trial and

a court appearance to make it perfectly clear to you that my behaviour was not even remotely similar to theirs. [224] There's also the fact that I'm afraid. Yes, afraid. I shall be completely frank with you. I'm afraid that, when the time comes, you will pull me down with them, a perfectly innocent man, and that at the moment you have given up hope. For to me you seem completely passive, Athenians, as though you were just waiting for disaster to strike. You see terrible things happening to others, but you take no precautions for yourselves, and you appear not to care about the widespread corruption that has long afflicted the city.

[225] It's horrible—even surreal, don't you think? (Even things I'd planned not to mention are being dragged out of me.) You know Pythocles, of course, the son of Pythodorus—[*pointing*] there he is now. He and I had always been on perfectly civil terms, and to this day no unpleasantness has occurred between us. But now, ever since he paid Philip a visit, he turns aside when he sees me, and if for some reason he can't avoid an encounter, he takes his leave immediately, in case anyone spots him in conversation with me. But he hangs out with Aeschines in the Agora, discussing policy. [226] But this is all wrong, isn't it, Athenians? Isn't it perverse when those who have chosen to take care of Philip's business are so accurately observed by him that it was as though he were physically present? Each of them feels Philip's eyes on him here in Athens whatever he's doing, and behaves in a friendly or hostile fashion towards others as Philip wishes, while those who devote their lives to you, who long to rise high in your estimation, and who have stayed true to you, find you so deaf and blind that here I am today competing on equal terms with these accursed men in your court, despite the fact that you know the truth.

[227] Would you like to hear how this situation arose? I'll tell you—while asking you to pardon my candour. It's because Philip is, of course, a single entity, body and mind. This means that he *wholeheartedly* likes those who do him good and dislikes those who harm him. In your case, however, the main problem is that, if someone does the city good as a whole, you don't consider that he has done you good personally, and vice versa when someone harms the city. [228] Each of you finds other feelings more compelling, feelings that often lead you astray: pity, spite, anger, granting favours, and thousands of others. And so a man might avoid every other danger, but still not

escape those who'd like to silence him. And every time this happens, it undermines the city a little more, until it becomes a cause of comprehensive harm.

[229] I urge you, Athenians, not to succumb to these feelings today. Be sure to convict this man for the terrible wrong he has done the city. If you acquit him, what story will people rightly tell about you? 'Some men set out from Athens on an ambassadorial mission to Philip—Philocrates, Aeschines, Phrynon, Demosthenes.'

'And what happened?'

'One of them not only made no profit from the mission, but even spent his own money on ransoming the prisoners, while another was bribed to betray the city, and went around spending the money on whores and fish. [230] One of them, the repulsive Phrynon, sent his son to Philip when the boy was still too young to be registered as an adult,* while another did nothing that would disgrace either Athens or himself. One of them, despite having previously funded a dramatic production and paid for the maintenance of a warship,* still felt obliged to spend more, although he wasn't officially required to do so, because he didn't want to leave any of his worse-off fellow citizens in distress; while another, so far from saving any of the already existing prisoners, helped to ensure that an entire region fell to Philip, and that more than ten thousand hoplites and a thousand cavalrymen in all, allies of Athens, became Philip's prisoners.'

[231] 'Then what happened?'

'The Athenians had long been aware of the facts, and they detained the corrupt ones . . .'

'Yes, and then?'

'Well, they acquitted the bribe-takers who had brought disgrace down on themselves, their city, and future generations of citizens, in the belief that they were men of principle and that the city was being steered aright.'†

'And what about the prosecutor?'

'They regarded him as a crackpot with no understanding of the city's needs and a spendthrift with no better use for his money.'

[232] If you set such a precedent, Athenians, why would anyone bother to be honest? Why would any member of an ambassadorial mission refuse a bribe if, in addition to gaining nothing, he's going to be treated by you as if he were no more trustworthy than those of his colleagues who accepted them? Today, you're not only trying this

case. No, you're also laying down a law that will last for ever about whether any ambassador should disgrace himself by taking money and working for the enemy, or whether he should remain uncorrupted and unbribed, and do his best for you. [233] There's no need for depositions to corroborate any of the other points, [*to the Clerk of the Court*] but please call the witnesses to testify that Phrynon did send his son to Philip.

The witnesses' deposition is read out.

[*To the jurors*] So Phrynon sent his son to Philip for disgraceful purposes, but did Aeschines take him to court for this? No, Aeschines picked on a man who, through the accident of having been exceptionally good-looking in his youth, was led to live a rather reckless life, not suspecting for a moment that his appearance would get him into trouble. This was the man Aeschines took to court for prostitution.*

[234] But I almost forgot one of the most important points I wanted to mention, the matter of the entertainment and the decree. When I drew up the draft resolution for the first embassy, and again when I raised the matter in the Assemblies where the peace was the main item of business, nothing Aeschines and his cohorts had said or done had yet given the slightest indication of their wrongdoing. And so, in keeping with custom, I thanked them and issued them with the standard invitation to the Prytaneum. [235] And that's not all, by Zeus! I also entertained Philip's ambassadors, and did so in a particularly splendid fashion, Athenians. I could see that they were preening themselves on how sumptuous and splendid such affairs were in Macedonia, and my immediate reaction was to think that it would be a good start to get the better of them in this and put on a greater display of generosity.

This is what Aeschines will presently be referring to when he says, 'He personally thanked us; he personally entertained the ambassadors!' But he'll avoid saying precisely *when* I did these things. [236] It was before they had injured the city with their crimes, before their corruption was out in the open. The ambassadors had just returned from their first mission, the Assembly had yet to hear their reports, and no one knew either that Aeschines was going to speak in support of Philocrates, or what terms Philocrates was going to propose. So if Aeschines does bring up this business, please remember that it took place before their criminal activities. Afterwards, we became estranged and stopped working together. [*To the Clerk of the Court*] Please read the deposition.

The deposition is read out.

[237] [*To the jurors*] Now, perhaps Philochares and Aphobetus will testify on behalf of their brother. But there's plenty that you can fairly say back to them, and it must be said candidly, with no holds barred. [*To Philochares and Aphobetus*] Philochares, you are a painter of perfume-jar boxes and tambourines, while your brothers are just ordinary clerks. There's nothing wrong with this, but it doesn't have the dignity of generalship. Nevertheless, we have dignified you with ambassadorial missions and generalships, the highest offices in the city. [238] Now, it may be that none of you did any wrong, but that doesn't put us in your debt; you should really be in our debt, because we raised you up over many men who deserved high office more than you. So if one of you, while actually in office, committed a crime of this magnitude, wouldn't condemnation be more appropriate than acquittal? Much more, I'd say.

[*To the jurors*] But they may try to carry the day with their loud voices and lack of scruples, and with the help of the proverbial 'It's never a sin to help your kin.' [239] But don't let them get the better of you. Bear in mind that while it may be their job to protect their brother, it's yours to protect the laws, the entire citizen body, and above all the oaths you swore before taking your places as jurors. If they have begged any of you to acquit him, ask yourselves whether they mean that he should be acquitted if he's found guilty of crimes against the city, or if he's innocent. If they mean that he should be acquitted if innocent, I agree; but to ask for his acquittal generally and unconditionally is to ask you to perjure yourselves. Your voting may be secret, but it doesn't escape the notice of the gods. The legislator was perfectly well aware that, although none of these men will know which of you did them this favour, the gods will know, and heaven will know, who has cast a wrongful vote. [240] And so it makes more sense for each of you to gain from the gods the prospect of a good future for himself and his children by delivering the right and proper verdict, than it does for you to do these men a favour they won't even know or be aware of by acquitting a man whose own testimony declares his guilt.

[*To Aeschines*] Look, Aeschines, how could I come up with better evidence for the extent of your misconduct as ambassador than your own testimony against yourself? The fact that you felt obliged to ruin the life of a man who wanted to make just a fraction of your conduct as ambassador public knowledge proves that you expected a disastrous outcome for yourself if the jury learnt what you had done. [241] [*To the jurors*] If you look at it in the right way, you'll see that this act of his tells against him. First, it constitutes powerful evidence about his conduct as ambassador; second, the arguments he used as a prosecutor are just as relevant now against him. [*To Aeschines*] After all, surely it's only fair for others to insist on using against you exactly the same arguments that you felt justified in using when you prosecuted Timarchus.

[242] [*To the jurors*] Well, what did the jurors hear from him on that occasion? 'Demosthenes is going to defend Timarchus and denounce my conduct as ambassador. And then, if his sophistries succeed, he'll get big-headed and go around saying: "See how I distracted the jurors' attention from the matter at hand! See how I stole the case from them, and got away with it!" '* [*To Aeschines*] So *you'd* better not do any distracting; just restrict your defence to the charges against you. You've already had your chance to play the prosecutor and say whatever you liked when you took Timarchus to court.

[243] Lacking the ability to produce evidence to prove your case against the man, you even quoted epic verse to the jurors:

> No rumour, heard on many lips, altogether
> Perishes. She too is somehow a goddess.*

Well, Aeschines, here we have jurors who all agree that you profited from the embassy, so I suppose that in your case too 'no rumour, heard on many lips, altogether perishes'! [244] Then again, let's see how many more people recognize your guilt than his. Even some of Timarchus' neighbours didn't know about him, but the whole world agrees that you ambassadors profited from your mission. If rumour is true, then, the rumour on the lips of the people tells against you. And it was you who affirmed that the poet knew what he was talking about—that rumour is to be trusted and 'is somehow a goddess'.

[245] [*To the jurors*] He had a sheaf of iambic verses as well, which he also recited. For example:

> I never ask a man why he enjoys the company
> Of evil-doers. I recognize him for what he is:
> The same as those whose company he enjoys.*

His characterization of Timarchus included calling him 'a man who goes to cock-fights and hangs out with Pittalacus', and he concluded: 'You know what to think of such a person, don't you?' [*To Aeschines*] Well, Aeschines, those lines of verse you quoted will suit my purposes too, for use against you. I won't be making a mistake or distorting the facts if I tell the jurors: 'I never ask a man why, particularly when serving as ambassador, he enjoys the company of Philocrates. I recognize him for a bribe-taker, just as Philocrates is, by his own admission.'

[246] [*To the jurors*] One of the ways he tries to insult people is by calling them speech-writers and sophists,* but it's easy to prove that the terms fit him perfectly. Those verses he quoted come from Euripides' *Phoenix*, but neither Theodorus nor Aristodemus ever acted in that play, and they were the ones who invariably used Aeschines as their third-string actor. *Phoenix* used to be staged years ago, with someone like Molon as the star. But both Theodorus and Aristodemus often acted in Sophocles' *Antigone*, a play that contains some excellent lines that you'll enjoy hearing—lines which are perfectly familiar to Aeschines, since he often recited them on stage, but which he failed to mention. [247] You know, of course, that whenever a tragedy is performed it's the special privilege, so to speak, of the third-string actor to play tyrants and rulers. So let's consider some lines the poet wrote for Creon–Aeschines, which Aeschines forgot to apply to himself in the context of the embassy, and failed to include among the lines he recited to the jury. [*To the Clerk of the Court*] Go ahead, read the passage.*

Lines from Sophocles' Antigone *are read out:*

> No man can be fully known, soul and heart and mind,
> Until exposed by the test of rule and government.
> A man may guide the fortune of an entire city,
> But if he cleaves not to the best counsels,
> And if fear stops his tongue, he is the worst of men.
> That is my view now, just as it always has been.
> And a man who values a friend more than the land
> That gave him birth, him I discount utterly.
> As all-seeing Zeus is my witness, I shall not be silent

If I see ruin drawing near my subjects instead of safety,
Nor shall I ever call our country's enemy my friend.
For this I know: our country bears us safe,
And friends aren't hard to find if she sails on even keel.

[248] [*To the jurors*] Aeschines applied none of these lines to himself during the embassy. Bidding farewell to the wisdom of Sophocles, he discounted the city in favour of friendship and intimacy with Philip, which he found far more valuable and personally profitable. And when he 'saw ruin drawing near', in the form of the campaign against Phocis, he failed to sound the alarm or give a warning. On the contrary, he concealed the facts, colluded with the enemy, and stopped those who wanted to say something from doing so. [249] He forgot that 'our country bears us safe'. He forgot that it was on board this ship that his mother practised her rites and purifications, sheared her clients of their property, and raised Aeschines and his brothers to be such fine, upstanding men. He forgot that it was on board this ship of state that his father, the primary-school teacher (whose school, I'm assured by those old enough to remember, was by the shrine of the Hero Physician),* made a living, such as it was. He forgot that he and his brother were paid by the state to work as under-secretaries in government offices and were maintained at public expense for two years in the Round House once they had finally been promoted by you to the rank of secretary. He forgot that he was acting as a representative of this state when he was sent abroad as ambassador. [250] He paid none of this any mind, and so far from trying to ensure that the ship sailed 'on even keel', he caused it to capsize and founder, and did his best to have it fall into enemy hands. [*To Aeschines*] So does this not make you the 'sophist'? Yes, and a pernicious one too. Doesn't this make you the 'speech-writer'? Yes, and a damnable one too. You knew these lines by heart, having often performed them on stage, but you ignored them and instead tracked down lines from a part you've never played in your life and gave them a public hearing to help you injure one of your fellow citizens.

[251] [*To the jurors*] Now, what was it that Aeschines said about Solon? He said that the statue of Solon with his cloak thrown over his shoulder and his hand hidden inside was an example of the restraint practised by public speakers in those days, and he professed himself astounded and disgusted by Timarchus' immodesty.* But the people

of Salamis say that the statue was put up less than fifty years ago, and since Solon lived about two hundred and forty years ago, not only was the sculptor of this image not Solon's contemporary, but neither was his grandfather! Anyway, that's what Aeschines told the jurors, and he struck the same pose himself. [252] It would have been far more useful for his fellow citizens if he had displayed Solon's heart and mind, but he didn't even come close. After the revolt of Salamis, the Athenians decreed the death penalty for anyone who suggested they should try to regain the island, but Solon took that risk on himself. He made up and sung an elegiac poem on the subject, recovered the island for his fellow citizens, and wiped out their disgrace.* [253] But Aeschines did quite the opposite. Amphipolis, a place acknowledged to be yours by the Great King of Persia and all the Greek cities, was surrendered and sold by him when he spoke in support of Philocrates' proposal to that effect. Wasn't he the man to pose as Solon!

Then he compounded what he'd done in Athens when he went to Macedonia, where he failed to mention even once the name of the place which was the whole point of the embassy. He even admitted as much in his report to you. I'm sure you remember him saying 'I could have talked about Amphipolis, but I left it to Demosthenes.' [254] I stepped up and said that in fact he hadn't left it up to me to say any of the things he wanted to say to Philip. He'd sooner give a man some of his blood than allow him to contribute to a conversation in which he's involved! No, as I see it, he couldn't speak out against Philip because he'd been bribed and Philip had given him money precisely so that he wouldn't have to give up Amphipolis. [*To the Clerk of the Court*] Now please take Solon's poem—here it is. [*To the jurors*] This will show you that Solon too condemned people like Aeschines.

[255] [*To Aeschines*] It's not so much that you need to *speak* with your hand inside your cloak, Aeschines, but you really should keep it tucked away when you're acting as an ambassador! In Macedonia you held your hand straight out and disgraced your city, and then here in Athens you express lofty ideals. Do you think the paltry phrases you've practised and rehearsed will keep you from being punished for your monstrous crimes? Do you think that going around with a cap on your head and abusing me will save you?* [*To the Clerk of the Court*] Go ahead, please.

Solon's poem is read out:

If our city is destroyed, it shall not be by the decree of Zeus
  Or the will of the blessed, undying gods.
For Pallas Athena, spirited guardian, born of a mighty father,
  Keeps her hands spread over it.
No, in their folly the citizens themselves, tempted by money,
  Are intent on destroying our great city.
So too are the leaders of the people with their unjust policies.
  But their violence will bring grievous suffering,
For they know not how to curb their greed, nor how to arrange
  In peace a festive banquet from what they already have.
                    [One line omitted]
  Tempted into unjust acts, they grow rich.
                    [One line omitted]
  Not sparing the property of gods or city,
They rob and steal, one here, one there, and pay no heed
  To the sacred foundations of Justice.
Though silent, she knows what men do and have done before,
  And comes in time to exact payment in full.
There is no escaping this wound that is nigh the whole city,
  And foul slavery has fast come upon it,
Slavery that† stirs from sleep discord and civil war,
  The takers of many a fair youth's life.
For thanks to men of ill will our beloved city is fast being destroyed
  By conflict that only the unjust hold dear.
These are the evils at large among the people, and many
  Of the poor arrive in foreign lands,
Sold into slavery and bound with humiliating bonds.
                    [One line omitted]
Thus the common evil assaults every home, and no longer
  Can the courtyard door keep it out.
It o'erleaps the lofty wall and never fails to find its man,
  Even cowering in a corner of his chamber.
My heart commands me to explain to the people of Athens:
  There is nothing worse for the city than lawlessness,
But respect for law brings all things to order and certainty,
  And binds the unjust, time and again, with fetters.
The rule of law smooths obstructions, checks greed, reduces violence,

> *And causes the flowers of doom to wither;*
> *It straightens crooked judgements, tames deeds born of pride,*
> *Puts an end to acts of division and strife,*
> *And ends the bitterness of furious dissent. Under the rule of law*
> *All human affairs gain certainty and sound guidance.*

[256] [*To the jurors*] That's what Solon has to say about men like Aeschines, Athenians, and about how the gods protect the city. It may be wishful thinking, but I've always regarded the idea that the gods protect our city as true, and in a sense I think that everything that has happened today in the context of this audit demonstrates the existence of some kind of divine goodwill towards the city. [257] Look at it this way. A man committed terrible crimes while acting as your ambassador, surrendered territory where you and your allies should have been worshipping the gods,* and ensured that the man who responded by denouncing him was stripped of his citizenship. Why? So that he should meet with no pity or leniency for his own crimes. Moreover, in the course of prosecuting the man in question he made a point of slandering me, and later in the Assembly he kept threatening to bring charges and so on. Why? So that I, the person who has always been best placed to gain the most precise knowledge of his unscrupulous ways, should meet with the utmost indulgence from you as I prosecute him.

[258] Moreover, he has so far always managed to evade being brought to trial, but now he finds himself in court at a time when the future, if nothing else, makes it both impossible and dangerous for you not to punish him for having taken bribes. It is of course never inappropriate to condemn and punish traitors and bribe-takers, Athenians, but it would be particularly opportune, and universally beneficial, to do so now. [259] For Greece is in the grip of an epidemic, Athenians—an epidemic of such severity that it will take considerable care on your part to deal with it, not to mention plenty of luck. What I'm getting at is this. In the cities of Greece the most notable men, the preferred political leaders, are sacrificing their own freedom, the poor fools. They're voluntarily reducing themselves to slavery, while glossing it as 'being on good, friendly, and intimate terms with Philip', or the like. And what of everyone else, and the various civic authorities in each city, who ought to be punishing these men and putting them to death without delay? So far from doing so, they admire them and look up to them. Everyone takes them to be setting a good example!

[260] But look at how this epidemic of emulation, Athenians, has affected the Thessalians. Up until yesterday or the day before, it had merely brought their regional supremacy and their national prestige to an end, but now it is also robbing them of their freedom, since some of their citadels are in the hands of Macedonian garrisons. In the Peloponnese, it has caused massacres in Elis, where it drove those poor people out of their minds and infected them with such madness that, in pursuit of political power and Philip's approval, they slaughtered their own relatives and fellow citizens.* [261] And it hasn't stopped there. It has spread to Arcadia and plunged the region into complete chaos. Despite the fact that they ought to value freedom more than anything else (and as much as you, because you and they are the only autochthonous peoples in Greece),* they now, out of admiration of Philip, are erecting his statue in bronze and awarding him a crown. To cap it all, they've voted to make him welcome in their cities, should he come to the Peloponnese. And the Argives have done the same.

[262] There's no point in beating about the bush, by Demeter! This epidemic is spreading outwards in all directions and has reached us here, Athenians. Considerable caution is called for. While you are still safe, take the precaution of stripping those who first brought it here of their citizenship. Otherwise, watch out: you might recognize the validity of what I'm saying only when you've lost the chance to take the necessary steps.

[263] Look at the poor Olynthians, Athenians; they clearly and vividly illustrate the danger. The behaviour I've been describing was pretty much the only reason for their wretched downfall. Events there will enable you to see things clearly. When their resources consisted of no more than four hundred horse and a total fighting force of less than five thousand—this was before the synoecism of Chalcidice*— [264] the Spartans attacked them in strength with both a land army and a fleet. At the time, as you know, the Spartans were more or less dominant on land and sea.* Nevertheless, despite the sizeable attacking force, the Olynthians lost not a single town or fortress. In fact, they won a good number of battles, killed three enemy polemarchs, and brought the war to an end on their own terms. [265] But then some of them began to accept bribes, and the general populace foolishly or perhaps unluckily trusted these men rather than those who were true to them; then Lasthenes roofed his house with timbers

sent as a gift from Macedon, and Euthycrates paid nothing for his extensive herds of cattle;* then one man came home with sheep and another with horses, and the general populace, despite the fact that their interests were being undermined, not only failed to get angry or count this as punishable behaviour, but turned a blind eye, tried to emulate these men, rewarded them, called them real men.

[266] The situation deteriorated until corruption won out. By this time, the Olynthians had a thousand cavalrymen available and an army of more than ten thousand; all their neighbours were their allies; and you supported them with ten thousand mercenaries, fifty triremes, and a citizen contingent of four thousand men. But even this wasn't enough to save them. The war lasted less than a year and the Olynthians lost every city in Chalcidice to treachery. In fact, Philip was so swamped by traitors that he didn't know which offer to take first. [267] He gained five hundred horsemen, along with their weaponry, thanks to the treachery of their officers—more than anyone else in recorded history. The perpetrators felt no shame before the sun, before the land of their birth on whose soil they stood, before temples and tombs, before the disgrace that inevitably follows acts of betrayal. You see how people are unhinged and driven mad by corruption, Athenians. So you, the people, must keep your wits about you. You must not connive at such behaviour, but punish it in the public courts. It would be monstrous if you showed yourselves unwilling to punish the traitors in your midst, after having officially and thoroughly condemned those who betrayed the Olynthians. [*To the Clerk of the Court*] Please read the decree about the Olynthians.

The decree is read out.

[268] [*To the jurors*] It is universally held, jurymen, by Greeks and barbarians alike, that you did the right and proper thing when you voted to condemn those damned traitors. So since corruption comes before treachery and is what makes people turn traitor, you must regard anyone you catch taking bribes, Athenians, as a traitor as well. Traitors may surrender windows of opportunity, or political power, or troops—whatever they find it in their power to betray—but it is always an act of destruction, and all of them equally deserve condemnation.

[269] You are singularly well placed in this case, Athenians, since you can draw on your own history for examples. All you have to do is follow the practice of your ancestors, who fully deserve the praise you

bestow on them. Now is not the time to imitate the brilliant battles and campaigns they fought or their bravery, since you are at peace; but you can imitate their intelligence. [270] That is always desirable, whatever the circumstances, and it's no more troublesome or inconvenient to make good use of the mind than it is to make bad use of it. I mean, each of you is going to be here in court for the same amount of time whether the decision you reach and the vote you cast are sound or unsound—whether you match the good deeds of your ancestors and improve the general condition of Athens, or fall short of their standards and make things worse.

So what was their thinking about how to deal with traitors? [*To the Clerk of the Court*] Clerk, here. Take this and read it out. [*To the jurors*] It's important that you realize how carelessly you're behaving in matters that they judged to deserve the death penalty. [*To the Clerk of the Court*] Go ahead.

An excerpt from an inscription is read out.

[271] [*To the jurors*] As you've just heard, Athenians, the inscription says that 'Arthmius, the son of Pythonax, citizen of Zelea, is to be an enemy and foe of the Athenian people and of their allies, himself and all his kin.'* Why? Because he introduced the Greeks to Persian gold. Your ancestors, then, were taking steps to prevent anyone ever again being bribed to harm Greece, and this serves, as I see it, to highlight your failure to take steps even to protect your own city against the possibility of such harm from one of its citizens. [272] 'Yes, by Zeus, but the inscription was not set up in an especially prominent position.' I disagree. There's no part of the Acropolis that isn't sacred, and there's plenty of room up there, but this inscription stands just to the right of the great bronze statue of Athena, which was erected by the city, with donations from fellow Greeks, to commemorate victory in the war against the Persians.* At the time in question, then, justice was taken so seriously and punishing traitors was so highly valued that notice of the punishment due to criminals like Arthmius was taken to deserve the same placement as the memorial statue of the goddess. But now, unless you curb this inappropriate indifference of yours, you will be mocked, taken advantage of, and disgraced.

[273] Anyway, it seems to me, Athenians, that you would do well to imitate your ancestors not just in this way or that, but in all the steps they took. For instance, I'm sure you're all familiar with the story of

Callias, the son of Hipponicus, and the famous peace he negotiated
that everyone still talks about.* On land, the king of Persia was not
to come any closer to the coast than a day's journey by horse, and
none of his warships was to sail beyond the Chelidoneae Islands or
the Cyaneae Islands. Nevertheless, because Callias was thought to
have been bribed in the course of his mission, he came very close to
losing his life, and was fined fifty talents at his audit. [274] No peace
treaty entered into by the city before or since could possibly be held
to be better than this one, but as far as your ancestors were concerned
that was beside the point. It was their view that, while the favourable
terms were the result of their own courage and the city's reputation,
it was the character of the ambassador that determined whether or
not money changed hands, and they expected Callias to engage in
public business with integrity and without accepting bribes. [275]
They regarded bribe-taking as so harmful and contrary to the city's
interests that they refused to tolerate it whatever the circumstances
and whoever was involved. But you, Athenians, have seen one and
the same peace demolish your allies' fortifications and build houses
for your ambassadors. You have seen it rob the city of its possessions
and gain the ambassadors riches beyond their wildest dreams. And
yet instead of putting these men to death yourselves, you wait for
a prosecutor and in court rely on words to judge men whose crimes
everyone knows of from the evidence of their own eyes. [276] Anyway,
it's not only old cases that one might bring up and use as examples
to encourage you to take disciplinary action. Many such criminals
have been punished during the lifetimes of you who are here today.
The only ones I'll mention are one or two ambassadors who were
condemned to death for conduct that injured the city far less than the
mission we're considering today. [*To the Clerk of the Court*] Here, take
this decree and read it.

The decree is read out.

[277] [*To the jurors*] Those ambassadors, Athenians, the ones you
condemned to death in this decree, included Epicrates, who was
a good man, or so I'm told by people who were around at the time,
and often did the city sterling service. Apart from anything else, he
was a democrat, since he was a member of the Piraeus faction that
restored democracy.* But none of this helped him, nor should it have.
Anyone who undertakes affairs of state should be totally honest, and

should not first gain your trust and then take advantage of it to make things worse for you. Quite simply, he should never deliberately do you wrong.

[278] Now, if Aeschines and his cohorts left undone any of the crimes for which those earlier ambassadors were condemned to death, you may strike me dead here and now. Look at it this way. The earlier ambassadors 'disregarded their written instructions', as the decree puts it, in the course of their mission.* That's the first of the charges against them. Well, didn't Aeschines and his cohorts disregard their written instructions? Didn't they have the Phocians excluded from the treaty, despite the fact that their authorization said 'for the Athenians and the allies of the Athenians'? Didn't they receive the oaths of people sent them by Philip, although they had been instructed 'to administer the oaths to the city officials'? Didn't they constantly do business with Philip in private, even though they had been enjoined 'under no circumstances to hold private meetings with Philip'?

[279] 'Some of them were also found to have delivered false reports in the Council'—just as they did too, in the Assembly. And how were they caught? That's the key question. The very facts gave them away, because their reports have, of course, been perfectly contradicted by events. 'And of sending false dispatches as well'—just as they did too. 'And of telling lies about our allies and of taking bribes.' Well, Aeschines and his cohorts didn't so much tell lies about our allies as utterly ruin them, which is of course a far more serious matter. As for taking bribes, the case would remain to be made if they had denied it, but since they've admitted it they should of course have been arrested.*

[280] Well, Athenians, the people who drew up that decree were your fathers, some of them possibly still living. You see how things stand. Are you going to let Epicrates be banished and punished, a good democrat and a member of the Piraeus faction—or what about the recent ten-talent fine imposed in a famous case on Thrasybulus, son of Thrasybulus the democrat who came down from Phyle to restore democracy?* What about the man who counted among his ancestors Harmodius and your greatest benefactors, the ones who did you so much good that by law you include them in the libations offered at festival time in all your shrines, and whom you hymn and honour on a par with heroes and gods?*

[281] Are you going to let all these men suffer the legally stipulated penalty, unmitigated by clemency, pity, weeping children with the same names as the Benefactors, and so on, and then, just when you've got him in your power, acquit a man whose parents were Atrometus, a primary-school teacher, and Glaucothea, organizer of cultic revels for which another priestess was put to death?* A man who, following in the footsteps of his father and other members of his family, has consistently failed to do the city the slightest good? [282] Has any of them ever, over the years, provided the city with a single horse or warship? Has any of them served on campaign? Have they ever financed a chorus, undertaken any other form of liturgy, or paid a war levy? Have they ever shown patriotism or faced danger for the city?

As a matter of fact, even if he had all of these things to his credit, but not honest and uncorrupted service as ambassador, he would still deserve to die. But if he can claim neither the one thing nor the other, how can you not punish him? [283] Remember what he said when prosecuting Timarchus*—that a city which fails to act vigorously against criminals is no use at all, nor is a constitution in which the laws can be undermined by clemency and harassment; that you should not be moved to sympathy by Timarchus' elderly mother or his children, or anyone else, but should appreciate that, if you abandon the laws and the constitution, you will never find pity for yourselves. [284] Poor Timarchus has lost his citizenship for ever because he knew of Aeschines' crimes, but will you let Aeschines get away scot-free? Why would you do that? If Aeschines thought someone deserved such a severe punishment just for offences against himself, what about people—such as himself, as we have seen—who have seriously damaged the city's interests? How severely should you punish such people, given the oath you have sworn and the fact that you are here to see justice done? [285] 'Yes, by Zeus, but Timarchus' trial will improve the morals of the younger generation.'* Well, won't this one improve the morals of our public servants, and they are the ones who have the greatest effect on the city's fortunes?† You need to think of them too!

It's easy to demonstrate that Aeschines' purpose in ruining Timarchus was not the moral improvement of the younger generation. After all, Athenians, there's nothing wrong with their morals even now, and I pray that the city may never be in such a terrible state that our sons need Aphobetus and Aeschines to correct their behaviour! [286] No, the trigger for Aeschines was the fact that, while serving on the Council, Timarchus had proposed the death penalty for anyone caught supplying Philip with weaponry or naval equipment. Here's the proof. How long had Timarchus been making public speeches? A long time. But Aeschines had been in the city all that time, and had never previously found it offensive or shocking that a man like him should be speaking—not until after he had visited Macedonia and sold his services. [*To the Clerk of the Court*] Here, please take Timarchus' decree and read it out.

Timarchus' decree is read out.

[287] [*To the jurors*] In other words, the man who acted in your interests and proposed that Philip was not to be supplied with military equipment in wartime, on pain of death, was ruined and mistreated, while this fellow here, the one who made a gift to Philip of your allies' military equipment, took him to court and went on about rent-boys—and, by Earth and all the gods, was flanked by his two brothers-in-law as he did so! These are men the very sight of whom would make you cry out loud! There's the vile 'Nicias', who went to Egypt as a hireling of Chabrias, and the damned 'Cyrebion', who joins in festive processions unmasked.* Moreover, he was looking at his brother Aphobetus. What a topsy-turvy day that was, with all the talk about prostitution flowing back upstream!*

[288] Next, I'd like to show the extent to which this man's iniquity and lies have dishonoured our city. There's plenty I could say, but I shall focus only on what you already know. It used to be the case, Athenians, that everyone in Greece would take note of the decisions you made in the Assembly, but now it is we who go around with our ears to the ground, trying to find out what decisions have been reached elsewhere—what the Arcadians or the Amphictyons have resolved to do, where Philip is headed, whether he's alive or dead. Isn't that the kind of thing we do? [289] But what worries me is not whether Philip is alive, but whether Athenian will to condemn and punish criminals is dead. If all is well with you, I don't worry about Philip; but if in the future those who want to be his hirelings have nothing to fear from you, and those in whom you have placed your trust support their proposals, and men who in the past have consistently denied that they are working for Philip testify today on their behalf, then I'm frightened.

[290] [*To Eubulus*] For instance, Eubulus, let's consider your behaviour during your very own cousin Hegesilaus' trial, and during the recent trial of Niceratus' uncle Thrasybulus. Why both times did you refuse even to respond when you were called on to take the defendants' part for the first vote, and then, in the penalty phase, why, after rising to your feet, did you say nothing in support of the defendants, but begged the jurors' forgiveness?* Are you really going to stand up for Aeschines, when you don't do so for friends and relatives? [291] This is a man who evinced his hostility for you by speaking in support of Aristophon when Aristophon used his prosecution of Philonicus as a way to attack your policies.* But was it after you had terrified these jurors here by saying that, unless they voted for the motion proposed by the vile Philocrates and supported by Aeschines, they would have to go straight to Piraeus, pay a war levy, and use the Theoric Fund for military purposes,* as a result of which an equitable peace became a dishonourable one [292] and Aeschines and Philocrates have unleashed an orgy of destruction by their subsequent crimes—was that when you became friends? In the Assembly you cursed Philip and swore on your children's lives that you wanted to see him brought down. Are you now going to help his cause? How is your protection of men who were bribed by him going to bring him down?

[293] Why on earth did you take Moerocles to court for collecting twenty drachmas from every person who bought a mine lease? Why did you prosecute Cephisophon for stealing sacred funds, just because he was three days late in depositing seven mnas in the bank?* It makes no sense to do this and then, rather than bringing charges, to call for the acquittal of men who were bribed, who admit that they were bribed, and who have been shown beyond doubt to have taken the money in order to eliminate our allies. [294] The crimes committed by Aeschines and Philocrates are terrifying, and carelessness or indifference would be quite inappropriate, but the crimes for which you took Moerocles and Cephisophon to court are laughable.

[*To the jurors*] Look at it this way. Were there people in Elis who embezzled public funds? It seems highly likely. Were any of these people involved in the recent anti-democratic coup there? Not one of them.* And what about Olynthus? Could that kind of thief be found there—when there was such a place as Olynthus? Surely so. Well, were they responsible for Olynthus' destruction? No. What about Megara? Do you think there are no thieves there who help themselves to public money? There must be. And have any of them been found responsible for what happened there recently? Not one of them. [295] Who are they, then, the men who commit crimes of this magnitude and severity? They think themselves important enough to be called 'Philip's friends and intimates'; they aspire to military command and governorship; they expect to have pride of place. There was a case recently before the Three Hundred in Megara, with Perilas on trial for having gone to Philip, at which Ptoeodorus, the wealthiest, noblest, and most illustrious man in Megara, stepped up and asked the court to release the defendant. Didn't he send Perilas back to Philip? And didn't Perilas then return with mercenaries, while Ptoeodorus stayed at home and cooked up something fishy? That's right.*

[296] Nothing, absolutely nothing is riskier than letting an individual have pride of place in society. As far as I'm concerned, no one's life should be spared or forfeit at the whim of this or that individual. Acquittal or execution should depend on the facts, and in an Athenian court a defendant should get a verdict that fits the facts. That is the democratic way. [297] It's true that from time to time a number of individuals have gained power here—Callistratus, for instance, and then Aristophon, and Diophantus, and there were others before them. But where did they attain prominence?* In the Assembly. In the courts, so far, no individual has ever prevailed over you, the laws, or the oaths, so don't let Eubulus do so now. Caution is better than trust under these circumstances, and you shall hear an oracle to that effect—and oracles come from the gods, who are far better and more constant protectors of our city than its leading citizens. [*To the Clerk of the Court*] Please read the oracles.*

The oracles are read out.

[298] [*To the jurors*] You see the kinds of things the gods warn you about, Athenians? Now, if you were at war when they made these pronouncements, they are warning you to be on your guard against your generals, because in wartime the generals qualify as 'leaders'. If it was a time of peace, however, they are warning you against heads of state, and express concern that you might be led astray by the very people you trust to lead you.

'Keep the city whole,' says the god, 'that all citizens may be of one mind and give no joy to the enemy.' [299] Now, Athenians, what do you think would give joy to Philip? To see someone who has done so much damage spared, or to see him punished? Spared, of course. But the oracle warns you not to do anything that pleases the enemy. Zeus, Dione, and all the gods urge you to unite and punish those who serve the enemy's interests in any way—those who intrigue against the city from outside, and their collaborators on the inside. What the intriguers do is bribe, while the collaborators take bribes or protect those who have taken bribes.

[300] But even ordinary human intelligence allows one to see that there is nothing more dangerous and frightening than letting anyone in authority get close to people with non-democratic aims. How do you think Philip always got his way? How did he achieve his greatest successes? By buying them from people who offered them for sale; by corrupting the cities' leading politicians and influencing their views. [301] If you choose to take it, you have the chance today to make both of these approaches ineffective. All you have to do is, first, refuse to listen to politicians who testify on behalf of bribe-takers, which will show that, whatever they may say at the moment, they are not your bosses; and, second, punish, for all to see, the man who sold his services.

[302] You would have good grounds, Athenians, for being angry with anyone whose actions were designed to betray allies and friends, and to surrender windows of opportunity, which are critical to the success or failure of any enterprise. But never would your anger be more justified than if it were directed against Aeschines. This is the man who joined the ranks of those who mistrusted Philip and was 'the first and only person to see that Philip was the common enemy of all Greeks',* but then defected, turned traitor, and suddenly started to take Philip's part. Surely, this man deserves death many times over. [303] These are facts, undeniable even by him. Who was it who originally presented Ischander to you, saying he had been sent here by friends of Athens in Arcadia? Who cried out that you were sleeping while Philip was taking over Greece and the Peloponnese? Who delivered all those long and wonderful speeches, and read out Miltiades' and Themistocles' decrees and the oath sworn by the ephebes in the shrine of Aglaurus?* It was Aeschines, of course.

[304] Who persuaded you to send envoys almost as far as the Persian Gulf, on the grounds that, with Greece subject to Philip's intrigues, it was your duty to take precautions and look out for Greek interests? Wasn't it Eubulus who proposed the decree and Aeschines

who went off as envoy to the Peloponnese? Only he can know what discussions he had and speeches he made while he was there, but I'm sure you all remember what he told you in his report. [305] In his speech he called Philip a 'barbarian' and a 'fiend' over and over again, and he told you how happy the Arcadians were that Athens was at last waking up and noticing what was happening. He said that one thing had particularly upset him. On his way back home, he had met Atrestidas* returning from Philip, with about thirty women and children travelling along with him. He didn't know what to make of this, and asked someone he met on the road who the man was and who all those people were with him. [306] On hearing that the people were Olynthian captives Atrestidas had been given by Philip and was bringing back home with him, Aeschines said, he was horrified and shed tears of grief for Greece. If such terrible things could happen, it must indeed be in a bad way. And he recommended that you send a mission to Arcadia to denounce Philip's partisans there. For he said he had been told by friends that if Athens showed itself concerned and sent envoys, Philip's partisans there would be punished.

[307] The speech that Aeschines delivered on that occasion, Athenians, contained truly noble sentiments, nothing that could possibly dishonour the city. But after he had visited Macedonia and seen the man who was 'his enemy and the enemy of all Greeks', did his speeches run along the same or similar lines? Not at all! He told you to forget your ancestors, to make no mention of trophies, to ignore anyone who needed help. He expressed astonishment at the suggestion that you should include the Greeks in your discussions about the peace treaty with Philip, as if you had to satisfy anyone else where your private business was concerned. [308] He said, by Heracles, that no one was more thoroughly hellenized than Philip, no one a more formidable speaker, no one a truer friend to Athens. He said it was a disgrace that there were certain eccentric whingers in the city who abused Philip and called him a barbarian.*

How, I ask you, could the very man who had formerly expressed such noble sentiments now dare to say such things, unless he had been corrupted? [309] How could someone who had formerly felt loathing for Atrestidas because of the Olynthian children and women now bear to cooperate with Philocrates, who brought free Olynthian women here to Athens? But Philocrates is so well known for his disgusting habits that I don't have to say anything ugly or unpleasant about him now. I need say no more than that he brought women here, and you and all the bystanders know what happened next. You feel sorry for their misfortune and misery, I'm sure, but Aeschines didn't; he shed no 'tears for Greece' because of them—for the fact that they were violated, in an allied state, by ambassadors. [310] No, this corrupt ex-ambassador will shed tears for himself, and will probably produce his children and have them stand alongside him.* But if he does so, jurymen, you should remember that the children of many of your allies and friends are now homeless beggars, and that the catastrophe they have suffered is his fault. They deserve your pity far more than the children of a criminal traitor. Remember also that your own children have been deprived of a promising future by Aeschines and his cohorts, with their insertion into the peace treaty of the clause 'and for his descendants as well'. And remember, when you see him weeping, that you now have in your power the man who suggested that you send a mission to Arcadia to denounce Philip's partisans.

[311] Anyway, what you have to do now needs no mission to the Peloponnese, no long and expensive journey. All each of you has to do is approach this platform and vote in a spirit of piety, justice, and patriotism to condemn Aeschines. For this is the man—by Earth and all the gods!—who originally spoke, as I explained, about Marathon and Salamis, about battles and trophies, and then, as soon as he had set foot on Macedonian soil, changed his tune completely and told you to forget your ancestors, make no mention of trophies, ignore anyone who needed help, exclude your fellow Greeks from your deliberations, and all but demolish the city walls.

[312] Never in the past have you had to listen to more disgraceful views. I mean, no one in the world is so perverse or ignorant or anti-Athenian that, if he were asked, 'Tell me, is there anywhere in Greece, as it exists and is inhabited today, that would be called Greece or would be in the possession of its present Greek inhabitants, were it not for the courage displayed by our ancestors for their sake at Marathon and Salamis?'—no one would deny it, of course; everyone would say that all Greece would have fallen to the barbarians. [313] Not even our enemies, then, would fail to praise our ancestors and acknowledge the importance of what they achieved—and yet, for the sake of profit, Aeschines tells you, their descendants, to forget them. But what else do the dead have going for them? Praise for noble deeds is the inalienable right of those who have died noble deaths; they no

longer have to contend even with envy where they are. For trying to
deprive them of their privilege, Aeschines himself should now lose
his privileges as a citizen; that is the penalty you should impose on
him for your ancestors' sake. [*To Aeschines*] You vile creature, those
words of yours mocked and cheapened our ancestors' achievements;
in your speech you reduced everything they did to nothing.

[314] And all this has made you a landowner and a big man. [*To the
jurors*] That's another thing: before he did the city all that harm, he
used to admit that he had worked as a clerk; he was grateful to you
for the appointment, and his demeanour was modest. But now, after
harming the city in countless ways, he arches his eyebrows, and anyone who says 'Aeschines, the former clerk' is immediately his enemy
and accused of slander. He makes his way through the Agora with his
cloak hanging loose down to his ankles, keeping step with Pythocles,
and puffing out his cheeks. The message is that now he's a friend and
intimate of Philip, one of those who want to see the end of democracy
and regard the current system as rampant insanity. And this is the
man who until recently used to bow down before the Round House!

[315] I'd like to recapitulate for you how Philip recruited these
godless individuals and outmanoeuvred you. It's worth taking a
close look at the whole web of deceit. Philip wanted peace primarily
because his land was being raided by pirates and his ports had been
closed, depriving him of the revenue from all his goods. So he despatched those disarming speakers, Neoptolemus, Aristodemus, and
Ctesiphon, to act on his behalf. [316] But then, no sooner had we
envoys reached him than he paid Aeschines to support and work with
the foul Philocrates, and to get the better of those of us who were trying to do the right thing. He also wrote a letter to you, which he was
certain would gain him peace.

[317] Even so, he was still not in a position to do you serious
harm—not unless he could destroy the Phocians. But that was no
easy matter. It so happened that he found himself in a critical bind,
whereby he could either fail to bring his plans to fruition or be forced
into such blatant lying and oath-breaking that everyone in the world
would be aware of his wickedness. [318] If he accepted the Phocians
as allies and included them in his oath to you, he would immediately
and necessarily be breaking his oaths to the Thessalians and Thebans.
He had promised the Thebans that he would help them take over
Boeotia, and the Thessalians that he would help them regain control

of the Pylaea. On the other hand, if he refused to accept the Phocians as allies, which was his inclination, he felt sure that you would send troops to Thermopylae and block his passage—which is exactly what you would have done, if you hadn't been lied to—and that he would then be unable to advance through the pass.

[319] He didn't need any external advice to reach this conclusion; he had his own experience to draw on for evidence. The first time he defeated the Phocians,* when he annihilated their mercenaries and killed Onomarchus, the general in command, the Phocians found no help from anyone anywhere in the world except you—and yet he couldn't even approach the pass, let alone make his way through it or bring his plans to any kind of fruition. [320] So he was well aware, I should say, that it would be impossible for him to advance through the pass if you sent troops. Besides, at the time the Thessalians were fighting among themselves, with the Pheraeans initially reluctant to fall in line behind him, and the Thebans were in the process of losing a war: they had already been defeated in battle and a trophy had been set up at their expense. Under these circumstances, even an attempt on the pass would fail, unless he employed some ruse as well.

'How can I bring my plans to fruition,' he asked himself, 'and still avoid being caught in a lie or violating my oaths? Ah, I know. I must get some Athenians to deceive the Athenians. Then I'll avoid the taint of disgrace.' [321] Next, Philip's envoys warned you that his alliance with the Thebans and Thessalians made it impossible for him to accept the Phocians as allies,* and Aeschines and his cohorts took up the refrain and in their speeches said that it would obviously be improper for Philip to accept the Phocians as allies, because of the Thebans and Thessalians—unless, they said, he had his way and got peace, at which point he would do whatever we might ask him now to agree to. [322] By offering these prospects and inducements, they got the peace they wanted from you, which excluded the Phocians.

You also had to be prevented from sending troops to Thermopylae, despite the fact that you already had fifty triremes lying at anchor precisely in order to stop Philip if he took to the field. [323] How? What ruse would be employed this time? Using up all your time, and then springing a situation on you at such short notice that you wouldn't be able to launch an expedition even if you wanted to. There's no doubt that this was what Aeschines and his cohorts were up to. As for me, I'll remind you yet again that I was unable to leave Macedonia before them, and that, even when I hired a boat, I was prevented from setting sail.

[324] The Phocians also had to be induced to trust Philip and to surrender to him of their own accord, to save time and to make sure that you didn't pass any obstructive measures. 'It must be the Athenian ambassadors who convey the idea that the Phocians will be safe. That way, even if anyone in Phocis is suspicious of me, he'll surrender, because he trusts them. As for the Athenians themselves, I shall send for them, and then they'll think they're going to get everything they want and won't pass any obstructive measures.* At the same time, the report the ambassadors give will contain promises enough to keep the Athenians quiet whatever happens.'

[325] These were the ruses that enabled Aeschines and his cohorts to go about their orgy of destruction. May they die the worst of deaths! And so, almost immediately, instead of seeing Thespiae and Plataea resettled, you heard that Orchomenus and Coronea had been enslaved. Instead of the humiliation of Thebes and an end to its insolence and pride, your own allies' walls were razed to the ground and the demolishers were the Thebans, who were supposed to have been evicted from *their* city, as Aeschines told it. [326] Instead of returning Euboea to you in exchange for Amphipolis, Philip is further fortifying the island against you, and continues to intrigue against Geraestus and Megara. Instead of getting Oropus back, we're mounting an expedition to fight for Drymus and the farmland around Panactum— something we never did while the Phocians were safe.* [327] Instead of re-establishing the traditional rites in the temple of Apollo at Delphi, and seeing the sacred funds repaid, genuine Amphictyons are being driven into exile and forced off their land, while Macedonian barbarians are bullying their way on to the Council, when they have never before been members. And if anyone mentions the sacred funds, he is thrown from the precipice and his city loses its right of precedence in consulting the oracle.* [328] The whole business has been like a series of riddles for the city. He told no lies and got his way in everything; you expected your prayers to be answered and have seen quite the opposite happen; while apparently at peace, you have suffered worse than if you were at war; Aeschines and his cohorts have accepted bribes, and to this day have not been punished.

[329] It occurs to me that you might have known for some time that this was a simple case of bribery and that the whole affair has

enriched Aeschines and his cohorts. After all, there's plenty of evidence for it. And that makes me worried that I might be doing the opposite of what I intend; all this time I might have been irritating you with my attempts to make my case absolutely watertight, since you already knew the truth. Still, there's just a little more for me to say to you on the subject. [330] Would you set up a bronze statue in the Agora of any of Philip's envoys, Athenians? Or would you grant any of them any of the privileges you reserve for benefactors, such as the right to dine in the Prytaneum? No. But why not? I mean, you're not ungrateful people; you give others their due and do what's right. It's because you would say, quite rightly and fairly, that they acted throughout in Philip's interests, not yours.

[331] Now, do you think this response is unique to you? Do you imagine that Philip thinks differently, and that he has rewarded Aeschines and his cohorts so generously because in the course of their mission they did a good and honest job of promoting *your* interests? Hardly. You know how he treated Hegesippus and his colleagues on their mission.* Apart from anything else, he banished the poet Xenocleides—[*pointing*] there he is now—just for having made fellow citizens welcome! That's how he treats those who do an honest job on your behalf and speak their minds. It's his hirelings who receive the kind of treatment Aeschines and his cohorts received. Do you need any more witnesses or any further proof of this? Can any of you refute what I'm saying?

[332] Someone came up to me in front of the court not long ago and told me the most extraordinary thing—that Aeschines is planning to denounce Chares and expects to dupe you with this approach and the points he makes.* Now, so far from making much of the facts that on his every appearance in court, Chares has never been found to have done less than his best on your behalf, as a trustworthy and loyal servant of the democracy, and that it has been proved that all the opportunities he missed were the fault of those who have been bribed to work against your interests, I will make an extravagant gesture. Let's suppose that everything Aeschines will say about Chares is true. Even so, it's still absolutely ridiculous for him to be denouncing him. [333] After all, it's not as if I'm blaming Aeschines for anything that happened in the war; war is the generals' sphere of responsibility. Nor is he responsible for our entering into the peace treaty. I'm not interested in anything up to that point. What am I getting at, then? At what

point did he begin to be culpable, in my opinion? When he spoke in support of Philocrates' proposals for the peace treaty you were drafting, rather than supporting the proposers of the best policies; when he took bribes; when, later, on the second embassy, he wasted time and completely ignored your instructions to him; when he led the city astray and doomed everything by making us believe that Philip would do whatever we wanted; when, later again, he spoke in support of Philip, despite the fact that others were recommending caution where such an arch-criminal was concerned.

[334] These are my charges against him; please remember them. For if the peace were just and equitable, I'd be commending it to you; if these men hadn't taken bribes and then gone on to lie to you, I'd be thanking them and proposing crowns for them. Whether or not a general is guilty of wrongdoing towards you is irrelevant to the present audit. Was it a general who laid low Halus or the Phocians? Or Doriscus? Or Cersobleptes? Or the Sacred Mountain? Or Thermopylae? Who was it who opened a road for Philip through the territory of friends and allies all the way to Attica? Who has allowed Coronea, Orchomenus, and Euboea to fall into enemy hands? Who nearly did the same for Megara a short while ago? Who has built up Thebes' strength? [335] None of these places is insignificant or unimportant; none of them was ruined by any general; none of them is in Philip's hands because it was ceded to him by you as part of the peace accord. They were destroyed by Aeschines and his cohorts, by their bribe-taking.

If he tries to avoid the issue, if he digresses and changes the subject, this is how you should respond: 'We're not judging a general here. What you're talking about is irrelevant to the case. Don't try to shift responsibility for the devastation of Phocis on to someone else, but prove that it's not *you* who are responsible. And why are you reporting Demosthenes' wrongdoing to us now? The time for such accusations was his audit. You deserve death just for this. [336] Don't tell us what a blessing peace is, or how much good it will do us. No one's accusing you of getting the city to make peace. Prove to us instead that the peace we have isn't demeaning and disgraceful, that we were not subsequently deceived over and over again, that all is not lost. For these are the things you have been shown, to our satisfaction, to be responsible for. And why, even now, do you continue to express admiration for the man who has done us so much harm?' If you warn him off like this, he'll have nothing to say. He will raise his voice, but here it will do him no good; all those voice-training exercises will have been in vain!

[337] But perhaps I should say something about his voice as well. I'm told it's one of the things he's very proud of, and that he plans to overwhelm you with his acting skills. Now, when he was portraying the sufferings of Thyestes, or the Trojan heroes, you hissed him off stage, drove him out of the theatre, and almost stoned him to death, until in the end he gave up working as a third-string actor. It seems to me, then, that it would be remarkably odd behaviour on your part if you were to pay attention to him and his sonorous voice now, when it's not just some theatrical production he's ruined, but he has wreaked total havoc in state affairs of the first importance. [338] No, use your intelligence, rather than succumbing to a fit of foolishness. When you're assessing a candidate for the job of public herald, you have to consider the quality of his voice, but when you're assessing an ambassador, someone who expects to act as a state official, you look for integrity, and for someone who is proud when representing your interests, but sees himself as equal to his fellow citizens—as, for instance, I withheld my respect from Philip, but treated the prisoners of war with respect and did all I could to rescue them. Aeschines, meanwhile, was grovelling before Philip and singing paeans, and considers you his inferiors.

[339] Here's another point. When you find that a decent and public-spirited person has a way with words or a good speaking voice, or some such gift, you should all be happy and encourage his training, because it's a gift that also does everyone else good at the same time. But when you find such abilities in a bribe-taking villain who can't resist money, you should distance yourselves from him, and be a hostile and unreceptive audience, because it does the city no good if iniquity is seen as ability. [340] But you can see how much trouble the abilities for which Aeschines is famous have caused the city. Other abilities are more or less self-sufficient, but a skilful speaker is struck dumb if you, the audience, are unreceptive. That's how you should listen to Aeschines' speech, knowing that he is a bad and corrupt man, and that not a word he says will be true.

[341] I'd like you to appreciate that, however you look at it, Aeschines' conviction is a good thing, and not least because of the effect it will have on our relationship with Philip himself. There are

two alternatives. Either some time in the future he'll find himself compelled to treat the city fairly, in which case he'll have to change tack. At the moment, his method is to cultivate a few men while trying to deceive the majority, but if he sees that his chosen few have been killed, from then on he'll want to deal with you, the majority, seeing that you are fully in charge. [342] Or, if he remains just as rampageous and aggressive as now, by killing them you'll have rid the city of men who'd have done anything he asked them to do. I mean, if they behaved as they did when punishment was a distinct possibility, what do you think they'll do if they meet with leniency from you? Is there any traitor—a Euthycrates, a Lasthenes—they won't outdo? [343] And what about everyone else? They're bound to become worse citizens when they see that wholesale corruption gains people wealth, status, and the advantages of intimacy with Philip, while those who demonstrate their integrity and even spend some of their own money meet in some quarters with obstruction, hostility, and malice. No, you gain nothing by acquitting this man: people won't think the better of you for it, it would contravene your oath, and it won't make you more secure. Punish him, then. Make an example of him for everyone, here in Athens and elsewhere in Greece.

21. AGAINST MEIDIAS, ON THE PUNCH

In 348 the long-standing hostility between Demosthenes and a rich man named Meidias came to a head at the spring Dionysia festival. As well as the dramatic competitions, the festival included choral competitions between the ten Attic tribes. Each chorus had a *chorēgos*, or choral producer, whose role was to cover the costs of training and performance (pay, salaries for chorus members, musical support). The role involved considerable outlay; it also offered the opportunity to obtain a degree of prestige and popular goodwill. Demosthenes was acting as chorus-producer for his tribe. Meidias, having tried to obstruct Demosthenes' chorus in a number of ways, finally assaulted him. Demosthenes chose to prosecute him using a procedure called *probolē* (plural *probolai*), a preliminary hearing before the Assembly, available (among other things) for offences committed during a festival. The procedure had no immediate practical outcome beyond censure, since the Assembly vote was not followed by a penalty, but it did offer a very public expression of popular support and enormously improved the prospects for a subsequent courtroom trial. The choice of procedure may have had a political motive. Meidias was closely connected with the dominant political group headed by Eubulus, whom Demosthenes was harrying for what he considered their lacklustre policy against Macedon. The action allowed him to treat the incident as an offence against the festival, not just against him personally and to taint the leading faction by association. Demosthenes won the hearing in the Assembly, and then two years later decided to take the case to court in a public action.[1] But the story then becomes complicated. His enemy Aeschines says that Demosthenes 'sold for thirty mnas the outrage committed against him' (3.52). The claim is vague (probably deliberately so), but must imply some sort of settlement for money. We cannot trust Aeschines as a source against Demosthenes and recent critics are sceptical. But Demosthenes was visible enough both in the Assembly and in the courts to make a needless fabrication risky. Demosthenes may have reached an out-of-court settlement (as later sources believed), in which case this speech was never delivered;

[1] It is unclear whether the term *probolē* refers to the whole process, including the trial, or merely the preliminary hearing before the Assembly. In the latter case the plaintiff would then take the case to court in whatever public action was appropriate to the allegations. Though the fact that Demosthenes occasionally refers the term *probolē* to the Assembly hearing favours the latter view, it is also true that he never uses any term which would identify the court hearing as a separate action. He seems explicitly to rule out the most obvious action, the *graphē hybreos* (§§25–35), the indictment for 'outrage' (malicious assault), and the absence of a persistent emphasis on impiety rules out the *graphē asebeias*, indictment for impiety.

or he agreed on a small (for a toff like Meidias) fine at the penalty stage of the trial. Either way, despite the barnstorming rhetoric of this speech, he probably compromised. From 348 there was a slow movement towards peace and a rapprochement between some at least of the political factions. It is likely (and has often been suggested) that Demosthenes' compromise with Meidias was part of this burying of hatchets.

----

[1] The wanton insolence, jurymen, with which Meidias constantly treats everyone is, I'm sure, familiar to you all, just as it is to the rest of our fellow citizens. I acted exactly as any of you would have chosen to if you'd been assaulted: I brought a *probolē* against him for offences committed during the Dionysia—not just for the blows I received from him at the festival, but also for many other acts of violence that I suffered during my time as chorus-producer. [2] In the Assembly, honour and justice prevailed. To a man, the assembled people were so roused to fury and anger, and so concerned about the wrongs they now knew I had suffered, that they remained unmoved by the best efforts of Meidias and others acting on his behalf. They ignored the fact that these men were wealthy individuals, paid no attention to their promises, and unanimously censured him. Afterwards, many of my fellow citizens, including some who are here in court today, came up and asked me, urged me, to proceed against Meidias and have him examined by you. And, by the gods, they had two reasons for this, I think, Athenians: first, they were appalled at how I'd been treated; second, they wanted to punish him for the brazen, offensive, and unbridled way they had seen him behave on other occasions.

[3] Since this is how things stand, I have done my duty and pre-served for you everything that I should have kept safe,* and now that the case has come to trial, I'm here, as you can see, to act as pros-ecutor. I was offered a great deal of money, Athenians, to drop the suit, but I turned it down. I held out against all the pleas and the promises—and the threats, by Zeus—that I received. [4] The next step is up to you, and the more people he has pestered and solicited help from (I saw what he was doing just now in front of the court),* the more I hope to obtain justice. After all, I could hardly imagine that any of you would jettison the principles which motivated your earlier concern for me. Nor, seeing that you're under oath, would I expect you to cast your vote other than in accordance with the demands of

justice—unless you want to give Meidias permission to carry on with his abusive behaviour in the future.

[5] Now, Athenians, if I were accusing him of making an illegal proposal, or of misconduct as an ambassador, or something of that sort, any kind of personal appeal to you from me would, I think, be inappropriate. I believe that in such cases the prosecutor's only job is prove his point, while it's up to the defendant to make such pleas. But since this man corrupted the judges and unlawfully deprived my tribe of the tripod,* [6] since I myself have been struck and have suffered what must surely be worse treatment than any chorus-producer ever had to endure, and since I've come to court to try to secure a conviction for these crimes—the very crimes that the Assembly indignantly condemned in a burst of sympathetic anger—I feel no qualms about making an appeal as well. It's scarcely an exaggeration to say that I'm the defendant today, seeing that an insult that goes unpunished is a kind of personal disaster.

[7] The first thing I earnestly beg of you all, then, jurymen, is to give me a favourable hearing. But, second, if I prove that Meidias here has used violence not only on me, but on you, the law, and the whole community, I implore you to look after your own interests, as well as mine. For the fact of the matter is, Athenians, that although it was I who was the victim of physical violence and was treated like dirt on this particular occasion, the issue to be debated and decided today is whether or not *any* Athenian should be allowed to get away with committing this sort of casual violence towards people. [8] So if any of you formerly entertained the idea that this trial was motivated by a private quarrel, he should now bear in mind that it is in the public interest for a stop to be put to this kind of behaviour once and for all. I would urge him to pay careful attention, since the issue concerns the city as a whole, and to vote for whichever of us seems to have right on his side.

Let's begin, then, with a reading of the law governing *probolai*. After that, I'll try to clarify everything else. [*To the Clerk of the Court*] Please read out the law.

The law is read out.†

[9] [*To the jurors*] There's the law governing *probolai*, Athenians. As you heard, it says that an Assembly is to be held in the Theatre of Dionysus after the Pandia, and that at this meeting, once the

chairmen have dealt with the Archon's business, they are also to deal with any crimes or illegalities that might have been committed at the festival.* This is a good law, Athenians. It serves the public interest, as this very case testifies. I mean, since it's clear that there are people whose violence is hardly curbed at all by this deterrent, what do you think such people would get up to if there were no risk involved and they weren't liable to stand trial?

[10] Now, I'd like also to read you the very next law.* It will make it blindingly obvious that, where everyone else treads carefully, Meidias boldly rushes in. [*To the Clerk of the Court*] Please read out the law.

The law is read out.

[11] [*To the jurors*] Notice, jurymen, that in the first law the *probolē* is to be brought against 'those who commit crimes at the festival', but in this one you also allowed for *probolai* against people who try to recover overdue debts, or who take anything from anyone, or who resort to force.* In other words, so far from thinking it right that a person should be assaulted during the days of the festival, or that equipment supplied by him out of his own resources in fulfilment of a liturgy should be treated with violence, you even decided that property belonging to people who had gained it as a result of a legal verdict should remain, for the duration of the festival, at any rate, in the hands of the original owners, even though they had lost the case. [12] Now, Athenians, for all your leniency and piety—which may be measured by the fact that you postpone even the punishment of crimes committed earlier until after this period—I shall prove that, within precisely this period, Meidias did things that deserve the ultimate penalty. Once I've shown in detail all that I went through, starting at the beginning, I shall then tell you about the blows that he fetched me in the end, and you'll see that, from start to finish, he did nothing that does not deserve the death penalty.*

[13] Two years ago, no chorus-producer had been appointed by the tribe Pandionis, and it was time for the Assembly meeting at which the law requires the Archon to cast lots to assign each chorus-producer a pipe-player.* Harsh words were beginning to be exchanged, with the Archon blaming the Tribal Supervisors and the Supervisors blaming the Archon. But I stepped up and volunteered my services as chorus-producer, and it fell to me to be the first to choose a pipe-player. [14] Both my promise and my lucky break were universally

welcomed by you, Athenians, in the warmest possible terms; your cheers and applause were the kind you reserve for expressing approval and pleasure. As far as one could tell, Meidias here was the only one who was displeased, and throughout my entire liturgy he dogged my footsteps, constantly and maliciously making a major or minor nuisance of himself.

[15] Anyway, I shall pass over all the trouble he caused me by objecting to the exemption of our chorus members from military service, by getting himself proposed as a candidate for election as one of the supervisors for the Dionysia, and so on and so forth.* Although at the time every instance of his harassment and abuse made me no less angry than the most outrageous of his actions, I'm aware that the rest of you, who weren't involved, will probably consider them too trivial in themselves for a trial. I shall confine myself, then, to what will stir the same degree of anger in all of you.

[16] The actions of his that I'm going to mention are incredible and, speaking for myself, I wouldn't even have tried to prosecute him today if at the time I hadn't immediately made my case against him in the Assembly. He went under cover of darkness to my goldsmith's house with the intention, Athenians, of destroying the sacred clothing—I should say that I regard all clothing that has been made for the purposes of the festival as sacred, until it has served its purpose—including the golden crowns that I'd had made to adorn the chorus.* And destroy it he did, though he didn't manage to destroy it all. I defy anyone to claim that he has ever heard of an Athenian citizen attempting or executing such a deed! [17] But he didn't stop there: he also corrupted my chorus-trainer.* In fact, if that excellent man Telephanes, the pipe-player, hadn't been looking out for me at the time—he realized what was up, gave the man the sack, and decided to drill and train the chorus himself—we wouldn't have competed, Athenians. The chorus would have gone on stage untrained and we'd have been completely humiliated. Even that wasn't the end of his insolence. He had enough left in reserve to try to corrupt a crowned Archon, and he got the other chorus-producers to gang up against me. He yelled and threatened, stood right next to the judges as they swore their oaths, blocked off the green rooms—nailed them shut, when they were public property and he held no official position.* On and on it went; I couldn't tell you all the grief and trouble he caused me.

[18] Now, some of this happened in the Assembly or in the theatre

next to the judges, and for these events, jurymen, I have all of you as my witnesses;* and of course no statement can be considered more impartial than one whose truth is vouched for by a court in session. After suborning the judges for the men's contest,* he crowned, so to speak, his youthful exploits* with two more: he assaulted me, and he made himself primarily responsible for ensuring that the winning tribe failed to get the prize. [19] These were the abuses I and my fellow tribesmen suffered at his hands, Athenians—the festival-related crimes for which I brought the *probolē*.

Actually, that's far from the end of the story, and I shall go through his other crimes, or at least as many of them as I have time for, right away. I could mention countless other instances of offensive behaviour; I could show that many of you have been victims of his thuggery; I could point to the shocking and reprehensible acts this vile man repeatedly commits. [20] Some of his victims, jurymen, were terrified into silence by his aggression, his supporters, his wealth—by the whole package. Others tried to obtain justice, but failed. Others settled with him, as a way of making some money, I suppose. Those who made this concession did at least gain redress for themselves, but you have inherited the obligation to gain redress for the laws he broke when he wronged first those earlier victims of his, and now me and the whole community.

[21] Now, you should come up with just one penalty for all his crimes at once, whatever penalty seems right to you. But, after first proving that I wasn't the only one—that you too were victims of his violence—I shall go on to prove that he deserves to die many times over, not just once. [*To the Clerk of the Court*] Please take the first deposition, that of the goldsmith, and read it out.

The goldsmith's deposition is read out.

[23] [*To the jurors*] As I said at the start of my speech, Athenians, I have a lot to say about his crimes against others as well. I've drawn up a list of his abuses and insults, and I'll go through it all for you in a moment.* It wasn't a hard list to prepare, because I was approached in person by his victims. [24] But I'd like to start by telling you the ways in which I've heard he's going to try to deceive you. It's not just that I think this will make an essential preface; I also think it will be very educational for you. Why? Because any argument that

undeceives you will help you to vote in accordance with justice and your oath. It's of critical importance that you pay close attention to what I say, remember it, and have an answer for every point he makes.

[25] First, he will undoubtedly say, judging by the report I received of a conversation he had with certain close friends, that if my claims about how I've been treated are true I should have brought *private* suits against him: a suit for damages for ruining the clothing and the gold crowns, and for all his harassment of my chorus, and a suit for assault for the assault I claim to have suffered. I most certainly should not be putting him through a public trial, he'll say, and proposing penalties for him to suffer or pay. [26] But I'm quite certain, and you should be certain too, that if I hadn't brought a *probolē* against him, but had instigated a private suit, I'd have been faced straight away with the opposite argument. He'd be saying that, if there were any truth to my claims, I should have brought a *probolē* against him and taken steps to see him punished at the actual time of the offences. Since the chorus belonged to the city, the clothing was all being made for the festival, and I, the victim, was a chorus-producer, no one in my place could have chosen any form of retaliation other than the one that is enshrined in law for wrongdoing relating to the festival.

[27] I'm sure that's what he'd have said then. After all, it is of course normal for a guilty defendant to try to get out of being punished on the system currently in use by arguing that the alternative system should be used. But it's the job of sensible jurymen to ignore these arguments and punish each and every case of malicious abuse that comes before them. [28] So don't let him argue that, by law, I can bring private suits against him, as well as a public suit for assault. So I can. What he has to prove is that he's innocent of the charges I've brought against him, or that it wasn't a festival-related offence, because that's why I brought the *probolē* against him, and that's the issue on which you're to vote today. If I waive the chance of making money from private suits and entrust his punishment to the state—if *this* is the form of trial I've chosen, and it's one from which I gain nothing—surely it would be reasonable for me to expect your approval for that, not disapproval.

[29] Another argument I'm sure he'll rely heavily on is this: 'Don't betray me to Demosthenes! Don't destroy me to gratify Demosthenes! Are you going to destroy me just because I'm at war with Demosthenes?' I'm sure he'll repeat this kind of thing over and

over again, in an attempt to arouse hostility against me. [30] But that's a very tendentious way to put it. You never hand a criminal over to his accusers. Where there's a victim of a crime, you don't even let the victim suggest the form of punishment you are to apply. On the contrary, since legislation precedes crime, there's no telling who the future criminals and victims may be. And what do these laws do? They guarantee, for every citizen of Athens, that through them he'll be able to gain redress if he's the victim of a crime. In other words, when you punish someone for breaking the law, you're not handing him over to his accusers; you're affirming the law for your own good.

[31] Now, he's bound to say 'Demosthenes was the victim,' or something like that.* For this, there's a response to hand that is fair, impartial, and objective. The point is that it wasn't just me, Demosthenes, that he assaulted on that day, but also your chorus-producer. What's the significance of this? Look at it this way. [32] You know, of course, that 'Thesmothete' isn't the name of any of our Thesmothetes; each of them has his own name, whatever it may be. Now, anyone who physically or verbally abuses a private citizen will find himself defending a public suit for malicious abuse or a private suit for slander. But if it's a Thesmothete he abuses, he'll lose his citizenship rights once and for all. Why? Because the criminal in this case is additionally abusing the law, the crown that is the people's common property,* and a name that belongs to the city. For the label 'Thesmothete' identifies no single individual, but a city official.

[33] The same goes for the Archon too. If you physically or verbally abuse a crowned Archon, you lose your citizenship rights, but if you abuse him when he's out of office, you're liable to a private suit. And this applies not only to Thesmothetes and Archons, but to everyone to whom the city grants the right to wear a crown or some other honour.† The same therefore applies to me as well. If Meidias had committed any of these crimes against me at any other time, when I wasn't a city official, he'd be liable to a private suit. [34] But if it turns out that his criminal assaults were all committed against your official chorus-producer during holy days, he deserves condemnation and punishment by the state. So, you see, a chorus-producer was the victim, not just Demosthenes. This, along with the fact that it took place at a time of year when such acts are specifically interdicted by law, makes it the city's business.

Although you have to check the soundness of laws when you're in the process of passing them, what's important once they've been passed is to protect and enforce them. That's the right thing to do in any case, but it's also required by your oath.* [35] We've had a law about damages for a long time, and one about battery, and one about malicious abuse.* Now, any of these crimes could of course be committed during the Dionysia. If it were enough for the criminal to be punished under these laws, there'd be no need for this specific law as well. But it's not enough, and the proof is the sacred law you made just for Dionysus, covering the holy days. So if a man is guilty under those original laws *and* under this subsequent law—if he's just generally guilty before the law—should he therefore get off scot-free, or does he deserve a more severe punishment? A more severe one, I'd say.

[36] I've been told that he's been busy drawing up a list. He's been finding out who has ever been the victim of malicious abuse, and he's going to bring them up and tell you their stories. There's the Assembly chairman, for instance, who was apparently once struck by Polyzelus during an Assembly meeting; there's the Thesmothete who was struck not long ago, while rescuing the pipe-girl;* there are other similar cases. The idea is that showing how often terrible things happen to other people will make you less inclined to condemn what happened to me. [37] But it seems to me, Athenians, that it would make more sense for you to do the opposite, seeing that it's your job to take thought for the state as a whole. I mean, it will come as no surprise to any of you that there's a direct relationship between the frequency of such incidents and the failure to punish offenders, and that the only way to eliminate malicious abuse in the future is to make sure that every such criminal who falls into your hands receives the appropriate punishment. So, if the deterrence of future crime is a good thing, that gives you another reason to punish Meidias, and one that is all the more necessary given that these crimes are increasing in number and severity. But if he and all the rest are to be encouraged, you should let him off.

[38] Moreover, there's a far higher degree of culpability in his case, compared with the other victims on his list. The man who hit the Thesmothete, for instance, had three excuses: he was drunk, he was inflamed by lust, and the night was too dark for him to realize what was happening. And Polyzelus didn't mean to lash out, but

anger and his usual impetuosity got the better of him. There was no enmity between him and his victim; there was no malice in the act. But Meidias has nothing to offer in the way of mitigating circumstances. There's a long history of enmity between us; his assault took place knowingly in daylight; and he has clearly made it his mission to assault me on every possible occasion, not only on this one.

[39] In any case, I see no similarity at all between me and the other victims in respect of our behaviour. You'll find that the Thesmothete had no interest in the city and the law; he was indifferent to them, but was privately induced by a certain amount of money to drop the suit. And the man who was hit by Polyzelus did the same—he settled out of court, displaying his indifference towards the law and the city— and didn't even prosecute. [40] Now, these facts are important—for anyone who wants to use the present occasion to denounce these men. But for anyone who wants to defend himself against the charges I've brought, they are completely and utterly irrelevant, because you'll find that, contrary to them, I wasn't given any money nor did I try to get any. No, as an honest man should, I kept the right of punishment safe for the law, the god, and the city, and now I've handed it over to you. So don't let him bring these episodes up, and if he persists, don't listen to him. He's wrong.

[41] If he finds you resolute on this point, he'll be left with no defence. I mean, how will he explain his actions? What human, reasonable excuse will he give? Anger, by Zeus! Yes, I suppose that's what he'll say. And it's true that a man can attribute sudden actions of his, even when they're abusive in character, to the influence of anger, saying that he was carried away and wasn't thinking straight. But when he's known to have gone on and on constantly breaking the law over a long period, anger doesn't come into it. Of course not. Such a man is obviously acting with malice aforethought.

[42] Now that it's clear that he's guilty as charged, and that he acted abusively, we should take a look at the legal situation, jurymen. After all, you're under oath, as jurors, to uphold the law. Consider how much more severe the law thinks the condemnation and punishment of deliberate and abusive wrongdoing should be, compared with other forms of wrongdoing. [43] In the first place, all these laws about damages—let's start with them—stipulate a fine of double the damage for a deliberate offence, and just the single amount otherwise. This is as one would expect: the victim's entitlement to help is

unconditional, but the law prescribes a different degree of condemnation of the perpetrator depending on whether or not his actions were deliberate. In the second place, our homicide laws punish cold-blooded murderers with death, permanent exile, and confiscation of property, but grant involuntary murderers considerable clemency and leniency.*

[44] But it's arguable that the law punishes *all* instances of intentionally abusive behaviour severely, not just these cases. Otherwise, how does one explain the fact that someone who defaults on paying the penalty due on a private case does not become liable under the law to a private suit of ejectment, but has to pay an additional fine to the public treasury?* Or again, how else does one explain the fact that the city doesn't come to the help of the lender when a loan to which he's agreed (of a talent, or two, or ten) is misappropriated by the borrower, but if someone uses force to take something of very little value, the law requires him to pay an additional fine to the public treasury of the same amount that he owes his victim?

[45] The explanation is that the legislator regarded *all* acts of violence as crimes affecting the citizen body as a whole, even those who weren't directly involved. Few have strength, but everyone has recourse to the law; the legislator assumed that whereas a man who has agreed to a deal needs private means of redress, a victim of violence needs public assistance. That's why, where malicious abuse itself is concerned as well, he granted everyone the right to bring a public action and ruled that the entire penalty should be payable to the state. He regarded any instance of malicious abuse as a crime against the state, not just the victim; and he thought that the victim was adequately compensated by the punishment of the offender, and shouldn't receive money of his own as a result of such crimes. [46] But he went further, much further. He even granted the right to bring a public action on the victim's behalf if the victim of the abuse was a slave.* That is, he thought he should focus not on the identity of the victim, but on the nature of the act, and when he found an act pernicious he banned it altogether, never mind whether the victim was a slave or a free man. For there's nothing, Athenians, nothing at all that is less to be tolerated than malicious abuse, and nothing that deserves a more robust condemnation from you. But what could be better than hearing the law itself? [*To the Clerk of the Court*] Please take the law on malicious abuse and read it out.

The law is read out.

[48] [*To the jurors*] You can see what a merciful law this is, Athenians. It grants even slaves immunity from malicious abuse! 'Ye gods, why?' Well, suppose someone took this law to barbarian lands, to the places from where slaves are brought to Greece, and wanted to describe the city and sing your praises. He'd say: [49] 'There are people in Greece who are temperamentally so forgiving and merciful that despite all the wrongs you've done them, and despite their natural and ancestral hostility towards you, they still grant immunity from malicious abuse even to people they've paid good money for and bought as slaves. They've passed this law banning malicious abuse, and they've already put a lot of people to death for breaking it.' [50] Once this information had sunk in, don't you think the barbarians would by public consent appoint you collectively as their official representatives?* So here we have a law that isn't just well thought of in Greece, but would be well thought of abroad as well. When someone breaks it, then, what punishment do you think he deserves?

[51] Now, if I hadn't been a chorus-producer when Meidias treated me this way, Athenians, the only culpable aspect of his actions would have been their malicious abusiveness. But I was, and I think his impiety should properly be condemned as well, because, as you know, we perform all these choruses and hymns for the god. This is stipulated not just by the laws about the Dionysia, but also by oracles, in all of which, whether they come from Delphi or Dodona, you'll find it stated that choruses are to be instituted in accordance with tradition, that the streets are to be filled with the smoke of sacrifices, and that crowns are to be worn. [52] [*To the Clerk of the Court*] Please take and read the actual oracles.

Some oracles are read out.

[54] [*To the jurors*] Our city is blessed, Athenians, by these and many other oracles. But what conclusions should we draw from them? While they tell you to carry out the various sacrifices to the gods specified in each oracle, they also supplement every oracle you receive with the instruction to organize choral performances and to wear crowns in accordance with tradition.* [55] Think, then, about all the dances that take place, and about us chorus-producers. Obviously, on those days when we meet for the contest, all of us, from the eventual winner

to the eventual loser, are crowned, as enjoined by the oracles, for the sake of the city (as opposed to wearing a crown for oneself, as the victor does on the day of his celebration). It follows, then, that anyone who assaults any of these dancers or chorus-producers in a spirit of hostility, and does so during the contest in the god's sanctuary, is committing an act of impiety. What else could we call it?

[56] Besides, as you know, although you don't want foreigners to take part in the contest, you don't allow any of the chorus-producers to just challenge dancers and question them. You stipulated a fine of fifty drachmas for any chorus-producer who does so, and a fine of a thousand drachmas if he orders them to sit the performance out.* Why? To ensure that on the day no one with an ulterior motive challenges, harasses, or assaults anyone who is crowned and dutifully serving the god. [57] So, then, if even a man who performs the perfectly legitimate action of challenging a dancer is liable to a fine, what about a man who beats up a chorus-producer? Is this blatant infringement of the entire law code to go unpunished? But then what's the point of having noble, humane laws to protect the majority, if you, who constitute the administration, fail to condemn people for disobeying and violating them?

[58] Here's another point I'd like you to consider—and I crave your indulgence if I mention by name certain people who've fallen on hard times. The reason, I swear, is not to cast it in their teeth, but to show that generally in Athens people get by without using violence and being abusive and so on. So let's take Sannion, the trainer of tragic choruses, who was found guilty of draft-evasion, and suffered for it.* [59] After this misfortune of his, he was hired by a chorus-producer who was keen to win the tragic contest—I think it was Theozotides. At first, the rival chorus-producers were angry and threatened to stop him, but by then the theatre was full. When they saw that the crowd had gathered for the contest, they hesitated and relented, and no one laid a finger on him. In fact, in a magnificent display of pious tolerance from each and every one of you, he has been training choruses ever since, without even any of his personal enemies stopping him, let alone any chorus-producer.

[60] Then there's Aristeides, from the tribe Oeneis, who also suffered the same kind of misfortune. He's an old man now, and his dancing days may be over, but there was a time when he was the leader of his tribe's chorus. Now, you are of course aware that without

the chorus-leader the rest of the chorus falls apart. Yet none of all the rival chorus-producers over the years took advantage of the situation. No one went so far as to remove him or stop him. They couldn't just summon him to appear before the Archon, as though he were a forbidden foreigner, so in order to stop him working they'd have had to have laid hands on him, and no one wanted to be the first to carry out such an inexcusable act.*

[61] So, on the one hand we have chorus-producers, many of whom had bankrupted themselves on liturgies, with what they might well assume to be a sure-fire method of gaining victory, but none of whom ever dared to lay hands on people even when it was legally permissible, and instead behaved with such restraint, piety, and decency that, throughout the competition for which they were liturgists, they held back in view of your wishes, knowing how seriously you take the festival. And on the other hand, we have Meidias, who held no official position and wasn't out of pocket. Just because he was angry with someone, an old enemy, he struck this person a humiliating blow. Never mind that his victim was a chorus-producer, a liturgist, and an Athenian citizen: he displayed total lack of concern for the festival, the law, your response, or the god. What appalling and despicable behaviour, jurymen!

[62] Many men have fallen out with one another, Athenians, for both personal and political reasons, but no one ever went that far. Everyone else retained at least some self-control. For instance, there was a time, apparently, when the great Iphicrates had become the sworn enemy of Diocles of Pithos, and it also so happened that Iphicrates' brother Teisias and Diocles were rival chorus-producers. Now, Iphicrates was wealthy and popular, and he had the kind of opinion of himself that you'd expect in a man who had been honoured and rewarded by the state as he had.* [63] But he didn't sneak into goldsmiths' houses by night. He didn't shred clothing that had been made for the festival. He didn't bribe a trainer or interrupt a chorus's rehearsals. He didn't come close to behaving like Meidias. No, in deference to the law and the will of the people, he put up with watching his enemy gain the victory crown. Of course he did. It was his view that he should defer in such cases to the society within which, as he was aware, he had gained his prosperity. [64] Or again, there's the case of Philostratus of Colonae, who's well known to all of us. When Chabrias was on trial for his life over the Oropus crisis,* Philostratus

was one of the prosecutors, and the most savage of them all. Later, when Philostratus was a chorus-producer for the boys' competition at the Dionysia and won, Chabrias didn't hit him or steal his crown or, in short, trespass where he had no business.

[65] Anyway, plenty of people have fallen out with one another for plenty of reasons, and I could carry on with their cases as well, but no one I've ever heard about or seen has behaved with such extreme abusiveness. And here's something else for which I'm sure no one here can recall a precedent: one of the rivals in a case of personal or political enmity standing near by as the judges were being called forward, or getting them to repeat their oath after him. In fact, I doubt there is any precedent for using a festival like this, for a display of hostility. [66] The point is, Athenians, that there is some excuse for such behaviour in a chorus-producer who was carried away by ambition. But when a man deliberately seizes every opportunity to harass an enemy of his in an attempt to show that he can prevail over the law—*that*, by Heracles, is the behaviour of a tyrant and a criminal!

It does the city no good either. Suppose every chorus-producer knew in advance that 'With so-and-so as my enemy (Meidias or some other equally pushy and wealthy fellow), first, however good my performance, I'll be robbed of victory, and then I'll find myself humiliated at every turn and exposed to a barrage of insults.' Is anyone such a mindless moron that he would choose to spend a single drachma under such circumstances? I don't think so. [67] No, what always underpins a citizen's public-spiritedness and financial generosity in a democracy is, I think, the belief that he has the same rights and the same access to justice as everyone else. Well, Athenians, that's what Meidias has taken from me; even apart from his assault on me, I was also robbed of victory.

And yet I shall prove beyond the shadow of a doubt that Meidias could have got at me without resorting to bullying, abuse, or physical violence. He could have displayed his public-spiritedness to you by legal means, and he would have left me unable today even to open my mouth in his case. [68] When I offered my services in the Assembly as chorus-producer for Pandionis, Athenians, he should have got to his feet straight away and made the same offer to his own tribe, Erechtheis. We'd have been on a par then as liturgists, and that's how he should have tried to deprive me of victory—without resorting on that occasion, either, to abuse or physical violence. [69] That would have shown you respect, but that's not what he did. He didn't expend his youthful energy on any such project. No, after I had offered my services as chorus-producer—which you could see as the act of a madman (in the sense that it may be a sign of insanity to take on more than one can afford), or as an act of public-spirited generosity—he dogged my footsteps, harassing me openly and maliciously, until eventually he couldn't keep his hands off the sacred clothing, the chorus, or even my person.

[70] It would be a mistake, Athenians, if your anger at Meidias were insufficient to condemn him to the death he deserves. I mean, if a victim's self-restraint helps a man get away with unrestrained abusiveness, that's not right or fair. What's right is for you to punish the perpetrator, as one whose crimes are beyond the pale, and to show your gratitude to the victim by supporting him. [71] For it can't possibly be claimed that this kind of behaviour never has terrible consequences, and that I'm exaggerating after the event to make it seem frightening. That's not so at all. The story of young Euthynus, the wrestler, and Sophilus the pancratiast* is familiar to everyone, or is at least widely known. Sophilus was a strong man, swarthy—I'm sure some of you know who I'm talking about. Anyway, once in Samos town at some get-together (a private party, in fact), Euthynus thought Sophilus was insulting him, defended himself, and actually killed him. And many of you know of Euaeon, the brother of Leodamas, who killed Boeotus at a dinner party, a family gathering, in retaliation for just a single blow.

[72] It wasn't the blow that made them lose their tempers, you see; it was the indignity. Being struck is bad enough, but for a free man it's not as bad as being struck in an insolent manner. Hitting isn't a simple act, Athenians, and the victim may be hard put to describe some of what happened: the striker's stance, his look, his voice, when the blow was meant as an insult, when it was an act of hostility, when it was a deliberate punch, when it was a slap in the face. When men are unused to being treated like dirt, these are the aspects of the event that stir them up and make them act out of character. No one could describe these things in a way that would convey to his audience the terror of the situation in all its concrete reality, and make the assault as vivid as it was to the victim and the immediate witnesses.

[73] I would ask you, then, Athenians, in the name of Zeus and all the gods, to look at things rationally. How much more anger do

you think I was entitled to feel at the way Meidias treated me than that man Euaeon was, the killer of Boeotus, given his circumstances? He was struck by an acquaintance, who was drunk; he was struck in front of no more than six or seven people, also acquaintances, who were likely to reproach Boeotus for his actions and congratulate Euaeon for his forbearance if he exercised self-restraint after being struck; and he was struck in a private house where he just happened to have gone for dinner. [74] But I was assaulted in the early morning by an enemy who was sober and motivated not by alcohol, but by a desire to humiliate me; I was assaulted in front of a large crowd of both Athenians and foreigners; and I was assaulted in a sanctuary where, as a chorus-producer, my attendance was essential. It's true, Athenians, that I acted with restraint—or perhaps it was luck that prompted my decision to remain calm then, without getting carried away and doing irrevocable harm. Nevertheless, I have a lot of sympathy for Euaeon and anyone else who has defended himself against humiliation.

[75] I think many of those who judged the case at the time felt the same way too. At any rate, Euaeon was convicted by only one vote, I hear, and got by without tears, without appeals to a single juryman—without any attempt to ingratiate himself with the jury at all, in fact, great or small.* So I think we can assume the following: it wasn't the fact that he defended himself that caused those who condemned him to vote against him, but the fact that his self-defence was such as to cause death; and those who acquitted him did so because they allowed a victim of physical abuse more than the usual leeway for retaliation. [76] Well, then, given that I purposely didn't defend myself, not wanting things to go too far, from whom should I receive compensation as a crime victim? From you, I think, and from the law. This case should send a clear message to everyone else, that a man should sometimes refrain from lashing out in anger at abusive bullies, and should bring them before you instead, since you are the guarantors and guardians of legal protection for victims of crime.

[77] Well, jurymen, some of you are doubtless anxious to hear about the hostility between Meidias and me, in the belief that no one could treat a fellow citizen with such wanton violence unless he was owed redress for some great wrong in the past. I'd like next, then, to tell you the whole story from start to finish. A thorough account of our enmity will enable you to see how plainly he deserves to be

punished for this too. I'd better start at the beginning, I suppose, but it won't take long.

[78] When I initiated proceedings against my trustees to recover my inheritance, I was no more than a boy.* I didn't even know of Meidias' existence; I certainly wasn't acquainted with him—and I wish I still weren't! About three or four days before the hearings, Meidias and his brother burst into the house with a proposal for an exchange procedure for a trierarchy.* The brother's name, Thrasylochus, had been posted as the challenger, but in fact Meidias was responsible for everything, for all that happened. [79] The first thing they did was smash in the doors to our rooms, as if they had already been assigned the property by the exchange procedure. Then they began to curse in front of my sister, who was a young girl at the time, still living at home. Nothing could induce me now to repeat a single word of what they said, but it was the kind of filth that you might expect from the likes of them. They also called my mother, me, and the whole household names, some of them obscene. But the worst thing of all was not what they said, but what they did: they proposed to drop the suits against my trustees, as if they already had the right to do so.

[80] This may be old news, but I'm sure some of you remember. Back then, the whole city knew of the challenge, their designs, and their bully-boy tactics. Now, I was all alone in the world and just a boy at the time. I didn't want to lose the property that was in the hands of my trustees, and I was expecting to come away with not just the amount I did finally manage to recover, but everything I was aware of having lost. So I offered them twenty mnas, which was the sum for which they had contracted out the trierarchy.* Anyway, so much for their abusive behaviour towards me then.

[81] Later, I brought a private suit against Meidias for the slander,* which I won by default because he chose not to contest the case. I found him tardy with his payments, but I never laid a finger on any of his property, even though it was permissible.* Instead, I brought another private suit, this time for ejectment, but to this day I haven't been able to get the case to court, since he keeps coming up with all sorts of sly reasons for deferment.* Discretion is my watchword; I always choose to proceed like this, putting my trust in justice and the law. He, however, as you've heard, chose not just to bully and abuse me and my family, but also to take out his feelings for me on my fellow tribesmen. [82] [*To the Clerk of the Court*] To confirm

the truth of what I've been saying, please call the witnesses to these events. [*To the jurors*] Then you'll know the truth of what you've been hearing: that I haven't yet obtained justice for the wrongs he did me earlier, and that before doing so I've been the victim of further malicious abuse.

The witnesses' deposition is read out.

[83] I'd like you to listen next, Athenians, to an account of how he behaved over the court case—the one I won, I mean. His insolence and arrogance will be plain to see. As arbitrator* I got Straton of Phalerum. Now, Straton has to work for a living and lacks experience of public life, but basically he's not a bad sort and a perfectly respectable man. And that's precisely what has caused the poor fellow's ruin—his unwarranted, unmerited, and perfectly disgraceful ruin. [84] At last the appointed day arrived. All legal means had been exhausted—motions for deferment, counter-suits,* and so on—and there was nothing left to do. This man Straton, our arbitrator, first asked me to postpone the hearing, and then to adjourn it to the next day, but in the end, since I was still saying no and Meidias still hadn't shown up, and since it was getting late, Straton found against him.

[85] Night had already fallen and it was dark when Meidias went to the officials' chambers. He found them, as I was told by one of the bystanders, on their way out and Straton heading for home, having already handed in his default verdict. At first, Meidias had the cheek to try to persuade Straton to change his declaration from condemnation to acquittal and to get the officials to alter the written record. He even offered them fifty drachmas! [86] They were appalled, and neither they nor Straton wanted anything to do with this scheme of his. Meidias left, damning and blasting them—and what did he do? Something that will show you just how malicious he is. He first applied to have Straton's verdict annulled, but didn't take the required oath, so that he was returned as unsworn and allowed the verdict to become final against him.* Then, in an attempt to disguise what he was up to, he waited until the arbitrators' last session, which not all of them attend, [87] and persuaded the chairman to put the matter to the vote without recording the name of even one witness to the summons,* which was completely illegal. He had the arbitrator removed from office and disfranchised by bringing charges against him without either the accused or any witnesses present! In other

words, in retaliation for Meidias' losing a default verdict, an Athenian citizen has lost all his rights as a citizen and has become permanently disfranchised. It seems to be a risky business for someone who's been wronged by Meidias to prosecute him or arbitrate a case in which he's involved—or even to walk on the same street as him!

[88] The question to ask about this episode is: what was it that Meidias had suffered to make him hatch a plot to exact such savage retribution from a fellow citizen? If the way he was treated was truly reprehensible and unconscionable, he should be pardoned, but if it was nothing, it shows the brutality and savagery with which he treats everyone who crosses his path. So, what has happened to him? 'He's incurred a heavy fine, by Zeus, large enough to bankrupt him.' Really? The fine was only a thousand drachmas. [89] 'True, but even that amount hurts, when the fine to be paid is undeserved, and the injustice of it all made him forget that he was overdue with his payment.' Actually, he found out about the fine on the very day it was imposed (which, again, convincingly shows that Straton did nothing wrong), but he hasn't yet paid a single drachma of it. [90] More on that in a moment.

Now, he did of course have the option of applying to have the verdict annulled, which would have restricted his dispute to me, his opponent in the original suit, but he chose not to do that. Instead, to enable Meidias to avoid contesting a case with a fixed maximum penalty of ten mnas, for which he failed to appear as required—to avoid the risk of paying the penalty if he was found guilty (though he might have been acquitted)—an Athenian citizen had to be disfranchised and denied the opportunity to meet with clemency or defend himself or be treated fairly at all. Yet these rights are granted even to genuine criminals.

[91] But did he do what he had previously avoided doing *after* he had disfranchised his intended victim and you had allowed him to get away with it?* After he had seen through to fruition the brazen plan he had selected for the job? Has he paid the fine which was his reason for ruining Straton? Even today, he has yet to pay a single penny, preferring to undergo a suit for ejectment. One man has been disfranchised and ruined, while the other isn't even out of pocket, but still plays havoc with the law, the process of arbitration, and anything else he wants. [92] Moreover, while he has validated to his own satisfaction the verdict against the arbitrator, obtained without issuing a summons,

he is in the process of invalidating the verdict that went against him, despite the fact that I issued a summons, that he was aware of the summons, and that he failed to appear in court. And yet, if he expects arbitrators who decide against him by default to be punished so severely, how should you punish him, an open and insolent breaker of your laws? If disfranchisement—loss of legal rights and everything else—is the appropriate penalty for *that* offence, death seems a slight penalty for malicious abuse.

[93] [*To the Clerk of the Court*] To verify what I've been saying, please call the witnesses to these events, and read the law about arbitrators.

The witnesses' deposition is read out.

[94] And now read the law about arbitrators.

The law is read out.

[95] Please also call Straton himself, Meidias' victim. I suppose he's allowed to get to his feet.*

[*Straton stands; Demosthenes resumes addressing the jury*] Here you see a good man, Athenians, for all that he's not well off. He was an Athenian citizen, he served on all the campaigns that occurred while he was of military age, and he never did anything terribly wrong. Now he stands here in silence, since one of the many benefits of citizenship he has lost is the right to speak or complain. He's not allowed even to tell you whether or not it was *right* for him to have been treated like this. [96] This is what he's suffered at the hands of Meidias, with his wealth and arrogance, because he's poor and friendless and just one of the common people. If he had broken the law and accepted the fifty drachmas from him—if he had changed his declaration from a negative to a positive verdict—he'd still be in possession of his rights as a citizen and would be enjoying the same benefits as the rest of us without having come to any grief. And the reason why his life has been ruined so catastrophically by Meidias is just this: he paid more attention to justice than to Meidias; his respect for the law outweighed his fear of Meidias' bullying.

[97] When you find a man of such cruelty and heartlessness, a man who savagely retaliates against wrongs he can only claim to have suffered (for in reality he wasn't wronged at all)—when you find a man like this bullying a fellow citizen, are you going to let him get

away with it? When you find a man who displays no concern for the festival, the sacred rites, the law, or anything else, won't you condemn him? Won't you make an example of him? [98] What will you say, jurymen? By the gods, what justification or reasonable excuse will you offer for not condemning him? 'He's a foul brute, by Zeus.' Perfectly true—but surely you ought to condemn such people, Athenians, not protect them. 'He's rich.' Yes, but you'll find that his insolence is due as much as anything to the fact that he's rich, and so you'd do better to deprive him of the resources that support his abusiveness, rather than protect him because of them. I mean, leaving great wealth in the hands of such a bold and offensive man is tantamount to giving him resources to be used for undemocratic purposes.

[99] Are there any remaining reasons for acquitting him? Oh, compassion, I suppose. With his children by his side and tears in his eyes, he'll beg for mercy. That's the only possible remaining reason. But I'm sure you're aware of the fact that it's the victims of intolerable injustice who deserve compassion, not those who are being punished for monstrous crimes. How could it be right to feel pity for Meidias' children after his heartless treatment of the children of Straton here? On top of all their other troubles, they see that their father's catastrophe is beyond recovery. There's no debt he could pay to regain his citizenship;* no, he has quite simply been disfranchised by the force of Meidias' anger and abusiveness.

[100] So if you take pity on Meidias as though he were the victim, no bully is ever going to stop his insolence or be deprived of the money that makes it possible. Here we have a man of small means who has been completely ruined by Meidias for no good reason. Won't you even unite in condemnation of him? You must. No pitiless man deserves pity, no unforgiving man deserves forgiveness. [101] Everyone, I think, expects everything they do to be a kind of loan for their own benefit. Suppose, for instance, that I'm the sort of man who treats everyone decently, sympathizes with their troubles, and often does them favours. In a crisis or emergency, everyone should make the same kind of loan to me. Suppose someone else is a man of violence, heartless and inhumane: he should be paid in the same coin by everyone. [*To Meidias*] So, since that's the kind of loan you've made, that's also the kind of reward you should reap.

[102] [*To the jurors*] It seems to me, Athenians, that even had I no other charges to bring against Meidias—even if these were the least of

his crimes—you could use what I've already said to bring in a guilty verdict and sentence him to the severest of penalties. But that's not the end of the matter, and I hardly think I shall be at a loss to find more to say: he's created such a wealth of charges! [103] I'm not going to bring up the prosecution he brought against me for desertion, or his hiring as his agent for this job that vile and unprincipled man, 'Dusty' Euctemon. There's no need for me to bring it up because that sycophant failed to turn up for the preliminary hearing, and in fact the only reason Meidias hired him was so that the charge would be posted in front of the Eponymous Heroes for all to see: 'Euctemon of Lousia indicted Demosthenes of Paeania for desertion.'* I think he'd happily have included the fact that it was Meidias who had hired him, if it had been possible to do so. But I'm not going to bring that up. After all, by not proceeding with the prosecution Euctemon engineered his own loss of rights,* and I need no further satisfaction than that.

[104] But I shall mention something else he did, Athenians— a horrific and shocking act for which the term 'crime' seems inadequate: it dishonoured the entire community. When poor Aristarchus, the son of Moschus, found himself in trouble, facing serious charges, Meidias began by brazenly going around the Agora telling preposterous lies about me, to the effect that it was I who had done the deed.* But that was getting him nowhere, so he approached the men who were accusing Aristarchus of the murder (they were relatives of the deceased) and promised to pay them if they accused me of the crime. He felt no qualms about this: he let nothing—no sense of respect for gods or city—stop him making such an offer. [105] You'd have thought he'd have hesitated, in that company, before bringing calamitous ruin down on someone's head without a shred of justification, but there was only one thing he wanted—to find a way to destroy me—and he decided to leave no stone unturned. He felt, I suppose, that any victim of his abuse who saw fit to retaliate and refused to keep silent deserved to be banished and hounded to his ruin. He felt that such a man should be convicted of desertion, exiled for murder, and all but nailed up.* So you see? Once he's been found guilty of this too, on top of all his malicious abuse of me as chorus-producer, how could he possibly deserve to find you in a forgiving or charitable mood?

[106] These actions of his, Athenians, were the death of me, I'd say. First, at the Dionysia, he vented his malice on my equipment, my person, and my finances, and now, with his more recent actions and

activities, he's completed the list by abusing my city, my family, my rights as a citizen, and my prospects. If just one of his plans had succeeded, I'd have lost everything, even the right to be buried at home.* And for what reason, jurymen? Every one of Meidias' abuses is illegal, and yet if his victims are to be treated in these or similar ways when they try to defend themselves, it will be best to forget resistance, and just kowtow before those who abuse us, as barbarians do.*

[107] You need to see that I'm telling the truth about this loathsome brute's more recent activities [*to the Clerk of the Court*], so please call the witnesses to these events.

The witnesses' deposition is read out.

And please also find the law about bribery.

[108] [*To the jurors*] While he's finding the law, Athenians, I'd like to say a few words to you. In fact, I'd like to make a request, jurymen, in the name of Zeus and all the gods. As you listen to me, ask yourselves the following question: if it were *you* who were being treated like this, what would you do? How angry would you have been with the perpetrator? You see, although I found his festival-related abuses offensive, Athenians, the later ones I found far more offensive, and I was far more angry. [109] After all, how could one say, with hand on heart, that evil has a limit, that there's an end to impenitent brutality and malice, when one is faced with a man who feels neither regret nor remorse for his horrendous crimes and goes on to commit even worse ones? A man who uses his wealth not to improve some aspect of his personal situation without harming anyone else, but to banish and humiliate a man for no good reason, while congratulating himself on his affluence?

[110] Well, Athenians, that's exactly how Meidias has been behaving towards me. He falsely accused me of a homicide that had nothing to do with me, as was subsequently proved. He indicted me for desertion, when he himself has been a deserter three times over.* He tried to make out—I almost forgot to mention this—that I was responsible for the business in Euboea and the activities of his friend and intimate Plutarch, before the outcome made it perfectly clear that it was all Plutarch's doing.* [111] Finally, after I'd become a councillor, the charges he brought during my assessment* made things very dangerous for me, because instead of obtaining justice for the wrong I had suffered, I came close to being punished for matters that had nothing

to do with me. During this ordeal, thanks to the kind of harassment I've been describing to you, I had nowhere to turn, Athenians, even though I am not entirely without friends and resources.*

[112] Yes, perhaps this is another matter I need to raise at this juncture. The fact is, Athenians, that the playing field is not level: compared to the rich, the rest of us don't get a fair shake. No, we don't, we don't. They're given the dates they want for their trials, and their crimes are served up before you stale and cold, while if disaster strikes one of us, we come to trial fresh. They have witnesses prepared and waiting, and supporting speakers all of whom are ready to denigrate us. But, as you can see, I can't even find a few people who are willing to testify to the truth.

Anyway, a man could of course wear himself out moaning about this. [113] [*To the Clerk of the Court*] Please read out the law next, following my lead. Go ahead.

The law about bribery is read out:†
If any Athenian accepts a bribe, or gives one to someone else, or corrupts others by offering bribes, to the detriment of the people in general or of any individual citizen, by any manner or means, he and his children and his property are to lose their rights.

[114] [*To the jurors*] Now, Meidias is so unprincipled and unscrupulous that there's nothing he wouldn't do or say. Issues such as whether what he's saying is true or false, or whether he's dealing with a friend or an enemy, don't matter to him. And so, after accusing me of homicide and bringing that serious a charge against me, he still allowed me to conduct the entry rites for the Council, to perform the sacrifices, and to initiate the rites for you and the whole city;* [115] he still allowed me to lead the official delegation and take the collective offering to Zeus at Nemea* on behalf of the city; and he did nothing when I was one of the three chosen from the entire citizen body to perform the rites for the Reverend Goddesses and in fact to initiate the ceremony.* If there'd been a jot or tittle of truth in the charges he was trying to bring against me, would he have allowed me to do these things? Surely not. So this behaviour of his exposes the malice of his attempt to have me exiled from my homeland.

[116] Now, it was obviously after he had found it impossible to make me liable to this charge in any way whatsoever, despite all his devious attempts to make it stick, that he trumped up the allegation

against Aristarchus instead, as a way of getting at me. I'll mention only one incident relating to this. The Council convened to look into the matter, and in the course of the session he stepped up and said: 'You're in possession of the facts, aren't you, Councillors? And you have the murderer.' He meant Aristarchus. 'So what's the hold-up? Why are you still conducting an investigation? That's really stupid. Aren't you going to put him to death? Why don't you go to his house and arrest him?' [117] So he spoke, this unscrupulous monster, when he himself had visited Aristarchus' house the day before, and until then had been on just as good terms with him as anyone else. In fact, before his fall, Aristarchus had often pestered me to patch up my quarrel with Meidias.

Now, if his reason for speaking like this to the Council was that, in his view, Aristarchus had indeed brought about his own downfall in some respect or other—that is, he believed that Aristarchus was guilty as charged—he shouldn't have behaved as he did. [118] When people think that a friend of theirs has committed a crime, they impose upon him the moderate penalty of withdrawing their friendship, leaving punishment and legal proceedings to the victims and the perpetrator's enemies. But suppose we forgive Meidias this lapse. Even so, if we find that he treated Aristarchus as innocent by spending time under his roof chatting with him, and then began slandering and accusing him as a way of getting at me, does he not deserve to die ten times over, or rather ten thousand times over?

[119] To prove that I'm telling the truth—that the day before this speech of his he visited Aristarchus at home and chatted with him; that the next day he went to his house *again* (and this, Athenians, this really takes impurity to a new level),* sat as close to him as this [*Demosthenes demonstrates*], and, in front of many witnesses, gave him his hand; that this took place *after* that speech of his in the Council in which he had called Aristarchus a murderer and a number of other foul names; that he assured Aristarchus, calling curses down onto his own head if he was lying, that he had said nothing negative about him; that it didn't bother him to commit perjury even in front of people who knew the truth; and that he then asked Aristarchus to negotiate a reconciliation between him and me—for all of this I shall call witnesses who were present at the time. [120] But what a reprehensible, or rather amoral thing to do, Athenians—to call someone a murderer and then to turn around and swear that he had said no such thing, to

denounce a man for homicide and then to spend time under the same
roof as him!

Now, apparently, I'd be doing nothing wrong were I to let him off
the hook and betray your censure of him!* If I proceed against him,
however, I'm a deserter and an accomplice to murder, who deserves
to be crushed. But my view is exactly the opposite: if I'd let him off
the hook, I'd have been deserting, Athenians—deserting the cause of
justice. Indeed, I could plausibly have initiated proceedings against
myself for manslaughter, in the sense that my life would effectively be
at an end if I'd done that.

[121] [*To the Clerk of the Court*] Anyway, to confirm the truth of
what I've been saying, please call the witnesses to these events.

The witnesses' deposition is read out.

[122] [*To the jurors*] Has there ever been, or could there possibly be,
villainy that exceeds or even comes close to Meidias'? He deliberately
persecuted a man who was down on his luck, a man who had done
him no wrong—I say nothing about their friendship—while at the
same time he was asking him to negotiate a reconciliation between
him and me! Meanwhile, he was also spending money on trying to
have me exiled along with that man, when I had done no wrong!

[123] When it is a man's established habit, Athenians, to make
life even more miserable for innocent people who go to court to
defend themselves, I'm not the only one who should feel indignation and anger, while everyone else remains indifferent. Far from it:
you should all feel just as much anger as me. For if you stop and
think about it, you'll see that it's the poorest and weakest members
of society, Athenians, who are most likely to be treated badly, while
the filthy rich, with their propensity for abusive behaviour, are most
likely to escape punishment for treating others badly, by employing
hirelings to bring troublesome counter-suits. [124] No, you shouldn't
ignore this kind of behaviour. You must see that every time he uses
fear and intimidation to avoid being punished by one of us whom he's
wronged, he's denying us an opportunity to exercise our rights to free
speech and liberty.

Now, I managed to ward off his lies and misrepresentations—
there's always the chance that one of us might do that—without
being crushed in the process. But what will the majority do, if you
fail, in your official capacity, to make it dangerous for people to use

their wealth in this way? [125] A man should stand trial and defend himself in court against the charges brought against him, and only then retaliate against his accusers for the injustice of the charges. He shouldn't try to crush his opponent before the case comes to court, nor should he try to get off without a trial by trumping up charges against him. He shouldn't kick up a fuss about paying a penalty, but should avoid giving offence throughout the whole process.

[126] There, Athenians, you have an account of all the festival-related abuses I suffered, the beating I received, and how I managed to escape despite all his various plots against me and the ordeal I was going through. I've left out plenty of other instances—it would be hard to recount them all, I think—but the fact of the matter is that there's not one of his actions which is an offence against me alone. My tribe, ten per cent of the entire citizen body, was just as much a victim as I was of his festival-related crimes; the laws, which keep each and every one of you safe, were just as much victims of his malicious abuse of me and his plots against me; and the god in whose honour I was appointed chorus-producer was just as much a victim of *all* this wrongdoing of his, as was the sacred spirit of religious observance, whatever its precise nature may be. [127] It's important, then, for anyone who's concerned to sentence Meidias correctly, with a punishment that fits the crime, to see that what I'm saying doesn't apply only to me. Then he will feel the appropriate degree of anger. He should appreciate that Meidias' offences have affected everything at once—the laws, the god, the city—and should impose a penalty accordingly. And he should also understand that Meidias' supporters and assistants aren't just speaking on his behalf, but signalling their approval of what he's done.

[128] Well, Athenians, if Meidias' behaviour had otherwise been restrained and moderate, if I had been the only victim of this violence of his and his bully-boy tactics and none of my fellow citizens had suffered at his hands, I'd first have blamed my own bad luck, and then I'd have been worried that the self-restraint and humanity he displayed in the rest of his life might enable him to escape punishment for his abusive behaviour towards me. [129] But, in fact, many of you have been his victims, and have suffered so badly at his hands that I have nothing to worry about on that score. On the contrary, my concern is exactly the opposite, that once you've heard about all his

other victims, you might think: 'So what's all the fuss about? Have you been treated worse than anyone else?'

Now, it would be impossible for me to tell you everything he's done, and it would make for boring listening. Even if I were allowed both of our waters added together, his and mine, it wouldn't be enough for what remains to be said.* So I'll mention just the most serious and blatant episodes. [130] Actually, this is what I'll do. I'll read you all my notes, just as I wrote them out for myself, and whichever case you'd like to hear about first, I'll talk about first, and then your second choice, and so on, as long as you want to continue. There's a wide variety of cases: a large number of incidents of malicious abuse; crimes against his family; repeated failure to show the gods proper reverence. You'll find, in fact, that there's no area of life in which he hasn't persistently done things that deserve the death penalty.

Demosthenes' notes about Meidias' crimes are read out.

[131] That list, jurymen, covers incidents relating to people who just happened to cross his path on some occasion or other. I've left out other kinds of cases, because of the impossibility of recounting in one go the abusive acts that have taken him a long time to carry out. He's spent his entire life doing nothing else! But it's worth noting how big-headed he's become by now, as a result of having got away with all of this. It rather looks as though he tends to regard crimes committed by one individual against another as shabby, mean, and beneath his dignity.† Life will be unbearable, he tends to think, without the chance to insult an entire tribe, or the Council, or a whole section of society, or large numbers of his fellow citizens all at once.

[132] Countless incidents must remain unmentioned, but what about the expedition to Argura?* I'm sure you're all aware of how after his return from Chalcis he fulminated in the Assembly against the cavalrymen who had served with him there; you remember the denunciations and the claim that the expedition was a national disgrace. And you remember, of course, the harsh words he hurled at Cratinus for his part in this (though today, I've been told, Cratinus is going to support him). How depraved and cocky do you think a man has to be to alienate so many of his fellow citizens at once for no reason?

[133] [*To Meidias*] But, Meidias, is it a 'national disgrace' for men to make an orderly crossing with the appropriate equipment for confronting the enemy and supporting their allies? Or are *you*

the national disgrace, for praying, when you were drawing lots, that you wouldn't be selected for the expedition? For never once putting on your breastplate? For riding on a silvered mule-seat? For having cloaks, goblets, and containers of wine which the excise men tried to confiscate?* [*To the jurors*] That's the report that reached us in the infantry, anyway: our landing-point was different from theirs. [134] [*To Meidias*] And did you then go after the whole lot of them, just because Archetion or someone made fun of you for this? If what your fellow cavalrymen said about you and you accused them of saying about you was true, you deserved every bit of their scorn. After all, you were trying to harm and damage the reputation not just of the cavalry, but also of these people here, and indeed the whole city.

But suppose you were innocent and it was a case of people fabricating charges against you: even so, if the rest of the army failed to criticize these people and even enjoyed your discomfiture, they were clearly concluding, from the evidence of the rest of your life, that the cap fitted. So you should have behaved with greater moderation, and not launched a verbal attack on them. [135] But you threaten and harass everyone. You expect others to take your wishes into consideration, but you make no effort yourself to avoid hurting others. And I take this to be the most convincing, and most shocking, proof of your abusive nature, you monster—that you stepped up and denounced so many people all at once. Who else would have dared to do that?

[136] [*To the jurors*] In every other trial I can think of, jurymen, the defendant is accused of one or two crimes, but has an inexhaustible supply of arguments: 'Can anyone here really be certain that I did any such thing?' 'Have any of you actually *seen* me doing what I'm accused of?' 'There's no truth in it. These men are my enemies; they're telling lies about me; I'm the victim of false testimony.' And so on. But it's the other way around for Meidias. [137] You *all* know what he's like, I think. You're aware of his habitual insolence and arrogance, and I imagine some of you have been wondering for a while why you haven't heard me mention events that you personally know about.

It's clear, however, that quite a few of his victims are reluctant to testify about all the wrongs they've suffered because they're afraid of him—of his violent and restless nature, and of the resources that give this otherwise despicable creature his strength. He's dangerous [138] because unprincipled abusiveness, combined with power and wealth, is a wall that makes a man invulnerable to attack. If Meidias were stripped of his money, I doubt he'd be abusive, and if he is, I'm sure he'll be treated with utter contempt by you. Shouting and hurling insults will get him nowhere, and he'll be punished for his aggression just like the rest of us.

[139] But in fact, of course, he's protected by Polyeuctus, Timocrates, and 'Dusty' Euctemon.* These men are typical of the hirelings with which he surrounds himself, but there are others as well: he's put together a caucus of verifiers, who don't appear to be interfering with the democratic process, but are very ready to nod in silent approval of his lies. I don't suppose for one minute that they'll ever get a penny out of him, but there are some men, Athenians, who are just brilliant at being corrupted by the rich. They specialize in attending on them and testifying on their behalf. [140] All this is, of course, terrifying to the rest of us, who do the best we can on our own. That's why you should unite. Then, though they may have more resources—friends and money, for instance—than each of you on his own, they'll be no match for you collectively, and you'll put an end to their insolent ways.

[141] Now, he may try out on you an argument along the following lines: 'Why is it, then, that I got away with treating so-and-so in such-and-such a fashion?', or the same question with the name of another of his victims in the frame. I'm sure you're all familiar with the excuses people offer on such occasions for failing to help themselves. There are thousands upon thousands of them: lack of time, a reluctance to get involved, inability to speak in public, poverty, and so on and so forth. [142] But I don't think Meidias should make use of this argument today. He should prove himself innocent of every charge I've brought against him and, if he fails, that should just be a further reason for putting him to death. I mean, if a man is so powerful that, even when guilty, he can deny each of us, as individuals, a chance to get back at him, there should be no dissenting voices. Now that he's in our hands, he must be punished as a public enemy, for the good of all.

[143] Now, back in the time of Athens' golden age there was, we hear, a man in the city called Alcibiades.* Think of all the important public services he had to his credit—and then see how your ancestors dealt with him when he decided to turn offensive and abusive. The point of the story I'm going to tell is not to compare Meidias with Alcibiades—how stupid and senseless would that make me!—but to enable you to appreciate, Athenians, that qualities such as high birth,

wealth, and power become intolerable if they are accompanied by insolence.

[144] Alcibiades was, we hear, an Alcmeonid on his father's side. In other words, he was descended from people who were exiled by the tyrants for siding with the common people against them, and who then took out a loan from Delphi, liberated the city, and banished the Peisistratids.* On his mother's side, he was related to Hipponicus and therefore belonged to a family with a long record of service to the democracy. [145] As if these distinctions weren't enough, he also personally took up arms in defence of the democracy, twice on Samos and once in Athens itself,* proving his patriotism by risking his life, not by spending money or making speeches. Furthermore, he could boast of victories and crowns won at Olympia in equestrian events,* he was an outstanding military commander, and he was reputedly a first-rate speaker. [146] Nevertheless, the Athenians of the time, your ancestors, refused to accept that any of this gave him the right to lord it over them: they sentenced him to exile and sent him packing. This was a time when Sparta was strong, but your ancestors put up with everything—the fortification of Decelea against them, the capture of the fleet, and so on*—in the belief that involuntary disaster was better than choosing to be victims of abusive insolence.

[147] But did Alcibiades do anything as outrageously abusive as what Meidias has today been shown to have done? True, he struck Taureas, a chorus-producer, in the face, but that was one chorus-producer hitting another, and did not constitute an infringement of the law at issue today, because the law hadn't yet been passed.* He locked up the painter Agatharchus—that's another thing he's supposed to have done.* Yes, but he did so, we hear, because he caught Agatharchus in some reprehensible act. That's hardly classifiable even as a fault. He damaged the herms.* Well, even though all impious acts should be regarded as equally abhorrent, damaging things is rather different from the complete destruction of sacred objects, which is what we've found Meidias to be doing.

[148] So let's consider, by contrast, what sort of a person Meidias is and what kind of man this behaviour of his proves him to be. Now, seeing that you have in your hands a depraved, violent, and abusive man of utterly obscure origins, jurymen, you must realize that it wouldn't just be wrong, but immoral and impious as well to think that he deserves mercy or forgiveness or kindness. Why should he? 'For

his services as a general.' But, left to his own devices, he's no use even as an ordinary soldier, let alone as a leader of men. 'For his speeches, then.' But his public speeches contain not a shred of good advice, and his private speeches consist of nothing but personal insults. [149] 'For his family, by Zeus!' But everyone here knows the secret of his birth: it's like something from a tragedy! His birth was attended by a pair of opposite forces. On the one hand, there was his genuine mother, his birth mother, who was the most level-headed of people; on the other hand, there was his so-called mother, the woman who passed him off as her own, who was the most stupid person in the world. And here's the proof: the sensible one sold him as soon as he was born, while the stupid one bought him when she could have done better for the same price.* [150] This, then, is how he gained control of property that didn't really belong to him, and found a place in a city famed for having the best political system in the world. But even so, I think he finds the laws here completely intolerable and is incapable of adhering to them. The truly barbaric and god-forsaken side of his nature drags him forcibly on and makes it clear that he treats the privileges he currently enjoys as an Athenian citizen as though they did not really belong to him—as indeed they don't.

[151] Despite the fact that the life's work of this loathsome and unscrupulous individual has been so monstrous, his associates have approached me on several occasions, jurymen, advising me to give up, to drop the suit. When I refused, they didn't have the temerity to deny the frequency and magnitude of his offences, nor did they deny that he deserved to be punished, even severely punished, for what he'd done. They tried out the following argument: 'Imagine that he's already been convicted and sentenced. At what level do you expect the court to set the penalty? Don't you see that he's rich and is bound to talk up all his trierarchies and other liturgies? You'd better be careful, or he might get himself off the hook like that; he might end up making you a laughing-stock, by paying the city much less than what he's offering you at the moment.'

[152] My first response to this would be to say that I know you to be men of honour. I can't see you setting his penalty at a level of payment below what will make him stop his abuses. Best of all would be the death penalty, but otherwise the confiscation of all his property. Second, as for his liturgies and trierarchies and claims along those lines, this is my view. [153] What is it to perform a liturgy, Athenians?

Is it declaring, in every Assembly and at every other opportunity: 'We are the liturgists. We are the ones who pay the war levy up front.* We are the rich'? If that's all it takes, I concede that Meidias is the most conspicuous liturgist in Athens. At any rate, he wears us out at every Assembly with his tactless and tasteless rehearsal of the theme. [154] Perhaps we'd better try to see what it is to be a genuine liturgist. I'll tell you what I think, by means of a comparison between him and me, which I'm sure you'll agree is a fair way to go about examining him.

Meidias is about fifty years old, Athenians, or a little less, but he has performed fewer liturgies than I have, and I'm only thirty-two.* In fact, no sooner had I come of age than I served as trierarch; this was in the days when we trierarchs served in pairs, paid for everything out of our own pockets, and recruited the crews ourselves. [155] But Meidias had yet to perform a single liturgy when he reached the age I am now. His involvement dates from when the number of contributors officially became twelve hundred. Meidias and his ilk collect a talent from the twelve hundred and contract the trierarchies out for a talent apiece, and then the state provides the crews and donates the equipment. The upshot is that some of them actually spend nothing, though they appear to have done their duty and they gain exemption from any other liturgies.*

[156] Is there anything else to mention? He did once serve as chorus-producer for the tragic competition, while I was producer for the men's chorus.† Now, as everyone knows, I'm sure, the latter is far more expensive than the former,* and I volunteered for my liturgy, whereas he was appointed on that occasion after the threat of an exchange procedure, which means, of course, that he doesn't deserve any credit for it.* What else? I've laid on a festival dinner for the members of my tribe and I've been one of the chorus-producers for the Panathenaea, but Meidias has done neither of these things. [157] I was a syndicate leader for ten years,* matching the wealthiest men in Athens (such as Phormion, Lysitheides, and Callaeschrus), and paying war levies even though they were assessed not on the basis of my actual means (for I'd been robbed by my trustees), but on the basis of what my father was believed to have left me, which I was due to collect when I came of age.

So much for *my* services to the democracy. What about Meidias? As I speak, he has yet to lead a syndicate, even though no one robbed him of his inheritance and his father left him plenty. [158] Has he made his mark at all? What liturgies has he performed? What money has he spent on worthy causes? I know of nothing, unless we count the following: he's built a house at Eleusis which is so tall that it overshadows his neighbours; he drives his wife to celebrate the Mysteries (or anywhere else she wants to go) on a chariot with a pair of white horses from Sicyon;* he swaggers through the Agora with three or four attendants, making sure that passers-by can hear him talking about goblets, drinking-horns, and cups. [159] Now, I'm not sure how much benefit most of you gain from these objects, built or bought by Meidias to enhance his luxurious and extravagant lifestyle, but I do know that a lot of people, even ordinary folk, have been affected by the insolence these luxuries encourage in him. So when you come across such things, you shouldn't find them admirable or impressive, nor should you take it to be a sign of a public-spirited nature if a man builds a splendid mansion or purchases slave-girls galore or high-end tableware. No, you should look for a man whose hopes for distinction and whose ambitions are satisfied by things that you, the general populace, can enjoy too. You won't find this to be a feature of Meidias' character.

[160] 'But he did donate a trireme, by Zeus!'* Yes, and I'm sure he'll go on and on about it: 'I donated a trireme to the state,' he'll say. What to do, Athenians? If this was a public-spirited act, you should feel the appropriate gratitude and thank him for it—but you must stop short of letting him treat you with insolence. You should never allow that, whatever deeds and achievements a man may have to his credit. But if, on the other hand, we find that he acted out of cowardice, you need to be alerted to that. How will you know? I'll explain what happened. It won't take long, so I'll start at the beginning.

[161] The first such donations here in Athens were for Euboea.* Meidias wasn't among the first, though I was, with Philinus, the son of Nicostratus, as my co-trierarch. The second were for Olynthus; Meidias wasn't involved in this round either. A public-spirited man, however, would surely have put himself forward every time. The round in question was the third round of donations that took place, and this time he did contribute. But look at the circumstances. Even though he was there when the Council was receiving offers from donors, he remained silent at the time. [162] But then news began to arrive that our men were under siege in Tamynae.* The Council

recommended calling up all the rest of the cavalry, including Meidias, and *then* he stepped up at the next Assembly meeting, before the chairmen had even taken their seats, and made his offer—because he was afraid of being sent on the coming expedition.

The proof that this was an attempt to get out of military service and had nothing to do with the good of the city—and the evidence is so clear that he cannot even begin to deny it—lies in what he did next. [163] First, as the meeting progressed and the speeches went on, it began to look as though there would be no need for cavalry reinforcements; it became less likely that the expedition would go ahead, and Meidias made no attempt to embark on the ship he had donated. He sent Pamphilus in his place, the metic from Egypt, while he stayed here and spent the Dionysia doing what he's on trial for today. [164] Later, however, the general, Phocion, ordered the cavalrymen from Argura up to the front to relieve his men, and Meidias' ploy was exposed. At this point, the damned coward deserted his post; instead of taking to the field with the cavalry whose command he had once demanded from you, he boarded his ship. It goes without saying that, if conditions at sea had been at all dangerous, he'd have travelled by land.

[165] Niceratus, the son of Nicias, didn't behave like that, though he was an only child with no child of his own, and was in far from robust health. Nor did Euctemon, the son of Aesion. Nor did Euthydemus, the son of Stratocles. Each of them voluntarily donated a trireme, and none of them tried to get out of serving on the expedition in question. No, they supplied the city with seaworthy ships as a gift, a favour, and then dutifully took up in person the posts assigned them by law. [166] Unlike Meidias, the hipparch.* He deserted his legally assigned post, *and* he's going to count this as a benefaction, when it actually deserves official punishment! But, by the gods, I have no idea what to call this kind of trierarchy. Should we call it a public-spirited act, or is it more suitably seen as a version of the exemption from military service allowed tax-farmers and two-per-cent excise men, as a way to abandon one's post and evade one's military duty? Unable to find any other way to gain exemption from serving in the cavalry, Meidias has invented this new kind of two-per-cent exemption for cavalrymen.*

[167] Here's another point. All the other donating trierarchs provided an escort for the troops as they sailed back from Styra, with the sole exception of Meidias. Ignoring his fellow Athenians, he shipped

back vine-props, cattle, door-panels for his own use, and timber for his silver mines. For this loathsome individual, the trierarchy was not so much a form of service to the state as a business opportunity. You already know that most of what I'm saying is true, but I shall also call witnesses for you.

The witnesses' deposition is read out.

[169] Athenians, in a very short while he'll be bragging to you about his services to the state and all the things he's done. But even if they were as altruistic as he'll claim, rather than being as selfish as I'm showing them to be, it would of course still be a travesty of justice for him to use them to evade punishment for his malicious abuses. After all, you've had many generous benefactors in the past, even if their services weren't cut from the same cloth as Meidias'. They won naval battles, or captured cities, or erected trophies time and again for the greater glory of Athens. [170] But to my knowledge you never have, and never would, grant any of them the licence to assault their personal enemies whenever they feel like it and however they can. You didn't even let Harmodius and Aristogeiton do that, and no one has ever been granted more by you than them, in recognition of their supreme achievement. You'd have found it intolerable if an extra clause had been inscribed on their stele: 'Let them also have the right to assault whomsoever they may wish.' After all, the reason they received all the other honours from you was precisely because they *stopped* people acting abusively.*

[171] Another thing I want to prove to you, Athenians, is that you've thanked Meidias enough – enough not just for the services he has actually rendered (which were trivial enough), but for more, for the most outstanding services imaginable. You needn't think you owe this piece of filth anything. You appointed him—of all people!—treasurer of the *Paralus*.* Later, you made him hipparch, though he's incapable of riding through the Agora on ceremonial occasions, and you chose him for various religious positions, such as administrator of the Mysteries, state sacrificer, and purchaser of sacrificial cattle.* [172] By the gods, do you really think that having his innate depravity, cowardice, and iniquity remedied by official positions, privileges, and appointments is a trivial gift and favour? Take away his 'I've served as hipparch; I've been treasurer of the *Paralus*', and you're left with a worthless nonentity.

[173] There are further facts you should be aware of. First, while he was treasurer of the *Paralus*, he stole more than five talents from the people of Cyzicus. To avoid getting into trouble for this, he began to throw his weight around, harass folk there at every opportunity, and make a nonsense of the treaty, until he created a state of enmity between us and them, and kept the money for himself.* Second, after he'd been appointed hipparch, he impaired the cavalry's effectiveness by introducing new regulations (though he later denied that he had done anything of the sort). [174] Third, he was treasurer of the *Paralus* at the time of our expedition to Euboea, to confront the Thebans. He was assigned twelve talents of state funds, but when you asked him to set sail and provide an escort for the troops, he was no help at all. In fact, he arrived only after Diocles had already made his treaty with the Thebans.* This was also the occasion when he was overtaken at sea by one of the privately funded triremes, proving how well he had equipped the sacred one! Fourth, as hipparch—just wait till you hear this!—as hipparch, this brilliant and wealthy man didn't even venture to buy a horse (a horse!), but led the processions mounted on someone else's! It was Philomelus of Paeania's, in fact. Everyone in the cavalry knows about this. [*To the Clerk of the Court*] Please call the witnesses to these events. [*To the jurors*] Then you'll know that I'm speaking the truth.

The witnesses' deposition is read out.

[175] Now, I'd like to remind you, Athenians, of the past occasions when you've convicted people of festival-related offences after they'd been officially censured by the Assembly. And in some cases I shall be pointing out what they did to deserve your condemnation, so that you can compare their behaviour with that of Meidias. First, then—taking the most recent incident first—the Assembly censured Evander of Thespiae for offences relating to the Mysteries, after a Carian fellow called Menippus had brought a *probolē* against him.† [176] Well, what had Evander done, Athenians, to earn your condemnation? I'll tell you. After winning a commercial suit against Menippus, he couldn't find the man anywhere (or so he claimed), and grabbed hold of him when he was here celebrating the Mysteries. That was all he did to earn your condemnation, nothing else at all. At Evander's trial, you had no objection to the death penalty, but the plaintiff was persuaded to lower his sights. Still, you forced Evander to forfeit the whole sum

he had been awarded in the previous case, which was two talents, and you additionally awarded damages against him, to cover the expenses Menippus calculated he had incurred while attending on you and waiting here for your vote.

[177] So there we have a case where, as a result of a private dispute, a single individual paid a huge penalty just for breaking the law: there was no hint of assault as well. And the size of the penalty was appropriate, because it's your duty to protect the laws and your oath. Every time you sit as jurymen you hold these in trust from the rest of us, and it's your duty to keep them safe for all who come before you with right on their side.

[178] Here's another case of your judging an incident at the Dionysia a criminal act. You officially censured the man in question (who was acting as assistant to the Archon, his son), when all he did was lay hands on someone who wasn't entitled to a seat and exclude him from the theatre. I'm talking about the father of that excellent man Charicleides, who was Archon at the time. [179] Anyway, it was your view that the plaintiff had a strong case. His argument was: 'Suppose I had taken a seat; suppose I was breaking the rules, as you say. But what powers do you, or even the Archon himself, have under the law? You're supposed to tell the attendants to exclude me, not manhandle me yourself. If I still refuse, you're allowed to impose a fine, but you're certainly not allowed to lay hands on me yourself. There are invariably legal steps to take that fall short of assaulting a man.' That was his argument, and you supported it with your vote—though the case never came to court, because the plaintiff died.

[180] And here's another case where, after unanimous censure by the Assembly for a festival-related offence, when the case came to court, you put the defendant to death. I'm talking about Ctesicles, whose offence was hitting someone (a long-standing enemy of his) with a riding-crop that he had with him for the procession. He'd been drinking, but you decided that the issue was insolence rather than alcohol, and that he had seized the opportunity presented by the parade and his intoxication to commit the crime of treating free men as slaves.

[181] Now, everyone would agree, Athenians, I'm sure, that Meidias behaved in a far more reprehensible fashion than any of these men— and one of them lost what he had gained, while another actually lost

his life. Meidias behaved worse than any of them, and he wasn't on parade, he hadn't just won a suit, and he wasn't assisting the Archon either. There's no excuse: what he did was malicious abuse.

[182] Anyway, that's enough about these cases. But what about Pyrrhus the Eteoboutad, indicted for serving as a juryman while in debt to the state?* Some of you thought that he deserved the death penalty, and indeed he was put to death after being tried in your court, even though his attempt to claim the fee was driven by poverty, not insolence. There are plenty of other cases I could mention, where defendants were either put to death or stripped of their citizenship for far less serious offences. Then there was Smicrus, Athenians, whose penalty you assessed at ten talents, and Sciton was fined the same amount because he was judged to have made illegal proposals.* In neither case were you moved to mercy by their children or friends or relatives or anyone else who appeared on their behalf. [183] So don't let the world see you condemning one man for *proposing* illegal measures, and then extending the hand of mercy to another, who actually *did* something illegal. After all, the actions of a man who habitually abuses everyone he comes across are, generally speaking, harder to bear than his words and expressions. If you show no mercy when you have in your hands an ordinary citizen who's guilty of some crime—if you refuse to acquit him, and put him to death or strip him of his citizenship, but forgive a man his assault just because he's rich, you'll be making an exhibition of yourselves, Athenians, and I urge you not to. Why? Because it's wrong. The world needs to see you wielding anger impartially.

[184] There are other, equally important matters that I consider it essential to bring to your attention, and then, after saying a few words about them, I shall stand down. Your characteristic leniency, Athenians, is a great asset and advantage to criminals of every stripe. Listen to me now as I explain why Meidias doesn't deserve the slightest whiff of it. Everyone, I think, makes loans throughout their own lives. I don't mean just literal loans, where money is collected and you become a contributor, but others as well.* [185] Suppose, for instance, that a man is decent and kind, and readily feels sympathy for others: by all rights, in a crisis—if he finds himself in court, for example—he should be treated like that by everyone else. Another man may be an unscrupulous bully who treats others like the lowest of the low, scum, nonentities: by all rights, he should be paid in the same

coin by everyone. Well, if you stop and think about it, you'll see that Meidias has made the latter kind of loan, not the former.

[186] Now, he's going to display his children and shed bitter tears, I'm sure. He'll give us a long, humble speech, weeping and making himself as pitiful as possible. But the more he grovels, Athenians, the more he deserves your loathing. Why? Look at it this way. If he'd been that abusive and violent in his past life because he was utterly incapable of humility, he'd have deserved a degree of forgiveness because it would just have been his bad luck to have been made that way. But if he knows how to behave decently when he wants to, then he has *chosen* the opposite course, and it plainly follows that if he escapes punishment for this today as well, you'll later find him behaving in exactly the same way again.

[187] It's best for you to ignore him, then. You shouldn't take the present situation, when he's deliberately putting on a front, to be more authoritative or trustworthy than what you know of him from personal experience at any other time. I don't have children. I'm not in a position to have them stand by me while I weep and wail over the abuses I've suffered. Does that mean that in your eyes I, the victim, count less than the perpetrator? It had better not! [188] No, when he brings up his children and asks you to think of them when you vote, imagine that I've brought up the laws to stand by my side, and I'm begging and beseeching each of you to think of *them* when you vote. There are many reasons why, in justice, you should take their side rather than his. After all, you've sworn to uphold the laws, Athenians, and it's the laws that protect your rights as citizens and bring you all the blessings you possess. It's not Meidias who does this, nor his children.

[189] He'll claim, I suppose, that I'm a consummate politician. If a politician is someone who offers you what he takes to be the best advice, and does so without annoying or pressuring you, then I wouldn't refuse or deny the label. But we all know that, among our public men, there are some who are unprincipled and make themselves rich at your expense: if that's what it is to be a politician, I must not be one, because I've never taken anything from you, and in fact I've spent my entire fortune, apart from a tiny remnant, as a public servant. But even if I were the worst of this bad lot, it would still be his duty to punish me by legal means, not to assault me while I was performing a liturgy. [190] In any case, not a single one of our politicians

is supporting me today. I don't blame them for that, because nothing I've ever said in public has been designed to help them either. It's just that I made up my mind to focus only on *your* interests, in everything I say or do. Very shortly, however, you're going to see all the politicians lined up in a row next to him. But that's not right: how can he use the term 'politician' as a slur, but still expect their protection?

[191] I suppose he might also suggest that my whole speech today is a carefully contrived artifice. I admit it, Athenians: I have devoted thought to my speech. I see no reason to deny it. Yes, and I did the best job that I could. After all I've endured and am still enduring, it would be ridiculous for me not to take care over what I was going to tell you about it. But in fact my speech was written for me by Meidias! [192] For the true author of today's speech is the one who has supplied the facts that the words describe, not the one who has taken pains to ensure that what he says today is just. That's what I'm doing, Athenians; I'm the first to admit it. But in all likelihood Meidias has never thought about justice in any form in his whole life. If it had ever occurred to him to do so, even for an instant, he'd never have got it so wrong.

[193] I doubt he'll hesitate even to criticize the democratic Assembly. He'll repeat today the charges he came out with at the time of the *probolē*: that the Assembly was made up of men who had stayed at home rather than serve at the front, men who had left the forts deserted, and that the censure he received came from dancers, foreigners, and the like.* [194] All of you who were there, Athenians, remember how outrageously outspoken he became on that occasion: he was under the impression that he was cowing the entire Assembly into submission with his insults and threats, and with the glares he cast at whichever section was currently erupting in protest. And that, of course, is exactly what makes a nonsense of his tears today. [195] [*To Meidias*] You monster, whatever are you thinking? Do you expect pity for yourself or your children from these men here? Do you expect to find them sympathetic to your cause when you've publicly insulted them? No one in the world is so plainly riddled with arrogance as you are. After spending your life annoying everyone, even those who are of no importance to you, with your aggression, your tone of voice, your posturing, your acolytes, your wealth, and your assaults, are you suddenly to be pitied now that you're on trial? That would be a first in human history! [196] You'd certainly have opened up a rich vein—or

invented a neat trick, I should say—if you'd found a way to attract to yourself two complete opposites more or less simultaneously: hostility for your lifestyle, and sympathy as a result of your ruses. But it's impossible to conceive of a situation in which any degree of pity would be appropriate for you. Loathing, resentment, anger—these are the appropriate responses to your behaviour.

[*To the jurors*] But let's return to the point I was making before, that he's going to denounce the people and the Assembly. [197] When he does so, jurymen, I would ask you to bear in mind that this is the man who came before you in the Assembly and denounced his fellow cavalrymen. This was at the time of their expedition to Olynthus.* Now, however, things are the other way around: he's going to denounce the people before a gathering consisting in part of those who served at the front while he stayed at home.* So you have a choice: you can either agree with Meidias' description of you (and he had something to say about you whether you stayed here or served at the front), or, on the contrary, you can see that he never changes under any circumstances, and will never be anything but a god-forsaken brute. That's what I would call him, anyway—and it seems to suit a man who is loathed by his fellow cavalrymen, by his colleagues in the administration, and by his friends.

[198] Now, for better or for worse, the truth will out—and I swear by Zeus, Apollo, and Athena that what I'm about to say is true. When he was busy spreading the rumour that I had dropped the case, I gained the distinct impression that some of those who are, generally, perfectly happy to talk with him were finding him overbearing. And who could blame them, by Zeus? The man's unbearable! He's the only one with money, the only eloquent speaker. To him, everyone else is the lowest of the low, scum, not even a human being.

[199] So what do you think a man so steeped in arrogance will do if he's acquitted today? I'll tell you how you can reach an answer: by considering the evidence of what happened after he had been censured. After being officially censured—for dishonouring the festival, no less—anyone else, even if he faced no further trial or hazard, would take that to be reason enough to efface himself and behave decently at least during the period leading up to the trial, if not for the rest of his life. Anyone else—[200] but not Meidias. No, from that day onwards, he's done nothing but deliver speeches, fulminate, and blow off steam. There's an appointment to be made; Meidias of

Anagyrous is a candidate. He looks after Plutarch's interests and is in on his secrets; Athens isn't big enough to contain him. And throughout, whatever he's doing, the point is to demonstrate that 'The censure hasn't had the slightest effect on me. I'm not at all nervous or concerned about the coming trial.' [201] Athenians, when a man thinks it beneath his dignity to be nervous of you, when he thinks that belittling you enables him to cut a dash, doesn't he deserve to die ten times over? He's expecting you to be unable to handle him. He's rich and bold, big-headed and big-voiced, aggressive, unscrupulous. If he avoids punishment today, will you ever find him in your power again?

[202] As far as I'm concerned, he deserves the severest of penalties just for the speeches he keeps making, if for no other reason. He certainly times them well! I'm sure you know what I'm talking about. If we hear good news, the kind that makes everyone happy, it doesn't matter what the situation is: Meidias is never one of those who share the general pleasure and joy. [203] But if we receive bad news, unwelcome to everyone else, he jumps straight to his feet and delivers the first speech. He leaps on the opportunity, relishing the silence that grips the Assembly when you find events worrying: 'Yes, we know what you're like, Athenians. You don't undertake military ventures abroad; you see no need to pay the war levies. And then you find it surprising that things go badly for you? Do you really think I'm going to pay the levy, while you spend the money on yourselves? Do you really think I'm going to fund a trireme, while you refuse to embark?' [204] This insolent approach of his reveals not only a streak of bitterness, but also the hostility he feels for you, the common people, which he normally keeps buried inside. So when he gets up to his tricks and ploys, Athenians—when he weeps and wails and begs—you must interrupt him and say: 'Yes, we know what you're like, Meidias. You're abusive; you're free with your fists. And then you find it surprising that you should die a fittingly foul death? Do you really think we're going to put up with it, while you beat us up? Do you really think we're going to acquit you, while you refuse to change?'

[205] Now, the men who are going to support him, Eubulus and his cohorts,† will do so not so much because they want to do him a favour—by the gods, no!—as to make trouble for me, because, vehemently but wrongly, Eubulus claims, whatever I say, that there is personal enmity between him and me.* But great success can sometimes bring out the overbearing side of a man's character. Here's the

situation. Despite Eubulus' ill treatment of me, I still don't see him as my enemy, but he refuses to let me off even though I let him off. In fact, he even uses other people's trials to set up confrontations between us, and today he's going to step up and demand that I'm denied the legal protection that is the right of all citizens. All this surely proves that the man has got too big for his boots, and too powerful for the good of each and every one of us.

[206] Besides, Athenians, Eubulus was there at the time. He was sitting in the theatre when the assembled people censured Meidias, and was specifically called on to testify. And, as you know, even when Meidias begged and pleaded with him, he didn't get to his feet. Now, if he thought that the *probolē* had been brought against an innocent man, that was surely the time when, as a friend, he should have spoken up for him. But he can only have refused to testify then because he knew that Meidias was guilty, so if today he's going to appeal for clemency for Meidias, just because he too has a quarrel with me, it would be wrong of you to grant this request. [207] For in a democracy no single individual should be so powerful that a word from him can cause one man to continue to be abused and another to be acquitted.

[*To Eubulus*] No, if you want to hurt me, Eubulus—though, by the gods, I've no idea why you might want to—you have the power and the political clout, so punish me as you see fit, by legal means. But when I've been criminally abused, don't deny me the right to retaliate. If you can't find a legal way to hurt me, you could interpret that as a sign of my good character. After all, if you can't find anything to take me to court for . . . well, you have no difficulty with others.

[208] [*To the jurors*] Now, I've been told that a number of wealthy trierarchs, including Philippides, Mnesarchides, and Diotimus of Euonymon, are going to plead and importune you for Meidias' acquittal, and see no reason why this request of theirs should not be granted. I'd better not say anything derogatory about these men in front of you—that would be crazy!—but I shall tell you what ideas and thoughts should occur to you as they make this request. [209] What you need to bear in mind, jurymen, is this. Not that it will happen—or at least I pray it won't—but suppose these men were to take over the state, along with Meidias and others like him. And suppose that one of you, an ordinary member of society, were to injure one of them in some way, even not as seriously as Meidias has injured me. He would enter a court that was packed with these men—and do

you think he would find them in a lenient or forgiving mood? They'd
bend over backwards to do him a favour, wouldn't they? They'd listen
to a plea for mercy from one of the common people, wouldn't they?
Or would they immediately say: 'What an odious man! What a pest!
To think that he should insult us like this and still draw breath—a fellow who should be content if he's allowed to live!' [210] So don't treat
them differently from how they would treat you, Athenians. Respect
yourselves rather than their wealth or standing. No one stops them
enjoying the many advantages they possess, so don't let them stop you
enjoying the security which is the common property of all Athenian
citizens, under the law.

[211] Even though at the moment Meidias despises most of you
and stigmatizes you as beggars, he wouldn't be suffering anything terrible or pitiable if he had the same resources as most of you, and lost
the surplus that currently encourages his insolence. And it's certainly
wrong of his wealthy friends to tell you: 'Don't judge this case in
accordance with the law, jurymen. Don't help the victim. Break your
oath. Do us this favour.'* They may not employ those exact words,
but that's going to be the gist of every demand they make of you relating to Meidias. [212] But if they're his friends, and if an impoverished
Meidias is inconceivable to them—well, they're incredibly rich and
successful. Let them give him some of their own money. Then you
can do the right thing and vote in accordance with the oath under
which you came into court, and they can do their favours at their
own expense, without involving you in disgrace. But it's quite wrong
for you to betray your oath, while these men, with all their money,
are refusing to surrender a penny of it. [213] There's a sizeable cabal
of wealthy men here today, Athenians. Their wealth has also gained
them a reputation as men of substance, and they're going to come
forward and importune you. You must not betray me to any of them,
Athenians. Each of them is going to be focused on what is good for
him and for Meidias, and you should do the same: focus on yourselves, on the law, and on me, the person who is looking to you for
protection. You know what you think: don't change your minds.

[214] The point is, Athenians, that if the Assembly had acquitted Meidias after hearing the evidence at the time of the *probolē*, the
whole business would have been less serious. One could have found
consolation in the idea that no assault had taken place, that the incidents in question weren't crimes against the festival, and so on. [215]

But, as things are, there could be no worse result for me than for you to acquit him after all that's happened. You made it perfectly clear at the time the crimes were committed that all of you found them abhorrent, disgusting, and intolerable—so much so that when some of the super-rich, including Neoptolemus, Mnesarchides, and Philippides, began to demand of both you and me that we recognize Meidias' innocence, you shouted out 'Guilty!' And when Blepaeus, the banker, came up to me, you cried out 'Here we go again!', on the assumption that I was about to accept his bribe [216]—and so loud was your cry that the noise startled me, Athenians, and as I tried to escape from his grip I let go of my himation and was all but naked in my short khiton! Then, when you bumped into me after the meeting, you said things like: 'Make sure you press your case against the brute. Don't settle out of court. Athens is watching to see what you do.' His crime was censured as malicious abuse; the session at which this decision was reached took place in a holy sanctuary; I stuck to my task without betraying either you or myself. After all this, are you going to acquit him?

[217] Don't do it! It would bring nothing but disgrace. And I don't deserve that outcome from you—how could I, Athenians?—when I'm prosecuting a man who is and is known to be violent and abusive, and who has committed foul crimes during a festival, so that not just you but every Greek who was here in Athens at the time witnessed his malicious abusiveness. The Assembly heard the evidence—and what happened? They censured him and passed him on to you. [218] There's no way, then, for your verdict to remain unobtrusive and unnoticed; you're bound to be asked what decision you came to when the matter was brought before you in the Assembly. No, if you punish him, that will be recognized as the decision of prudent and honourable men who are determined to combat crime; but if you acquit him, it will look as though some other consideration weighed more heavily with you. For this isn't one of those affairs that concern only politicians: he can't do an Aristophon, who annulled the *probolē* against him by returning the crowns.* The charge is one of malicious abuse, and the trial is taking place because there's no way for him to undo anything he has done. So, under these circumstances, is it better to punish him now or later? Now, I'd say. For the verdict affects the community at large, as do all the crimes for which he is now on trial.

[219] Besides, it wasn't just me that Meidias was hitting when he hit me, Athenians. It wasn't just me he was assaulting when he assaulted me, but everyone whose ability to obtain justice for himself falls short of mine. Now, you weren't all acting as chorus-producers, so you weren't all beaten and bullied, but then, of course, as you're well aware, you don't all act as chorus-producers at the same time, and no one could ever humiliate all of you with a single punch! [220] But every time a victim fails to obtain justice in court, everyone in Athens should expect to be the next victim. You shouldn't ignore a crime of this severity, or wait until it's your turn to be abused; you must look well ahead and take precautions. Meidias may hate me, but everyone has some such enemy. Would any of you allow your enemy, whoever he may be, to treat you as Meidias treated me? I doubt it. But then it also follows that you shouldn't abandon me to his tender mercies, Athenians.

[221] Look: in a very short while, when the court rises, each of you will make his way home. Some of you will be in a hurry, perhaps, while others stroll at a more leisurely pace, but either way there'll be nothing to worry about. You won't be glancing over your shoulder. You won't be anxiously wondering who you might run into: will he be friend or foe, tall or short, strong or weak, and so on? And the reason for this equanimity is because in your heart you know, thanks to the security of your trust in the constitution, that no one is going to grab hold of you or assault you or hit you. [222] So you walk the streets in perfect safety—but won't you guarantee the same for me too, before making your way home? What reason do I have, after all that's happened to me, for expecting to survive, if you do nothing to help me now? 'Cheer up, for heaven's sake!' someone might say. 'You're not going to be assaulted any more.' But suppose I am: will you condemn him then, after acquitting him today? No, jurymen, don't abandon me—and don't betray yourselves or the law either.

[223] Consider the power those of you have who make up the juries of the popular courts, however many of you the state requires for any given session: two hundred, or a thousand, or whatever.* All Athenian affairs fall under your jurisdiction. But did you ever stop and wonder where that strength comes from? You'll find that it's not because you're the only citizens who are organized and armed, nor is it because you're fighting fit and in superb physical shape, nor is it because you have the most energy. Nothing of this sort is the reason:

your strength comes from the law. [224] And what is it that makes the law strong? Suppose one of us cries out in protest at some injustice he is suffering: will the law rush to his side and offer help? No. Laws are only words on a page: they can't do that. So where does their strength come from? It comes from you, every time you affirm them and give them the authority to respond to someone in need. In short, the law gets its strength from you and you get your strength from the law. [225] It follows, then, that you should help the law as readily as you would help yourselves if you were victims of injustice. Wherever you find an offence against the law, you should consider it a crime against the community as a whole. You should recognize that there are no mitigating circumstances: service to the state, compassion, the individual involved, rhetorical skill—nothing counts. If someone breaks the law, he must not be allowed to remain unpunished.

[226] Those of you who were spectators during the Dionysia greeted Meidias with boos and hisses when he entered the theatre, and gave every indication of your hostility even before you'd heard a word about him from me.* Before the case had been made, then, you were inclined to condemn him; you invited the victim to retaliate and applauded when I brought the *probolē* against him in the Assembly. [227] Well, the case has been proved. The assembled people, meeting on hallowed ground, have issued a provisional guilty verdict, and a thorough investigation has been conducted into this brute's activities. It has fallen to you to pass judgement on him, and you have the opportunity to settle everything with a single vote. You could help me, gratify the Assembly, deter crime, and afford yourselves security for the future—all by making an example of this man. Why would you hesitate?

For all the reasons I've given, but especially for the sake of the god whose festival Meidias blatantly sullied, cast your vote for his punishment. Both piety and justice demand it.

23. AGAINST ARISTOCRATES

Like *On the Crown*, this speech was composed for a trial arising from an indictment for illegal proposals (*graphē paranomōn*), in this case for the prosecution. It was probably delivered in 352/1, though it has been suggested that (as with the crown case) the charge was lodged several years earlier. The occasion was a proposal to grant special protection to the general Charidemus. Originally from Euboea, Charidemus had served as a successful freelance general in a career which had included fighting against Athens in the service of the Thracian kings Cotys and his son Cersobleptes, Athens' rivals for control of the Chersonese in the 360s and 350s. He was credited with engineering the cession of the Chersonese to Athens by Cersobleptes in the early 350s, for which he was rewarded with citizenship and a golden crown. Charidemus had made a lot of enemies and as a deterrent to attackers Aristocrates proposed that anyone who killed Charidemus should be liable to arrest in any allied territory and that a city or individual harbouring his killer should be excluded from the Athenian alliance. Though the immediate target is Aristocrates, the real target (as with the crown speech) is the honorand, Charidemus, and through him his Athenian associates. Our ancient sources say that the speech was delivered by a man otherwise unknown to us named Euthycles. Euthycles will not have been the only speaker. His attack is on two fronts. The first is alleged contravention of the principles and provisions of Athenian homicide law. The second is to argue that the proposal is disadvantageous to Athens. In the course of the former he expounds on the homicide laws, which makes the speech, despite some distortions, enormously informative. In the course of the latter he presents a Charidemus who is hostile to Athenian interests and duplicitous and gives a matching image of his sometime employer Cersobleptes. The case is not very strong; despite the speaker's fulmination, in prescribing the arrest of the hypothetical killer the decree allowed the accused access to due process. Though Charidemus probably was (as much by need as by character) devious and ruthless, the honours bestowed indicate that the Athenians found him useful.

Charidemus was later to align himself with the anti-Macedonian cause favoured by Demosthenes and was among the public figures whose surrender was demanded by Alexander after the destruction of Thebes in 335. He was eventually killed by the Persian king while serving for him against the invading Alexander.

———

[1] Athenians, I wouldn't want any of you to be under the impression that it's a personal grudge that has brought me to court today to prosecute Aristocrates. Nor am I lightly pitching myself into a feud; I take this risk only because of the severity of the error that has come to my attention. No trivial issue is concerned. The sole point of my efforts, if the way I see it is correct, is to keep you safe in the Chersonese and to prevent you being cheated out of control there yet again.* [2] Now, if you want to learn the facts of the matter and judge the case in accordance with the law, you must look beyond the terms of the decree and think about its consequences. After all, if all it took for you to recognize trickery was just hearing the words, you probably wouldn't have been duped in the first place. [3] But in fact this is one of the criminal aspects of the case—that some of our politicians are doing the best they can to allay your suspicions and put you off your guard, and tailor their speeches and proposals to this end. Please don't be surprised, then, if I show that the same goes for the decree in question too: it has been phrased in such a way that its purpose seems to be to offer Charidemus personal protection, but in fact it makes it impossible for us to justify our presence in the Chersonese and offer it secure protection.

[4] It would be only right, Athenians, for you to pay attention to what I have to say and grant me a favourable hearing. After all, I'm not one of those who make trouble for you; I'm not one of your trusted politicians.* But I am promising to prove that there's a lot at stake. If you work with me to the best of your ability, then, and pay close attention, you'll not only save the situation, but also smooth the path for any of us who thinks he's in a position to do the city good. And he's more likely to think so if he feels that it's not difficult to get a fair hearing from you. [5] As things are at the moment, however, many of us—inexpert speakers, perhaps, but better people than the experts—are so afraid of not getting a fair hearing from you that we don't even bother to turn our minds to political matters. Speaking for myself, I assure you, with all the gods as my witnesses, that I too would have hesitated to bring this indictment, if I didn't consider it quite disgraceful to do nothing, to keep quiet, when I could see that certain people had plans that would harm the city. Besides, I had already spoken out and denounced others for what I saw as their wrongdoing on an earlier occasion, at the time when I served as trierarch in the Hellespont.*

[6] I'm aware that in some quarters Charidemus is regarded as a benefactor of the city. But I know what he's done, and if I can find a way to tell you what I want about it, I'm sure I'll prove that, so far from being a benefactor, there's no one in the world more malevolent than him. He has gained, in other words, a completely unsuitable reputation. [7] Now, if the worst aspect of Aristocrates' decree, Athenians, was that it protects the kind of man I intend to prove Charidemus to be—and it's no ordinary protection, since it grants, in his case, a special and illegal penalty if anything happens to him—I'd have started with that, so that you could see how little he deserves to be the object of this decree. But in fact there's another, more pernicious consequence of the decree which you need to know about first, and must be borne in mind.

[8] First of all, however, it's essential for me to explain what it is that has enabled you to control the Chersonese, and control it securely. Unless you understand this, you won't be able to see where the wrongdoing lies. Here's the situation, Athenians. When Cotys died,* Thrace gained three kings instead of one: Berisades, Amadocus, and Cersobleptes. This led to their becoming rivals, and they began to court us and try to win our favour. [9] Now, there were people who wanted to put an end to this, Athenians. They wanted to depose the other kings and make Cersobleptes the sole ruler,* and they managed to get a preliminary resolution to this effect passed by the Council. The wording of the document actually makes it seem as though this was the last thing they wanted to see, but it was in fact their principal goal, as I'll explain.

[10] When Berisades, one of the kings, died Cersobleptes began to make war on Berisades' sons and Amadocus, in violation of his treaty with us and the oath he had sworn to ratify it. It soon became clear that Athenodorus,* who was related by marriage to Berisades, would side with Berisades' sons, and that Simon and Bianor would side with Amadocus for the same reason. [11] Cersobleptes' champions therefore put their minds to the question of how to take these men out of the game. The idea was to isolate Cersobleptes' rivals and leave Charidemus, who was trying to gain the throne for Cersobleptes, in complete control. The plan came in two parts.† First, they wanted to see you pass this decree into law, so that anyone who killed Charidemus would become liable to seizure. Second, they wanted Charidemus elected general, [12] not only because Simon and Bianor,

who had been awarded Athenian citizenship, were unlikely to take up arms against a general of yours (while, as an Athenian citizen by birth, Athenodorus wouldn't even contemplate it), but also because they would avoid the charges stipulated in the decree, which would certainly come the general's way in the event of Charidemus' death. In this way, they would both deny their opponents any allies and provide their own side with immunity, and then it would be easy for them to drive Cersobleptes' rivals from the country and make the monarchy theirs to dispose of.

[13] The facts themselves convict them of these plans and schemes. No sooner had they initiated hostilities than Aristomachus— [*Euthycles points*] there he is, Aristomachus of Alopece—arrived here as their spokesman. The speech he gave in the Assembly contained, among other things, praise of Cersobleptes and Charidemus, and a detailed account of their alleged respect for you. [14] He said that Charidemus was the only man capable of getting Amphipolis back for you,* and he advised you to make him general. But this preliminary resolution of the Council had already been drawn up and devised by them, so that, if you were won over by the assurances and hopes for the future that Aristomachus held out, the Assembly would immediately ratify the resolution and nothing would stand in their way.

[15] The human mind could not have come up with a more crafty or cunning plan for the expulsion of the other kings and the establishment of their own candidate as sole ruler. They intimidated those who had sided with Cersobleptes' two rivals and forced them to guard against the possibility of malicious and unwarranted charges, and they made it possible for the man who was trying to gain power for just one king to act without fear, when all his schemes were directly opposed to Athenian interests.

[16] This is not the only thing that shows that I'm right about the purpose of the preliminary resolution. The decree itself is pretty conclusive evidence. 'If anyone kills Charidemus,' it says, and then (without pausing to say anything about what his crime was, and whether or not his activities were good for Athens) it immediately goes on: 'he is liable to seizure and removal from allied territory.' [17] Well now, no enemy of ours, or his either, is ever going to enter the territory of our allies, as his assassin or for any other purpose, so it's not our enemies who are going to become liable to punishment under this clause, but people who are our friends, and are enemies of his

in so far as his endeavours oppose Athenian interests. It's someone like that who will be alarmed by this decree, and will guard against the possibility of being forced to become our enemy. And that's a description of anyone who wants to put us in his debt by restraining Charidemus when his endeavours oppose Athenian interests—such as Athenodorus, Simon, Bianor, and the Thracian kings.

[18] So, Athenians, there you have it: the purpose of the preliminary resolution is to trick the Assembly into ratifying it, and the reason we've brought this indictment today is because we want to stop it. Now, I've promised to prove three things: first, that the decree is illegal; second, that it harms Athens' interests; third, that the beneficiary of the decree doesn't deserve it. So, since you are the ones who are going to listen to me, perhaps it would be right for me to ask you to decide in which order you'd like to hear these three points.* [19] Which one do you think you'd like to hear me talk about first? The illegality? All right, then.

Now, I'd like to beg a favour of you all—a perfectly fair request, I'm sure. There may be people here, Athenians, who have been taken in by Charidemus, and who see him as our benefactor. I would ask those people not to give my account of the legal situation an unfavourable hearing, in a spirit of contentiousness. Don't make this a reason for denying yourselves the chance to vote in a way that doesn't make you oath-breakers. And don't deny me the chance to go through everything for you as I see fit. I'll tell you how I'd like you to listen to me, and you can decide whether or not it's a fair request. [20] As I discuss the legal situation, dismiss any thoughts about the beneficiary of the decree and his character, and focus your attention entirely on the question of the decree's legality. And as I prove what happened and explain how you were taken in by him, look at what he did and ask yourselves whether or not my account is accurate. [21] And as I consider whether it would benefit or harm the city to have this decree in force, ignore everything else and ask yourselves only whether or not my arguments on this topic are sound. If you listen to me like that, taking each point separately and not trying to think about everything at once, you'll gain a precise understanding of what you need to know, and it will greatly help me to get my points across. But none of my arguments will be long.

[22] [*To the Clerk of the Court*] Take these laws and read them out. They'll help me to prove the illegality of their proposal.

One of the laws of the Areopagus on homicide is read out:
The Areopagus Council is to judge cases of premeditated murder and
wounding, arson, and poisoning, if anyone kills by administering poison.

[23] Stop there, please. [*To the jurors*] You've heard both the law and
the decree, Athenians. I'll tell you how I think you will most easily
follow what I have to say about the illegalities. Ask yourselves to what
class the beneficiary of the decree belongs: is he a foreigner, a resident alien, or a citizen? It would be wrong to say he was a resident
alien, and it would be unfair to say he was a foreigner, since the gift
of the people, by which he became a citizen, should in all fairness
take priority. So, apparently, I'd better take him to be an Athenian
citizen as I talk about him. [24] By Zeus, do you see how open and
fair a speech I'll be giving? I'm allowing him membership of the class
which entitles him to the greatest respect. But I still don't think it
right for him to acquire illegal privileges which even those of us who
were born Athenian citizens don't have. Which illegal privileges? The
ones Aristocrates has included in his proposed decree.

What it says in the law is that 'the Areopagus Council is to judge
cases of premeditated homicide and wounding, arson, and poisoning,
if anyone kills by administering poison'. [25] Now, despite adding the
'if anyone kills' clause, the legislator provides for a trial and refrains
from stipulating what is to happen to the perpetrator until a trial has
taken place. And that was the right thing for him to do, Athenians: he
was taking thought for the moral status of the entire city. What do
I mean? Just that it's impossible for all of us to know who the killer is,
and the legislator thought it monstrous to believe this kind of accusation without a trial. He assumed that, since it is we who are going to
retaliate on the victim's behalf, we should have things explained to us,
until we understood what the culprit had done and were convinced
of his guilt. Punishment is morally acceptable only when you have
the full picture. [26] Another idea of his was that, before a trial takes
place, terms such as 'murder', 'temple-robbery', 'treason', and so on
name *charges*; only after someone has been judged and found guilty
do they name crimes. So he didn't see it as his job to stipulate what
penalty any given charge carried, but only that there should be a trial.
And hence he stated that the Areopagus Council was to judge cases
of murder, but he didn't state how defendants were to be punished if
convicted.

[27] So much for the law-maker. What about our decree-maker? He says: 'If anyone kills Charidemus.' He uses the same phrase as the legislator for the injury—'if anyone kills'—but that's as far as the similarities go. There's nothing in the decree about submitting to a trial, only that the alleged culprit is liable to seizure. Bypassing the court specified by the law, he hands the alleged culprit over to his accusers untried, for them to deal with him as they see fit, when his guilt or innocence is still uncertain. [28] And once they have him in their hands, they have the right to stretch him, torture him, and extort money from him. But the law immediately following the one I've just read explicitly and unequivocally states that nothing like that is to happen even to men who've been found guilty of murder. [*To the Clerk of the Court*] Please read out the law I'm talking about, the next one.

Another law is read out:
It is permissible to kill murderers within Athenian territory, or arrest them in accordance with the procedure stated in the table,* but not to maltreat them or force them to compensate, on penalty of a fine of double the damages. Any citizen may introduce the case to the Archons, according to their several jurisdictions, and the Heliaea is to adjudicate the case.

[29] [*To the jurors*] There you have the law, Athenians. Think about it. Do you see what a good law it is—how the legislator has taken pains to ensure that there's nothing immoral about it? The main thing to notice is that, though he uses the term 'murderer', it refers to a man who has already been sentenced. For, in truth, no one becomes liable to this description until he's been convicted and found guilty. [30] How can one be sure of this? Both this law and the one before it supply the evidence. The first law states that cases of *killing* are to be referred to the Areopagus Council. The second law introduces the *murderer* and stipulates how he is to be treated. In other words, where the issue is the charge, the legislator has called for a trial, and when the culprit has been found guilty, and therefore can be called a 'murderer', he makes provision for the punishment. So we should understand him to be talking in the second law about people who have already been found guilty.

And what is that he says? 'It is permissible to kill or arrest.' [31] And to hold in one's own home? Or to treat as one wishes? Not at all. How, then? 'In accordance with the procedure stated in the table.'

And what is that? You already know the answer. It is the Thesmothetes who have the power to impose the death penalty on people in exile for murder. Just last year, you all saw them take a man into custody from the Assembly.* So it's the Thesmothetes to whom we're supposed to entrust murderers who have been arrested. [32] But how does this differ from holding a murderer oneself? Because, Athenians, to hand the perpetrator over to the Thesmothetes is to give the law authority over him, but to hold him in one's own house is to claim such authority for oneself. In the former case, punishment will be directed by the law, but in the latter case, punishment will be at the whim of the arrester. And there's a huge difference, of course, between making the law responsible for punishment and giving that power to a man's enemy.

[33] 'But not to maltreat or force to compensate,' says the legislator. What does this mean? Well, you all know what not maltreating him means: not thrashing him, not tying him up, and so on and so forth. 'Not forcing him to compensate' means not taking any money from him, because in the old days people thought of money as compensation. [34] So the law specifies how a murderer, one who has already been found guilty, is to be punished and where this punishment is to take place: in the victim's own country. It expressly rules out other forms of punishment and other places. Our decree-writer, however—well, he doesn't recognize these distinctions at all. He takes a completely different tack. After 'If anyone kills Charidemus,' he says: 'he is liable to seizure wherever he may be found.'

[35] [*To Aristocrates*] What do you mean by this? By law, even those already found guilty can't be arrested except within Athenian territory, but you're proposing that a man should be liable to seizure without trial anywhere in allied territory? The laws do not permit seizure even in Athenian territory, and yet you're allowing him to be seized wherever he may be found? By making him liable to seizure, you're permitting everything that the law forbids: extorting money, maltreatment against a living person, detaining and injuring a man, killing him. [36] I can't imagine a bill with less legality than yours. I can't see how one could contain more preposterous proposals. You had two terms available—'killer' and 'murderer', the former applicable to someone under accusation, and the latter to someone who has been found guilty. In the rubric, you used the term for someone under accusation, and yet you propose that people who haven't had

their day in court should be punished in a way that the laws forbid
even for people who've been found guilty. What you've done is eliminate the intermediate stage. [*To the jurors*] Between accusation and
conviction, you see, comes a trial—which is simply missing from this
man's proposed decree.

[37] [*To the Clerk of the Court*] Now read out the next laws.

Another law is read out:
If anyone kills or is responsible for the death of a murderer who is avoiding
the border market and the Amphictyonic games and rites, he shall be liable
to the same penalty as the killer of an Athenian citizen, and the Ephetae
shall judge the case.

[*To the jurors*] You need to understand what the legislator was getting
at with this law, Athenians. I'll show you how much care he took to
ensure both precision and legality. [38] 'If anyone kills or is responsible for the death of a murderer,' he says, 'who is avoiding the border
market and the Amphictyonic games and rites,* he shall be liable to
the same penalty as the killer of an Athenian citizen, and the Ephetae
shall judge the case.' What does this mean?

The legislator thought that, if a man who has been tried and convicted in a homicide case flees abroad for safety, it's right to exclude
him from his victim's country, but wrong to kill him wherever he may
be found. What decided him was the certainty that if *we* kill people
abroad, others will kill people who have fled here. [39] If it were
permissible to kill him anywhere, it would destroy the last chance of
safety for everyone who has lost a case. What last chance? The chance
of moving and changing their place of residence from where their
victims live to a place where no one has been wronged by them. He
didn't want to see that hope destroyed, and he didn't want to generate an endless sequence of retaliations for crimes. So he wrote: 'if
anyone kills a murderer who is avoiding the border market.' What
does this mean? It means: as long as the murderer is keeping away
from the borders of his own country. For in the old days that, I think,
was where we and people from neighbouring countries close to the
borders used to meet, which is why he called it a 'border market'.

[40] And what about the Amphictyonic rites? Why did he also
exclude the murderer from them? He excludes him from everything
that was a part of his victim's life before he was killed—meaning
primarily his country and everything of importance there to both

religion and society—and he specified the border market as the limit of the exclusion zone. And so he also excludes him from the Amphictyonic rites, because, if the victim was Greek, those rites were part of his life. Why from the games too? Because everyone can attend the games that take place in Greece. They were a part of the victim's life just as they are a part of everyone's. So the killer has to stay away from them too.

[41] These, then, are the places from which the killer is banned by law. Now, if he's killed elsewhere, outside these places, the legislator has stipulated the same punishment as for killing an Athenian citizen. He didn't identify the fugitive by the name of his city, because the city is no longer part of his life, but by the name of the deed to which he owes his liability. That's why he says 'If anyone kills a murderer'. Then, in the course of stating the places from which the murderer is excluded, he mentioned the name of Athens, but only to ensure that the proper legal punishment is applied: 'He shall be liable', he says, 'to the same penalty as the killer of an Athenian citizen.' How different this is, Athenians, from the wording of the decree before us!

[42] But it's appalling for someone to propose that men the law permits to live in safety as exiles (as long as they stay away from the places I've mentioned) should be liable to seizure. It's disgusting to remove the benefit of the compassion which those unaffected by the crimes are likely to feel for people who are down on their luck. After all, no one knows for whom the benefit is being held in store: it could be any of us, since no man's future fortune is certain. As things stand, if Charidemus' killer (supposing that the murder had actually taken place) is killed in his turn by men who treat him as liable to seizure after he has fled into exile and while he is keeping away from the legally proscribed places, [43] his killers will become liable to a charge of homicide, [*turning to Aristocrates*] and so will you! The law says 'If anyone is responsible', and that will be you, because it was your decree that made the killing possible. So if the killer is killed and we let you and your kind get away with it, we'll be living in the company of polluted people,* or alternatively, if we prosecute you, we'll be forced to act contrary to one of our own resolutions. [*To the jurors*] Do you see how important it is for you to cancel this decree? There are solid, important reasons for doing so.

[44] [*To the Clerk of the Court*] Please read the next law.

Another law is read out:
If anyone drives, seizes, or carries off beyond the border the property of
a killer who has left the country, but whose assets remain unconfiscated,
he shall be liable to the same penalties as if he had acted within Athenian
territory.

[*To the jurors*] Here we have another good and compassionate law,
Athenians—and, once again, we shall find that Aristocrates is in
breach of it. [45] The subject is a killer who has left the country, but
whose property remains unconfiscated. In other words, the law is
talking about a case of involuntary killing. How do we know? Because
it says 'who has left the country', rather than 'who is in exile', and
because it specifically says that his assets remain unconfiscated,
whereas the assets of intentional murderers become state property.

[46] So, what does it say? 'If he drives, seizes, or carries off beyond
the border'. What does this 'beyond the border' mean? For all murderers, the 'border' is the limit of the country where his victim lived.*
The law allows his property to be driven and carried off from there,
but not from anywhere beyond the border. And anyone who breaks
this law is liable to the same punishment that he'd have incurred if the
wrongdoing had taken place at home: 'he shall be liable to the same
penalties as if he had acted within Athenian territory.'

[47] Now, if one were to ask Aristocrates—and it's not a foolish
question: don't think that—whether he knew that Charidemus' future
held death at someone else's hand rather than of natural causes, he'd
say no, of course. But let's assume him murdered. [*To Aristocrates*]
There are still further questions: do you know whether it was premeditated or accidental? Was the killer an Athenian citizen or a foreigner? Since it's impossible for you to claim to know these things,
[48] you ought, I suppose, to have qualified your 'If anyone kills' by
adding whether it was done deliberately or accidentally, justifiably
or unjustifiably, by a foreigner or a citizen. Then it doesn't matter
who the killer was: he still gets what the law stipulates as his deserts.
But, by Zeus, after writing down the name of just the accusation, you
shouldn't have leapt to 'he shall be liable to seizure'. Does your wording recognize *any* borders? I mean, you let the murderer be seized
and carried off from anywhere, despite the fact that the law clearly
forbids anyone or anything to be driven 'beyond the border'. [49] The
law forbids driving or seizure beyond the border, but the implication

of your decree is that anyone who feels like it can treat an accidental killer as one who is liable to seizure, and carry him off to the victim's country. But doesn't this make life very confusing? You're eliminating the motive, aren't you, when that is what makes any action good or bad?

[50] [*To the jurors*] Look: you find this distinction everywhere, not just in homicide cases. The law says 'If anyone strikes another, *initiating the act of aggression*', as if to say that no crime was committed if he was defending himself. The law says 'If anyone slanders another', but immediately adds '*with falsehoods*', as if to say that it was all right if he was speaking the truth. The law says 'If anyone kills another', but immediately adds '*deliberately*', as if to say that an accident is quite different. 'If anyone injures another, *with malice aforethought*'— everywhere we find the motive determining the nature of the act. [*To Aristocrates*] But you don't recognize it. You write just 'If anyone kills Charidemus, he shall be liable to seizure', whether or not it was an accident, justifiable, self-defence, legally permissible, or whatever.

[51] [*To the Clerk of the Court*] Now read the next law.

Another law is read out:
Under no circumstances are those who obtain a warrant against exiles to be prosecuted, if an exile returns to where he is forbidden.

[*To the jurors*] This is one of Dracon's laws, Athenians, as are the other homicide laws that I've cited for purposes of comparison. We need to see what it means. 'There is to be no prosecution', he says, 'of those who obtain a warrant against killers who return to where they are forbidden.'* There are two points of law here, both of which are infringed by Aristocrates' decree. First, Dracon permits a warrant to be drawn up against a murderer, while forbidding his seizure. Second, he permits a warrant to be drawn up against a murderer only if the murderer returns to where he is forbidden, not to any old place. [52] And where is he forbidden to go? Back to the city he's in exile from. And he makes this point with exceptional clarity by saying 'If anyone *returns*', a word that cannot refer to anything except the city a man is in exile from. I mean, it's impossible, naturally, for a man to *return* to a city from which he was never ejected in the first place. So the law allows a warrant, but only if the killer returns to where he is forbidden. Aristocrates, however, makes the fugitive liable to seizure even in places where it's perfectly legal for him to be.

[53] [*To the Clerk of the Court*] Now read another law.

Another law is read out:
If anyone kills another accidentally in an athletic competition, or by slay-
ing him in the road,* or unwittingly in battle, or after finding him with
his wife, mother, sister, daughter, or concubine kept for the begetting of free
children,* the killer shall not be sent into exile.

[*To the jurors*] Time and again, Athenians, Aristocrates' decree breaks
some law or other, but all these infringements pale into insignificance
beside his violation of the law I've just had read out. The law clearly
and simply states the circumstances under which killing is permissible, but Aristocrates ignores all that and jumps from 'If anyone kills'
to the punishment, without any mention of the circumstances. [54]
But look at the original legislator's careful distinctions, and you'll see
what a good and respectful job he did. If someone causes death in an
athletic competition, he specifically states that this is no crime. Why?
Because he focused on the killer's intentions rather than just the
event. And what was the killer's purpose? To defeat a living opponent,
not to kill him. If his opponent succumbed during the struggle for
victory through lack of fitness, Dracon regarded *him* as responsible,
and hence he assigned no penalty on his account.

[55] Or again, take 'If he kills a man unwittingly in battle'. There's
no pollution involved in this either, and exculpation makes sense: if
I killed a man, taking him to be an enemy soldier, I deserve to be forgiven rather than taken to court. 'Or', he says, 'after finding him with
his wife, mother, sister, daughter, or concubine kept for the begetting
of free children.' He finds a killer guiltless in such cases, and he's quite
right to let him off, Athenians. [56] Why? Look at it this way. The reason we fight our enemies is to defend our families from wanton abuse,
and in their defence Dracon even allowed us to kill friends, if they
violate and seduce members of our families in contravention of the
law. Friends and enemies aren't born friends and enemies: it's what
they do that makes them one or the other. So the law allows us to treat
men who act in a hostile fashion towards us as enemies and punish
them. When there are so many situations in which it's legitimate to kill
others, wouldn't it be shocking for Charidemus to be the only person
in the world who could not be killed under these circumstances?

[57] Suppose Charidemus left Thrace and came to live in a Greek
city. It's the sort of thing that's presumably happened to others in

the past. He would no longer enjoy the power which enabled him to get away with all his illegal activities, but his character and appetites would still drive him to try to carry on with them. But people will just have to keep quiet and let him get away with abusive behaviour, won't they? At any rate, with this decree in force, it won't be safe to kill him or punish him as the law allows. [58] Someone might take me up on that and ask: 'But where could this possibly happen?' But that doesn't stop me asking, in my turn, 'Who could possibly kill Charidemus?' Let's not bother with this. Since the decree we're examining is concerned not with an event that has already happened, but with something that may never happen at all—no one can possibly know—we can leave both possibilities in the same boat as regards the future. Let's adjust our expectations to the uncertainty, as human beings must, and pursue our investigation on the assumption that the future could go this way or that.

[59] Now, if you cancel the decree and he's killed, you can still avenge his death, by legal means. But if you leave the decree in place, and he stays alive, and he wrongs someone, it will be impossible for the victims of his abuse to obtain legal redress. However you look at it, this decree contradicts laws and it would be better not to ratify it.

[60] [*To the Clerk of the Court*] Read the next law, please.

Another law is read out:
If in self-defence one immediately kills a man who is forcibly and unjustly carrying off or seizing one's property, the killing incurs no penalty.

[*To the jurors*] Here are further conditions that make killing permissible: 'If in self-defence one immediately kills a man who is forcibly and unjustly seizing or carrying off one's property, the killing incurs no penalty.' By Zeus, do you appreciate what an excellent law this is? By including 'immediately' among the conditions that make killing permissible, he ruled out the time it takes to premeditate mischief. And with the words 'in self-defence' he's obviously extending the right to the victim and the victim alone. So the law allows a man to kill in immediate self-defence, but there's none of this in Aristocrates' version. He says just 'If anyone kills', even if it's a legally permissible killing.

[61] 'But this is sheer malice, by Zeus! I mean, who or what is Charidemus going to forcibly and unjustly carry off or seize?' No one

will be spared! Give a man an army and, as I'm sure you're aware, he seizes and carries off for ransom anyone he thinks he can overpower. By Earth and all the gods, isn't it monstrous, then, and blatantly illegal (in breach not only of written law, but also of principles common to all humankind), to forbid me to resist when someone is forcibly seizing and carrying off my property as though I were an enemy? But that will be the case, if it's forbidden to kill Charidemus even under these circumstances. If he commits the crime of forcibly seizing and carrying off someone's property, like some kind of brigand, the killer will be liable to seizure, even though, under these circumstances, the law finds him guiltless.

[62] [*To the Clerk of the Court*] Read the next law, please.

Another law is read out:
If anyone is responsible for subverting or altering this statute, be he in or out of office, he shall be disfranchised, and his children, and all he has.

[*To the jurors*] This law is perfectly explicit, Athenians: 'If anyone is responsible for subverting or altering this statute, be he in or out of office, he shall be disfranchised, and his children, and all he has.' Do you see the great and considerable care the legislator took on your behalf to ensure that the law will remain in force, without subversion or alteration? But this means little or nothing to Aristocrates, who's busy altering and subverting it. I think 'altering' is exactly the right term to use for what a man is doing to the law when he permits punishment without the involvement of the designated courts and beyond the border of the forbidden zone—when he denies people a fair hearing and makes them liable to seizure. And surely 'subverting' is correct when he drafts a series of clauses, every single one of which directly contradicts the terms of the laws.

[63] The laws I've mentioned aren't the only ones he's broken, Athenians—not by a long way. But there are too many for me to have compared them all with the decree. Here's a summary, though: he is in contravention of every single law there is relating to the homicide courts—the laws that regulate the summons, the witnesses' testimony, the litigants' oaths,* or some other aspect of the proceedings. The decree he has drafted contravenes them all. For when there's no summons, no testifying by witnesses, and no oath—when he jumps straight from charge to punishment and it's a punishment that is forbidden by law, how else can one describe it?

In fact, there are five courts, designated by the laws to handle all our homicide cases.* [64] 'By Zeus!' someone might object. 'But those courts are worthless, an unjust invention, whereas Aristocrates' proposals are good and just.' My position is exactly the opposite. First, I can't imagine that there's ever been anything worse for the city than this decree of his, and, second, I'm sure we'll find there to be no courts in the world that compare with ours for prestige and justice.

In this regard, I'd like briefly to mention some stories that bring our city a degree of admiration and esteem. I'm sure you'll enjoy hearing them too! I'll begin by returning to the gift that has been bestowed on Charidemus; you'll find this particularly instructive. [65] We made Charidemus a citizen, Athenians. By means of this gift, we allowed him to share in our rites, ceremonies, customs, and everything that constitutes the Athenian way of life. Now, we have many institutions here that stand out from what you find elsewhere, but one occupies a particularly lofty pedestal. This is the Areopagus court. There are more good stories to be told about it than about any other court—some traditional tales, others we've witnessed ourselves. It's worth listening to one or two of them, to make the point.

[66] First, then, in ancient times—or so the myths tell us—the Areopagus court was the only one where the gods chose to give and receive compensation for murder, and sat in judgement on one another's disputes. So we hear that Poseidon obtained satisfaction there from Ares for his son Halirrhothius, and that the twelve gods judged the case involving the Eumenides and Orestes.* Moving on from ancient to more recent times, the Areopagus court has proved to be the only one that no regime—tyranny, oligarchy, or democracy—has dared to deprive of its jurisdiction over homicide cases.* Everyone believes that in these cases a judgement reached by themselves would have less authority than one reached by this court. Moreover, in this court alone no convicted defendant and no defeated prosecutor has ever demonstrated the injustice of the final verdict.

[67] This is the bastion, with its garrison of legal punishments, that our decree-writer seeks to breach. He has made it possible for Charidemus to act as he pleases while he lives, and in the event of his death he has given the man's friends and relatives the right of sycophancy.* But think. You all know, of course, that in the Areopagus, the legally sanctioned and ordained seat for the judging of homicide cases, the prosecutor in a murder trial will begin by swearing an oath,

invoking obliteration, if he should lie, for himself, his family, and his house. [68] And you also know that the way in which the oath is sworn is extraordinary, and not used in any other context: he'll take the oath while standing over the entrails of a boar, a ram, and a bull, all duly sacrificed by the proper officials on one of the appropriate days, so that the sanctity of the whole proceeding is ensured not only by the timing, but also by the officiants. Even after swearing such a solemn oath, the prosecutor's word isn't just taken on trust, and if he's caught in a lie, he'll carry the taint of oath-breaking back to his children and family, and that's all he'll get out of the trial. [69] And even if the charges he's bringing seem justified and he obtains a conviction for murder, he gains no power over the condemned man. Punishment is up to the laws and the relevant officials, while the prosecutor is allowed no more than the right to watch the convicted defendant paying the legally ordained penalty. So much for the prosecutor's rights. As for the defendant, the oath-taking procedure is the same, but he's allowed to leave after delivering his first speech, and neither the prosecutor nor the court nor anyone else has the authority to stop him.*

[70] Why is this, Athenians? It's because those who originally introduced these regulations—were they heroes, perhaps, or even gods?—had no intention of oppressing people who had just lost a court case. They acted humanely and did what they could, within the bounds of propriety, to relieve the burden of their disaster. But now we can see that our decree-writer flouts all these fine principles; his decree contains not the slightest trace of any of them. And so here, first, is one court whose written regulations and unwritten principles are contravened by the decree.†

[71] Second, there's another court, the one by the Palladium,* which hears cases of involuntary manslaughter: we'll find that he subverts this one as well, and is in breach of its rules and principles. In this court too the proceedings consist of oath-taking, then speeches, then the court's decision, and again none of this appears in Aristocrates' decree. If the court finds the defendant guilty, neither the prosecutor nor anyone else gains power over him: he's the responsibility of the law. [72] And what does the law ordain? A man found guilty of involuntary manslaughter is offered certain specified times when he has to leave, by a pre-arranged route, and he has to remain abroad until he has obtained forgiveness from his victim's family.† Then he's allowed to return, but not just like that: there are various

things he has to do first, as directed by the law, such as sacrificing and undergoing purification.*

All of these legal provisions are right, Athenians. [73] It's only fair that the penalty prescribed for involuntary manslaughter should be less than for premeditated murder; it's only right to ensure that the killer can leave safely before ordering him into exile; it's sound practice for the returning killer to perform the appropriate rites and be purified in the customary ways; and it's good for the laws to have overall authority. Here, then, we have a series of precise and fair measures from the original legislators—and our decree-writer is in breach of every single one of them. So now there are two courts, both of high dignity and stature, with their procedural regulations handed down from time immemorial, that this unconscionable man has trampled underfoot.

[74] There's another court in addition to these, a third, the most sacred and awesome of them all: it hears cases where the defendant admits the killing, but contends that it was a lawful act. This is the court by the Delphinium.* Now, it seems to me, jurymen, that the very first question addressed by the men who originally established the regulations for these cases was whether they should consider every single case of murder a threat to society, or whether in certain cases it might not in fact have been the right thing to do. Bearing in mind that a panel of *divine* jurors had acquitted Orestes, a self-confessed matricide, they decided that murder was sometimes justified, because gods wouldn't have reached an unjust verdict. Having arrived at this conclusion, the next step was to write down and clearly define the conditions under which killing is permitted. [75] Aristocrates, however, recognizes no exceptions. *Anyone* who kills Charidemus becomes liable to seizure, even if it was a justified killing, permitted by law. But there are two attributes which apply to everything we do or say: justice and injustice. It's quite impossible for anything we do or say to possess both attributes at the same time: how could the same thing be both just and unjust? But we ask ourselves, about every act, which of the two it is, and we judge acts bad if we find them to be unjust, or good and honourable if we find them to be just. [*To Aristocrates*] But your 'If anyone kills' remains bare of qualification by either justice or injustice. You mention just the charge, unqualified, and then immediately add 'he is liable to seizure'. And so now we find you in violation of this court and its regulations, as well as the other two.

[76] [*To the jurors*] There's a fourth court as well, the one by the Prytaneum.* This is for cases where something like a stone or a piece of wood or metal has fallen and struck someone, and where someone else, without knowing who threw the death-dealing object, saw what happened and has the object in his possession. Here the objects are put on trial. Now, if it's unacceptable to deny inanimate and insensate objects a trial when they've become liable to such a serious charge, what about someone who may perhaps be completely innocent? All right, let's call him guilty, but he's still a human being, one of us. So it must surely be seriously wrong to make him liable to seizure, denying him a hearing and a verdict, for such a charge.

[77] There's yet another court, a fifth, the dignity of which he has violated, as you shall see. It's the one 'in Phreatto'. This, Athenians, is the court appointed by law for hearing cases 'If anyone in exile for involuntary manslaughter, who has not yet obtained forgiveness from those who expelled him, is charged with another, premeditated murder.' Now, the defendant in such cases is unable to come to Athens, but the legislator—the genius who masterminded the whole system we're looking at—didn't take this to be a reason for ignoring the case. He didn't feel, either, that, just because the man had done this kind of thing before, he should therefore treat the similar charge as certain. [78] No, he found a way simultaneously to avoid impropriety and to allow the defendant a hearing and a trial. What did he do? He took the men who were to judge the case to a place that was approachable by the defendant—to a certain spot outside town on the coast that he had picked, called 'in Phreatto'. And so the defendant approaches in a ship and gives his speech without touching land, and the judges listen and reach a verdict on land. If he's found guilty, he receives the punishment he deserves for premeditated murder, but if he's acquitted, his innocence of *this* crime doesn't clear his debt for the earlier murder.*

[79] Why has our legislator taken so much trouble over these regulations? Because he regarded it as equally impious to leave a guilty man at large and to make an innocent man liable to seizure before he's received a trial. But when so much effort has been taken to ensure that people who have already been found guilty of causing death get a hearing, a trial, and fair treatment in every respect, isn't it completely inexcusable to suggest that someone who hasn't yet been found guilty should be given up to his accusers—when it hasn't yet

been determined whether or not he did the deed, nor whether it was deliberate or accidental?

[80] There's also a sixth way to seek redress, which is flouted by Aristocrates' decree no less than the other five. Suppose someone is unaware of the procedures I've outlined, or the mandatory time for employing them has passed, or he has some other reason for choosing not to proceed in these ways. If he sees the murderer frequenting the sanctuaries or the Agora, he's allowed to arrest him and take him to the public prison, [*turning to Aristocrates*] but not to his own home or anywhere he feels like, as *you* allow. [*To the jurors*] And then, following his arrest, nothing will happen to him until he's undergone a trial. If he's found guilty, he'll be put to death, but a fine of a thousand drachmas awaits the man who arrested him if he fails to obtain a fifth of the votes.* [81] That's not what Aristocrates proposes, however: he wants the prosecutor to go ahead without risk, and the defendant to be given up straight away, without trial. And suppose a man, or even an entire community, tries to help; suppose someone tries to prevent the negation of such important regulations and the dissolution of such prestigious courts—courts that were instituted by gods and then for ever after have been available for use by men—and tries to rescue someone who's being abused and victimized. Aristocrates' proposal is that such a man should be excluded from the Athenian alliance, and once again he has denied him a hearing or a trial. Once again, a man is to be punished straight away, without a trial. It's impossible to conceive of a decree more riddled with iniquity and illegality!

[82] [*To the Clerk of the Court*] Have we got any laws left? Show me. [*Euthycles makes a show of searching for the document*] Here, take this one. Read it out.

Another law is read out:
If anyone dies a violent death, his relatives may take hostages on his account, until either they have been tried for the murder or they give up the killers. Up to three hostages may be taken, but no more.

[*To the jurors*] What an excellent and fair law, Athenians! It surely holds its own alongside all our other excellent laws. Let's examine it, and you'll see how sound and extraordinarily humane it is. [83] 'If anyone dies a violent death,' says the legislator. The first thing to note is that, by adding the word 'violent', he was subtly letting us know that he means us to think of the death as a criminal act. 'His relatives may take hostages on his account, until either they have been tried for the murder or they give up the killers.'* Excellent, as I'm sure you'll agree! He begins by insisting on a trial, and then, if they refuse, he orders them to give up the killers. If they reject both options, the law says that 'up to three hostages may be taken, but no more'.

Well, there's not the slightest correspondence between the decree and this law. [84] First, Aristocrates wrote 'If anyone kills,' without adding 'unjustly' or 'violently' or any qualification at all. Second, without pausing to call for a trial, he jumped straight to 'he is liable to seizure'. Third, while the law says that if the people of the land where the murder took place refuse to submit to a trial or surrender the perpetrators, up to three of them can be seized and taken hostage, [85] he lets them go scot-free. He has no interest in them at all, but focuses on the fugitives, who are already in exile, or so I suppose. Now, taking in a fugitive is one of the common principles of humankind, but Aristocrates wants to exclude from the alliance those who give a fugitive hospitality, unless they surrender the suppliant as one liable to seizure. So he doesn't qualify the killing at all; he says nothing about a trial; he omits any claim for redress; he allows culprits to be seized wherever they may be found; and he punishes those who take in fugitives, rather than the people of the land where the murder took place. Nothing could be clearer than that he's in breach of this law too.

[86] [*To the Clerk of the Court*] Read the next one, please.

Another law is read out:
It is also forbidden to propose a law that affects a particular man, unless the same law affects all Athenians.

[*To the jurors*] The law you've just heard, jurymen, is not one of our homicide laws, but it's as good as any of them. The man who composed this piece of legislation thought it important for every Athenian citizen to have equal access to the law, just as the constitution guarantees their equality in other respects too. That's why he wrote: 'It is also forbidden to propose a law that affects a particular man, unless the same law affects all Athenians.' But, as everyone knows, decrees should not contradict laws, and therefore when Aristocrates proposes personal privileges for Charidemus which none of you Athenians will get, it's obvious that he's in breach of this law. For it goes without saying that it must be illegal to include something in a decree that isn't permitted in a law.*

[87] [*To the Clerk of the Court*] Read the next one, please. Or is that all?

Another law is read out:
No decree, of the Council or of the Assembly, is to have greater authority than a law.

Put it down. [*To the jurors*] I don't think it will take much time or effort, jurymen, to show that the decree is in breach of this law. When a man has drafted a proposal that flouts every single one of our vast collection of laws, and uses a decree to settle some personal business, it is exactly right to say that he's expecting it to have greater authority than law.

[88] Now, I'd like you to consider a couple of decrees written for genuine benefactors of the city. You'll see that it's easy for a man to come up with legitimate proposals when he sincerely wants to honour someone and let him share in the advantages of citizenship. It's more of a struggle if he merely *pretends* that this is his purpose, when really he's aiming to dupe and deceive you. [*To the Clerk of the Court*] Read these decrees. [*To the jurors*] I don't want to take up too much of your time over this, so I've extracted the bits of the decrees that are relevant to this case. [*To the Clerk of the Court*] Go ahead, please.

Extracts are read out from some decrees.

[89] [*To the jurors*] You can see the similarity of approach these decrees share, Athenians, with their formulaic 'The punishment on his account shall be the same as if the killer had killed an Athenian.'* They leave the laws that govern these offences in force and even set off their dignity, in the sense that they count it as a gift to allow others to live as citizens under those laws. Not so Aristocrates. He does his level best to besmirch the laws, in the sense that the attempt to propose personal privileges for someone makes a nonsense of them, and he belittles even the gift of citizenship that you bestowed on Charidemus. I mean, on the assumption that you're content with the situation and feel yourselves to be in Charidemus' debt, he proposes that you should protect him as well, so that he can do whatever he likes with impunity. Don't you think what I'm saying about his schemes is right?

[90] Now, I feel confident that Aristocrates won't be able to disprove the blatant illegality of his proposal, but he's bound to try to

mitigate the most reprehensible part, the lack of provision anywhere in his decree for a trial even when someone is charged with such a serious offence. I don't think I need to say much about this, but I shall conclusively prove, from the wording of the decree itself, that it didn't even cross his mind that the accused should have his day in court. [91] Here's the evidence: 'If anyone kills Charidemus, he shall be liable to seizure, and if any city or person tries to save the killer, it or he shall be excluded from the treaty of alliance.' There's no 'If they fail to surrender for trial the man they have rescued', no such qualification or condition. But if he were offering a trial, instead of denying the chance of one, he'd have specified that the rescuers were to be punished only if they failed to surrender for trial the person they had rescued.

[92] Now, I'm sure he'll also make use of the familiar argument—in fact, I suspect he'll try very hard to trick you with it—that the decree has no force. It's no more than a preliminary resolution, and by law decrees of the Council expire after a year.* This means, he'll argue, that even if you acquit him today, the city will come to no harm from his decree. [93] I think you should respond by bearing in mind that Aristocrates' intention, in drafting this decree, was certainly not that it should become invalid and have no unpleasant consequences for you. After all, he needn't have written it in the first place, if his focus was on the best interests of the state. No, his intention was to deceive you and to allow certain people to put into effect schemes designed to harm your interests. It's *we* who have indicted the decree, delayed it, and invalidated it, and it would be absurd if the actions we've taken that should plausibly make you grateful to us made it safe for these people to act. [94] Besides, the situation isn't as straightforward as you might suppose. If Aristocrates were unique and there weren't others to make proposals that took equally little account of your interests, it might be all right. But in fact there are quite a few of them, and that's why it would be wrong if you didn't cancel the decree. Failure to condemn this one will boost their confidence and they'll all be drafting decrees next. And who will indict them? The relevant issue is not the expiry date for this decree, but the fact that if you let it off, that vote of yours will act as a grant of immunity to anyone who wants to harm you in the future.

[95] I'm well aware also, Athenians, that since Aristocrates isn't in a position to mount a straightforward or fair defence—or any kind

of defence at all, really—he'll try to deceive you instead with arguments such as that, after all, in the past many men have been the beneficiaries of many such decrees. But this is no proof of the legality of his proposal, Athenians, because for one reason or another you've often been deceived in the past. [96] I mean, if no one had happened to indict a decree that was subsequently condemned by the Assembly, it would be in force, naturally, but the proposal to ratify it would still have been illegal. Or again, consider a decree that was in fact indicted, but when it came to court either the prosecutors were suborned or they were unable to make their case, and so it escaped condemnation: that wouldn't stop it being illegal either.

'Are you saying that the jurors in this case compromised their oath?' No. 'What are you saying, then?' I'll explain. Jurors are under oath to vote in accordance with their honest opinion, but their opinion is formed by what they hear. They can have a clear conscience, then, as long as they cast their votes in accordance with their opinion, [97] because a juror's oath remains uncompromised as long as he isn't swayed by hostility or favour, or by any other unfair motive, to vote contrary to it. After all, failure to understand some point or other that is being explained isn't a punishable offence. No, it's the man who knowingly plays the jurors false and deceives them who is liable to the curse. That's why at every Assembly the herald calls down a curse not on the deceived but the deceivers:* 'If anyone lies to either Council or Assembly or Heliaea.' [98] So don't let yourselves be presented with a *fait accompli*; have the speakers explain why it's *right* for the decree to be ratified. Don't let them tell you that other juries ratified those other decrees; insist that they convince you today that their position is fairer than mine. And if they can't do that, I can't see how it could be right for you to give more authority to others' lies than to your own opinion.

[99] Besides, it strikes me as sheer impudence to argue that others have allowed decrees like this one in the past. [*To Aristocrates*] I mean, if you've imitated an illegal practice from the past, that's no reason for you to be acquitted. On the contrary, it's all the more reason for finding you guilty, in the sense that if any of your predecessors had been found guilty, you wouldn't have come up with this proposal of yours, and by the same token, if you're found guilty today, it will deter others in the future.

[100] [*To the jurors*] I hardly think, then, that Aristocrates will be able to deny that his decree blatantly contravenes all our laws. But

I've seen people contesting indictments for illegal proposals before, Athenians, and sometimes, even when they're guilty under the law, they try to argue—they *persist* in trying to argue—that their proposal is advantageous to you. But this strikes me as a naive argument, or perhaps I should say an impudent one. [101] Even if the proposal were fundamentally advantageous, it would still be disadvantageous in the sense that he's asking you to ratify a proposal whose legality even he is unable to prove, when you've sworn as jurors to uphold the law—and when keeping your oath is something all of you should regard as of critical importance. 'But it's a good argument, however impudent in this case.' Well, it's not an argument that he can make to you: even though his decree runs directly contrary to the law, its disadvantageousness exceeds its illegality!

[102] This is what I'd like to prove to you now, and in order to make my point clear as quickly as possible, I'll illustrate it first with a concept that's familiar to everyone. You know that it's in our interests for neither Thebes nor Sparta to be strong—for Thebes to be counterbalanced by Phocis, and Sparta by other states. That leaves us the strongest state, free of anxiety. [103] I'd like you to see that the same goes for the Athenian inhabitants of the Chersonese: it's in their interests for no single man in Thrace to be strong. No garrison can offer the Chersonese greater security than disarray and mutual suspicion in Thrace. Now, this decree of Aristocrates' offers protection to the commander of Cersobleptes' forces, but it makes the other kings' generals afraid of being accused of a crime, and so it weakens those kings and strengthens the other one, the single man.

[104] In case it strikes you as implausible for Athenian decrees to have such a powerful effect, I'll remind you of a familiar episode. Miltocythes had revolted from Cotys, the war had been going on for quite some time, Ergophilus had been replaced, and Autocles was about to sail there to take command. At that point, a decree was proposed here which convinced Miltocythes that he didn't have your support. He withdrew in alarm, and Cotys gained control of the Sacred Mountain and the treasury there.* And in consequence, Athenians, although Autocles was subsequently tried for having caused Miltocythes' rebellion to come to nothing, it was too late for the proposer of the decree to be indicted, and Athenian interests had been badly damaged.

[105] The situation today is much the same. I can assure you that,

if you don't cancel this decree, you'll undermine the confidence of the kings and their generals to an incredible degree. They'll believe that they've been brushed aside, and that you're inclining towards Cersobleptes. Now, if the result of this conviction is that they surrender their power when Cersobleptes attacks them at some point, you should be aware what the consequences will be of this too. [106] In the name of the gods, then, what do you think will happen if Cersobleptes goes on the warpath against us—and, once he can, he's more likely to do so than not? Won't we turn to those former kings in an attempt to use them to weaken him? And then suppose they reply: 'Athenians, not only did you not help us when we were under attack, but you also made us incredibly afraid of defending ourselves, when you passed a decree to the effect that if anyone kills the man—a man who is actively harming your interests as well as ours—he is liable to seizure. It's not right for you to ask us to help you, when it's your bad decisions that have got both you and us into this situation.' Right will be on their side in this argument, rather than ours, don't you think? I know I do.

[107] Nor can you claim that it was perfectly natural for you to have been misled and deceived. If nothing else had tipped you off and you didn't have a basis in your own past for understanding the situation, you could have looked at the example of those Olynthians.* How did Philip treat them? How are they treating him? He returned Potidaea to them, and not because the time had come when he was no longer able to keep it from them. That was why Cersobleptes returned the Chersonese to us,* but Philip took Potidaea in the course of a very costly war with us, and although he could have hung on to it if he'd wanted to, he handed it over to them without the slightest hesitation. [108] All the same, they remained in alliance with him only as long as they found him weak enough to be trusted, and in that capacity they fought us on his account. Eventually they came to realize that he had grown too great for them to trust, but they still refrained from decreeing that if anyone killed any of the men who had helped to establish his dominance, he was liable to seizure and removal from the territory of their allies. Far from it. [109] Instead, they got on good terms with us (and it will lead, they say, to an alliance), because they knew that there was no one in the world who was more keen to kill Philip's friends—and not just them, but the man himself as well. So is foreseeing the future something the Olynthians are good at, not

you? But you are Athenians, and it would be a disgrace for people who are reputed to be particularly expert at political deliberation to display less recognition than Olynthians of what is good for them.

[110] I hear that Aristocrates is also going to come up with a similar argument to one used by Aristomachus once when addressing the Assembly:* there's no way, he'll say, that Cersobleptes will ever deliberately provoke our enmity by trying to take the Chersonese. And anyway, even if he takes it and holds it, he won't profit from it. In peacetime, the land doesn't generate more than thirty talents, and at a time of war there's no income to be had from it at all. The ports produce more than two hundred talents a year, but under the circumstances they'll be closed. So people will wonder whether he's lost his mind: why would he choose small gains and war when he could have a better income and be on good terms with us?

[111] I could easily mention a dozen cases that, in my opinion, make scepticism a more reasonable response to this argument than believing it and allowing Cersobleptes to gain strength, but the one that springs to mind first concerns a man you know well, Athenians— Philip of Macedon. It was certainly far more profitable for him to draw an income from all Macedonia in safety than to draw one from Amphipolis with its attendant risks, and more desirable for him to get on good terms with you, who had been friends of his father, rather than with the Thessalians, who had once driven his father from their land.* [112] Even apart from that, another consideration, Athenians, is that we've never betrayed any of our friends, while the Thessalians have never *not* betrayed them! All the same, even under these circumstances, you can see what he chose: a reduced income, fickle friends, and danger, instead of a life of safety.

[113] Why on earth would he do that? It's not easy to see what sense it makes. The answer, Athenians, lies in the fact that you can't simultaneously have both success and good sense, the two chief blessings of life. There's no greater blessing than success, but good sense is second only to it and superior to everything else. Another part of the answer is that no successful man limits or curbs his desire to get more, which is why greed has often caused men to lose even what they had. [114] And the only person I need to mention in this context is not Philip or anyone else, but Cersobleptes' own father, Cotys. Whenever he had internal troubles, he used to send ambassadors here and was ready to do anything to gain your support. In those days, he

knew that there was no profit in making war on us. But as soon as Thrace was securely his, he began to occupy cities, go on the warpath, act like a stupid drunk (injuring himself more than us), take over the country—it was extraordinary! But, after all, men who undertake inappropriate ventures out of greed tend to ignore the worst-case scenario and focus on the gains success will bring them.

[115] In my opinion, then, the policy you choose should cover both possibilities. If Cersobleptes adopts the right attitude towards you, he mustn't suffer any wrong at Athenian hands, but if he begins to act aggressively, however stupid that would be, you need to make sure that he won't be too powerful to punish. I'm going to read you two letters sent by Cotys. The first was written during Miltocythes' rebellion, and the second, addressed to Timomachus,* was written after Cotys had made himself sole ruler and had destroyed your fortresses.

The letters are read out.

[116] Bear this example in mind, Athenians, and remember how Philip too used to say that the reason he was besieging Amphipolis was to hand it over to us, but then, once he had taken it, stole Potidaea from us as well. My recommendation, then, would be for you to seek the same kind of assurance that they say Philocrates, the son of Ephialtes, once demanded from the Spartans.* [117] The story goes that the Spartans were trying to trick him and were offering him whatever he would accept as a token of their good faith. He replied that the only acceptable token would be for them to convince him of their inability to wrong him in the future if they wanted to; he was certain that they would never stop wanting to, and therefore, as long as they had the ability to do so, he would remain unconvinced of their good faith. If you take my advice, you'll wait until you feel you can trust this Thracian to the same degree. There's no point in wondering what his attitude will be towards us if he gains control of all Thrace.

[118] An abundance of evidence makes another point easy to see: that proposing a decree like this, a decree of such wanton generosity, is an act of sheer insanity. It's as obvious to you as it is to me, Athenians, that, at the time when you made Cotys a citizen, you felt he was a friend of the city and had its best interests at heart. You even awarded him golden crowns, which you'd never have done if you'd thought him hostile. [119] Nevertheless, when the base and godless side of his nature emerged, and he began doing you terrible wrong, you

granted Athenian citizenship to his killers, Python and Heracleides of Aenus, and awarded them golden crowns as benefactors of the city. Now, suppose that, at the time when Cotys had seemed to be friendly, someone had drafted a decree to the effect that 'If anyone kills Cotys, he is liable to seizure.' Would you have surrendered Python and his brother, or would you have made them citizens in spite of this decree and honoured them as benefactors?

[120] And what about Alexander of Thessaly? When he had Pelopidas in custody as a prisoner of war, when he was public enemy number one in Thebes, when he was on such good terms with you that he asked you to supply him with a general, when he had your support and was the apple of your eye—by Zeus, what if someone had drafted a decree to the effect that 'If anyone kills Alexander, he is liable to seizure'? Would it have been safe for anyone to try to punish him as he deserved for his subsequent high-handed insolence?*

[121] But, leaving aside all the other instances that could be mentioned, what about Philip, the man we currently rate our main enemy? Remember when he caught some Athenian citizens trying to restore Argaeus?* He not only let them go, but made good all their losses, and wrote assuring us that he was ready to enter into a treaty of alliance and to renew his hereditary friendship with us. Suppose at the time he had asked for this favour, and one of the men he had released had drafted a proposal to the effect that 'If anyone kills Philip, he is liable to seizure'—how well we'd have been humiliated by now!

[122] Does this make things clear, Athenians? Do you see how people would have thought you crazy if you had in fact on any of these occasions ratified a decree like the one before us? It's as foolish to trust a supposed friend so completely as to deny oneself the chance of defence against any wrong he might try to commit, as it is to distrust a supposed enemy so completely as to make it impossible for him to change and be a friend if he wants to. In my opinion, we should guard against excess in both cases, when treating someone as a friend just as much as when treating someone as an enemy.

[123] I'm also absolutely convinced that, if you award these privileges to Charidemus, anyone with even the slightest reason for being thought your benefactor will expect to be granted them as well. Who do I mean? Simon, for example, Bianor, Athenodorus, countless others. Either we officially award these privileges to all of them, in which case, as I see it, we'll find ourselves unwittingly playing the role of

mercenary bodyguards, with the job of keeping each of them safe. Or we pick and choose, in which case the disappointed ones will have good grounds for complaint. [124] I mean, suppose Menestratus of Eretria or Phayllus of Phocis* or some other dynast were also to demand that you grant him these privileges—and of course we do often opportunistically befriend such men: shall we or shan't we let him have them? 'We shall, by Zeus!' In that case, how will we reconcile our claim to champion the cause of Greek freedom with the evident fact that we're protecting the lives of men who suppress the general populations of their states with private armies?

[125] If we grant such privileges to anyone—as I say we shouldn't—the criteria must be, first, that he should never have harmed us; second, that he will be too weak ever to harm us in the future even if he wants to; and third, that he should be someone whose motive genuinely is, and is universally recognized as being, self-protection rather than a desire to injure others with impunity. I won't bother to demonstrate that Charidemus is not to be counted among those whose conduct towards you has been blameless, nor among those who are motivated by the desire for self-protection. But listen to me now as I prove that he's not to be trusted in the future either. See if you find my argument sound.

[126] It seems to me, Athenians, that anyone who seeks Athenian citizenship because he's attracted by our customs and political system will make his home here as soon as he's won them as his right, and live the kind of life he's been wanting. But now consider a man who's not motivated by any such longing or desire, but is attracted rather by the advantage he'll gain from being known to be high in your esteem: I think—no, I'm absolutely certain that if he ever sees the prospect of greater advantage elsewhere, he'll make straight for that and ignore you altogether.

[127] Here's an example that will help you see what I'm getting at. After Python (the man we were just talking about) had killed Cotys, he didn't think it safe to go just anywhere, but came here and asked to be registered as a citizen. You were everything to him. But now he thinks he's better off with Philip, and so you're nothing to him and he's all for Philip. The point is, Athenians, that it's impossible, quite impossible, for anyone whose life is devoted to gaining advantage to be either reliable or moral. The only sensible way to deal with such people is to proceed with caution. That's better than first trusting

people and then denouncing them. [128] It follows, Athenians, that even if we assume the opposite to the truth—that Charidemus has always worked in our best interests, is doing so now, and will continue to do so in the future, and that he will never change his mind in this respect—even so, it's wrong to award him these privileges.

It wouldn't be so shocking if he was planning to use the immunity granted by the decree for some purpose other than supporting Cersobleptes, but in fact the man who will benefit from the use to which Charidemus puts the advantage afforded him by the decree deserves his trust as little as ours. That's the conclusion I've come to after thinking it over. [129] See if you find the points I make valid— and how very plausible my fears are.

This is what I think. Cotys was as closely related by marriage to Iphicrates as Cersobleptes is to Charidemus,* and, as I see it, the importance and value of what Iphicrates achieved for Cotys far outweighs what Charidemus has done for Cersobleptes . . . [130] Let's look at it this way. You are of course aware that there's a bronze statue here of Iphicrates, Athenians, and you know that he was given the right of free meals in the Prytaneum, as well as other awards and honours which contributed materially to his happiness. All the same, he still presumed to fight our forces at sea as Cotys' general. Protecting Cotys was more important to him than the honours you had awarded him here, but luckily for him your anger was more restrained than his presumption; otherwise, there can be no doubt that he would have been humbled more completely than any man on earth.* [131] Cotys owed Iphicrates his life and had practical experience of his loyalty, but, even so, once he felt safe and secure he made no effort to thank him, and so far from using him as the agent of some conciliatory gesture towards us, as a way of seeking forgiveness for his actions, he decided to put our last fortresses under siege. [132] When Iphicrates refused to take part, Cotys hired Charidemus instead and attacked our fortresses with both his native troops and the mercenaries collected by Iphicrates. This left Iphicrates so exposed that he went to live first in Antissa and then Drys. He didn't think it appropriate to come here to Athens, given that he had slighted us for the sake of the Thracian, a barbarian; but at the same time it wasn't safe for him to stay with Cotys, whom he could see had no interest at all in protecting him.

[133] Imagine a similar situation, then, Athenians, with Cersobleptes. Suppose that, strengthened by the immunity that is currently

being procured for Charidemus, he starts to consider him unimportant, and begins to wreak havoc and stir things up against us. Will the
fact that Charidemus was duped make you happy with the fact that the
strength the Thracian is employing against you is your own creation?
I sincerely hope not! What I think we have to do is this. If Charidemus
is aware of the danger and sees it looming in the future, but still does
his best to procure a decree for himself along the lines of the one in
question, [134] you should distrust him and his intrigues. But if he's
unaware of the danger, you have to take thought for his future as well
as for your own, in so far as you credit him with loyalty towards us.
After all, a true friend is not one who gratifies a well-wisher in ways
that will harm them both; no, he works with him for their mutual
benefit, and if he sees the future more clearly than him, it's his job
to arrange things for the best, not to treat momentary gratification as
more important than the future.

[135] Another conclusion my thinking has led me to is this.
Cersobleptes may be a fickle barbarian, but I can't see him failing to
take steps to ensure that he causes Charidemus serious harm. I mean,
when I take another look at the advantages Cotys was, without the
slightest hesitation, going to cause Iphicrates to lose, it seems altogether
unlikely that Cersobleptes will care at all about what Charidemus stands
to lose. [136] Cotys must have known that he would make Iphicrates
lose honours, maintenance at public expense, statues, the country that
had made him an object of envy—everything, I might almost say, that
makes life worth living—and he didn't hesitate for a moment. But
what, in all honesty, does Charidemus have that Cersobleptes might
have any reason not to deprive him of? There's nothing of his here
in Athens—no children, no statue, no family, and nothing else at all.
[137] So, given that Cersobleptes is innately fickle, and that the past
has shown how right it is not to trust him, and that there's nothing
in his current situation that might make him go against his innate
inclinations and spare Charidemus a thought, why ever would we help
him attain his goals, especially since they're designed to do us harm?
That would be nothing but sheer, downright stupidity, and I can see
no reason for us to act like that.

[138] So we gain no material advantages from the decree, but that's
not all: you must also see that the city's reputation will suffer if it is
known to have endorsed a decree of this kind. If it had been written for someone who was living in a constitutionally governed city,

Athenians, it would have been less disgraceful, though hardly something to be proud of. But in fact it's been written for Charidemus, who doesn't live in a city at all, but works as a general for a Thracian and commits many crimes under the protection of his kingship. [139] For, as I'm sure you realize, all these mercenary commanders want to seize Greek cities and set themselves up as rulers. Wherever they find themselves in the course of their footloose existence, they are, if the truth be told, the common enemies of all who want to live as free men in their own constitutionally governed cities. So is it right, Athenians, is it appropriate for you to be known to have voted protection for a man who is going to intrigue against whoever he comes across for his own selfish ends, and to have given notice that those who retaliate in defence of their own liberty are to be excluded from your alliance? [140] Personally, I don't think this is the right course, or worthy of Athens. How could it not be disgraceful for the people who rebuked the Spartans for giving the Persian king written permission to treat the Asiatic Greeks however he liked* to surrender to Cersobleptes the European Greeks and everyone Charidemus thinks he can subdue? But that is precisely the effect of this decree, in so far as it fails to specify what Cersobleptes' general may or may not do, and threatens all who retaliate with the direst consequences.

[141] Athenians, I'd like to relate a bit of history next, which will make even clearer the importance of cancelling this decree. There was a time when you gave Athenian citizenship to Ariobarzanes, and also to Philiscus, for Ariobarzanes' sake,* just as you recently gave it to Charidemus for Cersobleptes' sake. Philiscus chose the same career as Charidemus and began, under the protection of Ariobarzanes' power, to seize Greek cities. Every time his forces entered a city, they committed appalling crimes such as raping free boys and women. In short, he behaved exactly as you'd expect of a man who gained power after having been brought up in lawless conditions, without the blessings of a civilized community. [142] Now, there were in Lampsacus two men, one called Thersagoras, the other Execestus, and they felt about tyranny pretty much as we feel here. They killed Philiscus, which was no more than he deserved, because they wanted their homeland to be free. Now, there were politicians here at the time who represented Philiscus' interests. Suppose one of them had picked the time when Philiscus was the paymaster of the mercenaries based at Perinthus, when he was in charge of the entire Hellespontine

region, when he was the most powerful of the vice-governors, to draw up a proposal like the one before us today, to the effect that 'If anyone kills Philiscus, he is liable to seizure and removal from allied territory.' By Zeus, think what a scandal that would have been for the city! [143] I mean, Thersagoras and Execestus went to live on Lesbos, and if one of Philiscus' friends or sons had laid hands on them, they'd have been seized and deported in accordance with the terms of your decree. There's no other way to describe what you'd have done, Athenians: it would have been an inexcusable disgrace for you to erect statues in bronze of Athenian tyrant-slayers and award them the highest honours,* and then to have voted that people from somewhere else, who were just as loyal to their country as their Athenian counterparts, should be liable to seizure. Well, in Philiscus' case, I'm glad to say, you weren't duped and you avoided disgrace on that occasion. But if you take my advice, you'll be very careful in the present case: the clause 'If anyone kills Charidemus' remains unqualified, and so the outcome could turn out to be just as bad as I've described.

[144] Next I'd like to take a quick look at Charidemus' past, so that you can see the outrageous impudence of his supporters. And I can promise you this—with the hope that no one will find my promise offensive: I shall prove not only that he doesn't deserve the protection afforded by Aristocrates' decree, but also that what he does deserve is the most severe punishment—that is, if it's right to punish men who are hostile to the democracy, and spend all their time trying to misinform you and hamper your efforts. [145] But, in view of the fact that the man was first made a citizen, and then was later awarded golden crowns as a benefactor, it has probably occurred to some of you to wonder how you could so easily have been taken in by such a gross deception. Well, you can be quite sure that you *were* taken in, Athenians. What I'll do is explain why that was only to be expected. It's because you often get good ideas, Athenians, but fail to see them through.

[146] Here's the kind of thing I mean. If you were asked which you regard as the most pernicious of all the various sets of people in the city, you wouldn't pick the farmers or the businessmen or the miners or any such group. But I'm sure your agreement would be unanimous if someone mentioned those of our politicians whose speeches and proposals are for hire. So far, a good idea, but then things start to go wrong afterwards. [147] For even though you regard them as the

dregs of Athenian society, you've allowed them to guide what you think about particular individuals, and they judge a man good or bad by the criterion of their own personal profit, not by any honest or truthful standard. That's what the politicians have been doing all along in Charidemus' case, as you'll agree too, once you've heard what I have to say about his activities.

[148] Now, I don't count his early military career as wrongdoing, even though he fought against Athens as a light-armed soldier and a slinger, and I'm also going to make nothing of the time he spent as a pirate captain, raiding our allies. Why? Because, Athenians, calculations of right and wrong are always destroyed by harsh necessity, so one must not be too particular about such things if one is going to conduct a fair examination. But let me tell you about the harm he did us as soon as he became a mercenary leader and had some troops under his command. [149] The very first thing he did—this was after he had been hired by Iphicrates and had served under him for more than three years, when you replaced Iphicrates with Timotheus as general in Amphipolis and the Chersonese—the first thing he did was hand over to the Amphipolitans the hostages of theirs that Iphicrates had given him to guard—these were the hostages Iphicrates had received from Harpalus—even though you had ordered them brought to Athens. This action of his was what stopped us taking Amphipolis.* Second, he turned down Timotheus' offer to re-hire him and his men, and sailed off to Cotys with your triaconters, even though he was perfectly well aware that Athens had no worse enemy in the world.

[150] Next, when Timotheus decided to make Amphipolis the first field of operations, before the Chersonese—and also because he had found that he was unable to harm your interests in the Chersonese—Charidemus sold his services to the Olynthians, who were your enemies and held Amphipolis at the time.* He set sail from the Chersonese, with Cardia as his port of departure, to fight against us. He was captured by our fleet, but not punished for his failure to deliver the hostages and for deserting to the enemy—to Cotys, that is—with the triaconters. We were in the middle of a crisis, and needed mercenaries for the war against Amphipolis, and so, after an exchange of pledges, he fought on our side. [151] Now, he should have been grateful to you for having spared his life when by all rights he should have been put to death, but instead it was as though *we*

were in *his* debt, and he was awarded crowns and citizenship and so on, as you know. [*To the Clerk of the Court*] To confirm the truth of what I've been saying, please read the decree about the hostages, the letters written by Iphicrates and Timotheus, and then this deposition here. [*To the jurors*] You'll see that these are not just words and empty accusations; there's real substance to what I'm saying. [*To the Clerk of the Court*] Go ahead.

The decree, the letters, and the deposition are read out.

[152] [*To the jurors*] The letter and the deposition you've just heard prove that, of all the places in the world where he could have gone, Charidemus first sold his services where he expected you to be the enemy, and then, when he found himself unable to injure you there, he did the same again, and sailed for a part of the world where he would be acting against Athenian interests. They also prove that he must bear the burden of responsibility for your failure to take Amphipolis. So that's what Charidemus got up to first; now see what happened next.

[153] Some time later, during the war with Cotys, he wrote you a letter—though actually he addressed it to Cephisodotus,* because, knowing what he had done, he could hardly expect that we would be taken in by him. In this letter he promised to recover the Chersonese for Athens, but he had actually resolved to do exactly the opposite. It's important for you to see what this business with the letter was all about. It won't take long, and it will enable you to understand how this man has treated you from start to finish.

[154] At the time in question, his service with Timotheus was coming to an end. He left Amphipolis and crossed over to Asia, where the recent capture of Artabazus by Autophradates meant that it was Artabazus' sons-in-law who became his and his troops' paymasters.* Pledges were exchanged, but he scorned and violated the oaths he had sworn, and with the local inhabitants off their guard, since they assumed they were dealing with a friend, he took three of their cities— Scepsis, Cebren, and Ilium. [155] After this coup, he suffered the kind of mishap that shouldn't happen even to ordinary men, let alone to someone claiming to be a general. Although he had no presence on the coast, although there was nowhere else in his domain that could supply his men, and although there was no grain stored in the places he held, he stayed inside the towns, when he should have plundered

them and left, since he was committed to a criminal course anyway. But Artabazus, who had been released by Autophradates, gathered an army and arrived on the scene. He had supply lines running from inner Phrygia, Lydia, and Paphlagonia, which were all friendly to him, while Charidemus was left with no choice but to endure a siege. [156] When he saw how grim his situation was and understood that starvation, if nothing else, was going to force him to surrender, he realized (whether it was someone else's suggestion or his own insight) that his only chance of safety lay where it lies for all of us. And where is that? In your kindness, Athenians, if that's the right word for it.

So it was this realization that made him write you the letter, and it's quite a work of art. What he wanted to achieve by means of his promise to recover the Chersonese for you, and by making it seem as though Cephisodotus, as an enemy of Cotys and Iphicrates, wanted the same thing, was that you would supply him with a fleet, and then he could make good his escape from Asia. [157] But something happened straight away which exposed the whole business for what it was. What happened? It was Memnon's and Mentor's doing, the sons-in-law of Artabazus. They were young men, and had been enjoying the unexpected good fortune that accrued to them from their relationship to Artabazus. What they wanted, in the short term, was peace for the lands they ruled, and recognition for themselves, without warfare and risk. So, arguing that you would bring Charidemus back to Europe whether he liked it or not, and that there was nothing he could do about it, they persuaded Artabazus to forget about retaliating against Charidemus and to send him away under a truce.

[158] This was an extraordinary and unexpected reprieve for Charidemus, and under the terms of the truce, he was allowed to sail over to the Chersonese unescorted. But then, so far from attacking Cotys (who, according to his letter, would have collapsed before such an attack), and so far from working with you to recover the Chersonese, he once again sold his services to Cotys and put our last remaining fortresses, Crithote and Elaeous, under siege. And it's clear from the crossing he made that he had already decided on this course of action even while he was still in Asia and drafting the letter to you—in other words, that he was lying. For he departed from Abydus, which is always hostile to us and had been used as a base for the capture of Sestus, and landed at Sestus, which was in Cotys' hands.* [159] Now, given that his letter to you had already been sent,

there's no way that either Abydus or Sestus would have let him in, unless they knew that his letter was deliberately misleading and were party to the deception. They wanted you to keep his army safe during the crossing so that once it was across (which in fact came about when Artabazus granted it safe conduct) it would be available for them to use. [*To the Clerk of the Court*] To confirm the truth of what I've been saying, please read the letters—the one he sent and the ones written by the authorities in the Chersonese. [*To the jurors*] Then you'll see the truth of what I've been telling you.

One of the letters from the Chersonese authorities is read out.

[160] Think about his route from Asia to Europe: he started at Abydus and ended at Sestus. Do you think the inhabitants of either place would have let him in if they hadn't been in on the deception when he sent the letter to you? [*To the Clerk of the Court*] Now read his actual letter. [*To the jurors*] I'd like you to notice, Athenians, how extravagantly he praises himself to you as he tells you what he's done and promises more.

Charidemus' letter is read out.

[161] Fine words, don't you think, Athenians? A letter of great value—if only it were true! In fact, though, he wrote it to deceive you, when he had no idea that a truce was going to fall in his lap. [*To the Clerk of the Court*] Now read what he did after he got the truce.

Another of the letters from the Chersonese authorities is read out.

[*To the jurors*] Here the governor of Crithote says that after Charidemus had made the crossing, promising to recover our lost territories, our possessions were in greater danger than before. [*To the Clerk of the Court*] Show me another letter and read it.

Another letter is read out.

And another.

Another letter is read out.

[162] [*To the jurors*] You can see how the evidence from all sides shows that, after he had returned to Europe, he didn't march to attack Cotys, but to help Cotys attack us. [*To the Clerk of the Court*] Now read just this letter. Don't bother with the others. [*To the jurors*] After

all, you can already see that he has lied to you. [*To the Clerk of the Court*] Go ahead.

Another letter is read out.

Stop there, please. [*To the jurors*] Notice that, although in his letter he promised to recover the Chersonese, he sold his services to your enemies and set about depriving you of your last possessions there. And although in his letter he said that he had refused Alexander's ambassadors an audience, he ended up doing exactly what Alexander's pirates would have done.* What honest patriotism! Don't you agree? The man would never send a lying and duplicitous letter!

[163] There can hardly be any doubt that none of his professions of loyalty to Athens is sincere, but if the evidence has not yet made this clear enough, subsequent events will help. Cotys was killed by Python—I'm glad to say, since he was our enemy and a bad man. Cersobleptes, the present king, was just a boy at the time, as were all of Cotys' sons, and so Charidemus gained control because he was there with an army. By then Cephisodotus (the recipient of that letter from Charidemus) had arrived as our general, along with the fleet which had been going to rescue Charidemus, when his safety was in doubt and Artabazus was being uncooperative.

[164] Now, if Charidemus had really been sincere, Athenians, if he'd really been our friend, how should he have reacted to the arrival of a general who wasn't anyone he could claim harboured ill-will towards him, but was in fact the man he himself had designated as his friend and the recipient of his letter? Bear in mind that Cotys was dead, and Charidemus was in control. Shouldn't he immediately have restored control to us, helped us confirm the Thracian king in his position, and welcomed the opportunity to demonstrate his loyalty to Athens? [165] I'd say so. Well, did he do anything of the kind? Not at all. He spent seven whole months fighting us, making no secret of his hostility and refusing us even the courtesy of a conference.

At first, our squadron of ten ships put in at Perinthus, because they'd heard that he was near by. We wanted to arrange a meeting and talk things over, but he waited until our men were taking their morning meal and then made an attempt to capture our boats. He killed a lot of our sailors, and chased the scattering survivors into the sea with his cavalry and light-armed troops. [166] After that we set sail—not to attack any place or stronghold in Thrace. No, no one can

say: 'But, by Zeus, if he injured us at all, it was only in self-defence.'
That's not how it was. We didn't go anywhere in Thrace: we went
to Alopeconnesus, which is in the Chersonese and was therefore an
Athenian possession. It's a very long way from Thrace, a headland
jutting out towards Imbros, and teeming with brigands and pirates.

[167] Once we got there, we put these brigands under siege—at
which juncture Charidemus marched right through the Chersonese,
your property, and attacked us, in support of the brigands and pirates.
His blockade of our position enabled him to prevail on our general
and force him to act against your best interests, rather than being
prevailed on himself to fulfil any of his commitments and promises.
So he drew up the notorious pact with Cephisodotus, the one which
made you so furious that you dismissed the general from his post and
fined him five talents. In fact, he was only three votes short of being
put to death.* [168] But it's completely ridiculous, Athenians—I don't
know what else to call it—to have one man punished so severely as
a criminal and the other honoured even now as a benefactor *for the
same activities*! To confirm the truth of what I've been saying, you yourselves will act as my witnesses for what happened to Cephisodotus,
because it was you who judged his case and in your anger voted
to dismiss him. [*To the Clerk of the Court*] But for the events in
Perinthus and Alopeconnesus, please call the trierarchs to testify.

The trierarchs' deposition is read out.

[169] [*To the jurors*] So Cephisodotus was removed from command, and you found the pact he had made to be dishonourable and
illegal. The next thing that happened was that Miltocythes, who had
always been a loyal supporter of Athens, fell into Charidemus' hands,
betrayed to him by Smicythion. Now, putting people to death is not
the custom in Thrace, so what Charidemus did (such a *nice* man!),
knowing that Miltocythes' life would be spared if he were taken to
Cersobleptes, was hand him over instead to the Cardians, who were
your enemies. And they put to sea in a boat with Miltocythes and
his son on board; they cut his son's throat before his very eyes and
then had him walk the plank. [170] This atrocity enraged all Thrace.
Berisades and Amadocus joined forces, and Athenodorus, seeing
a favourable opportunity, entered into an alliance with them, which
put him in a position to make war. Taking advantage of Cersobleptes'
fear at this development, Athenodorus drew up an agreement

compelling him to swear to you and the other kings that rulership of Thrace would be shared and divided three ways, and stipulating that everyone would return your territory to you.

[171] At the annual elections you put Chabrias in charge of this war. But then what happened? Athenodorus had to disband his army because he hadn't received money from you and didn't have the resources for a war, and Chabrias set sail with only one ship.* And how did Charidemus react to all this? He repudiated the agreement he'd made with Athenodorus, persuaded Cersobleptes to do likewise, and drew up an alternative agreement with Chabrias which was even worse than the one with Cephisodotus. Compliance was Chabrias' only choice because, of course, he lacked an army.

[172] When news reached Athens, there was a furious debate in the Assembly. The agreement was read out and, in spite of the high standing of Chabrias and his supporters, you condemned this one too, and resolved, on Glaucon's motion, to appoint an ambassadorial delegation of ten from the citizen body. Their commission was to get Cersobleptes to commit himself once more on oath to his agreement with Athenodorus, or, failing that, to receive the oaths of the two kings and consult with them on how best to make war on Cersobleptes. [173] The ambassadors left, but wasted time and proved unwilling to act in a straightforward and honest manner on your behalf. Eventually things got so bad that when Chares returned from the expedition to Euboea with the mercenaries, you sent him to the Chersonese as general with plenipotentiary powers. Charidemus drew up yet another agreement, this time with Chares, and with Athenodorus and the kings as co-signatories. This is the best and most equitable of the three agreements. In short, he is a self-convicted opportunist where Athens is concerned; there's nothing sincere or honest about his policies.

[174] So here you have a man who is a friend only under compulsion, and whose loyalty to you waxes and wanes according to his estimate of your strength. Is this the kind of man you think you should allow to become strong, especially when it would be your own doing? You need to see that I've been speaking the truth, [*to the Clerk of the Court*] so please take the letter which arrived after the first agreement, and then Berisades' letter. [*To the jurors*] Nothing will help guide you to a correct conclusion better than the information these letters contain.

One of the two letters is read out.

[*To the Clerk of the Court*] And now the one from Berisades.

Berisades' letter is read out.

[175] [*To the jurors*] So that's how the kings formed their alliance, after the fraudulent agreement with Cephisodotus. By this time Miltocythes had been killed and Charidemus had given concrete proof of his hostility towards Athens. I mean, when the man whom he knew to be the most constant friend Athens had in Thrace fell into his hands, he handed him over to your enemies, the Cardians. What clearer proof could he have given of anti-Athenian sentiments? [*To the Clerk of the Court*] Now read the agreement Cersobleptes made later,* when he was frightened by the prospect of war against the Thracians and Athenodorus.

The agreement is read out.

[176] [*To the jurors*] This agreement was drafted and written by Charidemus, and affirmed by his oath, as you've just heard. But then, when he saw that Athenodorus had disbanded his army, and that Chabrias had arrived with just the one trireme, he refused to do any of the things he had undertaken to do, such as handing Iphiades' son over to you.* He repudiated all the other clauses of the agreement as well, and drew up this one instead. [*To the Clerk of the Court*] Here, read this one.

The agreement is read out.

[177] [*To the jurors*] Notice how he expects the money raised by both harbour-dues and excise duties to be his.* Notice how he talks as though the whole country belonged to him, with his insistence that his own excise officers are made responsible for the dues. And notice how he no longer mentions his promise to surrender the hostage, the son of Iphiades, whom he held for Sestus and had promised Athenodorus he would surrender. [*To the Clerk of the Court*] Take the decree the Assembly passed in response to all this. Read it.

The decree is read out.

[178] [*To the jurors*] Later the ambassadors reached Thrace. Here's the letter Cersobleptes wrote at that juncture, conceding nothing to

the justice of our cause, and here's the one written by the other kings. [*To the Clerk of the Court*] Go ahead.

Cersobleptes' letter is read out.

Now read the kings' letter. [*To the jurors*] See if you think they have no grounds for complaint.

The Thracian kings' letter is read out.

Do you get it, Athenians? Do you see how Charidemus' villainy and perfidy wax and wane? First, he was busy injuring Cephisodotus, and then he stopped out of fear of Athenodorus. Later he was busy injuring Chabrias, and then he came to an agreement with Chares. He has been inconsistent throughout; he has never acted with sincerity or honesty.

[179] Ever since then, he's been all smiles and trickery as long as you had an army in the Hellespont. But as soon as he saw that you no longer had a military presence there, he set about trying to depose and get rid of the two kings, and make himself the sole power in the land, since he knew from experience that he wouldn't be able to undo any part of his agreement with you until he had expelled them. [180] The easiest way for him to achieve his ends was to get this decree from you. If ratified (which is what we and this indictment of ours are trying to stop), it would leave the two kings plainly wronged, but their generals—Bianor, Simon, and Athenodorus—would have done nothing, out of fear of being falsely accused of a crime under the terms of the decree, and Charidemus, armed with the freedom of action afforded him by the decree, would make himself sole ruler and be a formidable enemy for us.

[181] Throughout, he has kept a close watch on his base of operations, Cardia. He has made a particular point, in every one of the agreements he's drawn up, of reserving it for himself, and in the end he openly stole it from you.* But why should men reserve a base to be used for the war against us if they harbour no hostility towards us, if they have sincerely and honestly chosen to be our friends? [182] I'm sure you all know, either with the certainty of personal experience or from listening to those with personal experience, that, given the geographical situation of Cardia, if Cersobleptes gets on good terms with his fellow Thracians, it's possible for him to march safely to the Chersonese in a day. Cardia in the Chersonese stands to Thrace as

Chalcis in Euboea does to Boeotia. Those of you who know its critical situation are also aware why he keeps it for himself and makes sure that you don't get it. [183] This is a place that you oughtn't help him ready for use against yourselves. You should bring all your strength to bear to stop him, to make sure it doesn't happen. After all, he's made it clear that he won't pass up any opportunity that comes his way. When Philip was at Maronea, Charidemus sent Apollonides to him, bearing pledges for him and for Pammenes.* If Amadocus, who controlled that stretch of territory, hadn't forbidden Philip from setting foot on his land, we would inevitably already be at war with the Cardians and Cersobleptes. [*To the Clerk of the Court*] Take Chares' letter, which will prove that I'm not exaggerating.

Chares' letter is read out.

[184] [*To the jurors*] In the light of these facts, what else can you do but distrust him? Don't be stupid and treat him as a benefactor. It's as wrong for you to be grateful for Cersobleptes' fraudulent professions of friendship, offered under compulsion, as it is for you to be grateful for the small sums Charidemus personally spends on our generals and politicians to arrange for official votes of thanks for himself to be proposed in the Assembly. It makes far more sense for you to resent the attempts he makes to harm Athenian interests wherever and whenever he has free rein.

[185] Everyone else who has ever received an award from you has been honoured for the good he has done you. Charidemus is the only one who's been honoured for trying but failing to harm you! In fact, though, you've rewarded a man like him more than sufficiently just by not punishing him as he deserved. But that's not how our politicians feel. No, in return for his personal gifts to them, they're happy for him to be a citizen and a benefactor, to be awarded crowns and so on. Meanwhile, the rest of you sit in a duped daze, wondering what's going on. [186] Finally, today, with this preliminary resolution, they made you his protectors—were it not for this indictment of ours. With the decree in place, the city would be doing the job of a hired hand, someone paid to look after him; Athens would be the protector of Charidemus. Wouldn't that be wonderful? By all that's sacred, for a man who was once a bodyguard in the pay of Athenian enemies to be guarded himself by an Athenian decree!

[187] I suppose I may be asked why, if I was so certain about all

this, and if I'd noticed some wrongdoing on his part, I did nothing about it. Why did I raise no objection when you were making him a citizen or when you were officially commending him? Why, in short, did I say nothing until this decree appeared? Athenians, I'll be completely frank with you. I knew he was unworthy. I was there when he was asking for these favours and I raised no objection. I admit it. [188] Why didn't I? The main reason, Athenians, is that I was the only one speaking the truth about him, and I expected to be overwhelmed by the sheer numbers of those who were glibly lying to you. Secondly, as Zeus and all the gods are my witnesses, it never occurred to me to begrudge him any of the awards he received for deceiving you. I didn't see that you would come to any great harm if you pardoned him his many crimes and encouraged him to do you good in the future.

These two considerations were sufficient for the grant of citizenship and the award of the crown. [189] But then I saw him also hatching a plot whereby, as long as he could supply himself with people here to lie to you on his behalf, none of our friends abroad who would have liked to do you a favour and stop him acting against your interests would be able to put up any kind of effective resistance. Which friends do I mean? Athenodorus, for example, Simon, Bianor, Archebius of Byzantium,* the two Thracian kings. That's when I stepped up and took him to court. [190] And I think that a man would be behaving like someone with a personal grievance or a sycophant if he argued against the awarding of honours which weren't going to enable Charidemus to cause the city any particularly serious harm, but like an honest patriot if he opposed a plan that would do Athens a great deal of harm. That's why I said nothing before, but am speaking up now.

[191] Now, they expect to put you off the scent with an argument along the following lines: 'It may well be that Cersobleptes and Charidemus acted against Athens' interests in the past, when they were enemies, but they're friends now and serve us well. We must forgive and forget. We didn't dwell on the harm even the Spartans had done us as enemies when we went to their rescue, and we were equally forgiving of the Thebans and, most recently, the Euboeans.' [192] But I can't see that this argument has the slightest relevance, except to a situation in which we were trying to block a proposal to send military help to Cersobleptes and Charidemus. But that's not the situation today; there's no such proposal before us. What we

have is men whose arguments are motivated by their desire to make
Charidemus inappropriately powerful, by getting you to award him
immunity, and in my opinion their behaviour is appalling. I mean, it's
hardly right, Athenians, for arguments that are appropriate for people
seeking rescue to be deployed on behalf of men who are working to
find ways to injure you. [193] And here's another point. There may
be some validity to the argument that, even if he used to do you harm
as an enemy, he has changed his profession to one of friendship, but
even so, that's not the case here. No, his worst deceptions date from
after he started to claim to be a friend, and so, even if you choose
not to hate him for his earlier actions, you should still be suspicious
of him for his later ones. As for forgiving and forgetting, my view is
this: it is unforgiving to rehearse past injuries as a reason for hurting
someone, but a man who's trying to find a way to protect himself and
avoid harm is merely being prudent.

[194] They'll probably try to suggest that, since the man has now
committed himself to friendship with us and wants to do Athens
a favour, we'll discourage him and make him doubt us if we condemn
the decree. I'll tell you how I feel about this, Athenians. Even if he was
genuinely and sincerely our friend, even if he intended to do us nothing but good, by Zeus, I still wouldn't think this argument deserved
a hearing. I don't think any friendship is worth perjuring yourselves
for, by casting a plainly unjust vote. [195] Since we've found him to
be a liar and a cheat, then it's a win-win situation for us if you vote
against him. Either he'll stop lying because he thinks he can no longer
get away with it, or, if his desire to be on good terms with us is genuine, he'll start trying to do us good, knowing that he can no longer get
his way by lying. It's in our interest, then, to vote against him for this
reason, even if none of the other reasons were sufficient.

[196] Here's another point that's worth thinking about, Athenians.
In the old days, how were honours assigned and awards given to genuine benefactors, both citizens and foreigners? If the old system seems
better, you should copy it, while if you think yours an improvement,
you can choose to carry on with it. The first point to notice is how
they treated all those men—men whose benefactions to the city tower
over those of today's generals—men like Themistocles, the victor at
Salamis, and Miltiades, who commanded the forces at Marathon.
They didn't erect statues in bronze or make an excessive fuss of them.
[197] 'So didn't they feel gratitude to their benefactors?' Yes, they did,

Athenians, a great deal, and they showed it in a way that demeaned neither them nor the recipients. Although they were all men of ability, they chose to promote these individuals and make them their leaders; and for men of sound thinking, men who are prepared to see things as they are, being awarded first place in an exemplary society is a far greater honour than a bronze statue. [198] The thing is, Athenians, that our ancestors didn't deny themselves any of their achievements. No one would have described Salamis as Themistocles' battle or Marathon as Miltiades': they'd have called them Athenian battles. But nowadays, Athenians, what one usually hears is that Timotheus took Corcyra, or Iphicrates massacred the *mora*, or Chabrias won the battle of Naxos.* The extravagance of the awards you give these men for their achievements makes it seem as though you're reluctant to claim any credit yourselves for those achievements.

[199] So our ancestors' system for rewarding citizens was both honourable and good for the city, and ours is wrong. What about rewarding foreigners? When Menon of Pharsalus contributed twelve talents for the war at Eion-by-Amphipolis, and supplied a cavalry contingent of three hundred of his own retainers, our ancestors didn't decree seizure for anyone who killed him. No, they gave him citizenship and considered that enough of an honour.* [200] Or again, when Perdiccas, the king of Macedon at the time of the Persian invasion, wiped out the retreating barbarians after the battle of Plataea and ensured that the battle was a complete disaster for the Persian king, whose enmity he provoked for our sake, they didn't decree seizure for anyone who killed him, but just made him a citizen.* In those days, in fact, Athenian citizenship was so highly valued all over the world that people were prepared to do you immense favours to get it, but nowadays it has become so degraded that not a few of the people who've been granted it have been more destructive of our interests than our open enemies.

[201] It's not only the award of citizenship that has become tarnished and debased. They all have, thanks to the corruption of our damned and despicable politicians. They casually toss out proposals for awards, and their avarice is so rampant that they sell Athenian honours and awards like peddlers hawking the most trivial of wares, cheapening them; and their many customers can have decrees containing whatever they want drawn up for them at a fixed price. [202] First, to start with recent cases, they decided that the notorious

Ariobarzanes should be rewarded as they saw fit, him and all three of his sons, and they also included two citizens of Abydus in the deal, Philiscus and Agavus, deadly enemies of Athens and men of the worst sort.* Then, when Timotheus was held to have performed an important service of some kind, they not only heaped him with the highest honours, but included Phrasierides and Polysthenes in the deal as well, pernicious brutes who hadn't even been born free and had been responsible for atrocities that any man of any sensitivity would shrink from mentioning.* [203] Then, finally, there's the present situation. They demanded whatever honours they thought appropriate for Cersobleptes, and while they were rushing that through, they included two others in the deal. One is the man whose troublemaking I've been telling you about, and the other, Euderces by name, is a complete unknown. So you can see my point, Athenians: this is why honours that once seemed important now seem trivial. And the process still has far to run. The usual rewards are no longer sufficient; apparently they don't feel properly rewarded unless you also provide each of them with personal protection.

[204] May I speak my mind openly, Athenians? It's you who must bear the burden of responsibility for the fact that things have got so disgracefully out of hand. You're no longer prepared to punish wrongdoers; even this practice has vanished from the city. But look at how your ancestors used to punish those who did them wrong, and see if it resembles current practices. [205] When Themistocles began to claim to be superior to them, they found him guilty of medizing and sent him into exile.* And Cimon they fined fifty talents for having altered the ancestral constitution without consultation; in fact, they came within three votes of condemning him to death.* That was how they treated their major benefactors, and they were right. They refused to sell these men their freedom and their pride in their achievements. They honoured them as long as they did right, and refused to submit to any attempt on their part to do wrong. [206] But this is not what you do, Athenians. You acquit men who are patently guilty of the worst crimes, as long as they tell a couple of jokes or some carefully selected fellow tribesmen of theirs ask you for this favour. And if you do actually find someone guilty, you assess the penalty at twenty-five drachmas.*

So, you see, in the old days it wasn't just that Athens as a state was wealthy and brilliant, but also that no individual citizen stood

out from the crowd. [207] Here's the proof: whereas the houses of
the celebrities of the time, men such as Themistocles and Miltiades,
were no grander than everyone else's (as those of you who know what
they're like can confirm), public buildings and their fittings were of
such quality and grandeur that no one subsequently has been able
to come close. Just look at these gatehouses, shipsheds, and stoas;
look at Piraeus, and everything else they built in the city. [208] But
every single politician nowadays has such enormous personal wealth
that some of them have built houses for themselves that are grander
than public buildings, and some have bought up more land than all
of you in court today own together. Meanwhile, the public buildings
you actually complete these days, from foundation to plaster, are
embarrassingly small and shabby. But can you tell me the gains we've
made as a city that we shall bequeath to subsequent generations that
compare to what our ancestors left us—the Chersonese, Amphipolis,
and a reputation for noble deeds?

The politicians I'm talking about are doing their very best to frit-
ter away this reputation, but they can't make it disappear, Athenians.
[209] Of course not. In those days the personal wealth of the man
appointed to take charge of the tribute, Aristeides, didn't increase by
so much as a drachma. In fact, he was buried at public expense when
he died.* You had more public money available to spend on important
projects than any other state in Greece, and this meant that if you
voted for an expedition that would take a certain number of months,
your troops left with pay for that many months. Nowadays, however,
it's our politicians who transform their poverty into wealth and who
have equipped themselves with ample funds for the foreseeable
future, while the state treasury doesn't have enough to last a single
day. No sooner is there a job to be done than you lack the means to
do it. In those days, you see, the people were the masters of the politicians, not their servants, like now.

[210] The fault lies with men who draft decrees like the one
before us today. They've accustomed you to belittle yourselves, and
to reserve your admiration for one or two individuals. Your ancient
reputation and assets devolve on to these few men, then, but you have
been completely disinherited. Others grow prosperous while you look
on, and your only role is to be duped. But how long and loud would
those men of old groan, who gave their lives for liberty and glory, and
left monuments testifying to their many fine achievements, if they

could see that now the city has the style and status of a servant—if they could see us trying to decide whether or not to grant Charidemus immunity. Charidemus! Ye gods!

[211] But the really terrible thing is not that our decision-making is worse than that of our forebears: after all, no one has ever come close to them for virtue. No, it's that it's the worst in the world. A couple of examples will show you the depths of our disgrace. Our neighbours on Aegina, a tiny island with nothing to boast of, have never to this day made Lampis a citizen, even though he's the largest ship-owner in Greece and built their city and their port for them. They haven't gone further than giving him exemption from the tax on resident aliens.* [212] And those damned Megarians are so proud that when the Spartans sent Hermon the helmsman to them, with orders that they were to make him a citizen—he had captured two hundred triremes fighting alongside Lysander in the course of our catastrophic defeat at Aegospotami—the Megarians replied that they would make him a Megarian when they saw that the Spartans had made him a Spartan.* [213] And then there's the way the people of Oreus, which takes up no more than a quarter of Euboea, have treated Charidemus, the same man we've been talking about today. His mother is a citizen of Oreus (I'm not going to identify his father, because I need no more than the essentials for my argument), but despite the fact that Charidemus is halfway there by birth, they haven't yet found him deserving of the other half. He is registered there as a half-citizen, in the same way that children with only one citizen parent are registered here at Cynosarges.* [214] Athenians, he's already had citizenship from you and various other honours—are you going to add immunity as well? What for? What ships has he captured for you, so drawing on to himself the unwelcome attention of those who lost them? What city has he taken and handed over to you? What dangers has he faced on your behalf? When has he chosen the same enemies as you? There are no answers to these questions.

[215] Finally, jurymen, before I step down, I'd like to say a few words to you about the laws that I've cited for the purposes of comparison. Remember what I say, and I think it will help you protect yourselves against any attempts on their part to mislead and deceive you.

The first law expressly states that the Areopagus Council is to adjudicate cases of murder. Aristocrates, however, jumps straight from 'If anyone kills' to 'he is liable to seizure'. Take careful note of that, and remember that allowing someone a trial is the complete opposite of making someone liable to seizure without a trial.

[216] Next, the second law forbids the maltreatment of, or the extortion of money from, even a convicted murderer. Aristocrates, however, allows all that: in making him liable to seizure, he allows his captors to do whatever they like with him.

By law, the perpetrator is to be handed over to the Thesmothetes, even if he's apprehended in the victim's country. Aristocrates, however, allows the perpetrator to be seized by the actual person bringing the charge, even if he's apprehended abroad.

[217] By law, killing is a permissible response to certain offences. Aristocrates, however, doesn't qualify the matter at all: even if the killing took place under permissible conditions, he allows the seizure of a killer who is innocent under the law.

By law, if a man has been arrested, the first step is for a claim for redress to be brought against him. Aristocrates, on the contrary, makes no provision for a trial himself, nor does he insist that those whom he thinks deserve compensation pursue the matter in court. He just says that the perpetrator is liable to seizure, and that anyone who tries to rescue him is immediately to be excluded from the treaty of alliance with Athens.

[218] By law, up to three hostages may be taken from the people of the land where the murder took place, if they refuse to stand trial. Aristocrates, however, immediately excludes from the treaty a man who refuses to surrender the killer before a trial and tries to protect him from seizure.

By law, no law may be introduced unless it is applicable to everyone. Aristocrates, however, has drafted a special decree for a single individual.

By law, a decree cannot have more authority than a law. Aristocrates, however, makes a nonsense of the laws by having a decree take precedence over every single one of them.

[219] Note these points carefully, and remember them as long as this session lasts. Pay no attention to the tricky arguments they'll come up with; don't let them get away with them. Tell them, instead, to show you where a trial is provided for in Aristocrates' decree, or where he stipulates how a convicted murderer is to be punished. For if he had provided either for the due punishment of a man who had

been tried and found guilty elsewhere, or for a trial to determine the guilt or innocence of the alleged perpetrator and whether or not the murder was justified, he'd have done no wrong. [220] But if, after inscribing the charge 'If anyone kills', he has omitted to add 'and is found guilty of murder' or 'and the verdict of the court is that he committed murder'; if he has omitted any clauses along the lines of 'he shall submit to the punishment for murder' or 'the punishment in his case shall be the same as if he had killed an Athenian citizen'; in short, if he has omitted everything that would have made his proposal legal and has merely written that 'he is liable to seizure', don't be deceived, but trust me when I say that no proposal has ever contained so many illegalities.

59. APOLLODORUS: AGAINST NEAERA

This speech (actually two, a brief introductory speech by the otherwise unknown Theomnestus, followed by a longer supporting speech by Apollodorus) has at most a dubious place in this volume. It has survived since antiquity under the name of Demosthenes, but was probably (like a number of other speeches in the corpus) written by Apollodorus. It is, however, one of the most fascinating speeches to have survived from fourth-century Athens and a collection would be the poorer for lacking it. The ex-courtesan Neaera is prosecuted for allegedly living in marriage with an Athenian citizen, Stephanus, which was illegal for a non-citizen. The stakes are very high, since the penalty on conviction was enslavement with confiscation of property. Neaera, however, is not the real target, but Stephanus. He and Apollodorus stand on either side of the faultline in Athenian foreign policy created by the rise of Macedon. Apollodorus belonged to a faction (probably the same as that of Demosthenes) which favoured assertive action against Philip, while Stephanus belonged to a more pragmatic group, on whose behalf he had prosecuted Apollodorus in the early 340s. The speech can be dated with confidence to the period 343–340, a time when the politicians hostile to Macedon were using the courts systematically to settle scores and adjust the balance of power in Athens in their favour (speeches 8, 9, and 19 belong to the same period). Most readers (with the luxury of time for pause and reflection, which the jury did not have) have found the case against Neaera unconvincing. Much of the narrative is devoted to the fascinating, but uncontentious, issue of Neaera's origin and career, and no real evidence is offered to prove that the children are Stephanus' offspring by Neaera and not by an Athenian wife; in the latter case Neaera was just a mistress, as Stephanus claims. But what the speech lacks in factual strength, it gains in emotional force from the blatant manipulation of prejudice, which it effectively if not deftly combines with a pronounced element of voyeurism.

───────────

[1] I had good reasons, Athenians, and plenty of them, for bringing this suit against Neaera and appearing before you today. We—my father-in-law, myself, my sister, and my wife—have been grievously wronged by Stephanus, and faced very grave danger because of him. This means that I shall be acting in this trial 'not as aggressor, but in self-defence'.* For it was he who initiated the enmity between us,

even though nothing we have ever said or done has injured him. The first thing I'd like to do is recount for you what he has done to us, to arouse in you a greater degree of compassion as you listen to my defence. In fact, we came extremely close to losing both our country and our citizenship.

[2] When the people of Athens decreed that for his services to the city Pasion and his descendants should be Athenian citizens, my father approved of the decision.* He married his daughter, my sister, to Pasion's son Apollodorus, and she is the mother of his sons. Apollodorus treated my sister and all of us well, and since he believed that as relatives we really should share everything,* I married Apollodorus' daughter. [3] Some time later, Apollodorus became a member of the Council. He passed his assessment and swore the customary oath.* But then the city found itself involved in a war.* The situation was so critical that victory would have enabled us to become the most powerful state in Greece, and we would have definitively recovered our possessions and defeated Philip. On the other hand, if we had been slow to help our allies and had let them down for lack of money to keep an army, we'd have destroyed them, gained a reputation for unreliability throughout Greece, and risked losing all that was left to us—Lemnos, Imbros, Scyros, and the Chersonese.

[4] We were about to march out at full strength to Euboea and Olynthus, when Apollodorus, in his capacity as councillor, proposed a decree to the Council, and brought it to the Assembly as a preliminary motion* to the effect that the people should decide by a show of hands whether the surplus funds generated by the administration should be used for military purposes or should go to the Theoric Fund. By law the surplus funds generated by the administration are to be used at a time of war for military purposes, but he still thought it important for the people to have the right to choose how to dispose of what was, after all, their own.* He was under oath, you see, to act, as councillor, in the best interests of the Athenian people. And at the time you unanimously testified that that was what he had done. [5] For when it was put to the vote, no one voted against the use of the surplus for military purposes, and even now, if the topic comes up, everyone admits that Apollodorus offered the best advice and didn't deserve to suffer as he did. You should reserve your condemnation, then, for the man who lied to the jurors, and not blame the jurors for having been deceived.

It was Stephanus who indicted the decree as illegal,* brought the case to court, produced lying witnesses to defame Apollodorus,† repeatedly made allegations that were irrelevant to the case, and made certain that the decree had no future. [6] Well, we can understand why he might feel he had to proceed like that, but when the jurors were voting to fix the level of the penalty, he refused to compromise, despite our pleas, and proposed a fine of fifteen talents. His intention was to see Apollodorus and his children disfranchised, and my sister and all my family reduced to utter poverty and destitution. [7] Apollodorus' estate was worth a little less than three talents, which meant that he couldn't pay such a large fine, and then, if he failed to pay off the debt by the ninth prytany, it would be doubled and he'd be registered as owing the public treasury thirty talents.* Once he was on the list of public debtors, all his existing property would be inventoried as belonging to the state, and after it had been sold, he, his children, his wife, and all of us, would be faced with the direst poverty. [8] And that's not all. His other daughter would never even find a husband. I mean, who would have married an undowered woman, the daughter of an impoverished public debtor? So you can see how much trouble he caused us all, even though he had never been injured by us. I'm very grateful to the jurors who judged the case at the time, because at least they didn't let Apollodorus be ruined, but fixed the fine at one talent, so that he could just afford it. But even so, it's only fair for us to try to pay Stephanus back in his own coin.

[9] For this was not the only way he did his best to destroy us; he also wanted to have Apollodorus sent into exile. He brought a false charge against him, alleging that once in Aphidna (where he was in pursuit of a runaway slave of his) he struck a woman and she died of the blow. He groomed some slaves, disguised them as men from Cyrene, and issued the proclamation at the Palladium for murder.* [10] And it was Stephanus who prosecuted the case; he swore on oath that Apollodorus had killed the woman with his own hand, and invoked obliteration, if he should lie, for himself, his family, and his house. But it *was* a lie: the event had never taken place, and he hadn't seen it or heard about it from anyone on earth. So when his lies and the falsity of the charge were exposed, and it became clear to everyone that he was the hireling of Cephisophon and Apollophanes,* and had been bribed to see to Apollodorus' banishment or disfranchisement,

he received no more than a few of the five hundred votes, and left court a perjurer with an odious reputation.

[11] Ask yourselves, jurymen, what was likely to happen. What would I have done with myself, my wife, and my sister, if in either of the two trials Stephanus' schemes had succeeded and Apollodorus had been punished? Sunk in the depths of disgrace, our lives would be completely ruined. [12] So we had everyone's support. People were coming up to me in private and urging me to seek revenge for what he had done to us. They were accusing me of rank cowardice if I failed to gain compensation for my immediate family—for my sister, father-in-law, nieces, and wife—and if I failed to bring to court the woman who made no secret of her disrespect for the gods, her disdain for the city, and her contempt for the law. They urged me to prove her guilt and make you responsible for dealing with her as you see fit.

[13] Now, Stephanus here tried to take my family away from me by tactics that were illegal and unconstitutional, and by the same token I have come here today to prove to you that he is living under illegal conditions with a foreign woman; that he has introduced someone else's children into phratry and deme; that he gives the daughters of courtesans in marriage as though they were his own; that he has offended against the gods; and that he is trying to deny the people of Athens its right to grant citizenship to whoever it wishes. For why would anyone in the future go to all the bother and expense of trying to gain citizenship as an award from the Athenian people, if he can get the same thing cheaper from Stephanus?*

[14] All right, then. I've told you of my illegal treatment at Stephanus' hands before I brought this indictment. Next, you need to know about Neaera—[*pointing*] there she is. You need to know that she is a foreigner, that she lives with Stephanus as his wife, and that she has committed many crimes against the city. I have a request for you, then, jurymen, which I think is not inappropriate from a young man who lacks experience of public speaking: I would like your permission to invite Apollodorus to speak on my behalf in this trial.* [15] He's older than I am, knows the law better, and has taken a keen interest in the whole business. Besides, he's another of Stephanus' victims, and so no one could object if he defends himself against his aggressor. As for you, I would ask you, once you've heard the finer points of prosecution and defence, to vote in accordance with the truth and in the interest of the gods, the laws, justice, and yourselves.

APOLLODORUS' SPEECH

[16] You've heard from Theomnestus, Athenians, about the injuries I've suffered at Stephanus' hands that have made me stand up before you today and prosecute Neaera. What I'd like to make perfectly plain to you is that Neaera is a foreigner and is living with Stephanus under illegal circumstances. First, then, the clerk will read the law which made it possible for Theomnestus to bring this indictment, and for this trial to come to court.

The law is read out:
If a non-Athenian man lives in marriage with an Athenian woman by any manner or means, any Athenian in good standing may bring an indictment before the Thesmothetes. In the event of a guilty verdict, the defendant himself and his property shall be sold, and one third of the proceeds shall go to the successful prosecutor. The same shall apply also if a non-Athenian woman lives in marriage with an Athenian citizen, and in the event of her conviction the man living in marriage with the foreign woman shall owe 1,000 drachmas.

[17] There you have the law, jurymen. It forbids a non-Athenian woman from living in marriage with an Athenian citizen, or an Athenian woman from living in marriage with a non-Athenian man, by any manner or means, or from producing citizen children. Anyone who breaks this law, a foreign man or woman, is to be indicted before the Thesmothetes, and if they are found guilty, the law states that they are to be sold into slavery. So what I'd like to do now is prove to you in thorough detail that Neaera here is a foreigner.

[18] All right, then. Seven young girls were acquired, each at a very young age, by Nicarete, who was a freedwoman of Charisius of Elis and the wife of his cook Hippias. She was expert at spotting the potential for beauty in young girls, and skilled at bringing them up and training them in their craft. This was her profession; she made her living by these means. [19] She addressed them as though they were her daughters, making out that they were free women, so that she could charge men the highest possible price to spend time with them, and once she had profited, in every case, from the years of their youth, she promptly sold the seven of them: Anteia, Stratola, Aristocleia, Metaneira, Phila, Isthmias, and Neaera here. [20] Later on in my speech, if you want and I have enough water remaining,*

I'll give you the details of each of their new owners, and how the girls obtained their freedom from the men who had bought them from Nicarete. But now I'd like to go back to the time when Neaera belonged to Nicarete and was working as a courtesan, her body for hire by anyone who wanted to spend time with her.

[21] Lysias the sophist, who was in love with Metaneira, was already spending huge sums on her, but that wasn't enough for him: he also wanted to have her initiated into the Mysteries.* His thinking was that, since all the rest of the money he spent went to her mistress, anything he spent on the festival and the Mysteries would earn him the gratitude of the girl herself. So he asked Nicarete to come for the Mysteries and to bring Metaneira with her, so that she could be initiated, and he guaranteed that he would see to the whole process. [22] When they reached Athens, Lysias didn't put them up at his own house, out of respect for his wife (who was his niece, the daughter of Brachyllus) and his mother, a rather elderly woman who was also living there. Instead, he had the two of them, Metaneira and Nicarete, stay with Philostratus of Colonae, an unmarried friend of his. And Neaera travelled with her mistress too; she was already working as a prostitute, but was rather young, having not yet reached puberty.

[23] To confirm the truth of this—that Neaera belonged to Nicarete, came to Athens with her, and was already in the business of selling her services to anyone who was willing to pay her price—I call on Philostratus himself to testify to you.

Philostratus' deposition is read out:†
Philostratus of Colonae, the son of Dionysius, testifies that he knows that Neaera belonged to Nicarete, who also owned Metaneira, and that they stayed with him when they came to Athens for the Mysteries from their home in Corinth; and that it was Lysias, the son of Cephalus, a close personal friend, who arranged for them to stay with him.

[24] Some time later, Athenians, Simus of Thessaly also came here with Neaera, for the Great Panathenaea. Nicarete came with her, and they stayed at the house of Ctesippus of Cydantidae, the son of Glauconides. While they were there, Neaera joined her mistress in communal drinking and eating, since she was a courtesan.* I have witnesses to confirm the truth of this. [25] [*To the Clerk of the Court*] Please call Euphiletus of Aexone, the son of Simon, and Aristomachus of Alopece, the son of Critodemus.

The witnesses' deposition is read out:
Euphiletus of Aexone, the son of Simon, and Aristomachus of Alopece, the son of Critodemus, testify that they know that Simus of Thessaly came to Athens for the Great Panathenaea, and that with him were Nicarete and Neaera, the defendant in this case; and that they stayed with Ctesippus of Cydantidae, the son of Glauconides, and that when there were many men in Ctesippus' house, drinking together, Neaera drunk along with them, since she was a courtesan.

[26] [*To the jurors*] After this, then, she was working openly in Corinth and became a celebrity. Among her lovers were Xenocleides the poet and Hipparchus the actor, both of whom hired her services and kept her. I'm not able to corroborate this by presenting Xenocleides' testimony, because he's forbidden by law from testifying in a trial. [27] When, at Callistratus' instigation, we set about rescuing the Spartans,* Xenocleides spoke out in the Assembly against the expedition. Now, before the war had started, he had bought the right to collect the two-per-cent tax, and he had to pay his instalments to the Council chamber every prytany.* He didn't join that particular expedition, then, because he was legally exempt, but Stephanus still indicted him for draft-evasion, and his wicked lies cost Xenocleides the case and his citizenship. [28] But don't you think it's terrible for Stephanus to deprive natural citizens, with a legitimate claim to citizenship, of the right to speak their minds, while he illegally and forcibly passes off as citizens those who don't belong at all? I now call on Hipparchus himself to testify to you. That way I will force him either to testify or to take an oath of disclaimer, as the law demands, or I shall subpoena him.* [*To the Clerk of the Court*] Please call Hipparchus for me.

Hipparchus' deposition is read out:
Hipparchus of Athmone testifies that he and Xenocleides hired Neaera, the defendant in this case, in Corinth, since she was a courtesan who worked for hire, and that in Corinth Neaera drank along with himself and Xenocleides the poet.

[29] [*To the jurors*] Next, two men became her lovers, Timanoridas of Corinth and Eucrates of Leucas. Since Nicarete was expensive and demanding—she insisted on their paying all the daily expenses of her household—they paid Nicarete thirty mnas for Neaera, so that they

owned her outright, according to Corinthian law, as their slave. She was theirs, then, and they spent as much time as they wanted with her. [30] Now, when they were about to marry, they told her that they didn't want to see her, their former courtesan, plying her trade in Corinth or under the thumb of a brothel-keeper. They said they'd be happy to take less money from her than they had paid and that they wanted to see her doing well, so they told her they would contribute a thousand drachmas, five hundred each, towards her freedom, and that she was to come up with the remaining twenty mnas herself and give it to them.

On hearing this, she summoned some of her past lovers to Corinth, including Phrynion of Paeania. Phrynion was the son of Demon and brother of Demochares, and, as the older among you will remember, he used to have a wild and extravagant lifestyle. [31] When Phrynion reached her, she told him what Timanoridas and Eucrates had said. She gave him the money she had collected from her other lovers as a loan to purchase her freedom, and all her personal savings, and asked him to add what was left to make up the twenty mnas, and pay it on her behalf to Eucrates and Timanoridas, so that she would be free. [32] Phrynion happily complied. He took from her the money her other lovers had contributed, added the remainder himself, and paid the twenty mnas to Eucrates and Timanoridas on her behalf for her freedom, on the understanding that she wouldn't ply her trade in Corinth. To confirm the truth of this, I call as witness someone who was there at the time. [*To the Clerk of the Court*] Call Philagrus of Melite.

Philagrus' deposition is read out:
Philagrus of Melite testifies that he was in Corinth when Phrynion, the brother of Demochares, paid twenty mnas for Neaera, the defendant in this case, to Timanoridas of Corinth and Eucrates of Leucas, and that after paying the money he went off to Athens, taking Neaera with him.

[33] [*To the jurors*] After bringing her back to Athens, Phrynion treated her in an obscene and dissolute manner. He used to take her with him everywhere, whenever he was invited out in the evening for a drinks party; she was by his side at all his drunken revels; and he had sex with her in public whenever and wherever he felt like it, ostentatiously showing onlookers what he could get away with. He used to take her to parties all over town, and once they went to the house of Chabrias of Aexone. This was in the archonship of Socratides,* on the occasion of Chabrias' victory at the Pythian games in the four-horse

chariot event, with the team he had bought from the sons of Mitys of Argos. When Chabrias returned from Delphi he celebrated the victory at Colias,* and many men there had sex with her while she was drunk, including the slaves who had served the meal. [34] To confirm the truth of this, I shall call witnesses who were there at the time and saw what happened. [*To the Clerk of the Court*] Please call Chionides of Xypete and Euthetion of Cydathenaeum.

The deposition is read out:
Chionides of Xypete and Euthetion of Cydathenaeum testify that they were invited to dinner by Chabrias, when Chabrias was celebrating victory in the chariot race, and that the party took place at Colias; and that they know that Phrynion was at this dinner, accompanied by Neaera, the defendant in this case, and that after Phrynion and Neaera went to bed they saw various men, including some of the servants, Chabrias' household slaves, get up in the night and go to Neaera.

[35] [*To the jurors*] Finding herself being humiliated by Phrynion's obscenity, rather than treated as lovingly as she had expected—finding that she wasn't getting what she wanted from him—she packed up his household goods, all the clothing and jewellery he had bought for her, and two slave-women (called Thratta and Coccaline), and ran off to Megara. This was the year of Asteius' archonship here in Athens, and the time of our second war with Sparta.* [36] She spent two years in Megara (the years of the archonships of Asteius and Alcisthenes), but she wasn't making enough money as a courtesan to maintain her household. She was extravagant, the Megarians are mean and stingy, and there were few visitors from abroad because of the war, and because the Megarians were on the Spartan side while we controlled the sea. At the same time, she couldn't go back to Corinth because she had been set free by Eucrates and Timanoridas on the condition that she wouldn't ply her trade there.

[37] The war came to an end in the archonship of Phrasicleides, with the battle of Leuctra between the Thebans and the Spartans,* and at that juncture Stephanus went to live in Megara. He took a room at Neaera's house, since she was a courtesan, and struck up a relationship with her. She told him about Phrynion's abusive behaviour, and everything that had happened, and gave him the property of Phrynion's that she had brought with her. She wanted to live in Athens, you see, but since she was afraid of Phrynion—she had

wronged him, after all—and knew his violent and haughty nature, she made Stephanus her protector.

[38] What Stephanus told her in Megara reassured her. He boasted that Phrynion would regret it if he laid a finger on her, and he promised to make her his wife, to introduce the children she already had to the phratry as if they were his own, and to make them Athenian citizens.* No one in the world would harm her, he said. And so he brought her back here with him from Megara, along with her three children: Proxenus, Ariston, and a daughter, who nowadays is known as Phano. [39] He put her and the children up in the little house he used to own near the Whispering Hermes, the one between the houses of Dorotheus of Eleusis and Cleinomachus, which Spintharus has now bought from him for seven mnas.* In other words, since this was the sum total of Stephanus' property, he had two reasons for bringing her here: not only would he have a beautiful courtesan for free, but she would earn money and maintain the household. For Stephanus had no source of income other than what he could earn by sycophancy.

[40] When Phrynion found out that she was living here with Stephanus, he went to Stephanus' house, taking some young men with him, and tried to carry her off. Stephanus opposed the seizure, as he was entitled to by law, on the grounds that she wasn't a slave, but then Phrynion required her to post bail before the Polemarch.* To confirm the truth of this, I shall call as witness the man himself, the one who was Polemarch at the time. [To the Clerk of the Court] Call Aëtes of Ceiriadae.

Aëtes' deposition is read out:
Aëtes of Ceiriadae testifies that, when he was Polemarch, Neaera, the defendant in the present case, was required by Phrynion, the brother of Demochares, to post bail, and that the men who went bail for Neaera were Stephanus of Eroeadae, Glaucetes of Cephisia, and Aristocrates of Phalerum.

[41] [To the jurors] So Stephanus went bail for her. While she was living with him, she continued to ply the same trade just as assiduously as before, except that she charged higher fees for her company, on the pretext that she now enjoyed a degree of respectability, as a married woman. And Stephanus became her accomplice in blackmail: if he caught a wealthy non-Athenian making love to her, someone he didn't know, he would accuse the man of having illicit

sex with her, lock him inside the house, and demand a great deal of money.* But this is no more than one would expect, [42] given that Stephanus and Neaera couldn't afford to meet their daily expenses, and it cost a lot to run the household. She had to earn enough to keep him, herself, the three children she had brought with her, two slave-women, and a male attendant, and matters were not made easier by the fact that she had become accustomed to living in comfort, since in the past other people had paid her bills.

[43] In those days, you see, Stephanus had no income worth men-tioning from his political career. He was still only a sycophant, one of those who raise their voices by the speaker's platform, who are paid to bring indictments and denunciations, and to put their names to other people's proposals. His political career didn't take off until he fell under the spell of Callistratus of Aphidna. After I've finished with Neaera—after I've shown that she's a foreigner, that she has griev-ously wronged you, and that she has offended against the gods— I shall tell you how and why Stephanus' association with Callistratus came about too.* [44] Then you'll be in a position to see that he deserves punishment no less than Neaera. In fact, he deserves to be punished more severely, and all the more so because, while claiming to be an Athenian citizen, he has shown utter contempt for the laws, for you, and for the gods. The measure of his contempt is that he doesn't even bother to curb himself for shame at his wrongdoing. No, his continued persecution of me and others in the courts has forced my friend here, Theomnestus, to bring him and Neaera to court on a grave enough charge to ensure that her background will be investi-gated and his iniquity exposed for all to see.

[45] Well now, after Phrynion initiated proceedings against Stephanus for opposing his seizure of Neaera and for receiving the property of his that Neaera had brought with her, some friends brought them together and persuaded them to submit the dispute to their arbitration.* Satyrus of Alopece, the brother of Lacedaemonius, acted as arbitrator for Phrynion, and Saurias of Lamptrae did the same for Stephanus. As the impartial arbitrator, they chose Diogeiton of Acharnae. [46] The arbitrators met in the sanctuary,* and after hearing an account of events from both men and from Neaera, they gave their verdict, which was accepted by both sides: Neaera was free and her own mistress, but she was to return to Phrynion everything she had taken with her, except for the things that had been bought

just for her—the clothing, the jewellery, and the slave-women; and she was to share her time equally between the two men, but any other arrangement reached by mutual agreement was also to be valid. Her expenses were to be paid by whichever of the two men she was with at the time, and the disputants were thereafter to be on good terms with one another and to bear no grudges. [47] That was the judgement reached by the arbitrators to settle the dispute between Phrynion and Stephanus over Neaera. To confirm the truth of this, the clerk will read out the arbitrators' deposition. [*To the Clerk of the Court*] Call Satyrus of Alopece, Saurias of Lamptrae, and Diogeiton of Acharnae.

The arbitrators' deposition is read out:
Satyrus of Alopece, Saurias of Lamptrae, and Diogeiton of Acharnae testify that they served as arbitrators in the dispute between Stephanus and Phrynion over Neaera and brought about a settlement between the two men, and that the terms of the settlement are as given by Apollodorus.

The settlement is read out:
Settlement was reached between Phrynion and Stephanus on the following terms: that each of them should have Neaera stay with him and have the use of her for an equal number of days per month, unless they come to some other agreement between themselves.

[48] [*To the jurors*] With the settlement in place, the men who had represented Phrynion and Stephanus at the arbitration and supported them through the whole business did what people usually do under such circumstances, especially when the dispute concerns a courtesan: they each went to dine with the man they had represented when it was his turn to have Neaera living with him, and ate and drank there in her company, since she was a courtesan. [*To the Clerk of the Court*] To confirm the truth of this, please call as witnesses their companions Eubulus of Probalinthus, Diopeithes of Melite, and Cteson of Cerameis.

The deposition is read out:
Eubulus of Probalinthus, Diopeithes of Melite, and Cteson of Cerameis testify that, once the dispute between Phrynion and Stephanus over Neaera had been settled, they often used to eat and drink in the company of Neaera, the defendant in the present case, both when Neaera was staying with Stephanus and when she was staying with Phrynion.

[49] [*To the jurors*] All right, then. Neaera was originally a slave; she was sold twice; she worked as a courtesan; she ran away from Phrynion to Megara; and when she returned to Athens she was required to post bail before the Polemarch as a foreigner. I've demonstrated the truth of all this, and it's been corroborated by witnesses. What I'd like to do next is show that Stephanus has also testified himself to her foreign status.

[50] Neaera's daughter—the one she brought with her when she came to live with Stephanus, and who was called Strybele in those days, but is nowadays known as Phano—was given in marriage by Stephanus, as though she were his own daughter, to an Athenian called Phrastor of Aegilia, with a dowry of thirty mnas. When she went to live with Phrastor, an industrious man who had grown rich through frugal living, she proved incapable of adjusting to his lifestyle. She missed the way things were done in her mother's household, and the unrestrained lifestyle there; no doubt she'd been brought up without any discipline at all. [51] Phrastor soon realized that she wasn't a decent woman and had no interest in obeying his wishes. At the same time, he had also found out by then that she wasn't Stephanus' daughter, but Neaera's, and that he had been tricked, above all when he had been betrothed to her. He had accepted her as the daughter of Stephanus, not of Neaera, supposing that she was his daughter by an Athenian woman he had been married to before Neaera.

All this made Phrastor furious and, feeling himself insulted and lied to, he threw the woman out of his house, pregnant, after just a year of marriage, and refused to return the dowry.* [52] Stephanus brought a suit for maintenance against him at the Odeum, under the law that stipulates that a man who divorces his wife is to return the dowry, or is to pay interest on it of nine obols per mna per month, and that the woman's guardian may bring a suit for maintenance at the Odeum on her behalf.* And Phrastor responded by indicting Stephanus before the Thesmothetes for betrothing to him, an Athenian citizen, the daughter of a foreign woman, as though she were a member of his own family.* Here's the law under which this suit of Phrastor's was brought. [*To the Clerk of the Court*] Please read it out.

The law is read out:
If anyone gives a foreign woman in marriage to an Athenian man as though she were a member of his own family, he shall be disfranchised,

and his property shall be confiscated, with one third going to the successful
prosecutor. Anyone in good standing may bring an indictment before the
Thesmothetes, as in a prosecution for masquerading as a citizen.

[53] [*To the jurors*] There you have the law under which Stephanus
was indicted by Phrastor before the Thesmothetes. In view of the
severity of the punishment to which he would become liable if he
were convicted of betrothing the daughter of a foreign woman, he
made a deal with Phrastor. He abandoned his claim to the dowry and
withdrew the suit for maintenance, and Phrastor withdrew his indictment from the Thesmothetes. To confirm the truth of this, I call on
Phrastor himself to testify; I shall compel him to give evidence as the
law requires.* [54] [*To the Clerk of the Court*] Call Phrastor of Aegilia.

Phrastor's deposition is read out:
Phrastor of Aegilia testifies that when he found out that Stephanus had
betrothed the daughter of Neaera to him as though she were his own daugh-
ter, he indicted him before the Thesmothetes in accordance with the law,
threw the woman out of his house, and stopped living with her, and when
Stephanus brought a suit for maintenance against him at the Odeum, he
came to terms with Stephanus, with the result that the indictment was
withdrawn from the Thesmothetes and so was the suit for maintenance
that Stephanus had brought against me.

[55] [*To the jurors*] Now let me produce further evidence that
Neaera is a foreigner—evidence supplied both by Phrastor and by
members of his phratry and his clan.* Not long after Phrastor had
divorced Neaera's daughter, he fell ill. In fact, he was in a very bad
way, in extreme distress. Now, Phrastor had long ago fallen out with
his family, and he remained angry and on extremely bad terms with
them. He was also childless, and he was comforted in his illness by
Neaera and her daughter. [56] They used to come and visit him,
since he was ill and had no one to take care of him; they brought him
things to make him feel better, and looked after him. I'm sure you all
know from your own experience how welcome a woman is at a time
of illness, by a patient's bedside. And so he was persuaded to take
back and to recognize as his own son the child Neaera's daughter had
given birth to after he had sent her away pregnant, when he found
out that she wasn't Stephanus' daughter, but Neaera's, and was furious at the deceit. [57] Why did he do this? For perfectly human and

comprehensible reasons. He was in a bad way and the chances of his survival were slim; he didn't want his relatives to inherit his property and he didn't want to die childless. And so he recognized the child as his own and took him into his home.

Now, I can prove, decisively and conclusively, that Phrastor would never have done this if he'd been well. [58] For as soon as he recovered from that illness, as soon as he was back on his feet and reasonably fit, he legally married a wife of citizen birth, the legitimate daughter of Satyrus of Melite, the sister of Diphilus. So there's your proof: he didn't accept the boy as his own voluntarily, but was pressured into it by his illness, his childlessness, their nursing of him, and the fact that he hated his family and didn't want them to inherit his estate in the event of his death.

You'll be even more convinced when you hear what happened next. [59] While he was still ill, Phrastor set in motion the introduction of his son by Neaera's daughter to his phratry and to the Brytidae, the clan to which he belonged. But his fellow clansmen rejected the boy and refused to register him. Their reasons, of course, were that they were aware of his wife's background (Neaera's daughter, I mean, his first wife), and knew that he had divorced her and that it was only his illness that had persuaded him to take the boy back. [60] Phrastor sued them for their refusal to register his son, and his fellow clansmen challenged him before the arbitrator to lay his hands on unblemished sacrificial offerings and swear that he considered the mother of his son to be a citizen woman who had been legally given to him in marriage.* In response to this challenge from his fellow clansmen before the arbitrator, Phrastor declined the offer and refused to swear the oath. [61] To confirm the truth of this, I shall call as witnesses some of the Brytidae who were there at the time.

The witnesses' deposition is read out:
Timostratus of Hecale, Xanthippus of Eroeadae, Eualces of Phalerum, Anytus of Laciadae, Euphranor of Aegilia, and Nicippus of Cephale testify that both they and Phrastor of Aegilia belong to the clan Brytidae, and that when Phrastor requested that his son be enrolled as a member of the clan, they vetoed the enrolment, because they knew that the mother of Phrastor's son was the daughter of Neaera.

[62] The evidence I'm presenting makes it perfectly clear: even those who are closest to Neaera—both Stephanus, her current

husband, and Phrastor, who was married to her daughter—have testified to her foreign status. Stephanus did so by refusing to go to court to defend Neaera's daughter, when he was indicted by Phrastor before the Thesmothetes for betrothing the daughter of a foreign woman to him, an Athenian citizen, and by abandoning his claim to the dowry instead of recovering it. [63] Phrastor did so by divorcing Neaera's daughter once he found out that she wasn't Stephanus' child, and by refusing to return the dowry. Then later he did the same again. This was when, thanks to his illness and childlessness, and the feud between him and his family, he was prevailed on to acknowledge the boy as his own and tried to get him enrolled in the clan. His fellow clansmen rejected the boy and challenged Phrastor to swear an oath, but he refused, because he preferred to avoid perjury, and later legally married another woman, an Athenian. There can be no doubt about the significance of these actions, and they prove conclusively that Neaera here has foreign status.

[64] Another way to see that Neaera is no Athenian is to consider the immoral ways in which Stephanus tries to satisfy his greed. Epaenetus of Andros, for example, had long been one of Neaera's lovers, and a very generous one; and because of his fondness for her he stayed with them whenever he was in Athens. [65] Stephanus cooked up a plot against him and invited him to the country, allegedly for a sacrifice. While they were there, Stephanus caught Epaenetus having illicit sex with Neaera's daughter,* and frightened him into promising to pay thirty mnas. He accepted as guarantors Aristomachus, the former Thesmothete, and Nausiphilus, the son of the ex-Archon Nausinicus, and let Epaenetus go on the understanding that he would pay him the money.

[66] But as soon as Epaenetus was out of his grasp and regained his liberty, he indicted Stephanus before the Thesmothetes for wrongful detention, under the law that states that anyone wrongfully detained for illicit sex may bring an indictment before the Thesmothetes for wrongful detention; and that if he secures the conviction of the man who detained him and the Thesmothetes decide that he was set up, he is liable to no penalty and his guarantors are released from their liability; but if the court decides that he *is* a seducer, the guarantors are required to hand him over to the man who won the case, who can do whatever he likes with him within the confines of the court, short of using a knife, seeing that he is guilty of illicit sex. [67] This

was the law that allowed Epaenetus to indict Stephanus. He admitted that he had had sex with the woman, but denied that it was illicit, on the grounds that she wasn't Stephanus' daughter, but Neaera's; that Neaera herself was aware of his relationship with her daughter; that he had spent a fortune on them; and that he supported the entire household whenever he was in Athens. In addition to these arguments, he also cited the law which forbids a man to be seized as a seducer if he is found with women who sit in a brothel or offer themselves openly on the streets,* and he claimed that that's what Stephanus' house was, a brothel—that prostitution was their business and their chief source of income.

[68] Faced with these arguments from Epaenetus and the prospect of being indicted by him, Stephanus realized that he would be exposed as a brothel-keeper and sycophant, and submitted his dispute with Epaenetus to the arbitration of the same two guarantors, on the condition that they were released from their liability, and that Epaenetus would withdraw the indictment. [69] Epaenetus accepted these terms and cancelled the indictment he was in the process of bringing against Stephanus. When the meeting took place, with the guarantors sitting as arbitrators, Stephanus had nothing to say to excuse himself, but made it clear that he expected Epaenetus to contribute towards Neaera's daughter's dowry. He brought up his own poverty and the woman's disastrous marriage to Phrastor; he explained that, having lost the dowry, he wouldn't be able to find another husband for her. [70] 'You've had the girl,' he said. 'It would be only right for you to do her a favour.' He came up with other specious arguments too, typical of a man pleading in difficult circumstances. The arbitrators listened to what the two men had to say and arranged a settlement between them, getting Epaenetus to agree to contribute a thousand drachmas towards Neaera's daughter's dowry. To confirm the truth of this, I call as witnesses the men themselves, who acted as guarantors and arbitrators.

[71] The witnesses' deposition is read out:
Nausiphilus of Cephale and Aristomachus of Cephale testify that they acted as guarantors for Epaenetus of Andros when Stephanus said that he had caught Epaenetus in illicit sex; and that after Epaenetus had left Stephanus' house and regained his liberty, he indicted Stephanus before the Thesmothetes for wrongful detention; and that in their role as

conciliators they reconciled Epaenetus and Stephanus; and that the terms of the settlement are as given by Apollodorus.

The settlement is read out:
The arbitrators reconciled Stephanus and Epaenetus on the following terms: that the business with the detainment should be forgotten; that Epaenetus should give 1,000 drachmas for Phano's dowry, since he has had the use of her many times; and that Stephanus should let Epaenetus have Phano whenever he is in Athens and wants to consort with her.

[72] So here was a woman whose foreign status was openly recognized, and Stephanus had even gone so far as to detain someone he caught with her for illicit sex. But that wasn't the end of his and Neaera's insolence and unscrupulousness. Not content with claiming citizen status for her, when they saw that the position of King Archon had fallen to Theogenes of the clan Coeronidae, a man from a good family, but poor and unworldly, Stephanus supported him through his assessment and helped him with the costs involved in taking up his post.* Having wormed his way into his confidence, he bought from him the position of Secretary to the Archon, and gave him Neaera's daughter in marriage, as though she were his own daughter. Do you see how little respect he has for you and the law? [73] And Phano used to perform the unnameable rites for you as the representative of the city;* she has seen things no foreigner such as her should see, and despite her alien status she has set her feet on ground that is forbidden to all the multitudinous population of Athens, except for the wife of the King Archon; she administered the oath to the Reverend Women* who assist with the rites; she was given in marriage to Dionysus; and as the city's representative she performed in honour of the gods the many solemn, secret ceremonies that have been handed down by our ancestors. When rites are so secret that no one is allowed even to hear about them, how could it not be sacrilege for a mere amateur actually to perform them? Especially a woman of this sort, with a history like hers.

[74] I'd like to go back to the beginning, and give you a more thorough and detailed account of these ceremonies. This will focus your attention on the question of punishment, and you'll see that the vote you cast, when you penalize impiety and punish the wrongdoers, defends not just yourselves and the law, but also the practice of religious observance.

In ancient times, Athenians, the city was a monarchy, and the king-ship went to the man who stood out in each generation thanks to his autochthony.* All religious rituals were the responsibility of the king, and his wife used to perform the most solemn and secret ceremonies, as you would expect from a queen. [75] Then Theseus formed us into a single community and established the democracy, but even when the city had become populous, the people still chose a king by a show of hands from a shortlist of candidates of sufficient calibre, and they passed a law that his wife should be an Athenian citizen and was to be a virgin when she married, having never been with another man. The reason for this law was to ensure that the unnameable rituals would continue to be performed in the traditional manner on the city's behalf, and to see that the gods were treated with due respect, with no omissions or innovations. [76] They inscribed this law on a stone stele and set it up in the sanctuary of Dionysus in the Marshes, next to the altar. The very stele stands there still, and the inscription, in the Attic alphabet, is just about legible.* This stele was a concrete token of the Athenians' reverence for the god, and a sacred trust that they bequeathed to future generations, showing what we expect of the woman who is to be given as a bride to the god and will perform his rites. And the reason they set it up in Dionysus' most ancient and holy sanctuary, the one in the marshes, was to restrict knowledge of what was written on the inscription to few people. For the sanctuary is opened only once a year, on 12 Anthesterion.*

[77] You can see, then, the impressive amount and quality of care that your ancestors devoted to these sacred and solemn rites. You should take them just as seriously yourselves, Athenians. You *must* punish people who in their arrogance think themselves superior to the law and have failed to show proper reverence for the gods. There are two reasons why they deserve punishment: first, they need to pay the penalty for their crimes; second, it will deter other people and make them think twice before offending against gods and city.

[78] I'd like to call for you now the Sacred Herald. His job is to assist the wife of the King Archon as she stands by the altar and administers the oath to the Reverend Women, equipped with their baskets, before they touch the sacrificial offerings. Then you'll hear the wording of the oath, or as much of it as you're permitted to hear, and you'll appreciate the solemnity, sacredness, and antiquity of the rites.

The oath of the Reverend Women is read out:
I live a consecrated life. I am pure and untainted by impurities, and espe-
cially by intercourse with a man. I perform for Dionysus the Theoenia and
the Iobaccheia according to ancestral custom and on the appointed days.

[79] Now you've heard as much of the oath and the traditional rites
as you're permitted to hear, and I've told you how the rites were performed, and the Reverend Women's oath administered, by the woman
Stephanus passed off as his own daughter and married to Theogenes
when he was King Archon. You're also aware that not even the women
who witness these rites are allowed to talk about them to anyone else.

The next evidence I want you to consider concerns a confidential
meeting, but the facts themselves, as I shall show, allow us to infer the
truth of what happened behind closed doors. [80] Some time after
the celebration of these rites, the appointed days arrived for the nine
Archons to go up to the Areopagus.* The Areopagus Council—which
often has a very important role to play to ensure that as a community we treat the gods with due observance—immediately launched
an investigation into the background of this woman Theogenes had
married, and the facts came to light. The rites were their principal
concern, and they set about punishing Theogenes, in secret session
and without any hullabaloo, to the limit of their authority, given that
they don't have discretionary power to punish fellow Athenians as
they might wish.* [81] They talked things over, expressed their dis-
pleasure with Theogenes, and proposed to fine him for having married such a woman, and for having let her perform the unnameable
rites for the city.

But Theogenes begged, implored, and pleaded with them for leniency. He said that he hadn't known that she was Neaera's daughter,
that he had been tricked by Stephanus. He had married her legally,
he said, on the understanding that she was the legitimate daughter
of Stephanus, and had made him his secretary and manager to compensate for his own unworldliness and naivety. He had assumed that
Stephanus was his friend, and that was also why he had become his
son-in-law. [82] 'I'll prove to you,' he said, 'beyond doubt or dispute,
that I'm not lying. I shall send the woman away, out of my house,
since she's Neaera's daughter and not Stephanus'. That should convince you to trust me when I tell you that I was tricked; but if I fail to
divorce her, by all means go ahead and punish me for my offences and

my impiety.' [83] Partly thanks to Theogenes' promises and pleas, and partly because the Areopagus Council pitied him for his naivety and believed that he really had been lied to by Stephanus, they relented. And his first actions on coming back down from the Areopagus hill were to throw the woman, Neaera's daughter, out of his house and to sack Stephanus from his cabinet for having lied to him. This brought his trial to an end: the Areopagites forgave Theogenes, excusing him on the grounds that he had been tricked. [84] To confirm the truth of this, I call as witness Theogenes himself; I shall compel him to give evidence. [*To the Clerk of the Court*] Please call Theogenes of Erchia.

Theogenes' deposition is read out:
Theogenes of Erchia testifies that when he was King Archon he married Phano, believing her to be the daughter of Stephanus, and that when he realized that he had been deceived, he threw her out and brought the marriage to an end, and sacked Stephanus from his post and forbade him to serve on his cabinet.

[85] Now here's the law that deals with these matters. Please take it and read it out. [*To the jurors*] This will allow you to see that not only should a woman of this sort, with her history, have had nothing to do with these particular rites—she shouldn't have seen them, she shouldn't have been responsible for the sacrifice, and she shouldn't have performed any traditional religious duties for the city—but she should also be barred from *all* religious observance here in Athens. For a woman with whom a man has been caught in illicit sex isn't allowed to enter any state-run sanctuary, even though the law permits foreign women and slave women to enter them as spectators and suppliants. [86] In other words, the *only* women forbidden by law from entering state-run sanctuaries are those with whom a man has been caught in illicit sex. If such a woman breaks the law and enters one of these sanctuaries, anyone can do whatever he likes with her, short of killing her, and will not be punished for it. Anyone who comes across her there is permitted by law to punish her for her crime.* The reason for refusing her any legal right of redress, however brutally she is treated short of death, is to keep our sanctuaries untainted by pollution and impiety. The law threatens women into living modest and proper lives, taking care of their domestic duties as they are supposed to, and teaches them that if they commit offences of this sort, they will find themselves evicted simultaneously from their husbands'

homes and from the city's sanctuaries. [87] You'll see that I'm telling the truth once you've heard the clerk read the actual law. [*To the Clerk of the Court*] Go ahead.

The law on illicit sex is read out:
Moreover, anyone who catches a man in illicit sex may no longer live in marriage with his wife; if he does so, he shall be disfranchised. No woman with whom a man has been caught in illicit sex shall be permitted to enter any state-run sanctuary; if she does so, she shall suffer any form of punishment short of death with no right of redress.

[88] [*To the jurors*] I'd like next, Athenians, to have the Athenian people themselves testify to how important they regard these rites and how much care they have devoted to them. The point is that in all respects the people have sovereign authority in the city. Although they therefore had complete freedom of action, they considered the grant of Athenian citizenship so valuable and prestigious that they made laws to regulate how they themselves go about making some-one a citizen when they want to. These are the laws that have been violated by Stephanus and others who have made the same kind of marriage. [89] You'll understand these laws better once you've heard them, and you'll appreciate how Stephanus and his ilk have debased the most valuable and prestigious gifts that are reserved for the city's benefactors.

The first point to note, then, is that, by law, the people aren't allowed to make anyone an Athenian citizen unless he has earned it by exceptional service to the democracy. Second, even when the people concur with the proposal and assent to the award of citizenship, the law doesn't allow the award to become valid unless at least six thousand Athenians cast their votes in favour in a secret ballot at the next Assembly.* [90] By law, the Executive Committee is required to have the ballot boxes in place and hand out the ballots to the people as they approach the meeting place, before the barriers have been removed and non-Athenians are allowed in.* That way, everyone thinks about the candidate for citizenship by himself, without external influences, and decides whether or not he qualifies for the award he is slated to receive.

The next step is that any Athenian citizen may, if he so chooses, initiate an indictment to block the proposal as illegal. He can go to court and argue that the candidate is unworthy and his citizenship illegal. [91] There have been cases in the past when the assembled people, misled by a petitioner's lies, granted citizenship, but then someone initiated an indictment for illegality, and when the case came to court the recipient of the grant was shown not to have deserved it and the court stripped him of his citizenship. It would be tedious to go through the many cases from the distant past, but you all remember how Peitholas of Thessaly and Apollonides of Olynthus were given citizenship by the Assembly and then the court stripped them of it.* [92] You can't have forgotten that episode; it didn't happen so long ago.

Now, the purpose of these naturalization laws was to regulate the process of gaining Athenian citizenship, and they did an excellent and effective job. Even so, the total was increased by one very important law, and it just goes to show how carefully the people ensured, for their own sake and for the gods, that the sacrifices offered on behalf of the city should be properly carried out. The law expressly forbids any naturalized citizen from becoming one of the nine Archons or a priest, though it allows their descendants to hold any office, with the proviso 'if they are born from a citizen woman who was legally married'.

[93] I'll prove to you, beyond doubt or dispute, that I'm right about this. I'd like to start with an account of the origins of the law, explain how it came to be passed, and tell you about the good men, committed democrats, for whom its provisions were intended. All this will enable you to see the contemptuous treatment our democracy's special way of rewarding benefactors is receiving, and you'll realize that many of your rights are being wrested from your control by Stephanus and others with the same kinds of marriages and children as him.

[94] The Plataeans were the only Greeks who came to help us at Marathon, Athenians. This was when, after subduing Euboea, Datis, King Darius' general, left Eretria, landed at Marathon in force, and began to plunder the land.* Even now, the mural in the Painted Stoa is a visible reminder of the Plataeans' bravery, with its depiction of them, distinguished by their Boeotian helmets, running straight into battle, each man as fast as he could. [95] Then again, when Xerxes invaded Greece* and the Thebans collaborated with the Persians, so far from abandoning their friendship with us, the Plataeans dared to be the only Boeotians to join the alliance. Half of their men fought and died at Thermopylae, resisting the invaders alongside Leonidas

and the Spartans, while the rest served on board our triremes, since they didn't have ships of their own, and fought beside us at Artemisium and Salamis. [96] They were also involved in the final battle at Plataea, fighting alongside us and the other liberators of Greece against Xerxes' general Mardonius. So they enriched all their fellow Greeks with the precious gift of freedom.

Later, the Spartan king Pausanias began to treat us with insolence. It wasn't enough for him that the Spartans had been honoured with sole command by the Greeks, and that we, who were the true champions of Greek freedom, were public-spirited enough not to dispute their command, in case it became resented by the allies. [97] Anyway, power went to the Spartan king's head, and when the Greeks who fought at Plataea and Salamis commissioned and set up a tripod in Apollo's sanctuary at Delphi to commemorate their victory over the barbarians, he inscribed the following words on it:

> This memorial was dedicated by Pausanias, leader of the Greeks,
> To Apollo, to commemorate his destruction of the Persian host.

It was as though he alone were responsible for the victory and the memorial, and they weren't joint efforts of all the allies.

[98] This made the Greeks furious, and the Plataeans, acting for the whole alliance, initiated a suit for a thousand talents against the Spartans before the Amphictyonic court, and forced them to erase the lines and write instead the names of the cities which had contributed towards the victory.* This was largely responsible for the persistent hostility the Spartans in general, and their royal house in particular, used to feel towards the Plataeans. In the short term, the Spartans were unable to do anything about it, but about fifty years later the Spartan king Archidamus, the son of Zeuxidamus, made an attempt to seize the city in peacetime.* [99] With Eurymachus, the son of Leontiadas and one of the Boeotarchs,* as his agent Archidamus launched the attack from Thebes, and the gates of Plataea were opened for him at night by Naucleides and some of his accomplices, who had all been bribed.

When the Plataeans realized that the Thebans had gained entry under cover of darkness—that the city had suffered a surprise attack at a time of peace and was in enemy hands—they began to form up and organize resistance. When it grew light, they found that there weren't very many Thebans, and they realized that only the advance guard had broken in. It had rained heavily in the night and the rest of them had been prevented from reaching the city by the Asopus, whose swollen waters had become virtually unfordable, especially in the dark. [100] When they realized, therefore, that the Thebans inside the city were not at full strength the Plataeans attacked. Battle was joined, the Plataeans prevailed, and they killed the Thebans before the rest could come up. The very next thing they did was write to us, to tell us what had happened, give an account of the battle and their victory, and ask us for help in the event of Theban raids on their land. When we heard what had happened, we raced to Plataea, and when the Thebans saw that the Athenians had come to protect the Plataeans, they went back home.

[101] The Thebans' failure and the Plataeans' execution of their prisoners of war enraged the Spartans and they marched against Plataea, though they had no good reason for doing so. They ordered all the Peloponnesians (except the Argives)* to send two-thirds of each city's forces, and instructed the remaining Boeotians, the Locrians, Phocians, Malians, Oetaeans, and Aenianes to take to the field at full strength. [102] With a huge army besieging the city, they offered terms: the Plataeans were to surrender the city (though they would keep their farmland and continue to cultivate it) and end their alliance with Athens. The Plataeans declined the offer, replying that they would not enter into negotiations unless the Athenians were involved, so the Spartans surrounded the city with a double wall and set about a two-year siege, marked by repeated assaults of every kind and description.

[103] Eventually, the Plataeans reached their limit; they were completely out of food and their survival hung in the balance.* They cast lots among themselves, and one group stayed behind to endure the siege, while the others waited for a wet, stormy night, left the city, scaled the siege walls without being spotted by the enemy troops, slaughtered the pickets, and made their way safely here to Athens, arriving unexpectedly and in a terrible state. Of those who stayed behind, the men of military age were all massacred when the city was stormed and taken, and the women and children were sold into slavery, except for those who had slipped away to Athens at the first indications of the Spartans' approach.

[104] These men, then, gave indisputable proof of their loyalty to our democracy and gave up everything for it, including their wives

and children. Let's look now at the process whereby you made them citizens. The decrees you passed will shed light on the legal situation, and you'll see that what I've been telling you is true. [*To the Clerk of the Court*] Take this decree and read it out, please.

The Plataean decree is read out:
On the motion of Hippocrates, it is decreed that from this day onward the Plataeans shall have Athenian citizenship, with the same privileges as other Athenians, enjoying all the sacred and secular rights that Athenians enjoy, except for any priesthood or ceremony that is specific to a particular clan; nor shall they be eligible for any of the nine archonships, though their descendants may. The Plataeans are to be distributed among the demes and tribes. Once this distribution has taken place, no Plataean shall be entitled to become an Athenian citizen, unless he obtains this as a gift from the Athenian people.

[105] [*To the jurors*] You can see what a good and fair proposal this is, Athenians, from a politician who was acting in the best interests of the Athenian people. He required the Plataeans who were receiving the award to undergo a preliminary assessment in court, one by one, to check that they really were Plataeans and to confirm their loyalty to Athens. This was a way of restricting the numbers of people who could gain citizenship on this criterion. Then the names of those who passed their assessment were inscribed on a stone stele, which was set up on the Acropolis next to Athena's temple, so that there was a record of the awards which could be consulted by future generations as a way of checking a particular person's lineage. [106] Also, to prevent large numbers of people in the future gaining citizenship by claiming to be Plataeans, he ruled that anyone who hadn't undergone an assessment and become an Athenian citizen at the time was not automatically entitled to become one later. Then, for the good of the city and its gods, he also made a point in the decree of explaining to them that by law they were not to hold any of the nine archonships or any priesthood, although their descendants may, 'if they are born from a citizen woman who was legally married'.*

[107] Shocking, isn't it? In dealing with your neighbours, people who are known for their unrivalled loyalty to Athens, you specified in exhaustive detail the conditions a man must satisfy in order to gain the award. Are you then going to let a woman who has blatantly prostituted herself throughout the length and breadth of Greece get

away with her shameless and disdainful behaviour towards the city and her offences against the gods, a woman who is a citizen neither by birth nor by naturalization? [108] Is there anywhere in Greece she hasn't whored? Is there anywhere she hasn't gone to ply her daily trade? She's been all over the Peloponnese; she toured Thessaly and Magnesia with Simus of Larisa and Eurydamas, the son of Medeius; she accompanied Sotadas of Crete to Chios and most of the Ionian seaboard; she was hired out by Nicarete while she was owned by her. But when a woman is subservient to this man and that, and goes around with anyone who gives her money, what do you think her job is? It's to minister to her customers' every pleasure, isn't it? But when everyone knows what she's like, when she's plied her trade all over the world, are you going to officially recognize her as a citizen?

[109] When you're asked if you're proud of what you've done, what will you reply? How will you absolve yourselves of unethical and impious conduct? Before she was indicted and brought to trial—that is, before everyone had the chance to know about her and her sacrilegious behaviour—she was in the wrong, but attracted no official attention. Some of you didn't know what she was like, while those of you who had learnt the truth expressed their irritation, but were unable actually to do anything, since no one had brought her to trial or provided them with an opportunity to express their opinion of her in a vote. But now all of you know what she's like, you have her at your mercy, and you have the power to punish her. Under these circumstances, the impiety would be yours if you failed to punish her.

[110] Suppose you acquit her. When you go back home, what are you going to say to your wives or daughters or mothers when they ask where you've been? 'In court,' you'll reply, and that will immediately prompt the next question: 'Who was on trial?' 'Neaera,' you'll say, of course (won't you?), 'for being a foreigner illegally married to an Athenian citizen, and for having married her daughter, a woman who had been caught in illicit sex, to Theogenes, the former King Archon. And then the daughter performed the unnameable rites for the city and was given in marriage to Dionysus.' You'll give a thorough account of the charges against her, explaining how well, memorably, and thoroughly the case for the prosecution developed, point by point. [111] And they'll ask, once you've finished: 'So what did you do?' And you'll say, 'We've acquitted her.' At this point the most

respectable women will be livid with you for treating her no different from them, for allowing her to enjoy the same civic rights and to participate in the same religious ceremonies. At the same time, your lax and casual attitude will give people the impression that you approve of her lifestyle, and foolish women will take this as a signal that they can do whatever they like without either you or the law stepping in. [112] In other words, it would have been much better for this trial never to have taken place than for you to acquit her now that it has. Prostitutes will have complete freedom to marry whoever they like, and to claim anyone at all as the father of their children. Your laws will have no authority, but courtesans will have the right to do whatever they want.

You also need to think about women of citizen birth, to make sure that the daughters of poor families don't become unmarriageable. [113] At the moment the state contributes an adequate dowry for a poor woman, if she's even moderately good-looking.* But if you acquit Neaera—that is, if you trample the law underfoot and make a nonsense of it—prostitution awaits the daughters of citizens who are too poor to be married, while courtesans will gain the dignity of free women if any old child of theirs is legitimate, and if they're allowed to take part in Athenian rites, enter Athenian sanctuaries, and enjoy Athenian privileges.

[114] As you cast your vote today, then, each of you should see it as a way of protecting his wife, perhaps, or his daughter or mother, as well as his city with its laws and sanctuaries. Each of you, with his vote, can prove that you're *not* putting his womenfolk on the same level as this whore, nor treating women who were properly and carefully raised by their families in a respectable environment, and who were legally married, as if they were no different from a woman who has been with many men, many times a day, living a life of gross indecency, satisfying their every desire. [115] Imagine that you're listening not to me or to those of my fellow citizens who are going to defend and support her, but to the laws and Neaera debating what she's done. As you attend to the prosecution, hear the voice of the laws themselves, which regulate the life of the city and which, as jurors, you have sworn to uphold, telling you what they'd like to see happen and how they've been violated by the defendants. And as you attend to the defence, remember the charges brought by the laws and the persuasiveness of their testimony, take a look at her [*pointing*], and

ask yourselves only whether she is Neaera and whether she has done what she's accused of doing.

[116] There's a precedent for you to bear in mind as well, Athenians: you punished the Hierophant Archias when he was taken to court and found guilty of impiety—of sacrificing in a way that violated tradition.* Among other things, he was accused of having used the altar in the courtyard at Eleusis—this was during the Haloa*—to perform a personal sacrifice for the courtesan Sinope of a victim she had brought, on a day when sacrifices were forbidden, and when it was the priestess's job, not his, to perform sacrifices. [117] Shocking, isn't it? An Athenian citizen of noble ancestry, a member of the Eumolpid clan, was punished because he was found to have offended against an established custom. The pleas of his family and friends did him no good, nor did all the services he and his ancestors had performed for the city, nor did the fact that he was the Hierophant: he was found guilty, and you punished him. But this woman Neaera has offended against the same god and treated the laws with contempt, so won't you punish her—her and her daughter?

[118] Speaking for myself, I wonder what on earth they'll find to say to you in their defence. Will they argue that Neaera has citizen status and is legally married to him? But you've heard evidence that she's a courtesan and was once a slave belonging to Nicarete. That he isn't living with her as his wife, but as his mistress? But the existence of her sons and their introduction by Stephanus to the phratry, and the marriage of her daughter to an Athenian, make it perfectly plain that she is his wife. [119] I feel sure that neither Stephanus himself nor anyone speaking on his behalf will be able to disprove the charges and the supporting evidence by showing that Neaera is an Athenian citizen.

I was told that the line of argument he would use in his defence is that he doesn't keep her as a wife, but as a courtesan, and that the children aren't hers, but their mother was another woman, a citizen, a relative of his whom he married before. [120] My response to this shameless nonsense, the contrived defence, and the carefully groomed witnesses, was to offer a detailed and fair challenge, which would have given you the whole truth.* I challenged him to hand over Thratta and Coccaline, the slaves who stayed in Neaera's service when she left Megara and moved in with Stephanus, and those she had subsequently acquired while she was living with him, Xennis and Drosis. [121] They know for sure that Neaera is the mother of Proxenus and Ariston—the one dead, the other still alive—and that Antidorides, the sprinter, and Phano, who was married to Theogenes the former King Archon, are also her children. If under torture it was revealed that Stephanus *had* taken a citizen woman as his wife, and that these children weren't Neaera's, but were his by another woman, an Athenian, I was ready to withdraw from the case and cancel the indictment. [122] What is marriage, after all? A man is married if he fathers legitimate children, introduces his sons to his phratry and deme, and marries his daughters off as his own. For we have courtesans for pleasure, concubines for looking after our daily physical needs, and wives for the procreation of legitimate children and to take good care of domestic matters. So if Neaera wasn't his first wife, and the mother of his children was this first wife, an Athenian citizen, and not Neaera, he had the opportunity to prove it with absolute certainty: all he had to do was hand over these slaves. [123] The clerk will now read to you testimony confirming that I issued this challenge, and the challenge itself. [*To the Clerk of the Court*] Read first the deposition, and then the challenge.

The deposition is read out:
Hippocrates of Probalinthus, the son of Hippocrates, Demosthenes of Paeania, the son of Demosthenes, Diophanes of Alopece, the son of Diophanes, Deinomenes of Cydathenaeum, the son of Archelaus, Deinias of Cydantidae, the son of Phormus, and Lysimachus of Aegilia, the son of Lysippus, testify that they were present at the meeting in the Agora when Apollodorus issued his challenge to Stephanus, asking him to hand over the slave-women to be interrogated under torture about the charges Apollodorus is bringing against Stephanus concerning Neaera; that Stephanus refused to hand over the slaves; and that the challenge is the one produced by Apollodorus.

[124] Now read the actual challenge that I issued to Stephanus here.

The challenge is read out:
This challenge was issued by Apollodorus to Stephanus, in relation to the indictment Apollodorus has brought against Neaera, that despite being a foreigner she was living in marriage with a citizen. Apollodorus was ready to have handed over to him for examination under torture Neaera's slave-women, those she already owned when she came here from Megara,

Thratta and Coccaline, and those she acquired later when she was living with Stephanus, Xennis and Drosis, who know for sure that Neaera is the mother of Stephanus' children—the children being Proxenus (who died), Ariston (still alive), Antidorides the sprinter, and Phano. And if the slaves confirm that these children are Stephanus' and Neaera's, Neaera is to be sold as stipulated by the law and the children are to be classified as non-Athenians. But if they confirm that the children are not hers, but that their mother was another woman, a citizen, I was willing to abandon my case against Neaera; and if the women suffered any injury from the torture I was willing to pay compensation for the injuries.

[125] [*To the jurors*] That was the challenge I issued to Stephanus, jurymen, but he turned it down. Don't you think, then, jurymen, that Neaera has already been tried by Stephanus in his mind? Don't you think he already knows that she's guilty of the crimes I've charged her with, that I've been telling you the truth, that the depositions I've provided are sound, and that he's going to tell you a pack of lies? His refusal to hand over the slaves for torture as I requested amounts to an admission on his part that he has no valid case to make.

[126] I have played my part, jurymen. In retaliation for their offences against the gods, as well as for my own sake, I have brought these people to trial and submitted them to your vote. For your part, you should appreciate that the gods, the victims of their crimes, will not fail to notice how each of you votes, and therefore you must uphold justice with your vote and exact vengeance above all for the gods, but also for yourselves. If you do this, when people consider this indictment, brought by me against Neaera for being a foreigner married to an Athenian citizen, they will unanimously think that you did a good job and gave the correct verdict.

PRIVATE AND GHOST-WRITTEN SPEECHES

27. FIRST SPEECH AGAINST APHOBUS, ON TRUSTEESHIP

Demosthenes was still a boy when his father died. In his will Demosthenes senior, a very rich man, made arrangements for the disposition of his property when his son came of age and also for the marriage of his widow and his daughter, Demosthenes' sister. The estate was to be managed in the interest of his son by three guardians chosen from among his close family and friends, Aphobus, Therippides, and Demophon. Aphobus and Demophon were also to marry Demosthenes' mother and sister, both of whom were provided with substantial dowries in the will. The marriages did not take place as instructed by the elder Demosthenes and presumably agreed in advance by the guardians, though Aphobus and Demophon kept the dowries. So relations must already have been bad by the time Demosthenes reached his majority. When he was given the accounts for the period of guardianship, Demosthenes received only a small fraction of the money he expected; he concluded that the estate had been defrauded and sued his guardians, beginning with Aphobus. He was successful and the jury accepted his assessment of ten talents' damages: see speech 28. (We do not know how much, if anything, he was awarded as a result of the suits against Demophon and Therippides.) It was for the successful litigant to obtain payment and we know that his guardians tried to thwart him; it is therefore unclear how much he recovered. Though it seems clear that the guardians did in fact collude against the estate, it is unclear how far Demosthenes was the victim of fraud and how far of mismanagement.

---

[1] If Aphobus had been prepared to do right, jurymen, or if he had referred our dispute to members of our family, there'd have been no need for all the bother of a trial. I'd have been happy to abide by their decision, and that would put an end to our quarrel.* But since he has refused to allow the decision to be made by people with intimate knowledge of our affairs, and has turned to you, who are completely ignorant of them, I have to try to obtain justice from him here, in your court. [2] Now, jurymen, I have no illusions about how risky it is for someone young and altogether inexperienced to get involved in a contest for his entire property with men who are not only competent speech-makers, but are also equipped with considerable resources.

But despite my many disadvantages, I firmly expect to obtain justice from you, and also to give an adequate speech myself—or at any rate an adequate description of what has happened, so that you are abreast of the facts in all their detail and aware of the issues on which you'll have to vote.

[3] I ask you to give me a favourable hearing, jurymen, and, if you decide that I've been wronged, to uphold justice for me. I plan to keep my presentation as short as possible, and so I'll start with the facts that most readily promote understanding of the situation. [4] Jurymen, my father, Demosthenes, left an estate worth almost 14 talents to me and my sister—respectively seven and five years old at the time—and my mother had also brought fifty mnas into the household.* He pondered what to do with us, and not long before his death he entrusted the whole estate to Aphobus here and Demophon, the son of Demon, who were his nephews (the sons respectively of his brother and his sister), and also to Therippides of Paeania, a life-long friend rather than a relative. [5] To Therippides he gave 70 mnas from my estate to draw the interest from until I came of age,* because he didn't want his management of my affairs to suffer through lack of money. To Demophon he gave my sister and 2 talents straight away, and to Aphobus himself he gave my mother with a dowry of 80 mnas, the house to live in, and my furniture to use.* His thinking was that if he bound them into an even closer relationship with me, this extra affinity would make better trustees. [6] So the first thing that happened was that they received this much of the estate's money for their own use, and took over the management of the rest of the estate. But after ten years of their trusteeship, they have made off with every-thing else and have handed over only the house, fourteen slaves, and 30 mnas of silver, with a total value of about 70 mnas.

[7] So, jurymen, there you have the briefest possible summary of their crimes. There could be no better witnesses to testify that I've correctly stated the value of the estate that my father left than the men themselves, in the sense that they concurred in the assessment that they should contribute on my behalf to the syndicate 500 drachmas per 25 mnas, which is as much as was paid by Timotheus, the son of Conon, or by any of the men with the highest assessments.* But I must also give you the details of how much of the estate was at work and how much was idle,* and the value of each of these two portions. This information will enable you to know for sure that never has an

estate been more shamelessly or blatantly plundered by its trustees than mine.

[8] I'm going to provide depositions from witnesses to show, first, that the trustees concurred on my behalf to this assessment of the contribution to be paid to the syndicate, and, second, that my father didn't leave me poor or with an estate worth only 70 mnas, but with one that was so large that even they couldn't hide it from the city. [*To the Clerk of the Court*] Take this deposition and read it, please.

A deposition is read out.

[9] [*To the jurors*] This deposition too shows the value of the estate, because 3 talents, which is the amount they agreed to contribute to the war levy, is the assessment for 15 talents.

Things will become clearer when I've told you what the actual estate consisted of. My father left two workshops, jurymen, each a pretty extensive business. One had 32 or 33 knife-makers,* worth on average 5 or 6 mnas apiece, with none worth less than 3 mnas. This workshop made him a net profit of 30 mnas a year. The other had a total of 20 bed-makers, who were security for a loan of 40 mnas,* and made him a net profit of 12 mnas. He left about 1 talent of money, which was out on loan at the rate of 1 drachma per mna per month, the interest on which generated more than 7 mnas a year.*

[10] That, as even Aphobus and the others will acknowledge, is the productive portion of the estate my father left me. The capital value came in total to 4 talents, 5,000 drachmas, and the annual profit was 50 mnas. In addition, he left ivory, iron (ready for use), and wood for bed-making, worth 80 mnas; dye and copper which had cost him 70 mnas; a house worth 3,000 drachmas; furniture, cups, golden jewellery, and clothing (my mother's trousseau), worth in all about 10,000 drachmas; and 80 mnas of coined money stored in the house. [11] That's the total of all the domestic assets. He also left 70 mnas on loan to Xuthus for maritime purposes,* and 4,500 drachmas on deposit at Pasion's bank,* 600 with Pylades, 1,600 with Demomeles, the son of Demon, and loans of 200 or 300 drachmas here and there, amounting to 1 talent. The sum total of these loans is more than 8 talents, 50 mnas; and the overall total is about 14 talents, as you'll see if you do the maths.

[12] That was the value of the bequeathed estate, jurymen. There's not enough water* for me to explain in one go how much has been

stolen—that is, how much each of them has taken individually and how much they're cheating me of together. These are matters that demand separate treatment, and so it will be best if I wait until my suits against Demophon and Therippides come to court before telling you what they have of mine. Today I'll tell you what their evidence proves that Aphobus has and what I know he has kept for himself. I'll start by proving that he has the dowry, the 80 mnas, and then I'll cover everything else. I shall be as brief as possible.

[13] Immediately after my father's death, Aphobus entered the house and began to live there, as stipulated by my father's will. He took my mother's jewellery, and the cups my father had left, and kept them for himself. They were worth about 50 mnas, and he also received from Therippides and Demophon money raised by the sale of the slaves, until he had the full amount of the dowry, 80 mnas. [14] Once he had all this, he sailed off to Corcyra as a trierarch,* but before leaving, in a list he compiled for Therippides, he acknowledged that these things were in his possession and that he had recovered the dowry. The principal witnesses to this are Demophon and Therippides, his co-trustees, but Demochares of Leuconoeum, my aunt's husband,* has also vouched for this admission of his, and so have a great many other people. [15] For, even though he now had the dowry, Aphobus was withholding my mother's maintenance. Demochares had words with him about that, and also about his decision to manage the estate himself, with the help of his co-trustees, rather than lease it.* In his response to Demochares, Aphobus didn't challenge the notion that he had the dowry, nor was he angry at not having received it. No, he admitted that he had it and added that he and my mother were having a little difference of opinion over some pieces of jewellery. He said that once he'd sorted this matter out, he'd see to my mother's maintenance and make sure that I was perfectly all right.

[16] And yet, if I prove that he made this admission in front of Demochares and everyone else who was there at the time, that he has received money from the sale of the slaves to make up the dowry, that in the list he compiled for his co-trustees he acknowledged his possession of the dowry, and that he moved into my house as soon as my father died, this will surely make it perfectly clear, given that the facts are agreed by everyone, that he has recovered the dowry, the 80 mnas, and that his denial of this just reveals his unscrupulousness. [17] To

confirm the truth of what I'm saying [*to the Clerk of the Court*], take the depositions and read them out.

The depositions are read out.

[*To the jurors*] This shows how he gained possession of the dowry. Now, the law stipulates that, in the event of his not marrying my mother, he should pay interest on the dowry at a rate of 9 obols per mna per month. I'm prepared to accept a rate of only 1 drachma per mna per month, however, which, if you add together the principal and the income for 10 years, comes to about 3 talents.*

[18] So I can prove that he's got *this* much, since he admitted it in front of all those witnesses. He's also kept another 30 mnas, the income from the workshop, and has resorted to the most unscrupulous tactics in his efforts to deprive me of it. The slaves my father left me generated an income of 30 mnas; half of them were sold, and so, proportionately, I should have got 15 mnas. [19] Now, Therippides, who was responsible for the slaves for seven years, declared an income of 11 mnas a year, 4 mnas less per year than the proper amount.* Aphobus, on the other hand, who was responsible for them for the first two years, showed no profit at all. Sometimes he said that the workshop was idle, sometimes that it wasn't his responsibility, but that the overseer was our freedman Milyas: since he had managed the workshop, I should get the accounts from him.

Well, if he repeats any of these stories today, it will be easy to prove him a liar. [20] He cannot claim that the workshop was idle, because he himself has submitted an account of the money he spent, not on food for the men, but on work-related items: ivory for the manufacture of knife-handles, and other materials, as he would if the workforce was active. Moreover, his accounts state that he paid Therippides for the hire of three of Therippides' slaves, who were in my workshop, but if there was no work going on Therippides shouldn't have received a fee and these expenses shouldn't have been charged against me. [21] On the other hand, if he says that work went on, but there was no market for the products, he still ought to show that he returned the products to me, and produce witnesses who were present when he did so. Failing either of these actions, then of course he must have the 30 mnas, two years' revenue from the workshop, since work was clearly going on.

[22] But perhaps he won't say any of this, but will claim that the

whole thing was under Milyas' management. But can we possibly believe him when he says that he bore all the expenses himself, more than 500 drachmas, and Milyas kept all the profits? It seems to me that the opposite would have happened: if Milyas really had been in charge of the workshop, he'd have borne the expenses, and Aphobus would have taken the profits, to judge by the unscrupulousness of his behaviour in general. [*To the Clerk of the Court*] So take these depositions and read them out.

Further depositions are read out.

[23] [*To the jurors*] So he's kept the 30 mnas from the workshop, and also eight years' worth of interest on this sum. At a modest rate of 1 drachma per mna per month, that comes to another 30 mnas. He's kept all that just for himself, and when added to the dowry it makes about 4 talents, including the principal.

Now what about the money he has stolen along with his fellow trustees? And there's also some money that, he argues, wasn't left me by my father at all. I'll give you all the details. [24] Let's take the bed-makers first, bequeathed to me by my father, but made to disappear by my trustees. There were 20 of them, security for a loan of 40 mnas, and I'll prove how unscrupulously and blatantly they're cheating me of them. No one denies that these slaves were part of the estate at the time of my father's death, and everyone agrees that they brought him 12 mnas a year. But, according to their declarations, I made no profit from them for ten years, nothing at all, and in his accounts Aphobus calculates their costs at almost 1,000 drachmas. What impudence!

[25] At no point have they passed over to me the actual men on whom they say this money was spent. Instead they come up with a completely inane tale, according to which the man who gave the slaves to my father as security is a thoroughly bad sort, who has failed to repay a number of loans and is heavily in debt.* They've even called quite a few witnesses to testify to these facts against him. But who has the slaves? How did they come to leave the house? Who abducted them? Or did they lose them in a lawsuit? They have no reply to any of these questions. [26] But if they were at all sincere in what they were saying, they wouldn't have produced witnesses to testify to this man's wickedness, about which I couldn't care less. No, they'd be trying to recover the slaves, they'd have identified the men who seized them, and they wouldn't have left any of them unaccounted for. But in fact

they're behaving in the most heartless manner possible: even though they agree that the slaves were bequeathed to me, even though they took possession of them, even though for ten years they've profited from them, now they're making the workshop disappear altogether. To confirm the truth of what I'm saying, [*to the Clerk of the Court*] take these depositions and read them.

Further depositions are read out.

[27] [*To the jurors*] I shall next produce evidence to show beyond the slightest shadow of a doubt that Moeriades was not insolvent, and that it wasn't a foolish mistake on my father's part to have done this deal with him. After Aphobus took over the workshop, as you've just heard from the witnesses, as a trustee it was his job to block any attempt to use these slaves for further loans, but instead he himself lent 500 drachmas to Moeriades with these slaves as security—a loan which, as he acknowledges, has been duly and fairly repaid. [28] But isn't it scandalous that I, who put up the earlier loan, should not only get no income from the slaves, but should lose the use of them as security too, while the man who made a loan secured on my property in a deal that was negotiated so many years after my earlier loan has recovered both the interest and the principal out of my estate, and has suffered no loss whatsoever? But to confirm the truth of what I've been saying, [*to the Clerk of the Court*] take this deposition and read it.

A deposition is read out.

[29] [*To the jurors*] Think about how much money these men are stealing where just the bed-makers are concerned: the principal was 40 mnas, on which 10 years' worth of income is 2 talents, since they were getting 12 mnas a year from them. Is that an insignificant amount, from such an obscure source that miscalculation might well have taken place? Isn't it perfectly clear, rather, that they've stolen almost 3 talents? Since this theft was committed by all of them together, I suppose I should recover a third of that from Aphobus. [30] And they've done pretty much the same, jurymen, with the ivory and iron that my father left as well. They don't declare these materials either. But my father owned both bed-makers and knife-makers in considerable numbers, so it's inconceivable that he wouldn't have left iron and ivory. He was bound to have stock; no work could have taken place without it.

[31] So we have a man who owned more than fifty slaves and ran two businesses. One of these businesses alone, the bed-factory, used easily 2 mnas of ivory a month, and the knife-factory used at least the same amount of ivory again, and iron as well. But they claim he left no ivory or iron. What impudence! [32] Actually, they make it easy for you: they expose their own fraudulence. My father left enough materials not only for his own artisans' work, but also for resale to others. This is proved by the fact that during his lifetime he himself used to sell these materials, and after his death Demophon and Aphobus carried on retailing them from my house.* [33] But how much should we suppose was left by my father, when it was plainly enough for all these workers and was also being sold by the trustees? A small amount, or in fact much more than I have included in the charge? [*To the Clerk of the Court*] Take these depositions here and read them out.

Further depositions are read out.

[*To the jurors*] No mention here of more than a talent of ivory, or of the income from it. They've made this completely disappear as well.

[34] And that's not all, jurymen. I shall also prove by reference to what they acknowledge they've received, as demonstrated by the accounts they've submitted, that the three of them have more than 8 talents of my money, and that Aphobus personally received 3 talents, 1,000 drachmas of this. In doing so, I shall reckon their expenses separately, at a higher rate than they assume,* and I shall deduct the payments they've made to me from what they've received. This will enable you to see how few scruples they bring to their work.

[35] Here's how much of my money they acknowledge receiving. Aphobus: 108 mnas (but in a moment I'll show that he actually has more). Therippides: 2 talents. Demophon: 87 mnas. That makes a total of 5 talents, 15 mnas. Now, some of this—almost 77 mnas, the income from the slaves—didn't come in a single tranche, but they still immediately received not far off 4 talents. Add ten years' interest, at the rate of 1 drachma per mna per month,* and you'll find that, including the principal, it comes to 8 talents, 1,000 drachmas.

[36] The cost of my upbringing should be deducted from the 77 mnas generated by the workshop. Therippides spent 7 mnas a year on this, and I acknowledge having received this amount. So, since in ten years they spent 70 mnas on my upbringing, I'm crediting them with the balance of 700 drachmas, in keeping with my assumption

that their expenses were greater than they allow. But we must still deduct from the more than 8 talents what they handed over to me when I came of age, and the amount they paid to the city as part of the war levy. [37] So, then, Aphobus and Therippides paid me 31 mnas, and in their accounts they state that the contribution they made on my behalf to the war levy came to 18 mnas. I shall overestimate this sum too, and call it 30 mnas, so that they have no grounds for querying it. Subtract this 1 talent from the 8, and you get 7 talents. It follows that, by their own admission as to what they've received, they must have this amount. Even if they steal everything else from me by denying that they have it, they should have repaid this much, because by their own admission they earned this much from my property. [38] But is that what they're actually doing? No. They declare no interest on this money, and claim that they've spent all the principal and the 77 mnas as well. Demophon has even entered my name as in debt to him.* Isn't this flagrant and outrageous effrontery? Isn't this unrestricted avarice? If such extreme behaviour doesn't strike you as reprehensible, I don't know what will.

[39] As for Aphobus, then, since he acknowledges the receipt on his part of 108 mnas, he has not only this amount, but also ten years' interest on it, which comes to more or less 3 talents, 1,000 drachmas. To confirm the truth of this, and to show that in their accounts of their trusteeship each of them acknowledges having received the stated amount, but enters it as all spent, [*to the Clerk of the Court*] take the depositions and read them.

Further depositions are read out.

[40] [*To the jurors*] Well, jurymen, I think you have all the information you need on this; you know how much each of them has stolen and you're aware of their criminal cunning. You'd have been even better informed if they had been prepared to give me the will my father left. My mother tells me that it itemized my father's entire estate, specified the funds these men were to draw on to receive their legacies, and gave instructions about leasing the estate. [41] Whenever I ask to see the will, however, they admit that my father left one, but don't produce it. The reason for this is that they don't want anyone to know how much my father's estate was worth before their thievery, so as to make it seem as though they never received their legacies. But they failed to take into account how easily they would be convicted by

the facts themselves. [*To the Clerk of the Court*] Take the depositions containing their answers to my questions, and read them out.

Further depositions are read out.

[42] [*To the jurors*] Here we have a man* who agrees that there was a will in existence, and testifies that the 2 talents were given to Demophon and the 80 mnas to Aphobus, but denies that the will made any mention of Therippides' 70 mnas, or stated the value of the bequeathed estate, or left instructions about leasing the estate. But then, of course, it's not in his interest to acknowledge these things. [*To the Clerk of the Court*] Now take the defendant's answer sheet.

Another deposition is read out.†

[43] [*To the jurors*] Here's another* who concurs that there was a will, and adds that the money raised from the sale of the copper and the dye was paid to Therippides (though Therippides fails to mention it), and the two talents to Demophon. As for *his* legacy, he agrees that it was specified in the will, but he doesn't want us to think that he received it, so he says that he disputed it. There's not a word from him either about the value of the estate, nor anything about leasing it. Again, it's not in his interest to acknowledge these things.

[44] Despite their attempt to make the estate disappear from the will, then, we can still infer the value of what my father left from the amounts that each of them says was given to the others. If my father spent 4 talents, 3,000 drachmas on giving two of them dowries amounting to 3 talents, 2,000 drachmas, and the other the use of 70 mnas, it's surely obvious that the estate from which he set aside this amount—the estate he was trying to leave me—wasn't small, but worth at least double that amount. [45] After all, it wasn't his intention to leave me, his son, a pauper, while making these men, who were already rich, even richer. No, the great value of the bequest was precisely why he gave Therippides so much money and Demophon the use of 2 talents, even though my sister wasn't yet going to be living with him as his wife. That way, he would achieve one of two things: either their legacies would encourage them to be better trustees, or, if they turned out bad, they'd meet with no mercy in your court for having wronged me so grievously after being entrusted with such great sums.

[46] As for the defendant himself, in addition to the dowry, he also got the female slaves; and, since he's living in the house, if he's ever

asked to account for them he says it's no one's business but his own. He's so mean that he's even failed to pay my teachers, and he's behind in his payments of the war levy—though they're charged against me in his accounts. [*To the Clerk of the Court*] Now take these depositions and read them.

Further depositions are read out.

[47] [*To the jurors*] How could it be clearer that he has plundered the entire estate and has made off with everything, however small? So many witnesses and pieces of evidence have confirmed it: in the list that he compiled for his co-trustees, he acknowledged that he received the dowry and has that amount in his possession; he has exploited the workshop, but declares no income from it; [48] some of the other property he has sold, without paying me what he got for it, and the rest he has kept for himself and made disappear; even his own accounts show how much he stole. And that's not all: he has made the will disappear, sold the slaves, and managed my estate worse than my worst enemies would have. I can't imagine how it could be any clearer.

[49] When the case came before the arbitrator,* Aphobus had the barefaced cheek to say that he had given the money on my behalf to his co-trustees Demophon and Therippides, to pay off a very large number of debts, and that they had received a lot of my property. But he couldn't prove the truth of either of these assertions. In the first place, he failed to provide documentary evidence that my father had left me in debt, just as he failed to produce as witnesses the men he said this money had been paid to. In the second place, the amount of money he entered to the credit of his co-trustees was much less than the amount we know that he received himself.* [50] The arbitrator questioned him on these points, one by one. He asked him how he ran his own estate: from the profits, or by spending the capital; he asked him whether, if it were his own estate that was in the hands of trustees, he'd have accepted this account from them, or would have insisted on being given both the principal and the accumulated income. To these questions Aphobus made no reply, but tendered a challenge: he said he was ready to prove to my satisfaction that my estate was worth 10 talents, and that if it fell short of this amount he would make up the difference himself. [51] I asked him to prove it to the arbitrator's satisfaction, but he didn't. He also failed to show that his co-trustees

had returned my property (otherwise, the arbitrator wouldn't have found against him), but he submitted a deposition by a witness along these lines, and he'll have something to say about that presently.

So if today he repeats the claim that I do have my property, ask him who made it over to me, and require him to produce witnesses for every item. [52] And if he says I have it in the sense that he is taking into account what is due to me from each of the other two trustees, he'll obviously be talking about a sum that is only one third of the correct amount, and he still won't be proving that I actually have it, because, just as I proved how much he has in his possession, so I shall also show that each of the other two has no less than that.* And this means that, instead of taking this line, he should claim that either he himself or his co-trustees has repaid me. Failing that, I can't see why you should take any notice of this challenge of his, because he's still failing to prove that I have my property.

[53] He found himself in considerable difficulties with the arbitrator throughout. He was challenged point by point (as he's being challenged here today), and in response he had the audacity to tell a truly preposterous lie. He claimed that my father had left four talents for me buried in the ground, and had made my mother responsible for this money. And why did he say this? Either I'd be expecting him to repeat the claim today, and then I'd have to spend time arguing about it, time that would be better spent bringing my other charges against him to your attention. Or I'd assume that he wasn't going to repeat it, and say nothing, and *then* he'd say it, to make me seem rich and less deserving of your sympathy. [54] He felt he had a right to say these things, but he didn't introduce testimony to support any of it. He just asserted it dogmatically, expecting the arbitrator to believe him.

When asked what he's spent so much of my money on, he says he's been paying off debts on my behalf. This is an attempt to portray me as insolvent, but apparently, when he feels like it, he portrays me as rich—*if* my father left such a fortune at home. But a number of considerations readily show that this can't be right, that nothing like this happened at all. [55] If my father didn't trust these men, it goes without saying that he would neither have entrusted the rest of the estate to them, nor told them he had left a cache of money. He'd have been completely crazy to tell them about the hidden money if he wasn't even going to make them trustees of his visible property.

Alternatively, if he had no reason to doubt them, he wouldn't have entrusted the bulk of the estate to them and kept this amount out of their hands. Nor would he have given the money into my mother's care, and then given her in marriage to the defendant, one of the trustees. It doesn't make sense to use my mother to try to keep the money safe, and then make a man he distrusts responsible for both her and the money.

[56] Besides, if there were any truth to the story, don't you think he'd have married her? She'd been given to him by my father, and he already had her dowry, the 80 mnas, on the understanding that he would marry her, but then he married the daughter of Philonides of Melite. Had there been 4 talents in the house, in my mother's possession, as he claims, don't you think he'd have leapt at the opportunity to get control of it by getting control of her? [57] Having disgraced himself, along with his co-trustees, by the manner in which they plundered the visible estate, which even many people here knew my father had left, is it likely, given the opportunity, that he would keep his hands off money about which you'd never know anything? Of course not. The story is a pack of lies, jurymen, every word of it. My father gave them all the money he had to leave, and the only reason he's going to use this story is to make you feel less sympathy for me.

[58] I have by no means exhausted what I could say about him, but there's one fundamental charge that comprises them all, and allows me to undermine all his arguments at once. He could have avoided all this trouble if he had leased the estate in accordance with the following laws. [*To the Clerk of the Court*] Take the laws and read them.

Laws are read out.

[*To the jurors*] These laws enabled Antidorus to make more than 6 talents from 6 years of leasing an estate worth 3 talents, 3,000 drachmas. Some of you actually saw this, because Theogenes of Probalinthus, the man who rented Antidorus' estate, counted out the money in the Agora. [59] What about me? Considering the time and the terms of Theogenes' rental, in ten years I should probably have more than tripled the capital of 14 talents. So ask Aphobus why he didn't do it. If he says that it was better for the estate not to have been leased, have him show that I've been paid, not double or triple, but just the principal in full. But if they've made over to me not even 70 mnas out of 14 talents, and one of them also listed me as owing him money, how can we accept a single word of what they say? We can't, obviously.

[60] So the estate I inherited was as large as you heard at the beginning, and just one third of the capital generated an annual profit of 50 mnas. Now, even if they didn't want to lease the estate, all these men had to do, to satisfy their insatiable greed for money, was leave things in place and from this income they could have paid for my upbringing, managed their obligations to the city, and have some left over to save as well. [61] They could have invested the other two-thirds of the estate and, if they needed money, taken modest amounts from the profits for themselves; this would have done me a good turn too by keeping the capital intact and increasing the estate from the income. But they did none of these things. All they did was sell one another the most valuable slaves and make the rest disappear, thus removing even my ongoing income and ensuring that they themselves were provided with a good income from my property. [62] And then, once they had taken all the rest in this underhand way, they ganged together to argue that more than half of the money hadn't been left to me at all, and so the accounts they've submitted assume that the value of the estate is five talents. But it's not that they fail to show an income from this money and declare only the capital. No, their barefaced claim is that this capital has all been spent. And their effrontery doesn't even make them blush!

[63] But how would they have treated me if I'd been their ward for longer? Not that they would have a reply to this question. After ten years I've recovered just this small amount from two of them, and then I'm listed as in debt to the other one. Why shouldn't I feel resentment? It as plain as a pikestaff: if my father had died when I was one year old and I'd been their ward for an extra six years, I wouldn't even have got this small amount from them. After all (assuming for the moment that their accounts of their expenditures are correct), the money they've made over to me wouldn't have lasted the full six years. Either they'd have paid for my upbringing themselves—or they'd have let me die of hunger.

[64] Other bequeathed estates, worth one or two talents, have doubled or tripled in value as a result of being leased, until they've been required to perform liturgies. My estate, however, which had regularly financed triremes and contributed substantially towards war levies, won't be able to pay even small amounts now, thanks to their unscrupulous

behaviour. What could be more shocking? It's impossible for me to make their behaviour seem more monstrous than it already is. They've made the will disappear, hoping that no one will notice. They've managed their own estates from my profits, used my money to plump up their own capital reserves, and completely destroyed all my capital. It's as though they had a major grievance against me!

[65] Let's look at what *you* do. Even when you convict people of offences against the city, you don't confiscate all their property; you leave them something, out of pity for their womenfolk and children.* But the difference between these men and you may be measured by the fact that even after receiving their legacies from us, with the help of which they could have done an honest job as trustees, they've treated us in this outrageous fashion. So far from feeling sorry for my sister, they didn't moderate their behaviour at all: although my father thought she deserved two talents, she's now going to get nothing of what was due to her. It's as though my father bequeathed us bitter enemies rather than friends and relatives; they care nothing for family ties.

[66] There's no one in the world worse off than me. I lack the resources either to find a husband for my sister or to manage the rest of my estate, and I don't know what to do about either of these problems. And then the city is also pressing me to pay a war levy. This is as it should be, because the estate my father left me could have coped with it, but these men have taken all my inheritance. [67] And now I've put myself in great danger, trying to recover what's mine. If Aphobus is acquitted (as I trust he won't be), I'll owe the one-sixth fine of 100 mnas.* If he's found guilty, the amount of his fine remains to be assessed, and he'll pay it not from his own funds but from mine; but my fine is fixed, and that means that I'll lose not only my patrimony, but also my citizenship, if you don't take pity on me.*

[68] I beg you, then, jurymen, I beseech you, I implore you, to remember the law and the oaths you took as jurors, to uphold justice for me, and not to prefer his pleas to mine. It's not criminals you should feel sorry for, but people who've been unexpectedly brought low—not men who are so brutally misappropriating someone else's property, but me, because for so long now I've been denied my inheritance and abused by these men, and now I'm in danger of losing my citizenship. [69] I think my father would groan out loud if he saw that the dowries and legacies he gave these men were putting me, his

28. SECOND SPEECH AGAINST APHOBUS, ON TRUSTEESHIP

The jury found for Demosthenes in the suit against Aphobus. Where there was no fixed penalty, it was for the jurors to decide. In such cases the litigants each proposed a penalty and the jurors chose between them; they could not propose their own compromise. In most cases time was set aside for separate speeches on the assessment proposals. This is Demosthenes' speech for his own proposal of ten talents. The time available is limited; hence the brevity of the speech. The tone is dramatically different from speech 27. Though Demosthenes revisits the arithmetic needed to nail the accused on factual grounds, there is a much stronger emotional thrust in this speech, necessary to convince the hearers of the need to choose his own higher assessment and to induce them to ignore Aphobus' appeals for sympathy. Aphobus in reply claimed that he could not afford the ten talents and proposed a penalty of one talent. The jurors voted for Demosthenes.

------

[1] A great deal of what Aphobus has been telling you consists of appalling lies, but I was particularly offended by one of the things he said, and that's the first point I shall try to refute. This is his assertion that it was because my grandfather owed money to the state that my father did not want his estate to be leased out, thinking it might be risky.* According to him, anyway, that was my father's reason, but he didn't provide any testimony at all to prove that my grandfather died in debt. In fact, he waited until the last day before submitting testimony to show that he became a debtor at all, and now he has reserved the evidence for his second speech, on the assumption that this will enable him to get away with a distorted account.* [2] So if he does have the testimony read out, pay close attention to it. You'll find that the evidence he has supplied proves only that my grandfather became a debtor, not that the debt is still outstanding.

So this is what I shall try to refute first, this point that he's so mightily proud of—this point that I dispute. If I'd been given the opportunity before and hadn't been ambushed by time, I'd have supplied witnesses to prove that the money was paid in full and that my grandfather discharged all his obligations towards the state. But instead I shall prove by argument, beyond the shadow of a doubt, that he was not in debt, and that we weren't running any risks in exposing our property to public scrutiny.

[3] In the first place, you see, Demochares, whose wife is my mother's sister and therefore Gylon's daughter, has never made any secret of what he's worth: he funds choruses, takes on trierarchies, and carries out all his other liturgical obligations without feeling that he's running any risks. Secondly, not only did my father himself conceal none of his property, but his estate included 4 talents, 3,000 drachmas, which, in the depositions they've submitted against one another, Aphobus and the others admit was mentioned in the will and was received by them. [4] In any case, Aphobus himself and his fellow trustees made the amount of money that had been left to me in my father's will public knowledge by making me the leader of the syndicate, with my contribution assessed not at a paltry level, but at 500 drachmas per 25 mnas.* But if there were any truth to what Aphobus has been saying, he wouldn't have done that; he'd have been *extremely* careful not to do that.* As it turns out, then, Demochares *and* my father *and* the defendants themselves appear to have acted openly without the slightest fear that they were running any such risk.

[5] The strangest thing of all is that, while claiming that my father refused to lease his estate, they never produce the will in question, which would have put the matter beyond doubt, and then they expect to be believed by you anyway, even though they are withholding such an important piece of evidence like this. What they should have done, the moment my father died, is call in a large number of witnesses and tell them to seal up the will, so that, in the event of any dispute, it would have been possible to refer back to this document and discover the whole truth. [6] But in fact they chose to have other documents sealed up, which hardly mentioned the bequest, since they were only notes, but didn't seal or hand over the actual will which gave them authority over those sealed documents and all the rest of the property, and absolved them from blame for not leasing the estate. Oh, yes, it's a very credible tale they tell!

[7] But here's something that I, at any rate, find perplexing. [*To Aphobus*] You say my father didn't want you to lease the estate or reveal how much money was involved. But did he mean you not to reveal the amount to me, or not to reveal it to the city at large? I mean, you seem to have done the opposite to what he wanted: you've made

the estate public knowledge, but you've made it disappear completely from my sight. Nor have you disclosed the value of the property on the basis of which you assessed and paid the contribution to the war levy.* Why don't you show us what the estate in question was, where you made it over to me, and who witnessed you doing so?

[8] Of the 4 talents and 3,000 drachmas, you received 2 talents and 80 mnas,* so you didn't include *this* amount in the assessment you made on my behalf to the state, because at the time it was yours. But there's no way that what you handed over to me—the house, the fourteen slaves, and the 30 mnas—could have formed the basis for as hefty a contribution to the war levy as you agreed to pay to the syndicate. [9] No, there's no escaping the conclusions that the bequest was much larger, that you've kept it all for yourselves, and that the danger of your theft being exposed is what induced you to invent such a pack of lies. Sometimes you refer to one another's testimony for support, but then, in your depositions, you accuse one another of having the money. You claim that you didn't receive much, while submitting accounts showing considerable expenditures. [10] All three of you were jointly made my trustees, but since then you've been scheming individually. You've made the will disappear, which would have revealed the whole truth, and the statements you make about one another are riddled with inconsistencies.

[*To the Clerk of the Court*] Take the depositions and read them all, one after another, to the jury. They need to bear in mind the depositions as well as my arguments, to gain a more accurate sense of what these men are like.

Some depositions are read out.

[11] [*To the jurors*] There you have the assessment they made on my behalf, and it is appropriate for estates worth 15 talents, but the property the three of them have handed over to me isn't worth even 70 mnas. [*To the Clerk of the Court*] Now read the next ones.

Further depositions are read out.

[*To the jurors*] So much for the dowry. Not only do his fellow trustees testify that Aphobus received it, but so do others, to whom he admitted as much. But he has given me neither the dowry nor the maintenance. [*To the Clerk of the Court*] Take the rest of the depositions and read them.

Further depositions are read out.

[12] [*To the jurors*] So, after managing the workshop for two years, he paid Therippides what he owed him for the slaves he hired, but he hasn't paid me the 30 mnas he received as income from the workshop in these two years, neither the principal nor the interest. [*To the Clerk of the Court*] Take another one and read it.

Another deposition is read out.

[*To the jurors*] This shows that, after taking for himself these slaves and the others who were given to us along with them as security for a loan,* he has included in his accounts the large sum he spent on them, but shows no profit from them at all. In fact, he has made the men actually disappear, when they were bringing in a net profit of 12 mnas per year. [*To the Clerk of the Court*] Another one, please.

Another deposition is read out.

[13] [*To the jurors*] This shows that he sold the ivory and iron—but he now denies that they were included in my father's estate either, which is to say that he's trying to defraud me of the value of these items as well, and they were worth about a talent. [*To the Clerk of the Court*] Now read these ones, please.

Further depositions are read out.

[*To the jurors*] This shows that, leaving everything else aside, he has in his possession 3 talents, 1,000 drachmas. So he has kept 5 talents of the principal. Including the interest, even if it's assessed at only 1 drachma per mna per month, he therefore has in his possession more than 10 talents. [*To the Clerk of the Court*] Read the next ones, please.

Further depositions are read out.

[14] [*To the jurors*] So the depositions they submitted against one another show that the ivory and iron were included in the will and were received by them. Now, Aphobus admits that my father asked him to come and that he went to the house—but he denies that he went inside to meet the man who had asked him to come for a meeting, or came to any agreement with him about these items.* All that happened, he says, is that he heard Demophon reading out a document and Therippides saying that my father had made these arrangements.

In fact, however, he was the first to enter the house and reach an agreement with my father about *all* the items included in the will.

[15] The point is, jurymen, that when my father realized that his illness was terminal, he called the three of them to a meeting. He had his brother Demon sit down next to him, and he entrusted us to them for safe-keeping, as he called it. He offered my sister straight away to Demophon, along with two talents as her dowry, and betrothed her to him; and he made all three of them joint trustees of me and his money, enjoining them to lease the estate and work together to keep his property safe for me. [16] At the same meeting, he also gave Therippides 70 mnas, betrothed my mother to the defendant on the understanding that her dowry was 80 mnas, and sat me on the defendant's lap. But there is no one in the world who feels less bound by a sacred trust than Aphobus. Even though he had gained control of my property on these terms, he conspired with his fellow trustees to rob me of all the money—and now he expects you to take pity on him, when what he and the other two have repaid me amounts to less than 70 mnas, and he has been trying to find ways to get even this amount back.

[17] For example, not long before I was due to come to court to prosecute them, they got at me by working up a demand for an exchange procedure. I could either have agreed to the exchange, in which case I wouldn't have been able to take them to court because those cases too would belong to the man who had proposed the exchange.* Or I could have refused outright, in which case I would have been completely ruined by undertaking a liturgy with insufficient resources. It was Thrasylochus of Anagyrus who performed this service for them. Without considering the consequences at all, I agreed to the exchange, but excluded him from my property, hoping that this would gain me a trial to decide which of us would be exempt.* But I didn't obtain the hearing I wanted, and so, since the dates set for the trials were fast approaching and I didn't want to lose my chance to prosecute them, I paid for the liturgy by mortgaging my house and all my property, so that I could appear before you in court and put these men on trial.

[18] Do you see how terribly they have wronged me from start to finish? And do you see that I'm still being injured by them now, because I'm seeking to right those wrongs? Is there any man here who wouldn't feel indignant that, in addition to the property worth more

than ten talents that he inherited, the defendant has also taken property worth the same amount from me? Is there anyone who wouldn't take pity on me, seeing that I've not only lost all my inheritance, but have been robbed by these crooks even of what little I got? Suppose you were to return any verdict in this case other than the right one, what resources would be left me? The property I gave as security for the loan? But that belongs to the lenders. The remnants of the estate? But they belong to Aphobus, if I incur the one-sixth fine.* [19] Jurymen, I beg you, don't cause us so much distress. Don't leave my mother, my sister, and me caught up in a calamity we've done nothing to deserve. That's not what my father wanted for us when he made his will. He wanted my sister to be married to Demophon with a dowry of 2 talents, and my mother to become the wife of this heartless monster with a dowry of 80 mnas, and me to carry out my liturgical responsibilities to you in his stead.*

[20] Help us, then, help us, not just because it's the right thing to do, but for your own sakes, as well as for us and my dead father. Save us, take pity on us, for they have shown me no pity, these relatives of mine. We have turned to you for refuge. I implore you, in the name of your children and your wives, in the name of the blessings you enjoy. So may you have joy of them, if you don't ignore me and don't make yourselves the agents of undeserved suffering for my mother by denying her the last hopes that remain to her in life. [21] At the moment, she expects me to obtain justice here in your court, and then take over responsibility for her and arrange my sister's marriage. But if you give the wrong verdict (as I trust you won't), how do you suppose she'll feel, when she sees that I have lost not only my inheritance but my citizenship,* and when our impoverishment denies her any hope that my sister will find an appropriate position in life?

[22] It would be as wrong for me to fail to obtain justice here in your court, jurymen, as it would be for Aphobus to keep all that money which is not rightfully his. You may not yet be familiar enough with *me* to know what to expect in the future in terms of my attitude towards you, though you might reasonably expect to find me no worse a man than my father; but you're familiar with the defendant, and you are well aware that, so far from using the large estate he inherited to distinguish himself in your service, he has even been proved to be a thief, stealing what does not belong to him.

[23] So bear this in mind too, as well as remembering everything else I've been telling you, and then cast your vote on the side of justice. The witnesses and arguments you've heard, as well as what is likely given the defendants' admissions that they took possession of my entire estate, give you enough to be certain of the facts. They claim that they have spent the money when they haven't; they've kept it all themselves. [24] All these considerations should make you treat us well, because you can be sure that if you enable me to recover what is mine, I will of course happily fulfil my liturgical obligations, grateful to you for doing what was right and returning my property to me, whereas Aphobus will do no such thing if you give him control of my property. I mean, it would be unrealistic of you to imagine that he will be prepared to perform liturgies for you when he denies possession of the property that would make him liable to them. No, the chances are that he will conceal it, to make it look as though you did the right thing in acquitting him.

35. AGAINST LACRITUS

This case arose out of a trading loan. Athens was heavily dependent on imported grain to feed the population, especially grain from the Black Sea area. The importance of the trade is reflected in the Athenian concern to have a set of maritime staging posts stretching up the Aegean as far as and including the Thracian Chersonese. In the fourth century, by law (cited at the end of this speech, §§50–1), an Athenian resident could not lend money on a grain shipment other than to Athens, and maritime loans in the Athenian financial market could not be made on a cargo of grain to any other city. By the middle of the fourth century there was a special fast-track procedure to allow disputes relating to sea trade to be resolved quickly to avoid impeding trading activity. The conditions for access to the procedure were that one of the parties must be a ship's captain, the loan must be on a voyage to or from Athens, and there had to be a written contract. The standard type of loan was made on the security of the ship or the cargo, with the condition that the loan was written off if the ship failed to return safely. Lending on sea trade was therefore risky; but the risk was offset by the scale of the interest, which was dramatically higher than interest on landside loans, especially when one considers that these are short-term loans. The high interest also introduces an element of insurance (since it allows for intermittent losses), for the lender at any rate; the borrower was much more exposed. The speech was delivered not in the main but in a subsidiary hearing. The plaintiff, an Athenian named Androcles, who has lent money on a trading venture, has brought a suit alleging breach of contract. The defendant, a resident alien from Phaselis (in what is now south-west Turkey), has countered with a plea that the action is invalid (a *paragraphē*). The loan was made not to Lacritus but to his brother, who is now dead. Lacritus claims that he has no part in the contract and that he cannot therefore be sued under the special maritime trade procedures. He also claims that he has rejected the inheritance and therefore cannot be sued either for money as the debtor's heir. It is therefore important for the speaker to implicate Lacritus in the loan agreement and to counter his claim that he has no connection with the borrower's estate. The speech probably dates from *c*.350.

———

[1] It's not as if the Phaselites are up to new tricks, jurymen; it's just business as usual for them. They're expert at this. They borrow

money in the commercial district,* and then, no sooner is the money in their hands and a maritime contract drawn up than they forget all about contracts and legalities and the obligation to repay debts. [2] For them, repayment is no different from losing money that is their own, and they concoct schemes and counter-pleas* and excuses to avoid it. They are the most underhand and dishonest people in the world. Witness the fact that, of all the people who fetch up at our port, both Greeks and foreigners, there are regularly more suits against Phaselites than all the rest put together. [3] That's what they're like.

Now, jurymen, I lent money to Artemon, the defendant's brother, on terms stipulated by the mercantile laws, for a voyage to the Black Sea and back to Athens. Artemon died before he had repaid the loan, so I've brought this suit against Lacritus, as stipulated by the same mercantile laws under which I made the contract. [4] For he is Artemon's brother, his sole heir, and the possessor of all the property Artemon left here and in Phaselis as well. And what law could he possibly point to that granted him the right to hold his brother's property and manage it as he saw fit, but not to repay money he has that belongs to someone else, and instead to claim that he was not his brother's heir and that his brother's affairs are none of his concern? [5] This gives us the measure of Lacritus' unscrupulousness.

I am asking you, jurymen, for a favourable hearing in this matter and, if I prove that his wrongdoing injures you no less than me, the lender, I hope you will uphold justice for me. [6] I had not the slightest acquaintance with these men myself, jurymen, but Thrasymedes, the son of the well-known Diophantus of Sphettus,* and his brother Melanopus are my friends—my closest friends, in fact. They approached me in the company of Lacritus—I suppose they had got to know him somehow, but I don't know the details—[7] and asked me to lend his brothers Artemon and Apollodorus money for a voyage to the Black Sea, to set them up in business. Now, jurymen, Thrasymedes had no idea either that these men were crooks. He took them to be respectable men—the kind of men they pretended and claimed to be—and believed that they would do everything that Lacritus here was promising and assuring us they would do. [8] As it turns out, Thrasymedes had been thoroughly duped; he had no idea what sort of beasts he was dealing with in these people. And I was persuaded by Thrasymedes and his brother, and by Lacritus, with his assurances that I would receive nothing but fair treatment from his brothers. So, along with a guest-friend of ours from Carystus, I lent thirty mnas in coined money.

[9] Jurymen, I'd like you first of all to hear the contract under which we loaned the money, and the testimony of witnesses who were present when the loan was made. Then we'll move on and I shall show how they acted against us in the matter of the loan like burglars. [*To the Clerk of the Court*] Read the contract, and then the depositions.

The contract is read out:

[10] *Androcles of Sphettus and Nausicrates of Carystus loaned 3,000 drachmas of coined money to Artemon and Apollodorus of Phaselis for a voyage from Athens to Mende or Scione,* and from there to the Bosporus and, if they wish, on up the left-hand coast to Borysthenes, and then back to Athens, at a rate of 225 drachmas per thousand, or 300 per thousand if they leave the Black Sea for Hieron after the rising of Arcturus,* the loan being secured by 3,000 jars of Mendaean wine, to be conveyed from Mende or Scione in the galley owned by Hyblesius.* [11] *The borrowers offer this amount of wine as security, and guarantee that they are not currently in debt to anyone else with this as security, nor will it be so used for additional loans.* The borrowers shall bring back to Athens in the same ship, as their replacement cargo, the full quantity of goods from the Black Sea. If the goods reach Athens safely, the borrowers shall repay the lenders within twenty days of their return to Athens the amount due under the contract in its entirety, apart from the value of anything jettisoned with the unanimous consent of everyone on board or anything used to pay off hostile forces,* but otherwise in its entirety. And the borrowers shall give the security intact into the charge of the lenders, until they have repaid the money due under the contract.* [12] *If they fail to repay the money within the stipulated time, it shall be permissible for the lenders to use the goods as security for another loan or even to sell them at the going rate. If there is any shortfall in the sum due to the lenders under the contract, the lenders singly or collectively shall recover the money from Artemon and Apollodorus, and from all their possessions landed and maritime, wherever they may be, just as if they had lost a court case and had defaulted on the fine.* [13] *If they do not manage to enter the Black Sea, they shall wait for ten days after the rising of the Dog star,* unload the cargo wherever there is no right of seizure against Athenians, and after returning to Athens they shall repay the interest included in the*

previous year's contract.* If the ship transporting the goods is lost, but the goods acting as security are saved, the remainder shall be shared among the lenders. On this issue nothing else shall have greater validity than this contract. Witnessed by: Phormion of Piraeus; Cephisodotus of Boeotia; Heliodorus of Pithus.

[14] Now the depositions too.

A deposition is read out:
Archenomides of Anagyrus, the son of Archedamas, testifies that Androcles of Sphettus, Nausicrates of Carystus, and the Phaselites Artemon and Apollodorus deposited an agreement with him for safe-keeping and that the contract is still in his keeping.*

Now the witnesses' deposition.

Another deposition is read out:
Theodotus (metic with citizen tax privileges),* Charinus of Leuconoe, son of Epichares, Phormion of Piraeus, son of Ctesiphon, Cephisodotus of Boeotia, and Heliodorus of Pithus, hereby testify that they were present when Androcles lent Apollodorus and Artemon 3,000 drachmas of coined money, and that they know that the contract was given to Archenomides of Anagyrus for safe-keeping.

[15] [*To the jurors*] This, jurymen, was the contract under which I lent the money to the defendant's brother Artemon, with Lacritus encouraging me and assuring me that I would receive nothing but the fair treatment stipulated by the contract under which I made the loan. Lacritus even drafted the contract himself and was a co-signatory of the finished document, because his brothers were rather young, hardly more than boys really, but *he* was Lacritus of Phaselis, a big shot, a student of Isocrates.* [16] It was he who arranged the whole business, and he told me to deal exclusively with *him*. He promised to do right by me throughout, and said he'd be staying in Athens while his brother Artemon would sail and see to the cargo. At this point, jurymen, when he wanted our money, he described himself as Artemon's business partner, as well as his brother, and was incredibly persuasive. [17] But as soon as they got their hands on the money, they divided it up among themselves and did what they liked with it. In everything they did, big or small, they ignored the contract under which they had obtained the money, as became clear subsequently—and throughout,

Lacritus was the ringleader. I shall show, by reference to each clause of the contract, that everything they've done is culpable.

[18] In the first place, the contract states that they borrowed the 30 mnas from me on security of 3,000 jars of wine, on the understanding that they already had security for another 30 mnas. In other words, the total cost of the wine came to about 1 talent, including the expenses incurred in making arrangements for it.* And these 3,000 jars were to be taken to the Black Sea on the galley owned by Hyblesius. [19] That's what's written in the contract, jurymen, as you've heard, but instead of the 3,000 jars, they loaded fewer than 500 jars into the ship. Instead of buying all the wine they were supposed to, they did what they liked with the money, without intending for a moment to load the '3,000 jars' into the ship as they were contractually obliged. [*To the Clerk of the Court*] To confirm the truth of this, take the deposition of their fellow travellers on the ship.

The deposition is read out:
[20] *Erasicles testifies that he was the helmsman of the ship owned by Hyblesius, and that he knows that Apollodorus brought on board 450 jars of Mendaean wine, and no more, and that Apollodorus carried no other portable cargo on the ship to the Black Sea.*

Hippias of Halicarnassus, son of Athenippus, testifies that he was on board Hyblesius' ship as its first mate, and that he knows that Apollodorus of Phaselis carried on the ship from Mende to the Black Sea 450 jars of Mendaean wine and no other cargo. Hippias' deposition was made out of court* in the presence of: Archiades of Acharnae, son of Mnesonides; Sostratus of Hestiaea, son of Philippus; Eumarichus of Hestiaea, son of Euboeus; Philtades of Xypete, son of Ctesius; and Dionysius of Cholleidae, son of Democratides.

[21] [*To the jurors*] That's how they behaved, then, in the matter of the 3,000 jars of wine they were supposed to take on board. The first clause of the contract was the first clause they broke and failed to carry out.

The next clause of the contract states that they offer these goods as security unencumbered, in the sense that they are free from debt on these goods, and will take out no additional loans secured on these goods. This is perfectly explicit in the contract, jurymen, [22] but what did they do? They took no notice of the terms of the contract and borrowed from a very young man, whom they tricked into believing that they were free of debt. They lied to us, surreptitiously borrowed using our goods as security, and tricked that poor young man who loaned them the money into believing that the goods on which they were borrowing were unencumbered. These are typical of their sneaky tricks—and all these schemes were devised by Lacritus. To confirm the truth of this, that they took out a further loan in breach of the contract, the clerk will read you the testimony of the lender himself. [23] [*To the Clerk of the Court*] Read the deposition.

The deposition is read out:
Aratus of Halicarnassus testifies that he lent Apollodorus 11 mnas of coined money on the security of the merchandise that Apollodorus was carrying in Hyblesius' ship to the Black Sea, and on the goods bought there for the return journey, and that he had no idea that Apollodorus had borrowed money from Androcles, otherwise he would not have lent Apollodorus the money.

[24] [*To the jurors*] You can see how devious these people are. The next clause in the contract, jurymen, states that when they've sold their cargo in the Black Sea, they are to buy goods with the money raised, load them in the hold instead, and bring them back to Athens as a replacement cargo. When they reach Athens, they are to repay the money to us within twenty days in good coin. Pending the payment, until we have the money in our hands, we are to have control of the goods, which they are to give us intact. [25] This is quite unambiguous in the contract. But here more than anywhere else they reveal their barefaced insolence, and show that they didn't take the contract seriously at all, but saw it as a discardable piece of rubbish. They didn't buy a replacement cargo in the Black Sea, and left the hold empty for their return journey to Athens. So when they came back from the Black Sea, there was nothing we, the lenders, could confiscate or hold as surety until we recovered from them what was ours, since they entered the harbour of Athens empty-handed.

[26] The way we've been treated is quite extraordinary, jurymen. In our own city, when we're guilty of no crime and haven't lost a law-suit in their favour, we've had our property seized by these men from Phaselis, as if Phaselites had been granted right of seizure against Athenians.* I mean, they're refusing to pay back what they were given, and there's no difference between this and taking by force what

belongs to someone else. Speaking for myself, I've never even heard of anything more disgusting than what they've done to us—and yet they acknowledge receiving the money from us! [27] Although every *disputed* point in a contract requires a legal decision, jurymen, when the terms are acknowledged by both parties and the matter is covered by a maritime contract, everyone considers it closed, and both parties should abide by the terms of the contract. But these Phaselites haven't fulfilled a single clause of our contract. Straight away, right from the very start, they schemed and plotted to act fraudulently, as has been unequivocally shown not just by the witnesses, but also by their own actions.

[28] I must now tell you about the very worst thing Lacritus did— I say 'Lacritus' because he was in overall charge. When they returned here, they didn't put in at our port, but moored at the Thieves' Cove instead, which lies outside the boundaries of the official port. Anchoring at the Thieves' Cove is no different from anchoring at Aegina or Megara, in the sense that you can leave for any destination at a time of your choice.* [29] The boat lay at anchor there for more than twenty-five days. As these men were walking one day around the Exhibition Area,* we came up and spoke to them. We asked them to make sure that we got our money back as soon as possible. They agreed and said that they were trying to do just that. And while we were in their company we kept our eyes on them to see if they were unloading anything from the ship or were paying any harbour dues.*

[30] After a while, even though they had been in town for quite a few days, we hadn't seen any evidence of unloading, or found that they had paid any dues in their name, and so at this juncture we began to get more insistent in our demands, and eventually we got quite heavy. Then, Lacritus, Artemon's brother, said that they couldn't pay us because everything had been lost—and added that he could justify their failure to pay! [31] This did not go down well with us, jurymen, but anger got us nowhere: they couldn't have cared less. Nevertheless, we asked them how the goods had been lost, and Lacritus told us that the ship had foundered while sailing from Panticapaeum* to Theodosia and that all his brothers' cargo that had been in the hold at the time of the wreck had been lost. The cargo had consisted of salted fish, Coan wine, and various other items, they said, all of which was replacement cargo they had been going to bring back to Athens, if it hadn't been lost on the boat.

[32] Well, that's what they said. But you need to hear what disgusting liars these people are. In the first place, they had no financial interest in the ship that was wrecked; someone else had lent them money secured on the freight from Athens to the Black Sea and on the ship itself. The name of the lender is Antipater, a native of Citium.* In the second place, the Coan plonk (eighty jars of wine that had turned sour) and the salted fish were being transported on the ship from Panticapaeum to Theodosia for some farmer, as provisions for his labourers. So why do they come up with these feeble excuses? It's not right.

[33] [*To the Clerk of the Court*] First take Apollonides' deposition, showing that Antipater was the one who lent money secured on the ship, and that the wreck had no effect on the defendants at all, and then the depositions of Erasicles and Hippias, showing that there were only eighty jars of wine on board.

The depositions are read out:
Apollonides of Halicarnassus testifies that he knows that Antipater, a native of Citium, loaned money to Hyblesius for a voyage to the Black Sea on the security of the ship owned by Hyblesius and on the freight destined for the Black Sea. He further testifies that he has an interest in the ship himself, along with Hyblesius, and that slaves owned by him were on board; his slaves were present when the ship was wrecked, and they told him that at the time of the wreck, on the leg of the journey between Panticapaeum and Theodosia, the ship held no full cargo.

[34] *Erasicles testifies that he joined Hyblesius on the voyage to the Black Sea as the helmsman, and that he knows that between Panticapaeum and Theodosia the ship held no regular cargo, and that there was no wine on board belonging to Apollodorus, the defendant in the present case,* but that about 80 jars of Coan wine were being carried for someone from Theodosia.*

Hippias of Halicarnassus, the son of Athenippus, testifies that he was on board Hyblesius' ship as its first mate, and that between Panticapaeum and Theodosia Apollodorus had 1 or 2 containers of wool loaded on to the ship, and 11 or 12 jars of salted fish, and two or three bundles of goatskins, but nothing else. Hippias' deposition was made out of court in the presence of: Euphiletus of Aphidna, son of Damotimus; Hippias of Thymaetadae, son of Timoxenus; Sostratus of Hestiaea, son of Philippus; Archenomides of Thria, son of Straton; Philtades of Xypete, son of Ctesicles.

[35] [To the jurors] See how brazen these men are! Try to remember, jurymen, if you've ever known or heard of wine being imported on a commercial basis from the Black Sea to Athens, especially Coan wine! On the contrary, wine of all kinds—from Peparethos and Cos, from Thasos and Mende and so on—is exported from our part of the world to the Black Sea, while they send us other things.

[36] We didn't let up, but kept trying to find out from them if any of the cargo had survived the wreck in the Black Sea. Eventually, Lacritus replied that 100 Cyzicene staters had been saved,* but that his brother had lent this money in the Black Sea to a Phaselite ship-owner, a fellow citizen and friend of his, and couldn't recover it, so that this too was as good as lost. [37] That's what Lacritus said, but it's not what the contract says, jurymen. The contract tells them to load replacement cargo and bring it back to Athens, and not to lend our property to whoever they feel like in the Black Sea without our say-so, but to bring it to Athens and hand it over to us intact, until we've recovered the money we lent. [To the Clerk of the Court] Read the contract again.

The contract is read out again.

[38] [To the jurors] What does the contract say, jurymen? Does it tell them to lend our property, and to a man we've never met, a total stranger? Or does it tell them to load replacement cargo, bring it to Athens, let us inspect it, and hand it over to us intact? [39] The contract refuses to allow anything greater authority than its terms; it doesn't allow even a law or decree to undermine its authority.* But Lacritus and his associates completely ignored the contract right from the start, and used our money as if it were their own. Such cunning sophists! Such dishonest people!

[40] Now, as the lord Zeus and all the gods are my witnesses, if a man pays Isocrates' fees and wants to be a sophist, I've never held it against him, jurymen, or criticized him for it. I'd be crazy to let that kind of thing bother me. But, by Zeus, I don't think that in their arrogance self-styled experts should covet and steal other people's property, trusting in their rhetorical skill. That would be sophistry indeed, of a foul and despicable kind. [41] Lacritus here, jurymen, has come to court today trusting not in the justice of his cause, but in his eloquence. Even though he knows full well how he and his associates behaved over this loan, he doesn't think it will be hard for him

to find arguments to justify an unjust cause, and he expects to lead you down any side alley he wants. This is, after all, what he claims to be good at; he even draws students by professing to teach just these skills, and charges fees.*

[42] The first people to whom he gave this training were his own brothers—and you can see how it's a training in iniquity and dishonesty, jurymen. He taught them to borrow money on maritime loans in the commercial district and to keep it for themselves, without repaying it. Can you imagine worse people than this—than the man who teaches such skills and those who want to acquire them? Anyway, since he's smart, and trusts his eloquence and the thousand drachmas he paid his teacher, [43] ask him to show *either* that they never got the money from us, *or* that they did receive it and have paid it back, *or* that maritime contracts should not be binding, *or* that there was some good reason for the money they were given to be used for a purpose other than the one stipulated in the contract. Let him convince you of any one of these alternatives, whichever he likes. And if he succeeds in convincing you of it, when you are the ones who decide cases involving maritime contracts, I too will concede his brilliance. But I'm sure he won't be able to find a convincing argument for even one of these points.

[44] Besides, jurymen, in the name of the gods, what do you think would have happened in the opposite situation? Suppose, rather than his brother dying in debt to me, it was me who had died owing his brother a talent or 80 mnas or thereabouts. Do you really think, jurymen, that Lacritus would be relying on the same arguments he's bombarded us with today? Would he be claiming that he was not his brother's heir or that his brother's affairs were none of his concern? Don't you think he'd be demanding the money from me with just the same ruthlessness that he's employed in getting money from all his brother's other debtors, in Phaselis or wherever? [45] And if one of us, in defending a suit brought by him, had dared to bring a counterplea alleging that the case was inadmissible, I'm absolutely sure he'd be waxing indignant to you, protesting that to vote a mercantile case inadmissible would be monstrous and illegal.

[*To Lacritus*] Well, Lacritus, if you think it's all right for *you* to do that, why won't it be for me? The legal system is the same for all of us, isn't it? We all have the same rights in mercantile cases, don't we? [46] [*To the jurors*] But he's so obnoxious. There's no one in the

world more steeped in iniquity. I mean, he's trying to persuade you
to vote this mercantile suit inadmissible even though this is the time
of year when you hear mercantile cases.* [To Lacritus] What is it you
want, Lacritus? Isn't it enough that we're being robbed of the money
we lent you? Do you want to see us in prison as well, for failing to
pay the fine we'll also have incurred?* [To the jurors] [47] But what
a scandal, jurymen! What a dreadful disgrace for people who loan
money within your commercial district for maritime purposes, and
are being robbed, to be hauled off to prison by the very people who
borrowed the money and are robbing them! [To Lacritus] That's what
you're trying to persuade the jurors to allow, Lacritus.

[To the jurors] But, jurymen, where should we go for justice in cases
involving mercantile contracts?* To which official should we present
ourselves? At what time of year? Should we go to the Eleven? But
they bring before the court burglars, thieves, and other criminals
facing the death penalty.* [48] Should we go to the Archon? But the
Archon's assigned sphere of responsibility is heiresses, orphans, and
parents, isn't it? All right, then, by Zeus, we'll go to the King Archon.
But we're not gymnasiarchs, nor are we indicting anyone for impiety. Then the Polemarch will introduce the case? Yes, if it involves
a slave's dereliction or a resident alien's lack of a sponsor.* Then
we're left with the generals. But they appoint trierarchs; they're not
responsible for introducing mercantile cases. [49] [To Lacritus] I'm
a merchant, and you're the brother and heir of one of the merchants
who received a mercantile loan from us. In which court should the
case be heard? Tell us, Lacritus, as long as what you say is honest and
legal. But no one has such skill with words that he could say anything
honest in your situation.

[50] [To the jurors] This isn't the end of the horrors Lacritus has
been putting me through, jurymen. Even apart from having my
money stolen, he'd have made things extremely dangerous for me if
the contract I'd made with them hadn't come to my help and testified
that I gave the money for a round trip to the Black Sea and back again
to Athens. For as you know, jurymen, the law comes down hard on
an Athenian who conveys grain to any destination other than Athens,
or who lends money for a shipment to any commercial district other
than the one in Athens. You know how very severe the penalties are
for these activities. [51] [To the Clerk of the Court] Better still, read the
law out, then they'll know what's what.

The law is read out:

No Athenian or metic resident in Athens (nor any person over whom they exercise control)* may advance money for any grain vessel unless it is going to convey grain to Athens . . . [and so on: there are clauses covering every eventuality]. *If anyone advances money in contravention of this law, the money may be the subject of a denunciation or an inventory presented to the supervisors of the commercial district in the same manner as has already been described for the ship and the grain,* and he shall have no right to bring an action to recover any money advanced for a voyage to anywhere other than Athens, nor is any official to introduce a court case involving this money.*

[52] [*To the jurors*] You can see how strict the law is, jurymen, but we're dealing here with the most disgusting individuals in the world. Even though the contract explicitly states that the money must be brought back to Athens, they allowed what they had borrowed from us in Athens to be taken to Chios. This is how it came about. While they were in the Black Sea, the Phaselite ship-owner was trying to borrow money from some fellow from Chios, and the Chian said that he wouldn't lend the money unless the loan was secured on all the goods the captain had with him, with the consent of the previous lenders. And they allowed these goods, which belonged to us, to act as security for the Chian, and put everything in his name. [53] So they sailed out of the Black Sea with the Phaselite owner and the Chian lender on board, and they anchored at Thieves' Cove,* not at the official Athenian port. And by now, jurymen, the money that was loaned in Athens for a voyage to the Black Sea and back has been taken to Chios by these men.

[54] As I suggested at the beginning of my speech, then, you are the victims of their wrongdoing just as much as we are, the people who lent the money. Look at it this way, jurymen. How could you not be victims when someone sets himself up as superior to your laws, makes maritime contracts null and void, and has sent the money he got from us off to Chios? No, of course such a man wrongs you too.

[55] My words are addressed to Lacritus and his colleagues, jurymen, since they were the ones to whom I gave the money. It will be up to them to make their case against that Phaselite ship-owner, their fellow citizen, the man to whom, they say, they lent the money without our permission and in violation of the contract. We have no

knowledge of the deal they made with him; only they know. [56] But what we're asking, jurymen, and it seems only fair to us, is that you support us, the victims, and punish these men for their cunning and devious schemes. If you do this, you'll find that your vote has done you good: you'll rid yourselves once and for all of the underhand schemes of unscrupulous men, who from time to time employ their wiles on maritime contracts.

36. FOR PHORMION, A COUNTER-PLEA

This trial sheds fascinating light on Athenian society and business life. The defendant, Apollodorus (the prosecutor in ps.-Demosthenes 59), was the son of a remarkable man named Pasion. Pasion began as a slave clerk in a bank and was eventually freed by his owners. He rose to become a very rich banker himself, and after assiduous donations to the city was rewarded with the (rare) gift of citizenship (59.2). The plaintiff, Phormion, had been Pasion's slave in the bank, but was in turn freed to become a banker himself, and he too was rewarded with Athenian citizenship. When Pasion died, Apollodorus was already an adult, but his brother Pasicles was still a minor. In his will Pasion arranged for Phormion to marry his widow, Archippe, and to act as guardian of Pasicles. The estate was to be left undivided until Pasicles reached his majority. In the event, the guardians became concerned by Apollodorus' expenditure and divided up the estate, except for Pasion's bank and a shield factory, which were leased by Phormion for a monthly rent until Pasicles came of age, when the two sons were given the choice between the two commercial operations.

The case (which was part of a protracted legal dispute between Apollodorus and Phormion) arises out of complaints from Apollodorus about Phormion's handling of the estate. Phormion has lodged a special plea (*paragraphē*),[1] counter-suing on the basis of formal flaws in the prosecution, and arguing that the case should be dismissed; the present speech was delivered in this counter-action. Though speeches in such cases have to argue the technical grounds, both defendant and plaintiff (as in the previous speech) also argue the main case at length, the former to avoid the impression that he is evading justice on a technicality, the latter because it may be his only chance to argue the case.

The date has been plausibly fixed as about 350. The speech is delivered not by Phormion, but by a supporting speaker, who does not identify himself. Apollodorus lost the case and sued at least one of Phormion's witnesses for false testimony. Demosthenes changed sides and wrote a speech (Demosthenes 45) for Apollodorus. By this time he was becoming hawkish about Macedonian expansionism, as was Apollodorus (who was also politically active), and the rapprochement may have a political base.

---

[1] See note on 35.2 for this action.

[1] As all of you can see for yourselves, Athenians, Phormion's linguistic skills are so limited that he's completely helpless.* People like me, his friends, have to do the talking. We'll tell you what we know—he's often told us about the case—and explain the situation, and then, once you know the facts and understand the rights and wrongs, you'll be able to give the right verdict† and abide by your oath.*

[2] This counter-plea of ours is not meant to be an evasive waste of time. No, the reason we brought it was to give Phormion the chance to clear his name once and for all, and to find in your court a definitive release from his troubles. Everything he's done other people would find perfectly satisfactory and convincing, without resorting to one of your courts: he's helped Apollodorus greatly; [3] he duly discharged all his obligations and handed over all the properties belonging to Apollodorus for which he had been responsible; and subsequently he was found not to be liable to any charges. Despite all this, as you can see, Apollodorus, motivated by personal animosity, has brought this malicious and unwarranted suit for 20 talents. So I'll try to give you a thorough account of Phormion's dealings with Pasion and Apollodorus. I'll keep it as short as possible, but I'm sure it will enable you to see that Apollodorus' action is motivated by sheer malice. In fact, once you've heard what I have to say, I'm confident you'll see that the suit is inadmissible and throw it out.

[4] The first document you'll hear, then, is the contract under which Pasion leased his bank and shield workshop to Phormion. [*To the Clerk of the Court*] Take the contract, please, and the challenge,* and these depositions.

The contract, the challenge, and the depositions are read out.

[*To the jurors*] So, Athenians, there you have the terms of the contract under which Pasion leased the bank and the shield workshop to Phormion, who had by then set up on his own account.* You need to hear and understand how Pasion also came to owe the bank the 11 talents.* [5] It wasn't poverty that led him into this debt, but industry. Pasion's landed property was worth about 20 talents, and in addition he had more than 50 talents of coined money out on loan. Eleven of these 50 talents had been invested from money deposited in the bank. [6] So when Phormion took over the operation of the bank and gained the deposits, seeing that, until he'd been granted citizenship, he wouldn't be able to recover the sums Pasion had lent on the security of land and housing,* he preferred to have Pasion himself as his debtor for these 11 talents, rather than the men to whom Pasion had loaned the money. That's why Pasion's name was entered in the lease as owing 11 talents, as you've just heard in the deposition.

[7] So you've heard the personal testimony of the chief clerk of the bank explaining how the lease came about. Next, you should see the arrangements Pasion made for his property when he fell ill. [*To the Clerk of the Court*] Take the copy of the will, and this challenge,* and these depositions from the people with whom the will was deposited.

Pasion's will, the challenge, and the depositions are read out.

[8] [*To the jurors*] After Pasion had died, under the terms of this will, Phormion married Pasion's wife* and became one of his son's trustees. Now, Apollodorus proved rapacious, and saw no reason not to spend freely from the capital that was jointly his and his brother's. The trustees calculated that when the time came, as stipulated by the will, for them to subtract everything that Apollodorus had spent from this joint fund and divide what was left evenly between him and his brother, there would be nothing left, and so they decided, in the interests of the boy, to divide the property straight away. [9] They divided it all up between them, except what Phormion had leased, and they kept up their payments to Apollodorus of half of the income from this leased property.

So far, then, he had no possible grounds for complaint against Phormion about the lease. I mean, if there had been any grounds for complaint, the time to show his dissatisfaction was then, straight away, not now. And he can't claim that he hasn't been paid the rent that subsequently came due either. [10] [*To Apollodorus*] Otherwise, when Pasicles came of age and Phormion's lease ended, you wouldn't have released him from all charges; you'd have been demanding immediate repayment of anything he owed you. [*To the jurors*] To confirm the truth of this, and to show that Apollodorus accepted the division of the property with his brother, who had still not come of age, and that they released Phormion from the lease and all future charges,* [*to the Clerk of the Court*] take this deposition.

The deposition is read out.

[11] [*To the jurors*] As soon as they had released Phormion from the lease, Athenians, they divided the bank and the shield workshop between themselves. It was Apollodorus' right to choose, and he chose the workshop rather than the bank. But if there was personal capital of his in the bank, why would he have chosen the workshop rather than the bank? The workshop generated less of an income than the bank—1 talent as opposed to 100 mnas—and was a less attractive possession too, if he had some of his own money in the bank. But he didn't, and that's why it was sensible of him to choose the shield workshop, which is a risk-free venture, whereas investing other people's money is a risky way to make a profit.

[12] There's plenty of evidence that could be brought up to prove the malice and baselessness of Apollodorus' contention that there was some capital. But I think the strongest evidence of all that Phormion never received any such money is what was written in the lease: that Pasion *owed* money to the bank, not that he had *given* Phormion anything. Secondly, as we know, Apollodorus lodged no complaint at the time of the division of the property. Thirdly, Apollodorus subsequently leased the bank to others for the same amount of rent, which goes to show that there was no extra capital included in the lease. [13] I mean, if thanks to Phormion he was short of some of the capital his father had left, he should have come up with the same amount of capital from elsewhere and given it to the new tenants.

To confirm the truth of what I've been saying—that is, to show that Apollodorus subsequently leased the bank* to Xenon, Euphraeus, Euphron, and Callistratus, and also that he did not make any personal capital over to them either, but that they took a lease only on the deposits and the profits accruing from them—[*to the Clerk of the Court*] take their deposition.

> *The deposition of Xenon, Euphraeus, Euphron, and Callistratus is read out.*

[14] [*To the jurors*] This deposition shows, Athenians, that Apollodorus and his brother leased the bank to these men as well; that they didn't make any personal capital over to them; that they gave them their freedom in gratitude for their great services;* and that they didn't take either them or Phormion to court at the time. As long as his mother was alive, who was fully aware of the situation, Apollodorus found no cause for complaint in Phormion's behaviour over anything.

After her death, however, he brought a baseless suit against him not just for the 2,000 drachmas she'd bequeathed to the children she'd had with Phormion, but for 3,000 drachmas more of coined money, and a short khiton, and a slave-girl.* [15] Even then, however, we'll find, he made no mention of the charges he's bringing today. He let his father-in-law and brother-in-law arbitrate (along with Lysinus and Andromenes), and they persuaded Phormion to make Apollodorus a present of the 3,000 drachmas and the additional amount, and to have him as a friend rather than an enemy. So Apollodorus received 5,000 drachmas in all, and at the temple of Athena for the second time he released Phormion from further charges.* [16] But now, as you can see, he's in court again, with a raft of made-up accusations and grievances dating (this is the worst aspect of it) from the past—grievances about which he was silent earlier. [*To the Clerk of the Court*] To confirm the truth of this, please take the record of the judgement that was made on the Acropolis, and the deposition of the people who were present when, on receipt of the money, Apollodorus proved ready to release Phormion from all further charges.

The judgement and the deposition are read out.

[17] [*To the jurors*] There, jurymen, you have the judgement made by Deinias, whose daughter is Apollodorus' wife, and Nicias, whose wife is the sister of Apollodorus' wife. So he's received the money, and released Phormion from all further charges—and still he has the impudence to bring a suit for such an enormous sum of money! It's as though all these people had died, or he expected the truth to remain hidden!

[18] So, Athenians, you've now had a thorough account of all Phormion's dealings and transactions with Apollodorus. Now, since Apollodorus has no way to justify his case, I imagine he'll repeat the preposterous statement he made at the arbitration meeting:* that, under Phormion's influence, his mother destroyed the papers,* and that, with them lost, he has no way to establish his case in detail. [19] But there's powerful evidence to prove that this is false, that the accusation is untrue. Look at it this way, Athenians.

In the first place, who would accept a division of his father's estate unless he had papers to show what his patrimony consisted of? No one, of course. [*To Apollodorus*] But in the eighteen years since you accepted the division of the estate, you've plainly never

brought charges relating to the missing papers. [20] [*To the jurors*]
In the second place, even if he shrank from accusing his mother of
having destroyed the papers, why wouldn't he have mentioned it to
Pasicles when Pasicles, having come of age, was gathering the trustees' accounts?* Then Pasicles could have done something to bring
the facts to light. [*To Apollodorus*] In the third place, on what papers
did you base the suits you brought? [*To the jurors*] You see, he's succeeded in recovering a great deal of money from not a few of his
fellow citizens by taking them to court with a charge sheet that reads:
'So-and-so injured me by failing to pay back money which the papers
my father left show him as owing.' [21] But if the papers have vanished, on what papers were the suits he brought based?

To verify what I've been saying, I've already mentioned that he
accepted the division of the property, and you've heard depositions
to that effect. And the clerk will now read to you depositions relating
to these suits of his. [*To the Clerk of the Court*] Take the depositions,
please.

The depositions are read out.

[*To the jurors*] So in these suits he acknowledged the receipt of his
father's papers. His only other option, you see, would have been to
admit that the charges he was bringing were baseless, or that he was
suing men for what they did not owe.

[22] To my mind, Athenians, Phormion's innocence is proved by
a great many considerations, the most important of which is that
Pasicles, Apollodorus' brother, hasn't taken him to court and hasn't
joined his brother in accusing him of anything. [*To Apollodorus*] But
why would Phormion have refrained from defrauding someone who
was still a boy when his father died, and whose property he managed
as a trustee, only to steal from you, when you were a 24-year-old adult
at the time of your father's death, and would easily and immediately
have obtained justice for yourself for any injury you suffered? That's
just not possible. [*To the Clerk of the Court*] To confirm the truth of
what I've been saying, that Pasicles feels he has nothing to complain
about, take his deposition.

Pasicles' deposition is read out.

[23] [*To the jurors*] Now, what about the critical issue, the inad-
missibility of the case? Certain facts have already emerged from my

account that you need to take into consideration when addressing this issue, and I would ask you to bear them in mind. First, Athenians, a final accounting had taken place and Phormion had been released from the lease of the bank and the workshop. Second, there had been an arbitration hearing, and again Phormion was released from any further charges. Third, the law forbids suits on matters where a release has been granted. [24] Fourth, despite this legal prohibition, Apollodorus was making malicious accusations and initiating a suit against us. These were the circumstances under which we put in a counter-plea, as permitted by law, to have the suit thrown out.

This is the issue on which you are to vote, and it's important that you understand it, so the clerk will read you the law I was referring to, and a series of depositions from people who were present when Apollodorus released Phormion from the lease and from all future charges. [*To the Clerk of the Court*] Take these depositions, and the law.

The depositions and the law are read out.

[25] [*To the jurors*] As you've heard, Athenians, the law says 'There shall be no suit' under certain conditions, among which are all cases where a man has been granted a release or discharge. This is how it should be. I mean, if it's right that cases which have already been tried should not be re-tried, it must be even more right for there to be no trial where a release has been granted. After all, a man who has lost a case in your court may argue that you were misled, but a man who has granted a release and discharge has, in effect, decided against himself. This means that, if he were later to prosecute a case on the same issue, he would be accusing himself, but what charge could he reasonably bring against himself? There is none, of course. That's why the legislator started the list of conditions where 'There shall be no suit' with all cases where a man has been granted a release or discharge. And both of these apply to Phormion, because Apollodorus has granted him both release and discharge.* You have already heard testimony that confirms the truth of all this, Athenians.

[*To the Clerk of the Court*] Now please take the statute of limitations.

The statute of limitations is read out.

[26] [*To the jurors*] As you can see, Athenians, the law is perfectly clear and explicit about how much time has to pass.* What Apollodorus

wants, however, after more than twenty years,* is for you to allow his own baseless prosecution to take precedence over the laws you swore to uphold as jurors. Now, you have to safeguard all our laws, of course, but especially this one, Athenians, [27] because its sole purpose, as far as Solon was concerned, was, I think, to rid you of sycophants and their unwarranted prosecutions. Five years was enough time, he thought, for people with genuine grievances to obtain redress, and he also believed that nothing would expose false pleas better than the passage of time. At the same time, bearing in mind that neither the signatories of a contract nor its witnesses are immortal, he made this law to stand in for these people, to serve as a witness to justice in cases where no others are available.

[28] Personally, jurymen, I have no idea what Apollodorus can do to respond to this. He can't have supposed that, if you saw that he hadn't been cheated out of any money, you'd condemn Phormion for marrying his mother. He knew as well as many of you do that Socrates, the famous banker (who had been freed by his masters just as Apollodorus' father was), married his wife to his former slave Satyrus.* [29] Another banker who did the same thing was Socles, who gave his wife to his former slave Timodemus, who's still alive today. And people in the banking business do this elsewhere, Athenians, not just here in Athens. On Aegina, for instance, Strymodorus gave his wife to his slave Hermaeus, and when she died he had him marry his daughter instead.

Many examples of the practice could be cited, [30] and it makes sense. I mean, it would be disgraceful for *you*, Athenians, who are citizens by birth to prefer any amount of money to good birth, but what about people who've been granted citizenship of Athens or elsewhere, and who were considered to deserve this honour in the first place because of their success as businessmen and the fact that they were richer than others? They have to protect their fortunes. [*To Apollodorus*] That's why your father Pasion gave his wife, your mother, to Phormion. He wasn't the first or the only man to have done this; he wasn't debasing himself or you, his sons; he simply saw that the only way for his business to survive was for him to bind Phormion closely to the family. [31] If you look at how much good this did, you'll realize what a sound idea it was of your father's; but if you snobbishly look down on Phormion as a relative, you should be careful: you might be making a fool of yourself.*

Suppose someone were to ask you what sort of a man you consider your father to have been: 'A good man,' you'd answer, naturally. 'Well, then, whose character and lifestyle in general more closely resemble Pasion's, do you think: yours or Phormion's?' 'Phormion's,' you'd reply. I'm sure you would. So you're looking down on a man who more closely resembles your father than you do for having married your mother? [32] But this was done at your father's bidding and behest. [*To the jurors*] It's not just his will that makes this clear, Athenians, but [*to Apollodorus*] you yourself have testified to it. When you requested your share of your mother's property, you acknowledged the legality of her marriage to Phormion, with whom she had had children, because if he had married her illegally, without having been bequeathed her, his children by her didn't count as heirs and by that token weren't entitled to a portion of her estate. [*To the jurors*] You've already heard testimony confirming the truth of this—that he accepted a *quarter* of his mother's estate and forfeited the right to bring any further charges in the future.*

[33] Given his inability to justify himself on any point, Athenians, he resorted at the arbitration meeting to barefaced lies. It's better for you to hear about them from me first. The first is that there never was a will, and that the supposed will is nothing but a fake and a forgery; the second is that the reason he made no protest at any point earlier, and didn't raise a court case, is that Phormion was prepared to pay him a generous rent, and promised to go on paying it. 'But he's stopped,' he says, 'and that's why I'm prosecuting him now.' [34] Well, these statements will both be lies, if he makes them, and his own actions will prove him false. Look at it this way. When he denies the authenticity of the will, ask him how he gained the tenement as his inheritance, which was bequeathed to him in the will? He can't treat the clauses of the will that benefited him as valid and the rest as invalid. [35] And when he says that he was led on by Phormion's promises, remember that we've already produced as witnesses the men who rented the bank and the workshop for a long time after Phormion had given them up.* But he should have prosecuted Phormion on the spot, when he leased the businesses to these new tenants, if there was any truth to the charges he's bringing against him now—but released him from then. To confirm the truth of what I've been saying—that he received the tenement-house as part of his inheritance under the will, and that not only did he see no need to

bring any charges against Phormion, but even thanked him—[*to the Clerk of the Court*] take the deposition.

The deposition is read out.

[36] [*To the jurors*] He moans about his poverty and how he's lost everything, so you need to know how much money he got from rents and debts. I'll tell you; it won't take long. The papers left by his father have enabled him to recover debts amounting to 20 talents, and he's kept more than half of this, because he often cheats his brother out of his share as well. [37] As for income from rents, he made 80 mnas a year (160 mnas being the total rent) for the 8 years when Phormion had the bank, which comes to 10 talents, 40 mnas; and for the next ten years, when they leased the business to Xenon, Euphraeus, Euphron, and Callistratus, he made 1 talent a year.* [38] In addition, for almost 20 years, he's had an income of more than 30 mnas a year from his share of the original property, which he managed himself. If you add it all together—his original share, the recovered debts, and the rents – you'll find that he has made more than 40 talents, and that's not counting Phormion's gift,* what he inherited from his mother, and 2 talents, 3,600 drachmas that he has taken from the bank and not repaid.

[39] [*To Apollodorus*] I suppose you'll say that all this money has been spent on service to the city, and that you don't deserve this treatment after the generosity of your liturgies. But some of the money you spent on liturgies came from the joint fund, so you and your brother incurred that expense together. And the money you spent later wasn't even 20 mnas a year, well short of your income of 2 talents a year. So don't blame the city, and don't try to tell us that money you wasted on your shameful extravagances was spent on public service. [40] [*To the jurors*] It's important that you understand just how much money he's made, Athenians, and how much he's spent on liturgies. An itemized list will be read to you. [*To the Clerk of the Court*] Take this list here, and this challenge, and these depositions.

The list, the challenge, and the depositions are read out.

[41] [*To the jurors*] You can see how much he's made and, on top of what he's earned by leasing the bank and the rest of the property Pasion left, he's also owed many talents, money which he's recovering freely or by litigation. These debts were owed to Pasion, and now

Apollodorus and his brother have taken them over. You've also heard how much he's spent on liturgies—an insignificant fraction of his income, let alone his capital. But he'll still boastfully going on about all the times he's financed a trireme or a chorus. [42] I've exposed the lies he's going to tell about his financial position, but I have to say that, even if he were completely honest, I still think that the best solution (as well as being the most just) would be for Phormion to perform liturgies for you from his own resources rather than for you to give his money to Apollodorus and get only a little back, while Phormion is reduced to extreme poverty and Apollodorus arrogantly squanders money on his usual pursuits.

[43] [*To Apollodorus*] As for Phormion's enriching himself from your father's estate, and the questions you said you were going to ask about how he came to be so wealthy, you are uniquely disqualified for this line of questioning, because your father, Pasion, also got rich the same way—not by luck or inheritance, but by giving practical proof of his integrity and honesty, and so gaining the trust of his masters, the bankers Antisthenes and Archestratus. [44] In the field of commerce and finance, it's a remarkable thing to find diligence and integrity coexisting in the same man. Pasion was born that way; it wasn't passed on to him by his masters, and Phormion didn't get it from your father either. (After all, if it had been up to your father, he'd rather have made *you* good!) If you don't know that a businessman's most profitable asset is his trustworthiness, you know nothing. Besides, Phormion has given your father, you, and your family in general many proofs of his usefulness. But then, who could fathom the depths of your greed and your nature?

[45] I'm surprised you don't also factor Antimachus into your calculations, the son of your father's former owner Archestratus. He lives here in Athens and he's not doing as well as he might, but he doesn't take you to court. He doesn't take it as a personal slight that you wear a fine woollen cloak, that you've bought the freedom of one of your courtesans and have married off another (even though you already have a wife), that you go around with three slaves in attendance, that you parade your debauched lifestyle even before people you pass in the street, while he's living in dire poverty. [46] Nor is he unaware of Phormion's position. But if you think you have a claim on Phormion's property because he was once owned by your father, Antimachus' claim must be stronger than yours. I mean, your father belonged to

his father, and so, by this reasoning, both you and Phormion belong to Antimachus.

You're so crass that you force people to say the kinds of things about you that you'd be right to hate them for saying. [47] You disgrace yourself and your dead parents, and you insult the city. Your father, and subsequently Phormion, gained certain privileges because they enjoyed the kindness of these Athenians here,* but instead of cherishing and valuing these privileges, as a way of enhancing their glory for both the givers and you, the receivers, you cheapen them, mock them, and deprecate them. You almost tell the Athenians off for having made a person like you a citizen. [48] And your derangement—I don't know what else to call it—is so far advanced that you fail to see that even now we're doing you a favour in insisting that, since Phormion has received his freedom, it means nothing that he once belonged to your father. It's *you* who are arguing against yourself, in insisting that Phormion could never be your equal. For the privilege you assign yourself in claiming superiority to him will be used to the same effect against you by the men who originally owned your father. In fact, to show that Pasion too was once owned, and was then freed, just as Phormion was freed by your family, [*to the Clerk of the Court*] take these depositions, testifying that Pasion belonged to Archestratus.

The depositions are read out.

[49] [*To the jurors*] So the original saviour of the business, the man who made himself indispensable to Apollodorus' father and also did Apollodorus himself enormous favours, as you've heard—this is the man Apollodorus wants to see sentenced to a crippling fine and unjustly turned out of house and home. [*To Apollodorus*] That's all you would achieve, because a close look at his wealth will show you who its owners are—or will be if these jurors are misled into the wrong verdict, as I trust they won't be.* [50] Look at Aristolochus, the son of Charidemus: there was a time when he owned some land, but now it's in many hands, because he was in debt to many people when he acquired it. Look at Sosinomus and Timodemus and all the other bankers who were dispossessed when the time came for them to settle their debts. But you don't see any need to consider anything, not even your father's plans, though he was a far better and more intelligent man than you in every respect.

[51] Your father—I swear this by all that's sacred—your father felt that Phormion was so much more important to you, to him, and to the family business that, even though you were an adult, he made him, not you, a trustee of half the estate and gave him his wife. And while Pasion was alive, Phormion had his respect. [*To the jurors*] This was no more than Phormion deserved, Athenians. [*To Apollodorus*] The other bankers were all ruined even though they weren't paying rent, but owned their businesses outright, whereas, despite paying 2 talents, 40 mnas in rent, Phormion kept the bank safe for you. [52] Pasion was properly grateful for this, but it means little or nothing to you. Instead, in defiance of the will and the curses your own father wrote into it,* you harass Phormion, prosecute him, and bring baseless accusations. My good fellow—not the right term for you, perhaps!—when will you stop? When will you realize that honesty is more profitable than wealth? Look at you, for instance: according to you—let's assume you're telling the truth—you've lost the fortune you inherited; but if you'd been a man of worth you wouldn't have spent it in the first place.

[53] No matter how I look at it, I swear by all that's sacred that I can't see any reason why the jurors should believe you and vote against Phormion. What on earth might induce them to do so? Because you're bringing the charges soon after the crimes were committed? No: it all happened years and years ago. Because you kept a low profile in the intervening period? Hardly: everyone knows how constantly busy you've been, not only prosecuting high-profile private suits like this one, but also trumping up public suits and prosecuting . . . well, who didn't you prosecute?† Didn't you take Timomachus to court? And Callippus, who's now in Sicily? And then Menon, Autocles, Timotheus, and plenty of others?* [54] Do you expect us to believe that a man like you would have chosen to seek redress for offences against the state which hardly affected you at all, before doing so for the private offences you're currently prosecuting? Especially if these private offences are as serious as you say. So why did you prosecute these men and do nothing about Phormion? Because he wasn't doing you any harm: your current prosecution is, of course, baseless.

[*To the jurors*] So, Athenians, I don't think it's at all irrelevant for me to produce witnesses to verify what I've been saying. After all, when every suit he brings is malicious and unwarranted, what are we supposed to think about what he's doing today? [55] In fact,

Athenians, I also think it's relevant for me to give you a good sense of Phormion's character, his honesty and kindness. A repeat offender, you see, might very well be guilty of an offence against Apollodorus today; but when a man has never wronged anyone, and in fact has frequently helped others, it would be completely out of character for him to be guilty of an offence now. Apollodorus would be the only man in the world to have been wronged by him. Anyway, once you've heard these depositions, you'll know what both these men are like.

The depositions are read out.

[56] [*To the Clerk of the Court*] Now read the depositions that show what a bad piece of work Apollodorus is.

The depositions are read out.

[*To the jurors*] So is that what Phormion is like? See what you think. [*To the Clerk of the Court*] Go ahead.

The depositions are read out.

Now read the evidence of how much good Phormion has done Athens.

The depositions are read out.

[57] [*To the jurors*] You can see how extremely valuable Phormion has been to the city and to many of you, Athenians. In neither his private nor his professional life has he ever harmed anyone, and he's not wronging Apollodorus now. This is the man who begs and implores and requests your protection, and we, his friends, add our pleas to his.

Here's something you should be aware of. You've heard evidence, Athenians, that Phormion has raised enormous sums of money for Athens, sums greater than his own personal fortune or anyone else's. The point is that, among people who know what's what, his credit is good for such enormous sums and for more besides, far more. It's the fact that he's trusted like this that enables him to do good, whether he himself or you are the beneficiaries. [58] Don't throw all this away! Don't let this vile man ruin things for you! It would set a shameful precedent if you were to allow despicable sycophants to take the money of hard-working, unassuming men. That money will do you far more good in Phormion's hands. You can see for yourselves, as well as from the depositions you've been hearing, how good a friend he is to those in need. [59] And his intention in these cases has never been to make a profit; he has acted simply out of kindness and a good heart. A man like this shouldn't be sacrificed to Apollodorus, Athenians, and you shouldn't wait until he has no need of it to feel sorry for him. Now is the time, when you're in a position to save him. I can't imagine that there could be a better time for you to show your support of him than now.

[60] Much of Apollodorus' speech will consist of the empty words of a sycophant, and that's how you should treat it. Get him to prove to your satisfaction either that his father didn't make this will; or that there's another lease in existence, beside the one we're using as evidence; or that at the final accounting he didn't release Phormion from all future charges, in accordance with the judgement made by his father-in-law and acceded to by Apollodorus; or that the law permits prosecution in cases that have been settled in this way. Get him to try to prove anything along these lines. [61] And if his only recourse is to make slanderous and abusive accusations, don't listen to him, and don't let his loud-mouthed impudence mislead you, but bear in mind and remember everything we've told you. If you do, you'll be acting as your oath demands and you'll save Phormion, which is the right thing to do. By all that's sacred, it's no more than he deserves.

[62] [*To the Clerk of the Court*] Take this law and these depositions and read them out:*

The law and depositions are read out.

[*To the jurors*] I don't know that I need to add anything else. I think you've followed what I've been saying. [*To the slave in charge of the water-clock*] Pour the water away.*

39. AGAINST BOEOTUS, ON THE NAME

This speech was written for a private suit between two half-brothers, Mantitheus and Boeotus, sons of a politician named Mantias. The family background, especially Mantias' relationships with the two mothers, is confused. Mantias had refused to acknowledge Boeotus as his legitimate son. Boeotus on reaching manhood sued Mantias to compel him to acknowledge him. Thanks to Mantias' naivety and some deft manoeuvring by Boeotus' mother, Plangon, Boeotus succeeded and Mantias introduced him to his phratry under the name Boeotus. But Mantias died before he could admit Boeotus to his deme and Boeotus had himself admitted under the name Mantitheus, the name of his paternal grandfather. He has continued to use this name. Mantitheus is suing Boeotus to compel him to revert to the name under which Mantias acknowledged him. Mantitheus bases his argument on the potential for confusion and the consequent practical problems for both of them and for the city; but it is difficult not to detect more emotional rivalries and family bitterness at work as well. The nature of the suit is a puzzle. Mantitheus speaks of harm or damage several times; so this may be a suit for damages (*dikē blabēs*). It would be an unusual use of the action, which normally relates to financial loss. But this may have been the only action available to him. This is one of those rare cases where we know the result. A later inscription, recording the payment of a debt owed by their father, lists both brothers under the same name; so Mantitheus lost his case. The next speech in modern editions of the corpus (speech 40, which is not generally accepted as the work of Demosthenes), was written for another suit between the brothers relating to their maternal dowries. We can date the speech confidently to 348.

---

[1] I assure you, jurymen, in the name of the gods, that it wasn't love of litigation that prompted me to bring this suit against Boeotus. I'm also aware that many people will find it strange for me to be taking someone to court for having chosen the same name as me.* But the consequences of leaving the matter unremedied left me no choice: the case must be judged in your court. [2] If he hadn't claimed my father as his own, it would be fair to say, I suppose, that it's no business of mine what he wants to call himself. But in fact he took my father to court. He drummed up a gang of sycophants to support him—people like Mnesicles, who's probably known to all of you, and Menecles,

the scoundrel who procured the conviction of Ninus*—and went to court with the claim that he was my father's son by the daughter of Pamphilus, and that he had legitimate grievances—that, in fact, he was being deprived of his citizenship.*

[3] I shall tell you the whole truth, jurymen. My father was afraid to go to court in case he was confronted there by someone with a grievance against him from another context, as happens in politics. He had also been tricked by Boeotus' mother, who had of her own accord promised that if he offered her an oath on the matter, she would decline it, and that would be the end of it.* She had him deposit some money with a third party, and on these conditions he offered her the oath. [4] But then she accepted the challenge, and swore that my father was the father of Boeotus, and of his brother as well, her other son. Once she had done this, the boys *had* to be introduced to the phratry and there was nothing he could say or do about it. So he introduced them, recognized them as his own, and, to get to the point, at the Apaturia he enrolled the defendant here as 'Boeotus', and his brother as 'Pamphilus'.* I was already on the register as 'Mantitheus'.

[5] My father happened to die before their enrolment as demesmen, but the defendant presented himself before the deme for assessment, and registered himself as 'Mantitheus', not 'Boeotus'. I shall first produce witnesses to verify what I've been saying, and then I shall explain how harmful this action of his is, not just to me, but to you as well.

The witnesses' deposition is read out.

[6] There you have testimony about the process of our enrolment by my father. What I'll do now is show that, since the defendant chose not to abide by this arrangement, it was right, and indeed essential, for me to bring this suit against him.

My father had recognized the two of them as his sons, and I had accepted and become reconciled to only a third of the inheritance that had all been mine.* Under these circumstances, it would be sheer stupidity on my part—it would make no sense at all—for me to quibble about a name, unless I would incur great dishonour and the charge of unmanliness if I changed my name, and unless there were plenty of good reasons why it's quite impossible for us to share a single name.

[7] [*To Boeotus*] The first question, since I should address state before personal business, is this: when there's a job to be done, how will the state assign it to us? 'The usual process, of course: our fellow tribesmen will propose us.' So they'll be proposing 'Mantitheus of Thoricus, the son of Mantias' to serve as chorus-producer or gymnasiarch, or to lay on a festival dinner for his tribe. Then how will anyone know whether they're nominating you or me? You'll say it's me and I'll say it's you. [8] Suppose next the Archon, or whichever officer is hearing the case, summons us to his office. And suppose we don't respond to the summons, nor perform the liturgy. Which of us will be liable to the legally prescribed penalties?

How will the generals enrol us if they're registering members of a syndicate or appointing a trierarch? If the city is launching a military expedition, how will anyone know which of us has been conscripted? [9] Or suppose some other officer—the Archon, the King Archon, the Festival Games Committee—needs someone to serve the state in some way, how will they be able to tell which of us they're appointing? By Zeus, perhaps they'll add 'the son of Plangon' to the entry if it's you who are being enrolled, and *my* mother's name if it's me.* But that would be unprecedented. Where's the law that justifies such an addition, or that allows any names to be entered in the registry, beside the name of the subject, other than those of the father and the deme? And since both our names are identical, the result will be complete chaos.

[10] And if 'Mantitheus of Thoricus, the son of Mantias' were invited to judge a competition,* what would happen? Would we both go? How will anyone know whether it's you or me he's invited? By Zeus, suppose a lottery is being held by the city to assign offices—membership of the Council, membership of the board of Thesmothetes, whatever. How will anyone know which of us has been selected? Perhaps the ballot will have a distinguishing mark on it, the kind of mark one would put on any other piece of property. But even this won't help most people know which of us the ballot belongs to. He'll say it's him who's been selected, and I'll say it's me, [11] and the only option will be for us to go to court.

So the city will convene a court for each of our cases, and we'll lose the right shared by every citizen to hold office if selected by the ballot. Instead, we'll pitch into each other and whichever of us wins the argument will hold office. But would it be better for us to rid ourselves of the resentment we feel for each other, or to create fresh reasons for loathing and slander? For fresh reasons are absolutely bound to arise whenever a dispute occurs between us, whether it concerns offices or anything else. [12] And what if—we must consider all possibilities—what if one of us is selected and the other one persuades him to swap and gets selected like that? But this is no different from one man wielding two ballots. Are we then to be allowed to get away with something that by law is punishable by death?* 'Of course, because we wouldn't do it.' Well, I know *I* wouldn't, but even so it's wrong for people to be liable to such a severe penalty if it can be avoided.

[13] [*To the jurors*] All right. So much for the harm to the city. What about me personally? Just look at the terrible effect it has on me, and see if my argument makes sense. If you thought what you've just been hearing was bad . . . well, the effect on me is far worse. You know that, while Menecles was alive, Boeotus was close to him and his circle, that the people he's close to now are no improvement at all over Menecles, and that he shares their ambitions and wants to be known as a clever speaker. (And who knows? Maybe he is.) [14] Now, suppose that, as time goes on, he tries to imitate Menecles and his friends—that is, to raise indictments, disclosures, warrants, and summary arrests*—and that as a result of one such case he comes to owe the state money. We're only human, after all, and you are expert at moderating the behaviour of these clever speakers when they get above themselves. Under these circumstances, would it be he or I who was registered as a debtor? 'Good heavens, everyone will know which of us it is.' [15] All right, but suppose—it's a possibility, after all—suppose the debt remains unpaid for many years: why would it be his sons who would become listed as debtors rather than mine? The entry will have the same name, with the same father, the same tribe, and so on. And suppose someone brought a suit of ejectment against him:* the prosecutor in the case might acknowledge that his business wasn't with me, but once he's won the case and listed Boeotus as a public debtor, why would the name on the list be his rather than mine? What if he were to fail to pay a war levy? [16] Or what if the name were to become tainted by the threat of some other legal action, or generally by an unsavoury reputation? Who in the population at large will know which of us deserves this reputation, when there are two men called 'Mantitheus, the son of Mantias'?

Or again, what if he were taken to court for draft-dodging? What if he were serving in a chorus when he was supposed to be serving in the army?* After all, not long ago, when everyone else went to Tamynae, he remained behind. He stayed on here, celebrated the Pitchers, and danced at the Dionysia, as all of you who were in town at the time know. [17] On the army's return from Euboea, he was charged with desertion and, as taxiarch of the tribe, I was forced to receive the charge and lodge it against my own name, 'Mantitheus, the son of Mantias'. And if wages had been available for the law-courts,* it goes without saying that I'd have brought the case to trial. Anyway, if the jars hadn't already been sealed, I'd have produced witnesses to verify this.*

[18] Well, then, what if he were charged with being an alien?* He has made a lot of enemies, and the way in which my father was compelled to adopt him did not go unnoticed. Before, when my father was refusing to recognize him, you believed Boeotus' mother; but, with his blood, he'll make a nuisance of himself at some point, and then you'll change your minds and realize that it was my father who was telling the truth. And what if he were to allow a case to go by default, because he anticipated being convicted of bearing false testimony for the favours he does these cronies of his? Do you see how much it harms me, Athenians, to be linked for my entire life with his infamous behaviour?

[19] I'd also like you to see that it's perfectly realistic of me to find the situations I've been describing frightening: first, Boeotus has already been taken to court a number of times, Athenians, and, even though none of the cases had anything to do with me, I become tarred by the same brush; second, when you appointed me to an administrative position, he claimed that the position was his. The name has been responsible for much unpleasantness in my life. I shall call witnesses for the details, so that you can be certain of the truth.

The witnesses' depositions are read out.

[20] You can see what happens, Athenians; you see how much distress this thing causes me. Even if it weren't distressing, even if it weren't quite out of the question for us to have the same name, it can't be right for my father's unwilling recognition of Boeotus to gain him some of my money, and for me to lose the name my father gave me of his own free and unforced will. I can't see how it could possibly be right.

To prove to you that my father not only had my name inscribed in the phratry registry—you've already heard testimony about that—but also gave me my name during the tenth-day ceremony,* [*to the Clerk of the Court*] take this deposition too.

The deposition is read out.

[21] [*To the jurors*] As you can tell, Athenians, *I* have been in possession of this name all my life, while my father, when he had no choice in the matter, enrolled the defendant here in the phratry as 'Boeotus'. So there's a question I'd like to put to him here, in court: [*to Boeotus*] if my father hadn't died, what would you have done at your assessment by the deme? You'd have allowed him to register you as 'Boeotus', wouldn't you? But it hardly makes sense to bring a suit to gain something that you then later try to block.* And yet if you'd allowed him, he'd have enrolled you in the deme with the same name that was written in the phratry registry. But, by Earth and all the gods, isn't it sheer disrespect to claim that he's your father and then to try to invalidate measures he took during his lifetime?

[22] [*To the jurors*] When the case came before the arbitrator,* Boeotus had the barefaced cheek to say that my father had held a tenth-day ceremony for him as well as for me, at which he gave him the name 'Mantitheus'. What's more, the witnesses he produced to verify this were people who . . . well, if they were close to my father, this was the first anyone knew about it. But, as you all know, of course, no one would conduct a tenth-day ceremony for a child he didn't honestly consider to be his, nor, once the ceremony had gone ahead and he had displayed the kind of affection a father might feel for a son, would he have dared to deny it later.* [23] Even if he had fallen out with the boys' mother, he wouldn't have hated them, if he thought they were his. It's far more usual for a husband and wife to find their children a reason to make up, than it is for them to find their mutual grievances a reason for also hating their children.

Well, this isn't the only consideration that enables you to see that, if he tries out this argument in his speech, he'll be lying. No, indeed: before he began to claim that he was a member of my family, he used to go to the Hippothontis tribe to train for the boys' chorus.* [24] But it's not credible that his mother would have sent him to Hippothontis if, as she claims, she had been badly treated by my father—if he subsequently denied having held a tenth-day ceremony that she knew

had taken place. Can anyone here believe this story? Of course not.
[*To Boeotus*] I mean, you could just as well have gone to train with the
Acamantis tribe, and then at least there would have been a semblance
of consistency between your tribe and the alleged naming ceremony.
[*To the jurors*] To confirm the truth of what I've been saying, I shall
call as witnesses his fellow students, who know the facts.

The witnesses' deposition is read out.

[25] His acquisition of a father, and of birth into the Acamantis
tribe instead of Hippothontis, came about as blatantly as I've
described, thanks to his mother's oath and the naivety of my father in
offering it to her. But this is not enough for Boeotus. He has also taken
me to court two or three times to try to recover some money, on top
of the malicious and baseless suits he had brought against me earlier.
But you all know, of course, what kind of a businessman my father
was!* [26] I won't go into that. But if the oath sworn by the mother
of these men was honest, she exposes Boeotus' sycophancy in these
suits, because [*to Boeotus*] if my father had such an extravagant lifestyle that he kept another woman, your mother, even though he was
married to my mother, and maintained two households, how could he
possibly have left any money?

[27] [*To the jurors*] I'm sure, Athenians, since he has no way to justify his case, that Boeotus will rehearse his usual claim that my father
slighted him—at my instigation, apparently. He insists on his right
to bear the name of the paternal grandfather, as being the eldest son.*
I'll address this issue briefly; I think it's better for you to be properly
informed about it. Before he became a member of my family, I used to
see him around, as one does, and I was sure that he was younger than
me—quite a bit younger, to judge by appearances. Now, it would be
foolish of me to insist on this, [28] but I have a question for Boeotus
here: 'When you chose to dance in the Hippothontis tribe, before you
began to claim that you were my father's son, what name might you
have said you were entitled to? You might have said "Mantitheus",
but that wouldn't give you grounds for claiming to be older than me,
because in those days you didn't even think you had a relationship
with my tribe, so how could you have laid claim to a relationship with
my grandfather?' [29] Besides, Athenians, no one here knows how old
we are: I'll say I'm older and he'll say he is. But you all know how to
reckon justice, and this is how: they have been his sons ever since my

father recognized them as such, but he had already enrolled me in his deme as Mantitheus, before he introduced Boeotus to the phratry. It seems, then, that justice joins age in assigning me the privilege of this name.

[30] [*To Boeotus*] Well, then, suppose you were asked: 'Boeotus, how did you come to be a member of the Acamantis tribe and the deme Thoricus, and the son of Mantias? How did you get a portion of the inheritance?' You could only reply: 'Because Mantias adopted me before he died.' And to the question, 'What evidence or proof do you have of this?', you'd reply: 'He introduced me to the phratry.' And to the question, 'Under what name did he introduce you to the phratry?', you'd reply: 'Boeotus,' since that was the name under which you were introduced. [31] But it's extremely bad form to deliberately reject the name that has gained you citizenship and a share of the inheritance, and take another name instead. Suppose my father were to rise up and ask you either to stick with the name under which he adopted you, or to claim another man as your father: that would be a reasonable request, don't you think? Well, that's exactly what I'm asking of you: either choose another patronymic, or keep the name my father gave you.

[32] Oh, but you claim, by Zeus, that the name 'Boeotus' was given to you as an insult and a slight.* [*To the jurors*] But he and his brother were often heard to say, when my father was refusing to recognize them, that their mother's family was no worse than my father's, and 'Boeotus' is the name of his mother's brother. So, when my father was compelled to introduce them, since I had already been registered as 'Mantitheus', he introduced the defendant as 'Boeotus' and his brother as 'Pamphilus'. [*To Boeotus*] I mean, can you point to any Athenian who has given the same name to two sons of his own? If you can, I shall concede that my father gave you this name as a slight. [33] And yet, if you were the kind of person who could force him to adopt you, but never made any effort to please him, you didn't behave as a true son should towards parents; and since you didn't, you deserved not just to be slighted, but to be put to death. It would be truly monstrous if the laws protecting parents were to apply to people regarded by the father himself as his children, but were ineffective against people who force their way into a family where they are not wanted.*

[34] You are a most difficult man, Boeotus! The best thing would be for you to stop *everything* you're doing, but otherwise I beg you,

in the name of Zeus, to do at least this for me: stop making trouble
for yourself; stop raising malicious suits against me; be happy that
you've gained citizenship, property, and a father. No one is trying
to take these away from you; I certainly am not. You claim to be my
brother. Why don't you also act like a brother, and then people will
believe that we're related? But if you intrigue against us, take us to
court, envy us, and abuse us, people will believe that you've pushed
your way in where you don't belong, since you don't treat us like
family. [35] Even if it really were true that my father was failing to
recognize you when you actually were his son, I'm not to blame. It
wasn't up to me to know who his sons were; it was up to him to show
me who to consider my brother. Before he recognized you, I didn't
think of you as a member of the family either; but then he recognized
you, and since then I have done so. You want proof? You have a share
of the estate he left on his death; you take part in our rites and ceremonies; no one summarily excludes you from them. What more do
you want?

[*To the jurors*] If he says that he's being terribly treated and accuses
me with tears of grief in his eyes, don't believe a word he says. These
things are irrelevant to our current argument, and you shouldn't pay
attention. Your response should be to point out that he can obtain
redress just as easily under the name Boeotus. [36] [*To Boeotus*] Why
are you so quick to pick a fight? Please stop. Don't be so implacably
hostile towards me. I don't behave like that towards you. You might
not be aware of it, but even my present request that we not share
a single name does you rather a lot of good. Leaving all other considerations aside, it's inevitable, as long as there are two people with the
name 'Mantitheus, the son of Mantias', that anyone who hears the
name will ask which of us is meant. And if he wants to refer to you,
he'll describe you as the one Mantias was forced to adopt. Is that what
you want? [*To the Clerk of the Court*] Take these two depositions and
read them, to show that my father gave me the name Mantitheus and
him the name Boeotus.

The depositions are read out.

[37] [*To the jurors*] The only remaining points I think I should make,
Athenians, are that you'll be keeping your oath if you give the verdict
I'm asking for, and that he has himself confessed that his name should
be Boeotus, not Mantitheus. You see, when I initiated this suit against

'Boeotus of Thoricus, the son of Mantias', at first he responded to my challenge and had postponement oaths sworn for him, using the name 'Boeotus',* and in the end, when there was no longer room for evasion, he let the arbitrator decide against him by default. But, by all the gods, what do you think he did next? [38] He moved to nullify the arbitrator's decision, calling himself 'Boeotus'. But if the name 'Boeotus' had nothing to do with him, he should have allowed the original case, brought against 'Boeotus', to go by default, and then later he should never have used the name 'Boeotus' in any attempt to have the decision nullified. So since he has admitted that his name in law is Boeotus, what can he expect from you, who have sworn to vote in accordance with the law? [*To the Clerk of the Court*] To verify this, take the petition of nullification and this formal complaint.

The petition and the complaint are read out.

[39] [*To the jurors*] If he can point to a law that allows children to decide their own names, it might be all right for you to give the verdict he's asking for. But since the law, which you all know as well as I do, not only gives parents the right to name the child in the first place, but also allows them to deregister* the child and publicly disinherit him, and since I've shown that my father, exercising his legal right, named the defendant 'Boeotus' and me 'Mantitheus', do you have any choice but to give the verdict I'm asking for?

[40] Now, where there are no laws, you've sworn to vote 'in accordance with your honest opinion',* and this means that even if there didn't already exist a relevant law, the honest vote would have been a vote in my favour. I mean, is there anyone here who has given the same name to two sons of his own? Not all of you yet have children, but when you do, will you do that? Of course not. [41] But it follows that it's your duty according to your oath to decide my case in keeping with the opinion you have as to what is right for your own children. And so what I ask of you, Athenians, is that you comply with your honest opinion, the law, your oath, and Boeotus' own admission. This is not an unreasonable request, and I think it a fair one, whereas what he wants you to do is both unreasonable and unprecedented.

54. AGAINST CONON, FOR BATTERY

Ariston, the plaintiff in this much-admired speech, has brought a private action for battery (*dikē aikeias*) against a middle-aged man named Conon. As Ariston tells the story, the attack in question was both unprovoked and was the culmination of a series of thuggish acts by Conon's family against him. He had first encountered Conon's sons while on garrison duty and had been subjected to violent and humiliating treatment by them. The incident in question took place some time later, while he was walking one evening in Athens. He was set upon this time not by the sons but by Conon himself with some roughneck friends of his and seriously injured in the beating that followed. The fleeting reference to public services (*leitourgiai*) at the close and the fact that Conon is on familiar terms with some prominent Athenian public figures indicate that (like almost all the litigants we encounter in the surviving speeches) both plaintiff and defendant belong to the upper end of the socio-economic spectrum. The date of the action is uncertain, but is likely (see the note on §3) to be either in the early 350s or the late 340s.

---

[1] I was assaulted by Conon here, jurymen, and was so badly hurt that for a very long time no one in my family and no doctor expected me to pull through. But I survived and recovered against the odds, and now I've brought this suit against him for battery. All the friends and relatives I consulted said that his actions made him liable both to summary arrest as a highwayman and to an indictment for malicious abuse,* but at the same time their advice was that I shouldn't take on more than I'd be able to handle, and they warned me against being seen to complain more than a young man should about what happened to me. I followed their advice, and that's why I've brought this private suit,* but I'd have much preferred to bring him to trial on a capital charge. [2] You'll forgive me for this, I'm sure, all of you, once you've heard what I've been through. For however horrendous the original assault was, his brutality since then has been no less terrible. So I'm asking all of you equally, please, to give me a favourable hearing as I tell you what I've been through, and then, if you think that I've been wronged and the law has been broken, to uphold justice for me. I'll give you a thorough account of the whole business, from start to finish, and keep it as short as possible.

[3] Two years ago, I left Athens for Panactum, where we had been assigned garrison duty.* Conon's sons had their tent near by. If only they hadn't, because that was how we first became enemies, how the conflict between us started. Here's what happened. They regularly used to spend the whole day drinking, starting straight after the mid-morning meal, and they persisted in doing this for the whole term of our service, whereas our behaviour away from the city was no different from here. [4] By the time everyone else was starting to prepare dinner, then, Conon's sons were already belligerently drunk. Most of their abuse was reserved for the slaves who were attending us, but they got around to us in the end. Claiming that our slaves were smoking them with their cooking-fires and that everything they said was insolent, they used to hit them, empty their latrine pails over them, urinate on them, and so on and so forth—the whole gamut of malicious brutality. We were upset by this, and at first we remonstrated with them,† but they jeered at us and carried on, so we went and told the general. This delegation to the general was made up of every man from my unit; it wasn't just me without the others.

[5] The general roundly told them off not only for their abusive behaviour towards us, but also for their overall conduct in camp, but this didn't shame them into stopping in the slightest. That evening, in fact, as soon as it had become dark, they burst in on us. They began with insults, but ended by lashing out at me. The racket and din they raised in the vicinity of our tent was so loud that the general and the taxiarchs arrived, along with some of our fellow soldiers, and kept us from suffering irreparable injury or indeed doing *them* an injury under the provocation of their drunken belligerence. [6] Things had gone too far for there to be anything but bad blood and hostility between us after we returned here, as you would expect. But, as the gods are my witnesses, I didn't see any need to take them to court or make an issue of anything that had happened. I simply decided to be careful in the future and to make sure that I had nothing to do with people like that.

What I'd like to do first is produce the depositions of people who witnessed the events I've been talking about, and then I'll tell you what the defendant did to me. After that, you'll be in a position to see that the man who ought to have condemned the original offences has himself taken the lead in far worse crimes.

The depositions are read out.

[7] So those are the incidents I chose not to make an issue of. Not long afterwards, however, I was out for my usual evening stroll in the Agora with Phanostratus of Cephisia, a member of the same age-class as me.* We were close to the Leocorium,* near Pythodorus' establishment, when we were overtaken by Ctesias, one of the defendant's sons, who was drunk. When he caught sight of us, he let out a yell, and after muttering drunkenly to himself something that we couldn't make out, he carried on up the hill towards Melite.* As we discovered later, they were drinking there, at Pamphilus the fuller's place; Conon was there, some Diotimus or other, Archebiades, Spintharus the son of Eubulus,* Theogenes the son of Andromenes, and quite a few more. Ctesias stirred them into action and marched them into the Agora. [8] It so happened that we had turned round at Persephone's sanctuary,* and were once more walking more or less by the Leocorium itself, when we met. In the mêlée one of them— someone I didn't know—went for Phanostratus and pinned him down, while Conon, Ctesias, and Theogenes attacked me. At first, they tore off my himation, and then they tripped me up and beat me down into the mud. Their kicks and assaults split my lip and closed my eyes, and they left me too battered and bruised to get to my feet or make a sound. But as I lay there I could hear their offensive talk. [9] Basically, it was all filth, some of which I would hesitate to repeat here, but I will mention one thing, because it proves Conon's malicious insolence and indicates that he was the ringleader of the whole business. He kept making a crowing sound, like a victorious cock, and the others encouraged him to beat his elbows against his sides as though they were wings.

Afterwards, I was carried home by some passers-by in a state of undress, because they had gone off with my himation. When I reached my doorway, there was screaming and shouting from my mother and her serving-girls, and they struggled on with me to a bath-house to be washed, and then inspected by doctors. I shall call witnesses to confirm the truth of what I've been saying.

The witnesses' depositions are read out.

[10] It so happened, jurymen, that a relative of mine, Euxitheus of Cholleidae—[*pointing*] there he is—was walking home from dinner,

along with Meidias,* and they met me before I'd got far from home. They accompanied me on the way to the bath-house and were there when the doctor was fetched. I was so weak that the people there didn't want me to be taken all the way back home from the bath-house; they decided to take me to Meidias' house for the night, and that's what they did. [*To the Clerk of the Court*] Take these depositions. [*To the jurors*] You'll see from them how many people know about the assault.

The depositions are read out.

[*To the Clerk of the Court*] And take the doctor's deposition too.

The doctor's deposition is read out.

[11] [*To the jurors*] You've heard, then, what a terrible state I was left in by the beating and the assault, and you've also heard testimony to the same effect from all the eyewitnesses present. That was the immediate result, but it was not the end of it. The doctor said that he wasn't particularly worried about the bruising and cuts on my face, but I was plagued by constant fevers and racked by severe pains all over my body, especially in my sides and belly, and I lost my appetite. [12] According to the doctor, it was fortunate that a purging of a very large quantity of blood had spontaneously taken place (which was agonizing for me and caused me great distress), because otherwise internal suppuration would have occurred and I'd have died. It was the discharge of blood, he said, that had saved my life. To confirm the truth of this as well—that the beating I received from these men brought on an illness that all but killed me—[*to the Clerk of the Court*] read the depositions of the doctor, and of the people who used to visit me.

The depositions are read out.

[13] [*To the jurors*] I think it's clear to you now from all the various evidence you've heard that this was an abnormally severe beating, not a minor matter. Their flagrant assault almost cost me my life, and therefore you can see that the suit I've brought is far less serious than they deserve. Now, I imagine some of you are wondering what on earth Conon will dare to say in response. Well, I'd like to warn you about the argument I've been told he's ready to use, in an attempt to divert the issue away from the assault, away from what he's done, and to make the whole affair seem amusing and ridiculous. [14] He will argue

that the city is familiar with the phenomenon of the sons of perfectly decent men giving themselves names for fun—or what young people think of as fun—and calling themselves 'The Hard-on Club' or the 'Allcocks'.* He'll say that some of these young men, including his own son, take courtesans as their lovers, and that they often brawl among themselves over courtesans, and that this is just what young people do. And he'll portray me and my brothers as abusive drunks, uncharitable and sour-tempered.

[15] Personally, jurymen, however much I resented what they did to me, I'd be at least as unhappy and, if I may say so, I'd regard myself as no less abused, if you were to take this tale of Conon's about us to be the truth—if you are so unthinking that you believe what a man says about his own character, or what a neighbour alleges about him, while well-behaved people get no credit at all for their daily life and habits. [16] No one has ever seen us the worse for drink or behaving with arrogant abusiveness, nor do we believe that we are being at all uncharitable in expecting to receive compensation for the wrongs that have been done us. We agree that *his* sons are Hard-ons and Allcocks—and if the gods hear my prayer, they will see that Conon and his sons pay for this and all their disgusting behaviour. [17] For these are the people who initiate one another with the erect phallus, and what they get up to is too shocking for decent people even to mention, let alone do.

But so what? I'd be astonished if a man could be found guilty in your court of assaulting someone and beating him up, and yet get off without punishment—if there was *any* excuse or pretext in existence that allows that to happen. For the law does exactly the opposite: it has even found a way to prevent pleas based on necessity from escalating into something more serious.* For instance—and I should say that it's Conon who has forced me to research and find out about such things—take suits for slander. [18] The theory is that these exist so that people aren't tempted to hit one another when they're trading insults. Or take suits for battery. I've read that the reason for these is to ensure that no one, finding himself getting the worse of it, picks up a stone or anything like that to defend himself, but waits for legal redress. Or again, indictments for wounding exist to prevent wounding escalating to murder.* [19] It seems to me, then, that the provisions that have been taken for the least significant of these crimes, slander, are designed to avoid the final, terrible stage being reached—murder. That is, they are designed to make sure that a man should not gradually be led on from slander to hitting, from hitting to wounding, and from wounding to killing, but instead that each of these crimes should have a legal means of redress. Then they won't be judged by individual passion or whim.

[20] So that's how things stand under the law. Now, if Conon says, 'We're the Hard-on Club, and in our love affairs we punch and throttle at whim,' are you going to laugh and let him go? I very much doubt it. None of you would have laughed if you'd actually been there when I was being manhandled and stripped and assaulted. None of you would have found it amusing to see me leave home in perfect health and be carried back on a stretcher, or to see my mother burst out of the house, and hear the womenfolk screaming and shouting so loudly it was as though someone had died. In fact, some of the neighbours sent servants round to ask what had happened.

[21] Naturally, jurymen, justice requires that in general, here in court, assault should never be excused or left unpunished. Nevertheless, if an exception is to be made, it is people who can blame their abusive behaviour on their youth who should have such loopholes reserved for them. Not that they should get off scot-free, but the usual penalty should be reduced. [22] But when a man over fifty years old, in the company of younger people (his sons, in fact), not only did nothing to dissuade or discourage them, but was himself the ringleader and prime mover and the worst of the whole foul bunch, what penalty does he deserve for this? Personally, I don't think even death is adequate. I mean, suppose he had done nothing himself, but had just stood around while Ctesias, his son, did what we're finding his father guilty of today: you would still have to condemn him. [23] For if he has raised his sons to feel neither fear nor shame when they do wrong in his presence—when, in fact, they do things that in some cases earn the death sentence—is there *any* punishment that it would be unreasonable to suggest he might suffer? As a matter of fact, I think this shows that he felt no shame before *his* father either, because if he had respected and feared him, he'd have expected his sons to do the same.

[24] [*To the Clerk of the Court*] Take these laws now, the one about assault and the one about highway robbery. [*To the jurors*] You'll see that they are guilty under both these laws. [*To the Clerk of the Court*] Go ahead, read.

The laws are read out.

[*To the jurors*] What Conon has done makes him liable to both these laws, because he both assaulted me and robbed me. I've chosen not to sue under these laws, but that doesn't make him any less a criminal; it just shows my reserved and modest nature. [25] In fact, if I had died, he'd have faced a charge of murder and the consequences for him would have been disastrous. At any rate, the father of the priest-ess of Artemis at Brauron was banished by the Areopagus Council from the city even though he had unquestionably not laid hands on the deceased, because he encouraged the man who struck him to do so. And that was the right thing for the Council to do: when people are set on committing a crime, for whatever reason—drunkenness, perhaps, or anger—if bystanders actually urge them on instead of stopping them, there's no hope for anyone who falls into the clutches of vicious bullies. He'll just have to suffer their assaults until they leave off. That's what happened to me.

[26] I'd like to tell you now what they did at the arbitration meeting. This will give you further insight into their insolence. They stretched things out past midnight by refusing to either read the depositions or hand out copies; instead they just took our witnesses to the stone* one by one to swear their oath, and they drafted completely irrelevant depositions, such as that Ctesias was Conon's son by a courtesan and had been treated this way and that. And I swear, jurymen, in the name of the gods, that absolutely everyone there found these tactics of theirs despicable and disagreeable. Finally, they felt the same way themselves, [27] and so, when they had had their fill and grown tired of doing this, they issued a challenge, designed to delay things and prevent the sealing of the jars,* to the effect that they were prepared to hand over some slaves for questioning about the beating, and they wrote down the slaves' names.

I suspect that today they'll devote most of their speeches to this, but I'd like you all to appreciate that, if the point of their challenge was to allow the torture to go ahead,* and they believed that this would prove their innocence, they wouldn't have made the offer when the arbitrator's judgement was about to be announced, and it was the middle of the night, and they had run out of excuses. [28] No, right at the beginning, before I brought the suit, when I was still ill and confined to my bed, with my survival uncertain, and I was telling all my visitors that Conon was the one who had struck the first blow and that most of the assault had been his doing, *that* was when he would have come straight to my house with a crowd of witnesses and have offered to hand over his slaves. And at the same time he'd have invited members of the Areopagus Council to attend, because, if I had died, the case would have been heard by them.* [29] Alternatively, if he really was unaware of the seriousness of the situation and, because he had this proof of his innocence (as he'll claim today), was completely unprepared to face danger of this magnitude, then when I was back on my feet and had issued the summons, he would have made it clear at our first meeting with the arbitrator that he was making the slaves available. But he did none of these things. To confirm the truth of this, and so that you can see that his challenge was a delaying tactic, [*to the Clerk of the Court*] read this deposition. [*To the jurors*] It will help to make things clear.

The deposition is read out.

[30] When he brings up the torture, then, bear the following facts in mind: the timing of his challenge; his reason for it—procrastination; and those early days when he evinced not the slightest desire to make use of this 'proof of his innocence', and failed either to offer it or request it.

The whole business was exposed at the meeting with the arbitrator, just as it's being exposed here today, and it was clear to everyone that he was guilty as charged. [31] He therefore introduced a false deposition, and listed as his witnesses men whose names I'm sure you'll recognize too. Listen: 'Diotimus of Icaria, the son of Diotimus, Archebiades of Halae, the son of Demoteles, and Chaeretius of Pithus, the son of Chaerimenes, hereby testify that they were returning from dinner in the company of Conon; that they came across Ariston and Conon's son fighting in the Agora; and that Conon did not hit Ariston.'* [32] They must have expected you to trust them unthinkingly, without working out the truth, which is, first and foremost, that Lysistratus, Paseas, Niceratus, and Diodorus, who have explicitly testified that they saw everything that happened to me during the assault, including my being hit by Conon and stripped of my himation, had absolutely no reason to lie about what they saw. After all, these were people who were strangers to me and it was sheer coincidence that they were there when it happened. Second, if I hadn't been treated this way by Conon, I'd never have reprieved the men whom even my opponents agree took part in the beating, and have chosen to take action first against a man who had never laid a finger on me. [33] Why on earth would I do that? No, the man I'm suing is the man who struck the first blow, the worst of the offenders. He's the one I hate and want to see convicted.

As you can see, then, my entire case is built on the truth and what is known to be the truth, whereas if Conon hadn't come up with these men as witnesses, he'd have nothing to say, and he'd find himself convicted on the spot by his silence. But since they're his fellow symposiasts, and have often joined him in similar acts of violence, it would be sensible to expect their testimony to be false. If things come to such a pass that some people, having stifled their consciences, brazenly and openly bear false witness, and the truth does no one any good at all, it will be a complete disaster.

[34] 'But they're not like that, by Zeus.' Really? I imagine that many of you know Diotimus and Archebiades and Chaeretius—[*pointing*] that grey-haired man over there. In the daytime they scowl and claim to be behaving like Spartans, and wear thin cloaks and single-soled sandals, but when they meet and get together there's nothing they leave undone, however wicked or disgraceful. [35] And filled with vim and vigour they say: 'Why wouldn't we testify for one another? Isn't that what friends are for? What is there to be afraid of in the charges he'll bring against you? If some of his witnesses say they saw him being beaten up, we'll testify that no one laid even a finger on him. If they say he had his himation torn off, we'll testify that they started it. If they say his lip had to be stitched, we'll say that you had your head or something broken.' [36] But some of the testimony I've provided comes from doctors, and that's more than they've got, jurymen. Their supply of evidence against us will come from no one but themselves. But, as the gods are my witnesses, I could never find the words to describe how ready they are to do whatever it takes, to go to any lengths. But you need to know the kinds of activities they occupy themselves with, [*to the Clerk of the Court*] so please read these depositions. [*To the slave in charge of the water-clock*] And you there, stop the water.*

The depositions are read out.

[37] [*To the jurors*] Do you think that burglars and muggers have the slightest qualms about giving false testimony for one another

on a scrap of paper? These people are accomplices in viciousness, iniquity, unscrupulousness, and insolence, for, as I see it, whatever they do is characterized by these qualities. And I assure you that what you've just heard are not the last or the least of their criminal activities, but there's no way we could have located all their victims.*

[38] Now, I think it's better if I warn you in advance about the most unscrupulous thing of all that I've heard he's going to do. I've been told that he'll parade his children at his side and swear on their heads, calling down horrible and hideous curses—so horrible that our informant was astonished to hear them.* Jurymen, it's impossible to defend oneself against such barefaced tactics. Why? Because, as I see it, the most honourable people, the ones who are least likely to tell a lie themselves, are most likely to be taken in by such tactics. But in order to assess someone's trustworthiness, it's important to take his lifestyle and character into consideration. [39] I shall tell you, then, how little notice he takes of things like oaths. Under the circumstances, I had no choice but to make enquiries and find out. I've been told, jurymen, that a man called Bacchius, who was condemned to death in your court, and Aristocrates (the one with defective eyes), and others like them, including Conon, were friends when they were young and called themselves the 'Triballians'.* Not only did they gulp down the offerings people had left for Hecate, but they also regularly collected the testicles of the pigs which are used to purify a space before a meeting and served them up to one another for dinner.* And there was nothing, my informant said, that they found simpler than making oaths and breaking them.

[40] If that's what Conon is like, he's not to be trusted even when he swears an oath, not in the slightest. No, it's a man who would not swear even an honest oath—a man who would not dream of swearing on his children's lives in a fashion that you do not sanction, but would endure anything rather than that—and who swears an oath, if he has no choice, in the traditional fashion—this man is more deserving of trust than someone who swears on his children's heads and passes through fire. [*To Conon*] So however you look at it, Conon, I'm more deserving of trust than you, and when I resolved to swear the following oath, it was not, as it was for you, a desperate attempt to escape punishment for my crimes. No, I did it for the sake of the truth, and to avoid being the victim of further assaults, since I had no intention

of losing the case to your perjury. [*To the Clerk of the Court*] Read the challenge, please.*

Ariston's challenge is read out.

[41] [*To the jurors*] That was the oath I was prepared to swear then, and today I swear for your sake, jurymen, and for the sake of the bystanders here, by all the gods and goddesses, that I did indeed suffer at Conon's hands the abuses for which I am prosecuting him, that I was beaten up, that my lip was badly enough cut to have needed stitches, that I was maliciously assaulted, and that these are my reasons for bringing this action. If my oath is true, may blessings attend me and may I never again have to go through anything like this. If my oath is false, may I perish utterly, myself, my kin, and my posterity. But in fact my oath is not false, however strenuously Conon insists it is.

[42] Jurymen, I have proved the justice of my case in full, and have appended an oath to that effect. All I'm asking is that each of you should feel on my behalf the same degree of anger for Conon that you would yourself feel for someone who had done to you what he did to me. And I ask you not to regard as merely a private matter something that could happen to anyone else too. No, every victim of assault should receive your support and his legal due, and you should withhold your favour from men who are bold and reckless while carrying out crimes, and shameless cheats when they are on trial—men who care nothing about what people think of them and the way things are traditionally done, and whose only concern is to avoid punishment. [43] 'But Conon will beg and weep.' Well, please ask yourselves who deserves your sympathy more: someone who has suffered as I have at his hands, if I leave court further abused by the loss of the case, or Conon, if he's punished as he deserves? Is it in the interest of each of you to connive at beatings and assaults, or to stop them? To stop them, of course. Well, if you acquit him, more and more of these crimes will be committed, but if you punish him, they will decrease in number.

[44] I could go on at some length, jurymen, about the services my father, during his lifetime, and my brothers and I have performed for the state—the triremes funded, campaigns fought, commissions carried out. And I could show that neither Conon nor any member of his family has done anything in this line at all. But there isn't enough water for that,

and in any case it's irrelevant. I mean, even if we were in fact unquestionably of less use to the state and worse people than Conon and his family, surely we still wouldn't deserve to be beaten up and assaulted. I don't know that I need to add anything else. I think you've followed what I've been saying.

55. REPLY TO CALLICLES, ON DAMAGE TO A FARM

This gem was delivered in a suit for damages (*dikē blabēs*) relating to a watercourse. It was written for the defence. The case turns around the building of a wall on the defendant's family farm to prevent water flowing on to the property. The plaintiff, Callicles, claims that the effect is to make the water flow instead on to his property and cause flooding. The speaker counters that the wall was built years before by his father. We know the name of the speaker's father (Teisias), but not his own. The speech seems to have been one of a number of disputes between them and the speaker claims that Callicles' motive in bringing the action is to gain control of his land. The date is uncertain but given the scale of the dispute (a minor squabble between neighbours), it is perhaps more likely to be an early work.

———

[1] So it's true what they say, Athenians: there really is nothing worse than a dishonest and greedy neighbour. And that's what I've got. Because he covets my farm, look how Callicles has persecuted me with his malicious and baseless suits. First, he arranged for his cousin to dispute my claim to the property, [2] but his scheme was exposed and I survived their conspiracy. So next he won by default two awards given against me by the arbitrator,* one in his own name for a thousand drachmas, and the other after he'd persuaded his brother Callicrates to proceed against me.* Now, I ask all of you, please, to listen carefully to what I have to say, not because you'll be treated to a display of eloquence, but so that the facts themselves can prove to you, beyond the shadow of a doubt, that I am the victim of malicious litigation.

[3] I have just the one reply, Athenians, to all their arguments, but it proves my innocence. It was my father who enclosed the land in question, just after I was born. At the time, their father, Callippides, was still alive. He lived on the neighbouring farm, and certainly knew the facts better than his sons, because Callicles was already an adult and was living in Athens. [4] In all these years, when it rained just as much as nowadays, no one ever came forward with any charges or

complaints, and no one stopped the project at the beginning on the grounds that my father was causing anyone damage by enclosing our property. No one protested or objected, even though my father lived on for fifteen years, at least as long as their father, Callippides.

[5] [*To Callicles*] And yet, Callicles, it was certainly possible for you and your family, when you first saw the watercourse being blocked, to have gone straight to my father with your complaint and said to him: 'Teisias, what do you think you're doing? Blocking the watercourse? But then the water will run on to our land.' Then, if he agreed to stop, there'd have been no unpleasantness between our families, and if he ignored you or something, there'd have been people there whom you could have used as witnesses. [6] By Zeus, what you should have done is shown the whole world the existence of the watercourse, if you wanted to prove my father's guilt with facts, not by mere assertion as now. Well, no one ever bothered to do anything of the sort. Otherwise, there'd have been no arbitration hearings for you to win by default, as you did against me recently, [7] and there'd have been no point in your litigious persecution of me. Instead, my father, with his intimate knowledge of the situation, would have shown in detail how things stood and refuted these witnesses with their facile testimony.

I suppose you've dismissed me as young and inexperienced, [*to the jurors*] but I've got the strongest possible evidence to wield against them all, Athenians: their own behaviour. Why did no one either protest or lodge a complaint? Why did no one ever even grumble? Why were they content to let themselves be wronged in this way? [8] This alone, I think, is enough of a reply to their charge, but you need to know about the case as a whole, Athenians. I'll try to make it even clearer that it was not wrong of my father to enclose the farm, and that everything these men have said against us has been a lie.

[9] Everyone, including them, agrees that the farm is our own private property. We can take that for granted. Now, Athenians, if only you could see the actual farm. It would be the best way for you to realize that they have no genuine case. That's also why the impartial men to whom I wanted to entrust the case for arbitration were people who knew the facts.* But that didn't suit my opponents, whatever they've been trying to tell you today. I'll clarify this too in a moment.

I beg you now, Athenians, by all that's sacred, to pay close attention. [10] My farm and theirs are separated by a road, and since the farms are surrounded by mountainous terrain, runoff water flows partly on to the road* and partly on to the farmland. To be precise, the water which runs on to the road carries on down the road where it finds free passage, but where it meets an obstacle it inevitably spills over the edges, and that's when it streams on to the farmland. [11] And indeed, whenever there was a downpour in the past, jurymen, water did run on to the farm. This was before it was my father's, when it was owned by a man who couldn't stand the countryside and was more of a city type, and so nothing was done about the problem. There were two or three such floods, which damaged the land, and the water was beginning to carve out more and more of a channel for itself. As I was told by people who knew, it was because my father saw this happening, and also because the neighbours were tending to use the farm for grazing their flocks and as a short-cut, that my father built the wall in question around it.

[12] These people, the ones who knew my father's reasons, will testify to the truth of this, but I shall also provide much more compelling evidence, Athenians. Callicles alleges that I'm causing him harm by blocking the *watercourse*, but I shall prove that what's being blocked is farmland, not a watercourse. [13] I suppose we'd be in the wrong if there were any doubt about our ownership of the farm and it was public land we were enclosing. But, as things stand, not only are they not disputing the fact that the farm is ours, but it is cultivated land, planted with olives, vines, and figs. But would anyone decide to plant trees in a watercourse? Of course not. Or again, would anyone choose a watercourse for his family burial plot? Again, of course not. [14] But both these things have happened, jurymen. Not only was the plot cultivated before my father built the dry-stone wall, but the tombs are old, pre-dating our ownership of the farm. But no evidence could be more compelling than this. The facts themselves clearly prove the point. [*To the Clerk of the Court*] Take these depositions now, please, and read them.

The depositions are read out.

[15] [*To the jurors*] What do these depositions tell you, Athenians? Don't they explicitly affirm that the plot was thickly planted with trees, and that it has tombs and everything you'd expect on a farm?

Don't they also affirm that the plot was enclosed while their father was still alive, and that neither he nor anyone else from the neighbourhood raised any objections?

[16] What about the rest of Callicles' arguments? It's worth going through them for you. First, then, ask yourselves if you've ever seen or heard of a watercourse existing alongside a road. I doubt there's even one in all Attica. I mean, why would anyone have made a course for water to flow through his own private property when it was going to flow in any case along the public road? [17] Second, would any of you—wherever you lived, by Zeus, in the countryside or the city—allow water that was running along a road to flood your land or your house? Of course not. On the contrary, if it ever threatens to force its way in, aren't we all in the habit of putting up a barrier or building a wall to stop it?

Well, what Callicles wants is for me to let the water run on to my land from the road, and then channel it back on to the road once it's passed his farm!* But this means that the next of my neighbours, the owner of the plot adjacent to his, will be the next to complain, because if Callicles' argument is justified in his case, obviously *all* my neighbours will be able to use it. [18] But it's already proving risky for me to direct water on to the road, so it would be very rash of me to release it on to my neighbour's land! When I've been taken to court and face a fixed penalty because of water running from the *road* on to Callicles' land, in heaven's name how will I be treated by people who claim damages from water running on to their property *from my land*? But if I'm not allowed to let water either on to the road or on to the land, in the name of the gods, what other option do I have, jurymen? Surely Callicles isn't going to make me drink it!

[19] You can see, then, what a dreadful bind these men put me in, and that's far from the end of it. Of course I want to win the case, but I'd be happy just to end up not owing any more money. I mean, if there *were* a watercourse to receive the water again, jurymen, perhaps it would be wrong of me not to let the water on to my land. There are unquestionably watercourses on other farms, where the system is the same as for domestic drainage:* the first in line waters his land first with the help of the watercourse, and then it's the next man's turn to receive the water, and so on down the line. But no one passes water on to me in this way, or takes it from me, [20] so how could what I have be a watercourse?

Callicles would be very far from the first to have suffered flood damage as a result of not taking precautions. And the worst thing of all is that he fetches huge boulders to stop the water running on to his farm, but he has brought an action against me for damages on the grounds that my father was wrong to build a wall when the same thing was happening to his farm! I tell you, if everyone whose property has been damaged by run-off water there were to sue me, I'd be bankrupted even if I were far better off than I am. [21] But Callicles and his family are different from the rest of my neighbours. Despite the fact that they've come to no harm (I'll be proving this to you in a moment), while plenty of others have repeatedly suffered considerable damage, they're the only ones who have gone so far as to sue. But they should have been the last to do so. They've brought this malicious suit against me for damage that was their own fault, if there was any damage at all. The rest of my neighbours at least can't be accused of doing this, whatever else they might have done. But to make sure I don't get everything muddled up, [*to the Clerk of the Court*], take my neighbours' depositions.

The depositions are read out.

[22] [*To the jurors*] It's preposterous, isn't it, jurymen? After all they've suffered, these neighbours of mine make no complaint and put up with their bad luck, just like anyone else who's suffered misfortune, but Callicles brings a malicious suit. And he's not entirely innocent himself. First, he extended his boundary wall to take in the roadside trees, thus making the road narrower; second, he threw all his rubble into the road. So now the road is higher and narrower than it was. Depositions I'll be presenting shortly will give you a fuller picture, [23] but what I'll try to show in the meantime is that he has brought this serious a suit against me without having suffered any loss or damage worth mentioning.

Before these men set about persecuting me, my mother and theirs were on good terms. They used to visit each other, as you'd expect given that they were country neighbours; in any case, their husbands were friends too, while they were alive. [24] One day, my mother paid their mother a visit.* Their mother was very upset and showed my mother what had happened. That's how we learnt all about it, jurymen. What I'm telling you is what I was told by my mother, and so may blessings attend me; but if I'm lying, may the opposite be my fate.

I swear, then, that this is what she said she saw and was told by their mother. Some barley had got wet, and my mother herself saw it drying out, but there wasn't even three medimni of it; and there was also half a medimnus of wheat. And a jar of olive oil had been knocked askew, but hadn't been cracked or broken. [25] That, jurymen, is all that happened to them, and for this I am defending a suit with a fixed penalty of a thousand drachmas! He says he rebuilt an old wall, but that shouldn't be added to my account, because it didn't collapse and wasn't otherwise damaged either. And so if I were to admit liability for all the damages—well, that was all that got wet.

[26] All right, then. My father was not at fault originally in surrounding the farm with a wall; years passed, and they never complained; others, who've suffered repeated and extensive damage, have nonetheless not brought charges against me; all of you here are in the habit of channelling water from your homes and farms into the road, rather than—for heaven's sake!—letting it in off the road. What more is there for me to say? You can now see that this suit they're bringing against me is obviously malicious, since I've done nothing wrong and they haven't suffered as badly as they say. [27] To prove that they've thrown rubble into the road and have made the road narrower by extending their wall, and to prove also that I offered an oath to their mother, and invited my own mother to swear the same oath, [*to the Clerk of the Court*] take the depositions and the challenge.*

The depositions and the challenge are read out.

[28] [*To the jurors*] I can't imagine how anyone could be more shameless. I can't imagine a more flagrantly malicious prosecution. I mean, after they themselves extended their boundary wall, after they've raised the level of the road, they're suing *others* for damages— for a thousand drachmas, in fact, with no appeal, even though all their losses together amounted to fifty drachmas at the most? Jurymen, just think of how many people have suffered flood damage to their fields, in Eleusis or elsewhere.* But, in the name of Earth and all the gods, none of them expects to recover the damages from his neighbours. [29] Consider my case too: I had every right to be angry at the narrowing and raising of the road, but I didn't make an issue of it. But these men are so full of themselves, it seems, that first they do wrong and then they raise malicious suits against the people they've

wronged! [*To Callicles*] But look, Callicles. If you're allowed to build a wall around your own farm, I suppose we are too. If my father injured you by building his wall, you're now injuring us by building yours. [30] [*To the jurors*] I mean, now that the water meets his wall of boulders, it's going to run back on to my land, and at some unforesee-able point in the future it will knock down my wall. But I still won't bring charges against them. That's just my luck, and I'll do my best to protect what's mine. You see, I think it's sensible of Callicles to be walling off his property—though I still consider his prosecution of me monstrous and the product of a sick mind.

[31] You shouldn't find his eagerness surprising, jurymen, or his boldness in bringing this false prosecution today. After all, earlier, when he persuaded his cousin to dispute my claim to the land, he pre-sented a forged contract, and now he has secured a default judgement against me by the arbitrator in another similar suit, by entering on the charge the name of one of my slaves, Callarus. They've capped their evil machinations with this new trick, you see, whereby they bring an identical suit against Callarus.* [32] But what slave would build a wall around his master's land except at his master's instructions? They've got no other grounds for complaint against Callarus, so they're pro-ceeding against him for a wall that my father built more than fifteen years before his death! And if I give up my land—if I sell it to them or swap it with them for another property—Callarus is in the clear; but if I refuse to let what's mine fall into their hands, Callarus is putting them through hell, and they go and look for an arbitrator who will award the land to them,* or a settlement which will enable them to take possession of it.

[33] Anyway, jurymen, if scheming sycophants are to have the best of it, I needn't have bothered giving this speech. But if you find people like Callicles offensive, and if you vote in accordance with justice—after all, Callicles has lost nothing and has suffered no wrong from either Callarus or my father—I don't know that I need to say more.

[34] But you should know also about his earlier scheme to get hold of my land, when he used his cousin as his proxy, and about the judge-ment he has now won from the arbitrator against Callarus (meant to hurt me, because I value the man), and about the go-ahead Callicrates has received to proceed against Callarus yet again. Depositions relat-ing to all these matters will be read to you.

The depositions are read out.

[35] I beg you, jurymen, by all that's sacred, not to let me be their victim. I haven't done anything wrong! I'm not especially concerned about the financial penalty, although that would be tough on us since we aren't well off. But their harassment, their persecution, is driving me right out of the deme. To demonstrate our innocence, we were willing to entrust the matter for arbitration to unprejudiced and impartial men who were acquainted with the facts, and we were ready to swear the customary oath.* We thought that this would be the best way to convince you, since you too are under oath. [*To the Clerk of the Court*] Take the challenge and the last of the depositions.

The challenge and the depositions are read out.

EXPLANATORY NOTES

1–3. THE 'OLYNTHIAC' SPEECHES

The numbers in the left-hand column refer to the speech and section numbers in the text.

1.5 *opened their gates for him*: in fact, when Philip captured Amphipolis in 357 and reduced it to the status of Macedonian possession, he did not deal harshly with the population. Pydna, an Athenian possession on the Gulf of Therme, was taken in the same year, betrayed to Philip from within; he enslaved the opponents of Macedon, but again dealt leniently with the rest of the population.

1.6 *war levies*: Athens generally avoided direct taxation of citizens. But in times of war a tax (*eisphora*) was levied on the property of the wealthy.

1.8 *Euboean expedition*: in 357, when an Athenian force successfully opposed Theban attempts to gain control of the island.

1.8 *gained Amphipolis then*: in 357, when Amphipolis found itself under threat from Philip. Demosthenes here skates over the reasons for Athenian inaction, for which see note on 2.6.

1.9 *and so on*: Potidaea in the Chalcidice was captured by Philip in 356 with the aid of Olynthus. The population was enslaved and the city given to Olynthus. Athenian support for Potidaea arrived too late. Methone, like Pydna, was an Athenian base on the Thermaic Gulf. It was besieged and captured by Philip in 355–354, though the siege cost him his right eye. An Athenian force made its way into the city during the siege, but a second force arrived too late to save the city, which Philip then razed; the population was ejected. Philip captured Pagasae in Thessaly in 353 after being invited to intervene in the Sacred War by the Aleuad dynasty of Larisa. An Athenian force under the general Chares was too late to prevent him.

1.13 *Pherae*: rival power to Larisa in Thessaly. Its ruler Lycophron surrendered the city to Philip in 352. Magnesia also was part of Thessaly.

1.13 *and so on*: Philip campaigned in 358 in Epirus against the Illyrians, and in Thrace against the Paeonians. Arybbas was king of the Molossians in Epirus. In 350 Philip reduced Molossis to a subject kingdom, but left Arybbas on the throne. For the attempt on Olynthus in 351, see the first note on 4.17.

1.19 *as you want*: Demosthenes refers obliquely to the Theoric Fund (see Glossary). At this date it received the surplus of the administrative funds of the city. See further the next note and the second note on 59.4.

1.19 *for military purposes?*: he is not making a formal proposal, but merely expressing a view. According to one ancient source there was a penalty clause in the legislation governing the Theoric Fund, prescribing death for anyone attempting to annul it. This may be a conjecture to explain Demosthenes' caution. But even if there was no specific penalty clause, the proposer of a decree was subject to the *graphē paranomōn*, the 'indictment for illegality' (see introduction to speech 18). Demosthenes' suggestion here seems to be that the Theoric Fund should be diverted in whole or in part to pay for soldiers on campaign.

1.20 *in return for service*: his 'single system' (explained more clearly at 3.34–5) is that state pay should be given only for service to the state as soldier or juror, or for attendance at the Assembly, not dispensed in handouts.

1.22 *Magnesia*: after Philip's victory over the Phocians at the battle of the Crocus Field in 352 he was voted *archōn* (chief official) of the Thessalian League. The present passage, which seems to describe a motion from the League, indicates that his retention of possessions acquired during the war, especially the important port of Pagasae, and his consolidation of his hold over Thessaly were not unopposed. In the event any opposition was ineffective. According to Diodorus of Sicily (16.52.9) Philip was compelled to march into Thessaly to settle things there; but he was soon back in the Chalcidice.

1.25 *fight you here*: though this may have looked like a wild exaggeration in 349, it proved to be the case eleven years later, when Athens faced Philip and his allies at Chaeronea in Boeotia just to the north of Attica. Demosthenes' attitude to the Thebans here reflects the political rivalries of the fifth and early fourth centuries; by the end of the decade Demosthenes had concluded that Athens needed the support of Thebes, if it were to have any chance of mounting a serious military opposition to Philip. This later pro-Theban policy is at the heart of his defence in speech 18.

1.27 *previous war*: probably the various military activities in the north (see note on §9 above) in the wake of Philip's territorial acquisitions at Athens' expense.

2.2 *under our sway*: probably refers especially to Amphipolis (see Introduction, p. xi) but also other Athenian bases and allies in the north such as Methone and Potidaea.

2.6 *open secret*: a major (though not the sole) reason for Athens' failure to protect Amphipolis from Philip was a deal according to which Philip would trade Amphipolis to Athens in return for Pydna. It was kept secret to prevent the people of Pydna, an Athenian dependency, knowing of Athens' readiness to betray them. The same Athenian trust in Philip's (ultimately false) promises made them rebuff an approach from Olynthus, alarmed by Philip's expansion, with the result that Olynthus made an alliance with Philip which lasted until his aggression in 349.

2.7 *on their behalf*: for Philip's intervention in Thessaly in 353 see Introduction, p. xi, and 1.12–13. The picture given here of Philip's strategy of making and keeping friends (on the basis of shared enemies) until it became convenient to absorb them is broadly accurate, though it ignores the facts that those dealing with him were also motivated entirely by self-interest.

2.11 *negotiate about Magnesia*: see note on 1.22.

2.14 *dissension and disarray*: Timotheus was an Athenian general influential in creating the second Athenian League. The campaign against Olynthus, for which he received Macedonian help, dates to the late 360s when he was active in the Chalcidice; it was this campaign which won Methone and Pydna for Athens. For Philip's capture of Potidaea with the Olynthians, cf. 1.9 with note. For his intervention against the ruling house ('the tyrant house' here) of Pherae in Thesssaly see 1.13 with note. It suits Demosthenes' purpose to present Philip as a useful subordinate, but in each of these cases Macedon was actually the senior partner in the fighting.

2.15 *ever achieved*: the description of Philip here as a man who rejects the easy path in pursuit of risk and glory owes much to the value system of the Greek epic hero. It is here contrasted with the situation of the people of Macedonia in a description which underscores the weakness of individualistic monarchy and complements the picture of the advantages which an autocrat enjoys at 1.4. The less flattering aspect of his individualism continues in the next section.

2.17 *Foot Companions*: the Macedonian heavy infantry. Though rhetorically useful, Demosthenes' assessment of their worth is a wild understatement. As well as underrating the seasoning effect of and the loyalty created by relentless campaigning, it glosses over Philip's military reforms, which involved both reorganization and radical changes to equipment and made the Macedonian army a formidable military machine.

2.19 *in your presence*: the dances envisaged probably include the lascivious *kordax*, associated in Athens especially with comedy. The account belongs to a strand of hostile descriptions of Philip's court (and that of Alexander) which persisted long after the fourth century. Though selective and biased (it ignores the pronounced element of ceremony and the social and political importance of the symposium for the Macedonian kings), it is probably not just invention.

2.19 *Callias*: the ancient commentators on this passage describe Callias as a state-owned slave who fled to Macedonia from Athens when 'condemned/convicted'. They may simply be extrapolating from Demosthenes' text. Macedonia did, however, offer a haven for those out of favour in Athens.

2.24 *the Spartans*: victory in the Peloponnesian War in 404 left Sparta the dominant power in Greece, but Spartan expansionism caused both anger and alarm. The result was the Corinthian War of 395–387, in which Athens joined forces with Sparta's disaffected allies. A peace brokered by the king of Persia left Sparta in the ascendant and aggressive.

It was this that led to the foundation of the Second Athenian League in the early 370s, which was aimed at Sparta. Demosthenes could have in mind any point in the period, or the whole of it.

2.28 *shipping they capture*: the reference is to the Athenian condottiere Chares, who captured these sites when employed by the rebel Persian satrap Arta-bazus in the late 350s. The Assembly habitually sent out commanders with inadequate funds to pay their forces, and the generals would raise the funds by whatever means they could.

2.29 *syndication*: the reference is to the organization of the payment of war levies (*eisphorai*) by syndicates (*symmoriai*) of those liable on grounds of wealth. There were 100 syndicates and the 300 wealthiest citizens were allocated among these as 'leader', 'second', and 'third'.

3.4 *Heraeum Fortress*: a fortified position on the Sea of Marmara. After returning from Thessaly, Philip campaigned in Thrace in 352 against the Thracian king Cersobleptes, in alliance with a number of Greek cities in the region. Athens had colonies in the Thracian Chersonese (modern Gallipoli) and so her interests were directly threatened.

3.4 *Maemacterion*: the Athenian month roughly corresponding to November; the months named immediately after equate to July, August, September.

3.5 *the Mysteries*: the Eleusinian Mysteries, a cult of panhellenic importance held at Eleusis in Attica, were devoted to Demeter and her daughter Persephone (generally called *Korē*, 'the girl'). Initiation, which lasted for six days in Boedromion, offered the worshipper the prospect of a better fate after death. The ritual was secret and consequently modern recon-structions remain to some degree hypothetical.

3.8 *his current opponents*: the Phocians. The Phocian seizure of the tem-ple at Delphi in 356 in response to manoeuvring from Thebes at the Amphictyonic League (which controlled the temple) had precipitated the Third Sacred War. The Phocians used the temple treasures to pay for mercenaries, but the funds were gradually exhausted. At this stage Athens and Thebes (firm allies against Macedon ten years later) were on opposite sides, since Athens was supporting Phocis against Thebes and Macedon.

3.11 *military service*: Demosthenes' aim is to dismantle the laws channel-ling the fiscal surplus into the Theoric Fund in preparation for a for-mal proposal to use the surplus for military spending. See also notes on 1.19. Unlike in the fifth century, when the Assembly could legislate by decree, the fourth-century democracy used a system of boards of 'legislators' (*nomothetai*), appointed when the Assembly identified the need for amendments, annulments, and fresh legislation.

3.12 *to repeal them*: the name associated especially with the Theoric Fund at this juncture was Eubulus, the leading figure of the day. Though ready to confront Philip if necessary and feasible, he favoured a policy of con-flict avoidance where possible.

3.16 *barbarian?*: the ethnicity of the Macedonians was contested already in the fifth century (as in modern times), and Demosthenes repeatedly treats Philip as a 'barbarian' (*barbaros*, the Greek term for a non-Greek). Our earliest Macedonian inscriptions are in Greek and it is likely that they spoke Greek by the fifth century. The north of the Greek peninsula was ethnically varied and it may be that Macedonia had a mixed population (especially as the kingdom itself had expanded significantly by the fifth century). But there is no good reason to doubt that the majority was Greek, including and especially the royal house.

3.20 *Corinthians and Megarians*: Athens had been in conflict with Megara as recently as 350/49 over the sacred land on the border between the territories. Relations between Athens and Corinth were generally good in the fourth century, though there had been friction in the 360s. Demosthenes' point, however, is less about specific events than about the readiness of the Athenians to engage in local disputes and ignore more distant interests.

3.21 *my namesake*: the general Demosthenes, active during the Peloponnesian War, unrelated to the orator. Nicias was also a leading Athenian politician in the same war. Pericles was the leading politician of Athens in the decades leading up to the Peloponnesian War. Aristeides served with distinction in the second Persian invasion of 480/479 and was instrumental in setting up the Delian League, for which he allocated the individual state contributions; his fairness in the latter task earned him the title 'the just'. Miltiades (§26) was responsible for the Athenian victory against the Persians at Marathon in 490.

3.24 *the Acropolis*: the brief eulogy adopts the tone used in the praise of Athens at the public funerals for war dead. The reserve of 1,000 talents was created by the Athenians early in the Peloponnesian War. The other details (Macedon as vassal, the Greeks as willing subjects of Athens in the fifth century) are a creative rewriting of Athenian history, as is the contrast between politicians past and present in the preceding and following chapters (a cliché already by the fifth century).

3.28 *during the war*: the fighting first against Sparta and then against Thebes as the balance of power shifted in the period 378–362; the allies gained are those who joined the Second Athenian League. The 'peace' is paradoxically the period of the Social War (357–355), when Athens found itself fighting against seceding members of the League while at peace with Thebes and Sparta.

3.31 *the Boedromia*: a festival in honour of Apollo and Artemis. For the wide use of the Theoric Fund, see 1.19.

3.34 *the state requires*: there was pay for jury service and (from late in the fifth century or early in the fourth) attendance at the Assembly. These would remain in place, while the diversion of the theoric money to the military chest would remove the allowance for attendance at festivals; the loss theoretically would be made good either by these sources of income or by military service. The lack of real opportunities to replace the lost doles probably explains Demosthenes' vagueness.

4. FIRST PHILIPPIC

4.1 *given their views*: at this date (352/1) Demosthenes was in his early thirties and not yet an established political figure.

4.3 *expect of Athenians*: Demosthenes certainly has in mind the hostilities against Sparta from the foundation of the Second Athenian League in 378, possibly also the Corinthian War of 395–387. See note on 2.24.

4.4 *than with him*: for Philip's subsequent capture of these cities, see note on 1.9.

4.7 *war levies*: see note on 1.6.

4.11 *he's ill*: while Philip was campaigning in Thrace in 352 (see 3.4–5 with note). The Athenians concluded (unwisely in the event) that the emergency had been averted and so scaled down their planned intervention in the region.

4.12 *for us*: for the idea cf. 1.10.

4.16 *half the cavalry*: fifty ships would be about one-sixth of the total fleet of up to 300. Not all of the 300 would be at sea or seaworthy and the aim here is to have a substantial but affordable naval force readied for action in the event of a hostile act by Philip. The large cavalry contingent (500) is intended to increase mobility.

4.17 *and Olynthus*: for Philip's dash on Thermopylae in 352 and the Athenian response, see Introduction, p. xi; after withdrawing from Thessaly he then moved against the Thracian king Cersobleptes in the Chersonese. We know little about the attack on Olynthus of 351; Olynthus had made peace with Athens and this may perhaps have been an opportunistic attempt to take the city with the aid of supporters inside or simply an attempt to intimidate.

4.17 *just the other day*: the Haliartus expedition took place in 395. Faced with a Spartan invasion, Thebes sought Athenian aid. It was a source of pride that Athens, though impoverished and unfortified after her defeat in the Peloponnesian War, still sent a force. In the ensuing battle the Spartan general Lysander was killed. For Euboea see note on 1.8, and for the expedition to Thermopylae, Introduction, p. xi.

4.19 *fight him unceasingly*: this force is distinct from the larger reserve force proposed above. It is a small mixed fighting unit designed to take to the field immediately and harry Philip constantly.

4.20 *mercenaries*: from the late fifth century mercenary troops played an increasing role in Greek warfare.

4.21 *for a fixed term*: unlike normal campaigns, where soldiers were called up for the duration of the fighting.

4.24 *in Corinth*: in the Corinthian War of 395–387.

4.24 *defeat the Spartans*: refers especially to Iphicrates' celebrated destruction of a Spartan hoplite unit (*mora*) using light-armed troops in 390. Chabrias' most famous exploit was the defeat of the Spartan fleet at the battle of Naxos in 376, but in this context Demosthenes probably has in mind his use of mercenaries to force the withdrawal of a Spartan invasion force in Boeotia in 378.

4.24 *our enemies*: refers to the service of the condottiere Chares under the rebel satrap Artabazus (see note on 2.28).

4.26 *two hipparchs?*: military officers and financial officials were elected by show of hands in the Assembly. The ten generals (at this stage elected one from each of the ten Athenian tribes) had overall control of the Athenian forces; the hipparchs had overall command of the Athenian cavalry. The other groups of ten had responsibility for the individual tribal contingents, the taxiarchs in the infantry and the phylarchs in the cavalry.

4.27 *sail to Lemnos*: a third hipparch distinct from the two mentioned above was elected to command the Athenian cavalry stationed on Lemnos, an Athenian possession. The Menelaus mentioned in the next sentence was probably a commander of mercenary cavalry. He is generally identified either with a half-brother of Philip of Macedon, whom Philip had unsuccessfully tried to kill on his accession, or with a tribal chieftain from upper Macedonia who had served with the Athenian general Timotheus in Chalcidice in the 360s. The point is that an unelected non-Athenian is commanding troops in the service of Athens.

4.28 *for each man*: the rates are not generous, 1 drachma per day for the cavalry (who would need to maintain their horses as well as themselves) and 2 obols (⅓ drachma) for the infantry and naval crew (20 mnas = 2,000 drachmas for a crew of up to 200). To put the figures in context, by the end of the fifth century a labourer could earn 1 drachma per day, while in the latter part of the fourth century an unskilled labourer might earn 1½ drachmas, a skilled man 2 or even 2½ drachmas. Demosthenes' 'the war itself will provide the men with everything else' is a roundabout reference to plunder of the local populations; hence his budgeting for 'rations alone'.

4.31 *etesian winds or winter*: the annual (etesian) winds (modern *meltemi*) which blow from a northerly direction across the Aegean Sea in summer and early autumn can seriously impede sailcraft, as well as throwing up severe storms.

4.34 *sacred trireme*: Philip's harrying of the islands in the 350s is mentioned by Aeschines at 2.72. His seizure of the *Paralus* (one of two state triremes, with the *Salaminia*) on its voyage from Delos to Athens has been dated either to 354/3 or to 352/1. Demosthenes' account does not suggest a very recent event. The raid on the Athenian grain ships at Geraestus in southern Euboea probably belongs to the same occasion.

4.35 *Methone . . . Pagasae . . . Potidaea*: for Philip's capture of these cities see note on 1.9.

4.36 *or gymnasiarch*: examples of the 'liturgy' (*leitourgia*) system which assigned expensive public duties to wealthy citizens in lieu of direct taxation. The chorus-producer (*chorēgos*) was responsible for defraying the costs of a chorus in the dramatic or choral competitions; the *gymnasiarchoi* were a board with responsibility for supervising torch races.

4.36 *trierarchs*: the trierarchy ('command of a warship') was one of the main Athenian liturgies. In the fifth century a wealthy citizen was given a ship by the state, which he maintained and commanded for a year. The system underwent a number of changes but for much of the fourth century the financial costs were met by the 1,200 richest citizens organized into syndicates (*symmoriai*); but captains were still needed and a man might still find himself appointed commander of a ship. The exchange procedure (*antidosis*) mentioned here allowed anyone selected for a liturgy to propose someone else on the ground that he was richer and had been erroneously overlooked; it took the form of a challenge to exchange properties; the individual challenged could either perform the liturgy, or accept the exchange of property and leave the challenger to perform the liturgy, or allow the issue to be settled by a court.

4.36 *independent slaves*: literally 'those living apart', the normal term for slaves operating independently of their masters, who would normally pay the owner a proportion of their income (including presumably pay for military and naval service).

4.36 *proxies*: Demosthenes refers not to official substitutes but to those (slave or free) who are induced by citizens to serve in their place, a corrupt practice mentioned by Thucydides 7.37.

4.37 *handling the crisis*: the mercenary forces which are supposed to be in place but which are off privateering (§24).

4.38 *it shouldn't be*: the text of the letter does not survive. Philip had evidently made overtures to the cities in Euboea in a letter which included harsh criticism of the Athenians as unreliable supporters, detailing their past failures.

4.47 *at his audit*: on completing office Athenian officials were subject to a two-part audit (*euthynai*) covering their financial management and their general conduct. Anyone could bring a charge. Demosthenes oversimplifies in presenting the troops as judges, since the judicial panels were selected by a carefully randomized process; but some of course might be on the panels.

4.48 *the free states*: after their defeat of Sparta at the battle of Leuctra in 371 the Thebans mounted a series of invasions of the Peloponnese, freeing Messenia (previously under Spartan domination) and encouraging the Arcadians to form a league centred on the new city of Megalopolis. The effect was to confine Sparta (previously the dominant military power of Greece) to the Peloponnese. It was in Sparta's interest to break up these new states.

5. ON THE PEACE

5.5 *grave errors*: in 348 Plutarch, the dictator of Eretria in Euboea, sought and obtained Athenian aid to put down a revolt. After initial success, including a victory in a difficult position at Tamynae, the Athenian force was eventually defeated; Athens had to acknowledge Euboean independence and pay a substantial ransom to secure the release of the prisoners-of-war.

5.6 *here in Athens*: Neoptolemus was a distinguished tragic actor in favour with Philip and one of a number of intermediaries who conveyed Philip's desire for peace in the manoeuvres which began in 348 and led slowly to the sending of the Athenian peace embassies of 346. His work as an actor made it easy for him to come and go between Macedonia and Athens. Demosthenes' attack belongs to the period before the truce between (most) Athenian factions which led to the peace; it seems to have been a hostile speech in the Assembly rather than a prosecution. Demosthenes' hostility did Neoptolemus no harm; he was still performing in Athens and Macedonia in the late 340s and 330s, including the festival at Aegae where Philip was assassinated in 336.

5.9 *the peace treaty*: after the Assembly agreed the Peace of Philocrates, a second embassy was sent to receive Philip's oath. Philip kept the ambassadors in the dark about his intentions as they accompanied him on his march south to settle the Sacred War. Hence the (mistaken) Athenian anticipations of a settlement hostile to their rival Thebes, including the refoundation of the Boeotian cities of Thespiae and Plataea, destroyed by Thebes in 373, and the restoration to Athens of the coastal town of Oropus on the border between Attica and Boeotia (controlled by Thebes since 366 but long a bone of contention) and of Euboea.

5.13 *the current peace*: a cryptic pointer to Demosthenes' strategy of maintaining the peace while looking for resources to prosecute a successful war. It was to be several years before he was in a position to pursue it actively.

5.14 *common war against us*: for the role of the Amphictyonic Council, see speech introduction. The dismissive reference ('currently calling itself the Amphictyonic Council') is a sop to Athenian resentment at Philip's membership, which had to be acknowledged. Athens, as ally of the defeated Phocians, could not afford to provoke a war with a body which comprised most of the states of central Greece, especially with Philip now in control of the pass at Thermopylae.

5.15 *one might think they are*: the Boeotians in general had a reputation for being dull-witted.

5.18 *what the Spartans did*: the Theban invasions of the Peloponnese in the early 360s had freed Messene and created a centralized Arcadia based on Megalopolis (cf. note on 4.48). In 353 Sparta attacked Megalopolis in a bid to restore its own former regional power, while Thebes was busy with the Sacred War. Megalopolis appealed to Athens, which declined to send aid. The Spartans were foiled by an alliance of Peloponnesian states. Demosthenes had argued for intervention on behalf of the Arcadians.

5.19 *Phocian exiles*: that is, politically prominent Phocians who could expect no mercy in the settlement of scores after the Phocian surrender to Philip. The Amphictyons had issued an edict forbidding any state from taking them in. The refugees in §18 are anti-Theban elements from the Boeotian cities under Theban control.

5.20 *the pass*: Thermopylae.

5.21 *a little territory*: the towns in Boeotia previously controlled by Phocis, mentioned immediately below.

5.22 *above all*: the four-yearly Pythian festival at Delphi, held in honour of Apollo, was second only to the Olympics as a pan-Greek international athletics festival. For Philip's presiding role, see speech introduction. The festival was open to all Greeks but only to Greeks. The prestige mattered. Macedonia had long been trying to catch up culturally with central and southern Greece and some Greeks denied that the Macedonians were Greeks at all (see note on 3.16).

5.25 *the Chersonese*: in the 350s the general Chares had established Athenian control over the Thracian Chersonese, except for the city of Cardia, strategically placed at the isthmus. Cardia was accordingly excluded from the treaty by which Cersobleptes accepted Athenian control of the peninsula. Though the Athenians regarded the Chersonese as their territory, Cardia was again excluded from their possessions under the Peace of Philocrates.

5.25 *Rhodes*: the Carian is Idrieus, satrap of Caria and brother of Mausolus and Artemisia (sister, wife, and successor to Mausolus). The Carians had been in effective control of these coastal islands since the Social War, when Mausolus had supported them in their revolt from Athens.

5.25 *detain our shipping*: Byzantium, subsequently Constantinople and then Istanbul, because of its situation on the Bosporus was able to interfere with grain ships travelling to Greece from the breadbasket of the Crimea.

5.25 *the shadow in Delphi*: adapts a proverb 'to fight over an ass's shadow', used of quarrels over trifles.

8. ON THE SITUATION IN THE CHERSONESE

8.2 *Philip's Thracian campaign*: Philip had been campaigning in Thrace west of the Chersonese since the summer of 342 against Cersobleptes, who had been expanding his own power in the region. The eventual result was that Philip became master of Thrace (including the Greek cities which had sought his aid against Cersobleptes).

8.5 *stipulated by the treaty*: though the Peace of Philocrates left Philip in
control of his conquests, it also acknowledged Athenian control of the
Chersonese; Philip's current involvement in the region was within the
letter of the treaty (which excepted Cardia from Athens' possessions),
but strained the spirit.

8.14 *Byzantium under siege*: Byzantium had been a major opponent of
Athens during the successful revolt of her allies (the 'Social War')
in 357–355 and was still unfriendly (her 'folly' here; cf. §16 'they're
crazy'). The capture of Byzantium by Philip would be a devastating blow to Athens, since it would allow him to obstruct and even
strangle the Black Sea grain trade on which the city relied to feed the
population. Demosthenes' prediction proved correct when Philip in
340 laid siege (unsuccessfully) to Byzantium, which allied itself to
Athens. In §66 (cf.9.34) Demosthenes treats an attack on Byzantium
as imminent; evidently there had been some friction between Philip
and Byzantium.

8.16 *the settlers there*: in the letter, Philip clearly complained of Athenian
aggression. A letter purportedly from Philip survives as 'speech' 12
in the Demosthenic corpus, and includes the claim (§11) that his presence in the Chersonese is for the protection of Cardia. Demosthenes is
almost certainly right that Philip would welcome an opportunity to take
the Chersonese. His opponents were arguing that Diopeithes and his
supporters were offering cause.

8.18 *to Philip*: the unspecified individuals are the opposing speakers. They
must have argued that the impossibility of supporting Diopeithes during the season of the etesian winds made it imperative to recall him.

8.18 *not long ago*: Athens had lost control of Euboea in 348 (see note on 5.5).
But earlier in 341 Callias of Chalcis, alarmed at Macedonian activity in
Euboea (including the capture of Oreus in the north-west of the island,
narrated by Demosthenes in 9.59–65), sought and obtained an alliance
with Athens as head of a league of Euboean cities. In 343 a coup by the
pro-Macedonian faction in Megara was thwarted by Athenian intervention.

8.21 *a citizen contingent*: for the system of war levies see note on 1.6. Demosthenes had been pressing for more active military engagement by citizen
soldiers (in preference to mercenaries) since the late 350s (4.16). The
reference to public money relates to the distributions from the Theoric
Fund, which Demosthenes had tried unsuccessfully to divert to military
use (see note on 1.19). He eventually succeeded in 339.

8.27 *Asiatic Greeks*: the first of these (alleged) allegations raises Diopeithes'
freebooting to the level of serious warfare. The second is for Demosthenes a spurious panhellenic zeal which represents any hostile act
against a Greek city as a betrayal of Hellenism.

8.28 *the Hellespont*: the alternative proposal of the opposing speakers. Joint
commands were common.

8.28 *stop him in his tracks*: as the next sentence makes clear, the document is
the text of an impeachment decree against Diopeithes. Impeachment
(*eisangelia*) was a public action (i.e. it could be brought by anyone) for
political offences. It was initiated either in the Council of Five Hundred
or the Assembly. Trials were held in the Assembly for much of the life of
the democracy but were transferred to the law-courts by the middle of
the fourth century.

8.29 *Paralus*: the *Paralus* was one of the two state triremes that could be sent
to escort Diopeithes back to Athens for trial, as had happened with
Alcibiades during the Sicilian expedition of 415–413.

8.35 *and so on*: in 342 Demosthenes had visited a number of states in north-
west Greece to drum up support against Philip, while associates of his
had visited cities in the Peloponnese. Even before the Peace of Philocrates the Athenians had been labouring unsuccessfully to assemble
a coalition against Macedon.

8.35 *he was away*: campaigning in Thrace, §2 above. We know of an illness
during Philip's earlier campaign in Thrace in 352 (cf. 3.4). Since Demosthenes presses the point about the illness, it is unlikely that he is con-
flating the expeditions; probably he was ill again in 342.

8.36 *threatening Sciathos*: Cleitarchus in Eretria in the south facing the coast
of Attica and Philistides in Oreus in the north facing the Athenian island
of Sciathos.

8.40 *from Olynthus*: Lasthenes and Euthycrates were Olynthian political figures widely believed to have betrayed Olynthus' interests to Macedon.
Both men survived the destruction of Olynthus and enslavement of its
population. After the Athenian defeat at Chaeronea the pro-Macedonian
Athenian politician Demades proposed Euthycrates as *proxenos* (roughly
equivalent to honorary consul) of Athens for Olynthus.

8.42 *greedy course of imperialism*: few outside Athens would recognize this
characterization, which owes much to the tradition of civic funeral eulogies of the war dead, in which Athens was regularly praised as a lib erator
both in mythic and in historical times. Athens had controlled a vast
empire for much of the fifth century and her handling of the Second
Athenian League had been sufficiently unpopular for her allies to revolt
in 357–355 (the Social War).

8.45 *silver mines*: at Laurium on the south-east coast of Attica, an important
source of Athenian revenue, since the mines were owned by the state,
which leased out the concessions.

8.45 *millet and spelt*: Demosthenes chooses lower-grade grains to dismiss the
value of the agricultural potential of Thrace. In fact the flatter parts of
Thrace were a significant source of wheat in their own right. 'In hell' in
the Greek is 'in the pit', *barathron*, a precipice in Athens where certain
types of criminals were hurled, or possibly their bodies after execution
(our sources are limited).

8.58 *help to Cardia*: see speech introduction.

8.59 *on their land*: for Philip and Oreus, see 9.59–65. For his shifting relations with Olynthus, see note on 2.6. For Pherae, see 1.12–13 and 2.14 with notes.

8.60 *obliterate it*: the claim, useful for immediate rhetorical purposes, may reflect Demosthenes' belief. In fact Athens was always less significant for Philip than he was for them and he continued to deal generously with Athens, in so far as his strategic objectives and ambitions allowed.

8.61 *crucify*: see note on 21.105.

8.62 *current subjection*: for the situation in Thessaly at this time see the second note on 9.26.

8.62 *a great deal more*: for Olynthus and Potidaea, see 1.9 with note.

8.63 *major war*: i.e. the Sacred War. Many in Athens had hoped for a settlement unfavourable to Thebes, but Philip consolidated Theban power in Boeotia; cf. 5.9 with note.

8.64 *Cersobleptes himself*: Cersobleptes had been excluded from the peace of 346, which allowed Philip to reduce him to the position of vassal. Philip only finally neutralized him as a threat in 342/1.

8.64 *admitting that Cardia is his*: that is, by making a formal complaint to Athens about its treatment of Cardia. The presence of a Macedonian garrison gave Philip de facto control of the city.

8.66 *advancing on Byzantium*: for Euboea see §36 above; for Byzantium cf. note on §14 above.

8.68 *timid and weak*: Demosthenes' opponents (allegedly) accuse him of cowardice for avoiding any formal proposal of hostilities, which would expose him to prosecution in a culture which used the law-courts as an extension of the Assembly and where the penalties for failed policy fell on political and military leaders. He glosses over the fact that over the past few years he and his associates had been assiduously prosecuting the proponents of peace.

8.70 *my other benefactions*: it was common practice (though in law-courts more than in the Assembly) to list public benefactions as a means of claiming goodwill. Demosthenes here employs a device known by ancient rhetoricians as *praeteritio* ('I shall not mention . . .').

8.74 *enslavement by the Thebans*: in 357 during a brief struggle between Athens and Thebes for control of Euboea. Demosthenes served as trierarch in this campaign (18.99; 21.161). Timotheus is carefully chosen; one of the great generals of the first half of the century, he played a major role in the resurgence of Athenian influence under the Second Athenian League. His career lasted from the 370s through to the Social War of 357–355. The words quoted may reflect the overall gist of Timotheus' speech, a memorable sentence, or Demosthenes' invention.

9. THIRD PHILIPPIC

9.1 *the peace treaty*: the Peace of Philocrates of 346.

9.2 *fellow citizens to punish*: the high-minded complaint ignores the fact that Demosthenes like every other Athenian politician was happy to use the courts to attack his political opponents.

9.6 *responsible for the war*: the reference is to Diopeithes and his supporters back in Athens; see speech 8, introduction.

9.9 *the money he spends*: a reference to the sums paid by Philip to his supporters in the various Greek cities, in this context a barely concealed allegation of bought treason against the proponents of peace, which becomes explicit later.

9.11 *forty stades*: a little over 7 kilometres. See also 8.59.

9.11 *to plead his case*: it suits Demosthenes to present Philip's hostility to Olynthus as sudden, duplicitous, and unprovoked. But the alliance had been unsteady: see note on 2.6.

9.11 *his march south*: see 5.9–10 for the speculation about Philip's intentions in 346 in relation to the Sacred War before he finally settled it in favour of Thebes.

9.12 *in Oreus*: for Philip's intervention in Thessaly against Pherae see 1.12–13 and 2.14 with notes. For Oreus see §§59–65.

9.13 *content to be deceived*: not just by Philip but by his (alleged) hirelings in Athens, that is, the proponents of peace.

9.15 *been sent out*: the settlers sent out with the commander Diopeithes in 341; see introduction to speech 8.

9.15 *by your general*: Chares. Doriscus stood at the mouth of the Hebrus opposite the island of Samothrace. Serrion (Cape Makri) is in the same area. Sacred Mountain is not Mount Athos, but the modern Tekir Dag on the Propontis/Sea of Marmara east of the Chersonese. Philip had promised not to invade the Chersonese while the peace of 346 was negotiated, but he used the interval between the first and second Athenian embassies to take these places, all outside the Chersonese. He kept his promise to the letter, but the effect was to surround the Chersonese with Macedonian strongholds.

9.16 *oath to the peace*: Philip had not in fact at this stage sworn to the treaty (that was the purpose of the second embassy), though Athens had. So he was not *technically* in breach of an oath, as the account at 18.26 acknowledges.

9.16 *sending help there*: for Philip's letter see 8.16 with note. The claim that Athens' claim to the Chersonese was universally acknowledged ignores the status of Cardia, which did not accept Athenian control. See introduction to speech 8.

9.17 *the Peloponnese*: for Philip's abortive intervention in Megara in 343, see the second note on 8.18. Demosthenes returns to his intervention in

Euboea at §§59 ff. For his intrigues in the Peloponnese, see §27 (Elis) and 19.260–1.

9.19 *destroyed the Phocians*: for Philip's intervention in the Third Sacred War and treatment of Phocis ('destroyed' overstates: see note on 19.59), see Introduction, p. xii.

9.19 *up for debate today*: for Byzantium, see note on 8.14.

9.23 *the battle of Leuctra*: the first Athenian empire in the fifth century ended in 404 with defeat in the Peloponnesian War, which would date the beginning here to 476; Demosthenes may be counting back from the defeat at Aegospotami in 405 which broke Athenian power, giving a beginning of 478/7, when the Delian League (the anti-Persian alliance which evolved into the Athenian empire) was founded. The Spartan hegemony is here dated from 404 to 376, when Chabrias defeated their fleet at the battle of Naxos; Demosthenes may prefer this date to 371, the year of the Spartan defeat at Leuctra, because the latter was a Theban success. The count in years underscores the point about persistent Greek resistance; hence the vagueness about Thebes, whose hegemony lasted from 371 to the death of the great general Epameinondas in battle in 362.

9.25 *ascendancy*: Demosthenes is dating from Philip's initial intervention in the Sacred War in 353.

9.26 *Thraceward communities*: the cities of the Chalcidic League headed by Olynthus. For Philip's other conquests in the north, see note on 1.9.

9.26 *every city*: after unrest in Thessaly (where there was discontent at the outcome of the Sacred War, which had left their neighbour Thebes strengthened) in 344 Philip had suppressed the ruling houses of Pherae and Larisa and set up a system of local governors based on the pre-existing fourfold regional division of Thessaly.

9.27 *obey me*: the tone is unlike Philip, who could be blunt but whose diplomacy was usually much more subtle.

9.27 *Ambracia*: in Epirus (north-west Greece). For his early expeditions in the west, see the second note on 1.13. He was back there threatening Ambracia in 342; Athens sent a force to oppose him.

9.31 *not Greek*: for Macedonian ethnicity, see also note on 3.16.

9.32 *the festival*: for Philip and the Pythian games of 346, see speech 5, introduction.

9.32 *some Greeks*: for suppressing Phocis and settling the Sacred War, Macedon was given the seats on the Amphictyonic Council and the right to precedence in consulting the oracle (the order was otherwise organized by lot) which had belonged to Phocis.

9.33 *tyrant*: on Porthmus and Oreus (both in Euboea) see §57 and §§59 ff.

9.34 *ally of his*: Naupactus on the north coast of the Gulf of Corinth had a chequered history, but from 367 it had been occupied by the Achaeans from across the water, though coveted by the Aetolians.

Echinus was a Theban foundation on the south coast of Thessaly. For Byzantium, see note on 8.14.

9.35 *in his hands*: for Cardia and the Chersonese, see introduction to speech 8.

9.41 *on the Acropolis*: Arthmius of Zelea was an agent sent by Persia in the fifth century with money to bribe Greeks; the circumstances are unclear, but the Athenian decree against him is a favourite in fourth-century orators. Demosthenes had already cited it in 343 (19.271), where the wording is given more loosely.

9.44 *the killing*: the words 'outlaw'/'outlawry' (*atimos* and *atimia*, literally 'lacking/loss of honour/rights') in classical Athenian law referred to the loss of (some or all) citizen rights; but there is evidence that earlier it meant something more extreme, lack of any rights including the right to life.

9.48 *return home*: Demosthenes perhaps has in mind especially the Spartan annual invasions of Attica in the early years of the Peloponnesian War. Four or five months would in fact be an unusually long invasion, but Demosthenes is giving the upper limit possible in a system based on campaign seasons and citizen militias, whose members would have to return to the farms.

9.50 *for a break*: though scholars have observed that Demosthenes exaggerates the contrast between past and present in military matters (fifth-century armies too had light-armed troops and fourth-century armies had heavy-armed troops), as he does in civic ideology and morality, it is true that Philip had radically changed Greek warfare. He made more extensive use of cavalry and the core infantry were less heavily armed than in the past, with much longer spears. His access to the mineral wealth of the north allowed him to professionalize his army instead of relying on semi-trained citizen militias and he made extensive use of artillery and other engines of siege warfare.

9.51 *decisive engagements*: Demosthenes returns here to ideas he had first raised ten years earlier in the *First Philippic*.

9.56 *the other side*: at 19.267 we learn that Euthycrates took over a force of 500 Olynthian cavalry to Philip.

9.56 *Apollonides into exile*: leader of the anti-Macedonian faction in Olynthus, exiled from the city in 351; he took refuge in Athens and was granted citizenship, though the grant was revoked for unknown reasons.

9.57 *preferred Philip*: as part of a proxy struggle for influence in Euboea, Philip had sent a mercenary force which captured Porthmus in 343, a move which alarmed Athens, since Porthmus was directly opposite the coast of Attica. For Plutarch, former tyrant of Eretria, see note on 5.5.

9.58 *and Cleitarchus*: see also 18.295.

9.59 *Euphraeus*: the others are mere names now; but Euphraeus had been a pupil of Plato. He found favour at the Macedonian court, but became a staunch opponent of Macedon.

9.64 *war levy*: Demosthenes' seminar on Euboean history is carefully tailored to prefigure the situation in Athens.

9.66 *Lasthenes*: on Lasthenes (and Euthycrates), see note on 8.40. Elsewhere it is Euthycrates who is associated with cavalry command (§56 above); either both commanded cavalry or Demosthenes confuses the two, or, most likely, he simply wants to squeeze in the name of another traitor. For their later careers, see note on 19.265.

9.71 *world-conquering ambitions*: the idea of an invasion of Persia had been in the air for some time; the Athenian orator Isocrates had even tried to enlist Philip to the cause. Whether Philip himself had any such notion at this stage is unclear. The Persian king, Artaxerxes Ochus, may conceivably have had suspicions on the score. But in any event Philip's designs in Thrace certainly threatened his interests and he was happy to support Perinthus when Philip besieged it in 340. Though the diplomatic activity recommended here did take place (Demosthenes went to the Peloponnese and his associate Hypereides to Rhodes), the Great King sent money rather than conclude an alliance.

9.73 *all that they ask of us*: for the force in Chersonese (and its funding problems), see introduction to speech 8.

18. ON THE CROWN

18.1 *listen to me*: near the end of his prosecution speech (3.201–2), Aeschines had urged the jurors not to listen to (what he presents as) an evasive defence from Demosthenes and to reject Ctesiphon's request to call Demosthenes as his supporting speaker.

18.3 *at a disadvantage*: an example of what the Greeks called *aposiopēsis*, literally 'falling silent'. Demosthenes avoids the bad omen of appearing to anticipate defeat.

18.6 *loyal democrat*: Solon, in the surviving fragments, presents himself as an impartial mediator between the masses and the elite, but by the early fifth century he had been recruited retrospectively to the democratic cause.

18.9 *decree*: the preliminary decree of the Council of 500, necessary for an item to be placed on the assembly agenda—in this case the proposal that Demosthenes be awarded a crown.

18.12 *if . . . are true*: the court cannot punish Demosthenes because Ctesiphon is the defendant, not him.

18.15 *deprive . . . of citizenship*: that is, by inflicting a huge fine, as was common in Athenian political trials. A debtor to the state was automatically deprived of his citizen rights until the debt was repaid.

18.17 *with the help of Philocrates*: Aeschines argued that Demosthenes colluded with Philocrates in pushing through the peace treaty in 346. Though Aeschines exaggerates, Demosthenes had found it convenient to support Philocrates, probably because he thought that a temporary cessation of hostilities would allow Athens time to obtain allies and recover her strength. See introduction to speech 5.

18.18 *the Phocian War*: the Third Sacred War of 356–346 (see Introduction, pp. xi–xii).

18.18 *at Leuctra*: the Theban victory at Leuctra in 371 broke both the dominance of Sparta in Greece and the myth of Spartan invincibility.

18.19 *military assistance*: Thebes was at the time in question Athens' strongest rival in central Greece. Demosthenes creatively retrojects the alliance of 339–338 back to the period of the negotiations with Philip in 346 in order to refashion Thebes as natural allies of Athens. In fact Thebes was keen to have Philip intervene to break the deadlock of the Third Sacred War and the Athenians were hoping for a settlement against Theban interests.

18.20 *our present troubles*: Demosthenes had attacked Aeschines for his role in the negotiations with Philip before the treaty was finally ratified in 346. See speech 19, introduction.

18.21 *Aristodemus, the actor*: a successful actor who had worked with Aeschines. After Philip's capture of Olynthus in 348 he was sent to Macedonia to negotiate the ransom of Athenians captured in the city; his report on his return that Philip was interested in peace set in motion the negotiations which led to the peace of 346.

18.22 *the other Greek states*: in 346 embassies were sent from Athens to invite the Greeks to join in the peace negotiations. It seems that no response had been received by the time the Athenians debated the peace, and Aeschines and Demosthenes are eager each to pin a charge of unseemly haste on the other.

18.23 *your famous voice*: before turning to politics Aeschines had been an actor (a theme to which Demosthenes returns later in this speech). His (evidently impressive) speaking voice is mentioned several times by Demosthenes, who was plainly a little nervous of his opponent's performative skills.

18.24 *Eurybatus*: an Ephesian entrusted with money by the Lydian king Croesus in the sixth century who joined his Persian enemy Cyrus. Aeschines had used the comparison against Demosthenes in 343 (2.137) and the latter evidently takes pleasure in hurling it back.

18.25 *receive his oaths*: after the Athenians voted for peace, a second embassy was sent to receive the oaths of Philip and his allies. Philip was at this time campaigning in Thrace against Cersobleptes and the envoys had to wait in Pella, the Macedonian capital, for his return.

18.27 *mocked . . . in his speech*: fortresses in Thrace captured by Philip. Aeschines 3.82 mocked them as insignificant places nobody had even heard of.

18.28 *reserve seats for them*: it was normal for envoys from foreign states to be voted seats of honour at theatrical events. Aeschines had represented Demosthenes not just as moving a decree for honorary seats, but also as fawning on the Macedonian ambassadors.

18.30 *if we'd taken ship*: roads in fourth-century Greece were generally poor and travel by sea was faster. Had the ambassadors travelled by sea, they could have gone directly or indirectly (after stopping at Pella) to the Hellespont (Dardanelles). But it is unlikely that they could have stopped Philip's expansion.

18.32 *as you had done before*: in 352 Philip decisively defeated a Phocian army at the battle of the Crocus Field, a victory which secured his hold over Thessaly. He followed up the success by advancing on Thermopylae, but was blocked by an Athenian force under Nausicles.

18.35 *enemy . . . former friends*: Phocis and Thebes respectively.

18.36 *at the time*: a colossal understatement. In the first four decades of the fourth century Athenian policy had alternated between pro-Theban/ anti-Spartan and anti-Spartan/pro-Theban. Athenian and Theban rivalry for regional influence had put them on opposite sides in the Sacred War. But Demosthenes is revising history in the light of the Athenian–Theban axis against Macedon in the 330s.

18.36 *chattels in from the countryside*: Callisthenes' proposal to bring Athenian property, wives, and children inside the city walls reflects the panic following the surrender of Phocis, which left no obstacle between Philip and Athens. Cf. 19.86, 125.

18.36 *gratitude for what he had done*: that is, settling the Sacred War (while Athens' support for the Phocians had incurred the hostility of the enemies of Phocis in the region).

18.39 *from Philip*: since Demosthenes is explicitly reading between the lines, it is difficult to identify the letter or reconstruct its contents. It evidently addressed Athenian dissatisfaction with the outcomes of the peace.

18.41 *farm their land*: as (presumably) a gift from Alexander; no detail is supplied and this may just be a slur.

18.41 *the person who was responsible for it*: after the sack of Thebes in 335 Alexander demanded the surrender of a number of leading opponents of Macedon in Athens, including Demosthenes; he was dissuaded by an Athenian delegation.

18.44 *Greeks as well*: in Illyris in 344 and Thrace 342–340.

18.51 *for being Alexander's friend*: a verbatim quotation of Aeschines 3.66.

18.52 *what they say*: there is an ancient tradition that Demosthenes deliberately mispronounced the word for 'hired hand', prompting the jurors to shout the right pronunciation to correct him, thus giving him the answer he wanted. But he didn't need to. Demosthenes was free to 'hear' the response he wanted from the mixed shouts of the jurors.

18.58 *submitted to his audit*: on the audit, see note to 4.47. For Aeschines' objection to Ctesiphon's decree, see note on §112.

18.67 *renowned and honoured*: an ancient commentator on the text notes that the eye was lost at Methone, the collar-bone injured campaigning in Illyris, the wounds to the arm and leg acquired in the campaign against Scythia of 339 (the thigh wound was actually inflicted by the Triballians, who attacked him on his march home and seized the booty). Despite his disdain, here as elsewhere Demosthenes recognizes a heroic quality in Philip.

18.70 *of their existence*: Amphipolis and Pydna were captured by Philip in 357, and Potidaea in 356. The island of Halonnesos became a bone of contention in the late 340s. It had been seized from Athens by pirates; these were then expelled by Philip. He offered to give it to Athens but the anti-Macedonian politicians insisted he must *restore* it. Doriscus like Serrium (see note on §28) was in Thrace. Philip captured the island of Peparethos in 340.

18.71 *take back their exiles*: the events in Euboea (from 343 to 341) are narrated at length in 9.59–65. Macedonian influence was checked in 341 when the Athenian general Phocion ousted Cleitarchus, leader of a pro-Macedonian faction who had seized power in 343. Philip laid siege to Byzantium in 340. For Megara, see the second note to 8.18. The exiles mentioned are pro-Macedonians ejected from their cities.

18.72 *'Mysian plunder'*: a proverb of uncertain origin connoting undeserved but passive victimhood: 'easy pickings', perhaps.

18.73 *seized our ships*: Philip's seizure of the Athenian grain fleet coming from the Black Sea in 340 to provision his army at Byzantium was the event which finally precipitated the Athenian declaration of war. See also note on 4.34.

18.75 *all of them together*: Demosthenes neatly bundles together decrees from different periods and different persuasions to show that opposition to Macedon was both widespread and lasting. Philocrates and Eubulus had resigned themselves to peace by the mid-340s, though Eubulus had earlier tried to orchestrate a united Greek front against Philip. Cephisophon likewise moved between the opponents and supporters of peace. Hegesippus and Aristophon were hardline opponents of Macedon throughout.

18.76 *Philip's letter*: evidently part of the diplomatic manoeuvring prior to the declaration of war in 340 or the commencement of hostilities in 339.

18.82 *proxy*: Demosthenes seems to suggest that Aeschines was formal representative, *proxenos* ('proxy' here), of Oreus (unlike modern consulates, Greek cities were represented abroad not by their own citizens but by members of the other city). Whether or not, it was not treason to entertain them on their missions to Athens.

18.82 *only when it's gone*: Demosthenes' venality is a leitmotif in Aeschines' prosecution speech against Ctesiphon.

18.94 *treated you before*: see note on 8.14.

18.94 *that is*: the proviso because there were examples of crowns voted to Athens by foreign states for the activity of Athenian generals, whose impact abroad would inevitably be more visible.

18.96 *on land and sea*: the Spartan victory over Athens in the Peloponnesian War in 404 left them the dominant power in Greece. They secured their power by planting a Spartan governor (*harmostēs*) and garrison to support quisling local regimes in cities under their control.

18.96 *the Decelean War*: in the last phase of the Peloponnesian War the Spartans established a permanent base at Decelea in Attica in 413, which effectively placed the city under siege by land. The Thebans took the opportunity to make cross-border raids. For Haliartus see the second note on 4.17. The expedition to help Corinth against the Spartans took place in the spring of 394.

18.97 *from the gods*: the ideal here is one that goes back to Homer; it presents a heroic vision of Athens' destiny, one derived from the tropes of the public funeral orations for the war dead.

18.98 *the Spartans*: in 369 the Thebans followed up their success of 371 at Leuctra by invading Sparta. The Athenians sent aid to Sparta. The reasons were less grand than suggested here, since Athens had every reason to thwart Theban ambitions, and the Athenian expeditionary force achieved little.

18.99 *to annex Euboea*: the Athenians expelled a Theban force from Euboea in 357, but to maintain their own influence rather than Euboean freedom. The campaign against Themison, tyrant of Eretria, dates to 366, when he seized Oropus from Athens (he subsequently handed it over to Thebes). Theodorus is otherwise unknown.

18.102 *fleet was falling apart*: the operation of the navy was based on citizen contributions, but the system was revised several times. In the fifth century a rich citizen could be required to maintain a ship at sea for a year. By the end of the century the burden was shared between two. In the 370s a system of financing by syndicates (*symmoriai*) was introduced. Demosthenes' reform of 340 adjusted the scale of contributions relative to wealth (§107).

18.103 *the required proportion of the votes*: in public cases, as a deterrent against frivolous prosecution, a prosecutor who failed to get 20 per cent of the votes cast was fined 1,000 drachmas and barred from bringing a public action in future.

18.103 *the second or third ranks*: the leading figures in the trierarchic syndicates; cf. the description of the war levy in 2.29, with note.

18.107 *those of you who are poor*: 'poor' is a relative term; even the less well-off members of the syndicates were in the top 4 per cent of an adult male population of perhaps 30,000.

18.107 *the temple at Munychia*: the temple of Artemis at Munychia in Piraeus, the Athenian harbour town. The placing of a branch wreathed in wool on an altar was a common gesture of formal supplication by those in distress.

18.110 *measures and activities*: that is, his conduct in the war which culminated in Chaeronea in 338.

18.112 *to audit his donation*: part of the formal basis of Aeschines' objection to Ctesiphon's decree is the alleged illegality of proposing a crown before Demosthenes' final audit. The validity of the objection is debated by scholars and the legal position may have been ambiguous. But even if Aeschines was right, the breach of the law was common enough for Demosthenes to have precedents (§114). The office for which Demosthenes was still unaudited at the time of the proposal was that of *teichopoios*, 'wall builder', one of a committee responsible for emergency repairs to the fortifications after Chaeronea, for which he had added a donation of his own to the funds made available by the city. With 'Board of Sycophants' Demosthenes parodies the formal procedure for checking the conduct of a magistrate after he demitted office, which was controlled by a board of Auditors.

18.120 *award in the theatre*: Aeschines also argued that it was illegal for an award to be announced in the theatre; but he himself admitted that the law allowed for exceptions (3.47).

18.121 *hellebore for your problem*: hellebore was believed to act as a purgative cure for madness.

18.122 *according to specification*: Aeschines (3.168–77) had listed the qualities of the true democrat and contrasted Demosthenes' origin, life, and career with this ideal. The reference to a statue may be especially sarcastic in view of the exchange at 19.251.

18.122 *standing on a cart*: a reference to the ritual abuse which took place in the Anthesteria festival in honour of Dionysus.

18.127 *Aeacus . . . Rhadamanthys . . . Minos*: legendary judges of the dead in the underworld.

18.127 *as you know*: Demosthenes quotes from the closing section of Aeschines' speech (3.260).

18.129 *improper language*: Aeschines' father was named Atrometus (literally, 'untrembling, fearless'). Demosthenes changes it to Tromes, 'trembler'. His father almost certainly was or had been a schoolteacher, but there is no reason to trust the allegation that his mother was a prostitute. The allegation of foreign or servile origin is a common smear in Athenian politics and probably has its roots in comedy. Aeschines in the prosecution speech claimed that Demosthenes was of foreign extraction.

18.130 *'Empousa'*: a shape-changing bogey of popular belief.

18.132 *set fire to the dockyards*: at 3.225, Aeschines alludes to this case in alleging that Demosthenes arrested people on charges of spying and had them tortured. Demosthenes is careful to stress that the torture had a legal base. This Antiphon must have lost his citizenship in the review of the citizen registers which took place in 346/5. Citizens were exempt from torture in any circumstances; so normally were (free) non-citizens, though the latter might be put to torture where state security was at issue.

18.134 *vote from the altar*: the ritual added solemnity and reflected the religious importance of Delos, a panhellenic sanctuary under Athenian control. The incident relates to an interstate dispute which went to arbitration. The sacking of Aeschines need not indicate suspicion of treason, as Demosthenes claims, but it probably does indicate unpopularity.

18.136 *he's accusing me of?*: that is, Aeschines (allegedly) engages in the kind of collusion he has alleged against Demosthenes.

18.136 *in the wrong*: Python of Byzantium came as envoy for Philip to Athens in late 344 or early 343 to convey Philip's willingness to amend the peace of 346 in response to Athenian dissatisfaction with its terms.

18.137 *in Thrason's house*: Aeschines 3.223–4 tells the story differently. Anaxinus was in town making purchases for Alexander's mother Olympias; Demosthenes tortured him and secured his execution for spying, though he had been Demosthenes' host at Oreus in Euboea.

18.139 *to prove it*: speeches in court were allocated an equal amount of time (measured by the water-clock) to ensure fairness. It was a common ploy to demonstrate one's confidence by inviting the opponent to use part of one's own allowance.

18.140 *the Amphissan decrees*: the events which led to Chaeronea. In 339 the Athenian delegation at Delphi learned of an attempt by the Locrians of Amphissa to accuse Athens of sacrilege. Aeschines countered the charge by accusing Amphissa in turn of impiety. Demosthenes blocked his attempts to get Athenian support for the action against Amphissa and instead Athens (with Thebes) supported Amphissa against an Amphictyonic force led by Philip. This led directly to Chaeronea, blame for which Demosthenes is trying to pin on Aeschines.

18.141 *the city's ancestor*: as father of Ion, eponymous ancestor of the Ionian Greeks, whose mother city Athens claimed to be.

18.142 *Phocians to destruction*: in 346 when Aeschines and others encouraged the Athenians to expect a settlement of the Sacred War favourable to Athenian interests.

18.143 *Elatea*: a town in Phocis. Demosthenes describes the shock at Philip's seizure of Elatea in §168 below. Its possession allowed Philip to control the pass at Thermopylae and therefore direct access to Attica, blocked only by Thebes. Hence the strategic importance of the latter.

18.146 *I'll say no more than that*: the generals were held to have mishandled the campaign.

18.147 *ask for his help*: as they had done in the settlement of the Third Sacred War and as they in fact did in 339.

18.149 *hands had gone up*: officials in Athens were appointed either by secret lot or (where expertise was required) by show of hands in the Assembly (the normal way of voting there). There is no need to take the claim seriously. At that time Aeschines' popularity was in decline, but he was still a seasoned politician.

18.149 *consecrated land*: Aeschines' charge against Amphissa was that they were cultivating sacred land on the plain below Delphi which had been set aside for the god Apollo.

18.159 *caught sight of him*: as from one under a curse.

18.169 *burnt the booths*: the market stalls made mostly of wicker, burned to act as a beacon in order to achieve maximum turnout for the assembly meeting next day.

18.169 *the hill*: the Pnyx, immediately south-west of the Agora, where the Assembly met. Since the Pnyx could hold no more than 6,000 people (Introduction, p. xviii), 'the entire population' is an exaggeration.

18.171 *the Three Hundred*: the richest echelon in Athens; see note on 2.29.

18.187 *Oenomaus of Cothocidae*: Aeschines repeatedly mocks Demosthenes' nickname, Battalus, which Demosthenes explained as due to a stammer as a child, while Aeschines connects it with passive homosexuality. Cresphontes, Creon, and Oenomaus are all tragic characters; Collytus is one of the rural demes (villages/districts) and the reference here is to a tragic performance at the rural Dionysia there. Athenians were known by name, patronymic, and deme, and Paeania and Cothocidae were the demes of Demosthenes and Aeschines respectively.

18.197 *on Thasos*: islands formerly under Athenian influence. Here as in Athens the now-dominant pro-Macedonians were evidently settling old scores.

18.204 *acquiescence*: in 480, when faced with overwhelming odds as the Persian army advanced south, the Athenians after heated debate abandoned the city, sent the non-combatants to places of safety, and put their trust in the fleet, a policy championed by Themistocles, who had earlier been instrumental in making Athens a maritime power (Herodotus 7.143–4). Of Cyrsilus we know no more than we are told here (Cicero repeats the story with embellishments: *De officiis* 3.48). Herodotus tells a similar story of a man named Lycidas (9.5), which suggests that we have here a flexible folktale.

18.208 *Marathon . . . Artemisium*: the four main battles of the two Persian invasions of Greece in the early fifth century.

18.209 *the current trial*: Aeschines 3.181–90.

18.210 *staff and token*: the jurors were allocated to courts at random to preclude corruption; this was done by giving them different-coloured staffs. Each juror was given a bronze token before he voted and once he had fulfilled his duty by voting he was free to collect his pay for jury service.

18.211 *where I broke off*: he resumes the narrative interrupted at §188.

18.216 *and the winter one*: little is known about these early battles in the conflict. The river is probably Cephisus, which flows between Phocis and Locris, and into Boeotia.

18.217 *ask Aeschines*: a superb example of what ancient rhetoricians called *dilēmma* (choice), where the opponent is offered two equally unacceptable propositions, either of which will damn him.

18.223 *Hypereides*: Hypereides had added a rider to Demomeles' original draft proposal, hence the plural 'decrees' for what is essentially a single document. The case came to trial in 334/3. Part of Hypereides' defence speech has recently been found on a reused medieval manuscript; its rhetoric resembles the present speech, pointing (unsurprisingly) to a shared rhetorical strategy and collaboration by the anti-Macedonians.

18.227 *behave like auditors*: Aeschines 3.59–61.

18.230 *seven hundred stades away*: about 126 kilometres or 80 miles.

18.234 *collected in advance*: that is, by the expropriations of generals needing to support their troops because of the periodic failure of Athens to fund its expeditionary forces properly. Demosthenes is thinking of the mid-340s.

18.238 *your ignorance*: Aeschines (3.143) had charged Demosthenes with making excessive concessions to Thebes in assigning two-thirds of the costs of the war to Athens. Athens in fact had to deal generously with Thebes in order to detach it from Macedon.

18.238 *provided by Athens*: at Salamis in 480. Ancient sources differ on the precise arithmetic (between half and two-thirds of the fleet), though where a hard figure is given, this is often 200. What is never disputed is Athens' disproportionate contribution as the leading naval power.

18.245 *cowardice*: Aeschines repeatedly accuses Demosthenes of cowardly behaviour at Chaeronea; possibly he did run, but so probably did many.

18.250 *proved to be legal*: a reference to *graphē paranomōn*; see speech introduction.

18.253 *Zeus at Dodona agrees*: Zeus had a major oracular shrine at Dodona in Epirus. There may be some truth in the suggestion that at this period, with the site at Delphi under Macedonian influence and Athens deprived of her earlier privileges there, Athenian consultation of Dodona increased, though consultation of Delphi continued and evidently most people had faith in the oracle there despite occasional doubts in some quarters (Aeschines 3.130). We know nothing of the particular oracular response here.

18.255 *Aeschines claims*: cf. Aeschines 3.114, 157–8.

18.259 *hocus-pocus*: despite the elements of parody, Demosthenes is describing genuine cult activities of a mystic and ecstatic character. There are overlaps with the Orphic and Dionysiac mysteries and with the worship of the Asiatic Cybele, though we should not try to identify it with any of these. The number of such cults in Athens had risen at the end of the fifth century. Though we know of cases of trials for impiety of (usually female) overseers of fringe cults which were felt to involve criminal behaviour, the allegation here is of undignified rather than subversive conduct.

18.262 *third-string actor*: despite Demosthenes' sneer that the third actor would never get the best parts, the position was not negligible and was presumably for most actors the first rung on the ladder.

18.265 *I was initiated*: presumably into the Eleusinian Mysteries. Though its content and ritual were secret (and so open only to initiates, whence the vagueness here), it was, unlike the kind of cult described above for Aeschines' mother, a major Greek festival.

18.267 *where the dead lie hidden*: the first line of Euripides' *Hecuba*, spoken by the ghost of her murdered son Polydorus; this and the next (of unknown authorship) quotation are designed to associate Aeschines with bad omens, and the second perhaps also with dissembling as a returning ambassador. The third (again of unknown authorship) neatly slips in mid-sentence from tragic quotation, referring to a character who was brought low by the gods, to the present moment, implicating the audience in a prayer for Aeschines' destruction.

18.268 *ransomed from the enemy*: it was common for ransom to be arranged for the release of prisoners of war (the alternative might be sale as slaves). Though he speaks generally here, Demosthenes may allude specifically to the Athenian prisoners he ransomed out of his own pocket on his second diplomatic mission in 346 (see 19.166 ff.).

18.271 *set eyes ... heard my voice*: as an allegedly polluted man who brings bad luck by contact or proximity.

18.279 *private crime either*: true, as far as we know, whereas Demosthenes had brought a prosecution on a political charge against Aeschines in 343.

18.282 *A deceiver*: Demosthenes refers to the ritual curse with which a herald opened the Assembly meetings, which included damnation for anyone attempting to deceive the people.

18.284 *informed against yourself*: perhaps by serving on the embassy to Philip, or perhaps by his general behaviour (cf. 18.291; 19.211, 240).

18.285 *funeral oration*: it was a distinctive Athenian practice to burn the battle dead at the battlefield, collect the bones, and bury all those who died in war in any year in a collective public grave. A distinguished orator was chosen to give a speech in their praise. A funeral speech by

Demosthenes survives as number 60 in the corpus; scholars are divided on its authenticity.

18.292 *in his speech*: the claim occupies the preamble to Aeschines' speech, 3.1–8.

18.304 *Thessaly and Arcadia*: that is, states which collaborated with Macedon or sat on the fence.

18.312 *redeeming his citizenship*: for the loss of citizenship to be temporary, Aristonicus (author of a decree honouring Demosthenes: §83) must have been a state debtor as a result of a large fine in a political case (see note on §15). Evidently he donated to the war effort (some or all of) the money he had saved to redeem his status.

18.312 *the trierarchic law*: that is, Demosthenes' trierarchic reforms of 340, described at §§102 ff.; the allegation is that Aeschines was bribed to thwart it in some way.

18.313 *of the tragic stage*: Theocrines, the defendant in speech 58 in the Demosthenic corpus (not by Demosthenes), comes across there as a mercenary sycophant.

18.319 *athlete from the past*: Philammon was a contemporary athlete; Glaucus of Carystus in Euboea was a famous boxer from the early fifth century.

18.322 *before the Amphictyons*: for Alexander's demand of the surrender of the leading anti-Macedonians in 335, see §41 above. The threat of trial before the Amphictyons may belong to the same incident, but it could have been made earlier, when the Amphictyons united under Philip in the war which led to Chaeronea.

19. ON THE DISHONEST EMBASSY

19.1 *during your allocation*: in the fifth century jurors were allocated to a court for the whole of the year. During the fourth century the Athenians introduced an elaborate system of randomized allocation on each day of jury service to obviate the risk of corruption, which had emerged as a problem towards the end of the fifth century. See also note on 18.210. The present passage, even if Demosthenes is inventing or exaggerating, indicates that outsiders were present, so that there was still some scope for attempting to influence the jurors.

19.1 *into court*: at the beginning of the administrative year (in midsummer) those empanelled as jurors for the year swore an oath, of which the most important clauses were to judge according to the laws and decrees of the Athenian Assembly and Council, and to give an impartial hearing to both sides.

19.2 *threatening others*: in 346 Timarchus brought an indictment against Aeschines for alleged misconduct as ambassador to Macedonia. Aeschines responded by charging Timarchus with having prostituted himself in his youth, an activity which brought loss of citizen rights. Aeschines won the case, thus blocking Timarchus' prosecution. Demosthenes deals at length with the Timarchus case at §§241–4 and 283–6. Evidently the affair still rankled.

19.3 *since the embassy*: three years; long enough for memories to be imprecise, a fact exploited by both Demosthenes and Aeschines, the former in trying to distance himself as much as possible from a peace which he had (if only for pragmatic reasons) supported.

19.10 *Ischander*: a tragic actor like Neoptolemus, but possibly also a tragic poet. The 'second actor' was the second in importance of the three-actor troupe standard in Greece. So Ischander was Aeschines' supporting speaker.

19.11 *Megalopolis*: Megalopolis was head of the Arcadian League, whose assembly was the Ten Thousand. The visit belongs to the unsuccessful Athenian attempts to assemble a Greek alliance against Philip in the period before the Peace of Philocrates.

19.12 *the situation in Macedonia*: Ctesiphon served on the first and second embassies to Philip in 346. He *may* be the man who proposed the crown for Demosthenes in 336 (speech 18). Aristodemus, like Neoptolemus, was a distinguished actor; he too served on both embassies to Philip in 346. He and Ctesiphon had (separately) served as envoys on unrelated matters in the period immediately prior to the peace negotiations and their reports that Philip wanted peace had influenced the Athenian decision to open negotiations

19.15 *the vile Philocrates*: Demosthenes refers to the two successive Assembly debates on 18 and 19 Elaphebolion (corresponding to March/April) in 346 on the proposed peace with Macedon. The resolution of the congress of the states of the Second Athenian Confederacy was presented at the first meeting; while leaving the final decision to Athens, it allowed for any Greeks to choose within three months to be included in the treaty. This would have converted the bipartisan peace into something broader.

19.17 *for the oaths*: treaties were invariably ratified with oaths, and so a second embassy was sent to Macedonia to receive Philip's oath.

19.17 *presented ourselves before the Council*: envoys sent to or from other states reported first to the Council.

19.20 *the business with the Amphictyons*: a vague reference to the Sacred War.

19.21 *were being resettled*: unlike Attica, which was a single state with Athens as its capital, Boeotia remained a region of separate city states, overshadowed and intermittently controlled by Thebes within the Boeotian League. Plataea, destroyed by Thebes in 427 but refounded in 387, was razed again by Thebes in 373, as was Thespiae soon afterwards.

19.21 *seize the temple*: in 356 the Phocians (in response to a crippling fine imposed by the Amphictyonic League for cultivating sacred land belonging to the temple) had seized the temple to use the money there for military purposes, thus initiating the Third Sacred War. Thebes had pressed for the imposition of the fine on Phocis. Aeschines treats this as a manoeuvre designed to precipitate precisely the reaction it provoked, but the Thebans probably wanted to weaken Phocis rather than provoke conflict.

19.22 *veiled allusion to Oropus*: Oropus, on the border between Attica and Boeotia, fluctuated between Athenian and Theban control. In 366 it had been seized from Athens by the Euboean tyrant Themison, who handed it over to Thebes. Though Amphipolis had not been Athenian since the 420s, the Athenians continued to regard it as theirs and deeply resented Philip's capture of the city in 357. So, according to Demosthenes, Aeschines hinted that, one way and another, he had gained important concessions from Philip.

19.25 *what was going on*: Demosthenes forestalls the obvious response, one he made with crushing sarcasm against Aeschines 13 years later (18.240-43): 'Why didn't you say anything at the time?' Aeschines (2.121-2) claims that Demosthenes praised his fellow envoys both in the Council and in the Assembly, rather than denouncing them.

19.31 *Timagoras . . . condemned to death by the Assembly*: one of two envoys sent to the Persian court from Athens in 367 BC. He spoke in support of statements made by the Theban representative, Pelopidas, and was prosecuted on his return by his colleague Leon, convicted, and executed.

19.34 *the Assembly met*: the Assembly at which the second embassy (sent to receive Philip's oath to the treaty) reported, on 16 Skirophorion (the last month of the Athenian calendar, roughly June in ours).

19.36 *and the Pharsalians*: in other words, the envoys were not being remiss of their own accord, but only acceding politely to a request from Philip. Halus, a small port on the Gulf of Pagasae, was at the time under siege from Philip's general Parmenion. Evidently the Athenian envoys had been instructed to take the oaths from and in the individual cities allied to Philip, as well as from Philip himself. Deviation from an ambassadorial brief could be very dangerous. At §175 Demosthenes claims that Aeschines remained with Philip a full twenty-four hours after the other envoys left Pherae.

19.39 *the prisoners*: Athenians taken prisoner when Philip captured Olynthus in 348. Demosthenes expands on this theme at §§166-72

19.50 *returned home*: a Spartan force had advanced to Thermopylae at Philip's invitation in the hope of a settlement unfavourable to Thebes (§§76-7 below), which might allow them to reverse the diminution in their power resulting from the Theban invasions of the Peloponnese after their defeat of Sparta at Leuctra in 371.

19.50 *anything of this sort*: Demosthenes' point is that the reference to the Amphictyons is a fiction, since there was no Amphictyonic levy present, just Philip and Phocis' enemies, Thessaly and Thebes. Though he presents this as a ruse of Aeschines and Philocrates, in fact the Assembly can have had no illusions in passing the decree; they were abandoning Phocis. Aeschines (2.137) claimed in response that Philip invited the Athenians to contribute a contingent to the Amphictyonic force which oversaw the settlement at Phocis, but that Demosthenes and his associates induced the assembly to refuse, arguing that the troops would be used as hostages by Philip. Demosthenes evades the issue in the next sentence. Proxenus was an Athenian general.

19.51 *when I wanted to*: though the envoys were technically Philip's guests, in practice it would be difficult to leave without his permission. At §174 Demosthenes claims that he tried to send a letter to the Athenians, but was overruled by his colleagues.

19.55 *Fortune*: since the peace was now to be valid for Philip's descendants as well, there would be no gain even if Philip happened to die. In practice, however, Greek treaties were regularly repudiated as necessary and so the clause was not unduly restrictive.

19.57 *what he has to say*: for timing in Athenian trials, see note on 18.139.

19.59 *doomed and lost*: the truce that brought an end to the Sacred War. The arithmetic is meant to show the causal connection between the Athenian resolution for peace with Philip, and the Phocian surrender. The peace between Athens and Macedon will certainly have convinced the Phocians that their cause was lost, but it would be surprising if they were not separately negotiating with Philip. The terms imposed by the Amphictyons, now including Macedonian delegates, were far less harsh than Phocis might have feared. They were to repay the sums plundered from the temple of Apollo and their cities were destroyed, with the populations distributed among villages.

19.60 *Dercylus*: a third embassy had been sent to Philip to convey the Athenian resolutions of 16 Skirophorion (§§48–9 above). Dercylus, who had served on the first two embassies, participated in this expedition, but Aeschines and Demosthenes did not (§§122–4). In the event the envoys learned of the surrender of Phocis when they reached Euboea and turned back.

19.61 *the Phocians' defences*: that is, the resolution of the Amphictyonic Council: see note on §59.

19.65 *enslave us*: in 404 at the end of the Peloponnesian War, Athens' enemies debated what to do with the defeated city. Thebes and Corinth wished to enslave the inhabitants. Sparta resisted on the grounds of Athens' previous services to Greece (probably also from a reluctance to see Thebes dominate central Greece). This is our earliest evidence for the Phocian support for the Spartan position; they too will have been reluctant to empower Thebes.

19.69 *Antipater and Parmenion*: two of the three envoys from Philip (the third was Eurylochus) who received the Athenian oaths in ratification of the peace treaty.

19.70 *the curse will prove this*: at the beginning of each Assembly meeting the herald pronounced a curse on anyone who misled the people. Using a common oath formula it called down the total destruction of the guilty individual, his bloodline, and his house (§71).

19.73 *do his job*: Hegesippus, also known as Crobylus ('Bun') from his old-fashioned hairstyle, was fiercely opposed to peace with Macedon. In 347 the Phocians had offered to hand over to Athens several forts controlling the pass at Thermopylae, which would have allowed Athens to block Philip's entry to southern Greece; a force was assembled under the general Proxenus. The Spartan king Archidamus also offered to take them over. As a result of internal dissent in Phocis the offer was withdrawn.

19.75 *or anyone else*: for the (largely ineffective) Athenian aid to Sparta in 369, see note on 18.98; for the expedition to Euboea in 357, see note on 18.99. For reasons why Demosthenes in 343 might curse the Euboeans, see notes on 5.5 and 19.22.

19.76 *within only five days*: at §60 above it was four days (inclusively) from the Phocian discovery of the Athenian decision and the surrender, eight days from the Assembly meeting to the surrender. Demosthenes has telescoped time for rhetorical effect. The deceit is more obvious to the reader than it will have been to the hearer.

19.79 *fearful or threatened*: for the Athenian colonists in the Thracian Chersonese (modern Gallipoli), see especially speech 8. The region was important for securing Athens' grain route to the Black Sea. The conclusion of peace secured the Athenian territories against attack by Macedon.

19.84 *wasted effort*: in 352 Philip decisively defeated a Phocian army at the battle of the Crocus Field, a victory which secured his hold over Thessaly. He followed up the success by advancing on Thermopylae but was blocked by an Athenian force under Nausicles.

19.86 *Diophantus and Callisthenes*: the decree of Diophantus proposed thanksgiving sacrifices after the success of the expedition to Thermopylae in 352. That of Callisthenes proposed that the Athenians bring their property, wives, and children inside the city walls during the panic which followed the surrender of Phocis; the details are given at §125. The juxtaposition emphasizes the contrast between 352 and 346. Demosthenes returned to the Callisthenes decree at 18.37.

19.87 *Porthmus or Megara*: to expand his influence in the Peloponnese Philip had intervened in the factional struggles in Megara earlier in 343. Athens and Macedon were also competing for influence in Euboea in support of different factions. As part of that struggle Philip had sent a mercenary force (see 9.58) which captured Porthmus in 343, a move which alarmed Athens, since Porthmus was directly opposite the coast of Attica.

19.92   *the generals' offences*: Aeschines' line (2.70–3) is that the peace was made necessary by the failure of Athens' military commanders to contain Philip.

19.94   *proposals . . . for hire*: Philocrates, the proposer of the peace. Earlier in 343 he was indicted by Hypereides (an associate of Demosthenes) and fled into exile.

19.95   *damned, unscrupulous clerk*: for Demosthenes on Aeschines' career, see 18.265; 19.199, 19.249. 'Clerk' is a not infrequent term of abuse in speech 18 (§§127, 209, 261).

19.103   *at a time of his choosing*: Aeschines had blocked the first attempt to prosecute him in 346 (see note on §2 above). But Demosthenes was one of his first accusers and must be responsible in part for the time-lag between accusation and trial, having evidently waited for a propitious political climate (see speech introduction).

19.111   *admission to the Amphictyonic Council*: after the surrender of Phocis in 346, as part of its punishment and Philip's reward the Amphictyonic Council agreed that the two votes on the council which had belonged to Phocis should be transferred to Macedon. For the Athenian reaction to the honours given to Philip and Demosthenes' attempt to contain it, see speech 5.

19.113   *by Zeus!*: It is not surprising that Demosthenes hurries over this point. In fact as a young man Aeschines had a distinguished military record. Aeschines gives a spirited response at 2.167–71.

19.114   *tortured slaves, for instance*: a slave, as a chattel, lacked legal personality. The evidence of slaves was only admissible in an Athenian court if extracted under torture. For the evidence to be admitted the agreement of both parties was required.

19.114   *gold coins at the banks*: Philocrates exchanged Macedonian gold coins (Macedon controlled the mines of Mount Pangaeum) for Attic silver drachmas. Athenian politicians received no pay for speaking in the Assembly and had only limited opportunities to earn money from public office, since the latter was for a fixed period and in most cases non-repeatable (as part of a democratic culture of rotating power). Politics was, however, still a potentially profitable activity. In a gift-giving culture it was normal for politicians to receive gifts from interested parties, at home and abroad. The practice could be dangerous, since a man could be prosecuted on the grounds that he had taken money against the interests of the city. From the present passage it seems that Philocrates injudiciously flaunted his acquisitions.

19.118   *liable to audit*: this must mean that the individual has already successfully passed the audit for his participation in the embassy.

19.120   *an entire day each*: all Athenian trials were settled on the day they came to court. But while several private cases could be tried in a day by a single panel of jurors, a jury panel would try only one public case in a day.

19.122 *oath of exemption*: an oath of disclaimer to the effect that one cannot perform a public function because of illness or some other impediment beyond one's control. Demosthenes does not explain the ground for his demurrer.

19.126 *ambassador*: after the third embassy turned back, the Athenians sent the same ambassadors, this time including Aeschines, to Philip at the Amphictyonic meeting in Delphi which decided the fate of Phocis. Aeschines and Demosthenes alike treat this as essentially a continuation of the third embassy; hence Demosthenes can attack Aeschines here as serving unelected on an embassy he had declined; Aeschines claims (2.94) that he said he would serve if able. If there was a procedural breach, evidently the Assembly acquiesced, since Aeschines was not prosecuted.

19.128 *the Pythian festival*: together with admission to the Amphictyonic Council (§111 above) Philip was rewarded by the Amphictyony with the presidency of the Pythian games for 346. For the hostile Athenian reaction see introduction to speech 5.

19.129 *by name*: in the latter part of the fifth century the Athenians built a new chamber for the Council in the Agora. The old chamber, instead of being demolished, became the public archive, under the name *Mētrōon* (shrine of the Mother of the Gods). It was supervised by a slave owned by the state.

19.134 *in the wrong*: by acquitting Aeschines; the reference is to the jurors' oath.

19.144 *even worse conditions*: for the two meetings of the Assembly, see §15. Demosthenes is almost certainly lying when he claims that it was Aeschines who secured an adjournment of the discussion to the second day (debate was heated and there was clearly no consensus), but almost certainly correct to say that Aeschines shifted his ground between the two debates, only coming down firmly for the terms of Philocrates' peace on the second.

19.147 *take Philip's money*: because, since this fantasy city was defeating Philip, the only way Philip could secure peace on favourable terms would be by bribing its ambassadors.

19.148 *an Iliad of woes*: a striking phrase, probably invented by Demosthenes. Orchomenus, Coronea, and Tilphosaeum were all in Boeotia, Neones in Phocis, Hedylium a mountain in eastern Phocis. Dates and details of the last two engagements are obscure, but they clearly involved unsuccessful Theban incursions into Phocis. Demosthenes is right to claim that the Thebans could make no headway; access to the treasure of the temple at Delphi gave the Phocians a huge fund with which to hire mercenaries.

19.154 *used up*: there were four scheduled meetings of the Assembly each prytany (for this term see Glossary). It would however have been possible to call an extraordinary meeting.

19.156 *the Sacred Mountain*: see note on 9.15.

19.162 *the witnesses who were there*: roads in fourth-century Greece were generally poor and travel by sea was faster. Had the ambassadors travelled by
sea, they could have gone directly or indirectly (after stopping at Pella,
which was nearer to the coast in the classical period) to the Hellespont
(Dardanelles). But since Doriscus is west of the Dardanelles and Philip
was travelling east, by the time they caught up with him, he would still
have captured Doriscus and half of Thrace.

19.162 *subsequent mission there*: in late 346 the Athenians sent Euclides (presumably with others) to protest against Philip's activities in Thrace.
This appears to have been a belated attempt both to protect Athenian
possessions in the Chersonese and to shore up their ally, the Thracian
king Cersobleptes.

19.163 *arrange truces for us*: unlike the envoy, the person of the herald was
inviolate; the herald was therefore needed to obtain safe conduct for the
envoys.

19.174 *Cersobleptes*: a Thracian king who had at one stage been involved in
a struggle with Athens for possession of the Chersonese, but had allied
himself with it in the shadow of Philip's expansionism. See further
speech 23. At the meeting of the Assembly on 25 Elaphebolion 346 he
was excluded from the oath-swearing for the peace; see also the first note
on 8.64. Demosthenes and Aeschines each try to blame the other for the
exclusion of Cersobleptes. Probably both acquiesced, as certainly did
the Assembly.

19.174 *Cardia*: for Cardia see introduction to speech 8.

19.176 *duly accountable*: a witness in an Athenian trial could be sued for false
testimony; the action was a private suit and had to be undertaken by the
opposing litigant. We are told at Demosthenes 46.9 that 'the laws do
not allow' a litigant to be his own witness. The present passage suggests
either that the rule was not stringently policed or that, as with false testimony, enforcement was left to the opponent.

19.176 *knowledge of the matter*: see Introduction, note 9.

19.177 *beginning of my speech*: this passage reads like a summing up and transition to the finale, and may well have served this role in the original trial.
What follows could be a later addition, or additional points from the
pre-trial draft intended for selective use once the basic case has been
made.

19.180 *less than Aeschines*: the first three were Athenian commanders of the
fleet in the north Aegean who were tried for failure to protect Athenian
interests in the 360s and 350s, as the Athenians struggled to cope first
with King Cotys and then his son Cersobleptes. Ergocles and Dionysius
were active in the 390s and 380s; they served in the north and were less
narrowly connected with Thrace, but it suits Demosthenes to present
Thrace as the graveyard of Athenian military careers and policy.

19.185 *heralds and embassies*: Demosthenes refers to the regular agenda items for Assembly meetings. The Assembly met forty times a year (four times per prytany, the units into which the civic calendar was divided) and only half had 'heralds and embassies' on the agenda. This in turn constrained the Council in its task of setting the agenda for Assembly meetings.

19.189 *the libations?*: the shared social and ritual activities (meals, which were rounded off by a libation, a drink offering to the gods, before any drinking began) which bound the ambassadors as colleagues and which (they say) Demosthenes has betrayed in prosecuting a fellow envoy.

19.191 *Adeimantus*: for Timagoras, see note on §31. Eubulus was the most powerful politician in Athens from the early to mid-350s until at least the mid-340s. Smicythus is unknown but a Tharrhex is known to have served on the Council in 354/3. Possibly Eubulus was a member of the Council that year and prosecuted one or more of his colleagues. Conon and Adeimantus were among the generals at Aegospotami; Athens' defeat there in 405 led directly to Sparta's victory in the Peloponnesian War. Conon escaped. Adeimantus was captured by the Spartans and was the only general not executed. He was widely suspected in Athens of having betrayed the fleet.

19.195 *Alexander*: Alexander was assassinated in 367. Philip took Pydna in 357. Apollophanes' family evidently fled to Olynthus to avoid reprisals. Apollophanes may have been murdered by agents of Macedon after Alexander's assassination or by Macedonian collaborators in Pydna in the run-up to Philip's capture of the city.

19.196 *one of the Thirty*: After the Athenian defeat in 404 in the Peloponnesian War, an oligarchic regime of thirty men was voted in at Athens and maintained with Spartan support. The regime was characterized by brutal repression and plunder, and was overthrown in 403 in a revolution led by a group of returning exiles who made their base in Piraeus.

19.196 *respectable*: in 348 Philip had razed Olynthus and sold the population as slaves. It was not considered decent for a respectable free woman to eat and drink in the company of men not related to her; this was for prostitutes, slave or free, and low-status female entertainers. Here the slavery is sufficiently fresh (two years) for the experience to be mortifying. She also comes from a city which had been an ally of Athens.

19.197 *Iatrocles*: one of the Athenians captured by Philip when he took Olynthus. He was subsequently released and served on the first and second embassies to Philip.

19.199 *inebriated revellers*: cf. 18.129–30.

19.204 *unsecured by oaths*: the claim that the peace was not ratified by oaths is obscure, since both Philip and his allies swore to it. It has been suggested that this relates to the proposals and counter-proposals for amendment to the peace in 344/3 when Philip sent an embassy to address Athenian complaints, though that never became a serious peace negotiation. Possibly the reference is to the failure of the second embassy to administer the oaths to the officials of Philip's allies in their cities as instructed; at §278 Demosthenes says that the oaths were administered to representatives chosen by Philip, that is, men of dubious authority.

19.209 *not long ago in Piraeus*: for meetings of the Assembly in Piraeus cf. §60.

19.211 *now exempt*: Aeschines seems to be arguing, in an attempt to forestall Demosthenes' attack, that the first and second embassies are one (merely a prolongation of the office of the ten original envoys) and so neither he nor Demosthenes is now liable to a second audit. However, the appointment to the second embassy followed a fresh election (even though the ambassadors were the same); and even if the argument were accepted, the audit for a combined embassy would be at the end, not after the first phase and before the task was completed.

19.213 *time afterwards*: that is, as the prosecutor, Demosthenes delivers his speech first, before the defendant, and has no further opportunity to speak afterwards.

19.223 *special privileges*: that is, the formal vote of thanks and the dinner: §31 above.

19.230 *registered as an adult*: in a culture which saw pubescent boys as sexually attractive to older men it was not considered decent for an immature boy to stay unaccompanied in the home of unrelated males. The implication that Phrynon was pimping his son is made more explicit at §233.

19.230 *maintenance of a warship*: see the first two notes on 4.36, and for changes in the trierarchy over time, see note on 18.102.

19.233 *for prostitution*: Timarchus; see the second note on §2.

19.242 *got away with it*: Demosthenes accurately reproduces Aeschines 1.175, where Aeschines presented Demosthenes as an unscrupulous teacher of rhetoric using the Timarchus case to impress his young pupils. Either the gibe embedded itself in Demosthenes' memory or Aeschines published the speech after the court case.

19.243 *somehow a goddess*: Hesiod, *Works and Days* 763–4, cited at Aeschines 1.129 in the context of his attempt to get round the absence of eyewitness proof of Timarchus' sex-life by persuading the jurors that Timarchus' reputation for immoral living could not be unearned ('no smoke without fire').

19.245 *company he enjoys*: from Euripides' lost *Phoenix*, fr. 812 Nauck, which was quoted at greater length at Aeschines 1.152–4. Pittalacus featured in Aeschines' speech as a man who had allegedly paid Timarchus for sex. Aeschines actually used the quotation to attack Timarchus' relationship with Hegesander. This could be a memory slip by Demosthenes; but since Hegesander was one of the politicians firmly opposed to peace with Macedon, Demosthenes might hesitate to associate him even by implication with the charges against Timarchus.

19.246 *speech-writers and sophists*: though the Athenians never had a system of paid advocates, they did have professional writers of speeches to be delivered by litigants as their own in court. The profession was legal, but subject to disapproval in a system which aimed at equality before the law. Demosthenes had been a very successful speech-writer (see Introduction). Aeschines had sneered at him for this at 1.94. He had also (1.125, 174) called Demosthenes a sophist, associating him with the professional teachers of rhetoric and tapping a vein of suspicion which had its origins in the fifth century.

19.247 *read the passage*: Creon's entrance speech from *Antigone* (lines 175–90). The part of Creon was too big for the third-string actor. Possibly on this occasion Aeschines was the second actor. But Demosthenes may himself inaccurately have given this role retrospectively to Aeschines in order to supply him with noble sentiments to betray.

19.249 *Hero Physician*: heroes were cult figures who had once been (or were believed to have been) ordinary mortals. They are often marked out by extraordinary aspects of their life or death (for good or ill). Unlike a god, who may be worshipped anywhere, a hero's cult is usually attached to his tomb. Though most heroes were known by name, some were known only by function, as here.

19.251 *immodesty*: in the prosecution speech against Timarchus (1.25–6) Aeschines contrasted the indecorous speaking style of Timarchus with the restraint of Solon, the lawgiver, visible in his statue on Salamis.

19.252 *their disgrace*: Solon played an active role in the Athenian struggle with Megara for control of the island of Salamis in the late seventh and early sixth centuries. In this and other areas (in an age before the rise of prose as an artistic medium) he used his talent as a poet to express his political views. There was no 'revolt of Salamis', but the detail allows Demosthenes to underline the contrast between Solon on Salamis and Aeschines on Amphipolis.

19.255 *save you?*: that is, mimicking Solon. One anecdote has Solon feigning madness (to evade a law which prescribed the death penalty for anyone raising the subject of the campaign for Salamis) and bursting into the Agora wearing a cap (possibly a traveller's cap, since the poem presents him as having come from Salamis) to recite a poem urging the Athenians to fight for the island. The few remaining lines of Solon's Salamis poem are fragments 1–3 West; it is not the poem Demosthenes goes on to quote.

19.257 *worshipping the gods*: that is, Delphi, which was in Phocis. The shrine remained open to all Greeks, however.

19.260 *fellow citizens*: civil war had followed a change of government earlier in 343 from democracy to pro-Macedonian oligarchy.

19.261 *in Greece*: the Athenians and Arcadians claimed that they were *autochthones* ('of the earth/land'), that is, that they were the original inhabitants of their region.

19.263 *synoecism of Chalcidice*: synoecism is the process of political (sometimes physical) unification of separate polities, whether voluntary or imposed. Demosthenes exaggerates, since we know from Thucydides (1.58.2) that some form of political concentration took place in 432. But our knowledge of Olynthus is limited and it may be that the process of unification was strengthened in the fourth century.

19.264 *on land and sea*: Sparta attacked Olynthus in 382 at the request of Macedon, in order to curb Olynthian expansion. The outcome was actually defeat for Olynthus and subordination to Sparta, but Demosthenes needs to enhance the contrast between the 380s and the fall of Olynthus in 348 which follows.

19.265 *herds of cattle*: for the Olynthian traitors Lasthenes and Euthycrates, see notes on 8.40 and 9.66. Both survived the destruction of Olynthus and enslavement of its population, and the anecdotal tradition places Lasthenes at Philip's court later. One fourth-century source puts Euthycrates in the Macedonian camp at Chaeronea.

19.271 *and all his kin*: for Arthmius of Zelea, see note on 9.41. The case is cited repeatedly by the fourth-century orators. Aeschines with relish uses him against Demosthenes in the case for the crown (3.258), and Demosthenes refers to him again at 9.41.

19.272 *the Persians*: the gigantic statue of Athena Promachos ('vanguard') created in the 350s by the sculptor Phidias and financed from the spoils of Marathon.

19.273 *still talks about*: the Peace of Callias of (probably) 449. The historicity of this peace treaty was doubted by some already in the fourth century BC and debate has continued in modern times. The islands mentioned are at the southern and northern limits of Asia Minor respectively.

19.277 *restored democracy*: Epicrates, a prominent politician of the 390s, served as ambassador to Persia and was prosecuted for bribery on his return. For the democratic restoration of 403, see the first note on §196.

19.278 *in the course of their mission*: the procedure used was impeachment (*eisangelia*) before the Assembly, reserved for serious political offences. To go forward, it required a proposal from the Council and a decree of the Assembly.

19.279 *arrested*: the admission of guilt consists of Philocrates' flaunting of his wealth (§114 above) and his flight when indicted.

19.280 *restore democracy*: the older Thrasybulus was active politically and militarily in the latter part of the fifth century and was one of the leaders of the democratic insurgency which ended the regime of the Thirty (see the first note on §196). Phyle was the original base of the rebels, before they moved to Piraeus. The son is otherwise unknown but evidently followed his father into a political and/or military career.

19.280 *heroes and gods*: Harmodius and Aristogeiton (the 'Benefactors') assassinated Hipparchus, brother of the Athenian tyrant Hippias, in 514.

They were captured and killed. Although the tyranny outlived them, they were revered as tyrannicides and their descendants continued to enjoy privileges in the fourth century. An ancient commentator on the present passage takes the unnamed descendant of Harmodius to be the general Proxenus.

19.281 *put to death?*: the ancient commentators identify the priestess as Ninus, whose trial and execution were a *cause célèbre* of which little is known. Later sources suggest that the main charge was of introducing foreign gods. Though alien cults were introduced into Athens and some were absorbed into the civic festival calendar, there was a risk, if the activity involved was felt (or could be argued) to be a threat to values or civic order. Many such trials appear to have been politically motivated.

19.283 *prosecuting Timarchus*: nothing in the transmitted version of Aeschines' *Against Timarchus* corresponds to this paraphrase by Demosthenes.

19.285 *the younger generation*: Aeschines did in fact offer this argument in his speech for the defence, at 2.180.

19.287 *unmasked*: 'Cyrebion' was the nickname of Aeschines' brother-in-law Epicrates. Fertility processions of the sort envisaged here often involved indecency and ritual abuse of individuals. To perform without a mask is to allow one's own character to be associated with the indecency. The other brother-in-law was Philon. His nickname may be derived from the great fifth-century general Nicias, whether ironically (as Demosthenes uses it here) or out of respect is uncertain. The reference to his hiring himself to the general Chabrias is meant to suggest homosexual prostitution, but may reflect no more than military service as a mercenary.

19.287 *flowing back upstream*: though 'rivers flow upstream' was proverbial for reversal, the primary reference here may be to Euripides' *Medea* 410, which uses the proverb to comment on the gap between male criticism of women and their own behaviour, since the point again is the hypocrisy of Aeschines' claim to the moral high ground.

19.290 *begged the jurors' forgiveness*: for Eubulus, see notes on 18.75, 19.191, and 21.205; for Thrasybulus, see the first note on §280; Niceratus was an Athenian politician, but we do not know why he should be mentioned like this, implying a special connection with Eubulus. Hegesilaus was one of the commanders of the force sent by Athens in 348 to aid Plutarch, the tyrant of Eretria in Euboea, to put down a revolt. The campaign was a failure. Evidently Eubulus was called as a witness in both cases, but declined to testify during the main part of the hearing (when the jury voted on the question of guilt), perhaps by taking the oath of exemption, and then took the stand after the defendant's speech when the penalty was being decided, but declined to say anything (it was common for a defendant to have friends and relatives take the stand and urge mercy). In cases without fixed penalties accused and defendant each proposed a penalty to the jurors, whose task was to choose between them.

19.291 *attack your policies*: Aristophon of Azenia is a remarkable case of political longevity; having begun his career at or before the restoration of the democracy in 403, he was still active in the 340s. He fiercely opposed the peace in 346. We know nothing more of his prosecution of Philonicus.

19.291 *Theoric Fund for military purposes*: see notes on 1.19.

19.293 *in the bank*: these cases are otherwise unknown. All mines in Attica were the property of the state, which leased out the extraction rights. Moerocles may have been one of the officials charged with leasing out the rights. He may have been accused of taking bribes. The accusation (*hierōn chrēmatōn klopē*, literally 'theft of sacred monies') against Cephisophon seems to be that he diverted for his own use money belonging to a shrine or intended for a civic cult. Demosthenes' point, elaborated in what follows, is that, compared with treason, these are small offences.

19.294 *Not one of them*: the point being that even embezzlement and other apparently serious crimes are not such as to cause really serious political strife.

19.295 *That's right*: Ptoeodorus and Perilas are listed by Demosthenes at 18.295 as agents of Philip in Megara (see also 18.48 on Perilas). Demosthenes' associate Hypereides says, in a recently discovered fragment: 'Ask each [member of the jury] whom they hate most of all in Megara. They answer you: Ptoeodorus.' Demosthenes' narrative of the trial of Perilas manages to imply that people like Eubulus who speak for Aeschines are part of a fifth column.

19.297 *attain prominence?*: Callistratus was a successful general and politician in the 370s and 360s. He was prosecuted in 361 in relation to the loss of Oropus and went into exile in Macedonia. He returned to Athens in 356 and was executed. For Aristophon, see the first note on §291. For Diophantus, see §§86 and 198.

19.297 *read the oracles*: as the reference to Zeus and Dione (his partner there) makes clear, the oracles cited come from the oracle of Zeus at Dodona in Epirus. See also note on 18.253.

19.302 *of all Greeks*: cf. §10 above.

19.303 *Aglaurus*: the shrine of Aglaurus was at the east end of the Acropolis. The *ephēbeia*, a kind of cadetship, probably an old rite of passage, was reorganized in the latter part of the fourth century as a period of military service, involving training and garrison duty, lasting for two years after an Athenian male reached the age of eighteen. Miltiades was the leader of the Athenian forces at Marathon and Themistocles was responsible for the Greek success at Salamis. They are cited here as heroes of Greek freedom claimed as models (and betrayed) by Aeschines, who in 348 had been one of those seeking to put together a Greek alliance against Philip. For Ischander see note on §10.

19.305 *Atrestidas*: an Arcadian soldier from Mantinea, who had presumably been serving with Philip as a mercenary captain.

19.308 *barbarian*: for Demosthenes Philip is always a *barbaros*, a non-Greek; see note on 3.16. This allows him to make free use of the fifth-century Greek struggle against the Persians at §§303 and 312–13.

19.310 *stand alongside him*: it was common for defendants to have family members (including women and children) appear on the rostrum to appeal for pity. Though Aeschines 2.184 invites political and other associates to speak for him, 2.179 suggests that vulnerable members of his family also joined in.

19.319 *defeated the Phocians*: at the battle of the Crocus Field in 352.

19.321 *as allies*: probably on the second day of the two-day debate, 19 Elaphebolion, when the Athenian decision was in the balance: Aeschines 3.72.

19.324 *obstructive measures*: for Philip's invitation to Athens to send a force, see §§50–1.

19.326 *were safe*: Panactum was a border post between Attica and Boeotia, and so probably was Drymus. The point is that even Athenian home territory is no longer safe.

19.327 *consulting the oracle*: Athens and Sparta both had rocks from which serious malefactors were hurled; it seems that there was a similar place and practice at Delphi. Whether this passage reflects a threat or a decree or an actual incident (and if so how accurately) or indeed merely hyperbole is unclear.

19.331 *on their mission*: Hegesippus' embassy was a response to the initiative of Philip in 344/3 (see note on §204). For Xenocleides see also the second note on 59.27.

19.332 *points he makes*: Chares was an Athenian general active from the early 360s until at least the 330s. In the 340s he served intermittently in the north Aegean, but had little success against Philip. He was one of the generals in the campaign of 338 which led to the defeat at Chaeronea. Aeschines does in fact attack Chares at 2.70–3. Aeschines there confirms the picture of repeated prosecutions of Chares which Demosthenes gives here. Generals were especially liable to prosecution in Athens. Acting at long distance, they were open to suspicion from an Assembly which tended to overestimate the prospects for success, while the need to pay their troops in the absence of sufficient funding from Athens led to appropriations which inevitably provoked complaints from allied cities.

21. AGAINST MEIDIAS, ON THE PUNCH

21.3 *kept safe*: comparison with the end of §39 clarifies this obscure statement: he has kept safe the people's right to punish Meidias.

21.4 *in front of the court*: the allegation becomes ironic, if it is true that Demosthenes never brought the case to court; it shows the degree to which such accusations are a rhetorical cliché designed to create prejudice.

21.5 *the tripod*: a bronze tripod (i.e. a cauldron with three legs) was the official prize for a successful *chorēgos*, and he could then set up the tripod he won at his own expense as a public monument, if he so wished. The ornate base for one of these dedications, set up by Demosthenes' contemporary Lysicrates, still survives in Street of the Tripods near the Acropolis in Athens.

21.9 *at the festival*: the Dionysia, not the Pandia. The Assembly usually met in the Pnyx, but could meet elsewhere. The meeting in the Theatre of Dionysus probably reflects both the connection with the festival and the anticipation of a large turnout. The Archon (that is, the eponymous Archon, one of the officials known collectively as the nine Archons) was responsible for the festival; hence the need for a report from him

21.10 *the very next law*: 'next' perhaps means no more than 'next in the documents to be read out by the clerk'. It is unclear, therefore, whether this is a subsequent clause in the law cited above (speakers will often use the term 'law' (*nomos*) for a single clause) or a separate law. Demosthenes' account of the provision suggests the latter. Whereas the one cited above dealt with the conduct of Assembly business, this one deals with conduct forbidden during the festival.

21.11 *resort to force*: the inclusion of debt-collecting in the prohibition of the use of force during the festival reflects the reliance of the Athenian laws on the individual; anyone collecting a debt, even one adjudicated by a court in his favour, had to exact payment himself. The prohibition has less to do with protecting individuals than avoiding unseemly behaviour which would offend the god.

21.12 *the death penalty*: the declaration of intention to tell the whole story is a cliché. Here it allows Demosthenes to create a crescendo of abusive behaviour (and of his own exemplary conduct) which both adds to the credibility of his version of the assault and stimulates hostility against the perpetrator.

21.13 *a pipe-player*: the *aulos* or double-reed pipe was the only accompaniment in the choral competitions. The allocation of order of choosing by lot (typical of Athenian democratic institutions) prevented any one producer from securing an unfair advantage by cornering the best player in advance.

21.15 *and so on and so forth*: the importance of the festival is reflected in the exemption from campaigns of anyone currently selected for choral service. Since one could not oppose the blanket exemption, Meidias was presumably (on this account) threatening some members of Demosthenes' chorus with prosecution for evasion of service by denying that they had actually been selected for duty. The effect would be to intimidate and disrupt. The alleged attempt to have himself elected as one of the ten festival supervisors who assisted the Archon was, Demosthenes implies, intended to secure further opportunities to disrupt. In fact, since the supervisors covered the costs of the procession with their own money, Meidias was probably seeking an opportunity to shine, like Demosthenes.

21.16 *made to adorn the chorus*: the details of the costumes (likely to be accurate, since there was a mass attendance at the theatre) give a sense of the sums which might be spent by an ambitious chorus-producer. The description of the garments as 'sacred' is a nice touch, designed like other claims in the speech to taint Meidias with impiety.

21.17 *my chorus-trainer*: since the producer was selected only on the ground of wealth, he needed specialist support and one of the first tasks was to appoint a professional trainer.

21.17 *no official position*: as commonly in the democracy, the judges were non-specialist Athenian citizens selected at random. A further ballot was taken to determine which of the judges' votes would be counted, to prevent interference (and possibly to allow for the god to intervene unseen), but blanket intimidation of the sort alleged (see further §65) would potentially nullify this. Precisely what Meidias allegedly nailed up (presumably through his stooges) is uncertain, either (as here) the preparation space of the chorus or the side entrances to the performance space. The aim is the same either way, to harass and disrupt.

21.18 *as my witnesses*: it is normal for speakers to treat the jurors, as representatives of the sovereign people, as continuous with the Assembly (here the meeting which voted on the *probolē*); here additionally they are identified with the theatre audience (plausibly, given the size of the theatre audience and the civic importance of the festival).

21.18 *the men's contest*: each of the ten Athenian tribes provided a chorus of men and a chorus of boys.

21.18 *his youthful exploits*: also at §69; not literal, but intended to aggrandize the sense of outrage at his conduct; Meidias was born in the 390s and at this time would be in his late forties (§154).

21.23 *in a moment*: he finally comes to the list at §130.

21.31 *or something like that*: in an attempt to argue that, since only an individual was the victim, a private suit should have been brought, not a public one.

21.32 *the people's common property*: the crown is the garland worn by an official in the conduct of his duties. The Thesmothetes (*thesmothetai*) were six of the officials known collectively as the nine Archons. The analogy is weak; the chorus-producer was not a city official.

21.34 *required by your oath*: the first clause in the oath sworn by the jurors at the beginning of their annual empanelment was to judge according to the laws.

21.35 *malicious abuse*: for these offences, see notes on 54.1.

21.36 *rescuing the pipe-girl*: from a drunk, as explained below. Pipe-girls were regular entertainers at symposia. His status as *thesmothetēs* is mentioned partly for identification, partly perhaps because Meidias is using it to present the assault on Demosthenes as less heinous. In fact, however, he was evidently acting in a private capacity in intervening (§39).

21.43 *clemency and leniency*: the penalty on conviction for intentional homicide was death with confiscation of property (though the accused could pre-empt the death penalty by going into exile voluntarily before his final speech). The penalty for unintentional homicide was exile, though the dead man's kin collectively could grant pardon, if they were unanimous.

21.44 *the public treasury*: the *dikē exoulēs*, action for ejectment, elegantly sup-plemented the Athenian reliance on the individual litigant with a degree of central coercion. It was up to the individual to collect property, goods, or money awarded to them by a court, but if he was obstructed he could bring the *dikē exoulēs*; if the action succeeded, the person barring was liable to pay an assessed sum to the claimant and an equal sum to the state, thus becoming a public debtor. And a public debtor was automatically deprived of his citizen rights until the debt was repaid.

21.46 *a slave*: several ancient sources remark on the paradox that the law against *hybris* (for which see the first note on 54.1) protected slaves. Since a slave lacked legal personality, the action would be brought by the owner. It is not clear whether the inclusion is to preserve public order (and perhaps protect poor free men, who might be indistinguishable from slaves in appearance) or to protect owner rights.

21.50 *official representatives*: that is, *proxenoi*. Ancient states were not repre-sented formally abroad by permanent diplomats. They selected a mem-ber of the host state to represent their interests as *proxenos*, literally (loosely) 'host'. It was a largely honorary position. See also note on 18.82.

21.54 *in accordance with tradition*: clearly the Dionysia was not specifically mentioned in the oracles that were read out, so that, somewhat des-perately, Demosthenes claims that every oracle also tells the people of Athens to continue with the regular events they already hold, so that he can slip the Dionysia in by implication.

21.56 *sit the performance out*: as with the prohibition on debt-collection at the festival (§11), and for the same reasons, anyone objecting to the status of a chorister cannot challenge him or demand that he sit out the competi-tion, but must act afterwards.

21.58 *suffered for it*: the penalty for military offences (failure to serve, leav-ing the ranks, throwing away one's shield) was loss of political rights. Either the trainer did not enjoy the same exemption from military ser-vice granted to the chorus or the charge related to evasion which was unconnected with a festival.

21.60 *an inexcusable act*: a disfranchised citizen or a foreigner exercising a right which he had forfeit was liable to seizure or summary arrest (*apagōgē*), but this was forbidden by the rules barring physical intervention at a fes-tival.

21.62 *as he had*: Iphicrates was one of the most successful Athenian generals of the fourth century, associated with the revival of Athenian political and military influence in the early decades of the century. His military career lasted from the 390s to the 350s.

21.64 *Chabrias . . . the Oropus crisis*: like Iphicrates, Chabrias was one of the great Athenian generals of the fourth century, associated with the revival of Athenian power in the early decades of the century after their defeat in the Peloponnesian War. His career lasted from the late 390s until his death in battle in 357. The prosecution relates to the loss of Oropus to Thebes in 366 (see note on 19.22). We know little of Philostratus.

21.71 *the pancratiast*: the pancratium was a particularly vicious form of wrestling. Unlike upright wrestling, in which the winner simply had to throw his opponent three times, the pancratium included ground wrestling, almost nothing was barred, and victory consisted in making the opponent concede defeat.

21.75 *great or small*: for the tendency of defendants to bring vulnerable relatives into court to appeal for the jurors' pity, cf. 19.281. Like all references to previous trials in the orators this is highly tendentious; there were no records of court hearings, only verdicts and memories.

21.78 *no more than a boy*: for Demosthenes' suit against his guardians, see Introduction, pp. viii–ix, and speeches 27 and 28.

21.78 *exchange procedure for a trierarchy*: a reference to the procedure of *antidosis*; see the second note on 4.36. For this particular occasion, see also 28.17.

21.80 *the trierarchy*: it was not unknown for individuals selected to perform the trierarchy to pay someone to undertake the practical aspects of the task, including acting as captain; this was perfectly legal, if not in the spirit of the system.

21.81 *private suit . . . for the slander*: the action for slander related to the insults used when they invaded the house. Slander (*kakēgoria*, literally 'bad speaking') was narrowly defined in Athens; only a few specified false allegations were banned.

21.81 *permissible*: if a litigant failed to turn up, the jury could give a verdict by default; he would then have a limited period to excuse himself and reopen the case. Since judgement had gone against Meidias, Demosthenes was in a position to seize what was owed to him, armed with the option of the *dikē exoulēs* (see note on §44).

21.81 *reasons for deferment*: it was possible for a litigant to delay an action by having someone swear on oath that he was unavoidably unavailable. On this basis trials could be postponed indefinitely, in this case allegedly sixteen to seventeen years.

21.83 *As arbitrator*: Athenian males were liable to civic service until the age of sixty. For all but the last year this consisted of military service. In the final year they were potentially liable for service as public arbitrators. To spare the courts' time many private cases automatically went to arbitration. The arbitrator's job was to encourage a solution acceptable to both parties and failing that to find for one party; the loser had the right of appeal to a court. This is to be distinguished from the private arbitration procedures described repeatedly in speech 59, where litigants agreed to submit to the adjudication of friends. The importance of the arbitrator's role is reflected in harsh penalties for abuse.

21.84 *counter-suits*: the procedure of *paragraphē*, 'counter-suit', was a means of blocking an action by countersuing the plaintiff for alleged procedural irregularity. See note on 35.2.

21.86 *against him*: an arbitrator's verdict given by default could be contested; again this required an oath to the effect that absence was unavoidable; failure to contest meant that the default verdict stood.

21.87 *witness to the summons*: it was for the arbitrators collectively to hear accusations against an arbitrator (ps.-Aristotle, *Constitution of Athens* 56.5–6). In cases which came before the courts, it was up to the plaintiff to serve summons on the defendant, and the summons had always to be witnessed. It is unclear whether the rules were the same in cases coming before the arbitrators.

21.91 *get away with it*: though the arbitrators collectively had the right to punish an errant arbitrator, including disfranchisement, there was a right of appeal to the courts. The present passage (where 'you' as often assimilates the current to the preceding jury panel) indicates that Straton took the case to court and the jury found against him. He may not be quite the innocent Demosthenes describes.

21.95 *get to his feet*: as a disfranchised citizen Straton could not address the court in any capacity (unlike a resident alien), but was evidently not barred from the premises.

21.99 *regain his citizenship*: unlike the temporary disfranchisement of a debtor to the state, which ended when he repaid the debt, disfranchisement imposed as a punishment was permanent.

21.103 *for desertion*: the statues of the Eponymous Heroes (that is, those after whom the ten Athenian tribes were named) on the west side of the Agora were used for the posting of public notices, including forthcoming trials.

21.103 *his own loss of rights*: to deter frivolous recourse to the courts the Athenians imposed penalties on conspicuous failure by prosecutors in public cases. Though some details are obscure, it seems clear that anyone who failed to obtain one fifth of the votes cast or who abandoned a case was fined 1,000 drachmas and lost the right to bring the same kind of action again.

21.104 *done the deed*: a *cause célèbre* which crops up several times in our sources. A young associate of Demosthenes, Aristarchus, was charged with the brutal murder of a political opponent, Nicodemus. He was a useful stick with which to beat Demosthenes.

21.105 *all but nailed up*: a reference to the punishment called *apotympanismos*, in which a criminal was nailed or chained to a board and left to die of exposure, not unlike crucifixion.

21.106 *the right to be buried at home*: permanent exile as a homicide (see §104 and note on 23.31) would preclude the possibility of burial in Attica.

21.106 *as barbarians do*: a reference to what the Greeks called *proskynēsis*, which has the orientalizing and pejorative connotations of 'kowtow'. It is a gesture of respect from inferior to superior. Though our texts sometimes speak explicitly of prostration, probably the basic gesture was kissing the hand, sometimes accompanied by a bow or inflected knee, more rarely full prostration. It occurs in Greek gestures towards gods, but between humans is associated with oriental despotism and servility.

21.110 *three times over*: the homicide accusation relates to the Aristarchus affair mentioned in §104. The charge of evading service was made by Euctemon (§103). Medias is treated as the orchestrator. For his alleged desertion, see §§162–4.

21.110 *Plutarch's doing*: for the abortive campaign which culminated in the battle of Tamynae, see note on 5.5.

21.111 *my assessment*: Demosthenes was selected for service on the Council for 347/6. All Athenian officials on selection for office were liable to a *dokimasia*, 'assessment', of their eligibility. Meidias lodged an objection to Demosthenes.

21.111 *friends and resources*: Demosthenes was both wealthy and (as a now prominent politician) well connected. This statement sits oddly with the attempt in the next paragraph to present himself as underdog.

21.114 *the whole city*: that is, the offerings at the beginning of the year (which in Athens was midsummer). All official bodies (and all officials) had ritual responsibilities in a society in which the sacred was embedded in the secular.

21.115 *Zeus at Nemea*: Demosthenes evidently acted as *architheōros*, leader of the festival delegation to the Nemean games. The role was both to lead the delegation and to defray the costs.

21.115 *the ceremony*: the Reverend Goddesses (*Semnai Theai*), associated with the *Erinyes* (Furies) at least from the early fifth century, had a cult at the base of the Areopagus hill.

21.119 *impurity to a new level*: homicide made the perpetrator impure and physical contact of any kind, including being under the same roof, contaminated others.

21.120 *your censure of him*; that is, the vote against Meidias in the Assembly hearing. See §2.

21.129 *what remains to be said*: on the water-clock (*klepsydra*) used to time the speeches in order to maintain parity, see Introduction, p. xv and note on 18.139.

21.132 *Argura*: a small town on Euboea, used by the Athenian cavalry as their base in the Euboean campaign of 348, for which see note on 5.5.

21.133 *tried to confiscate*: the 'excise men', 'one-fiftieth collectors' (*pentēko-stologoi*), were private individuals who contracted to collect the 2 per cent levied on imports and exports. The gibe is that Meidias travelled in such style that his equipment looked like trade goods.

21.139 *'Dusty' Euctemon*: Timocrates and Polyeuctus were a politically active father and son. Euctemon is presented above (§102) as a prosecutor for hire.

21.143 *Alcibiades*: one of the most glamorous and notorious figures in fifth-century Athens. He was controversial both in life and in death. Demosthenes' account illustrates the freedom with which distant (and sometimes not so distant) historical events are treated by the orators. Demosthenes accurately assesses Alcibiades' talent, suppresses his defection to Sparta, invents some details, and distorts others.

21.144 *banished the Peisistratids*: the Alcmeonid clan was already prominent in Archaic Athens and remained influential. They were exiled by the sixth-century tyrants, which established their reputation as anti-tyrannical, though in fact they intermittently worked with the Peisistratid regime. While in exile they contracted to rebuild the temple at Delphi after a fire. Whether they formally borrowed money for an expedition to overthrow the tyrants or used some of the money allocated to the rebuilding is unclear. Demosthenes' genealogy is confused. Alcibiades was an Alcmeonid on his mother's side, while Hipponicus was his wife's father.

21.145 *in Athens itself*: Alcibiades served in the east Aegean from 411 to 407, and the Athenian fleet was based at Samos; but talk of fighting on Samos and in Athens is poor memory, careless drafting, or invention.

21.145 *equestrian events*: in the four-horse chariot race at the Olympics of 416.

21.146 *and so on*: Alcibiades was exiled from Athens as a result of the religious scandals of 415; his exile was one of the main factors in the disastrous defeat in 413 of the Athenian expeditionary force against Syracuse. In exile he decamped to Sparta and helped them in their military efforts against Athens, including advising on the fortification of Decelea in Athenian territory to maintain a constant siege against Athens. Eventually recalled, he achieved some successes in the east Aegean, but was again exiled in 407 as a result of a failure of a lieutenant he had left in charge of the fleet, and of suspicion that he wanted to make himself sole ruler of Athens. The capture of the fleet took place after the Athenian defeat in the battle of Aegospotami of 405.

21.147 *been passed*: whether this statement is fact or guesswork is uncertain; certainly it is disingenuous, since the blows could constitute battery. A speech wrongly attributed to the fifth-century orator Andocides (4.20–1) alleges that Taureas had tried to remove one of Alcibiades' choristers as an alien (cf. §56).

21.147 *supposed to have done*: Agatharchus was a famous fifth-century painter. Ps.-Andocides (4.17) has Alcibiades lock him up to force him to complete a commission on Alcibiades' house. The ancient commentator on our passage claims that Alcibiades caught Agatharchus having sex with his (Alcibiades') concubine, which gave him the right to kill, abuse, or imprison under Athenian laws on seduction. This may, however, be an inference from the vague statement in the present passage.

21.147 *the herms*: a very mild treatment of a notorious fifth-century scandal. Herms (*hermai*) were tetragonal columns surmounted by a head of Hermes and usually with a phallus carved on the front, dedicated to Hermes. They stood at the entrances to houses and other buildings. In 415 almost all the herms in Athens were vandalized overnight. The event shook the city and in the ensuing attempt to track down the perpetrators Alcibiades was accused of involvement; he fled to Sparta to avoid a trial. Though he probably did engage in irreligious activities, he was almost certainly innocent of the mutilation.

21.149 *for the same price*: allegations of low or even alien birth are common in political oratory, as we have already seen in speeches 18 and 19. Here, as there, the aim is less to make a substantive point than to make the target into an object of collective mockery.

21.153 *up front*: Demosthenes refers to the syndicates organized for the payment of the war levy (*eisphora*); see note on 2.29. The wealthiest members paid the sum due in advance (the term was *proeisphora*) and then collected the sums due from the rest.

21.154 *only thirty-two*: if the text is sound, Demosthenes has cut five or six years off his age (he was born in 385/4 or 384/3) to enhance the contrast between himself and Meidias.

21.155 *exemption from any other liturgies*: the scam is simple but effective. The wealthy man is selected as trierarch; he is also (in this hypothetical situation) one of the people liable for the advance payment (see note on §153). He makes the advance payment for the maintenance of the ship and simultaneously, as trierarch, contracts out the command (which is legitimate—see §80 above—but should be at his own expense), for a cumulative sum of 1 talent; he extracts this sum from the other syndicate members, who are then covering both his syndicate contribution and the costs of his avoidance of the ship command. Since a man could not be liable for two liturgies in the same year, he gets exemption from other liturgies, thus avoiding any costs for the year.

21.156 *more expensive than the former*: the men's chorus in the tribal competitions numbered fifty, while the tragic chorus numbered only fifteen.

21.156 *credit for it*: for the exchange procedure (*antidosis*), see the second note on 4.36. The point is that Meidias allegedly dodged the duty and performed it only when forced to.

21.157 *syndicate leader for ten years*: that is, one of the people charged with advance payment and collection of the war levies (§153). For Demosthenes' loss of his inheritance, see Introduction, pp. viii–ix, and speeches 27 and 28.

21.158 *Sicyon*: Sicyon was celebrated for its horses. The origin and (matched) colour indicate both ostentation and profligacy. Though lavish expenditure on public duties was considered praiseworthy, there was a strong cultural resistance to conspicuous consumption. For the Mysteries, see notes on 3.5, 21.171, and 59.21.

21.160 *a trireme, by Zeus!*: the navy was the most expensive military arm. Voluntary donations (*epidoseis*) of ships or armour over and above the expensive liturgy duties offered a way for the wealthy to demonstrate civic spirit.

21.161 *for Euboea*: that is, for the campaign of 357 to prevent Thebes from taking control of the island; see 18.99 with note. For the threat to Olynthus in 349/8 and Athenian responses, see speeches 1–3.

21.162 *Tamynae*: for the campaign in Euboea in 348, see note on 5.5.

21.166 *the hipparch*: a sarcastic sneer; Meidias had previously served as one of the hipparchs, the commanders of the cavalry (see §171).

21.166 *exemption for cavalrymen*: another sarcastic gibe. Those who bought the right to collect the 2 per cent tax (see note on §133 above) were given exemption from military service (otherwise a legal requirement for Athenian citizens) to leave them free to do their job.

21.170 *acting abusively*: for Harmodius and Aristogeiton, see the second note on 19.280.

21.171 *the Paralus*: see note on 8.29.

21.171 *purchaser of sacrificial cattle*: the administrator of the Mysteries was part of the organization of the Eleusinian Mysteries, in honour of the goddess Demeter and her daughter *Korē* (Persephone); in origin a fertility cult, it had evolved by the Archaic period into a panhellenic festival which offered its initiates the hope of a better life after death. The cattle-purchaser was needed to secure the large numbers of sacrificial beasts needed for civic sacrifices. The role of sacrificer (like that of priest, which again was often an elective office) reflects the nature of Greek worship, which was focused on correct ritual rather than orthodox belief. It was not a calling but a function.

21.173 *kept the money for himself*: an ancient commentator on this passage dates the incident to the Social War between Athens and her allies (357–355). Meidias, we are told, seized goods from merchants from non-combatant Cyzicus.

21.174 *treaty with the Thebans*: Demosthenes refers again to the campaign in Euboea in 357, when Diocles was one of the commanders. The Athenian reaction to the Theban threat was very fast (five days according to Aeschines 3.85), which may (but need not) explain why Meidias was wrongfooted.

21.182 *while in debt to the state*: the Eteoboutadae were an aristocratic clan which traditionally supplied the priestess of Athena Polias (Athena of the City/Citadel). The lineage is mentioned as a potential mitigating factor not available in Meidias' case. State debtors were deprived of their political rights until the debt was paid. Jury service was confined to citizens and exercise of the right while barred was an offence.

21.182 *illegal proposals*: a reference to the indictment for making illegal proposals in the Assembly (*graphē paranomōn*); see introduction to speech 18. We know nothing else of Smicrus or Sciton.

21.184 *others as well*: this and the following section repeat and expand the idea in §101. It has been suggested that we may have the pre-delivery text, containing options between which Demosthenes would choose in performance.

21.193 *and the like*: Meidias means that the people voting were liable to loss of citizen rights for failure to perform their military duties (punishable by disfranchisement) and that the Assembly contained an admixture of people exercising citizen rights fraudulently. The 'dancers' are performers in the festival choruses; the allegation (if it is what Meidias had said) is presumably that these are people who had used service in the chorus to avoid military duty (see note on §15).

21.197 *expedition to Olynthus*: a continuation of the campaign of 348, already brought up in §§132–4.

21.197 *stayed at home*: to counter the anticipated attempt by Meidias to undermine the significance of the Assembly vote in the *probolē* hearing by criticizing its make-up, Demosthenes imagines an audience made up both of those who served and those who didn't, and seeks to alienate Meidias from both.

21.205 *between him and me*: it is disingenuous of Demosthenes to claim that there was no enmity between Eubulus and himself. Eubulus headed the leading faction, which favoured a cautious defensive policy and the avoidance of distant adventures, and Demosthenes had been harrying them aggressively over Olynthus.

21.211 *this favour*: it is common for issues of character, including public service, to be raised in Athenian trials. Speakers don't usually request a verdict as a favour; but there is an underlying assumption that good civic behaviour merits gratitude and that the civic benefactions of witnesses and supporting speakers will rub off on the litigant. Here Demosthenes counters by presenting such ploys as a blunt appeal to the jurors to break their oath to judge according to the laws.

21.218 *returning the crowns*: for Aristophon, see the first note on 19.291. The case here is obscure, but it seems that he either had in his possession crowns used in or intended for a religious festival, or was meant to supply them.

21.223 *or whatever*: the size of the jury panel reflected the nature of the case. For private cases the jury panel was 201 or 401 depending on the sum at issue. For public cases the panel started at 501 and increased in units of 500.

21.226 *from me*: presumably this happened on a subsequent day of the festival at which Meidias assaulted Demosthenes.

23. AGAINST ARISTOCRATES

23.1 *yet again*: after accepting Athens' claim to the area in 357, Cersobleptes had reneged, only to accept once more in 352.

23.4 *your trusted politicians*: since the speaker has prosecuted at least one case in the past, he cannot be a complete political novice. But his presentation of himself as politically inactive would make no sense if he had a high profile in public life. A public prosecution was a demanding task (and risky, since it might provoke retaliation in kind), and not one to be taken lightly by a novice. The natural conclusion is that he is a frontman acting for and supported by a political faction.

23.5 *in the Hellespont*: during the campaign of Cephisodotus in 360–359.

23.8 *When Cotys died*: Cotys was assassinated in 358.

23.9 *Cersobleptes the sole ruler*: Cersobleptes was later to become an object of sympathy for Athenians opposed to Macedon after his exclusion from the Peace of Philocrates in 346 and eventual reduction to vassal status by Philip. For much of the time from his accession, however, he was an obstacle to Athenian ambitions in the north and so his name here is toxic. He has a bad press in Demosthenes. But squeezed between his Thracian rivals and Athenian (then Macedonian) expansion, he was as flexible as he needed to be.

23.10 *Athenodorus*: an Athenian condottiere in the north, perhaps from a family of cleruchs. The pattern of forming marriage alliances with the local rulers is a common one with Greek condottieri in the region. The Thracian Greek condottieri Simon and Bianor, mentioned shortly, are further examples.

23.14 *Amphipolis back for you*: for the Athenian obsession with Amphipolis, lost to Philip in 357, see note on 19.22.

23.18 *three points*: a clever exercise in contrived extemporaneity. If the audience do react, they will not all shout the same thing, leaving the speaker free to pursue the order he intended all along.

23.28 *in the table*: Greek *axōn*, literally 'axle', the standard term for the objects on which Dracon's homicide laws were inscribed, probably rotating blocks made of wood.

23.31 *from the Assembly*: the penalty for unintentional killing was exile; though the penalty for intentional killing was death, it was open to the defendant to withdraw into exile unimpeded after his first speech. See §69. The Assembly arrest must relate to a person in voluntary or judicially imposed exile for homicide who returned illegally.

23.38 *Amphictyonic games and rites*: the border markets define the extent of Athenian territory from which the exiled murderer was barred. The extension of the excluded area to panhellenic rites and games barred him further from all ritual activity which might include Athenians.

23.43 *polluted people*: murder rendered a man unclean; it was dangerous to be in the company of such a person, since in Greek belief pollution could be transmitted by contact like an invisible contagion. This in turn made a man vulnerable to hostile action from the gods, who were more prone to recognize states and actions than intentions.

23.46 *where his victim lived*: Demosthenes treats this clause as forbidding both the seizure of property abroad and kidnapping the killer for rendition in Attica. Though this suits his purpose, since he is arguing against the seizure clause in Aristocrates' decree, the clause seems rather to mean simply that a homicide exiled for involuntary homicide could not have his property plundered in his place of exile, any more than his property could be plundered in Athens. It prevented the victim's family—or just an opportunist—from taking advantage of an exile's vulnerability to rob him. Demosthenes is right, however, to the extent that Aristocrates' decree (if accurately presented here) eradicates the differences between voluntary and involuntary killing and the protections accorded in the latter case.

23.51 *where they are forbidden*: the procedure is *endeixis*, one of a number of 'self-help' procedures (i.e. involving direct intervention by the initiator) allowed in Athenian law. It was available especially against those who illicitly exercised a right, including for the homicide presence in public places from which he was barred. It has been argued plausibly that this procedure often formed the first stage prior to seizure or summary arrest (*apagōgē*) by the intervening volunteer prosecutor.

23.53 *slaying him in the road*: the later lexicographer Harpocration explains this obscure clause plausibly as conferring the right to kill an assailant attacking 'in ambush', that is, a mugger or highwayman.

23.53 *the begetting of free children*: this clause was probably in effect a dead letter by the fourth century. It presupposes a society in which bastards have considerable rights; but by the late fifth century their inheritance rights (and possibly, though this is disputed, their political rights) had been dramatically reduced. In addition most concubines (*pallakai*, formally acknowledged mistresses) will have been non-Athenian females, whose children under Athenian law by Demosthenes' time did not have citizen rights; homicide in protection of such a relationship, though perhaps still legal, would not attract an empathetic response from a jury.

23.63 *the litigants' oaths*: oaths were unusually prominent in homicide cases. The litigants both swore at the beginning (that the accusation was/was not true) and that they would keep to the issue; the winning litigant swore at the end that he had spoken the truth. In addition all witnesses had to swear to the guilt or innocence of the accused.

23.63 *homicide cases*: as the speaker narrates at length in what follows, unlike other charges, which had a single court designated, homicide cases were allocated to courts according to a number of factors relating to the status of those involved and the nature of the accusation or defence. Cases of voluntary homicide (together with wounding, arson, and poisoning) went to the Areopagus. Involuntary homicide of citizens and any homicide of a slave or a foreigner went to the Palladium, together with cases of *bouleusis* (indirectly bringing about, literally 'planning', a death). The Delphinium tried cases in which the accused admitted killing, but claimed that it was allowed under the law. The court 'in Phreatto' tried cases in which a person exiled for involuntary homicide was subsequently charged with voluntary homicide, and the Prytaneum tried cases where the perpetrator was unknown or where the killer was an inanimate object or an animal.

23.66 *Orestes*: in a society where antiquity confers authority, it is an important part of the standing of the Areopagus that its origins could be traced to mythic times. When Halirrhothius, the son of Poseidon, raped the daughter of Ares, Ares killed him and was then tried for murder by the gods and acquitted on the Areopagus. Another foundation myth, dramatized by Aeschylus in *Eumenides*, has Orestes stand trial on the Areopagus for the murder of his mother Clytemnestra in revenge for her killing of his father Agamemnon. Demosthenes below (§74) makes the trial of Orestes on the Areopagus the justification (though not the occasion) for the creation of the Delphinium.

23.66 *homicide cases*: broadly true, though the statement conceals as much as it reveals, since the Areopagus had once played a major political role in Athens as an aristocratic council, before it was stripped of most of its powers and reduced to a homicide court in the 460s in the reforms which led to the creation of the radical democracy. Statements about the Areopagus in the orators are almost invariably positive.

23.67 *the right of sycophancy*: that is, harassing his killers with the threat of prosecution.

23.69 *the authority to stop him*: the right to withdraw after the first speech (presumably if the prospect of acquittal looks bad) is especially significant in cases of voluntary homicide, where the penalty was death with confiscation of property. It reflects the antiquity of the laws in question, which emerged in a period when the duty to pursue lay primarily on the family and the interest of the state lay mainly in removing potential discord and, more importantly, possible pollution. Such withdrawal also gave the defendant the chance to take himself off into exile: see notes on 21.43 and 23.31.

23.71 *the Palladium*: the name suggests proximity to a shrine of Pallas Athena, the patron goddess of Athens. The historian Cleidemus (fr. 18) located it on Ardettus Hill near the modern Olympic stadium. See further note on 59.9.

23.72 *undergoing purification*: pardon by the surviving kin applied only in cases of involuntary homicide (in the case of voluntary killing only the victim could pardon, before expiring); the fragmentary text of the Draconian homicide law re-inscribed in the last decade of the fifth century makes explicit what this passage implies, that unanimous pardon from all kin was required. The relatives' forgiveness ended the exile but, since killing incurred pollution, the killer also needed to be cleansed. This usually involved being sprinkled with the blood of a sacrificial victim.

23.74 *the Delphinium*: dedicated to the twins Apollo Delphinios and Artemis Delphinia, this temple was outside the city walls, ESE of the Acropolis.

23.76 *by the Prytaneum*: in the old Agora at the east end of the Acropolis. The court probably had primarily a ritual role, to ensure that pollution was removed as far as possible; in the case of inanimate objects, we know that they were cast beyond the borders of Attica.

23.78 *for the earlier murder*: the court 'in Phreatto' was probably located at Zea in Piraeus. Cases coming before this court must have been few. Despite the risk, the incentive for a man exiled for involuntary homicide to return to face trial on a (separate) charge of voluntary killing was that if acquitted he could subsequently take advantage of any offer of pardon from the kin of his original victim. Since a returning homicide could be killed without punishment, a mechanism was needed to keep the accused technically off Athenian soil.

23.80 *a fifth of the votes*: the procedure is *apagōgē phonou*, summary arrest for homicide. Technically the charge is not homicide, but breaching the exclusions imposed on anyone accused of killing (the Agora, the temples, ritual contact with others). As with other public actions, it was open to anyone to pursue, though with the usual penalty of 1,000 drachmas and loss of the right to bring a similar action again that fell on anyone pursuing a public action who failed to follow through on the prosecution or to obtain 20 per cent of the votes cast.

23.83 *give up the killers*: the procedure of *androlepsia / androlepsion* (literally 'seizing of men') relates to the homicide of an Athenian citizen committed abroad; the hostage-taking (presumably of citizens of the relevant state found in Athens) is intended to compel the surrender of the alleged perpetrator to Athens. Our sources give conflicting accounts of the identity of the hostages, making them citizens either of the city where the killing took place or of the city where the murderer resides. Demosthenes chooses the former, since it suits his purpose to oppose Aristocrates' decree to universal practice. The latter, however, makes more sense in practical terms. It is possible that the law did not specify, allowing for both.

23.86 *in a law*: in the fifth century the Athenians made no practical distinction between laws and decrees. But from the restoration of democracy in 403 laws, affecting the entire citizen body, took precedence over decrees, relevant to individuals or less than the entire citizen body (see §87). In practice decrees affecting individuals (usually awarding honours) were common. The ice under Demosthenes' feet is thin here.

23.89 *killed an Athenian*: the flaw here is that this clause can only apply to a non-citizen, while Charidemus had already been granted citizenship, as the speaker goes on to note.

23.92 *after a year*: that is, since a preliminary vote from the Council lapses after one year unless ratified by the Assembly, the interval between the vote and the trial (evidently at least a year) means that the measure has anyway lapsed. Aristocrates' claim, if real, is weak. The decree had been challenged while still active. The argument, if allowed, would allow any proposer of a Council decree to filibuster until a year had elapsed.

23.97 *the deceivers*: see note on 18.282.

23.104 *the treasury there*: Miltocythes was a Thracian general who revolted against the Thracian king Cotys (father of Cersobleptes) in 363. For the Sacred Mountain see note on 9.15.

23.107 *those Olynthians*: for Potidaea and Olynthus, see note on 1.9. At this date (352/1) Demosthenes could still see Olynthus as intelligently exploiting Philip; despite the contemporary *First Philippic* (speech 4), Philip is not yet for Demosthenes the unique threat to freedom he was later to become.

23.107 *to us*: that is, Cersobleptes acknowledged the reality on the ground after Chares retook Sestus for Athens in 353/2. See also note on §1.

23.110 *when addressing the Assembly*: presumably the same speech mentioned in §13, which induced the Athenians to elect Charidemus as general.

23.111 *from their land*: Demosthenes is misremembering or inventing. Philip's father, Amyntas III, was *restored* to power by the Aleuadae of Larisa in Thessaly, when he had been driven from Macedonia by the Illyrians in the late 390s.

23.115 *Timomachus*: one of the many Athenian commanders in the north; see note on 19.180. Presumably the first letter mentioned was conciliatory, the second belligerent, reflecting the way in which the attitude and behaviour of the Thracian kings change with circumstances.

23.116 *demanded from the Spartans*: Philocrates served as general in 390, during the Corinthian War against Sparta.

23.120 *high-handed insolence*: Alexander of Pherae in Thessaly came to power in 370. His attempts to gain control of Thessaly brought him into conflict both with Macedon and with Thebes. He captured the celebrated Theban general Pelopidas when Pelopidas went to Pherae as an envoy in 368. The late 360s saw him threatening Athenian interests in the Aegean with naval raids and even attacking Piraeus.

23.121 *Argaeus*: a claimant to the throne of Macedon who ruled for two years in the 380s during the second exile of Amyntas III. When Philip became king in 359, the Athenians gave military support to Argaeus' attempt to seize power, but were induced to abandon him by conciliatory gestures about Amphipolis by Philip.

23.124 *Menestratus . . . Phayllus of Phocis*: Menestratus was evidently tyrant of Eretria at this point; by the early 340s he had been eclipsed by another, Plutarch. Phayllus, with his brother Onomarchus, was one of the Phocian leaders in the Third Sacred War.

23.129 *as Cersobleptes is to Charidemus*: that is, son-in-law.

23.130 *than any man on earth*: Iphicrates seems to have remained in Cotys' service until the late 360s. Despite his military actions against Athens he was subsequently given Athenian commands in the Social War of 357–355.

23.140 *however he liked*: in a series of treaties with Persia in 412/11 Sparta acknowledged the Persian claim to the Greek cities of western Asia (which had belonged to the Athenian empire) in return for funding which eventually allowed them to defeat Athens in the Peloponnesian War. The parallel exaggerates the threat posed by Cersobleptes, but has a powerful emotional appeal.

23.141 *for Ariobarzanes' sake*: Ariobarzanes was the acting Persian satrap (governor) of Hellespontine Phrygia, who in 367 joined a widespread revolt against the king. He was supported by Athens but was betrayed and crucified in 360. Philiscus of Abydus was in the service of Ariobarzanes (Demosthenes calls him vice-governor below). He had been sent to Greece in 368 to broker a peace between the warring factions; when the attempt failed he used his (large) financial resources to support Sparta.

23.143 *the highest honours*: for the 'tyrant-slayers', Harmodius and Aristogeiton, see the second note on 19.280.

23.149 *stopped us taking Amphipolis*: the incident belongs to the early 360s. Details are obscure, but Harpalus is a Macedonian name and it has been suggested that the hostages had been given to Macedon to secure a treaty, and were then given to Iphicrates when some of the Macedonians changed sides. Athens notoriously failed to pay its mercenaries and it has also been suggested that this was the root cause of Charidemus' action. It is unlikely that the incident was as critical as Demosthenes suggests, since Athenian attempts to regain Amphipolis were generally unsuccessful.

23.150 *at the time*: to defend itself against Athenian attempts to reassert control Amphipolis allied itself with the Chalcidian League headed by Olynthus in 365 and accepted an Olynthian garrison.

23.153 *Cephisodotus*: a senior Athenian politician and general.

23.154 *paymasters*: hereditary satrap of Hellespontine Phrygia, Artabazus was originally sent to suppress the satraps' revolt but changed sides. Autophradates was satrap of Lydia.

23.158 *in Cotys' hands*: captured in 360. Sestus and Abydus face each other at the narrowest point of the Hellespont.

23.162 *would have done*: for the piratical raids of Alexander of Pherae, see note on §120.

23.167 *put to death*: evidently at the penalty stage (see Introduction, p. xvi) the prosecution favoured death and Cephisodotus proposed a (very heavy) fine.

23.171 *only one ship*: that is, Chabrias went to negotiate, not to fight, presumably in response to the promising noises from Athenodorus. The date was 358/7.

23.175 *made later*: this is the pact of §170, made in 358 with Athenodorus, not one of the sequence of three agreements with Athens (in the persons respectively of Cephisodotus, Chabrias, and Chares).

23.176 *over to you*: Iphiades was a leading citizen of Sestus; his son was held by Charidemus as a hostage.

23.177 *excise duties to be his*: 'excise duties' in Greek is *dekatē*, '10 per cent tax', a levy on shipping passing between the Aegean and the Black Sea on the vital grain route to and from the Crimea, made possible by control of the strait.

23.181 *stole it from you*: that is, minus the loaded language, Cardia was exempted from the territory ceded to Athens by Cersobleptes in the treaty of 352. Its position at the isthmus made it an ideal location for control of access to the peninsula.

23.183 *Pammenes*: Philip sought leave to escort the Theban general Pammenes with a force of 5,000, on his way to support Artabazus in the satraps' revolt, probably in 354/3. Amadocus, who controlled western Thrace, was in a position to block him.

23.189 *Archebius of Byzantium*: according to 22.60, Archebius handed control of Byzantium to the Athenian general Thrasybulus in 390. He would now be advanced in years; but in a world without a retirement age political careers could be long.

23.198 *the battle of Naxos*: at the battle of Lechaeum in 391 during the Corinthian War Iphicrates destroyed a Spartan battalion (*mora*) of heavy-armed hoplites using light-armed troops. The other two engagements belong to the early successes of the Second Athenian League. Chabrias defeated a Peloponnesian fleet at Naxos in 376; Timotheus brought Corcyra under Athenian control during a successful naval campaign in the west in 375.

23.199 *enough of an honour*: Eion, a Persian stronghold on the river Strymon in Thrace, was finally captured in 476/5 by the Delian League in the long counter-offensive after the Persian War which resulted in the fifth-century Athenian empire.

23.200 *made him a citizen*: Demosthenes is confused about names: the Macedonian king at the time in question was Alexander I ('the Philhellene'), and according to Herodotus (9.89.4), it was the Thracians who cut down the retreating Persians. But by the mid-fifth century the Macedonians were reshaping their past as Persian vassals and by the mid-fourth were claiming to have participated in the hostilities after Plataea (ps.-Demosthenes 12.21). Demosthenes finds it convenient to accept the Macedonian claim, since he is attacking a Thracian king; he would not have accepted this narrative a few years later, once he had recognized Macedon as an unprecedented menace to freedom.

23.202 *men of the worst sort*: for honours to Ariobarzanes and Philiscus, see §141. Agavus is otherwise unknown.

23.202 *shrink from mentioning*: Phrasierides is probably the man who turns up as an agent of Timotheus at ps.-Demosthenes 49.8 and appears as a trierarch in ps.-Demosthenes 50; Polysthenes is otherwise unknown. Both are presumably military allies of Timotheus. For Timotheus, see notes on 2.14, 8.74, and 23.198.

23.205 *sent him into exile*: Themistocles was ostracized (subjected to ten-year exile by popular vote) in the late 470s. While in exile he was recalled to stand trial for conspiracy with Persia ('medizing'). Rather than face a trial he fled to the Persian court.

23.205 *condemning him to death*: in 462 on his return from campaigning in the north-east Aegean Cimon was tried for allegedly accepting a bribe from Alexander I of Macedon, but not for 'altering the constitution'.

23.206 *twenty-five drachmas*: a ludicrously small fine for a major political offence (equivalent to about ten days' pay for an unskilled labourer).

23.209 *when he died*: for Aristeides, see note on 3.21.

23.211 *tax on resident aliens*: resident aliens ('metics') in many Greek cities were liable to a tax. In Athens, they paid a poll-tax of 1 drachma per month for the right to reside in Attica, and were subject to significant limitations on their rights relative to citizens (in particular they could not marry citizens or own land in Attica). Exemption from the tax was one of the honours which might be granted to non-citizen benefactors.

23.212 *made him a Spartan*: Hermon was the helmsman of the Spartan general Lysander at the battle of Aegospotami in 405. He was famous enough to feature in the commemorative statue later seen by Pausanias (9.7.6) at Delphi.

23.213 *Cynosarges*: marriages between citizens and non-citizens were forbidden by law in classical Athens (see 59.16). The offspring of such relationships were therefore bastards. Cynosarges was an Athenian suburb with a shrine of Heracles to which a gymnasium was attached. Its association with the offspring of mixed-race partnerships reflects Heracles' status as the son of Zeus by a mortal mother.

59. APOLLODORUS: AGAINST NEAERA

59.1 *in self-defence*: the line is an iambic trimeter, and may be either a quotation from a verse text or a proverb.

59.2 *approved of the decision*: for Pasion, see introduction to speech 36.

59.2 *really should share everything*: alludes to a proverb, 'friends share their possessions'.

59.3 *the customary oath*: all officials in Athens were subject to an assessment (*dokimasia*) of their qualifications for office before assuming their duties. Council members swore an oath which included a commitment to serve in the best interests of the Athenian people.

59.3 *involved in a war*: refers to the double crises in Euboea and Olynthus. For the Euboean campaign of 348 which culminated in Tamynae, see note on 5.5. For Olynthus, see Introduction, p. xi, and speeches 1–3.

59.4 *a preliminary motion*: a *probouleuma* from the Council was necessary to get an item on to the agenda for the Assembly.

59.4 *their own*: Apollodorus, like Demosthenes (see notes on 1.19–20), tried to divert the state money going into Theoric Fund for military use. The legal situation is unlikely to be as simple as suggested here, since Apollodorus was successfully prosecuted. It may be that the law was not entirely clear, that is, that there was a provision for the money to go to the military exchequer in times of war, but there was also legislation in place allocating the surplus revenue to the Theoric Fund without further specification. If the law was unclear, the sensible course (the one chosen by Demosthenes; see note on 3.11) was to use Athenian legislative mechanisms to clarify the law, rather than to ask the Assembly to choose, as Apollodorus did.

59.5 *indicted the decree as illegal*: for the action for illegal legislation (*graphē paranomōn*), see introduction to speech 18.

59.7 *thirty talents*: though the Athenians, like other Greeks, used a lunar calendar, the civic calendar was decimal, divided into ten 'prytanies' (*prytaneiai*). Failure to pay a debt to the state by the ninth prytany led to a doubling of the debt. Anyone listed in the state register as a public debtor lost his political rights (as did his heirs on his death) until the debt was repaid. The 'inventory' mentioned here is a legal action against people holding assets belonging to or due to the state. The prosecutor made up an inventory (*apographē*) of the property to be seized and sold, and presented a case to a court; in return he received a substantial portion of the proceeds of the sale, the rest going to the state. A debt on this scale would beggar almost any Athenian; but Theomnestus exaggerates Apollodorus' inability to pay, since it has been calculated that his inheritance was over 43 talents. Though he was a profligate spender (see speech 36), he must have had much more than 3 talents left.

59.9 *the Palladium for murder*: see 23.63 and 23.71. The Palladium tried cases of involuntary killing of a citizen and all cases of killing of a metic (resident alien), slave, or foreigner. The reference to Cyreneans suggests that the dead woman was a non-citizen.

59.10 *Cephisophon and Apollophanes*: for Cephisophon, see notes on 18.75 and 19.293. Apollophanes is otherwise unknown.

59.13 *cheaper from Stephanus*: the exaggeration (the means allegedly used to sneak Neaera into the citizen body could not be replicated on a large scale) appeals to the Athenian jealousy of the privileges of citizenship, which was given only for major benefactions to the state.

59.14 *in this trial*: for the role of the *synēgoros* see the first note on 36.1. Apollodorus lets slip in §121 that he is the real prosecutor and Theomnestus a straw man. The penalties for conspicuous failure in public actions could cause problems for an active politician like Apollodorus, who needed the courts for political prosecutions; so a front-man would be useful.

59.20 *enough water remaining*: for the water-clock (*klepsydra*), see p. xv and note on 18.139.

59.21 *the Mysteries*: Lysias is the famous speechwriter. The Mysteries at Eleusis in honour of Demeter and her daughter *Korē*/Persephone were celebrated in (our) September. Though the early stages in the prolonged initiation process were public, the final rites were secret and could only be divulged to another initiate. The cult promised its celebrants a better life after death. Initiation was open to slaves as well as free. See also notes on 3.5 and 21.171.

59.24 *a courtesan*: in a society which sought to protect the family reputation and bloodline by keeping its female members (at least at the upper end of the socio-economic scale) out of contact with males outside the kinship group, it was considered improper for a respectable woman to dine in male company. Females at large parties were usually prostitutes or entertainers, categories which could overlap.

59.27 *rescuing the Spartans*: see note on 18.98.

59.27 *every prytany*: taxes in Athens were not collected by officials, but by private contractors ('tax farmers') who purchased at auction the right to collect and made their profit from the difference between price paid and revenue. Xenocleides had contracted for the 2 per cent tax on imports and exports. Anyone having to pay instalments every prytany would have to be in Athens continually and so could not be absent for a campaign.

59.28 *subpoena him*: it was up to the litigant to secure his witnesses. Anyone asked to give evidence at an Athenian trial could either agree to the deposition submitted to the court by the litigant or decline to testify on the ground that he was not present and knew nothing of the matter. If he refused both courses the litigant could use the procedure of *klēteusis* (here translated 'subpoena'), which seems to have involved a proclamation by the herald demanding his testimony, and a fine of 1,000 drachmas for non-compliance.

59.33 *the archonship of Socratides*: 374/3. For Chabrias see note on 21.64.

59.33 *at Colias*: a headland at the southern end of the Bay of Phalerum.

59.35 *second war with Sparta*: Athens was at war with Sparta after the attempted seizure of Piraeus by the Spartan Sphodrias in 378. After a brief interval of peace in 374 hostilities resumed until 371. It is the latter period that is meant here.

59.37 *the Thebans and the Spartans*: at the peace conference in 371 Athens and Sparta clashed with Thebes over the autonomy of the cities of Boeotia and Thebes was excluded from the peace. A Spartan force invaded Boeotia and was defeated at Leuctra.

59.38 *make them Athenian citizens*: the speech deals only very vaguely with the children. §§118–25 represent the four offspring as Neaera's children by Stephanus, while here three of them are already born before she begins her permanent relationship with him. The vagueness makes one suspect that the case is weak on this point and that Stephanus is right to maintain (§119) that the children are his by an Athenian wife and that Neaera was only his mistress.

59.39 *seven mnas*: a relatively small price/value by Athenian standards. The figure is given to make the following account of Stephanus' use of Neaera to generate cash plausible.

59.40 *the Polemarch*: Phrynion is clearly bluffing to intimidate Neaera. He may be claiming her as his slave on the grounds of failure to repay the money he had contributed to the purchase of her freedom. But it is equally possible that he has no legal ground to offer and is simply taking advantage of her vulnerable position as an ex-slave freed in Corinth in a world where such acts (like much else) were generally witnessed rather than documented. Stephanus is following the standard procedure when someone is wrongly seized as a slave, which is to block the act and post bail for the appearance of the person seized before the Polemarch, the official who received cases involving metics (resident aliens).

59.41 *a great deal of money*: Athenian law granted rights of self-help against a man caught seducing a free woman. The woman's guardian could kill the perpetrator (in the case of certain female relatives, including a daughter), hold him to ransom, subject him to physical abuse, or bring a public indictment of seduction (*graphē moicheias*), whose penalty is unknown. The Greek term for the perpetrator is *moichos*, 'seducer'.

59.43 *I shall tell you . . . too*: the promise is never carried out. Like the similar promise in §20 it is probably a bluff designed to create the illusion of greater knowledge (and stronger factual base) than he actually possessed.

59.45 *their arbitration*: a case of voluntary private arbitration by friends and associates, as 36.16, not formal arbitration before a public arbitrator, for which see note on 27.49.

59.46 *in the sanctuary*: temple precincts were commonly used for such purposes. They offered space and some (though not complete) privacy, and lent a degree of solemnity and authority to the proceedings. We do not know which sanctuary was used in this case.

59.51 *return the dowry*: a dowry was not a gift and never legally belonged to the husband, though he had the use of it during the marriage; it had to be returned with the wife in the event of dissolution of the marriage. On her death it went to her sons.

59.52 *on her behalf*: for this law, see also the note on 27.17. The Odeum (literally 'singing/concert hall') was built by Pericles adjacent to the Theatre of Dionysus on the slopes of the Acropolis. Athens had few purpose-built courts and so various public buildings had to serve this purpose in addition to their other functions.

59.52 *a member of his own family*: this law complements that cited in §16. Again its purpose is to protect the privileges of citizenship.

59.53 *as the law requires*: Apollodorus threatens to use the process of *klēteusis*. See note on §28.

59.55 *his phratry and his clan*: by 'evidence' he means the actions of Phrastor and the deme in the following narrative, where (at least as Apollodorus tells it) Phrastor hesitated when asked to confirm the child's legitimacy and with it the marital and birth status of the mother, Phano.

59.60 *given to him in marriage*: for the oath challenge, see note on 36.4. Here Phrastor is challenged to affirm the child's legitimacy on oath. The arbitrator here is a public arbitrator, unlike the private arbitrators in §45. Phrastor has brought a private suit against his clan, conceivably a suit for damages. Membership of the phratry was confined to legitimate male issue. The same applies to the clan (*genos*). Though all Athenians would belong to a phratry, not all would belong to a clan, which was a smaller and more exclusive body.

59.65 *Neaera's daughter*: Athenian law gave a man considerable powers over anyone caught having sex with female relatives under his care and protection; see §66 and note on §41.

59.67 *on the streets*: the law exempts women who are commercially available, since its purpose is to protect the family bloodline.

59.72 *taking up his post*: the archonship was the oldest magistracy in Athens. It had been very powerful, but in the classical period the job was merely administrative. Each Archon was given 4 obols a day (two-thirds of a drachma), which will not have met his expenses; so financial help would be welcome for a man of modest means. The duties of the King Archon (Greek *Basileus*, literally just 'king') were largely of a religious nature.

59.73 *representative of the city*: little is known about the duties of the wife of the King Archon (the *Basilinna*, 'queen') beyond what we are told here. The sacred marriage to the god Dionysus during the Anthesteria festival probably had a role in guaranteeing fertility, hence the element of secrecy, which was common in such rituals.

59.73 *the Reverend Women*: fourteen in number, serving for a year and selected by the King Archon to serve alongside his wife.

59.74 *autochthony*: see note on 19.261.

59.76 *just about legible*: Old Attic was replaced in Athens at the end of the fifth century by the Ionic alphabet (from Ionia on the coast of what is now Turkey), with three extra letters. Though the stone could be worn, it is more likely that the paint which was used to fill the incised letters had faded, making the inscription difficult to read.

59.76 *Anthesterion*: the Attic month corresponding roughly with the second half of January and first half of February in our calendar.

59.80 *up to the Areopagus*: at the end of their year of office the Archons became members of the Areopagus Council for life. But since Theogenes is still in post, this looks more like a specific visit to report on the conduct of the festival.

59.80 *punish . . . as they might wish*: the Areopagus Council had been the most powerful body in Athens until it was stripped of its powers in the 460s, other than acting as a court in certain restricted cases, including homicide. The present issue evidently fell outside its competence.

59.86 *for her crime*: in contrast to the punishment of the male seducer, which could include death, this may look mild. But since religion was the only context in which a woman played a public role, her exclusion from all public rites was very severe.

59.89 *at the next Assembly*: usually voting in the Assembly was by show of hands. The procedure in this case (with secret ballot and the use of urns for the votes for and against) resembles that of the courts. Together with the quorum (again not the norm) this creates a high bar for enfranchisement and exemplifies the jealousy with which the Athenians guarded citizenship rights.

59.90 *non-Athenians are allowed in*: wicker barriers controlled access to the Pnyx where the Assembly met; once those eligible to attend and vote had been admitted, non-Athenians could enter to observe proceedings.

59.91 *stripped them of it*: Peitholas was a member of the ruling house of Pherae in Thessaly who joined the Phocian cause after Philip ousted them from power in the late 350s. Apollonides had led the anti-Macedonian faction in Olynthus until he was exiled in 351. That both would be honoured in Athens is understandable. The reason for the revocation of honours is unknown. But grants of honours to foreigners followed the shifts in influence of political groups in Athens and the revocation presumably reflects struggles between Athenian political factions.

59.94 *plunder the land*: in 490, when the Persian king Darius sent a punitive expedition against Athens for aiding the revolt of the Greek cities of Ionia from Persia. The narrative which follows is unusual. Unlike most historical accounts in the orators, which rely (with some inaccuracies and deliberate distortions) on popular tradition, this draws on Thucydides' accounts of the career of the Spartan Pausanias in Book 1 of his *History* (1.128–34) and of the siege and capture of the city of Plataea in books 2–3 (2.1–6, 71–8, 3.20–4, 52–68). Opinions differ whether the departures from Thucydides reflect an alternative source or (as seems likely, since they help to support Apollodorus' laudation of Plataean loyalty) are free invention.

59.95 *when Xerxes invaded Greece*: in 480, to avenge the defeat of Darius' expedition.

59.98 *towards the victory*: the inscription and re-inscription are fact. In Thucydides the Spartans themselves take offence and cause the inscription to be changed.

59.98 *in peacetime*: the incident opens Thucydides' account of the outbreak of war at the beginning of Book 2. The unprovoked attack in peacetime (and its failure) is fact. Thucydides has the Thebans, inveterate enemies of Plataea, initiate it.

59.99 *one of the Boeotarchs*: the Boeotarchs ('Boeotian commanders') were officials of the pro-Theban Boeotian League. Eurymachus is not a Boeotarch in Thucydides, merely a powerful Theban.

59.101 *except the Argives*: Argos was Sparta's traditional rival in the Peloponnese. The events narrated here actually took place two years after the Theban surprise attack: the siege of Plataea began in 429.

59.103 *hung in the balance*: again Apollodorus jumps two years, to the Plataean breakout in 427.

59.106 *legally married*: cf. §92.

59.113 *even moderately good-looking*: Apollodorus may refer to the law on heiresses. If a man died leaving only female issue, the estate and with it the heiress (in Greek *epiklēros*, literally 'attached to an estate' or 'with an estate attached') could be claimed by her nearest male relative. In the case of poor heiresses (where there was no financial incentive to make a claim) the nearest kin had to provide a dowry, if he refused to marry her. Apollodorus would then be exaggerating the reach of this law. Alternatively the 'dowry' may be a woman's citizen status, which always places her above the non-citizen in terms of marriageability.

59.116 *violated tradition*: religious ritual must be carried out exactly according to tradition, if the gods are not to take offence. Archias was aligned in the 370s with those who favoured Sparta over Thebes in foreign policy. It is likely that his prosecution (as often with impiety trials) was politically motivated. The Hierophant (always drawn from the Eumolpid clan) was the chief priest of the cult of Demeter at Eleusis and played a central role in the Mysteries.

59.116 *the Haloa*: a women-only first-fruit ceremony conducted at Eleusis in the month of Poseideon (January/February). Though chiefly in honour of Demeter and Persephone, Dionysus was also involved and gives Apollodorus his parallel with Phano.

59.120 *the whole truth*: for challenges, see note on 36.4, and for the challenge to torture slaves, cf. 54.27.

27. FIRST SPEECH AGAINST APHOBUS, ON TRUSTEESHIP

27.1 *an end to our quarrel*: the opening is a classic. Anyone litigating against family risks alienating the jury; later rhetoricians recommended that the plaintiff, as here, should transfer the blame to the defendant. The process resisted by the guardians is private arbitration.

27.4 *fifty mnas into the household*: that is, as her dowry. See note on 59.51. Fifty mnas is a little short of one talent (= 60 mnas).

27.5 *came of age*: an Athenian male came of age at eighteen. At that point he was subjected to an interview (*dokimasia*) by his deme, membership of which allowed him access to citizen rights and responsibilities. The 70 mnas are capital to be left untouched; Therippides gets the interest to repay him for his efforts during Demosthenes' minority. Loaned out at a rate of 12 per cent per annum (reasonable for a loan on land) this would bring in close to a talent-and-a-half of income over the ten years.

27.5 *my furniture to use*: the arrangements here seem slightly shocking to the modern reader. In a patriarchal society such as Athens the arrangement by Demosthenes senior for the remarriage of his widow will have seemed considerate. Legally a woman was a minor throughout her life and under the control/protection of a male guardian (*kyrios*). This was her father or his heir, and on marriage her husband. It was for the *kyrios* to arrange the marriage. Though our figures for Athenian dowries are patchy, on any reckoning the dowries for the mother and daughter, as with the interest-free loan to Therippides, are generous, supplemented in this case by rent-free use of the house.

27.7 *the highest assessments*: that is, the syndicate for the payment of the war levy (see note on 2.29). We know little about the financial operation of the system. The 20 per cent is not his tax liability, since at §37 Demosthenes estimates the total paid from his estate as either 18 or 30 mnas, that is, 2 per cent or 3.5 per cent of the capital value. How this relates to the figure of 20 per cent (500 drachmas is 5 mnas) given here is unclear. This could be the advance payment required from the syndicate leaders (see note on 21.153), that is, up to 20 per cent of the total property value. It has also been suggested that the 20 per cent relates to the total amount due from the syndicate falling upon Demosthenes' estate. But §9 seems to present the 20 per cent as a proportion of Demosthenes' own property.

27.7 *at work . . . idle*: that is, earning or not earning income.

27.9 *knife-makers*: manufacture in ancient Athens was based on workshops manned by slaves; hence the reference to the value of the cutlers here.

27.9 *a loan of 40 mnas*: like other property, slaves could be pledged as collateral for loans. Demosthenes senior was holding the slaves pending repayment of a loan made to their owner and drawing income from their labour in the interim.

27.9 *more than 7 mnas a year*: that is, 1 per cent per month (the standard way of calculating interest) or 12 per cent per annum, giving (on 1 talent = 6,000 drachmas) 720 drachmas (7 mnas, 20 drachmas) p.a. income.

27.11 *for maritime purposes*: out on loan to a merchant; see speech 35 for such loans.

27.11 *at Pasion's bank*: for Pasion, see introduction to speech 36.

27.12 *water*: on the water-clock, see p. xv and note on 18.139.

27.14 *as a trierarch*: probably in Timotheus' expedition of 375 (see note on 23.198).

27.14 *my aunt's husband*: it seems from what immediately follows that, in the absence of support from Aphobus, Demosthenes' mother was being maintained by her brother-in-law.

27.15 *rather than lease it*: if a guardian lacked the time, expertise, or inclination to manage an orphan's estate, he had the option of leasing out the property to someone else.

27.17 *about 3 talents*: the law is cited at ps.-Demosthenes 59.52. There we are told that if a man divorces his wife without returning the dowry, he can be compelled by a suit from her *kyrios* (see the second note on §5) to pay interest of 18 per cent per annum on the unpaid dowry, which thus becomes a high-interest loan. Demosthenes' argument here, unless he is reasoning by analogy, suggests that the law more generally made the possessor of the dowry liable for maintenance.

27.19 *4 mnas less per year than the proper amount*: slaves age and so one cannot assume (as Demosthenes must) that productivity will be maintained at the same level, unless the workforce is replenished.

27.25 *heavily in debt*: the argument from the guardians appears to be that the asset was used as security for multiple debts before or after it was pledged to Demosthenes senior by Moeriades (named below). At this point we must reckon with the possibility that not all of the losses to the estate were due to conspiracy by the guardians.

27.32 *from my house*: though Demosthenes lumps together ivory and iron in his account, it is clear from §33 that he actually only has evidence for the stocks and sales of ivory.

27.34 *higher rate than they assume*: the concession is designed both to underscore Demosthenes' reasonableness and to strengthen his position by presenting the defendants' accounting as fraudulent even on the most generous evaluation of their position.

27.35 *1 drachma per mna per month*: that is, 12 per cent. The final figure is wrong; it should be about 8 talents, 4,000 drachmas.

27.38 *in debt to him*: that is, in the accounts he presented at the end of the guardianship he claimed that he had discharged debts owed by Demosthenes' father, which now fall to Demosthenes as heir to the estate.

27.42 *a man*: Therippides, as the context makes clear.

27.43 *Here's another*: Aphobus. The point here is to exploit inconsistencies in their accounts to demonstrate that they convict each other of fraud.

27.49 *the arbitrator*: most private disputes in Athens came first before a publicly appointed arbitrator, whose role was to arrange a compromise solution or, failing that, to find for one party; there was a right to contest the decision in court, which Aphobus is using, having lost the arbitration hearing.

27.49 *he received himself*: Aphobus is claiming that he made payments to the other two guardians from the money he received so that they could pay off debts allegedly left by Demosthenes' father. Demosthenes' rejoinder is that the sums still do not tally.

27.52 *no less than that*: that is, Demosthenes is claiming 30 talents (10 from each guardian) and Aphobus would only be accounting for his 10. The response is not compelling. If Aphobus could prove that he had paid any money he received to his co-guardians, Demosthenes' claims would be against them only.

27.65 *their womenfolk and children*: Demosthenes is describing not a legal provision but (possible but not inevitable) jury behaviour; it was common for defendants to bring dependants into court to remind the jurors of the impact of their verdict or of too harsh a penalty.

27.67 *the one-sixth fine of 100 mnas*: in some private cases a losing plaintiff had to pay a sum of one-sixth of the sum at issue to the defendant (possibly if he failed to get a certain proportion of the votes); Demosthenes is claiming 10 talents, which is 600 mnas.

27.67 *take pity on me*: the link to the *epōbelia* (the one-sixth fine) is obscure. Possibly Demosthenes envisages the outcome of failure on his part to pay the *epōbelia*, resulting in a suit for payment by Aphobus. Anyone seeking to recover a penalty awarded by a court could bring a *dikē exoulēs* (suit for ejectment; see note on 21.44), and if he succeeded, his opponent owed the state a sum equal to that adjudicated to the plaintiff. A debtor to the state lost his citizen rights until the debt was paid. If this is correct, the logic is strained, which is why Demosthenes hurries the point through.

28. SECOND SPEECH AGAINST APHOBUS, ON TRUSTEESHIP

28.1 *it might be risky*: for Demosthenes' maternal grandfather Gylon, politically active at the end of the fifth century, see Introduction, p. vii. Aphobus is claiming that the will did not stipulate leasing the estate (see note on 27.15), because the estate included assets of Gylon's liable to seizure in payment of the debt, and the older Demosthenes did not want to run that risk.

28.1 *a distorted account*: at the end of the arbitration hearing the arbitrator put the evidence for each side into two separate urns, which were sealed for use in the court hearing (see also 54.27). No new evidence could be introduced in the trial. Aphobus put in the testimony at the very end of the arbitration on the final day of the process to catch Demosthenes unprepared and he has saved the argument for the second speech for the same reason.

28.4 *at 500 drachmas per 25 mnas*: see the first note on 27.7.

28.4 *not to do that*: because once the state knew that the family was still well off, it would have had grounds for reclaiming Gylon's alleged debt.

28.7 *the war levy*: at 27.9 Demosthenes notes that they assessed his property at a level which confirms his figure for the total value of the estate.

28.8 *2 talents and 80 mnas:* as dowries for Demosthenes' mother and sister: 27.5.

28.12 *security for a loan*: as explained at 27.9.

28.14 *these items*: Aphobus is arguing that he did not discuss any of the estate with Demosthenes senior, but learned of the will and its contents at second hand from his fellow guardians.

28.17 *proposed the exchange*: on the exchange procedure (*antidosis*), see the second note on 4.36. Aphobus is manipulating the system by trying to have the property transferred away from Demosthenes. Since Demosthenes' claims against his guardians related to debts due to his father's estate, his right to sue for them would pass to the new owner of that estate. Their aim may have been as much to intimidate Demosthenes as genuinely to force the property exchange.

28.17 *would be exempt*: Demosthenes calls the bluff by agreeing in principle but failing to implement, so that the case has to go to court.

28.18 *the one-sixth fine*: the *epōbelia*; see the second note on 27.67.

28.19 *in his stead*: a hint that, apart from being just, a decision in his favour will benefit the state, in contrast to his opponent (§§22, 24).

28.21 *my citizenship*: see the second note on 27.67.

35. AGAINST LACRITUS

35.1 *the commercial district*: Piraeus, the seaport of Athens.

35.2 *counter-pleas*: Greek *paragraphē*, a private action designed to block litigation; the defendant in a legal action countersues the plaintiff in a separate hearing, alleging that the suit is barred on technical grounds. If he succeeds, the initial prosecution is terminated (or the plaintiff must start afresh, depending on the nature of the objection); if his plea is rejected, the original suit goes ahead. Here the technical ground for *paragraphē* is the absence of a contract between Androcles and Lacritus.

35.6 *Diophantus of Sphettus*: an Athenian politician about whom we know little; he features incidentally in speech 19 as well.

35.10 *Mende or Scione*: in Chalcidice in the north.

35.10 *the rising of Arcturus*: that is, its heliacal rising in the middle of September. The interest rates are 22.5 per cent or 30 per cent. The difference reflects the attendant risk from bad weather. Even the lower rate is almost twice the percentage of loans on land (12 per cent). When we bear in mind that the latter rates are annual, while the maritime loans are per voyage, the difference is still more dramatic.

35.11 *additional loans*: this clause protects the investment of the lenders by giving them sole claim on the surety.

35.11 *hostile forces*: the jettison clause relates to goods thrown overboard to lighten the load and save the ship in a storm; the requirement of unanimity of those on board protects the lenders against fraudulent claims by the borrowers. The other clause relates to sums exacted by any hostile forces as the price of passage. Both clauses allow room for *force majeure*.

35.13 *the rising of the Dog star*: late July to early August. The clause allows for the possibility that bad weather might prevent the ship from getting to the Black Sea at all.

35.13 *the previous year's contract*: a puzzling detail. The Athenian year began in summer, but in any eventuality envisaged in this contract the loan would be repaid in what for the Athenians (though not to us) was the next year. The assumption may be (since the loan was not time-limited, but linked to mercantile activity) that a voyage aborted in this way will be resumed in the next sailing season and that the loan will carry forward. The contract directs the borrowers to a safe port where Athenian goods are not vulnerable to seizure, for which see note on §26.

35.14 *in his keeping*: it was common for contracts to be lodged with a third party, often a banker.

35.14 *metic with citizen tax privileges*: literally, 'subject to equal tax'. See note on 23.211.

35.15 *Isocrates*: the celebrated rhetorician and educator. The mention is designed to present the defendant as a trained speaker manipulating the system unscrupulously for his own ends.

35.18 *making the arrangements for it*: the arithmetic matters. If the loan represents only half the value of the cargo, then the lenders have a much better chance of recovering their investment with interest.

35.20 *out of court*: a reference to the procedure of *ekmartyria*, absentee deposition. Hearsay evidence was prohibited in Athenian courts. To allow necessary evidence from someone ill or abroad to be admitted to court, the witness deposed to a proxy witness, who then stood liable for the testimony in court. The frequency in this speech of this procedure probably reflects the fact that many of those involved are traders and therefore may well be away from Athens.

35.26 *right of seizure against Athenians*: Greek *sylē*. If a state or its citizens had a grievance against another, it might claim or grant (by 'letter of marque') the right to seize by force their goods in reparation.

35.28 *Thieves' Cove . . . a time of your choice*: a small cove outside the formal limits of the harbour at Piraeus, suitable for evading customs duty.

35.29 *Exhibition Area*: the area in Piraeus for displaying samples of goods for sale.

35.29 *harbour dues*: there was a 2 per cent tax on imports and exports.

35.31 *Panticapaeum*: capital of the Bosporan kingdom on the north shore of the Black Sea, an important source of Athenian grain.

35.32 *Citium*: a major port in southern Cyprus.

35.34 *the defendant in the present case*: a telling detail. If the text is sound (and if the document is genuine, as seems generally to be the case in this speech), it would seem that this deposition was collected by Androcles for a suit against Apollodorus, the third brother. How this bears on the suit against Lacritus is unclear. Conceivably Apollodorus, like Artemon, is dead, leaving Lacritus as the only living target (but we would expect to have been told of his death), or he is beyond Athenian jurisdiction, or he has already been sued, successfully or unsuccessfully. Or perhaps the suit against Apollodorus was ongoing, but unlike Lacritus he cannot claim that he was no party to the contract and so has no ground for a *paragraphē*.

35.36 *100 Cyzicene staters had been saved*: at Demosthenes 34.23 we are told that a Cyzicene stater was worth 28 drachmas. Rates varied with time and location, but if we assume the same value (the same place, the Bosporus, is at issue) this is 2,800 drachmas, 200 short of the loan, but (depending how far the plaintiffs did adhere to the contract) far short of the value of the cargo; so a venture designed to recoup something by lending the money might make sense.

35.39 *undermine its authority*: probably a standard clause in such contracts, since the point is made again at ps.-Demosthenes 56.27.

35.41 *and charges fees*: we do not know enough to determine whether this is true or merely a smear by association with Isocrates. Either way, it allows him to exploit in what follows the stereotype of the sophist as the man who argues the paradox.

35.46 *hear mercantile cases*: we know from Demosthenes 33.23 that the special maritime cases (see speech introduction) were only heard for part of the Athenian year (from autumn to early spring), so that merchants would be free to sail during the best sailing months.

35.46 *also have incurred*: in a *paragraphē* case the *epōbelia* (see the second note on 27.67) unusually fell on the loser (not as in other private cases a losing plaintiff), which is why Androcles can envisage having to pay if he loses, when he is the defendant in the special plea hearing. In mercantile cases anyone owing money as a result of the hearing was held in prison (which was in Athens a holding-pen rather than a form of punishment in itself), because the large number of foreign traders involved increased the risk of absconding.

35.47 *involving mercantile contracts*: the point is that there is no other court they can use. The argument is without force. All that the mercantile suits allowed was a fast-track procedure. It would be perfectly possible to bring a normal suit for damages. In keeping with the rhetoric he gives a carefully selective account of the jurisdiction of the magistrates he lists.

35.47 *facing the death penalty*: the Eleven had charge of the prison. Thieves, muggers, and similar offenders (known collectively as *kakourgoi*, literally 'wrongdoers') were liable to summary arrest. They were taken before the Eleven and executed without trial if they confessed, otherwise committed to trial and executed if convicted.

35.48 *lack of a sponsor*: the Polemarch was the receiving magistrate for plaints against non-citizens (see also 59.40). The cases listed are the *dikē apostasiou*, brought by a former master against a freed slave who failed to comply with any conditions attached, and the *graphē aprostasiou*, brought against a resident alien who did not have a citizen sponsor as required by law.

35.51 *over whom they exercise control*: that is, minors (women and children) and slaves. Although there were strict legal limits on a woman's contractual rights, in practice we do find women lending sums considerably over the limit. Slaves engaged in retail (though again technically they lacked legal rights) and we do have evidence for slaves directly engaged in shipping, as commanders of merchant ships, or as agents on board ship.

35.51 *the ship and the grain*: refers either to another clause in the law from which this extract is excerpted, or to another related law. For the 'inventory', see note on 59.7.

35.53 *Thieves' Cove*: the allegation may be that the alleged loan was on a cargo of grain being shipped to Chios, which would have contravened Athenian law. On Thieves' Cove, see note on §28.

36. FOR PHORMION, A COUNTER-PLEA

36.1 *completely helpless*: as an ex-slave of non-Greek extraction, Phormion has (or could be represented as having) limited Greek or limited fluency. The speaker is here explaining his role as *synēgoros*, supporting speaker. It was the norm in Athens for litigants to speak for themselves (there were no professional advocates). But they could bring in supporting speakers, who in extreme circumstances might present the whole case. Phormion has spoken a few words and then passed his case to his *synēgoros*.

36.1 *abide by your oath*: that is, the oath sworn by Athenian jurors at the beginning of the year to vote (among other things, but especially) according to the laws.

36.4 *challenge*: Greek *proklēsis*. Formal challenges (always witnessed) played a significant role in Athenian legal disputes. They could be issued either prior to legal action as a means of avoiding litigation or at any point up to the court hearing. They took various forms, an offer or demand for an oath (e.g. 39.3, 59.60), for the torture of slaves to extract testimony (e.g. 54.27, 59.120), or to fulfil or accept fulfilment of an obligation (e.g. 21.78). The avowed aim is to obtain evidence or to resolve the dispute. Since they are usually offered in the confident expectation that they will be declined, the real purpose is to give the challenger a moral advantage in court. Apollodorus is among other things contesting the terms of the lease and Phormion's challenge here probably offers or demands evidence relating to the terms.

36.4 *on his own account*: that is, he had by now been freed by Pasion and was in business independently from his former master.

36.4 *the 11 talents*: Apollodorus denies that Pasion owed any money to the bank; he treats this sum as working capital handed over to Phormion with the bank and therefore money owed to Pasion's estate by the bank.

36.6 *land and housing*: only citizens could own land. Phormion as a non-citizen could not lend or foreclose on land given as security for a loan. So Pasion had to be the creditor for any such loans and stand as debtor to the bank for the equivalent amount.

36.7 *and this challenge*: this challenge figures prominently in Apollodorus' suit for false testimony (Demosthenes 45). Since Apollodorus is contesting terms of the will, Phormion challenged him to open in front of witnesses a copy of the will lodged with a third party. Apollodorus refused and this probably contributed in no small part to Phormion's success in the special plea hearing.

36.8 *Pasion's wife*: for such arrangements, see the second note on 27.5.

36.10 *released . . . from all future charges*: the point is important. One ground allowed in the law for a special plea was prior adjudication, either by a formal hearing or by formal agreement by the parties themselves.

36.13 *leased the bank*: we learn from §37 that they leased both bank and factory; only the bank is relevant here.

36.14 *their great services*: though slaves lacked legal personality and could not technically own property or make contracts, in practice we find slaves (usually belonging to the class known as 'living apart', that is, away from their owners) by the fourth century engaging in commerce, sometimes for substantial sums. In this case we seem to have slaves of Apollodorus and Pasicles working in the bank (Euphraeus is mentioned as working alongside Phormion in the bank at Demosthenes 49.44, probably from the early 360s), following the same trajectory as that of Pasion and Phormion.

36.14 *a slave-girl*: Pasion had bequeathed money to Archippe (Demosthenes 45.28) as her own possession; in addition the dowry of 1 talent which Pasion gave her when she married Phormion would naturally go to the sons of her second marriage. Apollodorus must have claimed that the property mentioned was part of Pasion's estate.

36.15 *released Phormion from further charges*: a case of private arbitration in which friends are asked to mediate a settlement. Presumably the deal was sealed with an oath in the temple. Phormion claims that these were *ex gratia* payments, and Apollodorus was a difficult enough character to induce someone to make concessions (especially his mother's widower), but it is conceivable that he was in the right on this issue.

36.18 *arbitration meeting*: not the earlier private arbitration just mentioned but the public arbitration on the current suit; see the note on 27.49 for public arbitration.

36.18 *destroyed the papers*: Pasion's accounts, which would allegedly have enabled Apollodorus to refute the will offered by Phormion and his version of the terms of the lease.

36.20 *the trustees' accounts*: their accounts of their management of the estate during the period of Pasicles' minority.

36.25 *release and discharge*: the distinction between these terms is obscure and was already the subject of discussion in antiquity. The difference may be between giving and receiving discharge on settlement. But beyond this rhetorical flourish it plays no further part in the speech.

36.26 *how much time has to pass*: in many areas of the Athenian system there was a limitation (*prothesmia*) on the time-scale for legal action, often, as in this case, five years. Failure to sue before the deadline rendered a case inadmissible and again offered ground for a special plea.

36.26 *more than twenty years*: measured from the start of the lease in 371/0, before Pasion's death, rather than its end, when Pasicles came of age. Despite the exaggeration, Apollodorus was far outside the limit of five years (see previous note).

36.28 *his former slave Satyrus*: that is, like Pasion he made arrangements for the marriage in his will.

36.31 *making a fool of yourself*: Apollodorus' own origins do not permit him to despise the ex-slave Phormion.

36.32 *charges in the future*: a wife's dowry and any personal property not otherwise disposed were inherited by her sons. In a case such as this, any legitimate sons of Archippe were entitled to an equal share in her property. The reference here to release from charges indicates that the settlement of her estate (like much in Apollodorus' life) was rancorous.

36.35 *Phormion had given them up*: §13 above.

36.37 *1 talent a year*: the 160 mnas (2 talents, 40 mnas) mentioned here is for the bank and shield factory combined while the inheritance was undivided. The rent of one talent relates to the shield factory alone (§11), on which Apollodorus received the rent after the division of the inheritance

36.38 *Phormion's gift*: the 5,000 drachmas mentioned at §15.

36.47 *kindness of these Athenians here*: the grant of citizenship. The process by which citizenship was granted is discussed in speech 59. As often in the courts, the jury is viewed as identical with the Athenian people as a whole.

36.49 *as I trust they won't be*: the point is that the supposed wealth of Phormion is in fact the money of others deposited at the bank. If Phormion loses the case and there is a run on the bank, Phormion will be ruined without any benefit to Apollodorus. In fact Phormion was a very rich man, as the speaker acknowledges at §42 in noting his liability for liturgies.

36.52 *the curses your own father wrote into it*: Pasion evidently inserted a clause cursing anyone attempting to thwart his declared wishes. It may be that such clauses were common; equally it may reflect Pasion's distrust of his firstborn.

36.53 *plenty of others*: as an active politician Apollodorus was inevitably involved in public prosecutions. The men named are all Athenian military commanders.

36.62 *read them out*: possibly the law defining the conditions for *paragraphē* or the relevant part of it. The depositions could reiterate the account of the character of the parties, but it is more likely that they reaffirm the basis of the case for dismissal on the ground that Apollodorus has given formal release from complaints.

36.62 *Pour the water away*: a bravura flourish. The reference is to the use of the water-clock to time trials and the point is that the case is so patently right that the speaker does not need the full time allowance.

39. AGAINST BOEOTUS, ON THE NAME

39.1 *the same name as me*: in Athens a man's full name consisted of his given name, his father's name, and his local deme. So both were called *Mantitheos Mantiou Thorikios*, Mantitheus of Thoricus, the son of Mantias.

39.2 *the conviction of Ninus*: for this *cause célèbre*, see note on 19.281. An ancient commentator on that passage identifies her as a priestess (perhaps of a fringe cult) prosecuted (and executed) for allegedly 'making love potions for young men'.

39.2 *deprived of his citizenship*: citizenship depended on deme membership. Mantias' refusal to acknowledge Boeotus (and then his death) blocked this. Since citizen status required Athenian parentage on both sides and Boeotus could not prove paternity, Mantias' refusal also blocked anyone else from enrolling him in the deme.

39.3 *that would be the end of it*: that is, he arranged to issue a formal challenge (for challenges, see the first note on 36.4, and for the challenge to a female to swear cf. 55.27) inviting her to swear to the boys' paternity; she agreed that she would decline the oath in return for a sum of money, but then reneged and swore; with his bluff called, Mantias had little choice (perhaps none, if, as the text implies, the challenge stipulated that the oath would be decisive) but to acknowledge paternity. The incident was notorious and is mentioned by Aristotle at *Rhetoric* 1398b.

39.4 *as 'Pamphilus'*: the reference is to enrolment in the *phratria*, 'phratry' or 'brotherhood'. The annual Apaturia was the main festival of the phratries. Boeotus' brother Pamphilus was named after his maternal grandfather, a public figure of note early in the century.

39.6 *all been mine*: Athenian law had no principle of primogeniture. All legitimate sons shared equally in the estate. Mantias' acknowledgement of Boeotus and his brother reduced Mantitheus' inheritance by two-thirds.

39.9 *my mother's name if it's me*: Mantitheus never names his own mother. It is a general rule that speakers avoid naming female relatives and other respectable women, but are more ready to name female relatives of the opponent and women of bad character (Mantitheus did not have to name Plangon here). Thucydides' Pericles famously said that 'a woman's greatest reputation is to be talked about by men as little as possible, whether for praise or blame' (2.45.2), and it may be that casual naming was felt to expose a woman to gossip or suggest that she was known to more men than was appropriate.

39.10 *judge a competition*: that is, a dramatic or choral competition. Here as elsewhere Athens relied on ordinary citizens selected by lot from those who put themselves forward.

39.12 *punishable by death*: the law in question envisages attempts to pervert the selection process by inserting two tickets with one name. Here Mantitheus stretches it to fit a case in which one of the brothers is successfully balloted, but gives the office to the other. The example is highly contrived.

39.14 *summary arrests*: Mantitheus lists some of the main public actions (that is, available to the volunteer prosecutor) which might appeal to someone wishing (as Boeotus and his associates allegedly here) to exploit the system for personal gain, as a sycophant. These are in order: *graphē* (the generic term of a public action), *phasis* (available for a variety of offences, mostly commercial, and generally involving a financial reward to the successful prosecutor), *endeixis* (in which the initiator reports an offence to a magistrate before proceeding), and *apagōgē* (see note on 23.80); for the relationship between *endeixis* and *apagōgē*, see note on 23.51.

39.15 *suit of ejectment against him*: see note on 21.44.

39.16 *serving in the army*: the penalty on conviction for failure to serve without good cause was disfranchisement. For the exemption of choristers and choral producers from military service, see 21.15. 'Pitchers' (from the drinking-vessels used) was a day in the festival of the Anthesteria (in the month Anthesterion, January/February); the Dionysia took place in Elaphebolion (March/April). The dismissive tone here ignores the need for rehearsals. For the campaign which culminated in Tamynae in 348, see note on 5.5.

39.17 *available for the law-courts*: there must have been a strain on the exchequer arising from the military operations in Euboea and Olynthus, resulting in a suspension of trials through lack of money to pay the jurors. The taxiarch was the commander of the tribe's infantry contingent; it seems from the present passage that his duties might involve presiding over cases of alleged military offences.

39.17 *witnesses to verify this*: the sealing of the jars after the arbitration; see the first note on 54.27. The battle of Tamynae obviously took place between the arbitration and the court hearing.

39.18 *being an alien*: that is, with being an alien illegally exercising citizen rights, for which the penalty was enslavement and confiscation of property.

39.20 *tenth-day ceremony*: a father was not compelled to acknowledge a child as legitimate. If he chose to do so, this was done at a family ceremony held (usually) on the tenth day after birth.

39.21 *try to block*: since Mantias would have insisted on enrolling Boeotus under that name, had he lived, the defendant is presented as inconsistent in suing to secure enrolment while rejecting the name. Boeotus would probably reply that it was the enrolment, not the name, that he had sought.

39.22 *before the arbitrator*: that is, public arbitration; see the note on 27.49.

39.22 *deny it later*: Boeotus is claiming that Mantias acknowledged him as his legitimate son in infancy, that is, that Mantias had been married to Plangon. Mantitheus maintains throughout this speech and the speech for the dowry (speech 40) that Boeotus was the son of an ill-defined clandestine relationship. Mantias' capitulation makes more sense if he was at some stage married to Plangon. A bastard did not belong to his father's family and had very limited inheritance rights.

39.23 *the boy's chorus*: choral competitions featured in a number of Athenian festivals. Competition was between the ten tribes (individually or in pairs) and involved choirs of fifty men or boys. The point is that Mantias' tribe was Acamantis, not Hippothontis, so Plangon was perhaps acknowledging that Boeotus was not Mantias' son. But the point is weakened by the fact that, since Mantias had not yet acknowledged Boeotus as his own, Boeotus could hardly have danced for Hippothontis.

39.25 *what kind of businessman my father was*: the inscription (mentioned in the introduction to this speech) recording payment of debt by Mantias' sons, may indicate that his affairs were not in good order at his death. But his sons were still wealthy enough to be liable for liturgies, to judge by Mantitheus' arguments in the present speech. The mask of filial delicacy allows Mantitheus to make the point without elaborating.

39.27 *as being the eldest son*: Mantias' father was named Mantitheus and it was common for the eldest son to bear the paternal grandfather's name.

From the evasiveness of the argument about age in what follows it seems that Boeotus may well be older than Mantitheus and the marriage to Plangon the earlier.

39.32 *as an insult and a slight*: Boeotians had a reputation for dull-wittedness. But Boeotus may be arguing that Mantias insulted him by accepting him under a name from the mother's family, thus implicitly rejecting Boeotus' right to consider himself a member of Mantias' family. For the 'slight', see §27.

39.33 *where they are not wanted*: Athenian laws gave protection to a parent's rights to food and lodging and freedom from abuse in old age with a public action (the *graphē goneōn kakōseōs*, 'indictment for maltreatment of parents'), to ensure third-party intervention to protect the vulnerable, and with disfranchisement as the penalty for offspring on conviction.

39.37 *the name 'Boeotus'*: if a party to a legal action was unable to attend a hearing before an arbitrator or jury, he could swear an oath to that effect. The arbitrator or jury could either agree to postpone or elect to hear the case anyway and give judgement by default. It was possible in the latter case for the losing party to move for a retrial (in contrast, there was no appeal against a jury vote in a normal hearing). From ps.-Demosthenes 40.16–18 we know that Boeotus subsequently took the advice given by Mantitheus here in allowing cases brought against 'Boeotus' to go by default on the ground that this was not his name.

39.39 *deregister*: the reference here is to an obscure procedure called *apokēryxis*, which otherwise we know only from later lexicographers. It seems to have involved repudiation by proclamation of a herald and (despite the implication of this passage) to have been confined either by law or cultural resistance to serious misdemeanours.

39.40 *'in accordance with your honest opinion'*: that is, in the jurors' oath; see also 23.96.

54. AGAINST CONON, FOR BATTERY

54.1 *malicious abuse*: 'malicious abuse' translates the Greek *hybris*. Though moderns often associate hybris with offences against the gods, in common parlance it was used of all kinds of insulting or humiliating behaviour against fellow humans, ranging from words to violence (including rape). In practice its legal use was probably restricted to physical abuse. The precise definition of *hybris* as a legal term is contentious. Probably it involves either the intent to humiliate or gratuitous violence which demeans the victim. The singling out of Conon's alleged cock impersonation (§9) pointedly takes us into the region of self-indulgent violence. *Hybris* was subject to a public action, the *graphē hybreos*, 'indictment for *hybris*'; the penalty was determined by the assessment process and could result in a heavy fine to the state or in theory could even be death. The highwayman/mugger (*lōpodytēs*) was subject to summary arrest and execution either on confession or on conviction by a court; see the second note on 35.47. Since for summary arrest the perpetrator had to be taken in the act, this was not a practical option in Conon's case.

54.1 *this private suit*: Ariston has brought a private action, the *dikē aikeias*, 'suit for battery'. This was an easier case than the indictment for *hybris* both to present, in that the court time was shorter, and to prove, since the case turned on the question who struck first. A point he skates over is that in a private action such as this any compensation went to the plaintiff.

54.3 *garrison duty*: Panactum was one of several border forts between Attica and Boeotia. The detail may help to date the speech, since at 19.326 Demosthenes says that during the Sacred War (356–346) no expedition to Panactum had been necessary. This might suggest a date of 357 or 343 for the incidents narrated, and 355 or 341 for the hearing. But since the present case looks like routine garrison duty rather than an expedition, 19.326 may not be relevant.

54.7 *same age-class as me*: this may be no more than an indicator of similar age; but it may suggest that they were in the same age-group for military service and so he may also have been a witness to events at Panactum.

54.7 *the Leocorium*: the Leocorium was a shrine to the daughters of the mythical king Leos, who were sacrificed to save the city from a plague. It was probably located at the north-west corner of the Agora.

54.7 *Melite*: the high ground bordering the Agora on the west.

54.7 *Sphintharus the son of Eubulus*: Conon keeps good company. This Eubulus was the leading politician in Athens from the 350s into the 340s. Since Demosthenes was from the late 350s opposed to Eubulus' policy of cautious pragmatism in foreign affairs, the appearance of his name here may point to a political motivation on Demosthenes' part in taking the case and might indicate a date in the 340s. However, the presence of Meidias at §10 complicates any attempt to trace relationships.

54.8 *Persephone's sanctuary*: probably in the south-east corner of the Agora.

54.10 *Meidias*: possibly the defendant of speech 21.

54.14 *the 'Allcocks'*: it was common from at least the late fifth century for gangs of well-heeled young men to engage in antisocial behaviour and for such gangs to give themselves defiant names. See further the first note on §39. The first of the two names here, *Ithyphalloi*, has connotations of ritual indecency inappropriate in a non-ritual context. The second, *Autolekythoi*, is more elusive. A *lekythos* was an oil flask, used after exercise and bathing. The title could be 'men who carry their own oil flasks' (i.e. which a servant should do) or 'all oil flask', which in view of the phallic shape of the *lekythos* is likely to mean something like 'all penis'. Conon is dissociating himself from the fight and arguing that it was between Ariston and his son Ctesias, whom he presents as members of rival gangs.

54.17 *something more serious*: it is unusual to have such detailed analysis of law in a private case, and would probably arouse suspicion (especially in the mouth of a young man) in a culture which embraced the principle of amateurism in legal matters; so Ariston is at pains to excuse his legal knowledge and lay the blame for it on Conon; see also §39.

54.18 *escalating to murder*: wounding in Athens was covered by a public action, the *graphē traumatos ek pronoias*, 'indictment for intentional wounding'. From this and other contexts it is clear that wounding was differentiated from battery by the use of a weapon. It is also clear that the action covered not just pre-planned injuries but also those which were committed in the heat of the moment. §25 shows that the same broad definition applied to intentional homicide. It meant that the charge could be brought if the act itself was done voluntarily, irrespective of the end willed by the perpetrator. It was enough to commit an act whose potential consequences could be foreseen.

54.26 *to the stone*: witnesses did not routinely swear an oath, but an oath could be demanded or offered, in this case allegedly to play for time. The stone mentioned was in the Agora and was used for oaths from arbitrators and witnesses (ps.-Aristotle, *Constitution of Athens* 55.5).

54.27 *prevent the sealing of the jars*: at the end of the public arbitration the arbitrator had the evidence from both sides sealed in separate jars for use in any subsequent legal hearing. No additional evidence could be used in court. Conon on this account is desperately trying to delay the sealing so that he can assemble a case.

54.27 *the torture to go ahead*: for challenges, see the first note on 36.4. The present challenge was an offer by Conon to have his slaves questioned under torture. To be admissible in court the evidence of slaves had to be extracted under torture. The agreement of both parties was required; cf. note on 19.114. Though the orators are full of such challenges to torture, and equally full of claims about the reliability of such evidence, we have no instance of such a challenge being both accepted and ultimately carried out, which suggests that in practice litigants were unwilling to risk too much on such an unpredictable process.

54.28 *heard by them*: as the tribunal for charges of intentional homicide.

54.31 *did not hit Ariston*: this passage is very important for the validation of suspect depositions which survive as documents in the orators, since it gives what appears to be the standard form. Its presence is an embarrassment for Ariston, since it gives strong support (both in number and in the mature age of his witnesses) for Conon's account (whether or not his witnesses are telling the truth), while it is unclear how much evidence Ariston has (apart from his friend Phanostratus) to the actual attack as distinct from his condition afterwards. Hence his extended and vehement demolition job on their character. The Greek of the deposition is ambiguous and could mean 'Ariston did not hit Conon'; so it is conceivable, if unprovable, that the witnesses were trying to avoid downright lies while protecting Conon.

54.36 *stop the water*: for the water-clock, see p. xv and note on 18.139. The water flow was stopped while documents (such as depositions and laws) were read out in private cases, though not in public cases.

54.37 *all their victims*: in the absence of a police force or other investigating agency it was for the individual litigants to assemble the evidence needed for their case.

54.38 *astonished to hear them*: the most common oath was to swear destruction on self, family, and bloodline, as in §41. Conon's oath may be little more shocking than this. Though Ariston does not say so, it seems that Conon issued a challenge offering to swear an oath to the truth of his account.

54.39 *the 'Triballians'*: the name of a Thracian tribe; Thracians were viewed as wild and brutal and the name (like those in §14 above) is designed to flout convention, like the 'Mohocks' who terrorized London early in the eighteenth century.

54.39 *for dinner*: the feasts left for the goddess Hecate at the crossroads were sacred to the gods below. Most public meetings in Athens began with a purificatory sacrifice to make the space ritually clean. The victim itself became unclean. Either of these acts would shock and frighten the average pious Athenian. Ostentatious contempt for religion of this sort was also associated with elite gangs, most notoriously the 'Bad Luck Club' of the early fourth century, which made a point of dining on days of ill-omen.

54.40 *Read the challenge, please*: Ariston meets Conon's challenge with a counter-challenge to nullify any rhetorical advantage, rather like playing poker.

55. REPLY TO CALLICLES, ON DAMAGE TO A FARM

55.2 *by the arbitrator*: that is, the arbitrator found against the speaker in his absence. See note on 39.37 for judgement by default, and on 27.49 for public arbitration.

55.2 *to proceed against me*: it has been suggested that the brothers were co-owners of their land. All legitimate sons had an equal share in an inheritance, but they might choose not to divide it up, for personal or economic reasons. Since a jury's verdict ruled out bringing the same action again against the same person, the separate suits allow them to pursue the case more than once without having the suit barred.

55.9 *knew the facts*: that is, private arbitration in contrast to the formal public process in §2.

55.10 *on to the road*: the road was undrained, probably a dirt track, and served also as a watercourse.

55.17 *passed his farm!*: the speaker's farm obviously has a long frontage, extending beyond that of Callicles to run parallel to that of Callicles' neighbour further down the hill. It may have been a substantial holding.

55.19 *domestic drainage*: in a city street, each house's drain ran out of the courtyard and flowed down a gutter in the centre of the street, where it was
joined by water draining from houses further down the street. Similarly
(and this still happens in certain parts of Greece) farms may be watered by
channelling water from a stream on to each successive farm down a slope.

55.24 *paid their mother a visit*: a very revealing detail, suggesting that women
had considerably more freedom of movement than many of our sources
might appear to suggest.

55.27 *the depositions and the challenge*: for challenges, here a demand that Callicles' mother swear an oath, see the first note on 36.4. For the oath
administered to a female, cf. 39.3. Women could not appear in court, and
their witness testimony (including this oath if the challenge had been
accepted), if needed, was given by their male guardian. Oath challenges
offered a useful means of giving weight to women's evidence.

55.28 *in Eleusis or elsewhere*: the plain near Eleusis was (and to some extent
still is) subject to occasional flooding in the wet season from the river
Cephisus, which flows to the sea near by.

55.31 *identical suit against Callarus*: it is difficult to reconstruct the background
in detail. Callicles' cousin presumably claims to have a contract of sale,
or a loan on the security of the speaker's farm, which entitles him to
ownership. The allegation against Callarus seems to be that he oversaw
the building of (or built) the wall. It allows them further possibilities for
litigation on the same complaint without facing a demurrer (*paragraphē*;
see note on 35.2). Where an offence was committed by a slave on the
instructions of the master, the suit was brought against the master.
Where the slave acted on his own initiative, the slave was named in the
charge, but any financial penalty fell upon the master, who would also
(since a slave lacked legal personality) present the case in court.

55.32 *award the land to them*: this must be private arbitration, since litigants
did not get to choose the arbitrator in a case that went to public arbitration; and there was always an appeal to the courts from a public arbitrator. The reference to loss of the farm is puzzling. It has been suggested
that forfeiture of the property to the alleged victim might be part of the
penalty in a case such as this. The text, however, is explicit that the case
has a fixed penalty of 1,000 drachmas. What seems to be envisaged is
adjudication of the farm as compensation for substantial damages or
a negotiated settlement involving surrender of the property.

55.35 *the customary oath*: that is, the speaker issued a challenge offering to
swear an oath, presumably to the effect that his father built the wall.
Here the motif is neatly tied to a reference to the oath sworn by the
jurors in an attempt to align their sympathy with the speaker. The ending is abrupt but not unparalleled. Rhetorical handbooks recommended
skipping a formal epilogue where the issues are uncomplicated, and
Demosthenes may have felt that a formal ending would not sit well in
the mouth of someone claiming to be a youth unschooled in disputes.

TEXTUAL NOTES

5.24 Reading <οὐδ'> ὁτιοῦν (Cobet).

18.29 The text of the decree that occupies §29 is a later forgery. The same goes for the documents at §§37–8, 39, 54, 73–4, 75, 77–8, 84, 90–1, 92, 105, 106 (twice), 115, 116, 118, 120, 135, 137, 154, 155 (twice), 157, 164, 165, 166, 167, 181–7. The spurious nature of these documents was thoroughly demonstrated by J. G. Droysen, 'Die Urkunden in Demosthenes' Rede vom Kranz', *Zeitschrift für die Alterthumswissenschaft*, 6 (1839), 537–99, 699–720, 799–824, 910–65 (repr. in id., *Kleine Schriften* I. 95–256); for a brief discussion, and further bibliography, see H. Yunis, *Demosthenes: On the Crown* (Cambridge: Cambridge University Press, 2001), 29–31.

18.30 Conjecturing πλεύσασι (Waterfield).

18.104 Retaining συνεκκαίδεκα with the MSS. At any rate, this was what the author of the first of the spurious documents of §106 read.

18.159 Omitting κακῶν with some MSS.

18.289 This epigram has been more widely accepted than the other spurious documents embedded within the received text (see the note above on §29), but it is spurious: see D. L. Page, *Further Greek Epigrams* (Cambridge: Cambridge University Press, 1981), 432–5. The fact that Demosthenes goes on to quote one of its lines proves that this line is genuine (from, then, an otherwise lost epigram), but otherwise means only that the forger inserted that line into his forgery, just as the forgers of the other spurious documents inserted occasional snippets of authentic information.

18.311 Omitting χρημάτων (Blass).

19.110 By an early editorial error, which has become enshrined in the textbooks, no sections of this speech are numbered 105–9.

19.231 Reading εὐθυνεῖσθαι (Waterfield).

19.255 Reading ἤ with later MSS.

19.285 Punctuating with a question-mark. The OCT's full stop may be a misprint.

21.8 The documents accepted as genuine by the OCT here, and at §§10, 47, and 52–3, are spurious. See E. Harris's review of M. MacDowell's commentary in *Classical Philology*, 87 (1992), 71–80.

21.33 Deleting ἄδειαν ἤ (MacDowell).

21.113 This law is probably spurious, especially since all the other documents in this speech are spurious. But in this case it's impossible to be certain.

21.131 Reading αὑτοῦ (Buttmann).

21.156 Deleting αὐληταῖς, and retaining ἀνδράσιν (MacDowell).

21.175 Excluding the final sentence of §175 as a marginal scholion that has crept into the text. The interruptive sentence reads: 'The law about the Mysteries is identical to the law in question, the one about the Dionysia, and the former came into effect later than the latter.' Judging by the meaningless reference to 'the law in question', the scholion has become detached from its original context.

21.205 There is a gap in the text. Eubulus' name needs seeding in the paragraph, and this is the most likely place where it has dropped out.

23.11 A few words have dropped out of the text here, but the meaning is still plain enough.

23.70 Retaining παρὰ with the MSS.

23.72 Reading αἰδεσθῇ παρὰ (Blass).

59.5 It's possible that a clause from §9, but out of place there and deleted by the OCT, belongs here, as originally suggested by Sauppe. The clause specifies that Apollodorus was defamed 'for having been a public debtor for twenty-five years'.

59.23 Almost all the documents that accompany this speech have been found spurious by some editors, but they are mostly too brief to be sure, and I have therefore translated them all, while remaining suspicious particularly of the two settlement documents at §§47 and 71.

27.42 A misprint in the OCT makes this plural.

36.1 The OCT's ἄν is a misprint for ἂν.

36.53 Reading <οὐ;>. The omission of the question-mark by Dilts is probably a misprint.

54.4 Reading ἀπεμεμψάμεθα (Carey/Reid).

GLOSSARY

Agora the administrative centre of Athens, which also served as a market-place.

Amphictyonic Council the grouping of Greek states which oversaw the shrine at Delphi. It met twice yearly, in spring and autumn, and member states sent two delegates.

Archon a generic term for 'official', the term also denotes a body of nine public officials at Athens, of whom the Archon (who gave his name to the year, hence the term 'eponymous Archon' often used by moderns), *Archon Basileus* ('King Archon'), and Polemarch were the oldest offices; see also *Thesmothete*.

Areopagus Council a body composed of ex-Archons, originally an aristocratic body with wide-ranging powers, but from *c.*460 primarily a homicide court.

Assembly the sovereign body in classical Athens, open to all adult male citizens; it met on the Pnyx hill west of the Acropolis forty times per year.

audit *(euthunai)* the review of the conduct of an Athenian public official conducted at the end of his period of office.

clan (*genos*) a formally organized kinship group which traced its origin to a common ancestor, open only to male citizens, though not all citizens belonged to a clan.

cleruch an Athenian colonist (literally 'lot-holder', i.e. recipient of a parcel of land) settled in land under Athenian control. Such colonists retained their Athenian citizenship.

Council (*Boulē*) the body of five hundred which prepared business for the Assembly and carried out a number of executive functions, especially financial; its members, who served for one year, were chosen by lot, fifty from each of the ten Athenian tribes; an individual could serve no more than twice in a lifetime.

deme (*dēmos*) roughly 'parish', the smallest administrative unit of the Athenian state organization. Membership (not necessarily coinciding with place of residence) was transmitted from father to son and was open only to male Athenian citizens, who were admitted at the age of eighteen. It was the basis for naming (a man was known by his given name, patronymic, and demotic, as 'Demosthenes, son of Demosthenes, of Paeania') and for citizen status, since there were no state records of citizens, only deme lists.

Dionysia, the the 'Great' Dionysia (also called the 'City Dionysia', to distinguish it from a rural festival of the same name). A magnificent procession was followed by competitions in tragedy and comedy and competitive choral performances of men and boys. It took place in spring, when the seas were open and there were many foreigners in the audience. The Athenians used the event to display the power and wealth and cultural significance of Athens to the Greek world.

elegiac poem a poem in dactylic rhythm (i.e. based on the 'dactyl', $-\breve{}\breve{}$) consisting of alternating hexameters ($-\breve{}\breve{} - \breve{}\breve{} - \breve{}\breve{} -\breve{}\breve{} -\breve{}\breve{} --$ with variations) and pentameters ($-\breve{}\breve{} - \breve{}\breve{} - -\breve{}\breve{} - \breve{}\breve{} -$ with variations).

Eleven, the a body of officials who had charge of prisoners and executions.

Ephetae the officials (fifty-one in number) who manned the homicide courts other than the Areopagus; it is uncertain whether they were a separate group or a subset of the Areopagus.

etesian winds the *meltemi*, the winds which blow across the Aegean Sea from a northerly direction in summer and early autumn.

Executive Committee (*prytaneis*) the Executive Committee of the Council, fifty in number, formed by giving the representatives of each of the ten tribes responsibility in rotation each for one-tenth of the year. During their period of office the Prytaneis dined at state expense at the Round House (see below).

generals (*stratēgoi*) the senior Athenian military officers, ten in number, elected by show of hands in the Assembly (unlike purely administrative officers, who were selected by lot). In the fifth century they functioned as a board, but during the fourth they were each given specific responsibilities. The term is also (unsurprisingly) used in a non-technical sense of condottieri in Athenian pay.

guest-friendship (*xenia*) the semi-formalized relationship between members of different states (most often members of the elite), based on reciprocal hospitality and a solemn oath of friendship.

gymnasiarch in Athens, a person selected to meet the costs of his tribal team competing in the torch races.

Heliaea the jury courts of Athens, often simply called *dikastēria*, 'courts'; the popular courts, as opposed to the old aristocratic Areopagus Council.

himation/khiton the two standard items of Greek daily clothing. The himation was worn over the khiton. The himation was a length of cloth that could be as large as 8 feet by 6 feet (2.4×1.8 metres); it was draped around the body and over one or both shoulders, usually without a belt or pin. The khiton was a smaller oblong piece of linen or wool, usually worn at knee-length by men and ankle-length by women. For modesty's sake, it was fastened at one or both shoulders with a pin, and with a belt around the waist.

hipparch (*hipparchos*) one of the two overall commanders of the Athenian cavalry, subordinate to the generals.

hoplite a heavy-armed soldier, equipped with shield, helmet, breastplate, greaves, a spear, and a sword, usually fighting in formation.

khiton see *himation*.

King Archon see *Archon*.

liturgy (*leitourgia*) the (expensive, means-tested) public duty, such as the trierarchy (responsibility for a warship) or *chorēgia* (responsibility for a civic chorus), imposed on rich Athenians as a financial contribution to the state in a system which avoided direct taxation of citizens (except for levies in times of war). See further notes on 4.36, 18.102, and 21.155.

medimnus an Athenian dry measure, a little over 52 litres.

metic a resident alien in a Greek city. Metics did not count as citizens (in Athens, for instance, they could not own property or marry a citizen), though they were required to serve in the army and had to pay a residency tax. In Athens and elsewhere, they often made a living as businessmen.

mna see *talent*.

paean a Greek song (usually sung in unison and often performed by a chorus), especially but not exclusively associated with Apollo and Artemis, performed in a wide range of contexts—in religious festivals, but also, for instance, before battle or after victory and after meals.

Panathenaea the most important Athenian civic festival, held in the summer; it was expanded every fourth year (and called the Great Panathenaea) with the addition of athletic competitions which were inferior in rank only to the big four panhellenic athletic festivals.

phalanx a body of heavy infantry in battle formation.

phratry a subdivision of one of the old four Athenian tribes; by the classical period a religious and social unit, but still important in political terms to the extent that phratry membership, confined to legitimate male citizens, is cited in court as evidence of citizenship status.

Polemarch in Sparta, commander of a military division (*mora*); in Athens, one of the Archons (see above), originally a military leader, but by the classical period an official with certain legal responsibilities, especially for cases involving non-citizens.

Prytaneum located probably in the old Agora to the east of the Acropolis, this building served a number of functions, including dining visiting dignitaries and Athenians granted free meals as an honour (such as Olympic victors and, occasionally, politicians), and as a law-court.

prytany (*prytaneia*) a period of one-tenth of the Athenian year, named after the period of office of the Executive Committee of the Council (see above).

Pylaea the name given to twice-yearly meetings of the Amphictyonic Council (one at Delphi, one at Thermopylae) and the building at Delphi which housed the meetings.

Round House (*Tholos*) a circular building in the Athenian Agora princi-
pally used as the dining-hall of the Executive Committee of the Council.

sophist literally 'a practitioner of wisdom/skill', by the late fifth century
the word is applied chiefly to the (mainly itinerant) teachers of language, politics, rhetoric, and ethics who flocked especially to democratic
Athens. Its use as a sneer-word stems from their hair-splitting argu-
mentation and the suspicion that they taught people to be good at
arguing for its own sake, never mind the moral consequences. In 59.21,
applied to the speechwriter Lysias, it is not pejorative.

stade Greek unit of distance with some variation from state to state, but
roughly 180 metres.

stele a stone slab, usually inscribed or incised, used for permanent recording or memorialization, ranging from tombs to laws and decrees.

stoa a covered portico designed to afford shade in summer and shelter
from the rain.

sycophant a nebulous term much used by Athenian litigants to designate
opponents and enemies; the sycophant's activity ranges from misrepre-
sentation of the facts to persecution and, especially, malicious, mercenary, and baseless prosecution.

symposium a formalized drinking-party held (usually) at the end of
a meal.

syndicate (*symmoria*) a group of well-to-do citizens charged with
the collective discharge of a financial duty such as a war levy or the
trierarchy (see below).

talent/mna/drachma/obol units of coinage; the ratios are: 6 obols = 1
drachma, 100 drachmas = 1 mna, 60 mnas = 1 talent.

taxiarch commander of one of the ten tribal infantry units of Athens;
phylarchs were the cavalry equivalent.

Theoric Fund literally 'viewing'/'festival' fund, originally created to
enable the poor to attend theatrical performances, but by the mid-fourth
century also used to support attendance at other festivals and public
works.

Thesmothete the title of six of the nine Archons.

third-string actor (*tritagōnistēs*) the state at the civic drama festivals
allowed only three actors per play (easier in a theatre which used
masks), so the third actor was the lowest in the troupe, after the lead
(*protagōnistēs*, 'first player') and main support actor (*deuteragōnistēs*,
'second player').

triaconter a vessel with thirty oars.

tribe in Athens, one of the main subdivisions of the state, important as
the basis for military service, representation in political bodies such
as the Council, and musical and other competitions in civic festivals.

Originally four, they were rearranged as ten in the democratic reforms at the end of the sixth century.

trierarch, trierarchy an Athenian liturgy (see above). The trierarch was given a trireme by the state and was responsible for its maintenance at sea (including captaining it and paying the crew). By the end of the fifth century, as three decades of war took their toll, the responsibility was divided between two citizens, and by the middle of the fourth century we find the burden spread over syndicates (see above)

trireme the three-tiered warship which was the standard man-of-war in the classical period; propelled by oar or sail, it was usually kept within sight of shore and beached at night.

trophy after a battle, the victors set up a trophy (in Greek, *tropaion*, cognate with the verb meaning 'to turn') at the point on the battlefield where the enemy had turned and fled. The trophy was often a kind of manikin, mockingly dressed in armour stripped from the enemy.

INDEX OF PROPER NAMES

Certain categories of names have been omitted: place or deme names used merely for identification; personal names used merely as patronymics.

The Oxford World's Classics Website

www.worldsclassics.co.uk

- Browse the full range of Oxford World's Classics online

- Sign up for our monthly e-alert to receive information on new titles

- Read extracts from the Introductions

- Listen to our editors and translators talk about the world's greatest literature with our Oxford World's Classics audio guides

- Join the conversation, follow us on Twitter at OWC_Oxford

- Teachers and lecturers can order inspection copies quickly and simply via our website

www.worldsclassics.co.uk

American Literature

British and Irish Literature

Children's Literature

Classics and Ancient Literature

Colonial Literature

Eastern Literature

European Literature

Gothic Literature

History

Medieval Literature

Oxford English Drama

Philosophy

Poetry

Politics

Religion

The Oxford Shakespeare

A complete list of Oxford World's Classics, including Authors in Context, Oxford English Drama, and the Oxford Shakespeare, is available in the UK from the Marketing Services Department, Oxford University Press, Great Clarendon Street, Oxford OX2 6DP, or visit the website at www.oup.com/uk/worldsclassics.

In the USA, visit www.oup.com/us/owc for a complete title list.

Oxford World's Classics are available from all good bookshops. In case of difficulty, customers in the UK should contact Oxford University Press Bookshop, 116 High Street, Oxford OX1 4BR.

HORACE	The Complete Odes and Epodes
JUVENAL	The Satires
LIVY	The Dawn of the Roman Empire
	Hannibal's War
	The Rise of Rome
MARCUS AURELIUS	The Meditations
OVID	The Love Poems
	Metamorphoses
PETRONIUS	The Satyricon
PLATO	Defence of Socrates, Euthyphro, and Crito
	Gorgias
	Meno and Other Dialogues
	Phaedo
	Republic
	Selected Myths
	Symposium
PLAUTUS	Four Comedies
PLUTARCH	Greek Lives
	Roman Lives
	Selected Essays and Dialogues
PROPERTIUS	The Poems
SOPHOCLES	Antigone, Oedipus the King, and Electra
STATIUS	Thebaid
SUETONIUS	Lives of the Caesars
TACITUS	Agricola and Germany
	The Histories
VIRGIL	The Aeneid
	The Eclogues and Georgics
XENOPHON	The Expedition of Cyrus

Late Victorian Gothic Tales

JANE AUSTEN
Emma
Mansfield Park
Persuasion
Pride and Prejudice
Selected Letters
Sense and Sensibility

MRS BEETON
Book of Household Management

MARY ELIZABETH
BRADDON
Lady Audley's Secret

ANNE BRONTË
The Tenant of Wildfell Hall

CHARLOTTE BRONTË
Jane Eyre
Shirley
Villette

EMILY BRONTË
Wuthering Heights

ROBERT BROWNING
The Major Works

JOHN CLARE
The Major Works

SAMUEL TAYLOR
COLERIDGE
The Major Works

WILKIE COLLINS
The Moonstone
No Name
The Woman in White

CHARLES DARWIN
The Origin of Species

THOMAS DE QUINCEY
The Confessions of an English
   Opium-Eater
On Murder

CHARLES DICKENS
The Adventures of Oliver Twist
Barnaby Rudge
Bleak House
David Copperfield
Great Expectations
Nicholas Nickleby
The Old Curiosity Shop
Our Mutual Friend
The Pickwick Papers